Introduction to
Educational Psychology

Introduction to Educational Psychology

Hershel D. Thornburg
Department of Educational Psychology
University of Arizona, Tucson

West Publishing Company
St. Paul   New York   Los Angeles   San Francisco

Library of Congress Cataloging in Publication Data

Thornburg, Hershel D., 1936–
  Educational psychology.

  Bibliography: p.
  Includes index.
   1.   Educational psychology.   2.   Learning.   3.   Teaching.
I.   Title.
LB1051.T387   1984   370.15   83–23581
ISBN 0–314–77830–6

Copy editing: Sylvia E. Stein
Design: Janet Bollow
Illustrations: Brenda Booth
Production coordination: Janet Bollow Associates
Cover photograph: © Tim Jewett, EKM-Nepenthe
Composition: Dharma Press

Photo Credits

Photographs were provided courtesy of the Kino Learning Center, with the exception of those listed below.

10 Magnum Photos, Inc.; **22** © Fredrik D. Bodin, Stock, Boston, Inc.; **68** © Mark Godfrey, Archive Pictures, Inc.; **95** Bob Adelman, Magnum Photos, Inc.; **120** Shirley Zeiberg, Taurus Photos; **125** © Jack Prelutsky, Stock, Boston, Inc.; **129** Ginger Chih, Peter Arnold, Inc.; **134** © Randy Matusow, Archive Pictures, Inc.; **140** © John Maher, EKM-Nepenthe; **143, 146** George Pearce; **153** © Robert V. Eckert, EKM-Nepenthe; **164** © Alex Webb, Magnum; **176, 191** Elizabeth Crews; **195** © 1978 Sherry Suris, Photo Researchers, Inc.; **202** Elizabeth Crews; **210** Mimi Forsyth, Monkmeyer Press Photo Service; **215** © John Maher, EKM-Nepenthe; **218** George Pearce; **220** © Eileen Christelow, Jeroboam, Inc.; **221** James Carroll, Archive Pictures, Inc.; **231** Elizabeth Crews; **243** James H. Winkler; **255** George Pearce; **263** Elizabeth Crews; **275** Elizabeth Hamlin, Stock, Boston, Inc.; **286** Elizabeth Crews; **297** Anestis Diakopoulos, Stock, Boston, Inc.; **328** Elizabeth Crews; **332** Barbara Rios, Photo Researchers, Inc.; **334** R. D. Ullmann, Taurus Photos; **355** Michael Weisbrot, Stock, Boston, Inc.; **359** Peter Vandermark, Stock, Boston, Inc.; **367** Copyright © Abraham Menashe 1980, Photo Researchers, Inc.; **370** © Suzanne Wu, Jeroboam, Inc.; **386** Eric Hartmann, Magnum Photos, Inc.; **401** James H. Winkler; **420** Charles Harbutt, Archive Pictures, Inc.; **423** Robert V. Eckert, EKM-Nepenthe; **426, 430** Michael O'Brian, Archive Pictures, Inc.; **434** Joan Liftin, Archive Pictures, Inc.; **436** Elizabeth Crews; **437** Frank Siteman, Taurus Photos; **450** Charles Harbutt, Archive Pictures, Inc.; **456** James Carroll, Archive Pictures, Inc.; **460** Joseph Szabo, Photo Researchers, Inc.; **497, 504** © Ellen Thornburg; **509** George Pearce.

Contents

Scene from Teaching
$1 = 100 Percent Memory   49

Concept Summary 2–1
Elements of Reinforcement
Schedules   54

Concept Summary 2–2
Teacher Reinforcement Strategies
Upon Observing a Behavior   64

Application
The Range of Reinforcers   65

Concept Summary 3–1
Basic Tenets in Cognitive
Psychology   72

Concept Summary 3–2
Learning Processes:
Jerome Bruner   76

Scene from Teaching
Understanding Is More
Important: That's a
Fact   81

Concept Summary 3–3
Cognitive-Behaviorism
Comparisons   86

Application
Student Perceptions
as Reality   87

Chapter 4
Concept Learning

93

Concept Summary 4–1
Basic Concept Assumptions   102

Scene from Teaching
Earl Brightup:
A Conceptual Whiz Kid   107

Concept Summary 4–2
Concepts and Rules   108

Concept Summary 4–3
Different Strategies:
Equivalent Outcomes   110

Application
Decision-Making
Opportunities   113

Chapter 5
Observational Learning

119

Scene from Teaching
Go, Team, Go   125

Concept Summary 5–1
Steps in Observational
Learning   128

Concept Summary 5–2
Exemplars   130

Application
Modeling Music Awareness   136

Chapter 6
Development in Humans

Concept Summary 6–1
Strands of Developmental
Theory   151

Scene from Teaching
Move over PeeWee   164

x

Concept Summary 14–1
Potential Teacher Causes of
Classroom Management
Problems   425

Scene from Teaching
Teaching and the Exercise
of Control   437

Concept Summary 14–2
Identifying Behavioral Change
Reinforcers   442

Application
Contingency Contracts   446

Concept Summary 15–1
Plotting an IQ Score
on the Curve   466

Box 15–1
How to Construct Essay
Questions   476

Box 15–2
How to Write Multiple-Choice
Questions   478

Box 15–3
How to Write Matching
Questions   479

Box 15–4
How to Write Recall
Questions   481

Concept Summary 15–2
Norm or Criterion Statements   486

Application
Affective Measurement   490

Epilogue
The Future of Education

495

Box E–1
Dimensions of Effective
Schooling   502

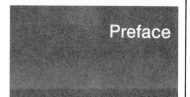

Historically, colleges and universities with teacher education programs have included a course in learning in their curricula. In many of these courses, however, students are introduced to the concepts and principles of learning without any clear insights or strategies as to how to apply them in classrooms. The application of learning theory is postponed until the students enter the teaching profession and are faced with many learning problems whose solutions are not readily apparent. In such cases, teachers often teach by trial and error or seek additional help. This book adds two dimensions not commonly found in educational psychology texts or in introductory educational psychology courses. The first dimension is instructional strategies to guide prospective teachers in using learning theory. The second dimension is actual classroom illustrations of the strategies.

This book closes the gap between when students are introduced to learning theory and when they begin to formulate a theory of instruction. I define learning on an operational plane, as well as on a theoretical plane, and then provide problems to which readers can apply the learning and instructional concepts being studied.

Although the primary audience for this book is undergraduate education students, it will also be useful at the graduate and the in-service level for many courses or school districts and serve as a resource for those seeking to improve their approaches to instruction through a better understanding of the principles and practical applications of current theory. Above all, this book provides future teachers and teachers presently in the field with insights into their everyday approaches in the classroom. It is *not* intended to provide educators with insights into experimental laboratory research on learning processes. For this reason, I have purposely not considered many experimental or research facets of the learning and teaching process.

When approaching a task of this scope, an author must rely on the supportive efforts of many others. Of foremost importance is the exchange of ideas with and the constant support base provided by my wife, Ellen, to whom this book is dedicated. In addition, two other people at the University of Arizona have provided significant input: Alice Schoenberger, my secretary, who is a manuscript typist par excellence, and Joyce Bell, a doctoral student who critically read the manuscript and facilitated my development of applied materials to use with students. I spent seven years, from 1975 to 1982, as a consultant to the Los Alamos, New Mexico, public schools. During that time, I not only developed my own thinking but was able to work out virtually all the applied examples used in this text. The relevancy of this text is enhanced considerably by actual field testing.

In preparation of the final manuscript, reviewers were most helpful. Their valuable insights and suggestions have contributed to the quality of this book. They were:

Henry R. Angelino
Ohio State University

Theodore Bayer
State University of New York (Albany)

Gloria C. Fauth
George Mason University (Virginia)

Robert A. Hicks
San Jose State University (California)

Robert L. Hohn
University of Kansas

Rita R. Keefe
Bowling Green State University (Ohio)

Don F. Keller
Clemson University (South Carolina)

Leonard K. Kise
Northern Illinois University

John L. Klem
Ball State University (Indiana)

Robert D. Smith
San Diego State University (California)

Helen I. Snyder
Pennsylvania State University

Suzanne Waller
University of Wisconsin, Milwaukee

Dennis A. Warner
Washington State University

Grover J. Whitehurst
State University of New York (Stony Brook)

Barry J. Wilson
University of Northern Iowa

In addition, I have never worked with an editor as capable as Clyde Perlee of West Publishing. His cogent approach to the task of codeveloping a book was refereshing and rewarding. Other personnel with West Publishing were also instrumental in the book's development. Of particular value to me were Carole Grumney, developmental editor, and Janet Bollow, who designed the book. The professional and technical assistance of the publishing firm were invaluable throughout the book's development.

Hershel Thornburg
Tucson, Arizona

Invitation
to Teaching

Understanding Behavior

This book is about **behavior**—yours and mine and all the people with whom we have contact. Behavior is a function of the mind, the signals it receives and the messages it sends to different parts of our systems telling them to behave in some way. The pilot who flies a jet is behaving, as is the hot dog vendor at the ball park, the person who cries when watching a sad movie, the adolescent who tries drugs, the priest who asks for divine guidance, the mother who breast feeds her child, the police officer who pulls someone over, the investor in the stock market, and the family that goes on a Sunday picnic. I was behaving as I wrote this book, and you are behaving as you read it.

Behavior
The observable responses of an organism or any of its parts.

Behavior is manifest in three ways: how we think, feel, and act. When we read about a political candidate, we are thinking about that individual. Our thought processes allow us to evaluate the candidate based upon information learned. We also develop an opinion about the candidate based on how we feel. The candidate's appearance, stage presence, or persuasive ability might influence our feeling. The combination of how we think and feel results in action. If we like the candidate, we will likely say positive things about him or her, trying to sway others' opinions. The ultimate action is to vote for the candidate.

To help students learn, to share our feelings, and to persuade another to act in a certain way, we must understand human behavior. To understand behavior, we must know what motivates it, what creates the need to do something, and how people can abstract meaning from their environment and integrate it into their personal lives. Once we understand the importance of behavior, we can begin to study it. Such study can increase our understanding of how behavior is learned.

Educational Psychology

Few studies are designed to test whether teacher behavior makes a difference in student learning. One that does (Brophy & Good, 1979) shows that teachers hold different expectations for different students. They do not treat all students alike. It is often easier or more expedient to ask questions of bright students. Teachers know that they almost

1

always answer correctly and faster than average or slow students. Calling on the fast learners may make the teacher's job easier, but what does it do to student learning? Providing corrective feedback to students who give wrong answers, and thus perhaps helping them get the correct answer, may actually serve the interests of more students than calling upon the bright students most of the time. Studies need to be designed to determine how teacher activity directly influences student behavior.

Gagne (1973, p. 113) has suggested that research on teaching should observe as variables "those events which support (or fail to support) learning." Such variables should include:

1. *Events that introduce or set the stage for learning.* Activities such as capturing student interest and directing student attention fall in this category.

2. *Events that guide the initial learning process.* This category includes verbal explanations, prompts and hints, and leading questions.

3. *Events that are designed to make what is learned memorable and generalizable.* Review questions and elaborations are two teaching strategies that could be used to support the retention and transfer of learning.

4. *Events that affect reinforcement.* This category includes instances of appraisal of student performance and the feedback that follows (teacher questions, quizzes, or student papers and the comments made on them).

Educational psychology established itself as a discipline by investigating learning and a variety of factors that affect it. The basis for understanding human conditioning is well established. However, the simple processes discovered at the turn of the century (Pavlov, 1903; Thorndike, 1898, 1903) and elaborated on between 1930 and 1960 (Hull, 1943; Skinner, 1938, 1953; Spence, 1956) only partially explain human learning as it manifests itself in the classroom. To understand teacher behavior, we need a more elaborate conceptualization and investigation of it. The need to understand teaching-learning processes is a primary goal of educational psychology today.

Educational psychology seeks to understand how people learn and how teachers instruct. As a science, it concentrates on the fields of learning, instruction, intelligence, motivation, development, perception, memory affectivity, measurement, evaluation, research, and statistics. Although much of educational psychology is based on the experimental model, it is not as exacting as experimental psychology, whose historical thrust was animal research. Human behavior is much more complex than animal behavior, and it is unlikely that research in school or classroom settings can account for all the variables affecting learning.

The psychological or educational researcher must deal with many variables in attempting to assess and predict behavior. Individual differences among subjects make prediction difficult. It is rarely possible to assert that a certain behavior will cause a certain result. The researcher may be able to state that in a situation highly similar to the one within an experimental study the same behavior is more likely to result, but humans always have the potential for unpredictable behavior.

Like educational psychologists, classroom teachers must recognize that they are working with many individuals, all of whom bring into classrooms different levels of learning and who may perceive and respond to teachers differently from their classmates. The more teachers understand the processes involved in both learning and instruction, the more capable they will be of providing consistently effective teaching for all their students.

Relationship of Research to Instruction

The historical basis upon which educational psychology was established as a science is its research on learning processes. Studies have yielded consistent results, have successfully been subjected to replication, and have been increasingly relevant to understanding human learning processes. Instructional research is not as well defined as learning research, although it must eventually become so if it is to have an impact on teachers' classroom instruction.

Frase (1977, p. 128) suggests that effective instructional research must be consistent and relevant: "By consistency of instructional research, I mean better definition of independent or dependent variables, better quantification in measuring those variables, and increased replication of findings. By relevance of instructional research, I mean doing research on instructionally relevant tasks and processes and relating those tasks and processes to an integrated conception of instructional development."

Classroom teachers tend to hold negative attitudes toward educational research (Gallagher, 1975a; Isakson & Ellsworth, 1979). There are three basic reasons why these perceptions may be held and why teachers may not use results of educational research to change their classroom practices.

The first reason is philosophical. Kerlinger (1973) has suggested that two broad views of science have impacted on educational research: the static and the dynamic. The static view is that science contributes systematic information to the world. Emphasis is on what we have and how we use it. Additional research only adds to our existing data base. Teachers are most likely to embrace this point of view. They want information that is useful. The dynamic view holds that there is more to be discovered. The present state of knowledge is important primarily because it provides the base for further theory and research. Educational researchers are likely to endorse this perspective. Thus, there may be a gap between educational research and classroom practices.

A second problem with educational research is the theoretical base from which it is derived. If instructional theory is a valid approach to teacher behavior, then instruction can be researched. Yet, thus far, research on instruction has yielded few useful results. Why? First, there is no broad consensus about what constitutes instructional theory. Research may be testing conflicting propositions and thus not improving theoretical constructs. Second, perhaps educational researchers do not see any urgent need for research on instruction. Certainly, however, research on instructional theory has yet to provide solid evidence in support of any one particular teaching approach.

Gage (1968) points out the difference between research on learning and research on instruction. Research on learning attempts to deal with all the conditions under which learning takes place. Research on teaching deals with a subset of those conditions, specifically, the conditions established by the teacher's behavior. Gage has elaborated on small segments of teacher behavior. He maintains that teachers can learn specific technical skills that they can use in the classroom and that researchers can analyze. Teaching methodology may thus be the primary determinant of successful teaching.

Content
The ideas that go into an experience a person is having. In school, subject matter makes up the experience.

The third problem is our inability to analyze the **content** of instruction and to identify student learning activities that maximize learning potential (Frase, 1977; Merrill & Tennyson, 1978; Tennyson & Park, 1980). **Content** is the subject matter of the course. As students move from simple verbal information to concepts or rules for problem solving, the content must be articulated in such a way that learning is sequential, that is, from simple to complex and nonconceptual to conceptual. This is a useful strategy for teachers and learners, but one that is limited in practice. To what extent do teachers articulate subject-matter content? Where is a block of empirical data that shows the importance of articulating content? How well do textbooks articulate their content? Where is the data base for this? The least research is in areas where it could generate a large information base that could potentially change teacher behavior. Subject-matter experts may have limited knowledge about learning processes and educational research, but they commonly write the textbooks used in schools. Drawing upon the limitation of undue dependency on subject matter, Glaser (1976) argues that the content of instructional materials should be organized on empirically based designs and not just according to traditional academic structures.

We also do not know how to structure classroom environments to help students learn. The usual assumption is that teachers direct students into learning activities. Their techniques are varied, and no large body of research shows conclusively which technique is best. We also have not sufficiently analyzed or investigated whether the diverse activities teachers use are content oriented or content relevant. The lack of investigation of such relationships creates an enormous deficit on the impact of research on teaching.

Educational researchers have conducted numerous studies on multiple aspects of the educational environment. Still, the data in instruction are somewhat weak. Better conceptualized instructional designs, more provocative research questions, and more concern by educational researchers about the functional nature of teacher-student interaction can enhance the relationship between research and instruction.

Teachers as Practitioners

Teaching is a complex and difficult task that requires ongoing preparation and revision, concern with students' academic and social needs, constant stage presence, often nothing short of intense performance, and a set of tasks and concerns that are often carried home. Because of diverse student demands, it is a practical job. Even though teaching is complex, it must be straightforward with each individual student.

Few classroom teachers have the luxury of theorizing, experimenting, or systematically collecting data on students and themselves that might subsequently change their behavior. Most develop individual styles with which they are comfortable and to which students respond. Each day they experience varying degrees of success and gain a sense of personal satisfaction from what they accomplish.

The practical aspects of teaching may take on a different dimension from the instructional design of teaching. Systematic approaches to instruction seem to increase students' academic learning rates (Berliner, 1980; McKenzie. 1980; Rosenshine, 1976). Nevertheless, teaching is an art. It involves interacting directly with students' feelings, minds, and expectations. Teaching consequently is highly intuitive. Yet teachers are obligated to exercise sound professional judgment, making decisions with minimal information and living with the consequences (Berliner, 1983).

Goals of Classroom Teaching

The underlying goal of classroom teaching is to increase the amount your students learn. Within the American educational system, this responsibility rests with the local school districts; so the ways and extent to which this goal is accomplished vary. The designated curriculum (academic content) is designed to increase student competencies. An increasingly important aspect of contemporary curriculum, although often poorly defined, is the social competencies students need to learn. Organizing instruction around these two learning thrusts increases the likelihood of effective learning occurring.

What are the best ways to teach individuals? The question is not fully answerable. The development of instructional models and experimental studies on instructional effectiveness are relatively new and limited. However, numerous approaches to teaching have been advocated (Bloom, 1974; Carroll, 1963; Gage, 1964; Gagne & Briggs, 1974; Glaser, 1962), and they all agree that an effective approach must be well designed and systematic. If we can specify teacher behaviors that can result in student learning, we can observe teaching-learning interactions to determine their effectiveness. By systematically observing teacher behavior, we can better determine what constitutes good teaching as it is reflected in student learning.

Academic Content

There is much that students must learn at each grade level. Goals are set, objectives are written, materials are presented, tasks are assigned, and students are evaluated as to their academic progress. The concep-

tualization of what is academic tends to remain traditional. Math, science, language arts, and social studies are the core academic subjects, with most other classroom activities being thought of as less academic. Academic teaching is often measured only in relation to these specific subjects.

A goal of classroom teaching is to place comparable importance on all activities that occur in a school day. Some subjects may require more time than others, but more time may not imply greater importance. All subject areas have content. To assume that areas such as physical education, art, music, health, and library do not is to relegate them to a lesser role. Teachers must carefully assess how effective they are in areas not traditionally thought of as having content.

The content of academic instruction must be specific as to learning activities for students and desired educational outcomes for teachers. Goals, when analyzed, are described as instructional objectives. They tell what a teacher will pursue and what students are responsible for learning once the instruction is completed. Thus, an important aspect of teacher behavior is to establish expected learning outcomes that are clear to the teacher and student alike.

Teachers must determine if the materials they use for instruction are appropriate. Textbooks are the most common resource, but they do not always meet teachers' goals. It is important that teachers not place undue emphasis on them. School districts have considerable curriculum materials, including audiovisuals, classroom computers, and other resources that aid instruction. Teachers must always ask whether such resources facilitate their instruction and increase the student's potential for learning.

Teaching Styles

The teacher's style sets the tone for classroom learning. Teachers can generate student enthusiasm, motivate students, appeal to their intellectual curiosity and creative sense, and control and structure the classroom so tightly that students respond only in "appropriate" ways. Just as students learn in many different ways, so teachers instruct in diverse ways. Some teachers provide **direct instruction,** which implies teacher dominance with limited student input. Others have more open classrooms where teacher-student verbal interaction is emphasized. Still others employ self-paced strategies where students are responsible for their own goal setting and the teacher functions primarily as a classroom resource. Regardless of the modality, it should increase learning. If it does not, a different teaching approach should be considered (McGreal, 1980; Peterson, 1979).

Research on direct instruction seems to support this approach as most preferable for academic achievement. Rosenshine (1979) has identified the following characteristics of direct instruction: (1) an academic focus, (2) a teacher-centered focus, (3) limited student choice of activity, (4) large group instruction, and (5) use of factual questions and controlled practice in instruction. He based his characteristics on the results of extensive studies done in California between 1972 and 1978 with second- and fifth-grade teachers (Berliner & Rosenshine, 1977; Denham & Lieberman, 1980; Fisher, Berliner, Filby, Marliave, Cahen, Dishaw, & Moore, 1978; Rosenshine, 1980). The results show that the more teachers are engaged in direct instruction of academics (defined as reading, math, science, and social studies), the more students learn. A commensurate amount of learning did not occur in areas these studies referred to as "nonacademic activities" (defined as music, art, story time, and sharing).

If the primary goal at the elementary level is to increase academic achievement, then teachers should engage students in as much academic direct instruction as possible. Some questions arise, however, in relation to the dominance of this style. Peterson (1979, p. 47) has concluded that, with

> direct or traditional teaching, students tend to do slightly better on achievement tests, but they do slightly worse on tests of abstract thinking, such as creativity and problem solving. Conversely, with open teaching, students do somewhat worse on achievement tests, but they do somewhat better on creativity and problem solving. Furthermore, open approaches excel over direct or traditional approaches in increasing students' attitudes toward school and toward the teacher and in improving students' independence and curiosity.

Another position contends that the effect of direct instruction is directly proportional to the learning style of the student, implying direct instruction is not the maximum learning style for all students (Janicki, 1979; Wright & DuCette, 1976). Research at the secondary level needs to be done to see if this teaching strategy holds or if it applies most effectively at the elementary level.

Direct instruction
The maintenance of student involvement in a learning task. Sometimes it is called "engaged time" or "time-on-task."

The varying emphases that different educators and psychologists place on teaching style are legitimate and relevant to the pursuit of understanding teacher effectiveness. Researchers help identify student characteristics and explain how they may operate in the classroom. Practitioners must make decisions on teaching and learning effectiveness as they interact with students each day. The combined understanding, when shared, should increase the quality of both research and practice.

The Learning Process

George Bauman, the principal of Jefferson School, decided to do something innovative for an in-service day scheduled for his staff: a "philosopher's field day." The teachers would be able to forget about the practical, everyday aspects of school and rethink the historical, philosophical, and theoretical roots underlying education.

Teachers made three brief presentations, followed by discussion periods. Ms. Petersen focused on the philosophy of John Locke, stressing students' impressionability and the importance of structuring their school environments in positive ways. Mr. Walters focused on Plato and on Aristotle's mind-body dualism, which stress the importance of academics in the realization of the self. Ms. Pawlowski presented a theistic perspective, indicating that, although academic education is very important, the primary aim of education is to help students become moral beings.

After lunch, a panel discussed whether teaching is an art or a science. This panel, made up of three classroom teachers, a school board member, a physician, a university professor, and a school administrator, was invigorating to the staff. The session stimulated the teachers to rethink how they do things in their classrooms.

This chapter focuses on the science part of teaching. It begins by tracing the history of learning from its initial scientific basis to its contemporary interpretations. I present various positions in an effort to emphasize how much the scientific study of human behavior can contribute to the educative process.

Key concepts in this chapter include:

- *A history of learning theory*
- *Stimulus-response learning*
- *Reinforcement theory*
- *Gestalt-cognitive learning*
- *Social learning theory*
- *Hierarchical learning*
- *Information processing*

A History of Learning Theory

Learning
The acquisition or modification of a response that results from experience.

Learning is generally thought of as a relatively permanent change in behavior that results from an individual's interaction with the environment. In school, learning is inferred from the student's ability to demonstrate knowledge and skills. It may result directly from the student's response to the teacher's instructional behavior. English and English (1958, p. 289) define learning more formally as a "highly general term for the relatively enduring change, in response to a task demand, that is induced directly by experience, or the process or processes whereby such change is brought about."

When we ask "How do we learn?" it becomes necessary to respond with theoretical statements. English and English (1958, p. 551) define **theory** as "a general principle, supported by considerable data, proposed as an explanation of a group of phenomena." Using theory as the base, educational psychologists can establish **hypotheses** ("if/then" assumptions), which they may then test in practical experiments to evaluate the validity of the theories. They also are often generated as a result of repeated experimentation. In short, a theory of learning states general laws or principles that describe the conditions under which learning takes place.

Theory
A principle or generalization that explains phenomena.

Hypothesis
A theoretical statement designed to explain observed behavior.

Lindgren (1980, pp. 300–301) lists the following requirements of an adequate theory of learning for teachers:

1. It must help us understand all processes of human learning.

2. It must extend our understanding of the conditions or forces that stimulate, inhibit, or affect learning in any way.

3. It must enable us to make reasonably accurate predictions about the outcomes of learning activity.

4. It must be a source of hypotheses, clues, and concepts that we can use to become more effective teachers.

5. It must be a source of hypotheses or informed hunches about learning that can be tested through classroom experimentation and research, thus extending our understanding of the teaching-learning process.

For years, learning theories were based on the findings derived from experimental research with animals. Animals were used as research subjects because it is easier to control the variables influencing the learning process. In the post–World War II years, however, there has been a significant shift in learning research toward the study of human subjects as scientists have learned how to control research variables more precisely. Research on human learning has confirmed much of the research originally done with animals, provided understanding of the complexity of human behavior, and assisted in the development of instructional theory.

The ancient Greek and Latin philosophers wrote the first descriptions of human behavior. Socrates, Plato, and Aristotle thought that the mind requires exercise, just as a muscle requires exercise. The more the mind is used, the more a person learns. Thus, they considered learning the use of intrinsic mental strength. This position remained dominant for over two thousand years. It took on a new perspective when St. Aurelius Augustine (354–430) and St. Thomas Aquinas (1225–1274) described people as naturally evil and believed that the discipline of the mind helped an individual overcome wrongdoing. The exercise of the mind was the central idea in all these early writings on learning.

A variation of the mental discipline theory, **natural unfoldment,** emerged in the writings of Jean Jacques Rousseau (1712–1778) and Johann Pestalozzi (1746–1827). They did not view people as basically bad. They believed that people are free, have autonomy, and are actively involved in their own development. These writers considered people responsible for the unfoldment of their own potential. In a sense, this view supports the concept of human development more than that of learning.

Natural unfoldment
Individuals, as they develop, unfold the capacity to learn without undue dependence on the environment.

The immediate forerunner of American experimental psychology was **associationism,** which refers to "ideas, feelings and movements . . . connected in such a way as to determine their succession in the mind or in the actions of an individual, or . . . the process of establishing such connections" (Drever, 1964, p. 21). Thus, associationism may be viewed as "any general theory within which it is assumed that learning starts with irreducible elements and the process of learning is one of combining these" (Bigge & Hunt, 1962, p. 277).

Associationism
The process of establishing connections between events in the mind.

Although many psychologists trace associationism back to Aristotle, the works of Thomas Hobbes, John Locke, and other British empiricists gave rise to the idea that an individual's understanding is influenced by previous experiences. Locke rejected the mental discipline idea, not believing human beings are innately good or bad. He proposed that the mind is blank at birth. According to his *tabula rasa* concept, the mind is highly impressionable and the nurturing environment, rather than heredity, is the basis for learning. Locke saw knowledge, morality, and personal values as derived from sense experience. Through internal reflection, we formulate complex ideas and learning occurs.

Locke's considerations gave rise in the nineteenth century to Johann Herbart's concepts of **apperception** (associationism), in which newly perceived ideas relate to and are added to ideas already in the mind. As the learner entertains new ideas, they find their way into consciousness and strive to maintain themselves. Herbart postulated that learning is facilitated by two principles: the **principle of frequency,** which holds that, the more often ideas enter the consciousness, the greater the chances of their remaining, and the **principle of association,** which suggests that, when several ideas gather in the mind, their combined strength determines when they will enter consciousness.

Apperception
Relating newly learned information, skills, or feelings to existing ones.

Principle of frequency
Ideas that enter consciousness with high frequency are better retained than those that enter with low frequency.

Principle of association
The combined strength of ideas in the mind increases their chances of entering consciousness.

Apperception, or Herbartianism, as it is frequently called, went virtually unnoticed until after Herbart's death in 1841. Some years later, German philosophers expounded it. In the 1890s, when some American students returned from studying in Europe, apperception spread throughout the United States and became very influential in teacher education. Herbart's ideas were carried into some of the more formal theories of learning advanced in the early 1900s. In a real sense, his theory was the forerunner of stimulus-response psychology.

Chapter 1
The Learning Process

13

Although theories about human learning have been available in various forms for two thousand years, E. L. Thorndike's animal research in 1898 must be considered the beginning of scientific experimentation on learning. In his research with cats, he was astonished by the overwhelming effect of reward on a cat's behavior. His theoretical position became known as **connectionism,** the term he used to indicate that a relationship between a stimulus (S) and a response (R) has taken place. This point of view remains as a dominant position in contemporary learning theory.

Within twenty years of Thorndike's experiments, Max Wertheimer, a German **Gestalt** psychologist, advanced a second major scientific explanation. He perceived all things as wholes, not as part of something else. Known today as **cognitive psychology,** interpretations of this theory discuss internal processes in perception, attitudes, and beliefs that people hold about their environment. Learning is acquired as our experiences interact within a meaningful environment and internal structures.

Although **stimulus-response learning** and cognitive learning are distinct, they are not as mutually exclusive as many have long held. Modifications of both systems, plus newer explanations of human learning, contain elements of both systems.

Stimulus-Response Learning

Connectionism

According to connectionism, now more widely known as stimulus-response (S-R) theory or behaviorism, learning is a process of "stamping in" or forming connections in the mind. Because the cats in Thorndike's research appeared aimless in their attempts to solve problems in a puzzle box, he came to view learning as a process of trial and error. He found that, when the cats came upon the correct response and were rewarded for it, the reward invoked a satisfied condition and thus reinforced (strengthened) the stimulus-response bond. The terms **satisfiers** and **annoyers** are essential to understanding Thorndike's laws of learning. "By a satisfying state of affairs is meant one which the animal does nothing to avoid, often doing things which maintain or renew it. By an annoying state of affairs is meant one which the animal does nothing to preserve, often doing things which put an end to it" (Thorndike, 1913, p. 2). Thus, attainment of a satisfier strengthens the connection between the stimulus and the response.

From this basic principle, Thorndike formulated his most significant law of learning, the **law of effect,** which states:

> Of several responses made to the same situation, those which are accompanied or closely followed by satisfaction to the animal will, other things being equal, be more firmly connected with the situation, so that when it recurs, they will be more likely to recur; those which are accompanied or closely followed by discomfort to the animal will, other things being equal, have their connections with that situation weakened, so that, when it recurs, they will be less likely to occur. (Bolles, 1967, p. 435.)

Connectionism
The reinforced association of a stimulus and response in the mind.

Gestalt
A configuration or pattern of a psychological phenomena that is a whole entity.

Cognitive psychology
The study of new patterns, knowledge, or ideas in a dynamic and meaningful way.

Stimulus-response learning
The specific input of a response into the brain due to some external stimulation.

Satisfier
A term used by Thorndike to describe something that is pleasant or rewarding to an organism.

Annoyer
A term used by Thorndike to describe something that is unpleasant or punishing to an organism.

Law of effect
The theoretical position that holds that a reinforced response is learned and will likely recur.

Thorndike's **law of exercise** states that connections, or S-R bonds, are strengthened with use and weakened by disuse. "Exercise strengthens the bond between situation and response" (Thorndike, 1913, p. 127). *Strength* is used to mean the likelihood that a response will occur when the appropriate stimulus is given; *weakness* indicates a low likelihood of response due to disuse.

Although Thorndike developed several subordinate laws, no others had such serious implications for learning. After thirty years of scientific analysis, his theory underwent several modifications, some of which he reported in *The Fundamentals of Learning* (1932) and the *Psychology of Wants, Interests, and Attitudes* (1935). His two most important modifications are:

1. In his law of effect, the concept of annoying states (punishment) was modified. "Rewarding a connection always strengthened it substantially; punishing it weakened it little or not at all" (Thorndike, 1932, p. 58). Thorndike found that, if the consequences of punishment influenced learning at all, they forced the learner to try alternative responses rather than to halt the established response.

2. Thorndike disavowed his law of exercise because he could find no virtue in use or practice alone. Because learning resulted from reward, practice could be effective only if accompanied by reward. Practice itself was meaningless.

Contiguity

During the period of Thorndike's research, Russian psychologist I. P. Pavlov was experimenting with dogs in his laboratory. Combined with the work of the American psychologist J. B. Watson, Pavlov's research gave rise to the theory of **contiguity,** which was a variation of Thorndikean theory. The contiguity theorists also regarded learning as a matter of habit forming or pairing of stimulus and response: A connection is formed between sensations and behavior when elements of the two occur in close proximity to each other. The major differences between the two theories were a matter of timing and the need for reinforcement. The contiguity theorists proposed that the individual learns best when there is an almost simultaneous occurrence of a stimulus and response. If such states exist, reinforcement is not necessary for learning. They also suggested that much learning results simply from a person's doing something at the time that an unrelated stimulus is provided. Whatever the person was doing may then become a habituated response to that indirect stimulus. Pavlov's original **classical conditioning** studies provide a better understanding of this idea.

Classical Conditioning   In Pavlov's view, the formation of an association between a stimulus and a **reflex** (response)—the primary learning process—depends on the time proximity between the stimulus and the response. He first demonstrated this notion in 1902 with his study of dogs. Pavlov noticed that, when a dog was presented with meat powder, it

Unconditioned response
The automatic response to a natural, external stimulus.

Unconditioned stimulus
An environmental event capable of eliciting an unconditioned response. For example, food eliciting salivation.

Neutral stimulus
Any event in the environment that is incapable of eliciting a response from an organism.

Conditioned stimulus
The deliberate pairing of a neutral stimulus with an unconditioned stimulus in order to condition a response.

Conditioned response
A response that is controlled by its specific pairing with a conditioned stimulus.

Respondent conditioning
The term used by Skinner to describe the phenomenon Pavlov discovered in classical conditioning.

Frequency
The more frequently an organism makes a response to a stimulus, the more likely that it will respond to that stimulus again.

Recency
The more recently an organism has made a response to a stimulus, the more likely that the response will recur.

would salivate. He interpreted the flow of saliva as an unlearned response, labeling it an **unconditioned response** (UCR), and the presentation of the meat powder an **unconditioned stimulus** (UCS). He used the term *conditioning* because he was dealing with the unlearned "state of being" of the animal and was attempting to elicit an inherent response of that state to something other than the stimulus (the meat powder) instinctively associated with a response.

Working with this unlearned S-R connection in the dog and persuaded that any response pattern could be learned with the appropriate, simultaneous stimulus, Pavlov set up experimental conditions to get the dog to salivate when presented with a **neutral stimulus** (something other than the meat powder). Using a tuning fork, a bell, or a flash of light as the **conditioned stimulus** (CS), Pavlov would present the conditioned stimulus and immediately follow it with the meat powder (the UCS). Within the time sequence that the neutral stimulus and the meat powder were presented, the dog salivated. And after several trials (usually eight or nine), the dog began to salivate at the sensory stimuli (CS) even before the meat powder was presented. Thus, learning occurred. This type of behavior became known as a **conditioned response** (CR), later referred to as **respondent conditioning** by B. F. Skinner (1938).

Behaviorism   J. B. Watson's experiment in 1903 was done with rats running mazes. He believed that rats instinctively ran the mazes without consciousness and advocated that human behavior was similar. He held a position comparable to Pavlov's, that learning is a process of conditioning reflexes (responses) through the substitution of one stimulus for another, but rejected the Pavlovian idea that learning involves only externally observable behavior. Watson proposed that learning is the process of associating relevant stimuli with human beings' existing innate responses. He viewed human emotional responses, primarily fear, love, and anger, as innate and set out to show that emotional conditioning patterns exist among humans.

In his most famous experiment, Watson conditioned a young child (reportedly eight or nine months old) to fear a white rat (Watson & Raynor, 1920). In a child this age, Watson conjectured that the sound of a loud noise (UCS) would trigger an unconditioned fear response (UCR). He set up his experiment in much the same way as Pavlov's classical conditioning experiments with dogs. He paired a conditioned stimulus (the white rat) with an unconditioned stimulus (the loud noise) in order to substitute a conditioned response (fear of the rat) for the unconditioned one (fear of the noise). In just seven trials spaced over a week, Watson established a fear response in the child.

Watson also attempted to describe learning according to the principles of **frequency** and **recency.** His principle of frequency states that the more frequently the organism makes a response to a stimulus, the more likely the organism will give that response to that stimulus again. The principle of recency says that the more recently an organism has made a response to a stimulus, the more likely that the response will occur again.

In light of these two principles, Watson maintained that reward was not necessary for learning and regarded reward as an illogical explanation for the establishment of S-R bonds.

Extended Contiguity   E. R. Guthrie extended the Watsonian theories to all types of learning and rejected Thorndike's law of effect (Guthrie, 1940). He suggested that learning may be explained in one simple **law of association:** "A combination of stimuli which has accompanied a movement will on its recurrence tend to be followed by that movement" (Guthrie, 1952, p. 23). Thus, in Guthrie's view, if an organism responds to a contiguous stimulus, it will likely respond in the same way on subsequent presentations. In other words, when a conditioned stimulus and a conditioned response are paired, they are learned. We learn not by reinforcement, or even by success, but by doing.

Law of association
Learning occurs by the contiguous pairing of a stimulus and a response.

Guthrie (1952, p. 30) went even further in revising earlier theories of contiguity: "A stimulus pattern gains its full associative strength on the occasion of its first pairing with a response." He proposed (1) that learning takes place in one trial, (2) that learning is not improved with practice, and (3) that no reinforcement (reward) is necessary for learning to take place. Guthrie contended that an individual learns by doing and that associations have nothing to do with whether an individual learns correctly or incorrectly. Associations are made only in the initial, one-trial stimulus and response, and reward does not strengthen the learner's subsequent responses in any way.

Another of Guthrie's important contributions focused on techniques for changing behavior. He felt that behaviors could be replaced, but rarely broken or extinguished. In this sense, Guthrie was a forerunner of contemporary behavior modification techniques. His strategies were

1. *Threshold method.* This strategy involves presenting a stimulus in ways that reduce the likelihood of the response occurring. A situation may be less intense, reducing the student's tendency to respond. A teacher's glare at a student in order to stop disruptive behavior may be reduced to a glance or brief eye contact. The strength of the stimulus is reduced but the effect is the same.

2. *Fatigue method.* This strategy involves presenting a stimulus so often that the individual tires of the response. It is a very good way to change behavior. Many factors that have fatigue potential in them occur in school and out. During the fall, football fans often tire of the football on television and may turn to another show or stop watching television in order to avoid the stimulus.

3. *Incompatible stimuli method.* This is the presentation of a stimulus that has previously evoked an undesirable response when the individual is unable to respond (Guthrie, 1952). For example, a mother who always receives a disrespectful response (undesired) when she tells her children to clean their room may write the children a note in church when they cannot talk back. If a stimulus is presented when an undesired response cannot occur, its strength weakens.

The most prominent American learning theorist during the 1930s was Clark Hull. He was a connectionist who used Thorndike's law of effect as a basic part of his learning theory. His system is centered on **habit** (response) as a factor in learning behavior. He held that learning takes place through conditioning and reinforcement, thus rejecting Guthrie's idea of contiguity and one-trial learning.

Two interesting contributions evolved from Hullian theory: **primary reinforcement** and the **habit-family hierarchy.** Hull's law of primary reinforcement is basically a restatement of Thorndike's law of effect. Reinforcers, which Hull specified as reducers of a **drive** (a basic physiological need), strengthen the stimulus-response behaviors they accompany; responses not accompanied by reinforcers are not strengthened and in fact may be weakened (Hull, 1943). Out of this law come two conditions to learning: (1) It is necessary for a drive to be reduced. If drive reduction does not take place, there is no reinforcement and no learning. (2) The drive does not have to be eliminated, only temporarily diminished in strength. In fact, the continuing drive serves as a motivator, and motivation is fundamental to learning. Hull maintained that, when drive-stimulus conditions exist, they facilitate the response, which in turn reduces the drive, and learning occurs.

Hull's concept of habit-family hierarchy views the organism as being born with a set of inherent habits that vary in their potential to occur. His hierarchy is the ordering of the responses by their greatest likelihood to occur. The greater the drive, and the more likely that a particular response will reduce it, the higher the response ranks on the hierarchy.

Kenneth Spence was a contemporary of Clark Hull and undoubtedly did more than any other theorist to maintain the significance of his work. Although Spence's theory was a modification of Hull's, the two were so much alike that their positions have commonly been referred to as the Hull-Spence theory of learning (Logan, 1959).

Initially, Spence was convinced that the Thorndikean law of effect (Hull's reinforcement principle) applied to both cognitive and affective learning, but his research experiments at the University of Iowa in the 1940s (Spence & Lippitt, 1940, 1946) caused him to modify his ideas so that they contained elements of both reinforcement and contiguity theory.

Spence (1956, p. 33) defined conditioning with his own **empirical law of effect:** "Responses accompanied or followed by certain kinds of events (namely, reinforcers) are more likely to occur on subsequent occasions, whereas responses followed by certain other kinds of events (namely, nonreinforcers) do not subsequently show a greater likelihood of occurrence." For Spence, learning behavior is based on **excitatory potential** (the strength of an organism's tendency to give a specific response to a specific stimulus). This potential is facilitated by the variables of habit strength (the frequency of prior S-R bond associations and the permanency of learning), primary drive, and secondary motivation or **incentive.** Like Hull, Spence proposed that habit strength depends ex-

Habit
The tendency to repeat or maintain a behavior.

Primary reinforcement
Responses are paired to stimuli if they are capable of reducing the drive.

Habit-family hierarchy
The ordering of response tendencies in an organism by their likelihood to occur.

Drive
The motivational state of an organism set up by deprivation in the organism.

Empirical law of effect
Kenneth Spence's theory that responses that reduce drive are more likely to recur than those that do not.

Excitatory potential
The strength of the likelihood that a specific stimulus will trigger a specific response.

Incentive
The increase in the motivational state of an organism due to the reinforcement of an emitted response.

Variations in Principles		
Theorist	**Reinforcement**	**Contiguity**
Thorndike	Necessary for learning	Not necessary for learning
Pavlov	Not necessary	Necessary
Watson	Not necessary	Necessary
Guthrie	Not necessary	Necessary
Hull	Necessary	Not necessary
Spence	Not necessary: optimal, facilitates motivation	Necessary

clusively on the number of times a response occurs. However, in contrast to Hull, Spence stated that the initial response must be contiguous with the presentation of the stimulus. He also suggested (1951) that reinforcement is not necessary for establishing and strengthening stimulus-response bonds. Rather, the function of reinforcement is to facilitate incentive motivation. Thus, in Spence's view, reinforcement serves motivation and subsequent additional learning, rather than strengthening already established S-R bonds.

Perhaps the greatest shift in emphasis in learning theory since the Hullian approach was the systematic views of B. F. Skinner (1938, 1953). Writing within Thorndike's tradition of reinforcement theory, Skinner emphasizes two types of conditioning—respondent and **operant.** In Skinner's theory, respondent conditioning is that behavior elicited by some identifiable stimulus. The learning condition required within respondent conditioning is contiguity, which is effective only if a response is emitted in the presence of the stimulus. The associative strength of the S-R bond depends on the classical conditioning of the response and the stimulus, the same principle as that held by Pavlov, Watson, and Guthrie.

Operant conditioning
The voluntary behavior of an organism that acts upon the environment. The result is that the organism learns.

Although respondent conditioning is basic to Skinner's theory of learning, his concept of operant conditioning is a departure from previous theory and is most important to contemporary learning theory. Operant conditioning is a person's response to the environment. In contrast to respondent conditioning, no specific or identifiable stimulus consistently elicits operant behavior. Skinner views most human behavior as operant. We emit varying responses to various stimuli situations; they are not elicited (triggered) from us by some specific external stimulus or inherent grouping of S-R associations.

The likelihood of recurring operant responses, or learning, is found in Skinner's concept of reinforcement. If behavior is reinforced, it tends to be learned and repeated. Skinner (1953) prefers to use the term *reinforce-*

ment rather than *reward*. He feels that reward carries with it the connotations of a pleasurable event (Thorndike's satisfiers); whereas he views reinforcement as neutral and as increasing the probability of response, rather than ensuring that response. Skinner (1953) does not see any real problem in reinforcing human behavior. Simply to tell the learner that he or she has made the right response or even the learner's own knowledge of the results (the rightness) of the response are sufficient reinforcement. Skinner's concept of operant conditioning is based on Thorndike's law of effect, which has been modified somewhat into today's concept of reinforcement theory (Table 1-1).

Skinnerian theory has made a great contribution to classroom learning. For example, his knowledge-of-results principle is a very useful theory of reinforcement for classroom learning, because, in many learning situations, the reinforcement does not necessarily have to come from the teacher—just knowing that the right response has been emitted is enough for the learner. Another highly effective part of his theory relates to contiguity of reinforcement—the immediacy with which reinforcement can occur. When it occurs soon after the response, the learner can continually progress in a logical, sequential way. We can see the practical incorporation of Skinner's theoretical principles in the teaching machine (1958), programmed textbooks, and computer-assisted instruction. His ideas, built in the tradition of both associationism and stimulus-response research, and more appropriately called reinforcement, continue to be a major influence in contemporary interpretations and practices of learning. I discuss them in detail in Chapter 2.

Gestalt-Cognitive Learning

During the first two decades of this century, German psychologists were developing a major theory of learning as an alternative to stimulus-response learning. Max Wertheimer began the work in 1912, and Kurt Koffka (1924) and Wolfgang Kohler (1925) continued it. Wertheimer believed **perception,** not the collective association of ideas, is the key to learning. People have whole, meaningful perceptions, attending to aspects of their environment that have a significance to them.

Perception
Awareness of one of the senses by external stimulation.

Wertheimer believed that everything is complete within itself. He recognized that some things are made up of multiple parts, but these parts are complete and not dependent on each other to form the whole. Thus, the parts are interrelated in ways so that the whole cannot be inferred from them. The parts are not summative, but dynamically interrelated. Thus, to Wertheimer (1923), the whole is always greater than the sum of its parts. Thus, a finished product is always greater than the components that make it up. In contrast, the stimulus-response psychologist defines the whole as the sum of its parts. The word *gestalt*, meaning form or pattern, represents Wertheimer's system, and his theory is known as Gestalt psychology.

Table 1–1   The Evolution of Thorndike's Law of Effect

Psychologist	Law	Definition	Source
Thorndike	Original law of effect	"When a modifiable connection between a situation and a response is made and is accompanied or followed by a satisfying state of affairs, that connection's strength is increased; when made and accompanied or followed by an annoying state of affairs, its strength is decreased."	Thorndike, *Educational psychology, vol. II: The psychology of learning*, 1914, p. 12.
Thorndike	Truncated law of effect	"Rewarding a connection always strengthened it substantially; punishing it weakened it little or not at all."	Thorndike, Reward and punishment in animal learning. *Comparative Psychological Monographs*, 1932b, **8** (39), p. 58.
Hull	Primary reinforcement	"Whenever a response is closely followed by the reduction of a drive stimulus, there will result an increment in the tendency for that stimulus on subsequent occasions to evoke that reaction."	Hull, *Principles of behavior*, 1943, p. 68.
Spence	Empirical law of effect	"Responses accompanied or followed by certain kinds of events (namely, reinforcers) are more likely to occur on subsequent occasions, whereas responses followed by certain other kinds of events (namely, nonreinforcers) do not subsequently show a greater likelihood of occurrence."	Spence, *Behavior theory and conditioning*, 1956, p. 33.
Skinner	Operant conditioning	"If the occurrence of an operant [response] is followed by presentation of a reinforcing stimulus, the strength [of the response] is increased."	Skinner, *The behavior of organism*, 1938, p. 21.

Source: Thornburg (1973), p. 18. By permission of the author.

The Joy of First-Year Teaching

Henry Franklin, the principal of Parkover Elementary School, holds a conference with each new teacher during his or her first year. The principal and the new teacher leave school for one day to get away from all interruptions and discuss how the teacher is adjusting to and enjoying the initial teaching experience. Last week Mr. Franklin had his conference with Michael Spradley.

Mike talked about how well he thought he was adjusting to his first year of teaching, alternating his evaluation between the adequacy of his college preparation and the nature of the school environment in which he was working. Generally, he felt that the skills he had learned in a teacher preparation program were most helpful but weighted the school climate in which he was now functioning as the more significant variable in how successful he had been thus far.

Mike commented to Mr. Franklin, "I remember the first few weeks of school. I was very fresh, not knowing exactly what was expected of me or what I could expect from students. My greatest apprehension was whether or not I could relate to the students. I felt slightly fragile because of the newness of it all, but I believed that I would be a good teacher; so that reduced my feelings of vulnerability." Mr. Franklin reinforced Mike's sense of security and stated that he felt Mike had made very good initial adjustments to the school environment.

After spending the morning exchanging ideas about how both Mike and Mr. Franklin could continue making Mike's teaching experiences successful, Mike remarked, "I am really fortunate because the experience of teaching is very fulfilling to me and I have good relationships with my students. In addition, I have developed some strong associations with several staff members."

When lunch was over, Mr. Franklin reviewed some of his expectations for Mike and tried to get him to think of ways to continue to build on his success. Mr. Franklin said, "You must learn to deal with the things that are frustrating to you as well as enjoy your pleasant times. What kinds of frustrations have you felt thus far?"

Mike cited the three things that disturbed him the most. First, he was surprised that so many students had little motivation to learn and wondered how he would be able to generate more incentives for them. Second, he could not understand why teachers talked so negatively about students, particularly in the teachers' lounge. Sometimes he avoided the lounge because of its negative atmosphere. Finally, he mentioned one boy who suffered from gross parental neglect and wondered what he might be able to do to help this student out. In addition, he questioned how many other students were in similar situations that he did not know about.

Mr. Franklin's experience was useful here. He reminded Mike that students come from diverse backgrounds and family situations and many of them get no real incentive for learning and experiencing in either their home or school environments. He suggested that, as Mike identifies students who need help, he ask the counselor or school psychologist for some suggestions. Mike was surprised that Mr. Franklin felt the same way about the teachers' lounge. Nevertheless, Mr. Franklin noted that this is an important environment for teachers and that the many dialogues and idea exchanges that occur there might offset the negative comments made. He was not justifying his teachers' behavior, only pointing out that this is one of many teacher behaviors and, to some extent, it is to be expected.

As the day drew to a close, Mike summarized his experiences as reasonably positive, fulfilling, and, at times, most exhilarating. He indicated that he fully intended to make a career of teaching. Mr. Franklin concurred that Mike seemed to have made a strong beginning in this school and suggested that many students would learn much from Mike. He encouraged Mike to think of ways to continue his positive experiences and was pleased that Mike was career oriented. The next day

Mike faced twenty-nine students; Mr. Franklin had to deal with several problems that had come up on his day away from school. At lunch time, they briefly exchanged notes and laughed. Indeed, today was another day of education at Parkover Elementary School.

What Do You Think?

1. Is the principal's strategy effective?

2. As a first-year teacher, would you like the opportunity to be evaluated on a highly personal basis as Mike was?

3. Is Mike still too naive about teaching to know whether he intends to pursue it as a lifelong career?

Laws of Organization

Wertheimer believed that the environment is organized in ways that are meaningful to individuals. He advanced the concept of **figure** to explain the things within our environment that stand out or are focused upon. A figure always stands in relation to the larger environment, which he called **ground.** We perceptually interact with the total environment (ground), from which specific events, ideas, or objects may stand out (figure). Classroom teachers, for example, may view the classroom as the teaching environment (ground), although from time to time they may attend specifically to one student (figure). The classroom is a perceptual whole. The student is both a whole and a part of that classroom. These perceptual relationships generate meaning to the learner.

Wertheimer's four primary laws of organization explain how perception operates. They are the laws of proximity, similarity, common direction, and simplicity.

Law of Proximity The greater the proximity of elements within a field, the more likely they are perceived to go together. In the classroom, teachers can organize instructional materials so that students perceive relationships between events. For example, a teacher might list the numbers one through twelve in a straight line, which students may recognize as the numbers one through twelve. A teacher may also arrange these numbers in a clockwise circle, which students may now perceive not just as numbers, but as the face of a clock. Figure 1–1 illustrates the **law of proximity.**

Law of Similarity Items with similar features (shape or color, for example) will likely be grouped together. Figure 1–2 illustrates this phe-

Figure
A Gestalt term used to describe phenomena in our environment that perceptually stand out.

Ground
A Gestalt term used to describe the total environment of which we are aware at any given time.

Figure 1–1
Arranging the numbers one through twelve to illustrate the law of proximity

Law of proximity
Our perception that things in the environment go together.

23

Figure 1–2

Grouping objects to illustrate the law of similarity

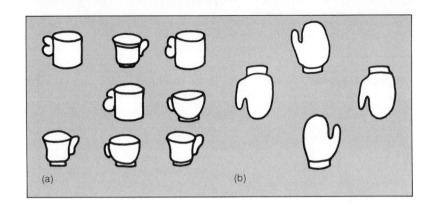

(a)   (b)

Law of similarity
The grouping together of objects or events in the environment that are perceived to go together.

Law of common direction
The belief that geometric shapes will be grouped together if they complete an object or concept.

Law of simplicity
The Gestalt explanation of symmetry in the environment. Environment is viewed as simple, regular patterns.

nomenon. If first-grade students were asked how many cups there are, would they be able to answer eight? The **law of similarity** implies yes, although a child who failed to see similarity among the three shapes of cups would not be as likely to give the correct answer. How many first graders would answer that there are four mittens in Figure 1–2? The mittens are more similar than the cups, but the student unable to see similarity between the mittens pointing in opposite directions is likely to respond incorrectly.

Law of Common Direction   This law states that a set of points will be grouped if they appear to complete or continue a series. Simple line drawings, geometric figures, two- and three-dimensional art, and architecture are examples of how the **law of common direction** operates.

Law of Simplicity   A learner sees the perceptual field in simple, regular patterns. Wertheimer stressed the characteristics of symmetry, smoothness, and regularity as important perceptual qualities. The **law of simplicity** operates where individuals are comparing objects or ideas with highly similar characteristics. For example, will a person who learns the shape "round" also generalize the concept to a "less round" figure, such as an egg or the moon when it is in three-quarter phase? Will a math student be able to perceive the relationships in repeating decimals? These learning possibilities fall within the scope of the law of simplicity.

Extensions of Gestalt Psychology

Koffka, who made an avid attack on Thorndike's connectionism, extended Gestalt psychology. He emphasized two laws of learning: proximity and closure (1935).

The law of proximity always deals with the relationship between objects. The greater the proximity between two things, the greater the likelihood of their being perceived as fitting or belonging together. Figure 1–3 illustrates this process. This is an example of a task that could be given to fourth graders. The students are given ten lines with varying proximities to each other (part A). The teacher asks the students to make rectangles out of as many lines as they can. According to the law of proximity, those with the narrower distance between them would be perceived as the ones to group. Part B illustrates that three rectangles would be completed. If the teacher asks the students to make rectangles using all the lines, then the students' perception is being qualified and the law of proximity is not the learning principle involved. The student response would look like part C in Figure 1–3. Understanding the concept "rectangle" is a more advanced learning state than perception. Students would have to understand this concept to solve the problem correctly.

The **law of closure** states that the more completely something is perceived, the more likely it is to be thought of as complete. Part D in Figure 1–3 illustrates this concept. The horizontal lines, even though short, are directional, telling the learner that there is a relationship between pieces or lines that complete the rectangle (something part A did not do). The horizontal (connecting) lines need not be complete—they are perceived as being related. This is an important aspect of the learning process. As learners perceive relationships between thoughts and actions, their learning increases. The relationship between ideas is an important process in the ability to complete an idea, thought process, or action.

Kohler gained recognition through his experiments with apes during World War I. Their ability to carry out simple problem-solving behaviors caused Kohler to advance the concept of **insight,** which has subsequently

Law of closure
The theory that things perceived to be complete are complete.

Insight
The sudden awareness of relationships between things.

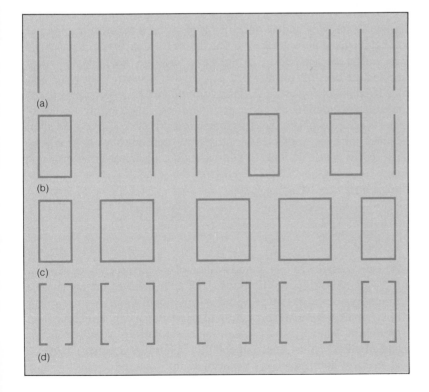

Figure 1–3
Examples of the laws of proximity and closure

become important in cognitive psychology. Insight is a sudden awareness or perception of relationships between things that heretofore seemed unrelated. In the vernacular, it is often called the "Aha!" or "Eureka!" phenomenon. The insight the apes used to solve problems caused Kohler to reject Thorndike's trial-and-error learning.

In one of his experiments, Kohler hung a banana from the top of the ape's cage, clearly out of reach. He put a box in the cage. If the animal moved the box into the right position, it could reach the banana. After several apes had solved this problem, Kohler designed a two-box experiment in which the apes had to stack one box on top of the other to reach the banana. This experiment proved to be much more difficult, and Kohler observed many errors in perception prior to the apes' learning to build the two-box structure in order to reach the banana.

A third type of experiment Kohler conducted involved placing the banana outside the cage. In the cage were sticks, which the apes could use to reach the banana. Some sticks were long enough to reach the banana (as in the single-box problem), and some had to be joined together to obtain it (as in the two-box problem). In this experiment, one ape eventually saw the relationship between the objects to be manipulated in order to gain food, a process Kohler called **insight learning.**

Insight learning
The theory that through perception people can put things together, which results in learning and problem solutions.

The advantage of these experiments from a gestalt point of view is that all the elements required are within the animal's perceptual environment. As Hill (1977) observed, it is different from stimulus-response experiments, where an animal runs a maze and is unable to see any relationship between the starting point and the end point. This contrast in experiments is not unlike many classroom situations. First, often within a classroom, only the teacher is aware of the desired learning outcome, leaving the students unduly dependent upon the teacher. If the teacher would state the goals-objectives for the day or the unit, the students would have greater understanding of the tasks. Second, students are often expected to see the relationship among things when they have only limited understanding of some of the components. Let us compare it with Kohler's stick experiments. The apes, regardless of their insight, would not have solved the problem by using only one short stick. If a second short stick had not been available, the problem would not have been solved. When teachers ask students to combine ideas or solve problems using multiple resources, they must be sure that the students have acquired the learning necessary to such solutions.

Field Theory

Life space
The totality of the individual in his or her perceived physical and psychological environment at any given time.

Kurt Lewin presented a major modification of Gestalt psychology when he introduced the concept of **life space** (1935). He believed that we live in a dynamic field of forces that move us toward a goal. Goals are not strictly learning goals, but depend on individual motivation and personality. Thus, his insightful learning was a means-end relationship where goals are identified and dynamic environmental forces propel a person toward a goal. In this system, a person's behavior at any given moment is the com-

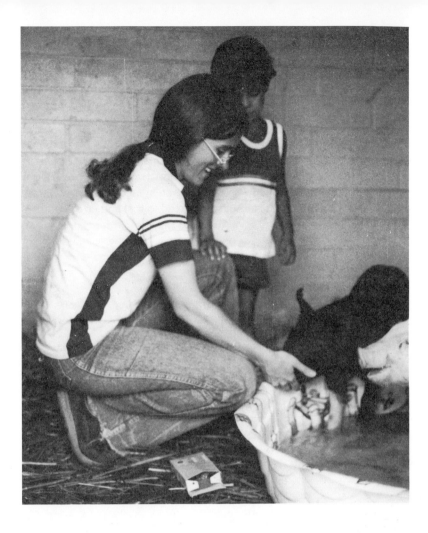

bined result of all forces operating simultaneously in the person's environment (Lewin, 1951).

In simplest terms, a person's life space is the immediate **psychological environment.** This environment is made up of the objects and events that the person perceives as important. Thus, we interact with our psychological environment. Because human behavior is goal oriented, it is always meaningful. Within our environment, there are both positive and negative perceptions and barriers that might impede progress toward a goal, just as there are forces that facilitate goal attainment. To Lewin, human behavior could not occur in a vacuum; thus, all behavior, whether positive or negative, facilitating or nonfacilitating, is goal directed.

Psychological environment
The objects, events, or attitudes within a person's environment that are perceived as important.

Cognitive Psychology

The contemporary movement that has its roots in Gestalt psychology is cognitive psychology. Concern focuses on the cognitive structure and the dynamics involved in learning and processing information. Insight is the basic sense of relationships between things. If you have insight into the environment, you can attach meaning to things. If you have meaningful relationships in the environment, higher level learning occurs. Bruner (1956) advanced this concept by indicating that learners continuously explore within the environment. In the process, they discover new ideas, meanings, and relationships. Ausubel (1968) has also advanced the idea that learning occurs only in a meaningful environment. Like his predecessors, Ausubel focused on the means-end relationship. He believed that, if the learner has a sense of purpose and direction, learning is more likely to occur. Ausubel contended that, where no meaningful pattern exists in our psychological environment, learning is reduced to trial and error.

Contemporary cognitive positions focus on **concepts** and **problem solving,** the subject of Chapter 4. Concepts are ways to categorize or internally represent multiple pieces of information. They imply understanding or comprehension. Concepts are important because things, either physical or functional, can be classified as the same group or set of events. Thus, we can efficiently process and store much information. Ausubel (1968) described this as concept formation, the mechanism by which the learner discovers relationships (the similarities within a class of objects) and gradually obtains a working concept through experience within or outside of the classroom.

Concepts are important because of their generalizability. If you understand (conceptualize) something and then encounter a similar situation, you can generalize your understanding from one learning situation to the other because you understand their similarities. This ability to understand is a function of the relationship between your state of knowledge and your present environment. When you interrelate the existing learning environment within your existing mental state, learning results.

The extension of concept learning is problem solving (the ability to make decisions or choices). Ausubel (1968) described such learning behavior as the extension of cognitive functioning beyond the information given within a situation. In order for this to occur, you must relate the immediate situation to your cognitive structure, which you learned through previously related and meaningful situations. The net effect is that you do not solve most problems independent of your existing cognitive structure, but rather by integrating or reorganizing the structure to cope with the problem at hand (Bruner, 1956).

Cognitive psychology accounts for higher level and more complex experiences than stimulus-response psychology. You perceive the psychological aspects of your personal, social, and physical environments, which encompass you cognitively, affectively, and behaviorally. As you perceive events within these environments as meaningful, you learn to conceptualize information, and acquire problem-solving strategies. In an increasingly complex world, where learning processes must consider myriad phenomena, cognitive psychology has the potential to explain meaningful human behavior in ways that are enriching and relevant to the learner. As Combs (1979) has observed, learning is a personal, human process; it is more than stimulus-response behavior and consequences. Education must move in meaningful directions because, by its very nature, learning is deeply human.

Concept
The internal representation of multiple ideas and attitudes by classifying them into previously established categories.

Problem solving
The ability to make decisions or choices by using multiple pieces of learned information.

Social Learning Theory

A major interpretation of reinforcement theory emerged in the 1960s with the **social learning** concepts of Albert Bandura. He was able to demonstrate learning from models, a phenomenon earlier theories did not conceive of. Bandura and Walters (1963) established that learning occurs through observing the behavior of others even though the ob-

Social learning theory
The formal term used to describe the various processes by which Albert Bandura postulates human learning occurs.

server does not act out (reproduce) the behavior. Bandura (1969, 1977a) believes that observing a model results in the following behaviors:

1. The learner (observer) may acquire new responses.
2. The learner may strengthen existing responses or may reduce the tendency to continue responding in some way (inhibition).
3. The learner may recall or reestablish already learned or forgotten responses.

Bandura (1965a) made it clear that social learning theory is not simply trial and error. He believes that individuals can greatly increase their response repertoire through imitation: "Almost any learning outcome that results from direct experience can also come about on a vicarious basis through observation of other people's behaviors and its consequences for them" (Bandura, 1967, p. 78). Thus, learning results from attending to a model as well as through reproducing the model's behavior.

I discuss Bandura's theory in detail in Chapter 5. Here I present some significant aspects of it to provide a broader perspective from which to view other learning theories and models.

Symbolic model
Something in the environment that is designed to represent the real things, for example, cartoon characters or situation comedies.

Self-reinforcement
The recognition of and satisfaction with our own behavior.

Affective learning
The process through which we acquire emotions, drives, or temperament associated with our feeling state instead of our thought processes.

Proximal goals
The ability to move toward goals that we have a desire to achieve.

1. Individuals learn from **symbolic models** as well as from real-life models. Bandura, Ross, and Ross (1963a) used film-mediated models to show that children exposed to aggressive models learn and demonstrate the same behaviors without reinforcement.
2. Bandura (1977a, p. 37) has demonstrated that "observational learning occurs through symbolic processes during exposure to modeled activities before any responses have been performed and does not necessarily require extrinsic reinforcement." Reinforcement may accompany the modeling process but is not required in order for learning to occur.
3. **Self-reinforcement** is important in modeling. Most stimulus-response explanations require external reinforcement. However, Bandura (1969) contends that self-reinforcement may be more important than external reinforcement, especially in older children and adults. The ability to evaluate your own behavior and be satisfied or dissatisfied with it is part of the self-reinforcement process, a characteristic of human behavior that sets humans apart from animals.
4. Bandura uses social learning to explain the acquisition of attitudes (**affective learning**) as well as intellectual skills (cognitive learning). His is the first major system of learning that accounts for learning equally in these two areas.
5. Bandura (1977b, 1982) has found that **proximal goals** serve in the development of self-perceptions of efficacy. Standards are needed against which people can judge their performance. This aspect of Bandura's model also bridges some of the differences between more traditional reinforcement and cognitive positions.

Social learning theory implies that people are strong models of behavior for other people, which is likely to be true in the child-adult

relationship. When you perceive another as significant, you are more likely
to observe and adopt much of that person's behavior. Teachers should not
underestimate the extent to which they serve as models for students. Much
student behavior aligns itself with teacher expectation, teacher behavior,
or desirable teacher characteristics.

Hierarchical Learning

Gagne's (1970b) **hierarchical learning** deals primarily with the prerequisite conditions of different types of learning, from simple to complex.
His theory relies heavily on the cumulative and orderly effects of learning. Although he writes within the S-R tradition, the complexity of human
learning brings Gagne (1965, p. 60) to consider a hierarchy: "The attempt is made to show that each variety of learning begins with a
different state of the organism and learning begins with a different ca-

Hierarchical learning
The arrangement of acquired
responses into a hierarchy from
simple to complex.

Chapter 1
The Learning Process

31

pability for performance." He proposes eight types of learning, which he considers cumulative because each more complex level of learning depends on the prerequisite knowledge or learning of a lower level of performance (Gagne, 1970b).

Gagne (1980) also suggests that the current shift of views toward learning from the older notion of connectionism—establishing S-R bonds—to a computer-based notion of **information processing** has some important implications for instructional strategies. Gagne's (1970a, p. 468) idea that stimuli are "processed in quite a number of different ways by the human central nervous system, and that understanding learning is a matter of figuring out how the various processes operate" can be related to instructional procedure in the following ways:

1. Each learner enters a new learning task with a different set of prerequisite skills. For effective instruction, the teacher must take into account what the learner does and does not already know. This means diagnostic testing.

2. The most important guide to assessing student needs for a behavioral objective is the related prerequisite skills and information that the student has not yet mastered.

3. Well-planned, periodic reviews of materials should be given to ensure retention.

4. Students should be taught strategies of **coding,** which involves presenting material so that the student can transform it into a form that makes it easier to process, then remember, later.

Because Gagne's model accounts for the various types of classroom learning more than most other contemporary learning theories, many of his concepts recur in my discussions of learning and instruction.

Information Processing

Another explanation of human learning comes from an information-processing model. No longer satisfied with studying external, observable behavior, some learning psychologists and educators started to study the internal cognitive processes that underlie human behavior. The concept originated in experimental psychology and computer technology and combined and interrelated linear sequences to process masses of information (Hilgard & Bower, 1975; Snow, 1980). The more recent approaches have shifted toward the cognitive approach, in which the processing of information into short- and long-term memory are the central issues (Atkinson & Shiffrin, 1971; DeCorte, 1980).

Two aspects of human behavior—conceptual learning and **complex learning**—cannot be effectively explained using the reinforcement model. Conceptual information is processed (encoded) in the mind so that it has meaning for the individual. It is also related to other existing concepts or information; thus, these interrelationships produce additional learning (more concepts). Human behavior is purposeful activity that

Information processing
The storing and retrieving of information in the mind. While in storage, information may interact, thus forming new capacities.

Coding
The translation of information, either verbally or visually, into the mind so it may be stored.

Complex learning
The acquisition of information or skills that contain multiple components, thus multiple behavioral potential.

32

varies in complexity. Complex actions or behaviors contain more components than simple ones. The greater the number of components, the
more they must be interrelated if they are to have meaning to the
learner. Complex behaviors are processed coherently in the mind so that
they are useful to the learner now and in the future. Several information-processing models account for the range of variables affecting
learning, memory, and retention (Bransford, 1979; Craik & Lockhart,
1972; Resnick & Glaser, 1976).

All models begin with input into the learner, whether this input is
labeled stimuli, information, perception, or instructional materials (see
Figure 1–4). According to Bransford, as the learner responds, the stimuli
are represented as **auditory information** or **visual information,** which
temporarily register on the senses. Some aspect of the sensory system
must pay attention to the information or it will not register and it will
disappear (Gage & Berliner, 1984; Joyce, 1979).

Bransford's model assumes that information that has registered on
the senses can enter **short-term memory.** "Though its retention in the
sensory register is limited, information can remain in short-term memory
indefinitely, provided that it is actively rehearsed" (Bransford, 1979, p. 37).

Auditory information
The term used in Bransford's
information-processing model to
describe learning that is initially
received through hearing.

Visual information
The term used in Bransford's
information processing model to
describe learning that is initially
received through seeing.

Short-term memory
The retention of learned material for
a very specific purpose for a short
duration.

33

Figure 1–4
*Bransford's information-processing
model of memory. [Source:
Bransford (1979), p. 37. By
permission of the publisher.]*

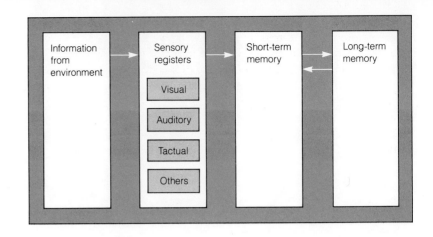

A variety of studies on short-term memory, many of which I discuss in Chapter 10, clearly establishes its usefulness and its limitations. Short-term memory has a specific usefulness, typically for a very brief time. For example, short-term memory is operating when you look up a telephone number to dial or remember a name throughout the evening at a party. The goal of most instruction is to have students process learning into **long-term memory.**

Long-term memory
The retention of learned material for an extended time through encoding of information into the mind.

Concept Summary 1–2

Learning Theories and Theorists	
Theorist	**Theory**
S-R Psychology	
E. L. Thorndike	Connectionism
I. P. Pavlov	Classical conditioning
J. B. Watson	Behaviorism
Edwin R. Guthrie	Contiguity (extended)
Clark L. Hull	Reinforcement theory
Kenneth W. Spence	Reinforcement theory
B. F. Skinner	Operant conditioning
Albert Bandura	Social learning theory
Robert M. Gagne	Hierarchical learning
Gestalt-Cognitive Psychology	
Max Wertheimer	Gestalt psychology
Kurt Koffka	Gestalt psychology
Wolfgang Kohler	Insight
Kurt Lewin	Cognitive-field
Jerome Bruner	Discovery learning
Davis Ausubel	Cognitive psychology
John Bransford	Information processing

Long-term retention or memory allows us to store and retrieve important information across an extended time frame. The more meaningful and conceptual information is, the more likely we are to store it in long-term memory. The storage capacity in long-term memory is unlimited. The critical element is whether the information is perceived as important enough to process it, thus increasing the amount of information in storage. I discuss teacher and learner strategies that are useful in transferring learning from short-term to long-term memory and in maintaining learned behavior across time in Chapter 10.

Do Humans Recapitulate History?

All processes start out as simple functions. Across time, people have discovered complex and integrated thoughts because simple thoughts were in place. However complex your current thought processes are, they are a result of an extensive learning history that includes simple facts and dynamic ideas. Stimulus-response learning is one way to explain the simple thought processes all of us have or have had. The countless thousands of pieces of information struggling relentlessly within our minds contribute to our learning dynamics. As we become increasingly older and complex, simple connections give way to more elaborate processes such as those cognitive theorists describe. However, our early and simple learning histories are essential.

No doubt Max Wertheimer was right when he said that E. L. Thorndike's simple connectionism does not account for a wide range of human capability. This observation did not negate what Thorndike did; rather, it posited that he did not do enough. Thus, a second major way to describe human functioning emerged. The realization that we are meaningful organisms that affect our environment, rather than simply being affected by it, was critical.

Now evaluate yourself. Do you see how most of your behaviors are related to meeting your personal needs or goals? Do you recognize that many of your personal traits are a result of your unique ways of assembling your ideas and experiences? Just as stimulus-response psychology has to recognize the important human cognitive functions, so cognitivists must realize that many complex thought processes are grounded in simpler processes. In the same way that a child gradually becomes a youth, an adolescent, then an adult, with increasing age come new abilities to function that are due partly to age, learning, experiences, and personal integration of all these factors.

Which then? S-R or cognitive? This argument has gone on for sixty years and will continue. In a sense, it is a moot point because the answer is not forthcoming and it is unlikely to impact on how we function. Let me give you an example.

When I was ten years old, like many ten-year-olds, I wanted to become a big league baseball player. Besides playing baseball every chance I had, I studied baseball and its history, learning as much about the game and its players as I could. Did you know that, in 1927, Babe Ruth, when playing for the New York Yankees, hit sixty home runs? Who cares, you say! Precisely! Why would a university professor still know an isolated piece of information thirty-five years later? Stimulus-response psychology would say I had been reinforced for that information so much that it has unbelievable habit strength. Cognitive psychology would say that, because I once aspired to be a professional baseball player, the information has meaning to me; thus, it is more than just a fact. What remains today is a relatively useless piece of information floating around in my head, and I cannot explain why it has been maintained for so long. So it is with most of us; our learning histories impact upon today as a result of learning in accordance with both theoretical systems. The dominant issue is how we use what we have learned, an issue largely determined by situational contexts.

I want you to follow the next three steps and go no further:

1. Identify a behavior you currently engage in regularly that you learned from either your father or mother.

2. Determine what kind of a personal need this behavior fulfills.

3. Evaluate whether you like the behavior.

You cannot take the fourth step unless you have completed the first three. When you have, try to analyze how you learned the behavior. Not an easy task, is it? In fact, you probably cannot describe how it did come about. But there are aspects of this situation you can describe, namely, steps one through three.

The purpose of this discussion is not to confuse you. Rather, it is to say that there are two major ways of learning that have been established historically. These systems of thought add to our understanding of human behavior even though we cannot always identify or isolate specific contributing factors. Throughout the chapter, I have tried to indicate the historical basis for much of our contemporary understanding of learning and the factors that affect it. Because of early learning experiences and our increasingly advanced states of knowledge, we can now explore the topic in greater detail. It is important that you understand the material in Chapter 1 as you work your way through Chapters 2 through 5, where I discuss contemporary learning processes.

Annotated Readings

Fishman, D. B., & Neigher, W. D. (1982). American psychology in the eighties: Who will buy it? *American Psychologist, 37,* 533–546.

> *The authors look at the field of psychology and its relevance in the 1980s, given the changes occurring in society and in the science of psychology. The article sets forth a planning model that contains nine action proposals for psychologists. Some conclusions include more applied research, more consumer-oriented results, and a better cost-effectiveness ratio. The authors conclude that the field of psychology may be required to undergo major shifts if it is to remain viable.*

Laosa, L. M. (1982). School, occupation, culture, and family: The impact of parental schooling on the parent-child relationship. *Journal of Educational Psychology, 74,* 791–827.

> *Laosa looks at the impact of parental interaction with children on the children's ability to learn and advances two hypotheses: (1) that our successful schooling experiences will affect how much, as a parent, we will interact with our children and (2) that parental behavior will have important consequences for a child's acquisitions of cognitive skills, learning strategies, and personality characteristics. The primary focus is a conceptual and empirical examination of the impact of schooling on the parent-child relationship.*

Peterson, P. L., Swing, S. R., Braverman, M. T., & Buss, R. (1982). Students' aptitudes and their reports of cognitive processes during direct instruction. *Journal of Educational Psychology, 74,* 535–547.

> *These researchers investigated students' ability to recall information learned from direct instruction. They administered a stimulated recall interview schedule to fifth- and sixth-grade students. Results of the study revealed that student understanding of the direct instruction material was related to achievement. Students who reported using cognitive strategies, such as relating information being learned to previous learning, did better on the achievement test than those who did not report such strategies.*

Ripple, R. E. (1982) The many faces of educational psychology. *Bulletin of the Hong Kong Psychological Society,* No. 7, 35–46.

> *The author summarizes the field of educational psychology within the behavioral setting. He presents the various components (for example, teacher characteristics, learner characteristics, and subject matter) in a dynamic, interactive model describing how the model can be applied to diverse behavioral settings, including within the context of Chinese culture and educational settings. It is a most intriguing application of our understanding of educational psychology.*

Scandura, J. M., Frase, L. T., Gagne, R. M., Stolurow, K. A. C., Stolurow, L. M., & Groen, G. J. (1978). Current status and future directions of educational psychology as a discipline. *Educational Psychologist, 13,* 43–56.

> *This is a very comprehensive document prepared by leaders in the field of educational psychology. Its purpose is to describe and forecast the field. It focuses on national needs relevant to the discipline of educational psychology, the current status of educational psychology as a discipline, promising advances in educational psychology, and recommendations for the future of the field. For individuals desiring an overview of the field of educational psychology, this article is most important.*

Sprinthall, N. A., & Thies-Sprinthall, L. (1980). Educating for teacher growth: A cognitive developmental perspective. *Theory into Practice, 19,* 278–286.

The authors conceptualize the need for teacher training and teacher growth with the goals of cognitive developmental psychology. References are made to the works of Jean Piaget, Lawrence Kohlberg, Jane Loevinger, David Hunt, and William Perry as different ways to conceptualize human development. Further discussion focuses on how to match students' learning environments to various stages of development, as represented by the previously cited theorists. This article is well conceived in light of the emerging national interest in human development as an explanation of human learning.

Reinforcement Theory

Sally Jones is a first-year teacher at Glenwood Elementary School. She teaches in a self-contained fifth-grade classroom. As the school year develops, Sally observes that the variance in student learning is enormous. If she is going to be effective, she will have to use small group and individualized instruction. In order to maintain learning in several smaller groups, she decides to use reinforcement to keep students actively involved in the subject matter. On the whole, Sally is pleased with the results of her effort, although she has observed that one small group (two boys and three girls) is not doing as well in science as when they were in large group instruction.

One day Sally decides to have a meeting with the school principal and the curriculum supervisor to discuss her strategies and ask if they have any ideas about why one group has started learning less in science. She is surprised and confused by what ensues.

Mr. Markham, the curriculum supervisor, tells Sally that so many different teachers have tried so many different things across the years that virtually anything can work or not work. He suggests that Sally alter her science teaching by moving back into large group instruction, at least in that subject area. He does not believe in reinforcement; he thinks fifth graders ought to be motivated enough to work on their own. He said, "This reinforcement stuff is a bunch of bunk. They either get it or they don't."

Ms. Leifer, the principal, commends Sally on her attempts to make learning more relevant and likely to occur, although she is worried about how taxing small group and individualized instruction is for Sally. She also suggests one explanation for the students' lower learning rate that Sally had not thought about: "Maybe this particular group of students is not getting reinforced as much or as consistently as they had been used to. In other words, in moving from group to group, you may inadvertently be giving less attention to this group than you realize."

As a result of the meeting, Sally has two perspectives to consider, although she clearly favors Ms. Leifer's ideas. She knows reinforcement works because she has repeatedly used it successfully. She also believes that small group and individualized instruction helps meet student needs better than large group instruction. It is really a matter of Sally continuing to work with students, trying different

41

reinforcement strategies with different groups until she hits upon the right combination for each one.

Reinforcement can be a useful instructional tool. To use it effectively, you should understand the underlying theory. To help you do so, this chapter discusses:

■ *Respondent conditioning*
■ *Operant conditioning*
■ *Methods of response management*

Conditioning is the process whereby we influence organisms (human and animal) to behave in certain ways. When a behavior occurs, we must infer that learning has occurred. For stimulus-response theorists, this established behavior is always observable. They do not make inferences as to the causes (reasons) for behavior; they assume that a person's behavior is dependent on the environmental conditions in force at the time. For example, assume that two eight-year-olds had a fight on the playground and as a result learned to dislike each other. The dislike is a learned behavior. According to S-R theory, either student could serve as a stimulus to evoke the dislike feeling in the other if it manifests itself some way, such as verbal abuse, negative body language, or physical confrontation. The environmental conditions must exist in order for this dislike to occur. Dislike is never inferred; it must be observed.

Skinner was the first learning psychologist to incorporate Pavlov's classical conditioning and Thorndike's trial-and-error learning into one theoretical framework. He labeled Pavlov's concepts *respondent conditioning* and Thorndike's, *operant conditioning*. Skinner recognized these systems as two different kinds of learning and placed greater emphasis on operant conditioning because he believed it best accounts for most human behavior. In this chapter, I discuss both respondent and operant conditioning, emphasizing the latter because it typifies behavior manifested by learners in school environments.

Respondent Conditioning

Respondent conditioning is the simplest type of human learning. Through laboratory experimentation with dogs, Pavlov (1927) determined that organisms have a strong, involuntary stimulus-response relationship, which he called reflexive behavior. He termed the components of this untrained relationship, or pairing, the unconditioned stimulus (UCS) and unconditioned response (UCR). A UCS is any stimulus that has the ability to elicit a response in an organism on a regular and measurable basis and without prior training. A UCR is the behavior the organism exhibits in reaction to the UCS.

Pavlov's famous learning procedure, which became known as classical conditioning, involved substituting a controllable stimulus for the UCS. The controllable stimulus, which he called the conditioned stimulus

(CS), did not originally elicit a response from the organism but came to do so by being paired with the UCS. In Pavlov's experiments, the pairing of the two stimulus events occurred with the CS (a sound) first and the UCS (food) just momentarily delayed, the process of contiguity. After several pairings of the CS (a sound) with the UCS (food), Pavlov noticed that the subject would respond (salivate) to the auditory stimulus (CS) without the presence of the food (UCS). Pavlov called this new response the conditioned response (CR), conditioned because the dog learned a new response or behavior that is conditioned upon the presentation of the previously neutral stimulus (a sound), now the CS. In effect, the CS signals the organism that the UCS is about to appear. The dog salivated when hearing the CS because it anticipated that the UCS was immediately forthcoming. Pavlov demonstrated that reflexive (involuntary) responses could be conditioned—that is, could be learned in relation to new stimuli.

Figure 2–1 shows two models of respondent conditioning. The solid lines represent bonding relationships; the broken lines represent the

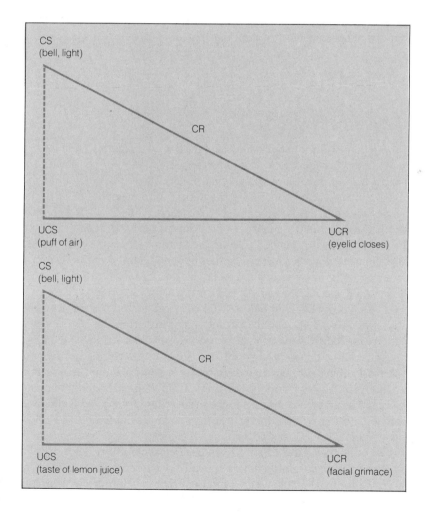

Figure 2–1
Examples of respondent conditioning. [Source: Thornburg (1973b), p. 82. By permission of the author.]

principle of contiguity. Generally, such conditioned responses are learned within ten trials. On the average, Pavlov's dogs took nine trials to learn the CS-CR relationships, and the child subject of Watson's (Watson & Raynor, 1920) conditioned emotions experiment took seven trials. The learned CS-CR response tends to be retained if it is useful.

The idea of respondent conditioning, particularly for human learning, focuses on the CS-CR relationship. Early in development, the infant demonstrates certain reflexive responses that arise out of physiological needs. When babies have a physiological need, such as hunger or physical discomfort, they make some automatic, involuntary response (usually crying) so someone will fill the need. If the sound of an alarm clock accompanies an infant's morning hunger pains or the discomfort of wet diapers, it may become associated with the unconditioned response (crying). The child may later respond in the same way to the secondary event (the sound of the alarm), regardless of whether the physiological need exists. Thus, the child establishes a CS-CR relationship.

Respondent learning is not what students commonly experience in a classroom. Teachers are not in a position to set up a deprivation state in students' learning. Respondent conditioning is reflex based, and the school curriculum is designed around nonreflexive behaviors. The knowledge-building type of learning that does occur in the classroom is more adequately described by operant conditioning.

Operant Conditioning

Thorndike first formulated reinforcement theory. From his early experiments with cats, he found that, after exploring various possibilities of escape from a puzzle box, they would finally hit on the solution to the door latch and escape. The more frequently Thorndike put the cat in the puzzle box, the quicker it tended to escape. Out of such behavior, Thorndike developed the law of effect. The cat's escape (response) from the box (stimulus) produced a satisfying state of affairs (reward or reinforcement) for the animal, thus increasing the likelihood of the response recurring under the same stimulus conditions. Essentially, a specific response to a specific stimulus is stamped into the cat's brain.

This type of learning differs from respondent conditioning in three ways. First, although operant learning may result from the stimulus of a basic physiological need, the response in operant learning is voluntary, not reflexive; it depends on what the organism elects to do. Second, operant learning is often suggested to an organism, as in the case of a teacher providing the student with stimuli; whereas respondent learning is elicited as an involuntary response to an external stimulus. Third, and perhaps most important, the response is acquired differently. In Pavlovian learning, the CS is paired with the UCS and a response is made until it is associated with the CS. In Thorndikean learning, a stimulus elicits a response and then reinforcement (reward) occurs to create an associative bond for that stimulus and response. Thus, in Thorndikean learning, reinforcement is contingent on the response; in Pavlovian learning, an external stimulus evokes the response.

Recognizing this important difference—that reinforcement is contingent on the response—Skinner elaborated on Thorndike's law of effect, calling this type of learning operant conditioning. Skinner used the word *operant* to indicate that the organism operates on the environment, altering it in some way by its selection of a response. Once the organism makes a response, its behavior is reinforced either by the satisfaction of the altered environment or by another, independent stimulus presentation (that is, a new stimulus that is not directly associated with the original stimulus).

Reinforcing Stimulus

In contrast to earlier theorists, Skinner advanced the idea of a second, reinforcing stimulus: When an emitted response is followed by a stimulus, this stimulus reinforces the immediately preceding response, thus increasing the probability of that response. Skinner (1938, 1953) considers respondent conditioning relatively unimportant to human behavior. Operant conditioning is the better explanation of human learning patterns because they are voluntary. The range of learning possible in conditioning is limited only by the person's capabilities and interests.

Skinner believes that behavior occurs without any specific, external eliciting stimulus. The cause of operant behavior is within the organism. Nevertheless, the learning and maintenance of emitted behavior depends on the consequences of the operant. Thus, although the frequency of respondent behavior is determined by the frequency of the eliciting stimulus, the frequency of operant behavior is determined by its consequences (the activity in the environment that follows it).

In some respects, Skinner's model of learning might be thought of as R-S learning because the learner emits a response (R) and is subsequently reinforced by a stimulus (S). In the classroom, a student may turn a painting (response) in to the teacher and subsequently receive either a grade or a verbal comment (reinforcing stimulus).

A **reinforcer** is any event or stimulus that increases the likelihood or strength of behavior. Skinner used the term *reinforcement* rather than reward (the term Thorndike used) because he viewed it as neutral; anything that increases the probability of a response is a reinforcer. Knowing you have the right answer, feeling better about yourself because of something you did, or your favorite team winning a game are all reinforcing.

Reinforcer
Any event that follows a response that increases the likelihood of its recurring.

Primary Reinforcer Some stimuli are able to reinforce behavior without the organism having had any previous experience with them. These are called **primary reinforcers** and include food, water, sex, and self-preservation events. Although primary reinforcers are essential in laboratory experiments with animals, they are not thought to be as powerful in producing learning in humans.

Primary reinforcer
Any event that satisfies a physiological need of an organism.

45

Secondary Reinforcer   The maintenance of much human behavior depends on **secondary reinforcers,** which include such events as acceptance, praise, privileges, money, and grades. For example, a child may pick a flower for his or her mother. The mother's smile, thank you, embrace, or other type of acceptance will be reinforcing to the child. Picking a flower for mother is a pleasurable event (mother's acceptance/reinforcement).

Some secondary reinforcers may be tied to primary events. For example, children may be hungry and "act up" until fed. If they are fed (primary reinforcement) when they act up, they learn that acting up is a way to get fed. The acting up becomes a secondary reinforcer. If parents eventually stop the feeding whenever acting up occurs, then the acting up will lose its secondary reinforcing power.

As children become older, they may come to prefer certain foods. Thus, acting up will take on a new dimension. They must not only be fed (primary reinforcement), but must be fed certain things (secondary reinforcement)—those preferred foods. For adults, eating patterns may take on secondary reinforcement characteristics. For example, if you usually eat dinner between 6 and 6:30 P.M. but one day are satiated at 5:30, you may be famished by 7 P.M. This is physiologically impossible, but psychologically you may be full or hungry within such a time frame. Thus, the pattern of eating at a certain time is a result of secondary reinforcement. The need to eat becomes psychologically rather than physiologically based.

In classroom environments, teachers use and students seek secondary reinforcers. Teachers use praise, grades, and special privileges to arrange classroom environments to increase student learning. They tend to repeat those events that produce or maintain the desired student behavior and stop using those that do not.

Positive Reinforcer   Most reinforcers are positive; they bring about satisfaction. A **positive reinforcer** is any event that follows a response that is satisfying to the individual and increases the probability of the response recurring.

Positive reinforcers include praise, feedback (Skinner's knowledge of results), food, and tokens (for example, gold stars, points earned toward privileges, green stamps, candy, or gum). Anything the learner perceives as pleasant, rewarding, or acceptable is a positive reinforcer. In school, a student may strive to make good grades, to be popular, or to become a class officer, a committee chair, or an athlete. A student also does things to gain attention from peers and teachers. These activities are rewarding and are continued because they have proven to increase and maintain behavior.

Negative Reinforcer   A **negative reinforcer** is the withdrawal of an event that the person perceives as annoying or aversive. The result is an increase in the probability of a response recurring. Negative reinforcement strengthens behavior, thus it is reinforcing. In common usage, positive and negative are opposite. In learning psychology, this is not the case. **Punishment** is the opposite of positive reinforcement, and negative reinforcement is a second way of reinforcing a behavior. Because negative

reinforcement follows an event that a person might wish to stop, it is called negative. It is the removal of an unpleasant event or an annoying stimulus from a person immediately following a behavior.

The concept of negative reinforcement can be illustrated by a visit to the dentist. Let us say that the dentist is preparing to give you an injection. Upon seeing the syringe, you have an anticipatory pain response that you manifest by saying, "I don't really mind shots; it is the sight of the needle I can't stand." In the interest of your comfort, once the injection is administered, the dentist removes the syringe from your sight. What has happened? First, the stimulus (syringe) evoked the response (verbal statement). Second, the dentist removed the syringe (negative stimulus) from your sight as soon as possible, thus reinforcing your fear of pain (Thornburg & Thornburg, 1974). Not having to deal with the situation reinforced your tendency not to deal with it on subsequent occasions.

Implicit within the resolution is the assumption that the illustrated behavior is undesirable and the person providing the negative reinforcement would like to avoid reinforcing the behavior when possible. The dentist's technique should be to ignore the patient's comment, lay the syringe back down on the dental tray, and move on to the next step in the dental procedure. It is all right if the dentist later removes the syringe from the patient's view. The fact that other events have occurred between the demonstration of a patient's fear (verbal statement) and the removal of the syringe from the patient's sight (now a neutral stimulus) means that no negative reinforcement is occurring and that the dentist did not inadvertently reinforce the patient's fear.

In summary, both positive and negative reinforcement increase the likelihood of learning. A positive reinforcer is added to a response, thus increasing its likelihood. A negative reinforcer is the removal of a negative stimulus following the response, thus increasing its likelihood. Positive is more common and more preferable. It is the optimal way to increase learning. It is more important, however, for teachers to remember that many teacher-perceived undesirable student behaviors are the result of the teacher's negative reinforcement. Although such teacher behavior may be inadvertent, it is nevertheless reinforcing. Teachers need to be aware of the potential for this behavior and how they can minimize its occurrence.

Examples of negative reinforcement that often occur within the school environment include:

1. A child becomes ill before a test (negative stimulus). He is sent to the nurse's office (avoids test), which reinforces the tendency to become ill in subsequent test situations.

2. An adolescent female fears participation in physical education class when it is conducted in a gymnasium. She brings a note from her parents saying that she is menstruating and should be excused. Being excused reinforces her avoidance behavior when physical education is being held indoors.

3. A teacher looks over the shoulders of a reading group (negative stimulus). The reading rate decreases. When the teacher goes to the next group (removal of negative stimulus), the reading rate increases.

Positive and negative reinforcements increase our response potential. They are illustrated in Figure 2–2, along with two types of events

Figure 2–2
Types of reinforcement and their effects on maintaining behavior

	ADD	REMOVE
PLEASANT STIMULUS	Positive reinforcement: increases likelihood of behavior	Time out: decreases likelihood of behavior
AVERSIVE STIMULUS	Punishment: decreases likelihood of behavior	Negative reinforcement: increases likelihood of behavior

$1 = 100 Percent Memory

Margie Sellers is in the fourth grade at Blenmar Elementary School. She is an attractive nine-year-old with an outgoing personality. In school, she is average to below average, has trouble being attentive, and is particularly poor on any learning task that depends primarily on memory.

Margie's worst subject is spelling. On Monday, Ms. Stone gave the fourth grade a list of twenty-one words to learn. The students wrote the words on Wednesday and again on Friday, unless they made 100 percent on Wednesday. On Friday, Ms. Stone was surprised when Margie jumped out of her seat and rushed to her desk to have her spelling paper graded. This was totally out of character for Margie, but she was anxious for immediate feedback as to how well she had done.

The teacher explored this new enthusiasm with Margie and found out that she had talked her father into giving her $1 if she made 100 percent on her spelling

test each week. This had motivated Margie to study more conscientiously than ever before in spelling. After a month, Margie had achieved four successive 100 percent scores. This pattern of behavior continued throughout the school year, and there were few weeks when Margie did not learn all her spelling words.

The word got around among the students, then teachers, and, as usual, to the principal's office. Ms. Foster called Ms. Stone in for a conference, indicating that she considered it morally wrong for a student to get paid for doing schoolwork. Ms. Stone pointed out that it was not the school or the teacher who was rewarding Margie, but her father, and, right or wrong, it had increased Margie's attentiveness in school and her industriousness in regard to spelling.

In retrospect, Ms. Stone was not sure that Margie's motivation to succeed in spelling was generalized to any of her other subject areas. Nevertheless, the token reinforcement system helped Mar-

gie turn her most difficult subject into her highest achievement area.

What Do You Think?

1. Is the principal right and should Margie's parents be called in for a conference?

2. Should the issue of learning take precedence over morality?

3. Could Ms. Stone use a similar, yet nonmonetary, reinforcement strategy to motivate other students to study?

49

Time out
The withholding of a positive
reinforcer for a specific time in order
to reduce the tendency to respond.

designed to decrease the response rate—punishment and **time out,** which is a type of punishment. I discuss these two important concepts later in this chapter.

Stimulus Discrimination

Discriminated stimulus
The presentation of a specific event in order to establish a specific response.

Although Skinner believes that many responses occur without any identifiable stimulus, it is possible to bring a response under the control of a **discriminated stimulus.** In early Pavlovian experiments, laboratory dogs learned to respond to specific, discriminated stimuli. In operant behavior, the same phenomenon occurs. Under the control of a discriminated stimulus, the probability of a response is high only in the presence of a discriminated event.

Operant experiments have included placing rats in an experimental apparatus containing a lever, a light, a food tray, and a food-releasing mechanism. Food is released into the tray when the animal presses the lever. The animal is brought under the control of the discriminated stimulus when it is trained to press the lever only when the light is on. The animal is reinforced only when the light is on; if it presses the lever when the light is off, no food is released. The discriminated stimulus controls the operant because the operant has been reinforced in its presence.

There are numerous teaching situations in which it is desirable, or necessary, to build discriminatory learning in the student. For example, a teacher may give out work sheets on grammar usage. Students must complete the first work sheet and the teacher must correct it and assign a proficiency level (discriminated stimulus) before the student can go on to the second work sheet. Teacher reinforcement is contingent upon student response. If the student is not at the designated proficiency level, no reinforcement is forthcoming. Thus, student behavior (operant) is brought under the control of the discriminated stimulus. Discrimination is most likely to occur when the teacher presents the student with a specific stimulus and reinforces only if the student makes the correct response.

Stimulus Generalization

Two highly similar stimuli may evoke the same conditioned response (Guttman & Kalish, 1956; Kimble, 1961; Razran, 1951). This phenomenon readily occurs as the organism seeks to reduce a physiological need. For example, stimulus generalization might occur in the case of a young child who is taken to the doctor's office and receives a painful injection. The UCS (needle in the arm) elicits a UCR (withdrawal and crying), and the sight of the doctor (CS) may elicit these same fear reactions of withdrawal and crying (CR). Other stimuli that are in some way similar—the sight of dentists, lab technicians, nurses, and others in white coats—may also elicit the fear reactions.

In stimulus-response learning within the classroom, it is common for the teacher to present similar, but not identical, stimuli to which the student must learn to make the same response. In learning lower- and uppercase letters, such as "b" and "B," the student is expected to be able to recognize and respond to both forms of "b" as the same letter. The phenomenon of stimulus generalization may also occur without teacher planning. For example, if a student is presented with a red apple and responds that it is an apple, the student is also likely to respond "apple" when presented with a yellow apple. The two stimuli are similar enough to trigger the same response. Generalization can occur with stimulus-response learning only when stimuli are closely related in appearance or other characteristics.

Stimulus generalization may also be counterproductive in classroom learning. For example, learners may mistake the letter "d" for "b" or respond in the same way to two different but similar geometric figures. Poorly presented discriminated stimuli can result in poorly defined or incorrect generalizations by the learner.

Schedule of Reinforcement

The **schedule of reinforcement** tells you when a consequence will be delivered.

Continuous Schedule   Early animal experiments used a **continuous schedule**—every correct response was reinforced. **Ratio schedules** indicate how many responses must be made before one is reinforced. The decision to reinforce is based on the number of responses occurring. Continuous reinforcement is provided on a ratio of 1:1. Learners usually respond to a 1:1 ratio by accelerating their response rate in subsequent presentations of the stimulus.

There are several problems inherent in continuous reinforcement. First, as Ferster and Skinner (1957) have documented, a continuous schedule is not necessary for a response to be maintained. Second, when learning moves out of the animal laboratory, it is virtually impossible to establish and maintain a continuous reinforcement schedule. Humans often emit multiple responses before receiving a single reinforcer. Third, within the school context, it is functionally impossible for a teacher to reinforce every student's response. In fact, if every student depended on the classroom teacher for reinforcement after each response, the learning rate would drop off significantly unless the teacher could keep up with the demand. Fourth, as we mature, we become increasingly self-reliant and less dependent on external reinforcement. The range of individual behavior would become severely restricted if this were not the case.

Intermittent Schedule   The alternative to a continuous reinforcement schedule is intermittent reinforcement. In **intermittent schedules,** the reinforcement occurs with varying frequency; it is not applied after every response. Ferster and Skinner (1957) researched two major types of intermittent schedules: ratio and **interval.** In the laboratory, an animal might be put on a 5:1, 25:1, or any other schedule. A 25:1 ratio means that twenty-four nonreinforced responses must occur before a response is reinforced. In humans, ratio schedules are based on actual behaviors.

Schedule of reinforcement
The arrangement of reinforcements and responses in a systematic way that ensures response maintenance.

Continuous schedule
The application of a reinforcer following every response.

Ratio schedule
The systematic application of a reinforcer following a number of responses.

Intermittent schedule
The application of reinforcers at varying frequencies following responses or time intervals.

Interval schedule
The systematic application of a reinforcer following a given time period.

51

Interval schedules indicate the amount of time that must elapse before reinforcement is forthcoming. The number of responses within that time frame is of no concern. The time interval becomes the basis for maintaining behavior. Thus, interval schedules are based on time elapsed and not on actual behavior.

Reinforcement can also follow **variable** and **fixed schedules.** When a variable schedule is in effect, the number of responses or amount of time from one reinforcement to the next is irregular, although it may approximate an arithmetical mean or average. When the variable schedule is dependent on actual emitted responses, it is called a **variable ratio schedule** of reinforcement. When the variable is dependent on time elapsed, it is called a **variable interval schedule.** Fixed schedules are applied after a pre-established number of responses have occurred or a designated time frame has elapsed. In each case, they are constant from one reinforcement to the next unless the schedule is abandoned in favor of another. A schedule built around a fixed number of responses is called **fixed ratio;** one dependent on fixed time elapsed is labeled **fixed interval.** The understanding of reinforcement schedules is very important to the classroom teacher.

Fixed Ratio Reinforcement Schedule   In the fixed ratio reinforcement schedule, the learner is reinforced after emitting a fixed number of responses. The decision to reinforce and the frequency with which reinforcement occurs is based on the learner's behavior. The idea is to maintain a high learning rate in students without applying reinforcement continuously. If students do not expect to be reinforced every time, yet know they will be reinforced with a predictable frequency, they anticipate the reinforcement and keep their learning rate up. In a fixed ratio schedule, reinforcement strengthens the preceding responses and motivates subsequent responses.

There are two advantages to fixed ratio schedules. First, the learner maintains a higher response level with a low amount of reinforcement. A reinforcer is expected as a result of personal behavior at established, predictable times. Second, because students are responding at a much higher frequency than they are being reinforced, the use of fixed ratio reinforcement decreases the likelihood of **extinction,** the reduction of a response tendency due to a lack of reinforcement. In fact, a teacher could set such a high response-to-reinforcement ratio (50:1, for instance) that extinction becomes nonfunctional.

If students expect much teacher attention and reinforcement, it might be desirable to increase learning while decreasing student dependency on the teacher for reinforcement. Let's say students are used to being reinforced after every response (continuous reinforcement schedule). The teacher might initially use a 2:1 schedule, that is, reinforce every other behavior. Once students learn to keep a high response rate with fewer reinforcers, the teacher can gradually move to different ratios (3:1, 5:1, 10:1, 20:1, and so forth), thus gradually reducing the students' dependency on being reinforced yet maintaining a high response rate.

Variable schedule
Reinforcers are given in a random, irregular pattern.

Fixed schedule
Reinforcers are given in a specific, regular pattern.

Variable ratio schedule
The learner is reinforced after several responses have occurred, the ratio being set around an arbitrary mean.

Variable interval schedule
Reinforcement is applied randomly, after an unspecified time lapse.

Fixed ratio schedule
The learner is reinforced after a predetermined number of responses has occurred.

Fixed interval schedule
Reinforcement is applied after a predetermined time has elapsed.

Extinction
The reduction of a response tendency by the withholding of reinforcement.

The disadvantages of fixed ratio reinforcement schedules are also twofold. First, fixed ratio reinforcement is external, provided by someone else. Attempts to increase the student learning rate should have a concomitant component—lessening learners' dependency on external reinforcers. Deci (1975) and Lepper and Greene (1978) have shown that external reinforcers may actually reduce intrinsic motivation to learn. Thus, teachers must use reinforcement judiciously, applying it more to those who need it to maintain a good learning rate than to those who demonstrate considerable internal drive. Second, if a student is on a fixed ratio, the teacher must keep track of this by using a tally sheet, golf counter, or some other device. To keep a tally and appropriately reinforce all students is a difficult classroom management task for most teachers; thus, variable ratio reinforcement schedules may be a preferable classroom practice.

Variable Ratio Reinforcement Schedule Variable ratio reinforcement schedules are also based on actual responses, although the ratio is set around an arbitrary mean. In contrast to the fixed ratio schedule, the teacher has more flexibility in administering reinforcers and avoids the necessity of specifically tallying student behavior in order to determine when to reinforce. Let us say a teacher has been reinforcing a student on a 5:1 fixed ratio schedule and decides to move to a variable ratio schedule, reinforcing once on the average of every five responses. The reinforcement might resemble this pattern: 3:1, 7:1, 6:1, 10:1, 2:1, 4:1, 5:1, 4:1. The number of reinforcements is basically the same as in the fixed schedule, although it has the advantage of giving the teacher greater flexibility and causing the student to make more responses than when placed on a fixed schedule. Students anticipate reinforcement; thus, they are motivated to keep the response rate up.

Although all the reinforcement schedules Ferster and Skinner (1957) describe use external reinforcers, the variable ratio schedule minimizes the chances of fostering student dependency. Students will work on their own, selecting many of their own reinforcers, because they know that teacher reinforcement is forthcoming, but they are not sure when. This type of reinforcement is highly resistant to extinction. Students on a high response reinforcement variable schedule show the highest maintenance response (**retention**) and the greatest resistance to extinction.

Retention
The maintenance of a learned response across time.

Fixed Interval Reinforcement Schedule In a fixed interval reinforcement schedule, reinforcement follows a specified time interval. The determiner of reinforcement is the time that has elapsed rather than the number of responses that have occurred. If the teacher decides to reinforce a student every twenty minutes, then reinforcement must be administered at twenty-minute intervals regardless of what the student does within that time frame. Whether students make fifty, forty, fifteen, or two responses, they are always reinforced once every twenty minutes. As in the case of fixed ratio, the teacher who has a student on a fixed interval schedule must systematically record time in order to administer the reinforcement.

Assume you are a tennis coach. After your tennis team has a good practice session, you say to them, "Everyone practice serves for fifteen minutes; then you can stop for the day." Is this really what you want to do? Are you interested in determining whether players can serve for fifteen consecutive minutes or whether they can serve many aces within that time frame? If you say, "After you have served twenty aces into each court, you can hit the showers," then you are making the reinforcer (the shower or end of practice) contingent on the players' actual behavior rather than on the amount of time spent practicing serves. The actual number of correct responses increases the skill level more than the amount of time spent working on the skill.

A teacher who gives a science test every Friday is using a fixed interval schedule. Report cards, commonly given at six-, nine-, or eighteen-week intervals, are another example. In both cases, as the time for the reinforcement draws closer, the learner's response rate increases. There is little uniformity of responding across a week or a six-week period. An inordinately high amount of responding occurs as the students move toward the end of the nonreinforcement period, an indication of anticipation of being reinforced. This is not surprising when we consider the interval between the behaviors and the reinforcer (Barth, 1979).

Elements of Reinforcement Schedules	
Type	Elements
Variable Ratio	Estimated around arithmetical mean Flexible teacher monitoring Learning rate high Extinction rate low
Fixed Ratio	Ratio same from reinforcement to reinforcement Strict teacher monitoring Learning rate above average Extinction rate low
Variable Interval	Estimated around arithmetical mean Flexible teacher monitoring Learning rate above average Extinction rate low
Fixed Interval	Based on same fixed time interval Strict teacher monitoring Learning rate average Extinction rate average
Continuous	Based on a 1:1 response ratio Constant teacher monitoring Learning rate high Extinction rate high

Variable Interval Reinforcement Schedule   Reinforcement is random—neither constant nor on a fixed interval of time—on a variable interval schedule. In some cases, a learner may be reinforced several times within a very short period; in other cases, the learner may go for an extended time period without any reinforcement. The effect of such a schedule seems to be greater response stability and more learning than with fixed interval schedules.

Teachers who use the "pop quiz" method are using variable interval reinforcement. At the end of a class period, regardless of the students' response rates, the teacher may give a pop quiz. On a variable schedule, students know that a pop quiz is likely, but they do not know when. The time frame is the class period; the variable is not knowing after which period a pop quiz will occur. The effect is to keep the student response rate high in anticipation of a pop quiz. Extinction is slow and very gradual for responses learned under this schedule.

Using the Schedules   All five schedules of reinforcement that Ferster and Skinner used in their animal experiments work with humans. All are capable of facilitating learning, although there are conditions under which any one of them is preferable. The following examples illustrate classroom situations that could easily occur.

It is the beginning of the school year and the introductory algebra teacher is introducing eighth-grade students to operations with real numbers. The prerequisite for this class is junior high general math. This is their first exposure to algebra. There are two important factors to consider at the onset. First, the mathematical operations involved in algebra are more complex than those in general math. Second, the terminology and problem-solving strategies in algebra are more abstract than in general math. Students will have to learn such concepts as singular and binary operations, real numbers, exponential notation, universal quantifier, existential quantifier, and equality. While they are learning concepts and rules that underlie basic algebraic processes, a continuous reinforcement schedule may be most effective. Students need much encouragement and feedback when they are initially learning material that is decidedly more complex (algebra as compared to general math) or different (abstract as compared to concrete). Once they learn these underlying concepts, they can be put on an intermittent reinforcement schedule.

High school sophomores are being taught how to type a business letter. They must learn the parts of a letter and their functions and how to proofread the typed letter. The teacher may place these students on a 3:1 ratio so that, after they have correctly typed, proofread, and corrected three letters, they may turn them in for feedback and evaluation. The motivation for the students is to accomplish in final, correct form three letters in order to gain information from the teacher as to personal progress. This fixed-ratio schedule is based on actual student behavior.

A third-grade physical education instructor works on the quality of body movement with a class. The progression of instruction may go from making flowing movements with specified body parts to making such movements using the whole body. Eventually, the students learn sequential movements, exercising a sequence of movement phases. Tumbling is a good avenue through which to sequence body movement. As the students begin to do tumbling exercises on the mats, the teacher can give verbal praise or encouragement. The speed with which several students tumble in quick succession makes it impossible to reinforce them on a fixed ratio schedule. However, variable ratio schedules work extremely well here. The teacher can provide the encouragement each student needs based on the student's behavior. There may be occasions when the tumbling movement is not up to the instructor's standard, but these can be ignored and the teacher can reinforce a subsequent behavior that more closely approximates the correct behavior. When students make many responses in rapid succession, the best way to maintain a high frequency of behavior is to use variable ratio reinforcement.

When time spent on a learning task is a critical variable in student learning, use a fixed interval reinforcement schedule. For example, fifth-grade students are in the library learning the Library of Congress system. Once they have mastered the main classes of the system of classification, the librarian or teacher might give the students time to work with the system. In a thirty-minute library period, the teacher might put students on a six-minute reinforcement schedule, moving from student to student, reinforcing each one at six-minute intervals. In a highly structured situation like this, it would be much easier for the teacher to monitor the time. In addition, where students are concentrating on a task that many might perceive as laborious, they would each be reinforced five times within the thirty-minute period.

A teacher of learning disabled junior high students is teaching sounds and blends as part of spelling class. They are learning the A, O, and I sounds and discriminating words by sounds. They also are learning two- and three-consonant blends. The majority of the class period is spent with students filling out work sheets on the vowels and consonant blends. The teacher may decide that each student will be reinforced twice during that class period, thus they would realize that the teacher is attending to their work. For one, this may be at the second and seventeenth minutes, for another, at the eleventh and fortieth minutes. This variable interval schedule has a minimum of two teacher reinforcements per student per class period, regardless of the actual number of student responses that have occurred.

Punishment

Punishment leads to behavior, the suppression of behavior, or the selection of an alternative behavior. As Figure 2–2 shows, punishment is added to a response, that is, it occurs when an aversive stimulus follows a response. Figure 2–2 also implies that punishment is designed to decrease the likelihood of a response. There is considerable disagreement as to whether punishment eliminates behavior, although it does seem to decrease the likelihood or frequency of a response.

Historical Development Thorndike's original law of effect contained the principles of both positive reinforcement and punishment. He believed that, whereas satisfaction strengthens the response tendency, annoyance weakens it. When Thorndike (1932) advanced his truncated law of effect, he changed his position on punishment by stating that punishing a stimulus-response connection weakens it little or not at all.

Saying to his experimental subjects either "right" (presumed to be positive) or "no" or "that's wrong" (presumed to be punishing), Thorndike found that the response rate increased 20 percent under the positive feedback and 15 percent under the punishing feedback. Although contemporary research has brought the original Thorndike research into question, punishment does seem to decrease and/or eliminate responses, although its effect is not always predictable or necessarily permanent.

Estes (1944) did important research on punishment. He attempted to clarify the use of punishment within the concept of operant conditioning. Although Estes experimented on animals, he concluded that punishment leads to the suppression of behavior recurrence, but not to its unlearning. When he discontinued the punishment, the response began again. Estes concluded that a response may not be eliminated from an animal's response repertoire as a result of punishment alone. He also found that the aversive stimulus might have emotional effects on the organism that become another response, a finding similar to that of Estes and Skinner (1941) and Mowrer and Solomon (1954).

One of the first well-designed studies done with children yielded results similar to Estes's. Sears, Maccoby, and Levin (1957) found that a mother's punishment of a child was not successful in reducing dependency and/or aggressive behavior.

Solomon (1964) observed that individuals tend to avoid punishing people or situations, which led him to postulate that punishment might better be described as **avoidance learning.** Solomon described two types of avoidance learning: passive and active. In **passive avoidance learning,** we learn not to respond in order to avoid the aversive stimulus (for example, a child may avoid talking back to a parent in order to keep from getting punished). In **active avoidance learning,** we pursue an alternative behavior in order to avoid the punishment (for example, a child may decide to straighten up his or her bedroom in order to avoid the consequences of not cleaning the room).

Avoidance learning
The deliberate avoidance of a situation or individual that has been punishing.

Passive avoidance learning
Purposely not responding in order to avoid punishment.

Active avoidance learning
The pursuit of an alternative behavior to avoid punishment.

Limitations Punishment has at least six aspects that imply it is an ineffective procedure, especially when compared to positive reinforcement (Thornburg, 1973b; Thornburg & Thornburg, 1974). First, *it does not last.* As research has indicated, if the threat of punishment is severe enough, the student's behavior will be controlled for a while. However, when the punishing effect wears off, the behavior will likely reappear. We have only to think of our own experiences when growing up to recall that, when the strength of a punishment diminished, we began exercising a behavior again. In punishing situations, we may exercise passive avoidance behavior.

Second, *punishment does not teach an alternative response.* This may be its most serious limitation. School children often do not have the skills, either academic or social, to behave appropriately in the classroom. Will punishment teach them new skills? It is important to distinguish here between academic and social behaviors.

In teaching-learning situations, the teacher's goal is to increase the student's learning rate. Positive reinforcement is the best way to do this. What happens to a child who cannot remember dates, events, or times tables or to the child who does not understand a rule and therefore cannot solve a problem? Nowhere does learning theory or instructional design imply that students who do not learn at the expected rate should be punished. Nevertheless, this happens. Teachers write aversive remarks on students' paper, make ridiculing or sarcastic comments, negatively compare one student with others, and sometimes even invoke corporeal punishment. Given all we know about human behavior and the ways in which learning occurs, we can conclude that teachers should not use punishment as a response to insufficient academic learning.

Regarding social behaviors, there may be occasions when teachers may advantageously use punishment, although they should first analyze the disruptive behavior to determine if an aversive interaction is appropriate. For example, some children may be disruptive in class in order to gain the teacher's attention. Such behavior may violate classroom rules, but these children may have learned at home that the only time they get attention is when they disrupt what their parents are doing. Thus, their behavior seems appropriate and is consistent with other interactions they have had with adults. It would be difficult for these children not to react negatively or feel unfairly treated if the teacher punishes their disruptive behavior. The teacher could teach an alternative social behavior because these children may not perceive their behavior as inappropriate.

Children may also select, on their own, an alternative social behavior in order to avoid the possibility of being punished. Solomon (1964) calls this active avoidance behavior. Becker (1971) lists some alternatives a child or adolescent may choose when punishment seems imminent:

1. Cheating (avoiding the punishment that goes with being wrong)
2. Truancy (avoiding or escaping the many punishments that go with school failure, poor teaching, or punitive school administration)
3. Running away (escaping the many punishments parents can use)
4. Lying (avoiding the punishment that follows doing something wrong)
5. Sneaking (avoiding being caught misbehaving)
6. Hiding (avoiding being caught)

Third, *punishment is upsetting,* not only to the student being punished, but to the teacher and the rest of the class as well. It intensifies the emotional climate of the classroom, often engendering feelings of anger, frustration, dislike, and hostility. It strains the social relationship between the punished student and the teacher and often makes the student uncomfortable with the rest of the class.

Punishment also produces a second response, which is characterized by emotion. Skinner (1953) had observed that punishment can cause emotional responses such as crying, trembling, and changes in the circulatory and respiratory systems. Rimm and Masters (1974) have observed that punishment has the capacity to condition anxiety. If you are punished and subsequently are in a similar situation, you may become anxious, even though you are not about to be punished again.

Fourth, *punishment causes counteraggression.* It is not uncommon for students to "get even" with teachers for the way they are treated in school. Hostility may surface when students perceive it to be advantageous to them. Playing tricks on a teacher or turning student sentiment against the teacher are other counteraggressive activities.

Fifth, *punishment demonstrates punishment.* Students learn through imitation (modeling); they can thus learn to be punitive by seeing and experiencing punishment in their classroom. It is illogical to believe that students imitate only the appropriate behaviors they see.

Sixth, *punishment causes withdrawal.* Students often withdraw both mentally and physically from punishing persons or from places where punishment occurs. They may avoid coming to school or, while there, avoid academic and social interaction.

Time Out   Time out is a form of punishment. Generally considered less aversive than other punishment, it is a reinforcement procedure that is finding wider acceptance in the classroom. In time out, a positive reinforcer is withheld or discontinued. This withholding is considered punishing because the anticipated or earned positive reinforcement is being withheld in an attempt to change or eliminate behavior. When the reinforcer is resumed or students are returned to a reinforcing environment, they find that reinforcement is contingent upon their making the right response.

Many students perceive withholding a positive reinforcer as punishing and will abandon or alter the behavior that caused time out to be administered. Time out avoids the negative consequences and emotional possibilities of punishment. The number of opportunities for applying time out within the school environment are considerably greater than the number for applying punishment.

Time out and extinction are not the same. Extinction is the withholding of reinforcement following an undesired response. When the response is inappropriate, the reinforcement is *never* forthcoming when extinction is used. In time out, the reinforcement is withheld contingent on the appropriate response being emitted. The purpose of time out is not to withhold reinforcement, but to withhold applying the reinforcement until the correct behavior has occurred. Figure 2–3 diagrams the difference between extinction and time out.

Although time out is generally referred to as a form of punishment, it is not identical with punishment. In punishment, an aversive stimulus is presented. As illustrated in Figure 2–3, a teacher may reprimand a student for poking another student while in their reading group. This is adding an aversive event. In time out, the student is simply removed, thus the reinforcing environment (where poking can occur) is withdrawn.

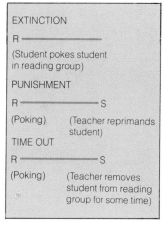

Figure 2–3
The difference between extinction and time out

Although teachers may understand the difference between punishment and time out, the logistics of moving the student out of a reinforcing environment often betray them. Teachers must remain neutral. Students may interpret a harsh voice, facial expressions, an air of impatience, or other body language as punishment, thus altering the effect of removing the student from the environment or even rendering it ineffective.

The teacher can never forget that time out, like other procedures, is a matter of student perception. Often teachers remove students from classrooms, having them sit in the hall for some length of time. If students perceive the classroom as a negative environment, their removal is negative reinforcement and not time out. Further, if a friend happens to walk down the hall while the student is sitting there, positive reinforcement may occur. If the teacher places the student in a time out situation too long, it may be perceived as punishment rather than time out. It is important for teachers to learn about their students and know what they perceive as reinforcers and punishers. Otherwise, it may be very difficult to determine the effects of any reinforcement strategy.

In summary, it is important for teachers to separate inappropriate academic behaviors from inappropriate social behaviors. Students often underachieve because they lack skills, understanding, or time to work. They should not be punished for this. Instead, teachers should work with students and determine the reasons for the lack of academic achievement. They could help students gain new understandings, set new goals, modify assignments, or define more realistic time frames in which to work. Punishment and time out should be used as classroom management techniques, not to make the teacher's job easier or to control student behavior, but to increase the likelihood that students will behave appropriately.

Additional Methods of Response Management

Reinforcement theorists use the concept of reinforcement to mean any consequences that increase the likelihood of a behavior occurring and recurring. Because individuals differ from one another and even within themselves from context to context, the effects of reinforcement vary greatly, especially when applied in a group setting. This has led to the interpretation that all reinforcers should be contingent upon the student emitting the correct response.

Shaping

In many cases in which a teacher desires to instill an appropriate behavior by applying reinforcement procedures, the desired behavior will not exist in the student's repertoire. How can a behavior be reinforced if it does not occur? One possibility is to reinforce an existing behavior that most closely approximates the desired behavior. Then, as response strength increases, only closer and closer approximations of the desired behavior are reinforced. This procedure is known as **shaping**—the application of differential reinforcement to **successive approximations** of a desired response (Skinner, 1953, 1968).

Natural shaping no doubt plays a significant role in the development of many of our social behaviors. For example, when infants are first acquiring a rudimentary vocal repertoire, parents are apt to reinforce very crude approximations of actual words. The adage that only a mother can tell that her infant's babblings mean "mama" attests to the fact that parents initially reinforce rather remote approximations of words. As the child grows older, there is a tendency for parents to require gradually better and better outcomes. A three-year-old who babbles in the same way an infant does is not likely to be reinforced.

In the classroom, teachers can use shaping to teach children to raise a hand and be recognized by the teacher before talking. First, the teacher should avoid recognizing students who speak in class without first raising a hand (extinction). Second, the teacher should reinforce any student behavior that approximates the teacher's expectation. Therefore, if a child raises a hand and then blurts out an answer, the teacher should reinforce the idea of raising the hand while pointing out that the student should still wait until called on. Thus, through ignoring undesirable behaviors and

Shaping
The reinforcing of a behavior that most closely approximates the desired response.

Successive approximation
The strategy used in shaping whereby an individual is reinforced for a series of responses, each gradually getting closer to the desired response.

reinforcing desired responses, the teacher may shape the student's behavior with an acceptable alternative. Shaping, which can be a slow and laborious procedure, is often coupled with other procedures, such as verbal instruction, which facilitate the shaping process.

Teacher Praise

Brophy (1981) has analyzed praise as administered by teachers to students. He has defined praise as the commendation of worth or expression of approval or admiration. He does not equate it with reinforcement, believing that praise goes well beyond feedback or teacher comments such as "okay," "right," or "correct." "Praise statements express positive teacher affect (surprise, delight, excitement) and/or place the student's behavior in context by giving information about its value or its implications about the student's status" (Brophy, 1981, pp. 5–6). Nevertheless, praise does serve as reinforcement. As teachers praise students, they are selecting the behavior they want to reinforce. It seems that it would be difficult for Brophy to develop rationale for praise not containing any reinforcement properties. However, it may be that praise goes beyond the minimal demands of a reinforcer. Brophy suggests that, in addition to its use as a reinforcer, praise has other meanings and functions.

Spontaneous Expression of Pleasure   Occasionally, students' responses are surprisingly insightful, or their assignments are surprisingly well done. This may cause the teacher to praise their accomplishments by expressing surprise or admiration. Ironically, this kind of praise, which is given spontaneously rather than as part of a systematic effort to reinforce, probably is the most reinforcing in its effects on students.

Balance and Justification   Regularly in dealing with habitual underachievers and occasionally in dealing with other students when they perform below their potential, teachers criticize students for sloppiness or poor effort or state that they are capable of doing (and expected to do) better work. Then, if performance improves, they praise the improved work. In a sense, this is just another example of teachers' efforts to reinforce systematically. However, it often has a special connotation: The teacher is not only praising the students but also justifying his or her own previous behavior. Such praise often communicates "See, you deserved my earlier criticisms" or "See, I said that you could do better, and I was right!" To the extent that teacher praise includes such messages, its effectiveness as a reinforcer probably is reduced.

Vicarious Reinforcement   The teacher's intention here is not so much to praise the desired behavior of the student to whom the message is directed as to change or control other students' behavior ("I like the way Susie has cleaned up her desk."). Unless the students singled out for such "praise" are very immature and teacher dependent, they are likely to feel manipulated or punished rather than rewarded by it.

Guidance and Avoidance   A related form of pseudopraise is used by teachers who realize that singling out a student's good conduct is not likely to reinforce that student, but who do so nevertheless because they want to avoid nagging, criticism, or even just the sheer monotony of repeated behavioral demands. Such teachers use "I like the way . . ." in order to provide guidance in positive language. Often this is part of a larger attempt to create a friendly, cooperative classroom atmosphere.

Transition Ritual   Much classroom praise occurs in situations where students are expected to show the teacher that they have finished an assignment before they can begin some other activity. Students may show off their work proudly at these times and elicit teacher praise. However, most students simply indicate that they have finished the assignment and that they want the teacher to certify that they are finished and thus eligible to begin self-chosen activities. In these situations, verbal praise tends to be perfunctory, and the teachers' nonverbal behavior communicates official recognition that the student can begin a new activity.

Consolation and Encouragement   In general, and increasingly in the higher grades, teachers deal with students rather impersonally, concentrating on the tasks of teaching and learning. When things go well, they keep moving along at a good pace, stressing the academic content under consideration and seldom stopping to praise the student or introduce other, more personal considerations. Most interactions with the best students are entirely academic in focus, although the students will occasionally be praised in public when they make an unusually creative or impressive contribution to a class discussion or in private through complimentary remarks in addition to grades.

Slower students, however, are often praised both publicly and privately. This is especially likely to be the case if they are cooperative and teacher dependent but slow and plodding, thus giving the teacher the role of a patient, helpful, or even protective tutor. The timing and quality of this praise makes it clear that teachers are not so much trying to reinforce specific behavior as to provide general encouragement and reaffirmation of the teacher-student relationship. Such praise appears grossly deficient from a narrow reinforcement purview. It sometimes even follows incorrect answers or generally poor performance, suggesting that the teacher is reinforcing error or failure rather than success. This sometimes may be the case. However, given that such praise is directed toward certain kinds of students whom teachers believe need encouragement, it may well be effective in the long run (Brophy, 1981).

Token Economy Systems

Another type of reinforcing procedure especially effective for children who are unresponsive to "natural" school reinforcers (grades, approval, and so on) is called the **token economy system.** The basic procedure involves the use of reinforcers that are originally neutral but acquire reinforcing

Token economy system
A reinforcement system wherein tokens of assigned point value are given for exercising certain behaviors.

Teacher Reinforcement Strategies Upon Observing a Behavior	
Situation:	A teacher observes Jerry shoving Charles while standing in lunch line. The teacher has previously observed that Charles occasionally bullies Jerry. What should the teacher do? The following strategies might result in the following behaviors.
Positive Rein-forcement	Acknowledge Jerry's assertive behavior and indicate you will talk with him about ways to channel it.
Negative Rein-forcement	Remove Charles from the lunch line.
Punishment	Send Jerry to the principal's office.
Extinction	Ignore the incident.
Time Out	Tell Jerry he will have to wait in the classroom until everyone else has gone through the lunch line.

power when they are established as discriminative stimuli for responses leading to existing backup reinforcers, such as privileges and tangible rewards. Initially, a token system involves selecting certain behaviors (academic tasks, appropriate social acts, and so on) and assigning them a value in tokens (poker chips, check marks, gold stars, play money, and so forth). A procedure is then set up whereby the child may "cash in" accumulated tokens for the existing backup reinforcers.

The advantages of a token system are that it uses a reinforcer (the token) that (1) can be quickly and easily delivered following an appropriate response, (2) will not satiate as long as the backup reinforcers are desirable for the child, (3) can be applied to a variety of appropriate behaviors, and (4) provides a way of reinforcing children for whom recognition and praise are not effective reinforcers. Token economy systems are generally used when modifying student behavior; so I discuss them more fully in Chapter 14.

Reinforcers work and reinforcing events occur in all our daily lives. So the better we understand them, accept that they exist, and appreciate their importance, the greater our chance of controlling their effects on our lives rather than being controlled by them.

Dependency on Secondary Reinforcers

The reason we go out of our way so often to let other people know what we have done or how well we have done it is probably to elicit their approval. It is very important to most people to have others recognize their effort, worth, products, and so forth. Social and academic structures set up numerous opportunities for individuals to be reinforced. Most of us understand being accepted, gaining praise, earning privileges, money, or grades, and being given tangible rewards. As a result, we often behave in ways designed to increase the chances of these things happening to us.

Students may be very achievement oriented in school. Their many schooling experiences have taught them that the more they accomplish what the teacher wants, the more rewards they receive. Thus, success-oriented students may generally be involved in work activity, carrying out several academic activities concurrently, and performing well on all

of them. Such students are described as "model students" because they are rarely disruptive, have minimal dependency on the teacher, yet successfully accomplish teacher-defined tasks.

Two children within a family may learn to interact differently with their father. One may believe that she must do things to demonstrate to her father that she is a good achiever. This may cause some degree of conforming behavior because her father's approval is very important. The second child may also seek approval, but in a less obvious way. What he achieves is related to father approval but is not deliberately brought to his father's attention. Both children need their father's approval, but their styles of gaining it are different.

A career woman may work very hard to gain tangible reinforcers within her occupation. It is often not simply a matter of demonstrating capability, but of earning the benefits that accompany the position if she is successful. Thus, salary increases, promotions, and fringe benefits are reinforcers that may motivate her to function in achievement-oriented ways.

Our environment is filled with secondary reinforcers. The extent to which they are important may vary tremendously from person to person. Still, they are important to all of us and we need to learn how to use them effectively.

Too Dependent?

Is it possible for a student to become too dependent on the teacher for reinforcement? A recent study done at the Far West Laboratory for Educational Research and Development (Ward, 1982; Ward, Rounds, Packer, Mergendoller, & Tikunoff, 1981, pp. 11–12) has found that this might be the case.

Students whose participation characteristics fit in the dependent category must be given frequent attention, feedback, explanation, and/or other assistance by the teacher, other students, or other adults (such as a teacher aide) in order to stay on task. The type of feedback, etc. that is needed varies across students. Some students need academic help. At most, they remember the directions for one step of an instructional task at a time and will need to have additional steps re-explained if they are to proceed with the task successfully. They respond to a series of simple questions better than to a single complex question. They attend to the teacher's instruction when in a small group, where the teacher can monitor their progress at each step and provide immediate assistance and reinforcement. In total-class instructional settings, they are inattentive.

Another subset of dependent students do not require the types of academic assistance outlined above. Rather, they are able to do the assigned task successfully—that is, know and can perform the academic work on their own—but will not proceed with a task unless given frequent reinforcement and approval by the teacher, their peers, or others. Some of these students bring completed work to "show" the teacher and receive a "Good," "Okay," "Keep going" response, or they show their work to their peers to obtain similar feedback. Others wait for the teacher or others to respond, doing no academic work in the meantime. If feedback is not received, they typically cease working on assigned tasks, sitting at their desks playing with various objects, looking around the classroom, or they begin wandering around the classroom. Since total-class instruction does not provide opportunity for reinforcement of individual students as readily as small-group instruction, these students also participate most successfully when working in a small group with the teacher. Four characteristics describe both types of dependent participation. The differentiation is in the type of feedback and assistance that is required. The characteristics are:

1. When working in a small group with the teacher, students are involved in the learning activity;

2. Typically does not attend to instruction that occurs in large group (e.g., total-class) situation; however, may remain on task if large-group activity includes manipulative tasks that are simple and are reinforcing in and of themselves (e.g., completing the activity demonstrates to the student that it was done correctly, without feedback from the teacher);

3. Needs frequent feedback and/or assistance from the teacher and/or others;

4. If feedback and/or assistance are not received, does not continue to be engaged in learning activity.

In the Ward et al. (1981) study, more students were described as dependent than nondependent. The demands such students make on teacher time are high and might result in teacher fatigue. If teachers are to reduce student dependence, they must do so gradually; the "cold turkey" approach will likely reduce student learning and increase student insecurity. Let's work through an example.

Marcia is an above average student. She has two older brothers who have "whizzed" through school and as a result were liked very much by their teachers. Marcia now has the same fifth-grade teacher as her brothers had. Although she is a good achiever, she is highly dependent on her teacher for reinforcement/support. Her teacher, recalling that Marcia's brothers were self-starters who made few demands on her time, decides that she will reduce Marcia's dependence on her. She sets up a reinforcement schedule for Marcia.

The teacher begins by drawing baseline data on Marcia for two weeks, which means that she records a rate of behavior before trying to alter it. Two findings resulted. First, she found she was reinforcing Marcia on a 1.3:1 ratio; that is, for every four responses Marcia made, the teacher was providing three reinforcers. Second, she found that Marcia's learning curve slowed between reinforcers. Thus, there was a direct relationship between Marcia's behavior and the time between reinforcers. In a work period, if the teacher could not get back to Marcia within ten minutes, no new learning occurred.

Having established this baseline, the teacher decided to put Marcia on a fixed ratio schedule. She began by putting her on a 2:1 ratio. She also reduced the time factor between reinforcers. In just two days, Marcia was completing two responses for every reinforcement. The teacher continued using the following schedule:

3:1 ratio	Days 3–4
3.5:1 ratio	Days 5–6
4:1 ratio	Day 7
5:1 ratio	Days 8–11
6:1 ratio	Days 12–14
7:1 ratio	Days 15–16
8:1 ratio	Days 17–19

On the twentieth day (the end of the fourth week), the teacher decided to switch to a variable ratio schedule through week five, using a variable ratio schedule of 8:1. Marcia's dependence began to decrease and her achievement rate increased. The teacher felt she had modified Marcia's learning rate and style.

Some students will be unnecessarily dependent on teacher reinforcement in order to learn. Teachers must devise a strategy to help them become more self-sufficient. Ignoring student attempts for teacher assistance will probably create a learning problem.

Bitterman, M. E. (1969). Thorndike and the problem of animal intelligence. *American Psychologist, 24,* 444–453.

> *This article is basically a treatise on Thorndikean learning principles. The author cites his own experimental research with goldfish as evidence that the law of effect as advanced by Thorndike some eighty years ago is still a fundamental law of learning. By providing degrees of positive reinforcement, Bitterman found that increasing a reward resulted in better performance of learning tasks. This phenomenon is comparable to Thorndike's satisfying state of affairs.*

Byalick, R., & Bersoff, D. N. (1974). Reinforcement practices of black and white teachers in integrated classrooms. *Journal of Educational Psychology, 66,* 473–480.

> *The researchers administered the Positive Reinforcement Observation Schedule to thirty black and thirty white female elementary school teachers. They found no differences in the types of rates of reinforcement between the two groups. They found in both groups that reinforcement was administered at a low rate, that teachers reinforced opposite-race children more than same-race children, and that boys were reinforced more than girls.*

Elms, A. C. (1981). Skinner's dark year and *Walden Two. American Psychologist, 36,* 470–479.

> *The author presents the reader with insight into Skinner's personal life, contending that he was undergoing an identity crisis when he wrote* Walden Two. *For individuals interested in better understanding the man behind radical behaviorism, this article is a must. Elms contends that Skinner's inner conflicts caused him to conceptualize an ideal society in* Walden Two, *one that could be realized only through widespread acceptance of behaviorism as the strategy for ensuring desirable human conduct.*

Hannafin, M. J. (1982). The effects of systematized feedback on learning in natural classroom settings. *Educational Research Quarterly, 7,* 22–29.

> *This article reports research done in three sixth-grade classrooms where students were given systematic feedback following math instruction. Results indicate that the students exposed to systematic feedback scored significantly higher than control students on a math proficiency test. The researcher interprets his findings as confirmation that comprehensive feedback programs in natural classroom settings are effective.*

Rescorla, R. A., & Soloman, R. L. (1967). Two-process learning theory: Relationships between Pavlovian conditioning and instrumental learning. *Psychological Review, 74,* 151–182.

> *The authors describe the history of two-process learning theory—classical conditioning and instrumental learning—and treat Pavlovian conditioning in detail. The article includes a rather sophisticated presentation of the evolution, evidenced in the learning paradigms of S-R, S-S, R-S, US-UR, and CS-CR, of different conditioning models. The authors point out the similarity between conditioned and unconditioned response systems.*

Watson, G. (1960). What psychology can we feel sure about? *Teachers College Record, 61,* 253–257.

> *The author presents fifty propositions about learning and its associated processes. Each points to a well-established fact of learning. Although the presentation of the material is somewhat awkward, in addition to being somewhat dated, this article is valuable for its demonstration of the application of psychological principles to classroom settings.*

Cognitive-Field Psychology

Nancy Abelman, principal of Lincoln Junior High School, had long been concerned about the lack of motivation that seemed to characterize so many students in the school and the resulting complaints of teachers, who were frustrated in coping with students' lack of interest. After reading an article titled "Self-Motivation and Self-Reinforcement: Strategies for Classroom Teachers," Abelman called a staff meeting to share some of the insights she had gained and to map out ways to approach the problem.

Abelman focused on three insights. The first was that students are more likely to approach a task with enthusiasm if the task is meaningful to them, that is, if it is significant or makes sense. This increases the likelihood that the students will understand what they are studying, and understanding, in turn, facilitates self-reinforcement because the students know they have done something well.

The second insight was that tasks or material that are relevant to the students' social environment promote self-motivation and self-reinforcement. Some school drudgery is a consequence of an out-of-date curriculum, and teachers must find ways to relate instructional content to student concerns.

The third insight was that a flexible classroom structure encourages self-motivation and self-reinforcement, and a rigid one is more likely to promote dependence on classroom teachers. Opportunities for self-exploration—the involvement of the self in the learning process—are enchanced by a less-structured classroom and are a third factor in student motivation and reinforcement.

Abelman and her staff agreed to share information and increase their awareness of things that could be done to promote a better educational environment. They realized that redesigning teaching materials was an ongoing, sometimes laborious process. Nevertheless, one of their goals was to become aware of alternative or new strategies that were needed to achieve the goals of education in an increasingly complex social environment.

These insights into the nature of motivation and reinforcement arise out of an area of psychology called cognitive-field psychology. This chapter discusses the content of cognitive-field psychology in the following ways:

- *Early gestalt learning*
- *Learning by doing*

- *Meaningful reception learning*
- *Using cognitive-field principles in the classroom*
- *Comparing cognitive and reinforcement theories*

Early Gestalt Learning

Cognitive-field psychology had its origin in Gestalt psychology as advanced by Wertheimer and two of his colleagues, Kohler and Koffka. Gestalt psychology can probably be summed up in the statement, "The whole is always equal to the sum of more than its parts." All experiences—all interactions—are complete in themselves and must be studied as integrated units. The components of the experience are interrelated in meaningful ways so that the whole cannot be inferred by examining its components. It is this relationship that makes learning relevant and meaningful.

Form Qualities

Form quality
The quality of a whole but not of its component parts.

Form qualities are characteristics of events that give them their relationship and significance, whereas independently they have no meaning at all. Recall the coloring books where children are given a series of dots to trace or connect by drawing a continuous line (see Figure 3–1). As they connect the dots, children suddenly perceive what the object is. They discover the whole (object) by interrelating the parts (dots). To children who have not yet reached that stage of perceptual organization, the page appears to consist of nothing but dots.

Music also illustrates how the relationship between parts determines our perception of the whole. Music is a series of notes that, when played in sequence and quick succession and at prescribed intervals, produces a melody. Notes played in that same succession but at, say, five-minute intervals have no melody and are likely to be considered meaningless by the listener. It is the successive proximity of the notes that produces the melody. Although the form of its presentation may change—a person may hear the music played on a piano or clarinet or hummed by someone on the street—the melody is recognized.

There are two general principles that govern form-quality relationships. The first is that perceiving something as a whole depends upon perceiving the parts in relation to each other. If the parts do not have the capacity to make the whole—if they lack form qualities—then we are not likely to perceive anything meaningful unless our perception distorts reality. Second, as the musical example shows, qualities can be transposed. The same quality may be perceived even though the collection of parts is different. Most of us would probably recognize a song played in a major key and then transposed to a minor key. Technically its parts are different, but its being played in melodic and sequential fashion makes it meaningful to us.

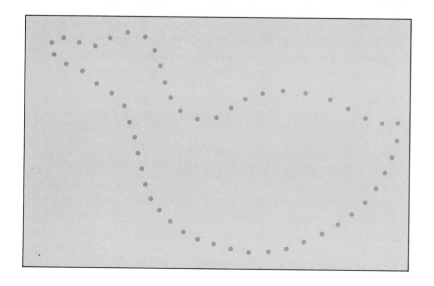

What happens if the learner perceives something as an organized whole and then tries to break it into its components? According to Gestalt theory, it loses its meaning. A teacher's desk is an organized whole. If you remove its drawers, top, and legs, you have a pile of wood, not a desk. This concept of organized wholes can be applied in the classroom. Students should learn how the parts interrelate to make the whole. To start with the whole and break it down into its parts runs counter to a person's perceptual ability and is an ineffective way to study organized wholes.

Perception

Perception has been defined as "the way one comes to know the world or the way one experiences the world of objects and events" (Weintraub & Walker, 1966, p. 1). There are two ways to approach perception. The first is to study it through the physics of sensory input, which is a major topic in psychophysics or the natural sciences (Graham, 1965; Weintraub & Walker, 1966). The second is to think of perception as the way we observe things and attach meaning to those observations.

According to cognitive psychology, learning requires that we be able to make certain perceptual discriminations called **differentiation of fields.** Kohler (1969) provided an interesting example of this concept in an experiment on the appearance of movement. Using two lamps and a straight rod in between, he placed the rod close to a screen, upon which shadows could appear. He used a double switch, which allowed the lamps to be turned on and off rapidly. The lamps projected shadows at different places on the screen. Kohler demonstrated that, when one lamp is turned on and off, followed by an on-off second lamp, a shadow appears and disappears at each place. However, when the lamps are turned on and off in rapid alternate succession, subjects perceive a single shadow moving

Differentiation of fields
The perceptual ability to discriminate among phenomena in the environment.

Basic Tenets in Cognitive Psychology

	Description	Example
Form Qualities	Discovering the relationship between parts and the whole	Teacher/pupils/furniture are total entities as well as a larger whole—the classroom
Perception	Ability to explore the environment through the senses	Belief that four fifteen-second commercials take longer than two thirty-second ones

back and forth across the screen. It is the rapid interaction of the two shadows that makes the observer perceive one shadow continuously moving and not two shadows appearing and disappearing. The rapid interaction altered perception, thus interfering with field differentiation.

As children develop an increased capacity for perceptual organization, their ability to learn increases. Weintraub and Walker (1966) observed that variations in learning from student to student can be attributed to three factors: illusions (the demonstrable differences between perception and physical measurement, such as something looking longer than it actually is), differences in individual perception based on age characteristics (that is, the older you are, the more accurate your perception), and differences in individual perception based on differing sensory capacities (hearing or sight, for instance). They believe these factors underlie our perceptions of the world, which we construct from the information available to us at the time. Our varying perceptual capacities affect the range and complexity of our learning.

Cognitive psychologists view learning as events individuals understand in the process of interacting with their environment (Bower & Hilgard, 1981). What we learn and remember depends on the total context of the event—psychological, social, and cultural. Thus, it is the interaction of the individual with a meaningful environmental context, not isolated pieces of information that have been reinforced, that results in learning. The impetus of cognitive psychology in the 1960s was carried by Jerome Bruner and David Ausubel, whose theories I discuss in this chapter.

Learning by Doing

Discovery learning
Awareness or understanding of objects, events, or symbols in our environment gained through personal exploration.

The concept of learning by doing, or **discovery learning,** was first advanced by John Dewey (1903), who emphasized the importance of students solving their own problems by examining multiple possibilities and trying them out. Dewey (1933) attempted to explain the modes of thought by which a person solves perplexing problems. Bruner has provided further insight into this process. According to Bruner (1960), effective learning occurs when students acquire a general understanding of a subject; that is, when they understand the structure of a subject, they see it as a related whole. They gain this understanding by building concepts, coding information, forming generalizations, and seeing relationships between things.

Understanding the structure of a subject does not mean that a subject must be taught at a complex level. Rather, the "curriculum of a subject should be determined by the most fundamental understanding that can be achieved of the underlying principles that give structure to that subject" (Bruner, 1960, p. 31). As students master the basic elements of a subject, they learn its underlying concepts and rules. Once they learn the concepts and rules, students can both solve problems and inquire into the subject more comprehensively, discussing new ideas and ways of doing things.

A good example is teaching sixth-grade students about the metric system. The underlying structure of the system is metric units. If students learn the concepts of meter, liter, and gram, they can then generalize to other metric units (milli, centi, deci, and kilo). This is more than a rote memory process. Students must first understand the value of these units, especially in relation to each other. They can then learn how to order two or more metric measures, an important concept that, in turn, will help them learn to multiply and divide by powers of ten and make conversions within the metric system. The understandings are the basis upon which the content is built.

According to Bruner (1966), academic content can be represented in three ways or at three levels of complexity: (1) by actions designed to achieve certain results, or **enactive representation;** (2) by images or graphs that stand for a concept, although it may not be fully defined, or **iconic representation;** and (3) by symbolic or logical propositions that are governed by rules or laws for forming and transforming propositions, described as **symbolic representation.**

Enactive Representation

Enactive representation refers to things we grasp through the senses and express through physical actions. There are many word-action relationships in this category; young children often define words in relation to the actions they associate with them. Spoons are to eat with; tricycles are to ride on; blocks are to build with. Enactive representation may also mean understanding the principles involved in one activity by referring to experiences with another activity. Bruner (1966, p. 45) uses the child's understanding of a balance beam as an example: "A quite young child can plainly act on the basis of the 'principles' of a balance beam, and indicates that he can do so by being able to handle himself on a see-saw. He knows that to get his side to go down farther he has to move out farther from the center."

Although the enactive mode of representation may be most dominant in childhood, it is not confined to children. Adults revert to this mode when they are learning something new or when something is hard to visualize. For example, a dental hygienist who wants to teach patients how to be more effective in brushing their teeth might use the following enactive activity. Because there is a high degree of similarity between a tooth and the surrounding gums in the mouth and the cuticle and fingernail on the hand, the hygienist might teach effective brushing by first having patients practice on their cuticle and fingernail, then transferring this action to their mouth.

Iconic Representation

This is a more advanced stage of thought in which things and events in the world are concretely represented. The action component characteristics of the enactive mode are no longer necessary. Most of the instructional

Enactive representation
The ability to represent environmental phenomena through one or more of the senses.

Iconic representation
An awareness of the concrete representation of phenomena in the environment.

Symbolic representation
The ability to represent environmental phenomena through symbols, primarily language.

materials designed for elementary education are concrete in nature: pictures of animals, maps of rivers and mountains. A student may engage in an activity such as drawing a barn without having to visit a farm. Also, the child is able to represent an event by a mental image. The child who grasped the relationship between a balance beam and a see-saw by being on the see-saw can now construct an image of the balance beam in his or her mind.

Symbolic Representation

Symbolic representation depends on language acquisition. Children at first use concrete symbols—a truck, an intersection, or the moon—to explain things. Visual image interacts with language and the concrete object becomes symbolically represented. As children move toward adolescence, they acquire abstract language and begin to represent an amazingly diverse set of phenomena abstractly. They can represent not only the world they experience in very abstract ways, but also the world of possible experiences, thus increasing their range of conceptual and problem-solving thought. Think of the question "What does love mean?" The child may describe love as "Mommy kissing daddy" or as other visible signs of affection. The adolescent may speak of the more abstract qualities of love, that is, "a strong feeling two people have for each other." Further, the adolescent may think of all the different ways love could show itself without having experienced these ways.

Intuitive thinking and **intrinsic motivation** are keys to learning (Bruner, 1971). Intuitive thinking, by which students discover reasons or answers for themselves, leads to a type of understanding that increases their desire to learn and makes them more self-reliant in learning. This intuitive process is complementary to intrinsic motivation, which Bruner (1971) describes as curiosity and competence. We are born with a strong curiosity drive that impels us to explore a variety of activities. Similarly, we maintain high interest in the things we do well and tend to avoid things we are unable to do well. It is, says Bruner, virtually impossible for teachers to maintain student interest in something in which the student does not feel competent.

There are several aspects of discovery learning that make it advantageous to the learner (Bruner, 1971). First, in discovery learning, there is an *increment in intellectual potency*. As learners' expectation of success increases, they are able to organize their thought processes conceptually with greater facility and solve problems in meaningful ways. Second, there is *greater emphasis on instrinsic than extrinsic reward*. Discovery learning is self-rewarding, as students know whether they performed well. Third, *at each discovery, new principles and strategies for discovering are learned*. These generalize to subsequent discovery learning situations and to students' out-of-school environments. Fourth, *students are more likely to remember the things they discover*. When they organize information in conceptually meaningful ways, they do so by selecting those processes that help them remember and recall material. Studies support the idea that long-term memory is better with conceptual than nonconceptual material

Intuitive thinking
The self-generated initiative to explore the environment and learn on our own.

Intrinsic motivation
An inner drive to explore and acquire without dependency on external incentives.

Learning Processes: Jerome Bruner

1. *Enactive.* The ability to abstract meaning from the environment through one or more of the senses. Within the first two years, such learning takes an action form, that is, a physical behavior results from the learning.

2. *Iconic.* The ability to internalize meaning through verbal representations and concept understanding. This is a dominant mode from early childhood through elementary school.

3. *Symbolic.* The development of elaborate concepts in the mind. This is initiated by concrete events and gradually broadened to include abstract events. Symbolic capacity overlaps with iconic thought, although abstractness is not likely to emerge prior to age eleven.

(Bransford, Barclay & Franks, 1972; Bransford, McCarrell, Franks, & Nitsch, 1977; Deci, Sheinman, Wheeler, & Hart, 1980; Dooling & Christiansen, 1977).

Meaningful Reception Learning

Meaningfulness
The extent to which learning is useful or purposeful in a person's life.

Logical meaningfulness
Material to be learned must fall within the learner's capacity to comprehend.

Potential meaningfulness
The capacity to relate new learning to what the learner already knows.

Meaningful learning set
The learner's intent to integrate new learning into his or her existing cognitive structure.

The concept of **meaningfulness** has become strongly associated with cognitive theory. Early Gestalt psychologists assumed that people learn only meaningful material. Osgood (1961, p. 91) calls meaningfulness the "single most important variable in human learning, verbal or otherwise."

Ausubel (1968) believes that, to be learned, material must have **logical meaningfulness,** that is, it must be within the bounds of an individual's learning capacity. Algebraic concepts, for example, would not fall within the learning capabilities of fourth graders, and the material would not have logical meaning. However, such material would fall within the capacity of most eighth graders; thus it would have logical meaning.

Learning is also meaningful if learners can relate a new task to what they already know. Ausubel (1977) defines this as **potential meaningfulness.** Learners possess the ability to relate the material in meaningful ways, and this meaningfulness increases if they can associate it with prior knowledge. The third condition for meaningful learning is the intent of the learners, that is, their desire to relate the material to their own cognitive structure or mode of thinking. This is also referred to as a **meaningful learning set.** These ideas are illustrated in Figure 3–2.

Several studies support the construct of meaningfulness. Bobrow and Bower (1969) compared a group of students who were asked to

(a) Meaningful learning or The acquisition of meanings	Requires	(1) Potentially meaningful material	and	(2) Meaningful learning set
(b) Potential meaningfulness	Depends on	(1) Logical meaningfulness (the non-arbitrary and substantive re-latability of the learning material to correspondingly relevant ideas that lie within the realm of human learning capability)	and	(2) The availability of such relevant ideas in the particular learner's cognitive structure
(c) Psychological meaning (idiosyncratic, phenomenological meaning)	Is the product of	Meaningful learning	or of	Potential meaningfulness and meaningful learning set

generate a linking sentence when given a noun pair with a group who only read an equivalent linking sentence. They found those who constructed their own sentence had better recall of the noun pairs than those who did not, presumably because the first group had to create a relational bridge between the two nouns. In another experiment, Anderson, Goldberg, and Hidde (1971) had one group of learners fill in blanks at the end of a sentence while a second group read whole sentences. The researchers found that those who filled in the blanks learned more, which they attributed to the process of giving meaningful representation to the words.

Ausubel recognizes that building relational bridges can become very complex. Situations in which a student may have to recall several rules to solve a complex problem are quite different from filling in blanks or constructing simple sentences that use a pair of words. The issue is the range of learner behavior this process represents. Ausubel sees adolescent and adult learners working with abstract propositions strictly on a verbal basis. They must be able to relate complex abstract verbal propositions to their existing cognitive structure without reliance on concrete-empirical props (Ausubel & Ausubel, 1966). A learner must have reached certain levels of intellectual maturity and subject-matter sophistication to do this. Elementary school children or individuals who are studying an academic area that is totally new do not have this capacity. Ausubel (1977) suggests that, to learn highly abstract concepts and principles, learners need concrete and specific examples.

Ausubel has derived several guidelines for teaching from his ideas about meaningful learning. First, teachers should structure material in ways that increase the likelihood of student learning; they should present the main ideas of a subject before presenting peripheral content. Second, teachers should emphasize correct definitions; preciseness is important when students are expected to understand the main ideas of a

Figure 3-2
Relationships among meaningful learning, potential meaningfulness, logical meaningfulness, and psychological meaning. [Source: Ausubel (1968), p. 39.

subject. Third, teachers should point out the similarities and differences in ideas. This helps the learner make distinctions and relate ideas in meaningful ways.

Rote Learning

Rote learning, according to Ausubel, is the opposite of meaningful learning. It is arbitrary, verbatim, and easily forgotten. Most rote learning is also nonconceptual. Thus, specific pieces of information must be memorized in order to be learned. Further, for rote learning to be recalled, the recall situation must be highly similar to the one under which the learning originally occurred. In contrast to meaningful learning, rote learning is not generalizable.

Rote learning can take place without any of the three characteristics of meaningful learning described earlier: logical meaningfulness, potential meaningfulness, and intent.

Learning mathematical times tables and places, people, and dates in history are examples of rote learning. Such learning, even though it has logical meaningfulness, is limited in its usefulness if the learner does not have the appropriate ideas to which to relate the material. Memorizing a list of the presidents of the United States is a marginally useful task and the list is less easily recalled than if this information is learned within its historical context as part of a meaningful whole, for example, the Revolutionary War or westward expansion. Finally, even if the material is both logically and potentially meaningful, if the learner's intent is simply to memorize it, then it has been reduced to a rote learning task. This possibility might be reduced if classroom teachers did no more than tell students why they are expected to learn an academic task (Taffel, O'Leary, & Armel, 1974), thus increasing student intent to learn.

As a counter to rote learning, Ausubel specified four types of meaningful learning: representational, concept, propositional, and discovery learning.

Representational Learning

Representational learning is very basic. It is the way children begin to make sense of the environment by associating symbols and objects and relating such learning to other symbols and objects. They are able to do this by attaching specific meanings to symbols and therefore being able to differentiate among them.

Representational learning
The attachment of symbolic meaning to objects in the environment.

Let's say a two-year-old child has been given a wagon, an object heretofore unknown to her. When the child looks at the wagon, the parent says the word *wagon*. According to Ausubel, two processes have occurred within the child's cognitive structure. First, she has visual representation from having looked at the wagon. Second, she has an aural representation from having heard the word *wagon*.

As the parent indicates to the child that the word *wagon* represents the object wagon, the meaning that the child attributes to the word *wagon* is the visual image elicited by the wagon. After one or more pairings of the symbol (word *wagon*) and the object (actual wagon), the symbol comes to stand for the object and the association has meaning.

The child is not learning a simple association but a general understanding, which Ausubel calls the proposition of **representational equivalence.** This essentially means that the child has processed the information and can generalize such learning to other events that fall within the same concept category. In other words, the child does not simply learn that, if the symbol wagon can represent the object wagon, then the symbol ball may represent the object ball, but rather that, if the object wagon can be represented by the symbol wagon, then *all* objects can be represented by symbols.

Representational equivalence
The ability to process new information or experiences by relating them to existing concept categories.

Concept Learning

We acquire concepts through two processes: concept formation and **concept assimilation** (Ausubel, 1968, p. 510). In speaking of concept formation, Ausubel states:

Concept assimilation
Learning the attributes of a concept or proposition, usually through abstract verbal representation.

> Concept formation is characteristic of the preschool child's inductive and spontaneous (untutored) acquisition of generic ideas (for instance, "house," "dog") from concrete-empirical experience. It is a type of discovery learning involving, at least in primitive form, such underlying psychological processes as discriminative analysis, abstraction, differentiation, hypothesis generation and testing, and generalization.

Thus, in concept formation, the learner discovers relationships and the similarities within a class of objects and gradually obtains a working concept through experience.

Concept assimilation is more characteristic of older children and adults. They learn "new conceptual meanings by being presented with the critical attributes of concepts by relating these attributes to relevant established ideas in their cognitive structures" (Ausubel, 1968, p. 511). Thus, as learners become aware of the various criteria that are the basis of all concepts and apply them to the ideas and information they have already acquired, they assimilate new concepts and conceptual meanings. (See Chapter 4 for an extended discussion of concept learning.)

Propositional Learning

Propositional learning involves combining or seeing the relationships between two or more lesser events or concepts and making a generalization that includes the properties of all. When concepts are restated into rules, principles, generalizations, or hypotheses, propositional learning is occurring. "An acre equals 43,560 square feet" is a statement of fact and a rather limited and nonmeaningful piece of information, but "to find the number of square feet in an acre, you must multiply the length by the width" is a generalization and is dependent upon knowing the concepts within the general mathematical rule, $A = l \times w$.

Discovery Learning

Meaningful reception learning
The ability to combine, relate, or reorganize ideas, concepts, and rules in order to generate new learning.

The preceding discussion has focused on what Ausubel calls **meaningful reception learning,** in which the content of what is to be learned is presented in final form; that is, the learner knows what is expected in the learning situation. There may be occasions when the learner must combine ideas, concepts, or rules in order to learn, but these are combinations of already learned materials and not the discovery of relationships. In contrast, in discovery learning, learners are not given the principal content of what is being learned; they must discover it before they can internalize the learning. This discovery results from the learner's active engagement in the rearrangement, reorganization, or transformation of materials. Many concepts are learned through discovery or by discovering new relationships by combining concepts. Once learning has occurred, it is internalized in the same way, by meaningful learning processes (Ausubel, 1960). Ausubel sees reception learning and discovery learning as complementary. Together they explain the mature individual's wide range of learning.

Using Cognitive-Field Principles in the Classroom

Bruner (1966, p. 40) considers his entire system of thought as a model for instruction rather than a model for learning. Instruction is "prescriptive in the sense that it sets forth rules concerning the most effective

Understanding Is More Important: That's a Fact

The parent-teacher conference centered around Lisa Unger's inability to recall multiplication facts. Lisa was a bright, ingenuous fifth-grade student who always wanted to go beyond the problem at hand. This annoyed her teacher, Mr. Feldman, particularly because Lisa commonly missed multiplication problems because of her inability to recall the facts.

As a result of the conference, the following information surfaced. Lisa was able to work out all the math problems Mr. Feldman gave. She could multiply two- and three-digit numbers and any problem that contained a zero was no problem at all—a skill not always shared by her classmates. It was clear that Lisa understood the concept of math, multiplication, and math problem solving. She simply mixed up the facts more often than it seemed she should, given how bright she was.

Mr. Feldman told Lisa's parents that Lisa was always into something other than what he had assigned. He attributed this behavior to Lisa's inability to disci-

pline herself. He concluded that, if Lisa could better control her "impulses," she would pay more attention and not make so many errors in multiplication. The parents agreed that this was a strategy the teacher should employ.

After two weeks of tighter controls on Lisa, Mr. Feldman observed that Lisa's overall performance had decreased rather than increased. The control decreased Lisa's self-motivation and, as a result, the quality of her work dropped off. Many teachers have students with Lisa's problem, which is not lack of control but lack of challenge by the material and boredom with the pace being set in the classroom. Lisa's priorities were different. She pursued higher level processes and wanted to be involved in things that were more challenging. Thus, she did not always attend to what she perceived as unimportant.

For Lisa and Mr. Feldman, there was never total resolution during the school year. He continued to believe that Lisa's failure to recall factual material was symptomatic of learning problems. Lisa continued to explore on her own

and engage in a variety of activities that often increased her learning and occasionally annoyed her teacher.

What Do You Think?

1. Should Mr. Feldman have insisted on Lisa's completing extra work in order to assure greater accuracy in facts?

2. Should Mr. Feldman have created more individualized and challenging assignments for Lisa?

3. Is it to be expected that this type of conflict will arise and never really be solved?

way of achieving knowledge or skill." To improve the potential for learning, he established four criteria for successful teaching-learning experiences.

First, "instruction should specify the experiences which most effectively implant in the individual a predisposition toward learning" (Bruner, 1966, p. 40). Here it is the interpersonal relations between the teacher and the learner that most affect the learning situation, although students' experiences with a subject also affect their willingness to learn.

Second, "instruction must specify the ways in which a body of knowledge should be structured so that it can be most readily grasped by the learner" (Bruner, 1966, p. 41). Optimal structure involves learning a set of propositions from which a larger body of knowledge can be generated.

Third, "instruction should specify the most effective sequences in which to present the materials to be learned" (Bruner, 1966, p. 41). Students seem to learn best when they move from simple to complex learning and from nonconceptual to conceptual. There is, of course, no universal instructional sequence for all learners; rather, the sequence may depend on prior learning and the learner's developmental stage, the nature of the instructional materials, and individual differences.

Fourth, "instruction should specify the nature and pacing of rewards and punishments in the process of learning and teaching" (Bruner, 1966, p. 41). Bruner does not deny the importance of feedback to learners, that is, giving learners immediate information about their success with the task. However, the teacher's goal is to shift emphasis from extrinsic, teacher-provided reinforcement to an intrinsic, self-reinforcement system and from immediate reward to deferred reward to increase the student's self-reliance.

Spiral Effect

Spiral effect
The organization of a school curriculum in progressively complex ways so students increasingly learn at higher conceptual levels.

Efficient learning capitalizes on the **spiral effect** within the structure of subject matter. This makes the sequence of instruction crucial and allows for the progressive development of curriculum across grade levels. For example, children in third grade may learn to form the simple past tense by adding "d" or "ed" to a verb, in the fourth grade learn to form the past tense with the helping verbs "have" and "is" and the past participle, and so on. The basic principles within a content area may be learned, reviewed, and restructured with each successive exposure to the content as it becomes increasingly complex. The better a school system has sequenced its content across grade levels, the more likely it is to gain maximum benefit from what has been learned about the spiral effect.

Categorization

Categorization
The organization and integration of new information with information that already exists.

Learning efficiency is also maximized through **categorization**—the process of organizing new information and integrating it with information that has been learned already. Learners need skills to appropriately sort and categorize the unending stream of information with which they are bombarded. "Cognitive mastery in a world that generates stimuli far faster than

we can sort them out depends upon strategies for reducing the complexity and clutter" (Bruner, 1971, p. 4). The better students conceptualize learning, the more likely they are to categorize learning in ways that are relevant and meaningful to them.

Comparing Cognitive and Reinforcement Theories

Historically, reinforcement and cognitive theories of learning have been viewed as mutually exclusive. Reinforcement theory is characterized by external reinforcement, external motivation, mechanical or rote learning, and limited generalizability. To some extent, research has supported these dichotomies. However, the classroom teacher may not make such clear distinctions and may find that effective teaching strategies include using dimensions of both systems of thought.

Reinforcement

Thorndike's law of effect clearly stated that reinforcement was necessary if learning was to take place. This law has not changed but its applications have. Ferster and Skinner (1957) demonstrated that there is less need for reinforcing learning than Thorndike and some of his followers envisioned.

As to types of reinforcers, Skinner's idea of feedback is similar to Bruner's, although Skinner (1968) believes that the purpose of feedback is to bring the student's behavior under the control of the reinforcement (1968), and Bruner (1966) thinks that reinforcement supports learning but does not cause it.

Reinforcement theory emphasizes external learning. As Maslow (1968, p. 685) states: "Reinforcement methods encourage extrinsic learning, i.e., learning of one outside, learning of the impersonal, of arbitrary associations, of arbitrary conditioning, of arbitrary meanings and responses." Cognitive psychologists believe that learning should be within the control of the learner, who learns by reasoning and exploring and only minimally by reinforcement (Elliott & Vasta, 1970; Taffel et al., 1974).

Reinforcement controls the individual's behavior. The assumption is made that learning not only occurs initially through reinforcement but is maintained through subsequent intermittent reinforcement. Skinner (1971) believes people are a collection of behaviors, structured and reinforced by the environment. Cognitive psychologists think people are inner driven, seeking relevant experiences, obtaining important goals, and carrying on internal interactions that make life purposeful and meaningful (Bruner, 1960; Lewin et al., 1944).

Motivation

The question here is whether individuals are self- or intrinsically motivated (the cognitive position) or whether motivation comes from the external environment (the reinforcement position). The issue of motivation has never been of much concern to stimulus-response psychologists, whose experiments in animal research have made limited use of the concept. In 1918, Woodworth introduced the term *drive* into experimental psychology, stating that, if an animal had no drive, it was useless to try to condition it. It was like trying to operate an automobile without gasoline. Drive became a major thrust in Hull's theory (1943), which posited a strong relationship among drive-stimulus-response-reinforcement. His experimental model required an animal to have a high drive, brought about by an induced state of deprivation, to gain the reinforcer in a conditioning experiment. Spence (1951) advanced the only major modification of this position when he said that reinforcement strengthens motivation, rather than the response. Both Lewin (1944) and Tolman (1938) criticized the mechanistic approach to motivation, partly on its assumption that animal and human motivation are the same; the latter, they stated, is goal directed and purposeful.

As early learning experiments with animals have been replaced by investigations into human learning, two major questions have surfaced: Does reinforcement motivate a person to continue acting in the ways that brought about the reinforcement? Are people primarily intrinsically or extrinsically motivated? (See Chapter 11 for a discussion of the broader issues of motivation.)

The cognitive position is that human motivation is more intrinsic than extrinsic. According to Bruner (1960, 1966) and others (Deci, 1975; Deci et al., 1980; Lepper & Greene, 1978; Lepper, Greene, & Nisbett, 1973), learners are energized by intrinsic motivation, which is based on the human need to be competent, self-confident, and self-reliant. When they are intrinsically motivated, they engage in a variety of learning and experimental activities without any regard to reinforcement or reward.

This energy is basic to Bruner's discovery learning, where students explore and reexplore their environment, finding new and different meanings in the process. If they are intrinsically motivated and perceive the school as an environment in which exploration can occur, then any limitations are imposed by self, teacher, or physical environment. Teachers who can arrange classroom environments so that challenging opportunities exist will find they need to spend little time extrinsically motivating or rewarding students. This is not an easy task, and, as Kolesnik (1976) has observed, student perception is a critical variable here. School environments must be optimal for students. If they see opportunities for involve-

ment, they will be involved. Activities that are too easy may be boring; those that are too hard may be ignored.

Generalization

"The first object of any act of learning, over and beyond the pleasure it may give, is that it should serve us in the future" (Bruner, 1960, p. 17). If this is to be achieved, then learning must occur in ways that are generalizable from one event to another, from one day to the next. Bruner and Ausubel, as well as their cognitive predecessors, emphasize relevancy and meaningfulness as key to understanding, which is then transferable to a variety of contexts. Bruner thinks this meaningful, highly transferable learning occurs primarily through self-initiative and discovery; Ausubel focuses on structuring the subject matter and teaching the relationships among concepts and principles.

Stimulus generalization
The ability of multiple stimuli to elicit one response.

Response generalization
The ability of one stimulus to elicit more than one response.

The stimulus-response position on generalization is much more limiting. **Stimulus generalization** occurs when more than one stimulus are capable of eliciting the same response. **Response generalization** occurs when more than one response are elicited by one stimulus. There must a high degree of similarity between the stimuli or the responses for generalization to occur. For example, an insulting remark and a shove may produce the same response—anger. But an insulting remark may produce multiple responses, such as anger, withdrawal, or retribution. Stimulus-response theory states that these specific responses have all been learned and are maintained through reinforcement.

Cognitive theory accounts for a much greater diversity of generalization in learning. Generalization occurs when we understand concepts and experiences through encountering and solving problems and applying this understanding to related problems. We transfer general reasoning skills developed in this process to a variety of academic areas and to behavior in the nonacademic areas of life as well. Generalization as it operates in cognitive learning is clearly more representative of the total learning experiences people have than it is within the framework of stimulus-response learning. (Strategies for problem solving are discussed in Chapter 4.)

Concept Summary 3–3

Cognitive-Behaviorism Comparisons		
Process	**Cognitive**	**Behavioral**
Reinforcement	Internal, optional	External, required
Motivation	Intrinsic, self-initiated	Extrinsic, teacher-dependent
Generalization	Conceptual, principle is transferred	Task specific, high stimulus or response similarity required

Student Perceptions as Reality

As most clinical psychologists tell us, perception is reality. In most human confrontations, the difference between people is attributable to one individual perceiving a situation to be different than another individual. Long-term problems, often described as chronic behaviors, are commonly a result of a person perceiving other persons, situations, or life experiences as negative, defeating, or punitive. It is not easy to reverse behavioral styles in people who generally perceive events in negative ways. This chapter focused on perception in cognitive areas, but perception is also a major factor in how students feel and act in school environments. Classroom teachers constantly encounter these aspects of student behavior within school contexts.

In the past decade, there has been considerable interest in the ways children make transitions into middle school/junior high environments. Studies generally investigate the students' perceptions of the school environment, anonymity, and/or victimization. "Perception of the school environment" refers to the extent that teachers exercise control. "Anonymity" is the students' perceptions of how well they are known or feel a part of the school environment. "Victimization" is the students' perceptions of how vulnerable they are in the school environment. Combining these perceptual dimensions provides some insight into how students perceive their school environment.

Several research studies have investigated these phenomena (Blyth, Hill, & Smyth, 1981; Blyth, Simmons, & Bush, 1978; Jones, 1981; Mitman & Packer, 1982; Thornburg & Jones, 1982; *Violent Schools–Safe Schools,* 1978). Most measured these student perceptions with paper and pencil scales that asked students to agree or disagree with the likelihood of conditions existing as reflected in the statements. Other studies asked students the same questions using the interview technique. Examples of items on the degree of control scale are

1. Teachers let other students get away with too much.

2. School is a dangerous place because no one controls students (see Blyth et al., 1981).

Examples from the anonymity scale are

1. Lots of kids don't know me in this school because it is so large.

2. At this school, the teachers don't seem to know who you are or what your name is.

3. This school has so many students in it that I feel I don't know lots of kids.

4. At this school most students don't seem to know who you are or what your name is (see Blyth et al., 1978).

Statements on the victimization scale include

1. It's always younger kids who get "picked on" in this school.

2. It is a shame that we all have to be so careful about protecting our personal property here at school.

3. There are too many students who threaten others here at school.

4. In this school, one has to worry about being "picked on."

5. Girls are more threatening to me than boys.

6. The school authorities don't do enough about kids who "shake down" other kids (see Blyth et al., 1978).

Examples from the negative peer cluster scale are

1. Older students may make fun of you.

2. Older students may bully or beat you up.

3. Older students will expect you to do things that you won't feel are right.

4. Personal possessions will be stolen (see Mitman & Packer, 1982).

Results of Studies

These instruments elicited three major findings about student perceptions. First, when individuals move from a familiar to an unfamiliar environment, their perceptions of lack of teacher control, anonymity, and victimization go up. Several studies have demonstrated this at several different grade levels. It is still uncertain as to whether these transitional perceptions, generally negative, are overcome relatively easily or if they may have long-term negative consequences.

Second, ninth-grade students in a middle school/junior high environment are likely to be perceived more negatively by the younger students in the school environment. Blyth et al. (1981, p. 107) report on this outcome:

Although we explored major domains which might be affected by the presence or absence of older students, we discovered that the students' perceptions of their school environment (in terms of the degree of control adults exercise, the degree of anonymity students perceived, and the extent to which students worried about being picked on) was the single domain most consistently affected by having older students in the school—particularly for females. Younger students, in general, perceived their school environment to be less controlled and more anonymous, and they worried more about being picked on when older students were present. This finding can be understood in terms of the sheer differences in student composition of the environment which students were perceiving. When ninth graders are in a school, the environment is made up of more physically mature students and the norms of behavior and misbehavior are probably quite different. Given the grade-related increases in substance use and dating/sexual behavior, for example, the environment can-

not help but reflect a higher overall involvement in such activities. In addition, it is likely that the presence of older students makes a difference in the types of rules which are created and how they are applied.

A third explanation for altering perceptions in this age range has to do with school size and living area. For example, Thornburg (1983) found that there is less negative perception in students who attend a smaller school (under three hundred students) than in those who attend a larger school (over seven hundred students). Similarly, rural students have fewer negative perceptions of their school environments than urban students.

What Schools Can Do

Research studies often provide information but virtually no suggestions as to the educational implications of their findings. The following ideas should reduce student apprehension, create a more positive school environment, and facilitate transition from one school to another:

1. In addition to the commonly held spring visit by the incoming fall students, have some general orientation meetings for students and their parents the first week of school. Such meetings should discuss the new school day, environment, and teacher expectations.

2. Identify for incoming students the potential problem areas or ways in which they may be victimized. If school officials let students know they are aware of potential trouble spots, they reduce the likelihood of those areas maintaining. Students need reassurance that they are not the only ones who know there are potential negative interactions in the school environment.

3. Incorporate a teacher advisement (old homeroom concept) program so that all students have at least one teacher with whom they can identify or turn to for help from time to time. Student perception of anonymity will decrease dramatically if they know there is an adult in that environment who cares.

4. Teachers should explain to students how and why their expectations are different. Too often teachers assume that, when students move into a middle level environment, they are aware of or should respond to the new school philosophies.

5. School districts should consider moving ninth graders into the high school. This not only changes the perceptual environment of a middle school/junior high, but places ninth graders with students with whom they are more developmentally matched.

In educational environments, the ability to perceive school environments positively is important. Students can be taught to understand and appreciate the social processes that go on and thereby develop themselves. Adequate perceptions or perspectives can be thought of as a skill that enables students to function maximally. In a socially impacted school environment where the range of social behavior is diverse, it is important to have a sense of self and not be unduly apprehensive about functioning in an environment that is, by definition, supposed to facilitate personal learning and development.

Annotated Readings

Ausubel, D. P. (1980). Schemata, cognitive structure, and advance organizers: A reply to Anderson, Spiro, and Anderson. *American Educational Research Journal, 17,* 400–404.

> *In 1978, Anderson, Spiro, and Anderson wrote an exhaustive article in which they attacked Ausubel's concept of advance organizers. In this article, Ausubel argues that the criticisms of his theory are unfounded. Because of the importance of this concept in learning practices, it is an interesting and informative article.*

Barringer, C., & Gholson, B. (1979). Effects of type and combination of feedback upon conceptual learning by children: Implications for research in academic learning. *Review of Educational Research, 49,* 459–478.

> *The authors review the literature on laboratory research that looked at various effects of verbal, symbolic, and tangible feedback on children's conceptual learning. Consensus from numerous studies supports the idea that verbal and symbolic feedback produce more rapid acquisition than tangible feedback. The authors conclude that these laboratory findings could likely be applied to classroom settings.*

Cunningham, P. M. (1980). Applying a compare/contrast process to identifying polysyllabic words. *Journal of Reading Behavior, 12,* 211–223.

> *The study was designed to investigate the likelihood of learning polysyllabic words. Fourth- and fifth-grade students were compared by giving one group a context of having learned one- and two-syllable words prior to learning the polysyllabic words. Results showed that these students did better than their control counterparts in learning the more involved words. The author concludes that readers might be able to identify an unfamiliar word by using an analogue or compare/contrast strategy.*

Light, P., & Simmons, B. (1983). The effects of a communication task upon the representation of depth relationships in young children's drawings. *Journal of Experimental Child Psychology, 35,* 81–92.

> *Attempts to represent the occlusion of a farther object by a nearer one are limited. Instead, most studies draw the objects side by side or one above the other. This experiment attempted to assess children's ability to produce view-specific drawings by creating a context that demanded such drawings. The experiments found age differences; that is, there were more view-specific drawings among seven- and eight-year-olds than among five- and six-year-olds. Apparently, the younger age group is developmentally limited in its ability to produce view-specific drawings.*

Luiten, J., Ames, W., & Ackerson, G. (1980). A meta-analysis of the effects of advance organizers on learning and retention. *American Educational Research Journal, 17,* 211–218.

> *The researchers analyzed the facilitative effect of advance organizers on learning and retention. They statistically evaluated 135 published and unpublished studies, comparing studies by grade level, subject area, organizer presentation mode, and subject ability level. The conclusion supported the facilitative effect on both learning and retention.*

Robinson, E. J., & Robinson, W. P. (1982). Knowing when you don't know enough: Children's judgments about ambiguous information. *Cognition, 12,* 267–280.

> *The researchers tested the extent to which children could make a correct interpretation if given an ambiguous message. Children were given both ver-*

bally and visually ambiguous messages and under both conditions failed to make correct judgments. The researchers contend that their results imply that children's failure to realize when verbal messages are ambiguous is but one aspect of a more general failure to realize when they have insufficient information at their disposal to guarantee a correct interpretation of what the world is like.

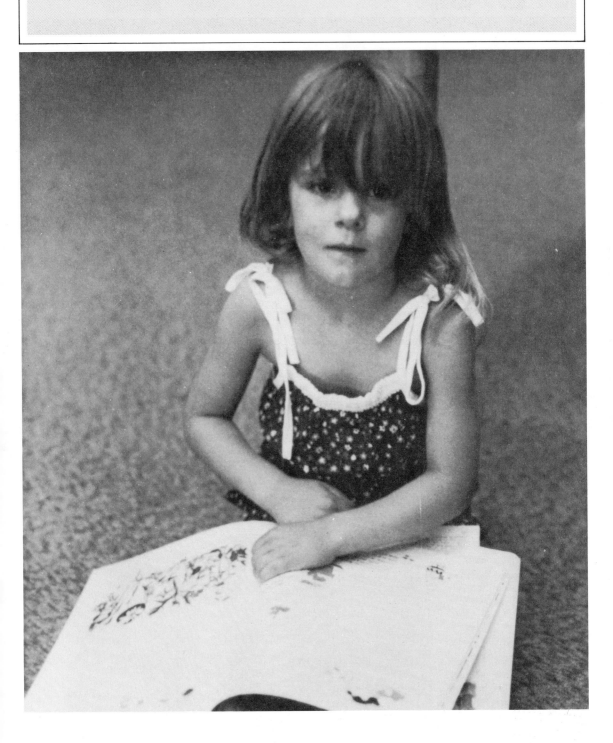

Concept Learning

The Shoreham school district is reevaluating its social studies curriculum. Two representatives from each of its twenty-two junior high schools have already attended an organizational meeting that was designed to open the channels of communication between schools and develop a plan of action. Two dominant points of view emerged at this meeting: that social studies should be taught from a chronological perspective and that social studies instruction should take a conceptual approach. Both groups have been asked to write a statement presenting their position and to be prepared to present and defend it at the next meeting.

At the next meeting, Mr. Glover, representing the group advocating the conceptual approach, presented his position first. He said that social studies needs a conceptual framework or overriding structure, made up of interrelated concepts, to which students can relate what they are learning. Their understanding of this framework allows students to see how they can apply something they learn about one aspect of life (such as kinship structure) to specific cultures (such as Asian or American). The ability to make such a transfer facilitates concept learning and results in students learning more about specific cultures.

Mr. Glover also cited what his group sees as the limitations in the chronological approach. For example, most dates, places, persons, or events are factual information. Outside their conceptual context, they are not very meaningful. Treating topics within a time period also tends to make them appear independent or unrelated. The chronological approach is too limited because important topics should be carried across multiple time frames. In essence, the advocates of the conceptual approach believe students learn more if they see the meaning and relevance in social studies content.

The chronological position was presented by Ms. Hart. She contended that students understand social studies better if they can see how an aspect of it, such as economics, unfolded across time. If students learn the economic base of the nation and how that base has developed across time, then they are better able to understand present-day economics. She argued that comparing the American economic structure in any given era with that of other countries would not yield the same understanding as comparing our own economic structure over three hundred years. In essence, the chronological

93

approach advocates believe that students learn more if they see how some aspect of the social structure has changed across time. Social studies should teach how history impacts on the present.

To decide whether social studies can best be taught by a conceptual approach, a historical approach, or a combination of the two, you must understand learning theory from the reinforcement and conceptual approaches. Chapters 2 and 3 and this one provide the information base you need to make such decisions.

Topics covered in this chapter include:

- *Concept acquisition*
- *Concept formation*
- *Concept teaching*

Concept Acquisition

A concept is an understanding of objects, symbols, or events that can be generalized to a variety of contexts, both familiar and unfamiliar. Concepts provide structure and meaning to the mind and are the framework within which we make sense of our experiences. Klausmeier (1977) sees concepts as the most important component of the maturing individual's cognitive structure. When we learn a concept, we have created a basis for interpreting new information and for retrieving what we have already experienced. Concepts also help us discriminate between objects, symbols, and events that represent the concept category and those that do not (Carroll, 1964; Gagne, 1977a; Williams & Carnine, 1981).

Two theoretical arguments that have persisted in education and psychology can help explain concepts and their role in human behavior. The first centers around the issue of language. The second originated in behavioral and cognitive psychology. In addition to these two broad theoretical issues, there are numerous interpretations of how concepts are taught and learned, an important consideration inasmuch as the instructor's ability to teach at a conceptual level is critical to students' learning concepts. At present, there are several major emphases on concept teaching. In this chapter, I discuss the behavioral approach, the cognitive approach, the developmental approach, the hierarchical approach, and concept mapping.

Language

Prelanguage position
The belief that children attach meaning to objects or events in the environment even though they cannot verbally represent them.

Advocates of the **prelanguage position** hold that verbal facility broadens our ability to represent something in our minds. Thus, the possibility of learning concepts prior to acquiring language is limited (Vygotsky, 1962). As concepts become more complex, we represent them mentally with language. This position holds that there can be no prelanguage concepts.

Its advocates believe that children perceive objects or events in their environment and attach meaning to them. Concept formation is the process of recognition, based upon perception (Lewis, 1963; Montessori, 1972; Nelson, 1977; Ricciuti, 1965). An implicit assumption within this view is that infants can devise sensory grouping, that is, they can relate things that have common perceptual properties. Those who view the infant's learning capacity as nonconceptual question the prelanguage position. They believe infants lack the developmental readiness to conceptualize (Kagan, 1966; Klausmeier, Ghatala, & Frayer, 1974; Piaget, 1952).

The **postlanguage position** holds that language, development, and/or prerequisite learning are essential conditions for concept formation (Ausubel & Robinson, 1969; Gagne, 1977a; Olson, 1970; Taba, 1967; Tennyson & Park, 1980; Travers, 1979). The mind must relate ideas in order for concepts to emerge. The perceptual or physical reference points are too limited or insufficient to build concepts that have the potential for broad representation. Thus, attaching meaning to words provides a broader base for conceptualizing. Research seems to confirm that concepts can be elaborately constructed through learning (Gagne & Wiegand, 1968; Markle, 1977; Markle & Tiemann, 1970), development (Kagan, Moss, & Siegel, 1963; Klausmeier et al., 1974; Levin & Allen, 1976; Vygotsky, 1962) and the acquisition of higher mental processes (Bruner, Goodnow, & Austin, 1956). I discuss each position in this chapter.

Postlanguage position
The belief that language is necessary if concepts are to be learned.

Learning

The behaviorists believe we acquire concepts through reinforcement, discrimination, and **hierarchical structures** (that is, one piece of infor-

Hierarchical structures
The arrangement of learning in a way where lower level skills are prerequisite to and facilitate the acquisition of higher level skills.

mation builds on another, with the accumulative effect being the learning of complex concepts). Ausubel (1968), Bruner (1960), and Gagne (1977a) have stated that ideas, objects, and events are highly conceptual and abstract and are interrelated as rules or propositions that facilitate problem solving. Concepts are not dependent on physical referents during their acquisition or retention stages. They are based on the cognitive capacity to combine and recombine ideas in ways that are relevant and meaningful to the learner. We learn concepts by maintaining relevance of all prior learning in light of new learning and everyday living experiences. In this chapter, I describe these conceptual processes as rules and problem-solving strategies.

Concept Formation

Concept formation is the ability to identify characteristics of events to which you are exposed and group or organize them in meaningful ways. Ausubel and Robinson (1969, p. 62) describe this process in a child who is left for a while to play with a variety of cubes:

> These cubes, we will suppose, differ in size, color, and texture. As a result of this concrete experience, the child discovers inductively the criterial attributes of the cube. Moreover, these attributes are embedded in a representative image of a cube, an image that the child has developed from his experience and can recall in the absence of real cubes. This process of inductively discovering the criterial attributes of a class of stimuli is called *conceptual formation*. When it is complete, the child is said to possess the concept of a cube, and the meaning of this concept is the representative image comprising the criterial attributes of this class of objects.

Ausubel suggests that children can learn concepts without knowing the concept name or word, in this case, *cube*. He considers the language the verbal representation of an already acquired concept. This process is illustrated in Figure 4–1. The word *cube* (stage II) is equated with the representative image "cube" (stage I). Ausubel and Robinson (1969) suggest that this two-stage process, formation of a concept and learning the concept names, is how we learn most concepts, although they recognize there are many occasions when these two stages occur simultaneously. The two steps have a strong relationship; thus, the concept will be more complete once the attributes of the concept and the language describing it have been learned.

Ausubel has suggested that, when children understand words, such meaning may be represented by **denotative** or **connotative understanding.** In the case of the object cube and the word *cube*, the verbal representation is what Ausubel calls denotative meaning. Connotative meaning refers to the personal, affective, and attitudinal reactions that the term elicits in a child, depending upon his or her experiences with the class of objects. He suggests that concept names such as "country" or "friend" may have connotative overtones, with the intensity or range of emotion varying from individual to individual.

Denotative understanding
The verbal representation of a physical object.

Connotative understanding
Learning the meaning of something in affective and personal ways, beyond any literal meaning.

96

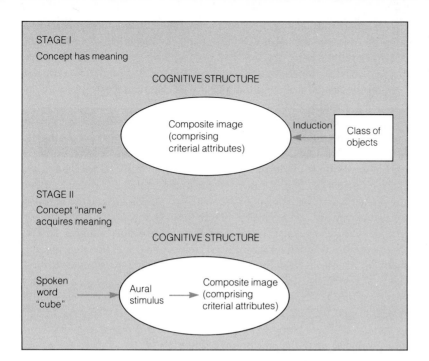

Figure 4–1
Two stages in learning of concept names. [Source: Ausubel & Robinson (1969), p. 62.]

Ausubel's connotative concept is important for three reasons. First, he has demonstrated that a person can learn something meaningful in two domains, the cognitive and affective. Second, he stresses the importance of affective learning, recognizing that affective concepts are an important part of learning. Third, he extends the idea of concept learning in more useful and relevant ways than those the behavioral model suggests. It is important not to underestimate these factors, especially because we need to learn concepts that are transferable and meaningful across our entire life span.

Concept Teaching

Behavioral Approach

When learners make similar responses to different stimuli, they have recognized the similarities of properties so that, even though the stimuli are different, they evoke the same response category. This is called generalization. For example, the child who learns the word *ball* when associating it with a typical ball that can be bought in a toy store may also use the word *ball* to describe a basketball, tennis ball, soccer ball, football, or golf ball. The category "ball" is formed as the word association is generalized to multiple instances.

Learners must also be able to discriminate between objects that fit a category and those that do not. If they are given objects in the environment that do not fit the category "ball," they should recognize this as a noninstance of ball. As Markle and Tiemann (1970, p. 42) put it, "the learner really understands a concept when he can correctly classify previously unmet bits of reality into two piles."

Behaviorists have focused on **concrete objects,** which are learned initially through the association of a term or action with an object—that is, through the learning of a single object or discriminate. For example, a teacher wants her students to learn the concept of round. She places a set of three objects ○ □ □ in front of them and says that a surprise is under one of the objects, but does not reveal which one. She has put the surprise under the round object and will continue to do so throughout the learning process. On the first attempt to find the surprise, the students lift the objects until they find the surprise under the round one. Then they identify the object as round. The learners have now associated the stimulus (round object and word *round*) with the response (lifting) and have been reinforced (surprise). To establish this relationship, the teacher presents the problem again, varying the position of the round object □ □ ○ ; □ ○ □ so that the learners come to respond to the round object and the word *round,* rather than to the placement of the objects.

When the students reach the point of always being able to identify any round object as a member of the category round, we infer that concept learning has occurred. In other words, learners operate at a conceptual level. They can discriminate among a variety of new sets of objects in order to identify and respond to other round objects. They understand the class of round objects and can identify and respond to an object of that class even though it is presented in an unfamiliar context. Further confirmation of the conceptualization of round can be demonstrated by providing learners with a variety of round objects that vary in size and context—for example, a quarter, a saucer, a volleyball, an automobile tire, a clock, and a propeller. If they recognize that each object is round, although they all differ in some respect, they have learned the concept.

Although reinforcement theory stresses objects, things, or ideas that have concrete representation, it is not restricted to this type of learning. Markle and Tiemann (1969; 1970, p. 42) point this out in regard to physics:

> Given a new example of "force," for instance, a student recognizes that this new example of force is *generalizing*. Given a bit of reality which a physicist would not classify as a force, the student who rejects it is *discriminating*. To really understand a concept is to be able to generalize all possible *instances* that might be presented and to be able to discriminate all possible *noninstances*, including those that bear a strong resemblance to the members of the class.

Markle (1977) makes two suggestions that have important implications for classroom teachers teaching concepts. First, no concrete instance is an example of only one concept. Second, a concept cannot be taught with a single example.

When you present students with new objects, they must realize that the way you present them is not the only way they will occur. Children and adults often limit their understanding of things because of misrepresentation, conventional labeling, or stereotyping. As Markle suggests, most objects elicit multiple rather than single classification responses. She cites a study she did in a college educational psychology class in which she showed a picture of a cow and asked students to classify it with the first label that came to mind. The overwhelming response was cow. When students were asked to provide a second label, animal surfaced. As additional labels were elicited, additional ways of classifying the object emerged. This object was not only a cow, but an animal, a farm animal, a mammal, and a quadruped. Classroom teachers should not lose sight of this important point. Few objects defy multiple descriptions; thus, teachers should develop the concept as completely as possible.

Markle has developed the concept of a **knowledge structure,** which states that any given concept you wish to establish in learners is also part of another concept or a more encompassing knowledge structure. Using the illustration of teaching the concept "dog," Markle (1977, p. 14) demonstrates the principle behind knowledge structure (see Figure 4–2):

> Using the all-time favorite example of what a concept is, the concept of "dog," let us embed it as a knowledge structure. It is a class that can be broken into several subsets, the names of the breeds, or into functional classifications such as "hunting dog." It is also a subset of many other concepts, such as "mammal" and "vertebrate" and "animal." These relations are hierarchical within the animal kingdom.

The concept learning that occurs in behavioral approaches depends on three processes: concreteness, generalizability, and discrimination. This type of learning is useful inasmuch as it provides concept definition and knowledge structures that can be elaborated. Table 4–1 compares conceptual and nonconceptual concept learning. The examples of the conceptual perspective seem to be an extension of the more concrete concepts, an idea I discuss further in the next section on cognitive approaches to concept learning.

Cognitive Approach

The impetus for the study of concept learning has come out of the work of cognitive psychologists. Bruner and Ausubel have investigated these processes and provided some working models for concept learning.

Figure 4–2
Part of the animal kingdom hierarchy. [Source: Markle (1977). By permission of the author.]

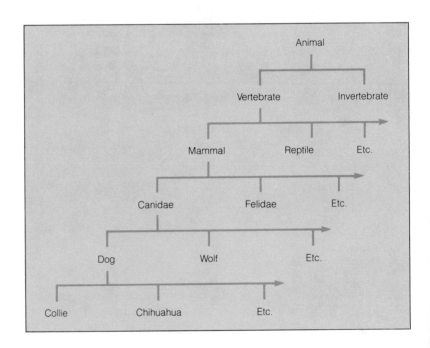

Table 4–1   Conceptual and Nonconceptual Learning Compared

Content	Nonconceptual Perspective	Conceptual Perspective
Arabic and Roman Numerals	Learner presented with systems and can discriminate between samples from each	Learner can equate numbers from both systems
Numbers 1 through 10	Learner knows their names and assigns names to numbers	Learner orders numbers according to their value
Primary and Secondary Colors	Learner recognizes primary and secondary colors	Learner describes differences between primary and secondary colors
Domestic and Wild Cats	Learner identifies domestic/wild cats by physical features	Learner classifies cats by known categories and subcategories

Bruner's idea of **categorization**/classification as a way to deal effectively with environmental complexity is important. Classification is the process of organizing information with previously learned information. The ability to place an object in a category is evidence that a concept has been formed. Categories or concepts are made up of objects, events, or ideas that are the same or highly similar.

Bruner et al. (1956) described **identity categorization** as the process by which we classify events as forms of the same thing. There is also an **equivalence category** wherein we respond to different things as if they were the same. In an identity category, the student would recognize that different makes of automobiles (Chevrolets, Fords, and Plymouths) are all cars. In the equivalence category, different objects (automobiles, buses, trains, ships, airplanes, horses, camels) are seen as equivalent, that is, all are considered modes of transportation.

Bruner et al. (1956) list five advantages to categorizing:

1. *Categorizing makes the environment a simpler place to interact.* Grouping objects so that we respond to classes of events rather than to everything we encounter is an efficient way to organize information and make it more meaningful.

2. *Categorizing facilitates our ability to identify the objects of the environment.* Seeing the similarities in things allows us to identify the myriad objects or events we encounter daily.

3. *Categorizing reduces the need for constant learning.* We do not have to develop new categories for everything we learn. The only time new categories are devised is when there is no previous knowledge in this content area. With concept categories, the similar attributes of things,

Categorization
The ability to process information into the mind, integrating it with already existing information.

Identity categorization
The ability to classify events that represent the same category.

Equivalence categorization
The ability to respond to different objects, events, or other phenomena as if they were the same.

whether concrete or abstract, allow us to classify many new or unfamiliar objects into known categories.

4. *Categorizing provides us with direction for subsequent activities.* Coming upon a road sign that says "Stop Ahead" or "Dangerous Curve" provides contextual clues for appropriate actions. We do not have to move ahead in order to know there is a stop sign or come upon a dangerous curve at normal speed to recognize its danger. Conceptual categories provide the learner with a preparedness to effectively deal with conceptual events.

5. *Categorizing improves our capacity to order and relate events.* It is the attributes of objects, events, or ideas that allow us to classify. When we place an object into a category, we relate it to our existing cognitive structure, thus enhancing that category and giving meaning to the newly related event.

Bruner et al. (1956) described three types of concepts: conjunctive, disjunctive, and relational. **Conjunctive concepts** are concrete and depend on an understanding of several attributes. Multiple experiences allow us to form conjunctive concepts such as ball, toy, car, or fruit.

Disjunctive concepts have multiple meanings, any one of which is sufficient to classify the object within a category as being representative of that category or event. Travers (1979, p. 334) illustrates the disjunctive concept using the strike in baseball. "A strike may be either a ball thrown by the pitcher that is over the plate and between a batter's shoulders and knees, or a ball at which the batter swings and misses, or a ball that the batter hits foul (outside of the playing limits of the diamond). Any one of these attributes enables the observer to classify it as a strike."

We form **relational concepts** when it is clear that multiple attributes or events are related in some way. As we relate them, new meaning emerges. Making a grade in this class is an example. There are several

Conjunctive conceptualization
The ability to place multiple objects in the same category because they have similar attributes.

Disjunctive conceptualization
The understanding of multiple meanings in any phenomenon that represents the concept category.

Relational concept
The ability to draw relationships between two or more concrete objects, commonly known as a "rule."

Concept Summary 4–1

Basic Concept Assumptions	
Concrete Concept	Learned by associating action with an object (word-action association)
Knowledge Structure	Recognition that any concept may also be included in additional concept categories (object is member of two or more classes of events)
Identity Categorization	Multiple events classified as a form of the same thing (object similarity)
Equivalence Categorization	Different things categorized as if they were equivalent (object dissimilarity; function similarity)

possible grades available, all of which exist because of the relationship between critical events, which could include test scores, term papers, and attendance. The combination of these factors determines your grade. Thus, test scores, term papers, and attendance are relational categories.

Hierarchical Approach

Bottom-Up Method   Robert Gagne's **learning hierarchy** approach has been instrumental in helping learners see the relationships between concepts in an ordered, hierarchical way. When we analyze student learning to the point of delineating an entire set of capabilities having an ordered relationship to each other, we have a learning hierarchy (Gagne, 1970a). Implicit is the idea that intellectual skills and concepts are arranged in a hierarchical order so that each subordinate skill is prerequisite to the skill immediately higher in the structure. This process explains the notion that simple concepts facilitate learning complex concepts to help learners function at a higher level. Gagne contends that we learn higher level skills more easily if we have learned the subordinate skills.

Learning hierarchy
The organization of a set of learned capabilities so they have logical relationships with one another.

Gagne's hierarchy takes into account a wider range of learning than any of the models discussed thus far. He recognizes that there is a wide range of nonconceptual learning, such as stimulus-response bonds and discriminations and the ability to recognize similarities and differences in objects or events, that occurs and is a necessary prerequisite for many concepts to emerge. Nonconceptual discriminations are typically learned by memory through reinforcement. Figure 4–3 shows their relative importance to the total learning hierarchy.

Gagne sees concepts and rules as being composed of simpler concepts and rules (1968, 1977a, 1980). These prerequisite concepts and rules are integral components that are organized into a higher level of learning. Figure 4–3 shows the relationship between concepts, rules, and higher order rules. These three hierarchical levels are ways of combining and representing multiple concepts of a variety of complexities into relevant and meaningful learning.

Gagne (1970a) states that, when a concept is learned through direct observation of physical objects or through an understanding of words that characterize the qualities or properties of objects, it is concrete. In this type of learning, a common identifying response may be made to several objects representative of the same class.

Relational concepts are formed by two or more concrete concepts. At this level, the learner is able to identify the functional relationship of two or more concrete concepts and to distinguish this relationship from others. "When the individual possesses the rule as a capability, he is able to identify the component concepts and to demonstrate that they relate to one another in the particular manner of the rule" (Gagne, 1970a, p. 1972).

When new problem situations occur, the learner combines two or more relational concepts to form a new rule that will lead to the solution. In other words, "problem solving may be viewed as a process by which the learner discovers a combination of previously learned rules that he can

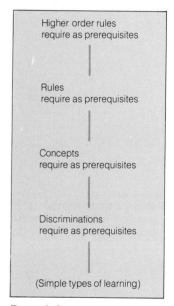

Figure 4–3
Intellectual skills arranged in order of increasing complexity. (From The Conditions of Learning, *2nd ed., by Robert M. Gagne. Copyright © 1970 by Holt, Rinehart and Winston, Inc. Reprinted by permission of Holt, Rinehart, and Winston, CBS College Publishing.)*

103

apply to achieve a solution for a novel problem situation" (Gagne, 1970a, p. 214).

Thus, the three levels of conceptual learning move from concrete to abstract and result in the emergence of complex, abstract thought. These three levels further imply a capability of intellectual functioning not found in nonconceptual learning. The learner's response repertoire becomes more flexible and less dependent on the immediate stimulus situation he or she encounters.

The teacher can best assist the learner in concept attainment by (1) establishing the prerequisite knowledge required for concept learning and (2) specifically teaching abstract properties or characteristics for classes of objects so that the learner acquires a basis for classification other than physical characteristics. Once students have learned a concept, they are no longer under the stimulus control needed with lower level learning. Their dependency on the teacher for appropriate stimuli is reduced, and spoken or written verbal instruction becomes sufficient. Students then become capable of generating responses internally and are free to apply concepts to a multiplicity of events or situations.

The requirements for reinforcements are not as demanding with concept learning for three reasons:

1. If they can maintain a conceptual response, students have had, over a period of time, sufficient acquaintance with the response.

2. The increased associative strength within the learner may itself be reinforcing.

3. The student may begin to supply internal reinforcers to the learning situation.

The following example helps clarify concept learning. The students in a geometry class have difficulty distinguishing different geometric shapes. Although they all know a triangle, they do not always correctly identify quadrilaterals, pentagons, hexagons, octagons, and decagons. What type of learning is involved here, and how can the material be more effectively taught? The problem provides an excellent opportunity to review the distinction Gagne made between discrimination learning and concept learning. At first glance, this learning task appears to fit the multiple discrimination category. In actuality, it requires that students operate at the concept learning level.

Multiple discrimination learning means that an individual is able to distinguish among several similar things on the basis of their physical differences. A triangle is distinctly different from an octagon. Therefore, students must first learn the physical properties and the name of each distinct shape. Then, when different shapes are presented to them as a group in a learning trial, students should be able to discriminate among them correctly.

What happens when students encounter new and differently composed triangles or octagons? They are no longer able simply to distinguish between the shapes already learned because these new figures are shaped somewhat differently. They must now have learned the conceptual properties that go into making a triangle three sided, a hexagon six sided, and an octagon eight sided. Learning what constitutes particular geometric figures implies understanding the concepts of figures. The multiple discrimination tasks are prerequisite to the concept learning task, but the former is restricted to observable physical properties while conceptualization infers some understanding of nonphysical, or abstract, properties. Therefore, such materials can be most effectively taught by stressing the nonphysical, identifiable properties that make one figure three sided and another eight sided—that is, the abstract properties of figures, such as space, area, proportion, angle, and geometric design.

If students understand what something is (a concept) and can relate it in a meaningful and functional way to another concept, we may assume they have learned a rule. In rule learning, it is not the complexity of the prerequisite concepts that is accentuated, but rather their relationship, which allows the rule to emerge. As students learn more and more concepts, they gradually come to use them in a variety of ways; thus, they form more rules. The learning of rules varies in complexity and is part of the learning of very young children, adolescents, and adults.

Rules are usually verbal statements. However, a rule is an "inferred capability" and a verbal statement is a "representation of a rule" (Gagne, 1970a, p. 193). Therefore, being able to verbalize a rule does not mean that learners understand it. Verbal statements are built on associations in which the learner combines several learned responses to make a logical statement. The statement does not, however, indicate any level of understanding or capacity to act. Rules are build on concepts, and the understanding of and implicit capability to act on these concepts determine whether the rule is learned. For example, the rule "Water is a compound of H_2O" is a verbal statement, but it is also characterized by certain concepts—"chemical," "elements," "hydrogen," "oxygen," "parts," and "compounds"— that must be learned if the rule is to be understood.

The accuracy and adequacy of rules depend on the students' level of concept attainment when they learn the rule. Thus, teachers must first specify and analyze the rule they wish the learner to acquire and then make sure that the learner has acquired the concepts that are essential to understanding and applying it. The rule will usually take the form of a verbal statement. If it does, the teacher must be certain that what the learner ultimately acquires is not merely this verbal utterance but rather a true conceptualization of the rule. The teacher can accomplish this by

Earl is a highly intelligent sixth-grade boy who always extends the teacher's presentation or classroom assignment to the next logical step. He never stops at the question asked or the work given. He not only answers the test questions, but often rewrites them for greater clarity.

Earl has a distinct advantage over most of his classmates. In addition to being highly conceptual, he has a great memory, is already using abstract reasoning, and is capable of building on almost any problem presented to him. By any standard, he is a gifted student—most describe him as a genius. In addition, he has a good personality, does not act superior to other students, and is socially interactive. In short, he has his multiple attributes in good perspective.

From time to time Ms. MacLeod, Earl's teacher in a self-contained classroom, feels threatened by Earl's presence. Such a student is most challenging, and it is easy to feel threatened, embarrassed, even inferior. But Ms. MacLeod has gradually learned not to get defensive when challenged, not to take Earl's corrections or persistence personally. Instead, she tries to create an environment wherein Earl can engage in high-level problem solving. The key is to move beyond continuously presenting more material at the same level of complexity and to provide Earl with classroom problems and assignments that require higher level processes. After about six weeks, Ms. MacLeod has begun to let Earl create many of his own assignments, a strategy that motivates him.

There are not such students in every classroom, but there are some students who have a percentage of Earl's potential. These boys and girls require greater challenges than normally emerge in the classroom. Teachers must be aware, encourage, and create positive learning environments for

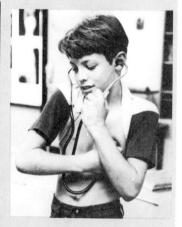

such students. In a real sense, it takes a gifted teacher to challenge a gifted student.

What Do You Think?

1. How much time should the teacher spend working with Earl?

2. Should students like Earl be given plenty of latitude in the classroom?

3. What type of student activities in classroom environments do you think would threaten you?

Concepts and Rules

1. As the component concepts that form a rule become relevant for the learner acquiring that rule, the concepts gain a greater level of meaningfulness.

2. A rule is conceptualized; by its emergence from two or more concepts, it holds a meaning independent of lower level responses.

3. A rule is productive; rule learning requires application, which may infer more meaningfulness than lower levels of learning.

4. Learners are more likely to retain rules than to retain lower level concepts. Therefore, repetition does not seem to be a necessary condition for learning rules.

---

reviewing the concepts that make up the rule to be learned. If the teacher finds that the student has not acquired one of the components, he or she must teach it.

Next the teacher should give students an opportunity to demonstrate the functionality of the rule by both applying it and stating what has happened. If the rule implies capability, as most do, learners can benefit by seeing it in operation. In addition, the recognition of successful performance has reinforcing value.

There is a minimal need for reinforcement at the concept learning level. As concepts are learned and combined into rules, they become more meaningful units. If the content is relevant to the learner, the combination of understanding, meaningfulness, and relevancy makes it more probable that learning will occur.

The relationship between concepts and rules in Gagne's hierarchical approach to concept teaching is not only relevant and meaningful, but it accounts for how previously learned intellectual skills facilitate new learning. We must retain learned concepts if we are to relate them in more highly structured ways, such as rules. I discussed these preexisting cognitive structures in Chapter 3. The importance of prior knowledge and its recall at the time of new learning continues to concern cognitive psychologists, especially those who are using the contemporary theoretical model of learning and retention known as information processing (Bransford, 1979; Glass, Holyoak, & Santa, 1979; Mayer, 1975).

Top-Down Method Ausubel's (1968) idea that learning is facilitated when learners have an organized set of inclusive ideas into which they can subsume new learning is somewhat different from Gagne's hierarchical framework. Whereas Gagne defines the concepts that are required to formulate a rule, Ausubel provides learners with the rule and then gets them to discover its relevant concepts. Gagne's approach has been referred to as "bottom-up" processing, and Ausubel's has been described as "top-down" processing (Rumelhart & Ortony, 1977). In both models, all learning is conceptual, meaningful, and capable of being related in order to acquire new learning and meaning.

The top-down approach assumes that, if a student learns an inclusive category, such as animals, the teacher can then teach the attributes of the category. Figure 4–4 illustrates this process. The inclusive category animals is conceptualized as having skin, being mobile, needing food, and breathing. **Inclusiveness** means that all members that fit the category have these characteristics.

Inclusiveness
The extent to which an idea best represents the understanding of that oncept category.

The next step is to discover classes of animals that are different in some ways, although they have common inclusive properties. Birds and fish are two such categories. The next step is to identify animals that fit one of the two categories. In Figure 4–4, canary and ostrich represent birds; shark and salmon represent fish. Learning at the conceptual level is indicated by being able to identify other animals that represent the categories birds and fish.

The final top-down process is to describe the defining characteristics of specific animals, such as the ostrich or salmon. This conceptual level allows students to encounter these objects on subsequent occasions and recognize them as members of the same class. This hierarchical network allows for interactions at multiple levels of complexity. Students can classify a canary as an animal before they have learned all the definitive characteristics of a bird. Once they have learned the concept "bird," the

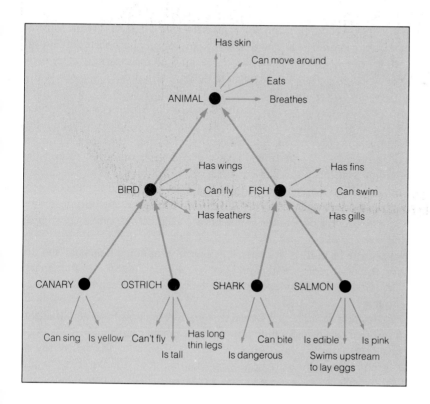

Figure 4–4
Hypothetical adult's knowledge about animals: Collins's and Quillian's network hierarchy.
[*Source: Collins & Quillian (1969), p. 242.*]

Different Strategies: Equivalent Outcomes	
Top-Down	**Bottom-Up**
1. Begin with the most inclusive idea	1. Begin with specific instance of a concept
2. Identify attributes of most inclusive idea	2. Develop concept category by exposure to multiple instances
3. Classify range of objects, ideas that represent inclusive idea	3. Show relationships between concept categories
4. Give specific instance of category classification	4. Demonstrate generalizability of conceptual relationships through problem solving

concept "canary" is more comprehensive. The top-down approach is more flexible than the bottom-up approach because the latter is restricted to previously learned concepts and rules.

Mapping

Concept mapping
The method of showing the relationship between concepts or ideas within the structure of subject matter.

The work on **concept mapping** is an outgrowth of Ausubel's principle of meaningful learning. He viewed learning on a continuum from rote (lower end) to meaningful (higher end). By relating all new learning to already existing learning, Ausubel was able to describe the process wherein learning becomes more meaningful (see Figure 4–5). Joseph Novak has gone one step further than either the top-down or the bottom-up approaches. He has devised a two-dimensional strategy that visually represents the relationship between concepts, rather than inferring them, as in hierarchical learning. Concept mapping is a way to demonstrate the relationship between concepts within the structure of subject matter. The two-dimensionality of the map allows for the representation of the various component concepts within an inclusive concept as well as the propositional relations among dependent concepts (Novak, 1979, 1980a; Posner & Rudnitsky, 1982; Stewart, VanKirk, & Rowell, 1979; E. Thornburg, 1981). Novak (1980a, p. III-1) assumes that concept mapping helps us "see the subject matter more clearly and learn the subject matter more meaningfully." Graphic representation of the relationship between ideas facilitates learning.

Novak (1980b) has observed that not all concepts have equal weight; some are more inclusive than others. In a concept map, the most inclusive concept is always at the top. The hierarchical arrangement is a way of showing how less-inclusive concepts (Ausubel's subsumption, see Figure 4–5) are related to the most inclusive concept. There may be many levels

LONG-TERM INFORMATION PROCESSING
ACCORDING TO AUSUBEL'S THEORY

Meaningful Learning   New knowledge is consciously linked to existing specifically relevant concepts and propositions in cognitive structure and incorporated into these concepts.

Learning moves higher on the rote-meaningful continuum when the following processes are facilitated.

THE ROTE-MEANINGFUL LEARNING CONTINUUM

Subsumption   incorporation of new knowledge into a specifically relevant existing concept or proposition.

Integrative Reconciliation   new learning that results in explicit delineation of similarities and differences between related ideas.

Superordinate Learning   new concepts or propositions acquired that relate the meanings of two or more related, less inclusive ideas.

Progressive Differentiation   elaboration and clarification of meanings of concepts or propositions occurring over time as new subsumption, integrative reconciliation and/or superordinate learning occurs.

Advance Organizer   a brief, meaningful learning task designed to help the learner link new specific knowledge to relevant concepts or propositions he/she already knows.

Rote Learning   Arbitrary, verbatim incorporation of new information into cognitive structure.

of relevant concepts. However, as concepts are mapped, each successively distant level is less inclusive. Using Ausubel's continuum, the most inclusive concept would be meaningful learning; the least inclusive would be less meaningful, possibly rote, learning. Examples are usually the least inclusive concept (Novak, 1980a, c).

Figure 4–6 graphically illustrates a two-dimensional concept map on metals. The most inclusive concept in the map is metals. The next most inclusive concepts are the major types of metals—natural and manmade alloys. Each successive concept level implies less inclusiveness. Finally, examples of metals, the least inclusive concept on this map, are given.

The map goes further than simply showing the relative degree of inclusiveness. It also depicts the relationships between concepts, thus demonstrating the logical connection between representative concepts. Manmade alloys can be metals. They also can be steel, brass, and bronze, all of which can be used to build cars, buildings, or create art. The interconnecting words are unique to concept mapping. Novak (1980c) observes that concept mapping also has motivational value because students recognize that they have some understanding of many relevant concepts but still have much to learn about the map.

When learners conceptualize information, they process it into their cognitive structures and use it in a variety of learning and experiential

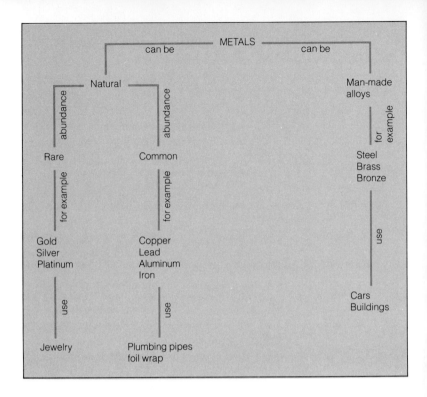

situations. One advantage of concept learning is its long-term retention and generalizability. Categorizing or classifying learning in relevant, meaningful ways facilitates learning in specific contexts and provides resources for functioning in subsequent contexts. Although nonconceptual learning is an essential part of the total learning process, concept learning is critical to competent, ongoing functioning, particularly when learners can both generate and assume responsibility for their own learning behavior.

Decision-Making Opportunities

Our decision-making capacity is increased by learning many concepts. We must all make numerous decisions every day. Here are two decision-making models and effective ways to use them. The focus is on early adolescents because it is at this age that the number of choices increase dramatically and decision-making skills are required in order to bring about successful resolution. The skills learned during the middle-level years of schooling will impact heavily on decision making in the adolescent years as well.

Critical Thinking Model

The critical thinking model is based on the assumption that individuals can weigh multiple information and determine appropriate action. Acquiring information and understanding content is essential if you are going to make decisions. Without such information you would be unable to consider all the options and consequences, thus limiting your decision making. The six steps of this model are:

1. *Identify the decision-making problem.* This step involves using conceptual categories to classify the problem at hand.

2. *Acquire decision-making information.* This step involves gaining as much information about an identified problem area as possi-

ble by listening, questioning, and so forth.

3. *Explore the options.* What decision-making options are available? The intellectual skills of comparing and contrasting are important here.

4. *Determine the reasonableness of the options.* To what extent do the options appear to provide an adequate solution? This requires using analysis skills.

5. *Select the appropriate action.* This requires determining which course of action will best solve the problem. Some judgment is required here.

6. *Evaluate the outcome.* Did the behavior solve the problem? This demands an understanding of and willingness to accept the consequences.

A group of eighth graders involved in a class session on substance use illustrates this process. Ms. Kelleher brings up the use of aspirin. After discussing what aspirin is, what it is designed to do, and its appropriate use, she shows the class three thirty-second commercials—one advertising a brand-name aspirin, one advertising Bufferin, and one advertising Tylenol. Working through the six steps in the critical thinking model, the students decide what they would take if they had a headache. Here are their questions for each step:

1. Identifying the decision-making problem: What are the different advertisements trying to do? Are they selling a product, promoting its use, implanting an idea, perpetuating drug dependence, providing data for an informed choice, or using propaganda techniques?

2. Acquiring decision-making information: What information is needed to determine which aspirin form to take? Is the information in the ads complete enough or should additional information be sought? Should you consult a physician or pharmacist?

3. Exploring the options: Identify the facts or underlying elements in each advertisement. Do the ads provide enough information so you can compare similarities and differences? Can you contrast the differences as a decision-making technique?

4. Determining reasonableness of the options: Does the product do what the ad claims? Is this true in all three cases? Are any of the ads misleading or are they fair representations?

5. Selecting the appropriate action: What criteria will you use to determine which of the three products to purchase? Are there elements of each ad that clearly show one preferable to the other two under certain conditions? Which of the three ads was the most convincing? Which ad seemed to be the most factual?

6. Evaluating the outcome: Will you now buy any of these products? What do you anticipate to be the outcome of having used the product? As a result of the product's use, reevaluate steps one through five and determine if your solution or decision-making abilities were appropriate.

Decision-Making Model

The decision-making model is more comprehensive than the critical thinking model; decision-making information is only one of its components, and as shown in Figure 4–7, it is interactive. Thus, the model implies that, even if the decision-making information exists, some other factor, such as developmental readiness, might not; so the problem would not be adequately solved. The following example focuses on using the model for moral decision making.

The first component in the model is *readiness for decision making*. It is designed to determine to what extent early adolescents are ready to make moral decisions about many behaviors in which they participate. Dating is an appropriate example here. Are junior high school–age early adolescents physically, emotionally, and socially mature enough to date? Is dating at this age an outcome of human development and natural curiosity or is it socially promoted? What happens inside the twelve-year-old who does not want to date but feels the pressure to attend a school

dance where the price of admission is bringing a date?

The model's second component is *sources for decision making*. As indicated, the most important decision-making source is within each individual. However, schoolchildren are heavily influenced by others—parents, peers, teachers, television, religion, society. These external sources facilitate decision making in three ways. First, they often are influential enough that they functionally tell someone what to do. Second, they are sounding boards off of which early adolescents can gain understanding or approval for behavior. Third, they can influence one's thinking enough to affect internal decision-making skills.

Decision-making information is the third component in the model. This is the conceptual aspect of

moral decision making. Cognitive development is an important aspect of moral development, as is understanding one's values. We learn values or moral precepts just like we learn academic content. We learn them when we perceive multiple instances of moral behavior to have common properties. Thus, when we learn that a certain category of behavior violates our internal beliefs, we view such behaviors as inappropriate or immoral. We also view as inappropriate any subsequent behavior from this category. This idea may be illustrated by working through the concept "deception."

To some individuals, deception means anything from an outright lie to withholding information from another person. The understanding of deception will vary among students in any given classroom. This is one reason

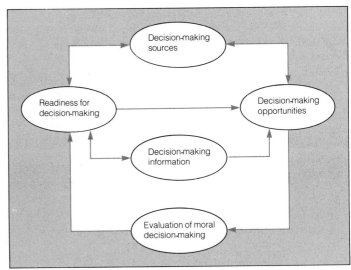

Figure 4–7
Model for decision making. [*Source: Thornburg (1981), p. 9. By permission of the publisher.*]

teachers see the concept manifested in so many different ways. Let us assume that the concept is being taught as "any misrepresentation of the truth." To confirm this concept, it is necessary to give instances of it, which could include lying, cheating, getting another student in trouble, getting help on homework when you should not have, and saying you did something you did not do. The greater and more diverse the examples, the more students are likely to understand the concept, which provides them with a better cognitive base for making moral decisions. In regard to the information component of the model, moral concepts can and should be taught as are cognitive concepts.

Decision-making opportunities, the model's fourth component, present themselves constantly. The appropriateness with which early adolescents make moral decisions is directly proportional to their moral decision-making skills. This is where the first three components of the model come into sharper focus. On the way home from school, Pat steals something from a convenience market. *Readiness*—was Pat prepared psychologically to steal and to accept the legal consequences of stealing? *Sources*—was it Pat's decision to steal? Did friends influence the decision? Had Pat stolen before without any negative consequences? *Information*—where did the idea of stealing come from? To what extent does Pat understand the concept of stealing? Has stealing, in any form, been modeled? The adequacy of the early adolescent's moral decision making is the summation of these multiple factors. Moral behavior is not as simple as reward or punishment. Individuals must approach the topic at a conceptual level.

The fifth component in the decision-making model is *evaluation.* Too often early adolescents judge morally appropriate behavior by its consequences. If one does not get caught, it is acceptable. Students must be provided with other types of consequences, some of which are conceptual in nature. For example, how does your behavior make you feel about yourself? To what extent does your behavior reflect the things you believe? These types of questions let the individual know that a behavior has more than immediate consequences and enhances the basis for decision making.

The model in Figure 4–7 is interactive. The readiness, sources, and information we have prior to making a decision affect the adequacy of our decision. The early adolescent's perception of adequacy in making a decision subsequently contributes to the readiness, sources, and information for forthcoming decision-making opportunities. The interaction of these components enhances the possibility of more effective decision making throughout life.

Annotated Readings

Bergan, J. R., Towstopiat, O., Cancelli, A. A., & Karp, C. (1982). Replacement and component rules in hierarchically ordered mathematics rule-learning tasks. *Journal of Educational Psychology, 74*, 39–50.

> This study investigated ordered and equivalence relations among hierarchically arranged fraction identification tasks to see if hierarchical ordering reflects the replacement of simple rules by complex rules. A total of 456 middle-class children in grades two through four were asked to identify fractional parts of sets of objects. The study revealed that children apply rules that are adequate for simple problems but that have to be replaced to solve more complex problems.

Canelos, J. J. (1982). The instructional effectiveness of three content-independent imagery learning strategies and visualized instruction of varying complexity. *Journal of Experimental Education, 52*, 58–68.

> This study examined the effectiveness of three imagery learning strategies—copying, relational, and hierarchical—for acquiring different outcomes when individuals received visual instructional information that varied in complexity. The levels of information to be acquired were list learning, spatial learning, general concepts, and relational concepts. The researcher found that the hierarchical strategy was the most effective in processing the different levels of information.

Champagne, A. B., Klopfer, L. E., & Gunstone, R. F. (1982) Cognitive research and the design of science instruction. *Educational Psychologist, 17*, 31–53.

> This position paper looks at the utilization of cognitive psychological theory in the design of instruction. Physics learning studies demonstrate that students' preinstructional world knowledge is often logically antagonistic to the principles of Newtonian mechanics taught in introductory physics. These conditions imply contradictory elements. By using results from cognitive research, semantic memory, and knowledge acquisition, a model that reconciles world knowledge and physics content has been proposed.

Lamiell, J. T., Foss, M. A., & Cavenee, P. (1980). On the relationship between conceptual schemes and behavior reports: A closer look. *Journal of Personality, 48*, 54–73.

> The researchers question the assertion that rated and self-reported behavior is almost entirely under the influence of preexisting conceptual schemes. They argue that the approach previously used to test this thesis is inadequate and propose an alternative. A resultant investigation indicated that presumed correspondence is neither as high nor as consistent as projected. Further investigations in social cognition may be required to determine the relationship between conceptual schemes and personal behavior.

Masson, M. E. J. (1982). Cognitive processes in skimming stories. *Journal of Experimental Psychology: Learning, Memory and Cognition, 8*, 400–417.

> Comprehension processes and memory representations associated with normal reading and skimming were investigated. Passages were selected on the basis of meaning or nonmeaning to the individual. Results indicated that, when skimming, readers have difficulty perceptually selecting from a passage information that is relevant to their goal in skimming. Such studies imply that, when reading for meaning, skimming is not likely to be an effective strategy.

Sternberg, R. J. (1982). Natural, unnatural, and supernatural concepts. *Cognitive Psychology, 14*, 451–488.

This study reports the results of five experiments designed to investigate information-processing consequences of concept naturalness and unnaturalness. An attempt was made to measure the effects of simplicity and entrenchment upon reasoning out such concepts. The investigator found in all five studies that simplicity and entrenchment affected ease of information processing, with two experiments indicating simplicity had a greater effect than entrenchment. The author concludes that ways in which individuals process nonentrenched concepts may provide insight into understanding human intelligence.

Observational Learning

5

Recognizing widespread concern about TV violence by adults and the often extensive viewing time of children, the Merryton PTA sponsored an evening with John Muller, a widely recognized authority on the effects of television on children. About eighty parents and fifteen teachers attended.

Mr. Muller said that TV's effects on children are still uncertain. Although studies have shown that TV violence increases aggressive potential, violence does not have the same effect on all children, even within the same household. He reminded parents of cartoon violence and suggested that they monitor the Saturday morning shows their children watch. In fact, Mr. Muller suggested that all family members carefully evaluate their TV viewing habits. "Remember," he said, "children get ideas about love, families, alcohol, friendship, hatred, prejudice, dreams, divorce, and rebellion from TV."

Children copy much TV behavior, but the speaker also addressed other modeling sources. He surprised many parents by emphasizing their importance as models. Family relationships have the strongest effects on developing children. Children's parents are the most powerful models in the world and thus should guide their children by explaining why they approve of some behaviors and disapprove of others. Parents should set aside time to communicate with their children and play an active role in their lives, modeling behaviors they want them to acquire.

Most parents left the meeting with an enhanced appreciation of their roles in their children's lives and a realistic perspective on the effects of television.

Many researchers have attempted to describe and explain observational learning, which can occur in an almost limitless number and variety of settings with an equally wide variety of models. This chapter discusses:

- *Modeling theory*
- *Self-determined consequences*
- *Teachers as models*
- *Television as a modeling source*

Modeling Theory

Observational learning theorists contend that learning can occur when one watches the behavior of others. Thus, direct participation in a learning act, an essential part of Skinner's theory, is not a requirement in **observational learning,** also termed modeling, imitation, or vicarious learning. Observational learning theory is flexible in that it holds that learning can occur without the individual having to act upon the environment.

Observational learning
The acquisition of behavior through the vicarious observation of that behavior in another.

Miller and Dollard (1941) stress that we can learn by imitating the behavior of others. Their model suggests that initial imitative learning occurs if some drive is reduced as a result of imitating the behavior. Writing in the tradition of behaviorism, they contend that performance and reinforcement are necessary in order for learning to occur.

Albert Bandura (1977a, p. 12) describes learning of modeled behavior as a process that "enables people to acquire large, integrated patterns of behavior without having to form them gradually by tedious trial and error." He emphasizes the rigidity of reinforcement theory and advances a theory that has greater flexibility, accounts for a wider range of human behavior, and gives credence to the individual's cognitive capacity.

Bandura's social learning theory suggests that much individual learning occurs *vicariously,* through observing another individual's response and then imitating it. Bandura delineates three characteristics of modeling that make his theory more flexible than reinforcement theory. First, he demonstrated that individuals can learn from verbal and visual models as well as from direct models (Bandura, Ross, & Ross, 1961, 1963a, b, c). Second, he observed that, with a modeled act, the observer learns not only the specific, targeted behavior but also the model's speech, mannerisms,

and attitudes (Bandura et al., 1963a; Bandura & Walters, 1963). Third, he demonstrated that a modeled behavior is unlikely to endure (be retained) unless it is effective when put into practice in everyday life (Bandura, 1976a). This wide range of outcomes through modeling caused Bandura (1971, p. 2) to specify limitations on behavioral theory:

> A valid criticism of the extreme behavioristic position is that, in a vigorous effort to eschew spurious inner causes, it neglected determinants of man's behavior arising from his cognitive functioning. Man is a thinking organism possessing capabilities that provide him with some power of self-direction. To the extent that traditional behavioral theories could be faulted, it was for providing an incomplete rather than an inaccurate account of human behavior. The social learning theory places special emphasis on the important roles played by vicarious, symbolic, and self-regulatory processes.

Before discussing the components of modeling theory, I shall discuss how Bandura's system differs from operant conditioning.

Modeling as an Alternative to Operant Learning

Operant conditioning requires both performance and reinforcement for learning through modeling to occur (Gewritz & Stingle, 1968; Miller & Dollard, 1941; Skinner, 1953). In contrast, Bandura stresses that learning occurs prior to performance and that reinforcement is not necessary until performance takes place.

Overt Performance   According to Bandura (1969), learning can occur through observation of modeled behavior; it does not require reinforcement to either the model or the observer. Bandura recognizes that humans have two representational systems: imaginal and verbal. Stimuli are coded into memory representation, which facilitates retrieval and reproduction. **Performance** is the transformation of these symbolic codes into behavior. Thus, imitative behavior can occur without any behavioral evidence.

Reinforcement   A significant difference in the two theories is the importance of reinforcement in the learning process. The operant model requires it; social learning theory minimizes its importance. Bandura has demonstrated learning without reinforcement. He does not think reinforcement is necessary prior to the reproduction phase of learning, and suggests that, even then, self-reinforcement is all that is required. Thus, vicarious and self-reinforcement are useful, but not mandatory, in observational learning.

Kanfer (1965) summarizes two outcomes of his vicarious learning studies. Observation of another person's behavior and subsequent reinforcement, coupled with the subject's inner rehearsal of the behavior, may represent an important way in which human beings learn. He concludes that individuals may be able to reinforce their own behavior in the absence of external feedback. Self-reinforcement may occur regardless of the quality of the response, a condition acceptable in modeling theory but unacceptable within operant conditioning.

Performance
The actual exercise of a behavior that has been learned and is in a person's response repertoire. In Bandura's theory, it is known as reproduction.

Symbolic Learning   Bandura believes that human learning has more complexity than operant learning theory attributes to it. He believes that the process of shaping is too laborious and not necessary in much learning. Bandura stresses that learning occurs in symbolic ways as well as through direct observation. In fact, a student should be able to learn by observing the symbolic code itself (Salomon, 1980). Visual and verbal representations are coded in the mind, thus learned. Learners represent visual and verbal behavior in a functional way. To be converted into cognitive functions, learning must be relevant and meaningful to the learner; otherwise, little attention will be given it and learning is unlikely to occur (Bandura, 1976b; Cole & Scribner, 1974).

Social Behavior   Bandura believes that social behaviors, social attitudes, and social values can also be learned through modeling. His work on aggression has established the impact that modeling can have on an individual's behavior. Bandura (1967, 1969; Bandura et al., 1963a, b, c) has not only established a causal link between viewing aggression and subsequently acting aggressively; he has also spurred much research on the effects of television on viewer behavior. The range of desirable and undesirable behaviors that children and adolescents have been taught includes (1) kindness toward others (Rosenhan, 1969), (2) affection (Fryrear & Thelen, 1969), (3) courage (Bandura & Menlove, 1968), (4) self-control (Bandura & Mischel, 1965; Stein & Bryan, 1972), (5) self-criticism (Thelen, 1969), (6) self-sacrifice (Bryan & Walbek, 1970), (7) peer involvement (O'Connor, 1969, 1972), and (8) inhibition of deviant behavior (Walters & Parke, 1964; Wolf, 1972).

Modeling explains a wide range of behavior. Learners are influenced by what they observe, either directly, through visual representation, or through verbal representation. They are not bound to specific, discriminated stimuli in order to respond or to reinforcement in order to establish a stimulus-response relationship. Rather, they can internally represent learning and build a response repertoire that will be available in a variety of learning and retention contexts. Because learners can select aspects of a model's behavior, there is greater flexibility in learning and less dependency on the environment for learning to occur.

Modeling Processes

Bandura delineates four processes that are essential to modeling: attention, retention, reproduction, and motivation. They are depicted in Figure 5–1.

Attention   The first step in the modeling process is **attention.** If a person is to learn from another person, he or she must pay attention to what the model is doing. Bandura (1977a) suggests that one must perceive accurately the significant features of the model's behavior. Those characteristics that have significance to the learner tend to be modeled. Thus, members of a group of students observing a teacher may attend to

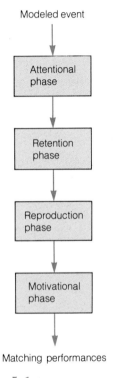

Modeled event

Attentional phase

Retention phase

Reproduction phase

Motivational phase

Matching performances

Figure 5–1
Analysis of observational learning. (Source: Albert Bandura, Social Learning Theory, © *1977. Reprinted by permission of Prentice-Hall, Inc., Englewood Cliffs, N.J.)*

Attention
The learner focuses on aspects of the model's behavior that the learner desires to imitate.

different behavioral traits and as a result acquire different learning. Bandura has found that attention is often given to those who have status or expertise, fit social stereotypes, or are heroes.

Bandura suggests that we model the behavior of people with whom we regularly associate. We can observe their behavior frequently and may give high credibility to consistent, repeated behaviors. Children model parents because they are a constant influence and tend to reward their children for the desired behavior. Relatives and teachers are two more sources to which children are continuously exposed. As a person moves into adolescence, peer groups become increasingly important, and individuals within the group may model another individual or the group behavior (Christen, McDaniel, & Doran, 1979; Johnson & Downing, 1979).

Some persons stand out in a crowd or attract others to them. We say such children and adolescents possess "leadership ability"; in adults, we call it charisma. Such individuals are stronger modeling sources than those who have less impressive personal dynamics and may stand out because they possess high competence (Gelfand, 1962), because they are considered to be experts (Mausner, 1953), because they are celebrities (Harper, 1980; Hovland, Janis, & Kelley, 1953), or because they are heroes or fit stereotypes (Christen, 1980; Glover, Christen, & Henderson, 1982). "The functional value of the behavior displayed by different models is therefore highly influential in determining which models people will observe and which they will disregard" (Bandura, 1977a, p. 24).

The media draw attention to some forms of modeling and seem to appeal to individuals of all ages. Bandura (1977a, p. 25) notes that "people today can observe and learn diverse styles of conduct within the comfort of their homes through the abundant symbolic modeling provided by the mass media." Television is a persuasive influence because one can easily attend to models and selecting one viewing possibility over another requires minimal motivation. Using a famous person to endorse a product is an attempt to induce the observer to emulate the modeled behavior by buying the product.

In classroom situations, teachers may enhance the modeling process. The science teacher may demonstrate an experiment and tell the students they will also have to demonstrate it to receive a passing grade. This will increase the students' attention. The fact that teachers are possessors of rewards and punishments causes many students to attend.

Retention   Bandura's concept of retention implies that if learners are going to reproduce a behavior without the continued presence of the model, they must symbolically process the behavior in memory. A modeled behavior that is not recallable is temporary. If learners can later use modeled behavior, it must be symbolically coded and processed into memory, according to observational learning theory. Bandura believes that individuals represent learning through one of two systems—**visual imagery** and **verbal coding.**

Many classroom experiences depend on visual imagery. First graders learn how to form letters in penmanship by looking at charts on the wall. Fourth graders look at an astronomy chart when trying to visualize the relationship among stars of the galaxy. High schoolers look at a schematic drawing when assembling parts of an automobile or an electronic device. The visual image is a modeled impression that may accompany learning. Thus, when a student must take a retention test or work on an automobile three months later, the images may be instrumental in helping recall the learning in order to perform accurately. Bandura suggests that repeated exposure to such modeling stimuli results in retrievable images when behavior is performed.

Verbal coding describes a wider range of school learning than visual modeling. When we can verbally code objects, events, or ideas that we observe, it is possible to represent this modeled behavior internally by symbolic verbal meaning. We cannot only see a train; we can describe it. Most human cognitive functions are represented verbally.

Bandura, Grusec, and Menlove (1966) studied the importance of verbal modeling by conducting an experiment containing three conditions. In one condition, the subjects verbalized the sequence of novel responses the model performed. In the second condition, the subjects were instructed to observe the model's behavior carefully. In condition three, the subjects were required to count rapidly while viewing a film (the counting presumably interfered with learning the model's behavior). Those who modeled the behavior by describing it in words learned the most and those who counted while observing learned the least. Such research led Bandura to believe that coding modeled activities into words or labels facilitates retention. Behavior is best learned by organizing and rehearsing the

Visual imagery
An impression that registers through the visual sense that accompanies learning.

Verbal coding
The internal representation of an observed behavior into memory.

Go, Team, Go

Franklin Stover was the only eighth-grade boy on the starting lineup of the junior high school football team in a large city that had junior high teams with an annual schedule of nine games. Using the plays of the high school their junior high fed into, the coaches were making the junior high program a training ground for high school players.

Frankie was fast, clearly talented, and "destined" to become a high school hero and eventually a professional star. He was the fans' favorite player on the team and all his teammates, including the older ninth-grade boys, admired him. Often the coaches used Frankie as an example of how something should be done.

It was the last quarter of game five of the season and Frankie had carried the ball in his halfback position thirty-five times already. The warm autumn afternoon contributed to his fatigue. On the next play, Frankie was "buried" by a sea of tacklers from the other team. The referee whistled the play over but Frankie did not get up.

Before the day ended, Frankie was having reconstructive surgery on his right knee. Even though he

was not in school the following Monday, he was the school hero. But, clearly, he was out for the rest of the season.

The rehabilitation process for Frankie was slow. The physicians would not let him play football in ninth grade, but they believed that, with his continued physical growth and an appropriate weight and rehabilitation program, Frankie would be ready to go by high school.

The attention Frankie received was incredible. His father, other adult males in the neighborhood, the high school coaches, and health personnel provided support for Frankie in a variety of ways.

As the first semester of his tenth-grade year approached, Frankie started to become frightened about having to play football, even though he had been given a clean bill of health by his physicians. Frankie sought out Mr. Long, his junior high school math teacher, because the two of them had always gotten along well. After several conversations, Mr. Long told Frankie that he would try to get the high school coaches to see why Frankie did not want to take a chance with his knee again. These

efforts were not successful, however, and Frankie succumbed to the pressure to play high school football. But he never lived up to the expectations of others. As a result, Frankie's high school years were more stressful and disappointing than they needed to be.

What Do You Think?

1. How motivating is it for Frankie to play football when all the other players look up to him?

2. To what extent do schools have the right to apply pressure on students to be athletes?

3. Should the school be involved in adjustment counseling when a "star athlete" does not live up to expectations?

modeled behavior symbolically and then enacting it (Bandura, 1977a, 1982; Jeffrey, 1976).

Reproduction The reproduction phase of Bandura's observational learning model focuses on actual behavior; it involves doing the behavior. Many students can internally represent something but may be hesitant to reproduce the behavior because they perceive it as unacceptable or inaccurate, or lack the confidence to let others observe their internal representation.

When we decide to behave, we select appropriate responses and organize them at the cognitive level. In this process, we "pull together" all the resources relevant to the behavior. If the skills and understandings exist, then the reproduced behavior will be representative of the modeled behavior. However, if we try to reproduce an imitated behavior but do not have the skill in symbolic representation, we will either not perform all the

required performance components or will perform them incorrectly. An example of this is high school students who learn how to drive using a driving simulator in the classroom. Some students perform extremely well in the simulated situation. To what extent do they perform equally well in an actual driving situation? If the simulator closely resembles actual driving conditions, the possibility of reproducing the act is high. If students learn all the relevant components in simulation, the chances of accurate reproduction are high. If students do not learn some driving components well in the simulated environment, they will probably be unable to reproduce them in an actual driving situation.

Modeling theory does not imply a simple, direct correspondence between an observed and a performed act. Rather, when we process observed behavior, it interacts with already existing information. As a result, the reproduction of observed behavior may be identical, qualitatively better, more comprehensive, slightly modified, highly dissimilar, or totally unacceptable.

Bandura addresses the issue of **corrective feedback** in this phase of his model. Teachers can use corrective feedback when a student's behavior is less than optimal. It allows the student to rethink the behavior without having the teacher either reinforce or punish it. Corrective feedback is an important teacher strategy because it avoids the negative implications of punishment.

Corrective feedback
Providing information to the learner on how to improve on a reproduced behavior that is less than optimal.

Motivation   Social learning theory holds that reinforcement increases the incentive or **motivation** to behave. Bandura believes that learning occurs during the retention phase and not during the reproductive phase. In social learning theory, in contrast to operant conditioning, you do not have to observe behavior to assume that it has been learned. Thus, a learner may reproduce only a small fraction of what he or she has actually learned.

Motivation
The term Bandura uses in place of reinforcement because he views the effects as facilitating motivation and not learning.

Reinforcement and punishment play a role in the reproductive phase. Bandura (1965b, 1977a) contends that behaviors that a learner anticipates will be rewarded are likely to be reproduced. Those behaviors that may bring punishment are not as likely to be reproduced. Two other factors enter in here. First, if a person finds a reproduced behavior to be self-satisfying, she is likely to maintain it (Hicks, 1971). Second, if an observer sees that a model is positively rewarded but the observer is not rewarded and is perhaps punished when he reproduces the behavior, the behavior is less likely to occur. Adolescents often experience such discrepancies when they reproduce a parent's behavior only to find the result is punishing rather than rewarding, as it is to the parent. It is difficult for many adolescents to understand why they should be punished when they see the same behavior being modeled by their parents. Drinking is an example of a heavily modeled behavior for which adolescents are often punished.

That modeled behavior can be learned but not reproduced can be seen in siblings, especially twins. If one twin models a behavior and reproduces it, only to be punished, the other twin, who also learned the behavior, may decide not to reproduce it, at least not under the same conditions. Bandura believes that the consequences of reproduced be-

Steps in Observational Learning
1. A person must attend to, observe, or interact with another person, image, or phenomenon (attention).
2. Upon observing another's behavior, a person must register it in the conscious mind. In effect, it is processed, internalized, or coded in relation to existing behavior potential (retention).
3. A person must engage in learned behavior by exercising it (reproduction).
4. A person must evaluate the effect of behavior on himself or herself by using internal or external criteria (motivation).

havior determine whether learned behavior will be reproduced. The key appears to be positive reinforcement. Bandura (1965b) demonstrated that, when positive incentives are introduced in observational learning, it is promptly converted into action.

Effects of Modeling

Bandura has discussed three effects of modeling: inhibition, disinhibition, and facilitation. These effects are related to the modeling process, but they warrant consideration independent of it.

Inhibition
The suppression of the reproduction of behavior because the observer sees its negative consequences on a model.

Inhibition   **Inhibition** occurs when an observer sees the model receive negative consequences for a behavior. Punishment is the most common type of aversive effect and it usually results in a reduction of modeled behavior. Teachers often punish a student in front of other students. This "example" is partly designed to help other students see the consequences of inappropriate behavior.

Suppressive effects in punishing situations counteract the tendency to respond to a modeled behavior. Rosenkrans and Hartup (1967) found that children who see aggressive behavior punished exercise very little aggressive behavior. In contrast, if they see aggressive behavior rewarded, they tend to exercise more aggression. Bandura (1965c) has found similar results. In studying modeling behavior, he found that rewarded behaviors increase the incentive to model the behavior and punished acts are not modeled as frequently.

Inhibition has also been found in studies that investigated modeling behaviors that may be considered wrong from a moral, social, or religious perspective. Observing others who are punished for wrongdoing inhibits such behavior in the observer (Benton, 1967; Lazarus, 1980; Walters, Parke, & Cane, 1965; Zimmerman & Ghoziel, 1974). The common recurring theme in numerous television shows, that the criminal is always caught or brought to justice, is designed to model inhibition for inappropriate behavior.

Disinhibition   It is equally possible to **disinhibit** behavior by observing a model. Children who see brothers and sisters "get away" with something, who see others steal without getting caught, or who see others "put one over on the teacher" are more likely to exercise the inappropriate behavior than to be inhibited.

The concept of disinhibition is related to consequences. Whether a model's behavior is desirable or undesirable, we are all more inclined to imitate behavior that is not accompanied by negative consequences. The observer may learn and reproduce an undesired response. An observed absence of negative consequences may also disinhibit a restrictive response, such as fear, and make the observer more behaviorally diverse and independent (Bandura & Menlove, 1968; Zimmerman, 1977).

Disinhibition
The reproduction of a previously inhibited behavior because an observer sees it in a model without negative consequences.

Facilitation   We have all learned responses we have never reproduced. If we see others engaging in such a behavior, we are more likely to reproduce it. Modeling can help us use the new behavior.

Facilitation and disinhibition are not the same. Disinhibition occurs only if a behavior has been previously inhibited. Facilitation occurs when an unlikely response becomes more probable because we see another person make it. Bandura indicates that learning occurs after an internal rehearsal of a behavior. For example, many people know slang or vulgar words but are inhibited from using them. Hearing such words used by someone they never expected to use them opens up the possibility that

Facilitation
The exercise of a learned response that has not previously been reproduced because the learner now sees it reproduced by a model.

Jimmy Tang, eight years old, watches his favorite baseball player get thrown out trying to steal second base on Saturday afternoon baseball. Next Monday, at his Little League game, Jimmy does not try to steal a single base, even though he is the team's leading base stealer.

Two junior high school students skip school to play video games because they both have older siblings in high school who have skipped school several times and have never gotten caught.

Judy watches her best friend, Denise, compliment the teacher on her dress. Judy has always wanted to compliment the teacher but has been afraid she would reject her. She sees the teacher thank Denise and thus decides to pay the teacher a compliment.

Which scene represents inhibition, facilitation, or disinhibition?

such behavior could be imitated. For example, parents may swear but verbally tell their children that swearing is inappropriate for children (the inhibition effect). Later, as the child moves toward adolescence and becomes more behaviorally independent, he or she may swear because of the continued influence of swearing by parents or by friends. At one point, a modeled behavior may be inhibiting; at another point, the same behavior may have a facilitation effect.

Parents are often astonished to see their child do something that they habitually do. Many children and adolescents have been punished for reproducing the modeled behavior of their parents (Thornburg, 1977). These demonstrated behaviors may be well established and the child or adolescent perceives a particular time to be opportune for reproducing the learning. Sometimes parents accept the behavior; sometimes they do not. In either case, parents are strong models for their children and serve to facilitate behavior.

Self-Determined Consequences

Self-regulation
The ability to monitor our own behavior by understanding its consequences.

Self-reinforcement
The ability to apply reinforcers, including self-punishment, to ourselves.

Self-motivation
Due to the application of self-reinforcement, we are motivated to engage in or avoid performance of behavior.

Social learning theory includes the concept of **self-regulation,** by which an individual exercises control over personal behavior by using **self-reinforcement** and **self-motivation.** We all determine what behavior we consider acceptable and then evaluate our own and others' behavior. The person who decides to diet may resolve to lose two pounds a week until reaching his desired weight. His eating patterns throughout the week will determine whether he reaches his goal. If he loses two pounds, self-reinforcement may cause him to maintain the behavior the next week. If he loses one pound, he may evaluate his behavior and determine to modify it in order to reach his goal. The process of evaluating personal behavior and administering self-reward or punishment is the way to regulate (Thoresen & Mahoney, 1974) and accept responsibility for one's own behavior.

Components of Self-Regulation

Bandura has selected three conditions necessary for effective self-regulation of behavior. Figure 5–2 summarizes the different components of self-regulation through the utilization of self-prescribed contingencies. The performance component focuses on the observation of self-behavior. We observe our behavior and evaluate it using combinations of the criteria Bandura lists in Figure 5–2. Observing personal behavior without having a basis for judgment as to its adequacy is somewhat meaningless. Therefore, we evaluate our behavior against our personal standards or values. Whether the behavior is rewarding or dissatisfying depends upon the personal standards against which it is evaluated (Bandura, 1978). This is where Bandura's self-response component interacts. If the behavior meets the standard, self-reinforcement generates self-motivation and behavior is maintained and perhaps increased if the behavior only partly meets the standard (as in losing one pound in a particular week). The extent to which a person believes the standard was met or not met determines what self-consequences are applied. If a person loses no weight or gains weight, self-punishment may be applied as an attempt to alter behavior.

In classroom situations, teachers often define acceptable behavior, both academic and social. As a result, students often apply external criteria

PERFORMANCE	JUDGMENTAL PROCESS	SELF-RESPONSE
Evaluative Dimensions	Personal Standards	Self-Evaluation Reactions
Quality	Modeling sources	Positive
Rate	Reinforcement sources	Negative
Quantity ⟶	Referential ⟶	Tangible Self-Applied
Originality	Performances	Consequences
Authenticity	Standard norms	Rewarding
Consequentialness	Social comparison	Punishing
Deviancy	Personal comparison	No Self-Response
Ethicalness	Collective comparison	
	Valuation of Activity	
	Regarded highly	
	Neutral	
	Devalued	
	Performance Attribution	
	Personal locus	
	External locus	

Figure 5–2
Component processes in the self-regulation of behavior by self-produced consequences. (Source: Albert Bandura, Social Learning Theory, © 1977. *Reprinted by permission of Prentice-Hall, Inc., Englewood Cliffs, N.J.)*

to determine the appropriateness of their behavior. Although behavior can be regulated by the interplay of self-generated criteria and external standards, the student who becomes too dependent on external criteria may use self-reinforcement and self-motivation less. Teachers often foster such behavior. It is important for teachers to help students reason through their behavior. Teachers often accept poor performance or assume that students can do no better. In effect, they reduce the students' sense of self-responsibility. In social learning theory, self-regulation is a way of being responsible for personal behavior and applying appropriate consequences for behavior (Bandura, 1978; Coates & Thoresen, 1979; Nelson, 1977).

Self-Motivation

Observational learning introduces reinforcement as a source of motivation. Reinforcement is not designed to strengthen behavior but to motivate people to expend the energy required to accomplish a desired performance. The net effect is to give us more control over our life and learning situations. Our capacity to think and behave serves as incentive to engage in activities over which we have control and that satisfy us. Although we may incorporate others' standards (Bandura & Kupers, 1964; Bandura & Whalen, 1966), behavior becomes self-regulated. Research has established two variables that affect the modeling process and that are important for classroom teachers to understand.

We tend to model behavior standards that we think we can meet. If standards are too low, students can easily perform the behavior and may not have the self-motivation to keep learning. If they are too high, students may abandon the behavior totally because they are unlikely to apply self-motivation to participate in a behavior that will lead to failure (Bandura, 1977a; Karoly, 1977).

Students do not tend to shy away from high standards, only from those they perceive as unattainable (Bandura, 1982). In fact, high standards may be a strong source of self-motivation (Bandura & Perloff, 1967; Leeper, Sagotsky, & Mailer, 1975). It is important for classroom teachers to learn about students so they can select performance criteria within students' behavioral ranges. If teachers achieve this goal, students can convert successful performance into self-reinforcement and self-motivation.

Locus of Control

Bandura (1977a) selected personal and external control as two of his judgmental criteria. Work in this area has been most revealing. Rotter (1966) conceptualized internal and external control as dichotomous characteristics, that is, within any given behavior, the two cannot coexist. He believes the effect of reinforcement on behavior depends in part on whether a person perceives the reinforcement as contingent on personal behavior or independent of it. He also believes that people perceive reinforcement differently if they think that their behavior resulted in reinforcement rather than that reinforcement simply occurred by chance. Rotter's social learning construct is consistent with Bandura's. The general construct refers to the extent individuals feel they have control over what happens to them.

Several studies have found a relationship between internality (the belief that one is responsible for one's own successes and failures) and academic achievement. Students who attribute success or failure to external sources, such as chance, fate, teachers, or powerful others, commonly show signs of lower academic achievement (Nowicki & Walker, 1974) or futility (Bandura, 1982). Social activities may also be better selected through self-determination (Strickland, 1965).

An important outcome of the locus of control research is the knowledge that we do have control over what happens to us. Therefore, we can both regulate behavior and generate rewards (self-reinforcement) and incentives (self-motivation) to continue involvement in a behavior or course of action. Classroom teachers need to recognize that their behavior can either encourage or discourage students to be unduly dependent on them (Deci, 1975). Students can exercise meaningful behaviors, and teachers should work at creating an environment in which such student-generated behaviors can surface. Students need teacher guidance, but they are not always dependent on teacher reinforcement and motivation in order to learn.

Teachers should help students see how consequences relate to their behaviors. Having students think through the following four steps will help them evaluate their own performance:

1. Be aware of one's own behaviors.
2. Relate one's behaviors to one's needs.
3. Determine if one's behavior was satisfying (Did it meet the need?).
4. Determine if the behavior should be maintained.

Teachers as Models

It has long been assumed that teachers are powerful models for students. Teacher contracts prior to World War II typically contained strong moral codes because school boards and communities believed teachers should always model desirable (morally correct) behavior for students. Although such codes rarely exist today, interest in teachers' impact on learners continues.

Several kinds of academic behavior have been researched to see what the modeling effect might be. Researchers have been able to establish that learning has occurred in the following areas: verbal information, motor skills, concept learning, rule learning, problem solving, and creativity (Rosenthal & Zimmerman, 1973; Zimmerman, 1977; Zimmerman & Kleefeld, 1977).

Teachers also model affective learning. They influence student behaviors by teaching children conservation, frugality, altruism, cleanliness, fairness, equality, self-discipline, consideration, and respect for others (Bandura & Mischel, 1965; Muuss, 1976). Altruism (behavior that benefits another person without any expected reward or reciprocity) is one frequently researched dimension of human behavior. What a teacher does influences students' behavior more than what a teacher says (Gagne & Middlebrooke, 1977; White, 1967). A study by Midlarsky, Bryan, and Brickman (1973) also showed that actions speak louder than words. When teachers advocated altruism but acted selfishly, their students, too, spoke of generosity but did not practice it.

Television as a Modeling Source

Bandura's (1969) concept of modeling has had a strong effect not only on learning psychology but also on studies of the media's impact. Bandura wrote that children and adolescents follow a model without being compelled or induced to do so and numerous studies corroborate this. People on television can model appropriate, inappropriate, or possible behaviors. The negative consequences of modeled behavior often have inhibiting effects. Critics of television often overlook its positive and diverse qualities.

Whether social behaviors are presented on TV programs as moral or immoral, violent or nonviolent, they are learned. Television as a

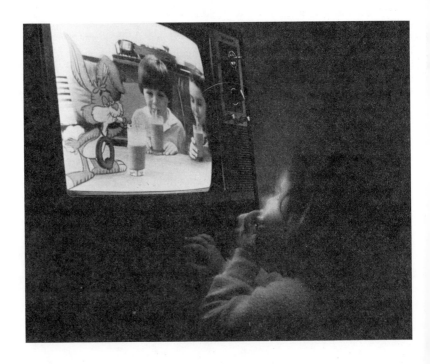

learning source has not been widely studied. Social scientists did not concentrate on the educational value of television until the appearance of shows such as *Sesame Street* and *The Electric Company*. The combination of entertainment, language, numbers, and concepts that they present has been a powerful stimulus to children. Yet how much learning occurs is in question because little effort has been made to coordinate program content with developmental capacity.

Salomon (1979) has found that the effects of media symbols on learning are related to their effects on the mastery of cognitive skills. He observed that, as frequent *Sesame Street* viewers tried to extract knowledge from the program, their mastery of skills improved, thus leading to increased knowledge. Salomon broke down this interdependence between program and viewer into three factors:

1. *Environmental factors*. The media's symbol system, the information they carry, and the learning task one is to perform

2. *Personological factors*. The learner's capabilities, mental schemata, and information preferences

3. *Behavioral factors*. The specific actions or behaviors one carries out while handling coded information

In essence, the media are a social and learning environment, as are parents, peers, schools, and the community. Our individual capabilities and the interest and attention we give to a show make a difference in the type of interaction that takes place. The behavior that results may be a direct result of watching something on television, a predisposed action prompted by television, or an internal rehearsal of a subsequent behavior. It is important to put behavior in an appropriate context here; it is an interactive effect and not a simple behavior enacted because of a powerful stimulus. Salomon (1979, p. 71) cogently stated this when he concluded from his research that "other things being equal, different symbol systems of the media address themselves to different parts of one's cognitive apparatus and require different amounts of mental translation."

Television is an important modeling source. Unquestionably, commercial television is designed to be entertainment, not the nation's teacher. But we all gain information, ideas, and attitudes from television. We would benefit greatly if we could better understand its messages and interrelate them with our existing cognitive and affective states. What we learn often seems so incidental that we pass it off as inconsequential; yet it is unlikely that television's effect on all ages is inconsequential. However, we cannot really say what these effects are because no studies have looked at television as a teacher and at its viewers as learners. The more the knowledge we gain from television parallels critical life events, the more we are likely to perceive television as reality. The viewer's perception is the salient variable that makes television both very powerful and difficult to ascertain.

The Ashland school board mandated that all third-grade students in the district be taught music awareness. The new program involves all music teachers, K–12, and is allocated ninety minutes per week for twelve weeks. The board earmarked in-service monies to hire a consultant to work with all the district's music teachers for one month during the summer to prepare the curriculum.

The consultant and teachers outlined what needed to be developed: (1) the philosophy of the music awareness program, (2) an articulated curriculum, by objective, (3) an evaluation package, and (4) implementation strategies. The following reflects the program development and the role that modeling plays in it.

Philosophy

The primary objective is to reach all third graders with the finest musical stimuli available to generate interest in and awareness of musical instruments and thus to enhance their future musical experiences. "Musical awareness" is defined as knowing the characteristic sound of each instrument. To enhance their musical awareness, students should have the opportunity to handle and experiment with musical instruments and hear good quality tone production, articulated sounds, and the range of the various instruments by listening to recordings and performances by staff mem-

bers, upper level music students, or community musicians. Other projected activities include field trips to concerts and rehearsals.

Instruction

The following units were designed for the music awareness program:

1. Introduction to instrumental music

2. Strings

3. Woodwinds

4. Brass

5. Percussion

6. Keyboard instruments

7. Additional instruments

Using the sequencing procedure of articulating curriculum from simple to complex and from nonconceptual to conceptual, the teachers developed the following unit on woodwinds, which is an example of how the curriculum was developed by objective:

III. Unit 3: Woodwinds
  A. Awareness
    1. The students will discriminate among woodwind instruments by sight and name.
    2. The students will learn that there are different groups within the woodwind family: single reed, double reed, and tone hole.
    3. The students will discriminate among wood-

wind instruments by the characteristics of sound (that is, pitch, duration, intensity, tone color).
  B. Familiarity
    1. A qualified person will demonstrate the production of sounds of woodwind instruments.
    2. The students will learn how to hold woodwind instruments properly.
    3. The students will be given the opportunity to produce sounds on woodwind instruments.
  C. Functions of woodwinds in musical groups
    1. The students will learn how woodwind instruments are used in various musical groups.
    2. The students will learn the role of each woodwind instrument within various musical groups.
    3. The students will learn to appreciate the function of woodwinds within musical groups.

Evaluation

The music teachers decided to give a pretest, then an equivalent form posttest, to see how much the music awareness program had increased students' knowledge of music. In addition, they decided to monitor student activity through the rest of their elementary years and into junior high to see if the music awareness program promoted greater long-term interest in music as determined by enrolling in music classes. The new longitudinal data would be compared against existing data on student interest in music prior to the program's inception.

In addition to cognitive knowledge and understanding, the teachers desired to test the student's ability to identify instruments and sounds via an audio tape. The following are examples of items given to students, in synchronization with the tape:

1. What kind of sound is this? (Unit 1)
   a. self
   b. nature
   c. machine
   d. musical instrument

2. Which instrument is playing? (Unit 2)
   a. violin   c. clarinet
   b. trumpet   d. drum

3. Which member of the string family is playing? (Unit 2)
   a. violin   c. cello
   b. viola   d. string bass

4. Which member of the double reed woodwind family is playing? (Unit 3)
   a. oboe   c. saxophone
   b. bassoon   d. English horn

5. Which member of the brass family is playing? (Unit 4)
   a. trumpet   c. French horn
   b. tuba   d. trombone

6. Which nonpitched percussion instrument is playing? (Unit 5)
   a. wood block   c. snare drum
   b. maracas   d. triangle

Implementation

The music teachers decided to divide the twelve-week program into two major sections: general awareness and in-depth exploration. They set this schedule:

Week 1. The program would be introduced and students would have a hands-on general orientation to various instruments.

Week 2. Music teachers would model different instruments, tone, quality, and so on by demonstrating on various instruments.

Week 3. Advanced students, from junior and senior high school, would model different instruments by demonstration.

Week 4. Community professional musicians would model different instruments and explain the role of music in their lives.

Weeks 5–6. Students would have more defined hands-on experiences. Such experiences would be governed in the following manner:

1. Students would select a specific area of interest.
2. Students would learn the history of music in the specific musical instrument area.
3. Students would learn all content relevant to their immediate experience with the specific instrument.
4. Students would learn the social and cultural significance of this specific musical instrument.

Weeks 7–12. Students would be assigned to the specific music teachers in their area of instru-

mental interest. They would go into considerable depth on the instrument, including learning some of the initial steps in playing it. The final week would include two field trips on which they could see how local amateur and professional musicians use the musical instrument they were interested in.

The program was a success. Its students did significantly better on posttest measures than on pretest measures. Five-year longitudinal data showed that the number of students enrolled in music courses increased dramatically, a finding that was attributed to the music awareness program. The program successfully employed the concept of modeling at several different levels. First, students listened to good music through some audio and visual tapes. Second, music teachers demonstrated various instruments for the students. Third, performing artists from the community came into the school and demonstrated their talent on various instruments. Fourth, students were taken on a field trip where they could observe performers. It is an example of how effective a program can be when it is designed to maximize learning potential (Thornburg, 1979b).

Annotated Readings

Bandura, A. (1982). Self-efficacy mechanism in human agency. *American Psychologist, 37,* 122–147.

> *This article focuses on self-efficacy in humans. Self-perceptions of efficacy influence thoughts, actions, and emotions. In causal tests done by Bandura, the higher the level of induced self-efficacy, the higher the performance accomplishments and the lower the emotional arousal. Bandura cogently argues the positive aspects of self-efficacy and how they affect different aspects of human behavior. This is an important, comprehensive article that speaks strongly for improving the human condition.*

Bandura, A. (1978). The self system in reciprocal determinism. *American Psychologist, 33,* 344–358.

> *Bandura believes that causal processes are appropriately conceptualized in terms of reciprocal determinism. Viewed from this theoretical orientation, psychological functioning involves a continuous reciprocal interaction between behavioral, cognitive, and environmental influences. He proposes reciprocal determinism as a basic analytic principle for understanding psychosocial phenomena within the individual, organizations, and social systems.*

Gould, D., & Weiss, M. (1981). The effects of model similarity and model talk on self-efficacy and muscular endurance. *Journal of Sport Psychology, 3,* 17–29.

> *The research study was designed to determine if observing a similar or dissimilar model who makes varying self-efficacy statements influences an observer's efficacy expectations and, in turn, his or her muscular endurance performance. Models were athletes and nonathletes, positive and negative in self-efficacy statements. Models who were similar to the subjects in the study and those who were positive had the strongest effect on the subjects' behavior. Thus, the modeling effect was positive.*

Moyne, J. A., & Kaniklidis, C. (1981). Models of language comprehension. *Cognition and Brain Theory, 4,* 265–284.

> *This article surveys recent work on the modeling of language comprehension. The article is basically a state of the art document that looks at language comprehension from two perspectives: (1) the parameters of human comprehension processes and discussion of theoretical issues concerning the nature, organization, and processing of information and (2) incorporation of observations drawn from the first perspective into a framework for categorizing and comparing models of language comprehension. The modeling effect in artificial intelligence is also a critical part of this overview article.*

Reiser, R. A., & Gagne, R. M. (1982). Characteristics of media selection models. *Review of Educational Research, 52,* 499–512.

> *This comprehensive article identifies and evaluates the learning effectiveness of the major features found in media selection models. The authors employ ten models, focusing on the characteristics across models. Features include the physical forms the models take, the ways in which they classify media, and the media selection factors they consider.*

Russo, N. F., & O'Connell, A. N. (1980). Models from our past: Psychology's foremothers. *Psychology of Women Quarterly, 5*, 11–54.

This provocative article reviews women's contributions to psychology, including the impact of female leadership and productivity on present behavior. The authors review significant women's contributions in the following areas: facilitative role of marriage, society, and the evolution of psychology. The authors synthesize these contributions by discussing how past developments provide foundations for the future.

Development in Humans

Mr. Li and Mr. Graff, the principal and librarian of Olema Elementary School, decided to put together a special literature section on the ways individuals develop for the parents in their school. Mr. Graff gathered all the popular books he knew of and had them available for people to look at during an evening parents organization meeting. They also asked Dr. Schweid, a local child psychologist, to make a forty-five minute presentation to parents, followed by a question and answer session.

Dr. Schweid described children as individuals who are developing through learning and experiencing things in the world. She stressed that children should be thought of as dynamic beings who grow physically and intellectually and, as they do, learn social behaviors, express emotions, learn values, and show affection toward others. Dr. Schweid listed major developmental events that happen in children's lives during their elementary school years and pointed out that, from around grade five on, children are increasingly adolescentlike in their attitudes and behaviors. Various comments sparked several questions, including the following:

- How much does heredity influence a child's development?
- Are the preschool years really the most formative in life?
- Is a child's temper inherited or is it learned from a parent?
- How are children supposed to learn appropriate social roles?
- Is there any chance that a growing child will go insane?
- How normal is it for children to fear things or have bad dreams?
- Will being around handicapped children affect a child's growth?

These questions were more than Dr. Schweid really wanted to answer. Yet, in a real sense, they are the kinds of issues that inspire the study of child and adolescent development because developmental researchers seek to discover how factors influence children in every aspect of their life.

The next day Mr. Li and Mr. Graff met to compare notes. In all, they felt that Dr. Schweid had been informative and that parents had asked very important and real questions and had indicated an interest in reading more about how they could understand their children and help them grow up.

Helping you understand human development is the purpose of this chapter, in which I discuss:

Development
The gradual increase in size and capacity of humans over time.

Structural development
Characteristics of humans that are directly related to biological development.

Growth
Quantitative change in human body characteristics.

Maturation
The nonobservable changes in human body characteristics.

Psychological development
Nonbiological aspects of humans that change over time.

Social development
The increased capacity to relate to others and the environment.

Emotional development
The emergence of the capacity to feel and express oneself in emotional ways.

Intellectual development
Gradual increase in thought processes.

Although people have been formally studying human behavior for over eighty years, only recently have theorists begun to reconceptualize and expand their beliefs about how individuals develop. **Development** is the living organism's movement over time in the direction of complexity of organization. In physical growth, there is the enumerable proliferation of parts—from the single cell at conception to billions of cells in the adult. Development implies that, as children increase in age, their capacity to function increases as well. Cessation of this increased capacity is the definitive criteria for moving from being an adolescent to an adult. The common range of physical development stretches from conception through adolescence.

Two terms used to describe **structural development** are **growth** and **maturation.** Growth is *quantitative* change in bodily characteristics, and its sequence is generally consistent among children, although growth rates may vary considerably. Regardless of its rate, growth is measurable. We could measure the height of a developing child, for example, at six-month intervals. These "measured sizes" would give us the child's height growth rate. We could also simply observe changes in height by looking at the child, but psychology is an exacting science, so we can do more than observe. We can measure actual change.

Maturation describes *qualitative* changes in bodily characteristics. Although qualitative changes imply a greater capacity for functioning, they are not as observable or measurable as quantitative changes. For example, it is easy to see that a four-year-old's hand is larger than that of a two-year-old. But the four-year-old's hand also has more-developed skeletal, muscular, and nervous systems, which make the four-year-old capable of more complex actions using the hand. This development is internal; the components that make up the hand become increasingly organized and interrelated with age.

Growth and maturation are highly coordinated physical processes. They maintain a biological balance in the body, which facilitates increasing integration among body parts. As they become differentiated and capable of autonomous functions, the separate systems come to function as an integrated, coordinated whole.

Children also develop psychologically. **Psychological development** may be partly affected or totally unaffected by biology. **Social development** includes learning to interact with others and to form friendships. **Emotional development** also begins during childhood. Expressions of this include feelings of love and affection, sharing, and security. **Intellectual development** is an increase in ability and achievement.

Most theories of human development ignore the ways in which children learn. Learning is brought about by environmental factors and is considered an outcome of development. As children develop, their capacity for learning increases; yet learning does not occur simply because children develop. It depends on external stimulation to which they can respond. In a real sense, development also depends on learning because, as children learn behaviors and use them, growth or maturation may be stimulated. To deny learning's role would be a mistake. As children develop and relate what they learn to their development, the two become interrelated, very much as growth and maturation. Learning is a major factor in human development.

Stages of Development

The study of human behavior across the life span focuses on critical growth periods at different times in life. Human behavior was originally viewed as having three major stages: childhood, adolescence, and adulthood. With increased scientific study, theorists have broken these three stages down considerably. Table 6–1 shows how stages are currently conceptualized. The age ranges shown in Table 6–1 approximate the time frames within which major development changes occur. Because growth and maturation rates vary, the best way to view these age ranges is as relative rather than absolute. In fact, the current view is that development is a continuous process from conception to death.

Perhaps the most accurate way to view human growth is as a progressive, continuous process throughout the lifespan. Functionally, however, stages help us better understand behavior within specific age ranges because they represent major shifts in emphasis. It is more helpful to a teacher or parent, for example, to know what can be expected of a three-year-old than to say that growth is continuing normally. Knowing what goals or tasks to expect within a specific stage and how each stage helps movement into another stage is essential to understanding human behavior.

There have been three established ways of looking at any stage of development. Recently, a fourth way has emerged.

1. *Normative characteristics.* The common ways in which people develop within an age range are the norms we define as the central characteristics of that stage. For example, early childhood (ages two to five) is dominated by the acquisition of language.

Table 6–1 Stages of Human Development

Infancy

Prenatal period	(conception to birth)
Neonatal period	(birth to 4 to 6 weeks)
Infancy	(4 to 6 weeks to 2 years)

Childhood

Early childhood	(2 years to 5 years)
Middle childhood	(6 years to 8 years)
Late childhood	(9 years to 11 years)

Preadolescence
(9 to 13 years)

Adolescence

Early adolescence	(11 years to 13 years)
Middle adolescence	(14 years to 16 years)
Late adolescence	(17 years to 19 years)

Youth
(19 years to 22 years)

Adulthood

Early adulthood	(20 years to 29 years)
Middle adulthood	(30 years to 49 years)
Adulthood	(50 years to 65 years)
Late adulthood	(66 years to 80 years)
Old age	(81 years and beyond)

Transitional adulthood
(60 years to 70 years)

Source: From *Development in Adolescence*, 2nd Edition by H. D. Thornburg. Copyright © 1982 by Wadsworth, Inc. Reprinted by permission of Brooks/Cole Publishing Company, Monterey, California 93940.

2. *Stage-specific experiences.* Familiarity with what is possible and expected at any stage allows those who work with children and adolescents to provide experiences designed to increase development. For example, we know the potential for abstract reasoning begins emerging around age eleven. It would be important to engage students in specific experiences designed to help them learn how to reason abstractly.

3. *Developmental deficiencies.* By knowing what to expect of children at various stages, we can identify those areas in which development is not taking place as expected. Immature and undeveloped behaviors can then be worked on. For example, a fifteen-year-old girl who has not begun to menstruate needs special attention. Professionals can often correct physical or psychological deficiencies.

4. *Transitional events.* In each developmental stage, there is a set of transitional behaviors. By viewing development on the life span continuum, we can understand gradual movement from one stage to the next. Identifying key transitional events helps us better understand movement from one stage to another (Thornburg, 1982a).

Characteristics of Development

In addition to being sequential, growth creates increasing complexity. Two-year-olds are obviously larger than six-month-old babies, but their language development, emotional expressions, and behaviors are also more advanced. The rate of psychological development varies more than the rate of physical development because the factors that influence it are more diverse. For example, vocabulary is integrated by the syntactical rules of language; emotions are affected by the attitudes and stability of others in the child's environment; and behavior is influenced by what the child perceives as appropriate actions. Therefore, as the child becomes increasingly complex, it is easier to observe psychological than physical differences.

The interrelation between growth and learning is another consideration. Developmental theorists see learning as an outcome of growth and maturation. What a child learns may facilitate or hinder maturation. At the same time, there are limitations on what a child can learn at each developmental stage. Growth and learning are so interrelated that most behaviors cannot be attributed solely to one or the other. Rather than view these processes as mutually exclusive, we increase our understanding of human behavior by recognizing the relative contribution each makes to actual behavior.

Increasing self-delineating is a third important characteristic. This relates to individuality. Heredity plays a major role in individual differences because we are all genetically different. Of equal importance is the environment. As children develop interests in others, they begin to see their own individuality. Conflict and competition with others point up differences. Our gender, nutrition, number of siblings, parents' personal-

ities, physical limitations, and parental love and affection are but a few of the environmental factors that contribute to our uniqueness.

A fourth characteristic is increasing self-control. Developing children learn to control their behavior and emotions and increase their capacity to endure frustrations and remain coherent even when highly excited or under stress. This emotional area develops more slowly than the rational thought area, primarily because our society stresses thinking more than feeling.

Increasingly rational thought occurs primarily because of a gradual increase in the capacity to think and secondarily because of the emergence of logic in the child. The conscious mind expands with age; so children gradually become aware of more things at once and their time perspective increases. Formal educational programs are probably the best facilitators of cognitive development.

Throughout the elementary school years, children become increasingly aware of personal choices. In many ways, childhood experiences help us learn how to become increasingly independent and self-determined, traits that gain prominence during the adolescent years. Independence is something most adolescents feel a need for. In order to become independent without resorting to rebellion, they must acquire the skills and ideas that help them become less dependent on others. This may be no more than parents allowing children to learn how to do something rather than telling them how to do it. Perhaps the best way to help children progress from dependence to independence is to allow them to participate in establishing guidelines for behavior and internalizing self-standards for behavior.

Types of Development

The five types of development that have been the subject of theory and research are biological, emotional, intellectual, social, and moral. They are all interrelated, although their interdependence does not imply proportionality. There will be growth periods when one aspect of behavior will predominate. Puberty, for example, will intensify awareness of the biological self. An eight-year-old who has just become a Christian may focus on moral development. The child entering first grade may find intellectual development to be dominant. But the prominent behavioral area is not the only functioning area. Developing children are interacting children, both within themselves and within the environment.

Biological

Heredity plays an obvious role in determining our gender, physical characteristics, structural differences, and development sequence and rate. Physical development is the observable characteristics of genetic transmission. Our basic sensory, neural, and motor structures depend on biological inheritance. Biological influence is not intended to refute the role of environment in human development, only to establish the importance of its contribution to the total individual.

The early **growth readiness** models advanced by G. Stanley Hall (1904, 1921) and Arnold Gesell (1928) state that organized growth patterns must occur before learning can contribute to development. For example, we cannot teach a child to ride a bicycle until the developmental readiness has emerged. Major evidence for the type of development comes primarily from studies of the development of children's physical and motor functions. Normative data on height, weight, and the range of biological behavior are additional ways to describe human biological dimensions. I discuss the physical characteristics of human development later in this chapter.

Growth readiness
The belief that biological growth must occur prior to an individual having the capacity to learn or behave in certain ways.

Emotional

Emotions describe behaviors related to the degree of feeling being expressed at the time. These may include expressions of love, happiness, anger, resentment, hate, satisfaction, or fear. Some people are more emotional than others, depending on their personal learning history and interactions. An infant's emotional life is relatively simple, but the adolescent may experience both complex and traumatic feelings. Emotions are primarily learned and represent the affective domain.

Although conceptualized as pertaining to personality rather than emotional development, the works of Sigmund Freud (1923, 1948, 1949) and Erik Erikson (1950, 1968) have provided the basic understanding of how the individual unfolds emotionally. Instinctual drives motivate behavior, some of which is undisciplined but most of which is controlled by the ego. I discuss human instincts later in this chapter.

Cognitive development may be viewed as a potentiality that is realized through interaction between genetic abilities and the environment. Intelligence is neither a static condition nor an energy reservoir waiting to be tapped. Heredity provides the parameters within which intelligence develops. Some individuals receive better genetic endowment, thus providing them a greater capacity for acting intelligently than those of lesser endowment. However, it must be recognized that a nonstimulating environment might prevent more adequate development of genetic potential, whereas a stimulating environment might enrich existing potential. Given that one's ability to act intelligently is a result of the interaction between heredity and environment, functional intelligence denotes degrees of competence in behavior that will vary at different developmental stages.

The work of Jean Piaget (1950, 1952) conceptualized intelligence as developmental. He believed that from birth through adolescence one's capacity to think increased due to age. To Piaget, intellectual development was the progressive internalization of different forms of logic. Progress in development is affected by the interaction of the child with the environment, although Piaget clearly believed human capacity was more attributable to development than learning. His position, as well as more recent advances, will be discussed in Chapter 8.

Social

Socialization is the process by which an individual learns and adapts to the ways, ideas, beliefs, and values of the culture. The child's primary social environments are the home and schools. As friends become increasingly important, they also influence an individual's behavior. The way we respond to others and adopt behaviors that we are told are socially correct is the way in which we become social beings.

Selman (1976, 1980) places social processes in a developmental context that parallels general cognitive development. Described as **social cognition,** the belief is that our affective or social development is concurrent with our cognitive development. Implications of such a system are that we can develop at the same pace socially, emotionally, and intellectually. I discuss this theory more fully in Chapter 8.

Social cognition
The ability to understand social phenomena in the environment because of the way they are cognitively presented.

Moral

Perhaps our thinking on moral development actually predates our consideration of all other types of development. Referred to as theological, religious, or spiritual, this aspect of individual behavior has been stressed for over twenty-five hundred years. In its elementary form, it is choosing right from wrong or good from bad. In the past two decades, moral behavior has been redefined and an elaborate theory has been advanced that views moral capacity as developmental, very much as intellectual development is viewed (Kohlberg, 1964). I also discuss Kohlberg's theory in Chapter 8.

Contemporary Influences on Development

Modern society is becoming increasingly complex, and this complexity has ramifications for human development. To understand developing individuals in contemporary society, we must identify the factors that influence their behavior.

Consistency
The extent to which a person's behavior is repeatedly the same or similar.

Norms, Values, and Roles

Consistency is important in understanding development. If a person's behavior is the same or similar from one instance to another, we can predict future behavior more reliably. The more erratic behavior is, the less accurately human behavior can be described.

Three terms are used to describe consistency in behavior: **norm, value,** and **role.** Norms refer to behaviors that are expected of most people. Because most people do something, it becomes a standard of

Norms
Expectations of human behavior that emerge from such sources as the family, school, religion, and society.

Values
The internal belief system of an individual that directly affects behavior.

Roles
Behavior that is expected of an individual in a specific situation.

149

behavior. Norms emerge in two ways. First, tradition has brought us many normative behaviors. For example, going to church on Sunday has become the expected behavior for most Western religions. Pledging allegiance to the American flag is an expected behavior of Americans.

Second, through scientific study, we have derived expected behaviors. For example, we measure the length of every newborn baby. Some babies are sixteen inches, others twenty-one inches, but by the time you average the length of all babies, you find the expected length is nineteen inches. Therefore, the norm for newborn babies is to be nineteen inches long. Human intelligence is another normative behavior. We give many people an IQ test and record their scores; then we average all scores to find out what is normal intelligence. An IQ of 100 is average, the norm around which most people fall. If you have an IQ of 85, you are below the norm. An IQ of 115 is better than the norm. The combined results of tradition and scientific observations tell people what is expected of them.

Values are what people believe in. They are internal belief systems that influence behavior. In American society, many values and norms are the same, although we should not make the mistake of thinking they are synonymous. Children learn many values from parents. We look again at the pledge of allegiance, which reflects the value of believing in America, the country, freedom, democracy, the things it stands for. People often recite this pledge at public events. If a person chose not to recite the pledge, others might view this person as un-American or unpatriotic. The pledge of allegiance represents a value (pro-American) and a norm (saying the pledge). It is often very difficult to know which is affecting our behaviors—values or norms. One way to distinguish between them is by remembering that values are internal beliefs and norms are others' expectations. In either case, they may result in a socially accepted behavior.

The 1970s brought new meaning to the term *role,* which refers to what is expected of us in specific social situations. Traditionally, roles have been divided up by the sexes. The male role has been one of breadwinner, protector, and masculinity. The female role has been one of wife/mother, benevolence, and femininity. Roles resulted in being able to do some behaviors and not others. Contemporary studies of human behaviors indicate that role expectancies may limit our abilities to function. For example, we have traditionally said that women are incapable of being business executives, but this was true only because society refused to allow women to prepare for and participate in this role. Today a significant number of women are business executives; so the limitation was due to role expectancy, not to being a woman.

Roles serve a useful purpose in that they describe what is acceptable behavior in a variety of contexts. The first grader learns what it means to be a first grader, including appropriate social behavior, cooperation, and respect. At the same time, roles can inhibit people by expecting them to conform without considering individual characteristics. Roles are important; they define much human behavior. But roles should not be stereotyped because that may discriminate against a person because of ability, age, sex, ethnic group, social class, or education. Several variations exist in norms, values, and roles today, and variations may become increasingly pronounced.

Strands of Developmental Theory		
System	General Trait	Key Theorists
Biological	Human behavior has a strong biological component that unfolds across time.	G. Stanley Hall Arnold Gesell
Personality	Human behavior is instinctual and is controlled by the ego, satisfaction of instinctual urges, and demands of society.	Sigmund Freud Erik Erikson
Cognitive	Human intelligence increases in capacity with age through adaptation to the environment.	Jean Piaget
Moral	Human moral capacity parallels cognitive development. As thought capacity increases, so does capacity to make moral decisions and evaluations.	Lawrence Kohlberg
Social	Social perspective taking parallels general cognitive thought with increased capacity to separate self from others and society.	Robert Selman

Culture

Culture is thought to be the prevailing or dominant influence in people's lives. The term describes a widespread influence on how we think, believe, feel, and act. The dominant social group within the culture generally has the strongest influence (Marden & Meyer, 1978). The more common something is, the more dominant it becomes. The dominant group tends to persist over time; therefore, it shares a past, language, and values, which enables it to influence economic, occupational, technological, and political decisions. It is common for the dominant culture to expect all of society to adhere to its values, perhaps even to the point of not tolerating anyone who holds different values.

The label **subculture** is generally applied to a group that does not endorse the dominant social attitudes and values. The past two decades have seen increased activities by subcultures. Many groups have pointed to past injustices, stimulating the American conscience to overcome prejudices and even make restitution for the past. Although the degree of success these subcultural groups have had is open to debate, one thing is clear: Subcultural groups are more viable than ever before in our society. They have found their roles in America, although many prejudices and injustices continue to prevail.

Culture
The dominant social influences in the lives of people.

Subculture
Social beliefs and behaviors that influence the lives of people to a lesser extent than does the dominant culture.

Since World War II, American society has changed tremendously. Through increased communication and technology, the privileges of a few have spread to many. Mass media brings our nation and the world before us, and the universality of human concern and behavior has resulted in cultural changes. All people are increasingly aware that the predictability of uniform behaviors in society is diminishing. The issue of individual representation in a changing culture is very real for children, adolescents, and adults.

Economics

Three changing areas directly related to economics are earning power, mobility, and social class. The affluence of the 1960s was the forerunner of the inflationary 1970s. The net result was more earnings yet less spending power. As people's lives become economically impacted, they give up things. Less economic flexibility often leads people to get involved in self-defeating activities. Diversity and enriched experiences are very important to developing children. These tend to disappear as disposable income decreases.

The 1950s and 1960s were highly mobile periods in America. In 1950, America was primarily a rural society. Today, over two-thirds of the population live in cities. But the 1970s saw reduced mobility, due in part to the recession. Less mobility is predicted in the 1980s. The majority of the population has already made its major shift to urban living, and the combination of high prices and fewer jobs will reduce mobility.

Many aspects define the term *social class*, but the most important one is income. Social class distinctions invariably give privileges to some and restrict others. The dominant culture is usually assigned middle-class and upper-middle-class rank. Minorities and subcultures, whose members' lives are characterized by low income, poor housing, inadequate living space, inadequate education, high unemployment rates, and feelings of powerlessness and hopelessness, are usually assigned lower-class rank.

Family Variations

The traditional family unit consists of a mother, father, and children. However, separation, divorce, one-parent families, step-parent families, nonmarriage living, and communal living are just some of the current variations on the traditional pattern. As family units become more diverse, each family member must learn to make new adjustments and develop new interactions. The issue of intact families versus other living patterns is a moral issue to many. Yet making people feel guilty if they are not in an

intact family does little to help them adjust their living patterns. This is especially true when developing children are made to feel bad about their family situation even though they have no direct bearing on it.

Divorce increases family stress, and, as a result, it may affect a child's behavior in out-of-family settings, such as school. Bohannan (1970) suggests several possible types of divorce and their effects: an emotional divorce where the problem is around a deteriorating marriage; a legal divorce, based on sufficient grounds; an economic divorce that focuses on personal and real property; a coparental divorce that deals with custody, visitation privileges, and new family structures; a community divorce that alters friendships and community interactions; and a psychic divorce that results in an identity crisis, particularly in regard to regaining personal autonomy. As parents feel the impacts of their decision to end their marriage, they transmit some of these feelings to their children, which often results in additional stress, acting out, and unpredictable or disruptive behavior in and outside of the home (Schoettle & Cantwell, 1980).

Divorce and separation are more common now than they have ever been in our society. Therefore, we must develop strategies to help children and adults who find themselves in this situation. Contrary to popular opinion, children and adolescents who find themselves in one-parent families do not necessarily have long-term adjustment problems in development. Similarly, they do not automatically know how to deal with these confusing situations.

The family unit faced stiff challenges in the 1960s and 1970s. In fact, its very nature was questioned so much that many people no longer viewed the family as a viable social unit in this society. The visibility of the family diminished as the concept of individuality surfaced. However, no other social unit has replaced the family. There is a growing awareness among social scientists that children learn social skills most successfully in a stable and secure family. "Stability" does not imply the nuclear unit; it does imply consistency in parental behavior and the ability to foster and respect the rights of each individual family member, whether child, adolescent, or adult.

Roles of Heredity and Environment

Humans, like the other living organisms, are basically biological, their life processes being tied to the biological system. Observable characteristics in children that depend on heredity include hair color, eye color, body build, height, weight, and, to some extent, intelligence. But as children increasingly interact with their environment, environmental influences come to play the dominant role in shaping development. A lively controversy concerning the roles of heredity and environment occurred among early child psychologists. Those who stressed heredity's role thought that the course of development was due primarily to the unfolding of an internal pattern predetermined by the genes and that the influence of environmental experiences was less important. The environmentalists believed that they could take any normal infant and determine the kind of adult he or she would become by controlling the experiences within the environment.

Heredity

The heredity position holds that the basic features of development exist as genetic blueprints that manifest themselves in a normal environment. One of the strongest advocates of this approach was Arnold Gesell, who established the Yale clinic of child development in 1911. Gesell and his associates carefully observed and described the child's physical and mental growth. He defined maturation as those developmental potentials that are genetically determined and represent movement toward the unfolding of inner tendencies, rather than the result of learning or experience. To illustrate, Gesell found that the ability to grasp objects (prehension) developed in the same sequence in all normal children under a wide range of conditions and experiences. This finding is more attributable to genetic factors than to environmental ones. Gesell stressed that the best environmental and training stituations can be devised only after we understand the child's maturational readiness.

Maturation has implications for teaching the young. First, it sets limits beyond which development and behavior potential cannot occur, regardless of the environment. As Gesell and Ilg (1949, p. 252) have pointed out, "This intrinsic growth is a gift of nature. It can be guided, but it cannot be created; nor can it be transcended by an educational agency." Maturation is generally gauged by the child's chronological age. To Gesell, learning's effectiveness depends upon proper timing; that is, if you are trying to teach children to read, they must be mature enough or have a readiness for reading.

Gesell illustrated the relative contributions of maturation and learning to climbing ability in a study of identical twin girls, one of whom was given training (twin T) and one of whom was untrained and served as a control (twin C). Because heredity was the same for both children, the direct influence of environment presumably could be studied by giving each twin different training. Twin T was taught stair climbing for twenty minutes daily from forty-six to fifty-two weeks of age, at which time she climbed the stairs quite ably. At fifty-two weeks, twin C could not yet climb the staircase; yet in one more week, she was mature enough to climb the stairs without the benefit of any training. After two more weeks, during which she did receive training, twin C was nearly as proficient at stair climbing as twin T, even though she had received much less training.

Gesell concluded that training is a slight and maturation is a powerful influence on the development of locomotor ability (Gesell & Thompson, 1929). Although extraneous variables were not as controlled in this study as in contemporary research, Gesell's basic point is generally accepted: Motor skills develop or mature in normal children in the same sequence and at an understandable rate under a wide variety of conditions, and premature training has little influence on such development and little beneficial effect.

Other studies support Gesell's contention. Dennis and Dennis (1940) researched Hopi Indian infants and found that, even though they were placed on a cradle board and highly restricted in movement, they learned to walk at the same age as those who were free of the cradle board. Gesell (1954) observed that infants cannot master grasping prior to developing an adequate neuromuscular pattern even though opportunities for grasping are given. Irwin (1960) found that, even though children were exposed to a regular reading program at thirteen months, they showed minimal improvement in their spontaneous vocalizations before seventeen months. The improvement beyond this point was great compared with children unexposed to a reading program. Irwin contended that the earlier slow progress is attributable to the children's lack of readiness to read between months thirteen and seventeen.

Environment

Perhaps the most extreme advocate of the influence of the environment was J. B. Watson, who rejected introspection and concern with mental states and emphasized the objective study of behavior. Watson was one of the first psychologists to carry out experimental child research. As a result of his research, Watson (1928, p. 41) wrote:

> The behaviorists believe that there is nothing from within to develop. If you start with a healthy body, the right number of fingers and toes, eyes, and the few elementary movements that are present at birth, you do not need anything else in the way of raw material to make a man [sic], be that man a genius, a cultured gentleman, a rowdy or a thug.

Having stressed the importance of a child's experiences and training, Watson believed the major responsibility for the success of the child's upbringing rested with the parents. In fact, Watson (1926, p. 82) felt that parents might not be qualified for the job and that structured environments were probably preferable: "Give me a dozen healthy infants, well-formed, and my own specified world to bring them up in, and I'll guarantee to take any one at random and train him to become any type of specialist I might select—doctor, lawyer, artist, merchant, chief, and yes, even beggarman and thief, regardless of his ancestors." Ongoing contemporary experimental child research attests to the absurdity of such boldness. It is not possible to produce a child prodigy through mere coaching; Watson's approach denies the child's inherent potential. The learning of complex ways to see, do, or understand things must correspond to the child's developmental level.

The environmentalist's position has had strong implications for education and society. It has become increasingly evident that an understanding of the child's developmental nature requires the study of complex situations to which individuals react. To the environmentalist, education becomes a virtually all-powerful way of shaping the child's character, and society can employ education to produce the kinds of people it needs. In the 1840s, Johann Herbart wrote that individuals learn or are shaped by the ideas that are presented to them and that teachers must provide students with those ideas. There is a striking similarity between Herbart's contentions and the ways parents, teachers, and society try to shape children today.

Interaction between Heredity and Environment

Child psychologists now recognize that both heredity and environment affect all aspects of development. Unquestionably, however, the influence of heredity varies in directness, that is, in the extent to which its effects cannot be modified or counteracted by the environment.

Each child has **phylogenic functions,** such as crawling, creeping, sitting, and walking, which have strong maturational bases. Training for these behaviors before the child is ready to learn them is basically ineffective. As Dennis and Dennis (1940) observed, even children in cultures where movements are restricted develop these functions. Smith (1966, p. 6) observed that the "influence of heredity on the species to which an individual belongs, certain anatomical or physiological deficiencies, the sequence of physical and motor development, sex, and eye color are relatively unmodifiable by environmental circumstances."

Environment, however, directly determines such things as the ability to swim, ride a bicycle, speak English or Spanish, roller-skate, or climb a mountain. These are **ontogenetic functions** for which training is essential. No hereditary potential can fully mature without an adequate environment.

Phylogeny
The evolution of a species or race.

Ontogeny
The evolution or development of the individual.

In recent years, there has been concern that children reared in culturally and educationally deprived environments do not have the same opportunity to realize their hereditary potential as nondeprived children. Within our society, research indicates that normal developmental sequences identified for motor skills (sitting and walking) and language skills (talking, listening, and reading) fail to proceed in family and school environments where such development is not encouraged. Individual differences such as readiness, motivation, intelligence, and learning are, to some extent, affected by deprived environmental states.

Heredity influences individual learning capacity, and maturation affects readiness to learn; thus, education must be properly timed and suited to each individual. Learning and experience can determine whether children develop to their full capacity. Environment shapes many aspects of personality, such as values and interests, and education must effectively produce desirable traits, knowledge, and skills within the developing individual.

Growth Readiness Model

The growth readiness model helps us gather information about individuals as they develop. It implies that (1) at given points, normative behavior can be described; (2) individuals can be compared with each other, enabling us to assess the range and variability in human behavior; and (3) what we know about individuals at given points provides an understanding of human capacity. The age-stage approach to human development views human potential within given age ranges. Thus, by collecting information on individuals, we can describe human characteristics or capacities at a given age or within an age range. Consequently, we know that infancy is different from early childhood, early adolescence from adolescence, and so on.

When a sperm provided by the male unites with an ovum provided by the female, fertilization has occurred. The cell resulting from the union is known as the zygote, the beginning of life during the germinal period (the first two weeks). During the first nine months of life, the new organism develops inside the mother (*in utero*), independent of and protected from the external world. After the two-week germinal period, the organism enters the embryonic state (two weeks to two months). During this period, the embryo increases in size ten thousand-fold over the zygote. Formative growth includes rudimentary eyes, ears, mouth, and brain, simple kidneys, liver, the digestive tract, the bloodstream, and a tubelike heart that begins beating toward the end of the first month (Jenkins, Shacter, & Bauer, 1966). During the embryonic stage, the organism is most susceptible to genetic mutation, which may be caused by some drugs, overexposure to radiation, and German measles in the mother. The organism does not totally develop until it moves into the fetal stage (two months to birth). By five months, the fetus weighs one pound and has formed all its body parts and organs. From the seventh month on, the fetus is characterized by steady growth and refinement of structure and function.

Between 265 and 280 days after fertilization, the child is born. Human infants have a long childhood; even compared with the higher mammals, they are slow to mature. Whereas the Rhesus monkey can grasp objects five days after birth, the human infant cannot do so until five months after birth. One study of the comparative rates of development showed that a chimpanzee raised with a child of approximately the same age learned how to eat with a spoon, open doors, control its bowel and bladder, and come when called sooner than the child (Kellogg & Kellogg, 1933).

Comparison of different groups of animals along the phylogenetic scale indicates that the more complex the animal, the longer the period of parental care. In contrast to lower animals, which mature rapidly and have many built-in patterns of behavior, the human infant starts with relatively few unmodifiable propensities and thus can profit greatly from experience. Learning the vast complexities of cultures takes time and is generally facilitated through instruction and modeling.

Growth is very rapid during gestation and the first year of life. The first general growth is throughout infancy. After infancy, the growth spurt levels off until the adolescent spurt, after which vertical growth tapers off and ceases in the early twenties. The period from six years to pubescence shows relatively stable growth. The child from six to twelve generally concentrates on the social, emotional, and intellectual skills characteristic of this age. The final growth period, from puberty through adolescence, covers the culminating physical and intellectual growth years. Three regularities describe the characteristic sequence of development: (1) from the head downward; (2) from the center outward; and, with some qualifications, (3) from massive general responses to more specific ones (from gross to refined movements).

There is a common sequence of growth through which all humans pass, but, because of the uniqueness of each individual growth pattern, rates differ. Psychological growth is also uneven, although patterns do exist. Ilg and Ames (1955) found that there were cycles of personality development as indicated by behavioral phases. For example, at chronological ages (CA) two, five, and ten years, the developing child tends to be good tempered, cooperative, and well adjusted. These are followed by ages two and a half, five and a half to six, and eleven, when the child seems at odds with self and others. There are also established periods of withdrawal and introspection (CA three and a half, seven, and thirteen), followed by the tendency to be outgoing, expansive, and adventurous (CA four, eight, and fourteen).

Although the meaning of these cycles is not fully known, they may represent alternations between differentiation and integration, learning new skills and consolidating them, and acquiring new knowledge and organizing it. Knowing the range of development at certain chronological ages can help parents and teachers understand the normality of such growth.

Tables 6–2, 6–3, and 6–4 provide overviews of the highlights of development from birth through the adolescent growth spurt. They pre-

Table 6–2 Normative Stages of Development

Physical and Language Development	Emotional Development	Social Development
Birth to 1 Year		
0 to 1 Month		
Birth Size: 7–8 lbs., 20 inches Feedings: 5–8 per day Sleep: 20 hours per day Sensory capacities: makes basic distinctions in vision, hearing, smelling, tasting, touch, temperature, and perception of pain Reflexes: sucking, swallowing, crying, hiccoughing, grasping, pupillary contraction	Generalized tension	Helpless Asocial
2 to 3 Months		
Sensory capacities: color perception, visual exploration, oral exploration Sounds: cries, coos, grunts Motor ability: control of eye muscles, lifts head when on stomach	Delight Distress Smiles at a face	Visually fixates a face Smiles at a face Soothed by rocking
4 to 6 Months		
Sensory capacities: localizes sounds Sounds: babbling, makes most vowels and about half of the consonants Feedings: 3–5 per day Motor ability: control of head and arm movements, purposive grasping, rolls over	Enjoys being cuddled	Recognizes mother Distinguishes between familiar persons and strangers No longer smiles indiscriminately Expects feeding, dressing, bathing
7 to 9 Months		
Motor ability: control of trunk and hands, sits without support, crawls (abdomen touching floor)	Specific emotional attachment to mother Protests separation from mother	Enjoys "peek-a-boo"
10 to 12 Months		
Motor ability: control of legs and feet, stands, creeps, apposition of thumb and forefinger Language: says one or two words, imitates sounds, responds to simple commands Feedings: 3 meals, 2 snacks Sleep: 12 hours, 2 naps Size at one year: 20 lbs., 28–29 inches	Anger Affection Fear of strangers Curiosity, exploration	Responsive to own name Waves bye-bye Plays pat-a-cake Understands "no no!" Gives and takes objects
1 to 1½ Years		
Motor ability: creeps up stairs, walks (10–20 months), throws a ball, feeds self, builds a 2–3 cube tower (18 months), makes lines on paper with crayon	Dependent behavior Very upset when separated from mother Fear of bath	Obeys limited commands Repeats a few words Interested in own mirror image Feeds self
1½ to 2 Years		
Motor ability: runs, kicks a ball, builds 6 cube tower (2 yrs.) Capable of bowel and bladder control Language: vocabulary of more than 200 words Sleep: 12 hours at night, 1–2 hour nap Size at 2 years: 23–30 lbs., 32–35 inches	Temper tantrums (1–3 yrs.) Resentment of new baby	Does opposite of what he or she is told (18 months)

Table 6–2 continued

Physical and Language Development	Emotional Development	Social Development
2 to 3 Years		
Motor ability: jumps off a step, rides a tricycle, uses crayons, builds a 9–10 cube tower Language: starts to use short sentences, controls and explores world with language; stuttering may appear briefly Size at 3 years: 32–33 lbs., 37–38 inches	Fear of separation Emotions, anger Differentiates facial expressions of anger, sorrow, and joy Sense of humor (plays tricks)	Talks, uses "I," "me," "you" Copies parents' actions Dependent, clinging Possessive about toys Enjoys playing alongside another child Resists parental demands Gives orders Rigid insistence on routine Inability to make decisions
3 to 4 Years		
Motor ability: stands on one leg, jumps up and down, draws a circle and a cross (4 yrs.) Language: asks questions, actively conceptualizes, complete sentences of 6–8 words (4 yrs.) Self-sufficient in many routines of home life Size at 4 years: 38–40 lbs., 40–41 inches	Affectionate toward parents Pleasure in genital manipulation Romantic attachment to parent of opposite sex (3–5 yrs.) Jealousy of same-sex parent Imaginary fears of dark, injury, etc. (3–5 yrs.)	Likes to share, uses "we" Cooperative play with other children Nursery school Imitates parents—beginning of identification with same-sex parent Intense curiosity, asks questions Interest in other children's bodies (3–5 yrs.) Imaginary friends (3–5 yrs.)
4 to 5 Years		
Motor ability: mature motor control, skips, broad jumps, dresses self, copies a square and a triangle (5 yrs.) Language: talks clearly, uses adult speech sounds, has mastered basic grammar, relates a story, knows over 2000 words (5 yrs.) Size at 5 years: 42–43 lbs., 43–44 inches	Responsibility and guilt Feels pride in accomplishment	Prefers to play with other children Becomes competitive Prefers sex-appropriate activities
5 to 6 Years		
Gets first permanent teeth (6 years) Motor ability: Draws recognizable person; jumps easily; throws objects overhand Language: Asks meanings of words; vocabulary approximately 3000 words Size at 6: 47–48 lbs., 45–46 inches	Basic emotions all established; gradually mature	Physical independence from parents

sent norms that show the various ages when motor, language, emotional, and social behaviors appear. Norms represent the summarized standards in a sample of children. They characterize an average tendency, represent average behavior for a given age, and provide reference points for describing the key stages in the sequence of development. Individuals vary in their rates of development; so some will exceed the norms and others will fall behind them. This individuality may be evidenced at birth; even

Table 6–3 Developmental Characteristics of Middle Childhood

Age (years)	Height (in.)		Weight (lb.)		Stanford-Binet Test Items	Motor Development
	Girl	Boy	Girl	Boy		
7	48	49	52	53	Child can detect in what way two things are similar: apple, peach	Child has good balance; can hop and jump accurately
8	51	51	60	62	Child can read a paragraph of seven or eight sentences and recall five or six major ideas	Boys and girls show equal grip strength, great interest in physical games
9	52	53	70	70	Child can observe card with two designs and after ten seconds draw the designs' main features	Psychomotor skills such as throwing, jumping, running show marked improvement
10	54	55	74	79	Child can repeat as many as 60 digits	Boys become accurate in throwing and catching a small ball; running continues to improve
11	57	57	85	85	Child can find similarities among three things: rose, potato, tree	Boys can throw a ball about 95 feet; girls can run about 17.5 feet per second
12	60	59	95	95	Child can recognize absurdities: we saw icebergs that had been melted by the Gulf Stream	Boys can run about 18.5 feet per second; dodge ball popular with girls

Source: Travers (1979), p. 65. By permission of the publisher.

infants have been observed to differ widely in activity level, interest span, and irritability. The norms in the tables describe the average, not the ideal, state. However, norms may be helpful in directing attention to advanced or slower development insofar as an individual is observed to deviate significantly from them. Some variation in development is of little consequence. Whether an infant's first tooth erupts at birth, at three months, or at six months (the norm) may be relatively insignificant. It is almost certain, however, that the lower incisors will erupt before the upper ones (Massler & Schour, 1958). Of greater consequence is that maturation in stature and intellectual ability by the time a child is five or six are somewhat indicative of subsequent adult standing (Bloom, 1964).

The stages of motor, language, emotional, and social development occur in much the same order in all individuals, although children proceed at different rates and some children even skip some developmental events. For example, some children go from sitting to standing and walking without an intervening period of crawling and creeping. There is probably more consistency in motor development than there is in language, social, and emotional development, primarily because of genetic influences on physical growth. Language, social, and emotional development are primarily learned; thus, they are most subject to societal and cultural variation.

Table 6–4 Sequence of Development of Primary and Secondary Sexual Characteristics

Boys	Age Span		Girls
Beginning growth of testes, scrotum, pubic hair Some pigmentation, nodulation of breasts (later disappears) Height spurt begins Beginning growth of penis	11.5–13	10–11	Height spurt begins Slight growth of pubic hair Breasts, nipples elevated to form "bud" stage
Development of straight, pigmented pubic hair Early voice changes Rapid growth of penis, testes, scrotum, prostate, seminal vesicles First ejaculation of semen Kinky pubic hair Age of maximum growth Beginning growth of axillary hair	13–16	11–14	Straight, pigmented pubic hair Some deepening of voice Rapid growth of vagina, ovaries, labia, uterus Kinky pubic hair Age of maximum growth Further enlargement, pigmentation, elevation of nipple, areola to form "primary breast" Menarche
Rapid growth of axillary hair Marked voice change Growth of beard Indentation of frontal hair line	16–18	14–16	Growth of axillary hair Filling out of breasts to form adult conformation, secondary breast stage

Source: Rice, (1978), p. 103. Reprinted by permission.

There are also some differences in development between boys and girls. Girls generally develop faster than boys and tend to be less physically active, more sensitive to pain, have less muscle tissue, be ahead in bone growth and appearance of teeth, be better in all aspects of language development in early childhood, and reach puberty about two years earlier. These developmental differences could impact on educational decisions; thus, it is important for school personnel responsible for curriculum to understand the developmental norms of boys and girls and any pronounced differences between the sexes in any given year in school.

Personality Development

Freudian Theory

Sigmund Freud maintained that human development is marked by a series of universal stages, which originate in the sexual instinct known as **libido.** In fact, Freud considered the sexual instinct a primary determinant of normal personality development. Freud's theory, which has a strong bio-

Libido
A person's sexual energy that strives for pleasure throughout the lifespan.

163

Move over PeeWee

It must be very exasperating to feel you cannot compete with others or have no desire to compete yet find yourself involuntarily in competitive situations. Many poor spellers have found themselves in spelling bees matched against a clear superior. Athletically, this was the case with Stanley Brown, who as a junior high school student found himself to be noncompetitive in basketball even though it was a sport he liked very much.

Stan was a scrappy player who was as good a shot as any on the team. The trouble was that he was not on the team. Even in junior high, four feet eight inches is pretty short for the basketball team. On weekends, Stan's friends always included him in neighborhood games and he always did fairly well. His outstanding shooting seemed to compensate for his size. But boys from several neighborhoods attended the same school; so the pool of players was larger and Stan was much too short. He resigned himself to the fact that he simply would not make the team.

When it came time for Stan to attend high school, he had not grown significantly. As a sophomore, he was only four feet eleven inches tall. He went out for the basketball team, but he did not make it because of his size. He had to resort to neighborhood games in his high school years as well.

Stan began to grow about midway through his junior year in high school, and by graduation he was six feet one inch tall. When he went to college, Stan decided to go out for the basketball team. His size was not a drawback then, and he was still scrappy and a good shooter. Much to his surprise, Stan made the team. In his sophomore year, he made the starting lineup. He was most gratified at making the team, but Stan still felt he had lost a lot because he had been unable to compete with his peers in his junior and senior high school years. The course of human development is unpredictable. Sometimes it works to one individual's advantage and sometimes to another's disadvantage.

What Do You Think?

1. Is the athletic structure in most secondary schools unfair to many students?

2. Should Stanley have selected a sport where size or head-on competition would not be as critical?

3. Should school counselors be assigned to athletic programs in order to assist students who simply cannot be competitive?

logical basis, explains the role of instinct in the child's behavior, societal control of human instincts, neurotic symptoms, and the tendency for adults not to remember events of the first six or so years of life. In order to deal with these various phenomena in a single theory, Freud regarded all areas of the body, especially the mouth, anus, and genitals, as capable of instinctual pleasure. These areas were aroused by the child's libidinal energies, a response that Freud (1923) considered to be a natural behavior in the child.

In his later years, Freud (1949) became convinced that, in addition to the universal striving for pleasure (libido), there was an instinct for death (Thanatos). The death instinct involved not only the wish to return to the state of nonliving but the urge to destroy others as well (aggression). The death wish counterpart is love (Eros), the desire to live. In effect, we have two competing urges—to live or love others and to die or destroy others. The death wish has not been as widely accepted as the sexual instinct, although the concept of aggression has been discussed throughout the twentieth century.

Out of the human instinctual nature, Freud constructed a three-part conception of personality. He perceived the newborn infant as simple, unrefined, and primitive. The child's actions were motivated by the pleasure principle alone. Freud called this early personality the **id.** As infants develop, they begin to learn through interactions with the world and to construct realities. This reality orientation level is the **ego.** Within the first year of life, these two personality sources come into conflict. When a child is hungry, for example, the id demands immediate gratification. Because the mother or father cannot always immediately respond to the child's demands, the ego begins to develop the idea that sometimes gratification must be delayed. Later, between ages three and four, the **superego** or conscience emerges. This conscience development is generally dependent upon social expectations. It, too, makes demands on the ego, sometimes generating guilt when there is no rational basis for it and sometimes creating an overly strict conscience.

Freud constructed the first theory that stressed the developmental aspects of experiences from birth to late adolescence. The first six years include a pregenital organization of the sexual urges. Following this is the latency period, which extends to puberty. Finally, the genital stage emerges. The first six years of life are divided into three stages: oral, anal, and phallic.

Oral Stage In the **oral stage** (birth to eighteen months), the mouth is the primary erotic zone. The child usually receives pleasure from stimulation of the lips and tongue, which may be derived by sucking at the mother's breast or on part of his or her own body, such as a thumb or toe. Any interference with the sucking (feeding) operation is thought to lead to frustration. "The infant's feeding experience is presumed to have not only short-term effects of relative satisfaction or frustration, but long-term consequences as well. Excessive gratification of oral impulses, too-intense frustration, or a combination of the two will lead to oral fixation" (Fergu-

Id
The personality dimension of the individual that seeks pleasure or basic satisfaction.

Ego
The personality dimension of the individual that tries to construct reality in the world, tempering both the id and the superego.

Superego
The personality dimension of the individual that is known as one's conscience. It incorporates social values and expectations.

Oral stage
The first of Freud's developmental stages that is characterized by gaining pleasure through stimulation of the mouth.

Human Nature According to Freud		
Sexual instinct (libido)	ID	Primitive, irrational, demanding, instinctual
Thanatos (death) and Eros (love)	EGO	Rational, reality oriented, civilized
	SUPEREGO	Conscience, socially oriented, demanding

son, 1970, p. 55). In normal development, oral stimulation is incorporated into adult sexuality (for instance, kissing).

Anal stage
The second of Freud's stages that is characterized by control over elimination of body wastes.

Autonomic process
The ability to function independently, thus gaining muscle control.

Anal Stage   By the age of two, children become aware that they can increase libido stimulation by eliminating or withholding feces; thus begins the **anal stage.** Elimination activity occurring in the anal region is an **autonomic process** for the infant and it is during this period that control of the anal sphincter is gained. Sexual pleasure now centers around the anal rather than oral areas, as was true in the earlier stage of development. With increasing sphincter control, the child develops toilet training habits.

With the beginning of toilet training, children must learn to regulate their reflexive impulses. For example, they are initially interested in their feces rather than disgusted or bothered by the smell. They learn these reactions later from adults. Social reinforcement often accompanies successful toilet training. Parents, and sometimes entire families, encourage an infant in this respect, often with extrinsic rewards. Being able to eliminate successfully allows the child to receive parental approval and avoid the shame that often accompanies unsuccessful toilet experiences, such as dirty diapers.

Phallic stage
The developmental period in which pleasure is derived by stimulation of the genital area.

Phallic Stage   In the **phallic stage,** which begins around three to four, the dominant stimuli arise for the boy from the penis and for the girl from the clitoris, the erectile organ of the vulva corresponding to the penis. Sensitivity in the vagina is not yet fully developed; thus, Freud chose the term *phallic* to describe the main feature at this developmental period for both boys and girls. Children commonly handle their own genitals and play exploratory games with others to find out about the sexual anatomy of other children.

Oedipus complex
A cross-sex attachment in the direction of a son toward a mother that results in pleasure.

Several things are crucial to Freudian theory throughout this period. The **Oedipus complex** occurs in most four-year-old males when they begin to form an association between their mothers and pleasure. Strong libidinal attachment goes to the parent of the opposite sex, and there is clear evidence that the child wishes to possess the parent exclusively and to dispense with the presence of the same-sex parent. The attachment of a girl to her father represents the same phenomenon and is known as the **Electra complex.**

Freud viewed such wishes by the child as resulting in high anxiety that arises from the **castration complex.** The boy fears his father. Because the father is a powerful, threatening figure, the boy's fear could be quite intense. In addition, Freud contended that much castration anxiety is a result of the boy's projection of hostility toward the father. The Oedipal situation begins to be resolved as the boy represses his desires for his mother and begins strongly identifying with his father.

The situation for the girl is more obscure. The first love object for both boys and girls is the mother who has cared for them and who, in the course of such care, has inadvertently provided some erotic stimulation. In the Oedipal period, the boy continues to love the mother, but the girl notices that she has no penis and turns to the father as the possessor of a penis and a suitable love object. Because the girl does not experience fear of castration, she does not have repressive motives similar to a boy's and may continue her attachment to the father for an indefinite period of time.

Freud held that the Oedipus complex is a universal phenomenon, which implies it is biologically bound. Anthropological evidence suggests that such a conflict may be culturally bound, thus denying its universality. A prominent cross-cultural study was done by Malinowski (1927) among the natives of the Trobriand Islands. Finding no evidence of father and son rivalry or conflict, Malinowski contended that the Oedipus complex depends on the culture of a society.

Latency Stage   Around six years of age, children begin incorporating more social mores and learn of prohibition against oral, anal, and genital stimulation. Such feelings usually thrust them into the **latency period,** a period of rest from the desire and fears that occurred during the phallic stage. Freud thought that during this time some libidinal energies were sublimated in order to exercise socially acceptable behaviors. There has been a consensus among Freudian proponents that this latency period extends until adolescence, usually considered to start around twelve years of age. It is possible that contemporary social-cultural stress has served to arouse the child's sexual urges prior to the physiological crisis known as puberty and therefore the latency period may no longer last for six or seven years (Thornburg, 1982a).

Genital Period   With puberty come renewed stirrings of sexuality and the need to make breaks from the infantile love expressed toward parents (the **genital period**). This renewal of sexual energy comes from physiological maturity. The genital organs mature; the endocrine system produces high concentrations of sex hormones; and the sexual exploration of one's own genitals or the genitals of a member of the opposite sex arouses much stronger feelings than at any time prior to puberty. Behavior includes heterosexual love with feelings of gratification replacing the feelings of shame or disgust that were experienced during the phallic stage. It is in this period that the adolescent reaches sexual maturity and develops a set of attitudes and behaviors toward members of the opposite sex.

Electra complex
A cross-sex attachment in the direction of a daughter toward a father that results in pleasure.

Castration complex
The Freudian position that male children abandon cross-sex attachment because of the fear of being castrated.

Latency period
The period roughly equivalent to the elementary school years during which a child abandons attempts at sexual pleasure and learns the mores, customs, and expectations of society.

Genital period
The resurgence of sexual energy triggered by physical and sexual maturation at the onset of adolescence.

Erik Erikson (1950, 1959, 1963) posited a contemporary version of psychoanalytic positions on personality. He hypothesized that evolution of developmental stages is controlled by the **epigenetic principle,** according to which the unfolding of stages is determined genetically. Erikson also considered the role of social factors in personality development. He outlined eight stages based on **psychosocial development.** Erikson sees normal personality development as being governed by a proper rate and sequence with respect to the instinctual urges endowed in different bodily zones (such as Freud's early stages) and interaction potentials within the social and physical environment that are affected by the inherent psychosexual functions of the bodily zones. Thus, Erikson's first five stages correspond with Freud's stages. Beyond this, Erikson's interest in personality change throughout the entire life cycle caused him to consider three stages in addition to those Freud suggested: young adulthood, adulthood, and maturity. Table 6–5 summarizes these stages, compares them to Freud's, and indicates their successful and unsuccessful resolutions. Erikson's first four stages approximate the age range known as infancy through childhood. The second four represent puberty onward.

Epigenetic principle
The belief that as genetically determined human capacity increases it is influenced by the prevailing social environment.

Psychosocial development
The capacity to function resulting from the interaction of one's instinctual urges and the social and physical environment in which one finds himself or herself.

Trust versus Mistrust Erikson states that ease of feeding and depth of sleep are basic signs of trust. This is the most fundamental phase because it lays the basis for the personality development to follow. It is important that the child experience minimum fear and discomfort. Inadequate physical care may generate feelings of mistrust.

Autonomy versus Shame or Doubt Purposeful behaviors such as controlling elimination, grasping, holding, crawling, and walking develop feelings of autonomy in the child. Such freedom, of course, is not equal to that characteristic of adolescence or adulthood. Children are beginning to see that they can function independent of adults in the environment. Nevertheless, they are acutely aware that in some things they are totally dependent, a condition Erikson describes as creating the potential for shame or doubt.

Initiative versus Guilt Initiative is characterized by the ability to organize behavior toward specific goals. Accomplishing goals gives the developing child feelings of power (Erikson, 1963). Some guilt seems inevitable during this period. One reason for this is the Oedipus complex; others arise from the child's own initiative, which often is not approved or accepted by others, including such things as breaking objects in the environment, conflict with age-mates, or not following rules set down in a classroom. Undoubtedly, it is the initiative experiences versus the guilt experiences that help the child emerge with knowledge of socially approved and socially disapproved behaviors (Erikson, 1968).

Industry versus Inferiority This age period corresponds to the time children are in elementary school. They urgently seek to win social ap-

Table 6–5 Erikson's Psychosocial Stages of Development

Stage	Age	Freudian Counterpart	Successful Resolution	Unsuccessful Resolution
Trust vs. Basic Mistrust	Birth to one year	Oral stage	Trust, optimism, trust in self	Mistrust, pessimism, easily frustrated, nostalgic
Autonomy vs. Shame and Doubt	1 to 3 years	Anal stage	Independent, self-assertive, flexible	Doubtful, ashamed, rigid, overcautious, overcontrolled
Initiative vs. Guilt	3 to 5 years	Phallic stage	Inventive, dynamic, ambitious, risk-taking	Inhibited, jealous, sexually afraid and blunted, guilty
Industry vs. Inferiority	6 to 11 years	Latency stage	Competent, hard-working, likes learning and achieving	Ineffective, wastes time, avoids competition
Identity vs. Identity Diffusion	12 through early 20s	Genital stage	Confident, has sense of self and future time perspective, sex roles defined	Sees self as phony, inconsistent set of loose roles, poor sexual identity, unsure of values and own future
Intimacy vs. Isolation	Young adulthood	—	Candid and open, shares self with others, tactful	Cool, isolated and remote, experiments sexually but with little commitment
Generativity vs. Stagnation	Middle adulthood	—	Productive, fosters the growth of the next generation	Unproductive, stagnating, old before one's time
Integrity vs. Despair	Later adultood	—	Understanding of life cycle, wisdom, principled ethics	Disgust with life, wish to "do it over again," fear of death, sees life as meaningless

Source: Alexander, Roodin, & Gorman (1980), p. 51.

proval through being achievers, a trait accomplished by being industrious in school. Because children's psychosexual urges are latent, they now concentrate their energy on learning and adopting skills of the culture. A feeling of inferiority results when they are incapable of learning proper skills or when they encounter much frustration in the process of trying to learn the skills. Because this period is characterized by much learning and skill acquisition, children can begin to gain a perspective of the workings of culture. If they dislike the social environment, alienation may occur. If they see submission as necessary for social approval, they may willingly give in to social and cultural expectations without questioning them. Movement toward identifying with peers indicates a need to consider the attributes and characteristics of others in striving.

Identity versus Role Confusion   As a result of puberty, which Erikson describes as a physiological revolution, adolescents question the continuities and regularities relied upon in earlier developmental stages. They must contend with three major factors in order to find identity here. First, the ego must accommodate sexual maturation and its accompanying urges. Second, adolescents must contend with physical growth, including appearance. Height, weight, body hair, sex organs, and facial blemishes are all part of this. Finally, adolescents seek some perspective on their functions as adult members of society, usually realized through selecting occupational goals and moving toward them. Erikson contends that role confusion may result if the adolescent's movement toward occupational status is thwarted. A lack of sex role identity may also lead to confusion.

Intimacy versus Isolation   If identity has been established, the late adolescent or young adult is now ready to pursue social intimacy as well as sexual intimacy with another person. Erikson saw this best realized in the ability to merge one's own identity with that of another individual without loss of personal identity. Erikson felt that an intimate relationship required self-discipline and ethical strength. It is more advanced than the search for ego identity. In ego identity, the love affairs through which adolescents pass contribute to their ego development as one identification succeeds another, and adolescents are aided in defining and revising their own definitions of their egos. In intimacy, their own identity becomes intimately involved with the identity of another person. Erikson felt that isolation could occur if a person's identity was too weak to sustain the uncertainties of intimacy; thus, the person will be unable to meet the demands of intimacy, which will seem too unreasonable and restrictive of personal freedom.

Generativity versus Stagnation   This seventh stage of human development, which begins around the mid-twenties, has not been advanced by any other writer on development. Erikson feels that, during adulthood, development goes beyond genital expression, and the individual who achieves a relatively happy genital adjustment does not have to view such experiences as ends in themselves. Now, in an adult, the genital expression becomes means toward a higher accomplishment: the production of children. Erikson (1963) contends that, if the adult does not feel this capability, stagnation may occur. Rappoport (1972) sees this as the middle-age crisis in which impoverishment, self-indulgence, and a feeling of the meaninglessness of life prevail.

Ego Integrity versus Despair   Erikson defines maturity as the forty-plus years. He feels that, as we move toward old age, we must have sustaining ego strengths or else despair will prevail. Such strength is called **ego integrity,** and its constituents are dignity, practical wisdom, belief in the order and meaning of life, acceptance of our own life pattern, and a

Ego integrity
The ability to interact with the social environment while maintaining a sense of self by perceiving both the self and society in a balanced perspective.

sense of continuity with the things that have gone on before our life and things that will follow after we are gone.

Although systematic research on human development has been done only since the early 1900s, much is already known about developmental trends in readiness, personality, cognition, morality, and socialization. Each is a critical investigative area in itself. Yet, in a real sense, all aspects of human behavior are integrally bound, and researchers and scholars must find better ways to synthesize, then communicate, this interrelatedness. Take, for example, the complexity of the six-year-old. By school age, a six-year-old has developed facility with physical skills, mastered speech sounds and grammar, refined thinking so that it is more concrete and logical, incorporated societal principles so that classroom integration becomes easier, and is motivated toward specific goals. The result is that the schoolchild typically learns, aspiring to increased independence and mastery, and exhibits cooperation and competition as well as functioning within the framework of sex-appropriate behaviors. To a great extent, the child's behavior reflects the teaching and internalization of adult values and standards.

Not only is each succeeding growth stage illuminated by the study of development, but the orderly process by which change occurs through time is also revealed. The human infant is born with fewer predetermined behavior tendencies than the lower animals and correspondingly matures more slowly. Experiences during prolonged infancy appear to have a formative influence on the course of development. Later experiences, as well as earlier ones, however, are also influential in shaping persons as they grow older. Educational plans, occupational pursuits, marital decisions, and basic adult values all have especially marked effects on later development. Changes with age continue throughout life—they are not confined to the school-age years, although they are particularly rapid and important during that period.

Much remains to be learned about the nature of human development, but already the applications of what is known are becoming more prominent in areas of cognitive and affective development, the topics of the next two chapters.

Fostering Physical Development

The rate of physical development beyond the first two years of life is rather gradual until boys and girls hit their growth spurt prior to puberty. The variance between boys and girls is not as great during the elementary school years as it is during the secondary level years. Nevertheless, there is considerable disagreement about the role of physical exercise in the elementary school years. For example, many persons who have been trained as physical education majors want to teach specific skills to these youngsters. Many teachers who are coaches believe that most skills can be learned through the sport or competition.

There have not been any widescale studies that indicate the appropriateness of providing elementary students with recess periods versus providing them with physical education classes. However, the recess period is generally thought of as free time, that is, unstructured and without direct teacher instruction. In contrast, physical education classes imply the actual instruction of physical or motor skills. As children move toward secondary schools, physical education classes become the more dominant mode, along with the addition of athletic programs in most junior and senior high schools.

In the mid 1970s, a physical education program called "Every Child a Winner" was developed in the state of Georgia. Its under-lying philosophy was that children in elementary schools need to be taught specific body movements and skills. Well-defined curricula were developed, field tested, and subsequently disseminated across the United States. Today, hundreds of elementary schools have adopted the "Every Child a Winner" program.

A unit entitled "Body Awareness" exemplifies this curriculum. Primary-level students learning about their bodies would be exposed to these content areas:

1. *Narrow/Stretched*
   Example: The ability to move through space while the body is in a narrow and stretched position

2. *Surrounding*
   Example: The ability to surround an object with a body part(s)

3. *Mirroring*
   Example: The ability to demonstrate a series of simple movements made by another individual/teacher

4. *Unison/Contrast*
   Example: The ability to make the same shape or movement at the same time

5. *Kick*
   Example: The ability to kick a moving target while the student is stationary

6. *Strike*
   Example: The ability to strike a moving or stationary object

7. *Throw*
   Example: The ability to throw a ball under- or overhanded

8. *Catch*
   Example: The ability to catch objects that have low and high trajectories

Once first-graders have learned skills associated with body awareness, they are ready to be taught the quality of body movement. One aspect of this is to carry out sequential motion. They would use bound and free-flow movements to imitate or create a sequence of movements. The following is an activities overview for teaching such a unit:

Activities for Sequential Flow of Movement (7 Days)

Definition—Sequential: Characterized by regular sequence of parts: Following; subsequent; consequent. In movement, the joining together of a series of actions is considered sequential. These phrases, which lead to dance making, have a definite beginning, middle, and an end. The teacher's responsibility is to lead the students to perform these sequences spontaneously.

Activities

Games

1. *Leap Frog.* This activity will give the students the idea of action

happening in a sequential manner. In this case, the action itself of leaping over each other is repetitious, but the total action is a sequence.

2. *Follow-the-Leader.* This game is better suited to the concept of mirroring but can be adapted to sequence. As the leader collects more followers and begins to add different actions, the students are adding parts to make up a series of movements or sequences.

Gymnastics

1. *Tumbling.* This is a good place to take advantage of the tumbling skills the students have already learned. Place a long series of mats in the gym and encourage them to put a series of stunts together. Give them enough time to experiment with different moves and patterns. The teacher should step in only if a student asks for help. There are many possible combinations of stunts, and the students' creativity will be their only limit.

2. *Apparatus.* The trampoline is a good place to point out a sequence of events. As soon as the basic moves are learned, they should be combined into a series of three or more stunts. This technique encourages smooth movement and a sense of accomplishment in being able to perform a routine. Ask the students to think about how a series of individual moves can be put together into a sequence of events.

Dance

When movement is joined, a sequence has been composed, and this phrasing is basic to dance. With proper guidance, children readily compose these phrases. The teacher should draw from concepts that the students have learned in prior years and earlier this year. Examples of moves to form sequences:

1. Travel by running, jumping, spinning through space in a free manner

2. Travel in a controlled manner through space, anticipating stops and hesitation

3. Combine free and bound movements.

4. Change directions, levels, pathways, and areas

5. Use fast or slow, sudden or sustained, or accelerating or decelerating action

6. Use light, fine movements and contrast them with heavy, firm movements

7. Allow the students to think of all the shapes the body can make, such as curled, twisted, open, and extended

The previous example represents a well-researched progression of motor skill development in young children, generally taught between grades one and three in schools. It is a clear example of how young children can learn specific motor skills and enhance physical development.

As children move toward adolescence, different capacities emerge and different social and educational expectations accompany them. There is still considerable selectivity in junior and senior highs in regard to athletics. Although most secondary schools have physical education classes, greater value is generally attached to the athletic programs. In a sense, many junior highs and most high schools have gifted physical programs for those who excel when placed in a competitive structure.

As students move into colleges and universities, new roles emerge. The dominance maintained in men's athletics is gradually giving way a little as women's athletics are emerging in more post–high school environments. Still, most major universities make physical education classes optional, or the classes are so specialized that general physical development is not maintained or enhanced. The competitive model remains dominant from secondary schools on, with an increasing number of women finding themselves in more competitive physical or athletic events. Fierce debates have been held about the general development of physical education and the more specific structuring of athletics. What is clear is that formal educational environments, from elementary school on, could incorporate educational programs specifically designed to develop motor skills and general physical awareness if they desired.

Annotated Readings

Adams, G. R., & Jones, R. M. (1981). Female adolescents' ego development: Age comparisons and child-rearing perceptions. *Journal of Early Adolescence, 1,* 423–426.

> *This study looked at the relationship between perceptions of parental socialization styles and ego development in female high school students. A total of 137 fifteen- to eighteen-year-olds responded to a child-rearing perceptions scale and an ego development scale. Results indicate that ego development is affected by age and by the female's perceived child-rearing experience. Ego identity seems to emerge in early adolescence and begin to consolidate in adolescence.*

Frankel, D. G., & Roer-Bornstein, D. (1982). Traditional and modern contributions to changing infant-rearing ideologies of two ethnic communities. *Monographs of the Society for Research in Child Development, 47*(4), 1–53.

> *The modernization of infant-rearing ideologies was investigated by interviewing grandmother and granddaughter generations of two ethnic communities, Yemenite and Kurdish Jews, about pregnancy and delivery, postpartum care of the mother and newborn, and infant care and developmental expectations. Results showed that both traditional and modern influences affect contemporary infant-rearing ideologies. Traditional differences in the emphasis on the mother-infant relationship, on cognitive development, on motor development, and on physical/biological effects on development and health, as well as relative differences in developmental expectations, all were reflected in the ideologies of the granddaughter generation.*

Juhasz, A. M. (1982). Early adolescents and society: Implications of Eriksonian theory. *Journal of Early Adolescence, 2,* 15–24.

> *The author integrates the concept of life span development, psychosocial development as discussed by Erikson, and the social environment into a social expectation model for early adolescent behavior. She stresses the embeddedness of human behavior in a social context and how it directly affects human behavior. The nature of self, our ideals and values, and expectations from the social order are interwoven into an identity statement. The author feels that early adolescents are actively searching for an understanding of themselves in relation to the larger social context.*

Peterson, A. C., Tobin-Richards, M., & Boxer, A. (1983). Puberty: Its measurement and meaning. *Journal of Early Adolescence, 3,* 47–62.

> *This article overviews the literature on the measurement of movement toward puberty, particularly with respect to hormonal and physical changes. A self-report device was administered to boys and girls to see how accurately they could predict the onset of pubertal change in themselves. Both sexes were asked to record information on their spurt in height, body hair, and skin changes. In addition, females were asked for information on breast development and menarche. Males were asked for information on facial hair and voice change. Results of the study indicated that young adolescents are capable of accurately predicting personal change. Results are interpreted in light of the effect such changes may have on cognitive and psychosocial development.*

Rose, R. J., & Ditto, W. B. (1983). A developmental-genetic analysis of common fears from early adolescence to early adulthood. *Child Development, 54,* 361–368.

> *A fear survey was given to some two thousand adolescents and adults, including over four hundred pairs of like-sex twins, to examine developmental patterns and genetic influences on common fears. Genetic effects were found for all factors, but their magnitude varied. The findings suggest significant genetic modulation of developmental patterns in the learning and retention of adaptive fears.*

Scarzoni, J., & Fox, G. L. (1980). Sex roles, family and society: The seventies and beyond. *Journal of Marriage and the Family, 42,* 743–756.

> *The literature reviewed for the 1970s decade is divided into studies of children and preteens, adolescents and young adults, and marrieds. The amorphous nature of the term sex role is discussed, and a model of gender-based decision making, applicable at both macro and micro levels, is offered as one way to specify relations between the sexes. Existing literature is then subsumed within the sex role model. The authors provide recommendations for continued research on sex roles.*

Intellectual and Cognitive Development

As part of an ongoing staff development program, the faculty at East High School heard a presentation by a university professor on how adolescents behave intellectually. The professor distinguished between the contributions of heredity and environment in human functioning. He pointed out the role heredity plays in human intelligence but indicated that environment had a stronger influence by the time students reached high school. As might be expected, his comments caused mixed reactions among the high school faculty.

The next day in the faculty lounge a lively discussion ensued between Jack Fogel, a social studies teacher, and Jim Branham, a physical education teacher. Fogel argued that heredity had little impact on adolescent behavior while Branham believed that heredity was the most important factor. Mr. Branham stated that he had seen so much "raw physical potential" in students during P.E. and athletics that had little to do with their environment, the type of family they come from, or their intelligence. Fogel alluded to heredity's contribution but argued that without appropriate environmental stimulation it did not make any difference what type of genetic potential a person has.

While the two were debating, Ms. Franover, the high school physics teacher, walked into the lounge. After listening to them for a while, she decided to join the discussion. She was a sports hobbyist, particularly interested in amateur athletics. She had been reading about the role of heredity in a recent issue of a sportsmedicine journal and decided to share with Mr. Fogel and Mr. Branham something she had read.

"There is little question but that genes set the potential for behavior, although the way in which the potential is realized may be due to the type of environment in which each individual functions. For example, genes predispose some individuals to short or long muscle fibers. The success of sprint and distance runners has now been tied to fiber size. Yet, without proper training, muscle size would be of little consequence." She shifted to a different example. "Some individuals are genetically predisposed to light skin, thus they sunburn easily. Yet, if one never sunbathes it would be hard to sunburn." Her point seemed well received; namely, that both heredity and environment play complementary roles in human development and adolescent behavior.

As in most robust dicussions, there was no universal agreement among these three individuals. Yet, they did concede that heredity and *environment may affect individuals in quite different ways. Heredity may predispose some adolescents to take advantage of environmental opportunities they have. Similarly, some environments may either foster or inhibit the expression of genetic traits.*

Topics covered in this chapter include:

- *Definitions of intelligence*
- *Theories of intelligence*
- *Stages of intellectual development*
- *Language development*
- *Differentiation of mental abilities*

Cognition
A general term describing all the ways in which people think; for example, knowledge, concepts, reasoning.

Cognition is the way the human mind learns, understands, and remembers knowledge. Cognitive science formulates and tests theories that relate to these dimensions of the mind, whether from an educational perspective, psychological perspective, computer science model, linguistics model, or philosophical model. Behavior has structural aspects that can be related to objects, events, other individuals, values, and personal dynamics. The study of cognition has been traditionally conceptualized as the study of human intelligence. Several theories or models of human intelligence have emerged throughout this century. Since the mid 1920s, the idea of human cognition being developmentally bound has been advanced by Jean Piaget. This chapter is primarily devoted to the development of intelligence, although we must look at the way our understanding of human intelligence has emerged over the years and relate developmental theory to it.

Human Intelligence

Definitions

Intelligence
A hypothetical construct that describes ways of behaving in humans and lower organisms.

Essentially, **intelligence** is a measure of how an individual behaves. The intelligence of the preschool child is frequently judged on the basis of alertness, attentiveness, motor ability, language ability, and "cleverness." During the educational years, estimations of intelligence are often tied primarily to the child's school achievement, although other factors, such as those mentioned for the preschool child, may enter into the estimation. The posteducation period usually brings a largely different kind of estimation, which is most frequently derived from occupational status, language ability, interests, and conversational topics.

Such definitions of intelligence are operational, that is, intelligence is being measured by the individual's behaviors, interpersonal interactions, and achievements. These are useful, but somewhat imprecise, measures. Parents of a cerebral-palsied child who have just been told their child's intelligence quotient and ask, "But what is his real IQ?" are intimating that there is a more basic intelligence, a capacity that cannot be actualized because of the child's impairment. Those psychologists who criticize current, largely operational intelligence tests on the basis of their being culturally biased against certain minority or socioecomonic groups are making the same point—that existing tests do not measure "real" intelligence. This view of intelligence as a potential capacity based on heredity and environmental factors may very well be the most theoretically correct. To view intelligence as an IQ score is too narrow because intelligence is a construct or process of human behavior.

Intelligence, then, may be defined in various ways. It has been defined as (1) the ability to do abstract thinking or, more precisely, (2) the ability to judge, comprehend, and reason. And it has been designated as (3) the ability to adapt to the environment or, more precisely, (4) the total ability of an individual to act purposefully and rationally in the environment.

Theories

The development of theories of intelligence has paralleled the development of intelligence tests. Although we now recognize that intelligence as a construct is more complex than its measurement as determined by a test, early thinking about theory and testing were often synonymous. With the advent of statistical analysis, the concept of intelligence as a single, unitary factor as measured by an intelligence test weakened. Statistical analysis techniques were used to show that IQ was useful in predicting individual achievement in certain learning activities, but it was less effective in accounting for the variances in an individual's abilities in a wide range of activities. Consequently, psychologists interested in intelligence and IQ testing have developed a number of theories to better explain the differences of abilities both within individuals and between groups of individuals. These theorists speak of individual intelligences rather than of intelligence.

Single-Factor Theory   The simplest theory of intelligence is that it is a single trait or characteristic. It is described as **monogenetic** because it is based on a single general (g) factor that is inherited. Terman (1918) believed this unitary factor was the individual's ability to verbalize and think abstractly.

Monogenetic
The belief that intelligence is based on a single factor that is inherited.

Multiple-Factor Theories

Spearman's "g" Factor   Charles Spearman (1927), a British psychologist, came to the conclusion that intelligence is composed of a **g** (general) **factor** and a large number of **s** (specific) **factors.** In a later formulation (Spearman & Jones, 1950), he amended his original thinking to reflect an overlapping of s factors into certain group factors. Spearman proposed that there is a controlling capability (the g factor) in all intellectual functioning, and this is the factor most intelligence tests measure. A

g Factor
The construct designed to explain a general basis for intellectual functioning.

s Factor
The construct designed to explain a wide range of specific traits that affect intellectual functioning.

person who is high in *g* factor tends to do well in a variety of tasks, and a person low in *g* tends to do poorly. He also suggested that there are specific abilities (the *s* factors) that are fairly insignificant in terms of total functioning but that overlap and form certain group factors—verbal ability, numerical ability, mechanical ability, attention, and imagination or creative ability—that are not always highly correlated with the individual's general capability, or *g* factor. For example, a student with below-average general achievement (*g* factor) might be exceptional in mathematics or creative ability. Thus, with this formulation, Spearman was able to explain the observed differences in an individual's overall achievement and his or her achievement in specific learning areas.

Guilford's Structure of the Intellect   A more extensive factor analysis of intelligence is that of J. P. Guilford (1956, 1967, 1972). Guilford conceptualizes the intellect as consisting of three major dimensions: the **contents of thought,** the **operations of thought,** and the **products of thought.** He subdivided each of these dimensions into a number of factors that, when combined in various interactions of thought, give a possible 120 different factors of intelligence. Approximately 100 of these factors have been delineated thus far (Guilford, 1973; Guilford & Hoepfner, 1971). Guilford's concept of intelligence is represented figurally in the three dimensions of a cube, as shown in Figure 7–1. This system is complex, but for our purposes in this chapter, we need examine only one of his dimensions: the contents of thought.

Guilford describes the contents of thought as the materials involved in thinking. He proposes four kinds of content. **Figural content** represents concrete objects, the things we perceive through the senses. Much of the

Contents of thought
Guilford's description of the kinds of things individuals think about; for example, school subject matter, experiences.

Operation of thought
Guilford's description of the way in which the mind functions that includes types of thinking, memory, and logic.

Products of thought
Guilford's description of the different types of intellectual experiences people have and how these experiences facilitate thinking.

Figural content
The ability to perceive through the senses.

180

young child's thinking, and some adult thinking, is figural in nature. The second type of content is **symbolic,** which includes letters, symbols, digits, or signs that have no real significance in themselves but have meanings attached to them. The symbol A, for example, has different meanings attached to it in the following situations:

He built an A-frame house.

$A = 1 \times w.$

He was playing A-sharp instead of A.

She received an "A" on her paper.

The meaning of each use of the symbol A is derived from the context and/or the figural referent that the symbol represents.

The third kind of content, **semantic,** is used in verbal thinking and verbal communication. For example, the word *apple* has meanings attached to it that enable us to visualize the figural referent, just as the abstract word *love* has meanings that allow two people to converse about the concept. The fourth kind of content is behavioral or **empathic,** which refers to essentially nonverbal thoughts that are used in social interactions. Behavioral content can be illustrated by the actions that would cause a child to say, "The teacher says she likes me, but I know she doesn't." Guilford has described this as a "social intelligence."

Cattell's g_c and g_f Factors   Cattell (1940, 1963, 1968) theorizes that the *g* factor of intelligence measured by intelligence tests is actually made up of

Symbolic content
The ability to learn letters, symbols, and other representations that have meaning attached to them.

Semantic content
The ability to attach meaning to concrete and abstract words.

Empathic content
Expression of personal thinking in social contexts.

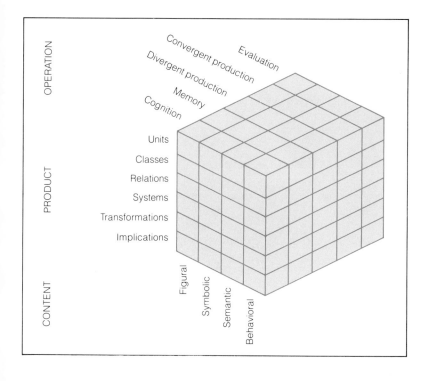

Figure 7–1
Guilford's Structure of the Intellect.
[Source: Guilford (1959), p. 471.
Copyright 1959 by the American
Psychological Association. Re-
printed by permission.]

Crystallized general ability
Cattell's theoretical construct that
accounts for the environmental
influences on mental functioning.

Fluid general ability
Cattell's theoretical construct that
accounts for heredity's influence on
mental functioning.

two factors. One *g* factor is the **crystallized general ability** g_c, which reflects the effect of culture upon the person's mental functioning. The g_c factor stretches across the whole range of cultural acquisitions and involves such materials as vocabulary, analogies, numerical skills, and habits of logical reasoning.

Cattell's second factor is the **fluid general ability,** g_f, which has little to do with the learned or experiential aspects of the culture but reflects the individual's inherent intellectual ability. This type of intellectual ability is thought to be measured by culture-fair tests, which, in essence, attempt to measure some general intellectual trait that is not culture bound, such as numerical reasoning or exercises of judgment. A person with high g_f possesses the ability to perceive certain problem situations that are not culturally related, to reorganize these perceptions, and to arrive at a solution more quickly than a person with low g_f. For example, excellent chess players usually possess a high g_f, which allows them to "see" whole patterns of strategic moves before they are made. People with little formal education can operate quite well in situations if they possess a high fluid general ability.

Individuals with a high level of crystallized general ability have different capacities. They are readily able to learn more astute responses to diverse problem situations, but high g_c may be fairly useless in a situation that does not fit the culturally acquired response pattern. However, a person often would not acquire skills connected with high crystallized ability if he or she did not possess the high fluid ability to perceive the problems to which the skills might be applied.

Cattell hypothesizes that the two different abilities, g_c and g_f, show a different growth pattern or curve. Fluid ability growth follows other biological maturational developments, reaching its peak in the individual at about fourteen years of age and declining slightly after about twenty-two years of age. Crystallized intelligence, however, continues to grow into adulthood and maintains its level for as long as adequate learning input continues. It is assumed that variations among individuals reflect different cultural opportunity, interest, and age because such variance will increase with experience and with the loss of fluid intelligence that accompanies aging. Both are ways of explaining the gradual acquisition of a broad range of knowledge.

Jensen's Mental Ability Levels   Arthur Jensen (1969) also hypothesizes that there are two levels of intellectual functioning. His research began when he examined the reasons for the rather limited effects of compensatory educational programs, such as Head Start and Higher Horizons, which were aimed at improving the educational success of children from lower socioeconomic classes. The primary purpose of these compensatory programs was to improve the participants' IQs, but evaluation studies showed little average gain, and follow-up studies have shown that most of the gains were not maintained through the first year of schooling (U.S. Commission on Civil Rights, 1967).

The basic premise upon which these compensatory programs were based was that the lower IQ of the culturally different child is due to a lack of preschool environmental stimulation and that a change in the environment would increase the IQ. Thus, most programs were aimed at broadening the experiential backgrounds of children by bringing them into direct contact with those experiences that were "normal" for middle-class preschool children.

Jensen rejects this environmental deprivation hypothesis as the cause of differing intellectual ability levels between the various socioeconomic and racial groups and proposes instead that the level of intellectual ability is primarily a function of heredity. He acknowledges environment as a factor but terms it a **threshold variable,** asserting that, if the environment is not *severely* restricted, changes in it will not make an appreciable difference in IQ. If the environment is severely restricted, as, for example, in cases where children have been maltreated by being shut in a room with no environmental stimulation, then changes in the environment will make a significant difference in the level of intellectual functioning.

Thus, according to Jensen, the primary variance factor in different mental abilities is heredity. Jensen (1969) hypothesizes that there are two levels of learning ability. Level I, **associative ability,** involves the registra-

Threshold variable
Jensen's term to explain that, unless the environment is severely restricted, environmental impact on intellectual ability is almost imperceptible.

Associative ability
The input of information that is straightforward, requiring little or no interpretation—such as learning a fact.

183

tion of stimulus inputs in the neural mechanism, the consolidation of these inputs, and the formulation of associations, with very little internal transformation of these inputs as they are emitted in the form of responses. Digit memory, serial rote learning, and paired-associate learning would be included at this level of intellectual ability. Level II, **conceptual ability,** involves the self-initiated transformation and elaboration of the stimulus input before a response is emitted. Concept learning and problem solving would be examples of this kind of ability, which is most truly measured by tests that are relatively "culture free" and high in the g factor.

Conceptual ability
The input of information that requires internal processing or transformation—such as explaining something.

On tests that measure level I abilities, Jensen and his coworkers found that lower-class children, regardless of ethnic and racial origins, did no more poorly than middle-class children. But on less culture-free tests measuring level II abilities, the lower-status children did not score as high as the middle-class children. Jensen concludes from this research that two kinds of abilities, associative and conceptual, are components of intellectual functioning. Through further research, he has developed the hypothesis that level I associative ability is necessary but not a sufficient requisite for the conceptual ability of level II. That is, he believes that high performance on level II tasks depends upon better than average ability in level I but that the reverse does not hold true. This hypothesis and the test results in his research suggest to Jensen that level I ability is distributed differently in the lower and middle socioeconomic classes as a result of hereditary factors (Jensen, 1974, 1982).

Concept Summary 7–1

Theories of Intelligence			
Theory	**Major Belief**	**Major Influence**	**Theorist**
Single Factor	Verbal ability, particularly abstract	Environment	Terman
Two Factor	G-factor in all intellectual acts	Heredity	Spearman
	S-factor in different intellectual acts	Environment	
Two Factor	Fluid in all behavior	Heredity	Cattell
	Crystallized in specific behaviors	Environment	
Two Factor	Associative in all behavior	Heredity	Jensen
	Conceptual in specific behaviors	Environment	
Multifactor	Multiple abilities: Figural Symbolic Semantic Empathic	Environment	Guilford

Jensen believes that lower-class children do more poorly in school because the schools tend to emphasize those skills connected with conceptual activities (level II abilities). His plea is that the schools recognize different types of learning abilities among various groups and provide methods of instruction that will capitalize on each learner's existing abilities. He believes that we can provide equal education for all children only when we recognize these differences and modify our instruction to account for them.

Piaget's Theory of Intellectual Development

Jean Piaget's writings (1950, 1952, 1960; Inhelder & Piaget, 1958; Piaget & Szeminska, 1952) reflect an interest in intelligence different from that of the preceding theoretical approaches. Instead of focusing on the measurement of intelligence or the components of intellectual functioning, Piaget's interest is in **cognitive growth,** the course of development of intellectual functioning. His earliest methodology for studying intelligence has been questioned by statistically oriented critics, and some of his writing is so general that his conclusions are untestable. In addition, the translation of his writings from French to English suffers from the difficulties inherent in all translations. Nevertheless, Piaget's theory of cognitive growth has probably spawned more research in the area of cognitive development than any other theory.

Cognitive growth
A general term used to describe the way in which intellectual development unfolds over time.

Much of Piaget's work derives from an interest in epistemology, the branch of philosophy that deals with the origin and nature of knowledge. He believes that the newborn child has no specific knowledge, but only a tendency to organize sensory information. As a result of experience, the mind generates classifications and discovers regularities, thus forming a mental organization into which information is placed.

Piaget offers several definitions of intelligence, all in somewhat general terms. For example, the concept that intelligence is a particular instance of biological adaptation (1952) reflects his training as a biologist. In another source (1950), he defines intelligence as a "form of equilibrium toward which all the structures . . . tend." Still another definition states that intelligence is a "system of living and acting operations" (1950). Thus, in these three definitions, Piaget suggests his concept of intelligence as a biological adaptation, involving mental activity, in which the person seeks equilibrium with the environment.

According to Piaget, cognitive development progresses from a unidimensional focus on immediate sensory perceptions to the capacity for multidimensional, multiperspective, and inferential thought (Inhelder & Piaget, 1958; Jarcho & Peterson, 1981). This undoubtedly results from the mind's ability to generate structure, function, and content (Brainerd, 1978). Structure is the pattern that cognition takes during mental growth, a way of organizing information so that rational behavior results. Piaget believes that structure takes on new forms at different points in development. Thus, he theorized stages of development, each of which is characteristically different from the others. Cognitive functions give direction and meaning to intellectual behavior. My discussion of moving the learner from simple to complex and nonconceptual to conceptual learning in Chapter 3 illustrates Piaget's concept of functions. Both structure and function are necessary to cognitive content—the specific intellectual act.

Cognitive content is the observable aspect of mental operations. Brainerd (1978, p. 18) addresses this issue:

> Cognitive contents are the specific intellectual acts that comprise intelligence at any given stage of development. Such things as a visual image, an auditory image, a mathematical concept, and an abstract symbol all are examples of cognitive contents. All of the problem solving and reasoning skills . . . e.g., object permanence, conservation, transitivity, are cognitive contents. Of the three concepts, structure, function, and content, cognitive contents are the only things that can be directly measured. Both structures and functions are inferred from the measurement of content.

Adaptation and Organization

Piaget's framework hypothesizes that all species inherit two "invariate functions"—**adaptation** and **organization**—that determine how any organism develops intellectually. Organization is a hereditary property that allows the organism to function within the environment through either physical or psychological mechanisms. Physically, organization involves the coordination of certain organs and systems in the body as it responds to the environment. Psychologically, organization involves the integration of the organism's sensory and cerebral structures in response to the environment.

The **invariate function** for adaptation is the inherent tendency of all organisms to modify behavior in response to the environment. How adaptation occurs varies from species to species, from individual to individual within a species, and from one developmental stage to the next within an individual. Regarding the latter, the newborn infant, uncomfortable in wet diapers, seeks to adapt (to relieve the discomfort) by crying. At a later stage, an infant may use nonverbal gestures. Still later, words may be involved in adaptation to the environment.

Adaptation consists of two complementary processes: **assimilation** and **accommodation.** Assimilation refers to the organism's incorporation of external reality into already existing psychological structures. Accommodation is the process by which the organism's psychological structures are modified to specific aspects of the environment. The two processes occur simultaneously and are essential to adaptation.

Assimilation   As a biologist, Piaget recognized that the body assimilates food. It is not a matter of adding new elements to the body, but of transforming them in ways useful to the body. He believed that this same principle applies to thought. People do not simply add a new thought or a

186

new piece of information. Rather, they evaluate it in light of their existing mental structure (Maier, 1978). Cowan (1978, p. 22) offers the following examples of assimilation at different developmental stages:

> A young infant is holding a rattle when her arm shakes and the rattle makes a pleasing sound. In succeeding days, every new object is shaken in the same way—hands, combs, rattles, beads, spoons full of food. Not all of these objects have rattle-qualities, but the child is cognitively transforming the objects by assimilating them (fitting them) into the shaking-an-object activity. In the process some aspects of the new stimuli are incorporated while others are ignored (e.g., size, color, shape).
>
> A four- to six-year-old usually fits the activity of counting into his or her ideas about quantity. For example, a row of six red checkers is placed in one-to-one correspondence with a row of six black checkers. The child agrees that there is the same number of checkers in each row. The six red checkers are then spread out and the child is asked whether that row has more, less, or the same number of checkers as the black row. The child answers that there are more checkers in the red row, an example of failure to conserve quantity.

When some children are asked how they know that the red row has more they first begin to count one row, placing a finger on each checker "one, two, three, four, five (they count a space in between), six, seven." Counting has been assimilated (molded) to the child's conception of quantity.

Eight-year olds, still conceptually egocentric, assimilate the world to their own point of view. Asked to draw a picture of a scene as it would be viewed by someone at a different location, they draw the scene as they themselves view it. Others' viewpoints are transformed to be identical with one's own.

Assimilation also occurs in adolescents and adults. The high school girl who is going out on a date may use several criteria for deciding what to wear. She may view herself as the "ideal," using information gained from a movie, TV show, magazines, her mother, her peers, or her boyfriend. She may create several "mental scenarios," each with different clothing and each anticipating her date's reaction to her. In reality, she will wear what she feels "best" or most comfortable with. Still, all these options and influences are assimilated into her final decision. Essentially, then, assimilation is one major way we incorporate information, skills, or experiences into our mental structures.

Accommodation Accommodation explains how we modify the psychological structure to take in new learning. As we eat food, our body releases chemicals, uses energy, and has muscle contractions, all of which are done to accept the food. In the same way, our mind restructures itself, even if only slightly, to take in new thoughts and ideas. In this sense, the existing mental structure is altered to accommodate new information. Again, Cowan (1978, p. 23) provides excellent examples of accommodation:

> The infant develops a behavioral pattern partly based on reflex sucking at the breast or bottle. When the infant attempts to assimilate a thumb to the sucking pattern, at first the hand motions are random and the sucking is not coordinated with them. Soon, however, the hand moves directly to the mouth, and then the mouth moves to incorporate the thumb. In this case, hand movements accommodate to the location of the mouth, while the mouth accommodates to the movement of the hand.
>
> The four-year-old who assimilated counting to his or her concept of numbers was also involved in some accommodation, most noticeably when modifying judgments of "the same" number of checkers because of a change in physical arrangement. The conceptual judgment accommodated to the perceptual data; this example illustrates that accommodative changes do not always produce more correct or adaptive responses.
>
> Accommodation at older levels can be seen in the fact that hypotheses (hunches, expectations) are often modified by feedback from observations and experiments. In fact, without direct feedback in a learning situation it is often difficult to produce any change.

Assimilation and accommodation are essential to maintaining equilibrium. This is a difficult task for the newborn baby, who may not be able to differentiate events adequately, the result of which is disequilibrium. Throughout the first year of life, this capacity emerges and the processes of assimilation and accommodation work in conjunction with each other to establish and maintain equilibrium (Bower, 1974; Bowlby, 1969). Cowan (1978, p. 27) synthesizes this process:

According to Piaget, newborns and young infants function in a continuous present; they do not yet have a symbol system that enables them to think about, imagine, or represent situations which are not being perceived. Once people or objects disappear from sight, sound, or touch, they are gone. (This idea disturbs some parents who believe that their babies are crying for *them*.) Because there is no conceptual notion of a permanent object, every time newborns interact with the world they transform events and are themselves transformed at the same time. For example, three-month-olds often attempt to grasp (assimilate) and this gives them a new view of the toy. As they move toward it, they change body position (accommodate) and this gives them a new view of the toy. Since they are unable to retrieve the image of the previous perception of the toy, the new view creates (conceptually) a new object to assimilate. Further attempts to assimilate result in further accommodations, and so on. Not until the age of about six to eight months does the infant establish a symbolic representative of a permanent object. Then the child is not always changed by events and he or she does not always transform events in some way.

Schemes

As individuals organize their thoughts and behaviors in order to adapt to the environment, they create new psychological structures, which Piaget called **schemes.** The schemes represent a kind of conceptual framework into which incoming environmental stimuli (inputs) must fit if the individual is to perceive and act on them. Although the processes of adaptation and organization are invariant, these schemes, which are represented through either sensorimotor or cognitive events, are variant; that is, they change as a result of experience. In other words, through experiences with the environment, individuals constantly create new schemes in order to continue the necessary process of organization and adaptation to the environment.

Schemes
Piaget's description of the way individuals represent things in their minds. Schemes are variant in that they change as a result of experience.

The first schemes are necessarily exemplified in the newborn infant's reflexes. As infants interact with the environment, certain readymade schemes that already exist (biological reflexes) begin to vary with circumstances and experiences. For example, the newborn's sucking scheme may be evidenced with any kind of object placed near an infant's mouth. However, as infants nurse, they begin to differentiate objects; some will bring on the sucking response while others will not. Thus, a new, more discriminatory scheme replaced the original reflexive scheme of sucking. This process is *cognitive growth.*

Stages of Development

Piaget hypothesizes that humans develop through a series of defined maturational periods and subperiods. The periods of interest to us are sensorimotor (birth to two years); preoperational, with subperiods of preconceptual thought (two to four years) and intuitive thought (four to seven years); concrete operations (seven to eleven years); and formal operations (eleven to fifteen years). Though Piaget has attached ages to each period, experiments by him and others have made the age boundaries less rigid. However, the developmental progression remains invariant.

Sensorimotor Development   At birth and through the first month of life, infants are unable to distinguish themselves from the world and depend mainly upon reflexes for interactions with the environment. They make orienting responses to light and sound, suck when their lips are touched, and grasp an object placed in their hand. However, contrary to the concept of the newborn being a passive organism, totally dependent upon stimulation from the environment, Piaget also records incidents that reflect some voluntary activity on the part of the infant.

The second stage of this period (one to four months) involves coordination. Piaget notes that the first coordination of schema very often is accidental in nature. For example, by chance, the child touches, then grasps an object in his or her visual range so that the "looking schema" is coordinated with the "reaching schema," which is then coordinated with the "grasping schema." When this has occurred, it may be repeated upon future stimulation, and the schemata become integrated into one. During this stage, a simple differentiation of objects begins as the infant responds differently to objects in the environment. The infant may also begin to repeat actions, such as smiling, when an adult responds by imitating that action.

During the third stage (four to eight months) of the **sensorimotor period,** infants firmly establish the distinction between themselves and the world beyond. In their actions upon objects, they show the first sign of intention and rudimentary means-end relationships. For example, they may perform motor acts that produce effects on the environment, such as kicking while lying in the crib to make toys move. Primitive concepts of object permanence, space, and time are also formed during this period, as evidenced by the child's momentary search for objects that are absent.

The first evidence of symbolic meaning is manifested during the fourth stage of this period (eight to twelve months). Children anticipate events from signs that predict, such as a reaction to the mother's putting on her coat to leave. True imitation also begins during this period, and children begin to react to novel objects in the environment in an exploratory manner.

During stage five of this period (twelve to eighteen months), children begin real experimentation leading to a concept of causality. Actions seem to represent a "What would happen if?" attitude, and means-end relationships take on new meaning with a focus upon the creation of new means (Elkind & Weiner, 1978).

In the final stage of this period (eighteen to twenty-four months), the child's experimentation becomes more internal. Before this stage, children try to gain ends by actively manipulating objects in the environment. During this final stage, the means for reaching ends seem to be manipulated mentally, or covertly. Children imitate complex types of presented behaviors as well as behaviors remembered from an earlier time. Both anticipation and memory become firmly established, which indicates a strengthened concept of time.

Preoperational Development The **preoperational period** (two to seven years) is typified by the development of schemes that represent the actual objects and people in the environment. For example, the development of language—internalized symbols that represent objects and people—takes place during this period. Thus, during the **preconceptual phase** of this period (two to four years), children achieve the capacity to form and articulate mental symbols that stand for absent things, people, or events. This ability frees them from previous intellectual ties to the here and now. It allows children to mentally represent things that previously were learned through actual experience. Internal imitation, which the child developed during the sensorimotor period, provides the basis for the formation of mental symbols, and meaning is attached to the symbols by their assimilation into existing schemes. This phase is termed *preconceptual* because these early concepts of language and symbols are primitive in nature and may be highly specific or too general. For example, the child's concept of "up" may be related only to being picked up and therefore serves primarily as a signal for a desired physical action rather than as a concept.

First reasoning is also exhibited during this phase. Piaget (1951) described his daughter's remark, "Daddy's getting hot water; so he's going to shave" as reasoning from having seen the two events occur consecutively in the past. Such **transducive reasoning**—the belief that, because two things are alike in one way, they must be alike in all ways—is typical

Preoperational period
The stage in childhood wherein individuals learn to symbolically represent objects, people, and events in the environment.

Preconceptual stage
A substage of the preoperational period that occurs in early childhood in which mental symbols are formed to represent absent objects, people, or events.

Transducive reasoning
The belief that because two things are alike in one way, they are alike in all ways.

191

in this period. Because the child's concepts are not yet clear, there are many "errors" from the adult's point of view, and these errors frequently are related as the cute stories that parents tell each other about their children.

During the **intuitive thought phase** of this preconceptual period (four to seven years), the child moves toward socialized behavior. This change is evidenced as four-year-old children who basically communicate with themselves begin to communicate with other people. As a result, their concepts of objects and experiences become more precise for they must be able to communicate these ideas to other people. This phase is termed *intuitive thought* because the process of arriving at answers concerning causality and rightness or wrongness is based on incomplete thinking. Children of this age make decisions on the basis of intuition rather than on the basis of logical reasoning. They can group objects into classes by attributes, but can attend to only one dimension at a time. For example, if they see a ball of clay made into a pancake shape, they are likely to say there is less clay in the pancake than in the ball because it is so thin. They have not yet learned the **principle of conservation,** which states that no change occurs in quantity of matter even though it may change in size, shape, or orientation.

Concrete Operations Development

The age span included in the **concrete operations period** is roughly equivalent to the time that the child is in elementary school (seven to eleven years). The most obvious change during this period is the child's ability to use written words and numbers. During the preceding stages, the spoken word came to symbolize people, experiences, and concrete objects. Now the written word or number possesses the same significance.

During this period, children also develop relational and combinational procedures whereby they are able to classify, order, and group. For example, children can perform additive, subtractive, repetitive, and equalizing functions. These abilities are in contrast to the preceding stages, when their attempts to systematize were incomplete and characterized by irreversibility of thought, transducive reasoning, and egocentric thinking. Thus, children develop the capacity for logical thought.

To illustrate the movement from the preoperational (prelogic) to the operational (logic) period, consider the example of a child presented with identical beakers, A and B, both filled to the same height with a liquid. Asked if the quantities of liquid are equal, the child agrees that they are. The liquid from one of the beakers is then poured into a differently shaped beaker C (see Figure 7–2). Asked the question of equality again, the preoperational child will answer no. The child at this preoperational stage can focus on only one aspect of the situation, either the height or the breadth of the liquid in container C in relation to the height or breadth of the liquid in container A. If the child centers on the height, A will appear to have more liquid. If the child centers on the breadth, then C will appear to have more liquid. If the procedure is reversed by pouring the liquid from C back into B, the child will then judge the two amounts of liquid as being

Intuitive thought stage
The ability to carry out simple problem solving without the corollary capacity to explain what one has just done.

Principle of conservation
The recognition that something remains the same in quantity although it may be manifested in different ways.

Concrete operations period
The developmental period wherein all the components required to carry out logical reasoning and offer verbal verification of such reasoning emerges.

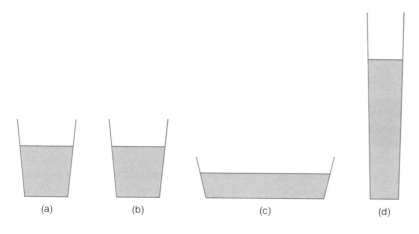

Figure 7–2
Conservation of Continuous Quantities. (Source: Herbert Ginsburg, Sylvia Opper, Piaget's Theory of Intellectual Development: An Introduction, © 1960, *p. 162. Reprinted by permission of Prentice-Hall, Inc. Englewood Cliffs, N.J.)*

(a)   (b)   (c)   (d)

equal. If a fourth beaker, D, of still another shape, is introduced and the liquid from B is poured into it, the child will again judge an inequality.

Children at the operational level have the ability to **decenter** (focus not on just height or breadth, but on both properties). Thus, they can judge equality between any combinations—A and B, A and C, or A and D. They recognize that transforming the shape of the liquid does nothing to the quantity.

During the concrete operational stage, children learn to master logical operations using concrete objects as referents. They begin to think according to some logical model of reasoning. Around age seven or eight, they become able to conserve. Conservation of mass tends to be the first conservation principle acquired, followed by conservation of weight and volume.

Another major thought process is **reversibility.** Piaget defined it as "the permanent possibility of returning to the starting point of the operation in question" (Inhelder & Piaget, 1958, p. 272). This ability to retrace intellectual behavior, or to see that an idea can be expressed differently, is also a significant step in the reasoning process. The ability to do reversible intellectual operations is basic to the process of carrying on logical deductions, a crucial factor in adolescent hypothesizing. The behavioral criterion for the existence of the reversible operation is the ability to conserve.

A major criticism of Piagetian theory has revolved around the issues of conservation and reversibility. Many researchers have argued that these operations begin earlier than age six or seven. Techniques such as verbal training (Belin, 1975; Kohnstamm, 1967), discrimination training (Gelman, 1969), hierarchical learning (Gagne, 1968), and modeling (Rosenthal & Zimmerman, 1978; Rosser & Brody, 1981) have all been cited as accelerating the acquisition of conservation skills. Two limitations can be observed: First, most of these studies have been successful within their specific investigation but less successful in generalizing the skills from one instance to another, although Rosser and others have demonstrated generalization in their studies (Rosser & Brody, 1981; Rosser & Horan, 1982). Second, most studies continue to support Piagetian contentions

Decenter
The ability to look at more than one property of a physical event.

Reversibility
The ability to retrace one's steps in an intellectual operation.

far more than any other findings (Bovet, 1969; Gallagher, Wright, & Noppe, 1975).

During the concrete operations period, the child also acquires the ability to perform **class inclusion** and **serial ordering operations.** Class inclusion refers to the ability to see something in two relationships, as an entity in itself and as a part of something. The ability to hold several pieces of information in memory and reverse the thinking process allows for the emergence of classification systems. Learning that all balls are part of the general category "balls" while also seeing that each individual ball is whole in itself is an example of class inclusion.

Seriation (ordering) takes place when an individual can impose some structure and order on things—for example, rank groups from large to small. During the concrete operational period, the child is able to order concrete objects on a hierarchy, such as tall to short in height, light to heavy in weight, or large to small in groups. The critical limitation of this ability at this stage is that all objects must be presented concretely. The child cannot engage in abstract mental ordering until the formal operations period.

Transition between Concrete and Formal Operations The process by which thought processes move from concrete to abstract symbols has not been well defined. It probably begins with the preadolescent's using concrete props to do abstract thinking. With use, concrete reference points gradually disappear as our abstract abilities become better defined. The developing preadolescent gradually learns symbols (words) that contain abstract components (functions within the mind), rather than concrete ones. Thus, a word such as *love* has an internal meaning within the mind. The verbal expression might be "Love is something two people feel about each other." In contrast, the concrete operational child might view love as

Class inclusion
The ability to see that something is complete within itself but is also a member of a larger classification system.

Serial ordering
The ability to assign value or structure to something, such as ranking or alphabetizing.

Concept Summary 7–2

Conservation and Reversibility	
Principle	**Example**
Conservation:	
The ability to realize that quantity remains the same even though it changes in size, shape, and so forth	Changing $1 into four quarters Changing a liquid into a solid Changing a rectangle into two triangles
Reversibility:	
The ability to reverse a mental operation	Changing four quarters back into $1 Changing a solid back into a liquid Changing two triangles back into a rectangle

Glen Holt: Tomorrow's Farmer Today

In 1960, Glen Holt was thirteen years old and in the eighth grade of a small rural school. There were only thirteen students in the eighth grade, and, by everyone's consensus, Glen was the least intelligent. In every subject area, whether on daily homework or more extensive tests, Glen always came up with the lowest score. Glen was also the tallest boy in class, but he was heavy set and disproportioned. These characteristics, combined with the fact that he was homely looking, made Glen the most picked on and laughed at student in the class.

One spring Monday morning when the teacher arrived after the school bus, he was surprised to see all the other students gathered around Glen and listening intently. Mr. Sklar stayed on the periphery and listened to what was going on. Glen had sold his calf at the county 4-H fair over the weekend for a handsome sum of money. All the students were buzzing about the money Glen had made.

When the bell rang, the students took their seats, but Mr.

Sklar changed the order of the day and asked Glen to explain his business venture to the class. As he did, Mr. Sklar asked Glen to put figures on the board. Once he had completed his story, with his teacher's help, Glen had written the following simple profit statement:

Initial Cost of Calf (Money loaned by his father at 3 percent)	$350.00
Cost of Feed (Money loaned by his father at 3 percent)	830.00
Sale Price of Calf	$3900.00
Interest Paid to Father ($1180 @ 3 percent for eight months)	26.55
Net Profit	$2693.45

Glen and his father were going to the bank after school to open a savings account. It was an exhilarating day for Glen. At least for one day in his eighth-grade year, Glen was perceived as intelligent by his peers.

Today Glen is married, has three children, and farms and ranches two sections of land in rural Kansas. Many of his junior

high school peers still live in the same area, and, when they get together in their small town, Glen is still the brunt of most jokes. Yet Glen lives a full and productive life. Indeed, Glen Holt is not as unintelligent as most people make him out to be.

What Do You Think?

1. What does an example like this tell us about intelligence?

2. What does this example tell us about school learning?

3. Does this example point out the need for more applied learning in the schools?

195

"Daddy kissing Mommy." One is a concrete event; the other is a mental abstraction. With the emergence of logic and reasoning in the concrete operations stage, the basis is formed for propositional logic (Ausubel & Ausubel, 1966; Elkind & Weiner, 1978; Mishra, 1983). Concepts and ideas take on expanded meaning when they are related to one another in new ways. As the preadolescent increases personal awareness of new thoughts and ideas, there is a tendency to abandon the concrete, less flexible thought patterns for the abstract, more flexible propositional logic.

Formal Operations Development   Although the final developmental period begins around age eleven, it is commonly thought of as characterizing adolescent thought. There are several significant differences between the child's and the adolescent's ability to think. Abstract thinking is the basic characteristic of the **formal operations period.** Further, this stage is typified by the transition from thoughts about reality to thoughts about possibility. Before acting on a problem, adolescents analyze the situation and process possible outcomes. They are also able to devise experiments to test these hypotheses so that they can reach a conclusion on the basis of these experiments. Concrete operational children can reason and hypothesize about current and concrete experience, but it is only during the formal operations period that they become capable of understanding and directly manipulating relationships between abstractions. Adolescents no longer need to base their reasoning on concrete or current experiences (Thornburg, 1982a). Their thoughts involve second-order constructs (operating on operations), abstract ideas, and understandings based on established verbal abstractions. Reality becomes secondary to possibility, and the form of the argument becomes as evident as the content.

Day (1981, p. 44) illustrates the difference between concrete and abstract thinking by using a scientific task often selected to measure formal thought. She presents subjects with a set of rods made of different materials (Plexiglas, wood, and steel) that also differ in diameter (thin, medium, and thick) and length (short, medium, and long). On a table she places a stand in which two rods can fit side by side parallel to the table. There are two equal weights that may be hung from the ends of the rods. Subjects receive the following instructions:

> Here are some rods that differ from each other. Some of these rods bend more than others. Find out what characteristics of the rods influence how much they bend. You can place pairs of rods in this stand to try to find out what influences bending. Tell me why you choose each pair of rods you test.

John, a child in the concrete operational stage, initially selects a long thin wooden rod and a short thick steel rod simply to find out what happens. After observing that the long wooden rod bends more, John concludes that long rods bend more than short ones. He makes no comment about the other differences. For the next comparison, John selects a long steel rod and a short Plexiglas rod of equal diameter. When he observes that the Plexiglas rod bends more than the longer steel rod, he comments that "glass bends more than steel" and does not notice that the Plexiglas rod is shorter than the steel rod. In the next comparison, John states ahead of time that he wants to test for the effect of diameter. He selects a thick Plexiglas rod and a thin steel rod. The Plexiglas rod bends more than the steel rod; so he concludes that thicker rods bend more. When he is asked if a comparison between a thick Plexiglas rod and a thin Plexiglas rod would be better, he argues that his comparison was better because the rods were "more different."

The performance of the ideal formal operational individual is noticeably different. Karen, for example, notes that length, material, and diameter might all be important. She selects a pair of rods that vary on only one characteristic—a long thin steel rod and a short thin steel rod—and states that she wants to see if length influences bending. She then goes on to test for the effects of material and diameter, using the control of variables strategy—that is, she makes sure the rods are the same except for the one characteristic she is testing (Day, 1981, pp. 44–45).

Reflective thinking, the ability to think about our own thoughts, is another major characteristic of the formal operational stage. It gives adolescents the opportunity to evaluate their own thought processes and determine ways to use their thinking abilities. Synthesis, another relevant characteristic of adolescent thought, is a type of combinative thinking described by Inhelder and Piaget (1958). Figure 7–3 presents a problem they used with formal operational thinkers to test its emergence in adolescence.

Inhelder and Piaget (1958) referred to two distinct stages within the formal operations period. The first, which encompasses the ages eleven through thirteen, reflects the transition between concrete and formal operations. As we move out of preadolescence and into adolescence, our cognitive structure is still growing. However, movement away from the use of concrete or environmental props occurs in the form of experimentation, hypothesis making, and synthesis and analysis of cognitive materials. Exploratory ideas begin to dominate the adolescent's thinking. Combinative thinking, for example, begins during this stage and may be facilitated by some concrete props.

This advance is completed during the next stage (ages fourteen through fifteen), when synthesis can be done without the need of environmental props (Keating & Caramazza, 1975). Two stages for the formal operations period of adolescence are designated because there are two distinct periods of time during which the mind goes through a state of reorganization and disequilibrium. The first stage is characterized by transition, and the second stage represents the final restructuring of the mind before it realizes its full growth potential. Intellectual processes in the latter stage are definitely more abstract and more reflective, and they include more self-generated thought about thoughts.

Extent of Formal Operational Thought   It is often assumed that, by the time an adolescent completes the fifteenth year of life, the capacity to think abstractly and carry out other complex forms of thinking exists. Piaget

Figure 7–3
Test of combinative reasoning in children and adolescents. This diagram illustrates the problem of colored and colorless chemicals. Four similar flasks contain colorless, odorless liquids: (1) diluted sulfuric acid; (2) water, (3) oxygenated water, and (4) thiosulfate. The smaller flask, labeled g, contains potassium iodide. Two glasses are presented to the subject; one contains 1 + 3; the other contains 2. While the subject watches, the experimenter adds several drops of g to each of these glasses. The liquid in the glass containing 1 + 3 turns yellow. The subject is then asked to reproduce the color, using any or all of the five flasks. [Source: Elkind & Weiner (1978). Reprinted by permission.]

1   2   3   4   g   1 + 2   1 + 3 + g

Table 7–1 Percentage of Individuals Completing Piagetian Tasks at Different Ages

Age (Years)	Stage				
	Pre-operational	Concrete Onset	Concrete Mature	Formal Onset	Formal Mature
5	85%	15%			
6	60	35	5%		
7	35	55	10		
8	25	55	20		
9	15	55	30		
10	12	52	35	1%	
11	6	49	40	5	
12	5	32	51	12	
13	2	34	44	14	6%
14	1	32	43	15	9
15	1	14	53	19	13
16	1	15	54	17	13
17	3	19	47	19	12
18	1	15	50	15	19

Source: Epstein (1979), p. 4. By permission of the publisher.

(1972, p. 10) pointed out that "all normal subjects attain the stage of formal operations [no later than] 15 to 20 years. However, they reach this stage in different areas according to their aptitudes and their professional specializations." Research has shown that the proportion of adolescents who function at the formal operation stage hovers around 50 percent (Arlin, 1975, 1980; Danner & Day, 1977; Peel, 1978; Ross, 1974; Tomlinson-Keasy, 1972).

Epstein (1979) measured both the onset of concrete and formal operations and mature thinking within each stage. Table 7–1 shows the dominant level of thinking for individuals ages five to eighteen. Epstein found that by age fifteen no more than 24 percent were capable of any formal operational thinking. Further, 15 percent were at the onset of such thinking; only 9 percent were mature formal operational thinkers.

The increasing evidence about formal operational thought will require developmental psychologists and educators to redefine this developmental construct and to rethink curricula for the ten- to fifteen-year-old. The explanation for this new evidence is unclear, although three factors warrant some discussion. First, there is much variability within the tasks that have been given to test formal operational thought. Second, studies focusing on subject-matter content have demonstrated considerable variance in abstract reasoning. Third, data on brain growth suggest that the period Piaget defined may be characterized by a plateau in brain growth. Thus, the capacity for formal operational thought may be limited by this biological fact.

Task Variability Inhelder and Piaget (1958) designed fifteen tasks, primarily involving physics and mathematics, to measure formal operational thought. Numerous studies have been done to verify their conclusions. In several of these studies, researchers have found that some tasks are more difficult to perform than others (Bart, Frey, & Baxter, 1979; Keating, 1978; Keating & Clark, 1980; Neimark, 1975; Protinsky & Hugston, 1980). This variability in task difficulty has caused most of these researchers to question whether these tasks are valid for assessing formal operational thought. Inhelder and Piaget recognized that some tasks were more difficult than others, but they argued that adolescents who have reached the formal operations stage should be able to complete all such tasks successfully. This assertion has now come into question and will continue to be investigated by researchers, especially those who argue that Piaget's tasks are too math and science oriented and may not apply to all aspects of cognitive functioning (Brazee, 1981; Nagy & Griffiths, 1982).

Subject-Matter Content   Another explanation of formal reasoning variability deals with content. In general, this position holds that the acquisition of logical thought and abstract representation is due to subject-matter exposure. Thus, a twelve-year-old who has learned abstract representation will think abstractly in a specific subject-matter area, whereas one who has not learned in the area will not think abstractly.

A series of studies (Linn, 1983; Linn & Pulos, 1983; Pulos, deBenedictis, Linn, Sullivan, & Clement, 1982; Pulos & Linn, 1981) has demonstrated the efficacy of content exposure to abstract acquisition. Basically, three characteristics of thought have emerged:

1. The greater the familiarity with the content of a task, the better the performance will be.

2. Specific training in a content area tends to increase performance.

3. Adolescents will generate alternatives for reasoning out problems rather than giving wrong answers.

Thus, they use subject-matter knowledge to solve the problem. Such findings call into question the assertion that abstract reasoning is due primarily to development and imply that learning is a significant variable in the adolescent thought process.

Brain Growth   Epstein (1974) demonstrated that the brain alternates between periods of growth and plateaus. Spurts of growth occur between ages two and four, six and eight, ten and twelve, and fourteen and sixteen.

Piaget's Stages of Intellectual Development	
I. Sensorimotor period	0–2
II. Preoperational period	2–7
A. Preconceptual thought	2–4
B. Intuitive thought	4–7
III. Concrete operations period	7–11
IV. Formal operations period	11–15

The plateaus are during the intervening periods. Of special significance here are the plateau period from twelve to fourteen and the growth period from fourteen to sixteen. Epstein (1978) has theorized that the ages twelve to fourteen are not characterized by new cognitive or mental growth. This is not to suggest that the brain is void of active intellectual thought, only that higher level cognitive skills are unlikely to develop. In actuality, the youngster can learn facts and information during a brain growth plateau as well as during a period of great brain growth and development of neural receptors. Epstein believes that problems begin when adolescents are presented with learning for which they have not yet developed neural receptors. To ensure that youngsters continue to learn facts and information successfully during a plateau period, it is necessary to teach within their existing thinking skills (those that exist when the student enters a plateau period).

Several researchers have demonstrated that far fewer adolescents reach the formal operations stage between eleven and fifteen than Piaget asserted. Work being done by learning theorists and cognitive scientists on ways to teach thinking and problem solving may demonstrate that Epstein's proposed limitations on adolescent thought could be neutralized through direct instruction (Nickerson, 1981; Sternberg, 1981; Vye & Bransford, 1981). At present, it is important to be aware that shifts in thinking between concrete (predominately elementary) and abstract (primarily secondary) are highly variable and will affect students' learning and performance capacity.

Language and Intelligence

Within seconds after birth, we are equipped with the potential to make sounds that render us distinctively human. This is the start of the development of enormous flexibility in language and thought. We have gained degrees of control over our environment as we have created and learned symbols that represent various phenomena in it. The degree to which we acquire the verbal capacity to function in our environment is one indicator of intelligence. There is a prevailing opinion that the greater our verbal fluency, the greater our intelligence. The extent to which this is true is questionable, but it does point out the significance of studying language development and intellectual development.

Linguistics is the scientific study of language. Linguists have described language on three levels: the phonological, which deals with individual sounds (phonemes) and combinations; the morphological, which deals with basic meaningful units (morphemes) and their combinations to form words; and the syntactic, which develops sentence patterns from words (Brown & Berko, 1960). Historically, linguists have studied the phonology and morphology of language. A more recent trend, which has been spurred by the work of Noam Chomsky, is the study of the syntax of sentences.

Chomsky hypothesizes that children have an inherent predisposition

to acquire language and that they hear sounds within their environment and operate upon them in order to elicit **implicit grammar** for those utterances. The child's ability to operate comes out of what Chomsky (1965) describes as a **language acquisition device** (LAD). The net result is grammatical competence. The LAD is a linguistic universal. Common to the species, it is thus part of inherent human linguistic competence and therefore is not learned.

Crucial to Chomsky's (1965) theory is the idea that competence is the language user's intrinsic knowledge of his or her language. It is called **generative grammar** because children inherently have some explicit and well-defined way of assigning structural descriptions to sentences. Language performance is the use children make of knowledge in concrete situations. Therefore, Chomsky's linguistic model is a competence model; it describes linguistic potential and not the actual production of language.

McNeill (1966) takes the position that, in order to explain children's language performance, it is necessary to show how that performance derives from competence. At any given stage of development, all that is necessary to explain performance is to infer what children must know. As they develop, they increase linguistic data. With concomitant intellectual

Implicit grammar
The formation of prevocal language based on the internalization of sounds perceived in the environment.

Language acquisition device
The universal, inherent ability to be linguistically competent.

Generative grammar
Language is composed of a large set of potential combinations, although only a few words/sentences are used in any specific setting.

growth, language becomes interwoven with thought and perception. Various stages of growth include increasing acquisitions of language.

Speech Acquisition

During the first few months after birth, infants' vocal apparatuses are not mature; they cry and gurgle but have little control over their vocalizations, many of which do not correspond with any phonetic classification. These prelinguistic utterances are the same for all children, even for those who are deaf. As the nervous system and vocal structures develop, children attain greater command over their vocalizations. They begin to babble at around five months and, unlike lower animals, babble repeatedly, appearing to experiment and play with sounds. Between eight and twelve months, they make nearly all the speech sounds that occur in any language (Menyuk, 1971; Palermo, 1978). Some of these early sounds are vowel sounds, especially *a* as in fat (Lewis, 1959). After emitting many vowel sounds, within the first year, children also utter some vowel-consonant combinations, such as *ba-ba, da-da,* and *na-na.* Not until they are three or four, when children have acquired the fundamentals of grammar and language sounds they may use as an adult. As late as four or five, they may be able to hear the difference between certain sounds without being able to pronounce them.

The first systematic attempt to assess the size of a child's vocabulary was done in 1926 by Smith; it placed the average number of words used or understood at two years at 272, with a vocabulary of over 2000 words developing by age five. It is thought that, once a child enters school, the word acquisition rate is around 1000 per year.

Normal children usually utter their first sentence between twenty-one and twenty-four months, although some normal children do not utter their first sentence until the twenty-seventh to thirty-first months. The sentences typically consist of two to three words, although their grammatical sequence may be inept. Such ineptitude does not mean that the sentences are haphazardly put together; rather, they may be put together according to a simplified set of grammatical rules that the child apparently deduces from adult speech in the environment. This problem is corrected by age four, when children have acquired the fundamentals of grammar and mastered the speech sounds made by adult models (Shatz & Gelman, 1973). Communication with others becomes more reciprocal and a period of consolidation and practice follows during the school years in which children extend their vocabulary, formalize the rules of grammar, and learn to write. The following four tasks are important in learning appropriate speech skills:

1. *Comprehension.* If children are to communicate with others, they must understand what is being said to them.

2. *Vocabulary growth.* This involves learning new words, associating meaning with them, and, in some cases, learning multiple meanings for words.

3. *Pronunciation.* Clarity of pronunciation is highly dependent upon the language models whom children imitate.

4. *Sentence formation.* Early sentences are composed primarily of nouns, with verbs and modifiers coming after three years of age.

Meaning Acquisition

Language is instrumental in intellectual development. Words are tools of communication and they provide the basis for increasing mental growth. Children do not grasp the full meaning of words all at once, but gradually, through development.

Words stand as symbols for objects. In building concepts and differentiating between classes of things, children initially tend to overgeneralize. Children also acquire complete understanding of concepts gradually for abstract words such as cold, hard, bright, and fair. Concepts are often built with words and numbers and may actually be more complex then they appear (Hyde & Jenkins, 1973; Winograd, 1972). A child who knows that one ice cream cone plus one ice cream cone makes two ice cream cones is applying an abstraction, expressed through verbal facility more than through conceptual understanding. Nevertheless, the idea of adding two objects together may be an example of rudimentary concepts and rules.

Children usually understand concrete words. It is not typical for four-year-olds to know that *bright* can describe a person, although they might know that a light is bright. As children move through the preoperational stage to the concrete operations stage, abstract words become more significant and descriptive of things in their environment.

Implications of Cognitive Development for Classroom Teaching

Although psychologists are clearly not in agreement on what intelligence is or on all the variables that affect intellectual functioning, the various theories do hold certain implications for the teacher. The effective teacher always takes account of individual differences in the classroom, and one of the prominent ways in which individuals do differ is in cognitive functioning. The concept of intelligences, rather than an intelligence, holds implications for teachers. If individuals possess different abilities, then teachers must take account of these differences in their *modus operandi.*

For example, if a child operates better figurally than symbolically, the teacher can help that student learn material through figural operations. Or, as Meeker (1969) has suggested, there may be strategies that the teacher can use to increase the child's ability to operate with symbols. Similarly, if there are different levels of mental ability, the teacher can assume that those students possessing a high level I ability but low level

II ability should do well on learning tasks representing structure but perhaps not as well in instructional situations (Jensen, 1969, 1974). The teacher then must continually vary the instructional methodology in an attempt to provide successful educational experiences for all students.

I stressed Piaget's work in this chapter. In his theory, intelligence is a matter of cognitive adaptation to the environment; so learning is but one adaptive factor in intellectual development. Children gain increasing capacities to function with increasing age. Initially, the primary intellectual activity is sensorimotor, which is the reaction to things within the environment through motor action. As children mature, objects in the environment begin taking on some meaning. This is symbolic activity, and intelligence increases through assimilation of new environmental experiences into existing intellectual structure or through the acquisition of new intellectual structures to accommodate environmental demands.

From ages two to eleven years, concrete objects serve as reference points for increasing intellectual capacity, because the mind has not yet matured to the point of abstract functioning. Not until early adolescence does symbolic representation become the characteristic thought process as the mind moves toward full adult maturity. Thus, while children are at the concrete operational stage or below, "telling" does not affect their schemes in the same way that actual interaction with people and objects in the environment does. Of course, the teacher telling a student can bring about changes, in that, through language, the child can verbalize what the teacher was telling. However, Piaget's conception of congitive development requires that children also be able to handle, manipulate, and experiment with reality, with concrete things, if real learning is to occur. In other words, for a child to develop a cognition, there first must be motoric understanding, which is followed by intellectual understanding and, finally, the level of verbal understanding. In Piaget's view, educational programs that attempt to start at the upper level tend to leave students with "empty verbalizations"—they may be able to repeat that "A hexagon is a closed figure with six sides" and still not be able to recognize or construct one.

In contrast to Piaget, a learning theorist is likely to consider intelligence as the outcome of environmental opportunities to function. Learning is viewed as a major factor in intellectual development. Gagne (1968, p. 181) stated, "Learning contributes to the intellectual development of the human being because it is cumulative in its effects." In short, intellectual functioning within Piaget's system is developmental; that is, one type of intellectual activity must necessarily precede another, from simple to complex thinking abilities. Learning theorists do not see intellectual functioning as restricted to developmental stages. Whatever the learning task, if it is presented correctly to the student, learning will occur. Effective human behavior is most likely a result of both learning and development. Learning tasks must be commensurate with the learner's ability to respond. Fortunately, the gradation of instructional materials makes this possible in most teaching-learning situations.

The Cognitive Development of a Concept

Although preschool children probably have never heard the word *transportation,* they are involved in various forms of it from infancy on. As they are able to walk, then move about freely, and acquire some language, transportation is represented to them in a variety of ways. For example, they travel with their parents in automobiles or airplanes (man-made motor forms of transportation); they ride in wagons, on tricycles, then on bicycles (man-made nonmotor forms); they are carried on their father's back (manpower); and they ride horses (animals). Each of their experiences is physical and eventually they attach language to the experiences; so they can verbalize wanting to be carried, ride a horse, or go in the car. This early type of exposure to transportation is the elementary basis for learning about transportation in more complex and systematic ways as they get older.

In the primary grades in school, children are specifically taught about transportation from early humans to the space age. They learn to categorize transportation by its various forms on land, water, and air. They learn numerous subcategories, such as natural or man-made, motor or nonmotor, slow or fast. Because elementary school children are basically concrete thinkers, they are given specific instances of these various categories and often are asked to identify various modes of transportation in which they are involved or see happening every day. The various classification systems depend on such abilities as conservation and class inclusion. Children are able to construct elaborate classification systems in which they can place a host of physical objects.

By junior high school, the concept of transportation can take on more abstract dimensions and focus on cultural relevance. Students can understand the broader term *transportation* and see all the types of classification systems they learned earlier as ways of delineating the more encompassing concept. Some teachers may delve into the history of transportation, its development, and its adaptations across the centuries. Advances in transportation can be viewed in the context of general technological growth so that students can see that the executive who took a month to travel from New York to London in the early 1800s can now fly there in a few hours. Other examples that show how transportation impacts upon people's lives could be brought up.

Students can also use their reasoning abilities to analyze contexts and determine which mode of transportation would be best under given conditions. For example, if a person wanted to vacation, he or she might drive, take a ship, or fly. The length of time available, the cost, and the traveler's personal desires could all be taken into consideration. Other examples might include transporting signals around the world via satellite, providing people with instant information in both print and nonprint forms.

Students could see how cultures depend on transportation and how, as advances in transportation occurred, certain cultural patterns have changed. They could learn the economic importance of a raft in the Phillipines, a kufa in Iraq, or a kayak among the Eskimos. They could learn how a business document can be flown across the United States in a matter of hours, thus affecting businesses and the economy. In short, by junior high the number of variations in the concept "transportation" can be explored extensively, a particularly important educational goal when students are given problem-solving situations and asked to discuss how transportation impacts upon the solution.

Annotated Readings

Brackbill, Y., & Nichols, P. L. (1982). A test of the confluence model of intellectual development. *Developmental Psychology, 18,* 192–198.

> *Longitudinal data from the National Institute of Neurological and Communicative Disorders and Stroke Collaborative Perinatal Project were used to test five confluence model hypotheses using direct empirical measures of birth interval as well as measures of family size, ability, and achievement. Results failed to confirm the importance of birth interval as a determinant of intellectual development.*

Christin, J. F., & Johnsen, E. P. (1983). The role of play in social-intellectual development. *Review of Educational Research, 53,* 93–115.

> *This article reviews studies in an attempt to assess the current status of play as an area of inquiry. The article begins with a discussion of the role of play in major developmental theories. Next, a number of experimental and correlational studies are reviewed. These studies are discussed in relation to their relative impact in the following areas: creativity, problem solving, language development, logical skills, and social knowledge.*

Fuson, K. C., Secada, W. G., & Hall, J. W. (1983). Matching, counting, and conservation of numerical equivalence. *Child Development, 54,* 91–97.

> *This study reports experiments done with children to see if experience at matching and counting improves their equivalence judgments in conservation of number tasks. Students in this study were between four and a half and five and a half years old. The matching experiment showed considerable improvement among the group exposed to matching problems. The counting experiment also found positive directions, but not as strong as in the matching experiment. Interestingly, students opted for the counting strategy more than the matching strategy, although the latter proved more beneficial.*

Linn, M. C. (1983). Content, context and process in reasoning during adolescence: Selecting a model. *Journal of Early Adolescence, 3,* 63–82.

> *The author proposed four models of understanding human cognition: Piagetian, mental ability, cognitive science, and philosophy of science. She also reports data from research that focuses on the content and context of thought. Essentially, the article suggests that the Piagetian notion of adolescent development is an unsatisfactory explanation of adolescent thought. Rather, it is more likely to be affected by familiarity with subject matter (content) or various situations in which an individual experiences the need to exercise different mental abilities (context). This is a most provocative article that contributes significantly to the literature.*

McCabe, A. E., Siegel, L. S., Spence, I., & Wilkinson, A. (1982). Class-inclusion reasoning: Patterns in performance from three to eight years. *Child Development, 53,* 780–785.

> *The performance of children aged three through eight years on a series of class-inclusion problems was examined in two studies. Three performance patterns were observed. Three- and four-year-olds responded in haphazard patterns and five- and six-year-olds tended to be consistently wrong in the classifications. The older children, ages seven to eight, showed a shift toward consistently correct responding, a finding that corroborates Piaget's notion of the emergence of this ability during the concrete operations period.*

Pulos, S., Karplus, R., & Stage, E. K. (1981). Generality of proportional reasoning in early adolescence: Content effects and individual differences. *Journal of Early Adolescence, 1,* 257–264.

A proportional reasoning task and a battery of eight cognitive styles, ability, and attitude measures were given to 248 adolescents in grades six through eight. The problems in the proportional reasoning task varied in content. The study showed that proportional reasoning was heavily affected by numerical content. This study did not verify many tasks designed like the Inhelder and Piaget tasks. The results suggest that young adolescents' proportional reasoning is more complex than was previously thought. It does not seem to be present in the general cognitive structure of most early adolescents.

Affective Development

The Redwood school district designated a Family Awareness Week during the first semester of the school year to increase faculty, staff, and student awareness of how families have changed and shall continue to change in contemporary society. Community resource people, school personnel, students, and many parents discussed the diversity of family structures and roles. Each contributed to increasing participants' understanding and acceptance of each other and families, regardless of their makeup. Students at all grade levels, kindergarten through twelfth grade, were given specific instruction on family change and listened to various resource people.

There are at least thirteen possible family configurations today. The traditional two-parent family with both biological parents is becoming less common. Other structures include single parents, two-career couples without children, blended marriages (generally two previously married individuals with families merging into a new family unit), and unmarried individuals living together with children. School Superintendent Chong noted that each type of family exists in the Redwood school system. The most common type is parent/stepparent, followed by both biological parents, then single parents.

Family roles were also discussed. Both parents of almost two-thirds of the students in this school district work. Ways for families to share responsibility was a major focus. Stress was placed on the multiple options people have and how all of these options could create positive living environments. Jack Elliott, a family life specialist, gathered some interesting data and distributed it to the staff so they could make students more aware of how things have changed. That information included the following:

1. By 1990, only 14 percent of all households will have just one working spouse. This compares with 43 percent in 1960 and 35 percent in 1980.

2. Whereas wives provide approximately 25 percent of the total family income now, they will provide 40 percent by 1990.

3. Within any given decade, at least one-third of the marriages will result in divorce and from one-third to one-half of all schoolchildren will spend part of their developmental years in one-parent family structures.

4. Mobility is projected to decrease because two-parent working families are more resistant to relocation than families with one breadwinner.

211

5. *By 1990, there will be an 800 percent increase over 1960 in the number of women with college degrees. They are pursuing self-employment at five times the rate of men and currently own some three million businesses in the United States.*

Although projects such as Family Awareness Week are difficult to evaluate in terms of their impact on individual behavior, the general consensus in the Redwood school district was that faculty, staff, and students all gained a greater appreciation of the diversity of families in society today. Everyone hopes the eventual outcome will be an increase in the capacity to function in school and family environments because participants gained a greater understanding of each other.

This chapter focuses on the kind of affective learning stressed during Redwood's Family Awareness Week. Key concepts include:

- *Components of affectivity*
- *Socialization*
- *Social cognition*
- *Processing affective responses*
- *Affective instruction*
- *Students' developmental characteristics*

Although throughout the history of learning psychology the primary emphasis has been on how people learn cognitively, there is increased interest today in affective learning. This interest seems apropos, given the complexity of contemporary society and people's responses to it. Society continues to emphasize the intellectual and occupational skills necessary to success, but many well-educated and successful individuals have very unhappy personal lives. The government and the media keep us informed about the economy, the jobless, and the underemployed, often comparing current statistics with days when things were better. But economic and occupational changes have not been as significant as changes in social, personal, and interpersonal problems. Maladjustment, divorce, excessive drug use, sexual exploitation, teenage pregnancy, child and spouse abuse, runaways, suicide, and mental illness are greater problems today than our economic and occupational woes. Yet who prepares children and adolescents to cope with these impending realities? Affective education is more important today than ever before. If we are to help people live productive, well-adjusted lives, we must teach them to deal with their total environment.

Components of Affectivity

Affective learning indicates the degree to which a person experiences emotional involvement. It is typically described within the framework of five levels of expression: interests, appreciations/preferences, attitudes, values, and social-emotional adjustments.

Interests

Interests are the behaviors a person performs when he or she is free to choose. Raths et al. (1966, p.69) describe interests as "those things which excite us, which occupy our minds and hands, and which cause us to spend time, money, and energy on them." Getzels (1966, p. 98) defines interests as the "disposition organized through experiences which impels an individual to seek out particular objects, activities, understanding, skills, or goals for attention or acquisition." Interests may be considered, then, to involve strictly a feeling state, although they do vary in intensity.

Interests
The behavior a person selects from freedom of choice.

Appreciations/Preferences

Appreciations are behaviors a person elects to perform based on feelings toward and understanding of activities a person chooses. A person may attend the opera not just because of interest in this type of music but because he or she understands how the story is developed both dramatically and musically. Appreciations involve both a feeling and a thinking state. The preference is based not only on how a person feels about the event, object, or person but on some knowledge as well.

Appreciations
The involvement in a high-interest activity because of one's understanding of it as well as preference for it.

Attitudes

Attitudes are the disposition to behave toward environmental objects in a positive or negative way. An attitude is more firmly developed than interests and appreciations because of this action tendency. If a student dislikes an academic subject, he or she may avoid studying it and thus not perform well. It is also possible that the student will associate dislike for the subject

Attitudes
The emotional disposition to behave in some way.

with the teacher and express a dislike for both. Therefore, attitudes involve not only feeling and thinking states but also a behavioral state. Because attitudes are a major way of behaving affectively, I discuss them in greater detail later in this chapter.

Values

Values are the consistent expression of attitudes to the point of internalization. In effect, the values characterize an individual's behavior. Although they are made up of the same three components as attitudes, values are more intense, complex, and lasting. For example, a person may have a positive attitude toward equal opportunity but express true values by speaking against a fair housing bill when he or she thinks that it could potentially devalue his or her property.

Social-Emotional Adjustment

Socio-emotional adjustment
The totality of one's feelings and expressions, often referred to as one's lifestyle.

Social-emotional adjustment, the most encompassing affective factor, describes an individual's ability to encounter, understand, and adjust to the social and emotional situations that arise within the culture in which he or she lives. The concept has strong implications for individual personality development and mental health, but it is too broad to be considered as a defined factor in the classroom. This social-emotional adjustment level is more akin to the complex of understandings, perceptions, and values found in the mature individual.

Attitudes are learned and are a function of the mind. For example, when we make an affective attitudinal response, our nervous system becomes highly active, and there is a strong "feeling" in the response. When we make a cognitive attitudinal response, it is more perceptual; we are expressing a belief that we have intellectually worked through. There-

Concept Summary 8–1

Levels of Affective Involvement	
Level of Expression	**Example**
Interest	Explores objects in a museum
Appreciation	Reads about special exhibit in museum before visiting
Attitude	Invites others to visit the museum
Value	Makes a contribution to the museum
Socio-emotional adjustment	Has feeling of inner satisfaction as a result of visiting the museum

fore, although it is an attitude response, it has a stronger "thinking" than "feeling" component. We usually express a behavioral attitudinal response through overt action or statements indicative of action. The predominant characteristic of the response is behavior, with thinking and feeling playing a lesser role.

Socialization

Socialization is the process by which we use mental processes to learn and adapt to the ways, ideas, beliefs, and values of our culture. A young child's society consists largely of the family. Thus, initial social behaviors are generally those of his or her parents. As the child develops, other sources, such as teachers, peers, siblings, the media, churches, and community organizations, become influential in the socialization process. As a result of learning, increased developmental capacity, and experiences, we gradually become more socially aware, sophisticated, and mature.

How we are socialized is culturally determined. Cultures select the goals, values, and behaviors that are acceptable for their members. The more fully that adult models accept social and cultural expectations, the more likely they are to teach children normative behaviors and values. When children enter school, they broaden their exposure to normative values and may select other models' behaviors. As they move into adolescence, peers become particularly strong alternative sources for social learning, sometimes to the benefit and sometimes to the detriment of the individual.

Socialization
Ways in which individuals learn about and act consistently with social norms, values, and roles.

Chapter 8
Affective Development
215

Davis (1944) contends that all socialization is accomplished through the continuous process of social reinforcement and punishment. One social mechanism that influences behavior is **socialized anxiety,** the anticipation or fear of punishment if we do not behave according to social expectations. This anxiety functions as our primary motivation to adapt to such demands. Although the contemporary social structure is relatively open, it still does not accommodate all individual differences. Thus, in many aspects of their lives, individuals may experience socialized anxiety from time to time, resulting in behavioral change and social conformity. If punishment is a potential consequence of behavior, the accompanying anxiety may reduce the likelihood of the behavior occurring (Wrightsman, 1977).

Socialized anxiety
The anticipation of punishment if behavior is not according to social expectations.

Aronfreed (1968) has conceptualized a person's reaction to unacceptable behaviors as having either an internal or external effect on the person. An **internal effect** could produce guilt, fear, or shame. An **external effect** could result in confession, restitution, or self-criticism in front of others. These adjustive mechanisms resolve such internal conflicts as anxiety or guilt. Table 8–1 summarizes Aronfreed's characteristics of reactions to unacceptable behavior.

Internal effect
Occurs when acceptable behavior results in guilt, fear, or shame.

External effect
Occurs when unacceptable behavior results in telling others or belittling oneself.

Table 8–1 Characteristics of Internal and External Reactions to Wrongdoing

Effect	Definition	Example
Internal		
Fear	Anticipation of unpleasant consequences associated with wrongdoing	An adolescent takes a beer from the refrigerator without permission and fears getting caught drinking it.
Guilt	A general anxiety associated with wrongdoing	An adolescent lies to a teacher even though he or she believes lying is wrong.
Shame	The feeling others may find out about one's wrongdoing	An adolescent steals something but never tells anyone about it.
External		
Confession	Telling of a wrongdoing, which terminates the negative anxiety	An adolescent prays to God for forgiveness.
Restitution	Payment in cash or service directly related to a wrongdoing	An adolescent repairs a fence that he or she damaged.
Self-criticism	Verbal criticism of self to others, which reduces anxiety	An adolescent belittles him- or herself in front of other adolescents.

Source: Aronfreed (1968), p. 90.

Table 8–2　Developmental Socialization: A Five-Stage Process

Task	Acquisition of Social Learning	Confirmation of Social Learning	Social Maturation	Social Integration	Finding Social Identity
Stage	Early and middle childhood	Preadolescence	Adolescence	Late adolescence and young adulthood	Adulthood
Age range	Birth–8	9–13	14–18	19–23	24 on
Task	Acquisition of social behaviors	Learned behaviors confirmed and solidified	Alternative social learning	Synthesis of self-social ideas	Finding one's social role
Primary influence	Parental	Parent/peer	Peers	Peer/society	Society
Peer influence	Minimal	Loosely defined	Strong	Strong	Loosely defined
Stage transfer	Facilitates	Solidifies	Breaks away Facilitates	Facilitates	Interrelates

Source: Thornburg (1973c), p. 21.

Socialization Stages

Once infants can knowingly interact with their environment, approximately one month after birth (Brazelton, 1977; Gander & Gardiner, 1981; Lipsett, 1975), social development begins and continues throughout the life span. As they grow and society changes, individuals must develop adaptive skills. Socialization, like other aspects of human behavior, is developmental, which means that our capacity for social learning increases with age. Table 8–2 presents a conceptual model of human socialization, indicating the age ranges during which socialization capacity increases. Too many variables affect social learning to mention here, but the sequence of social development seems to be the same, although the rate of the emergence of new capacity may vary.

The following general characteristics reflect major factors or processes involved in social development and learning (Thornburg, 1982a, pp. 124–125):

1. The family is the primary source of the child's initial social learning.
2. The family is the dominant influence in socialization for the first eight years of life, although increasing amounts of responsibility are delegated to the school. The media is also playing a more influential role in early life.
3. Education in morality and social values begins early and becomes a major aspect of socialization.

4. Throughout childhood, there is a high degree of consistency between values and behavior.

5. In early adolescence, new social influences from peers facilitate broader social learning and advanced moral thinking. The potential for a growing discrepancy between values and behaviors exists.

6. Maturation and identity resolution become the major socialization tasks during adolescence. They are characterized by alternative social learning and open conflict between values and behavior.

7. During young adulthood, integration into the larger society is the major socialization process. This integration is facilitated by the full development of moral values and by considerable restoration of value-behavior consistency.

8. Adult socialization involves identifying with society in such a way as to gain ego strength and accept the adult role. There is a high degree of consistency between values and behaviors. Each of the socialization stages conceptualized in Table 8–2 has unique characteristics and involves such basic processes that the fundamental socialization within each must be learned before the individual can progress to the next stage. The central characteristics of each stage are as follows.

Social Learning Acquisition   During infancy, the primary source of gratification is the family; thus, children learn to place importance on adult affiliation. Although preschool children extend their interest to others, their interaction with the family is not significantly reduced (Baskett & Johnson, 1982). It is during this time that parents explain many things to their children. By the time children have moved through the preschool years, regardless of whether they have been in nursery school, parents still basically dominate children's social behavior.

During childhood, some interaction with peers goes on, although it is limited. Outside adult influences by teachers in the primary grades tend to teach and reinforce parental and social values in the child, rather than presenting alternatives. Friendships at these ages are usually loosely defined, heavily influenced by models, and generally with children of the same sex. When formal social learning does occur, children tend to use parents more than teachers as reference points.

Social Learning Confirmation   In the pre- or early adolescent stage, individuals try out through direct experiences many of the things they previously have been taught. At the same time, parental influences begin to give way to peer influences as the peer group becomes a stronger social-ization source (Bowerman & Kinch, 1959; Kurdeck & Krile, 1982; Thorn-burg & Gould, 1980).

Early adolescents are concerned about finding out whether the things they have been taught are true and important. Through personal curiosity, they test ideas to determine their validity. This new ability is facilitated by their increasingly outgoing nature. Their desire to be popular causes them to associate with others of similar interests or values. Such associations result in some variance from early parental teachings. The feasibility of the alternatives and the satisfaction they derive from experiencing them will help determine whether adolescents dismiss or incorporate earlier teach-ing. This interaction with peers begins challenging parental interactions as the primary socialization influence (Condry & Siman, 1974), and, during the end of the preadolescent period, the influence of peers becomes highly visible (Kandel & Lesser, 1972; Konopka, 1973).

Social Maturation   Satisfactory interaction with others in the environ-ment is a primary accomplishment in adolescence. High school enroll-ment brings adolescents into contact with a diverse group of peers, teachers, and social expectations. Among peers, same-sex identification gradually becomes cross-sex identification. Membership in peer groups symbolizes acceptance, which adds to personal identity.

Social Integration   By college age, most of the basic tasks of adoles-cence have been accomplished, and the influence of peer groups breaks down after high school in favor of a growing awareness of the need to integrate into society. Most individuals carry the prevailing values and behaviors of adolescence into this stage. However, adults and social ex-pectations increasingly come to influence decision making as the individ-ual functions in the larger society. Young adults begin to learn the social processes that will allow them to function in a variety of social contexts.

Social Identity   When we begin to play responsible roles and have successfully integrated into society, we experience a high degree of stability and identity with society. We have achieved mature social identity when we can see ourselves and society as interrelated without becoming so absorbed by our social roles that we lose our personal identities.

Stages in Moral Development

We form a very elementary idea of what is right and wrong during the social learning acquisition stage. Because morality is an externally defined construct, it often is the basis for our social teachings, especially to preschool-age children.

Research on the development of values and conscience in the child has been going on for some time; the definitive work is Jean Piaget's *The Moral Judgment of the Child* (1932). As a developmental psychologist, Piaget interpreted cognitive and affective development as corresponding. Two primary ideas dominated his thinking, and several studies done since are somewhat supportive of them: First, early in children's experiences (at preschool age), they interpret the observable consequences of their behavior and base their value judgments on this external evidence. Second, as children move toward ages nine to eleven, they begin to **cognize**—that is, to internalize the rightness and wrongness of things.

Piaget (1948) distinguished two types of moral development: **heteronomous,** in which a person accepts rules that come from authority, and **autonomous,** in which a person believes that it is acceptable to modify the rules to fit the needs of a specific situation. If evidence from

Cognize
The ability to think about the rightness or wrongness of something.

Heteronomous moral development
The acceptance of external rules learned from an authority.

Autonomous moral development
The internalization of external rules to the point that they can be modified in specific situations.

Fouled in the Act of Shooting

Sometimes teachers have to make very difficult decisions, especially when the issue of fairness to students is concerned. This was particularly true in the case of Timmy Gaines, a handsome, twelve-year-old seventh-grader with an outgoing personality. But Timmy had something else that complicated his interactions with the teacher and students. Timmy had leukemia.

The problem became most difficult for Mr. Hansen, Timmy's teacher, when Timmy decided to try out for the junior high basketball team, because Timmy bled easily, a condition that could be brought about by stress or fatigue. His parents, not wanting Timmy to be different from the other boys, strongly encouraged him to go out for the team. Mr. Hansen, who was also the basketball coach, felt he should not discourage Timmy from trying out, but he worried about what might happen to Timmy in practice or a game if he were hurt or became tired.

Mr. Hansen decided to discuss Timmy's limitations with the other boys on the team so that they would better understand Timmy's condition and not make undue demands on him. This open relationship between the coach, Timmy, and the other players worked out well, and Timmy had a successful experience at basketball, sometimes playing as much as half of a game.

The basketball team had a successful season. In fact, the junior high was playing Mobley for the county championship. It was in the final seconds of the game; Timmy was playing; and, as he attempted a basket, he was knocked to the floor by an opposing player. The coach immediately called time out. After some deliberation, it was decided that Timmy could stay in the game and take his two free-throw shots. Timmy stood at the free-throw line and the first shot hit the edge of the rim and dropped in. The score was tied. The crowd yelled enthusiastically. One more free throw and the championship was theirs. Mr. Hansen was not that optimistic, however. He had observed that Timmy barely had the energy to shoot the first free throw. His suspicion was verified. Timmy's second shot missed the basket entirely and in ten seconds the game went into overtime. Mobley played extremely well during the overtime period and eventually won the game.

In the locker room, Timmy began to cry. He was reacting to the crowd's boos and his own disappointment about missing the shot. It was at this point that the open relationship paid off. Mr. Hansen and the players gave Timmy support and encouragement, reducing his stress and making him feel better about how well he had played all season long. The other boys knew Timmy had given his

best effort and they seemed to admire him for his courage.

Timmy lived for two and one-half more years. His warmth and his openess in dealing with his illness helped him form rewarding relationships with other boys in the school and made Timmy's school experiences extremely valuable.

What Do You Think?

1. How many people in the school environment should know about the health of a student (principal, special services personnel, classroom teachers, students)?

2. Should students like Timmy be encouraged to live as normal a life as possible in the school environment?

3. Whether Timmy or a student with no health problems, should junior high students be exposed to the pressure of winning in athletic competition?

Box 8–1 Kohlberg's Levels and Stages of Moral Growth

Preconventional level
The description of moral development that is based on one's perceptions of the physical consequences of action.

I. Preconventional Level

At this level, the child is responsive to cultural rules and labels of good and bad, right or wrong, but interprets these labels either in terms of the physical or the hedonistic consequences of action (punishment, reward, exchange of favors) or in terms of the physical power of those who enunciate the rules and labels.

Stage 1. Punishment and Obedience Orientation The physical consequences of action determine its goodness or badness, regardless of the human meaning or value of these consequences. Avoidance of punishment and unquestioning deference to power are valued in their own right, not in terms of respect for an underlying moral order supported by punishment and authority (the latter being stage 4).

Stage 2. Instrumental Relativist Orientation Right action consists of what instrumentally satisfies one's own needs and occasionally the needs of others. Human relations are viewed in terms like those of the marketplace. Elements of fairness, reciprocity, and equal sharing are present, but they are always interpreted in a physical, pragmatic way. Reciprocity is a matter of "you scratch my back and I'll scratch yours," not of loyalty, gratitude, or justice.

Conventional level
The ability to describe moral behavior in terms of what is right or wrong regardless of one's actions.

II. Conventional Level

At this level, maintaining family, group, or national expectations is perceived as valuable in its own right, regardless of immediate and obvious consequences. The attitude is not only one of conformity to personal expectations and social order, but of loyalty to it, of actively maintaining, supporting, and justifying the order, and of identifying with the persons or group involved in it.

Stage 3. Interpersonal Concordance of "Good Boy-Nice Girl" Orientation Good behavior is what pleases or helps others and is approved by them. There is much conformity to stereotypical images of what is majority or "natural" behavior. Behavior is frequently judged by intention—"he means well" becomes important for the first time. One earns approval by being "nice."

Piaget's research is accurate, it is appropriate to conceptualize moral growth as developmental.

Kohlberg (1971, pp. 290–291) enlarged on this idea, delineating three levels and six stages of moral growth. The first four stages are very rule and authority bound; thus, they correspond to Piaget's concept of heteronomy. The final two stages are more relative, or situation bound, corresponding to Piaget's concept of autonomy. I present Kohlberg's outline in Box 8–1.

Box 8–1, continued

Stage 4. "Law-and-Order" Orientation   There is orientation toward authority, fixed rules, and the maintenance of the social order. Right behavior consists of doing one's duty, showing respect for authority, and maintaining the given social order for its own sake.

III. *Postconventional, Autonomous, or Principles Level*

At this level, there is a clear effort to define moral values and principles that have validity and application apart from the authority of the groups or persons holding these principles and apart from the individual's own identification with these groups.

Stage 5. Social Contract, Legalistic Orientation   This level generally has utilitarian overtones. Right action tends to be defined in terms of general individual rights and standards that the whole society has critically examined and agreed upon. There is a clear awareness of the relativism of personal values and opinions and a corresponding emphasis on procedural rules for reaching consensus. Aside from what is constitutionally and democratically agreed upon, the right is a matter of personal "values" and "opinion." The result is an emphasis upon the "legal point of view," but with an emphasis upon the possibility of changing law in terms of rational consideration of social utility (rather than freezing it in terms of stage 4, "law and order"). Outside the legal realm, free agreement and contract is the binding element of obligation. This is the "official" morality of the American government and Constitution.

Stage 6. Universal Ethical-Principle Orientation   Right is defined by the decision of conscience in accord with self-chosen ethical principles appealing to logical comprehensiveness, universality, and consistency. These principles are abstract and ethical (the Golden Rule, the categorical imperative); they are not concrete moral rules, such as the Ten Commandments. At heart, these are universal principles of justice, of the reciprocity and equality of human rights, and of respect for the dignity of human beings as individuals.

Postconventional level
The understanding of morality in relation to individual rights and specific situations.

Kohlberg (1971) wrote that each of his moral stages is prerequisite to each successive stage. He did not find any formal moralizing by children before age four, the preconventional level, during which they are generally well behaved and responsive to cultural labels of good and bad. Parents' or other significant individuals' responses to children's behavior determine whether they will retain the behavior. Children tend to do what they want to do and then wait for physical consequences, such as punishment or reward. They interpret punishment as bad and reward as good, abandoning behavior that evokes punishment in deference to authority. At this stage, children obey rules essentially in order to avoid punishment. Kohlberg wrote that the punishment and obedience orientation stage begins to dominate children's thinking around age seven (Piaget's concrete operations stage). By that age, early parental influences are well established, and children have had some exposure to formal schooling.

Kohlberg's system has influenced much research as well as the design of moral education programs in schools. Instruction generally involves the discussion of social, moral, or ethical dilemmas in which students are asked to decide what is the most appropriate behavior and provide their rationale. Kohlberg (1975) believes that moral/ethical dilemmas should create a contradiction. In essence, contradictions cause students to think about the situation, usually on more than one moral level. When students consider the multiple aspects of moral/ethical situations, more advanced moral thought can evolve (Rosenkoetter, Alderman, Nelson, & Ottaviano, 1982). Kohlberg (1975, p. 675) offers the following suggestions for moral instruction:

1. Exposure to the next higher stage of reasoning
2. Exposure to situations posing problems and contradictions for the child's current moral structure leading to dissatisfaction with the current level
3. An atmosphere of interchange and dialogue combining the first two conditions in which conflicting moral views are compared in an open manner

Rosenkoetter et al. (1982) investigated the effect of specific teacher training in Kohlberg's system on student moral learning. The study evaluated the effectiveness of classroom moral dilemma discussions. Sixth graders' moral reasoning was assessed before and after an eight-week moral education program. Students taught by teachers with extended training demonstrated greater moral maturity than students whose teachers had limited training. Similarly, classes instructed by teachers who were skilled in assessing students' levels of moral reasoning were more effective.

Research also substantiates that prosocial behavior exhibited in the classroom is likely to be maintained if either the teacher or peers notice or reinforce it (Bar-Tal, Raviv, & Shavit, 1981; Eisenberg, 1979; Eisenberg, Cameron, Tryon, & Dodez, 1981). Whether students exercise a prosocial behavior, such as altruism, justice, or concern for others, or follow a socially prescribed behavior to avoid negative consequences, they clearly learn morality and their teachers and friends influence the maintenance of moral behavior.

Social Cognition

Social cognition
The thinking process by which individuals learn about their affective world.

Recent literature has focused on **social cognition,** the process by which individuals learn about their social world. Underlying social cognition is the belief that children and adolescents apply cognitive abilities to non-

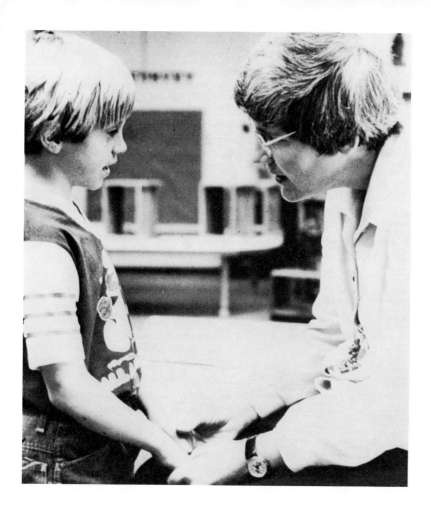

cognitive contexts (that is, their interpersonal world). It is believed that social cognition has structure, just as academic cognition does, and that this structure is organized and constructed out of the person's interaction with the environment (Turiel, 1983). Social cognition is developmental in nature because, with increasing age, we view others people in increasingly complex and abstract interpersonal ways (Montemayor & Eisen, 1977).

Piaget's demonstration of intellectual development is based on how the child handles the physical world. Social cognitivists believe that general cognitive principles derived from these observations can be applied to social processes as well.

One of the most influential developments in social cognition has been the work on social perspective taking by Robert Selman at Harvard University. Following Piaget's model of intellectual development, Selman (1980) constructed a development model of perspective-taking ability, which he believes is the heart of social cognition. He has differentiated four levels of social perspective development, corresponding to different age groups. I describe these levels in Box 8–2.

Box 8–2   Selman's Levels of Social Perspective Development

Level 0: Undifferentiated or Egocentric Perspective Taking

Concepts of Persons: Undifferentiated   At this level, young children do not clearly differentiate people's physical and psychological characteristics. They can observe and recognize feelings and thoughts in others, but the confusion between the subjective-psychological and the objective-physical leads to confusion between acts and feelings or between intentional and unintentional behavior.

Concepts of Relations: Egocentric   Selves and others are clearly differentiated physically but not psychologically. Children at this stage cannot recognize that another may interpret the same situation differently, although they recognize that people may see things differently.

Level 1: Differentiated or Subjective Perspective Taking

Concepts of Persons: Differentiated   At level 1, the key conceptual advance is that children can now clearly differentiate physical and psychological characteristics. This means they can distinguish between intentional and unintentioanl acts and have a new awareness that each person has a unique, subjective psychological life. Still, children at this stage will see another's thoughts, opinions, or feelings as unitary, not mixed. They cannot understand, for example, that a person may speak angrily but feel fear.

Concepts of Relations: Subjective   The subjective perspectives of self and others are clearly differentiated and recognized as potentially different. However, another's subjective state is still thought to be understandable by simple physical observation. The child has yet to understand that two people's perspectives are reciprocal—that one affects the other (for example, that the child's pleasure in receiving a gift will make the giver feel good). Where there is any understanding of two-way reciprocity, it is limited to the physical, such as the child who receives a blow striking back. The child sees that people respond to action with like action.

Level 2: Self-Reflective / Second-Person or Reciprocal Perspective Taking

Concepts of Persons: Self-Reflective / Second-Person   Key conceptual advances at level 2 are the growing child's ability to step mentally outside him- or herself and take a self-reflective or second-person perspective on his or her own thoughts and actions *and* on the realization that others can do so as well. Children now realize that people can feel more than one thing at a time, such as curiosity, fear, and happiness. Because of this, they understand that both they and others are capable of doing things they may not want to do. They also understand that people have a dual social orientation: visible appearance, possibly put on for show, and the *truer*, hidden reality.

Concepts of Relations: Reciprocal   The level 2 child recognizes that each person is unique and therefore that people will have different perspectives.

Box 8–2, continued

A new two-way reciprocity is the hallmark of level 2 concepts of relations. It is a reciprocity of thoughts and feelings, not merely actions. Level 2 children can put themselves in another's shoes and realize the other will do the same. However, they also recognize that the outer appearance–inner reality distinction means that people can deceive others as to their inner states, which places accuracy limits on taking another's inner perspective. So both people are still relatively isolated; each sees self and other but not the relationship system between them.

Level 3: Third-Person or Mutual Perspective Taking

Concepts of Persons: Third-Person   The young adolescent thinking at level 3 sees people as systems of attitudes and values fairly consistent over the long haul, as opposed to randomly changeable assortments of states, as at level 2. The critical conceptual advance is toward ability to take a true third-person perspective, to step outside not only one's own immediate perspective, but outside the self. Level 3 children develop an "observing ego," which enables them simultaneously to see themselves as both actor and object acting and reflecting upon the effects of action and to realize that others do the same.

Concepts of Relations: Mutual   The third-person perspective on relations that is characteristic of level 3 simultaneously includes and coordinates the perspective of self and others; thus, the system or situation and all parties are seen from the third-person or generalized other perspective. People thinking at this level see the need to coordinate reciprocal perspectives and believe social satisfaction, understanding, or resolution must be mutual and coordinated to be genuine and effective. They view relations more as ongoing systems in which thoughts and experiences are mutually shared.

Level 4: In-Depth or Societal Perspective Taking

Concepts of Persons: In-Depth   Two new notions are characteristic of level 4 social perspectives. First, the person understands that actions, thoughts, motives, or feelings are psychologically determined but that they cannot always be comprehended by the observing ego of level 3. Thus, we see, whether or not it is so named, the generation of a notion of the unconscious. Second, there emerges at level 4 a new notion of personality as a product of traits, beliefs, values, and attitudes, a system with its own developmental history.

Concepts of Relations: Societal-Symbolic   The individual now understands that two people can share perspectives at the level of superficial information, of common interests, or of deeper, unverbalized feelings and communication.

Selman's system, like Kohlberg's, provides insight into the way we develop affectively. One system deals with moral decision making, the other with social decision making, but, in a real sense, the two are parallel constructs that often interact. Thus, many social behaviors or interactions have moral components. Similarly, many moral attitudes and values are social in nature. These two systems of thought describe ways in which individuals develop, ways that are contiguous with cognitive development. In educational environments, the ability to interact socially is important. Students can be taught to develop an understanding and appreciation of the social and moral processes that go on around them and thereby achieve a more developed self. Social cognition can be thought of as a skill that enables people to function in social environments in positive and satisfying ways. The nature of behavior that might typify various moral and social development stages is summarized in Table 8–3, which provides greater understanding of the parallelism in the two systems as humans develop across time.

Processing Affective Responses

Many school situations focus on affective learning. Some subject areas, such as social studies, music, and art, may present as much affective as cognitive information. Teachers' expectations of student conduct typically result in their teaching prosocial behaviors and values. In reality, the opportunities for affective learning in school environments are unlimited.

Most theories of affective learning parallel those of cognitive learning, but affective theory is more complex because it invariably involves three processes—affective, cognitive, and behavioral. Attitudes and values involve all these processes; so they have become the primary focus in affectivity. Reinforcement theory and modeling explain how a simple affective response might be learned, and these strategies work. Yet conditioning simple affective responses seems too limited because most human behavior is more complex. Teachers and other adults can be extremely effective classroom models for attitude learning and particularly in the socializing functions within a school. Representational models, such as films, may also be effective (Bandura et al., 1963a). Gagne and Briggs (1979) have observed that human models can also be read about; thus, literature may be an important source for affective learning.

The literature emphasizes parents, teachers, and television as effective models (Hoffman, 1975). Although modeling theory does account for a broader set of behaviors than reinforcement theory, it also fails to get at the interactions in the mind. The extent to which students emulate modeled behavior often gets translated into dichotomies such as right or wrong, prosocial or antisocial, moral or immoral, and acceptable or unacceptable. These dichotomies may more accurately represent behavioral manifestations than interrelationships of affectivity. Theorists tend to investigate affective characteristics in isolation. Although it may increase our understanding of specific affective processes, it does

Table 8–3 Parallel Structured Relations between Selman's Social Role Taking and Five of Kohlberg's Moral Judgment Stages

Social Role-Taking Stage	Moral Judgment Stage
Stage 1 Egocentric Viewpoint (average age range 3–6)	Level I Preconventional *Stage 1* Heteronomous Stage
Child has a sense of differentiation of self and others but fails to distinguish between the social perspective (thoughts, feelings) of other and self. Child can label other's overt feelings but does not see the cause-and-effect relation of reasons to social actions.	Judgments of right and wrong are based on good or bad consequences and not on intentions. Moral choices derive from the subject's wishes that good things happen to self. Child's reasons for his or her choices simply assert the choices, rather than attempting to justify them.
Stage 2 Social-Informational Role Taking (average age range 6–8)	*Stage 2* Individualism, Instrumental Purpose, and Exchange
Child is aware that other has a social perspective based on other's own reasoning, which may or may not be similar to child's. However, child tends to focus on one perspective rather than coordinating viewpoints.	Child focuses on one perspective, that of the authority or the powerful. Child understands, however, that good actions are based on good intention. Beginning sense of fairness as equality of acts.
	Level II Conventional
Stage 3 Self-Reflective Role Taking (average age range 8–10)	*Stage 3* Mutual Interpersonal Expectations, Relationships, and Interpersonal Conformity
Child is conscious that each individual is aware of the other's perspective and that this awareness influences self and other's view of each other. Putting self in other's place is a way of judging his or her intentions, purposes, and actions. Child can form a coordinated chain of perspectives, but cannot yet abstract from this process to the level of simultaneous mutuality.	Moral reciprocity is conceived as the equal exchange of the intent of two persons in relation to one another. If someone has a mean intention toward self, it is right for self to act in kind. Right defined as what is valued by self.
Stage 4 Mutual Role Taking (average age range 10–12)	*Stage 4* Social System and Conscience
Child realizes that both self and other can view each other mutually and simultaneously as subjects. Child can step outside the two-person dyad and view the interaction from a third-person perspective.	Right is defined as the Golden Rule. Do unto others as you would have others do unto you. Child considers all points of view and reflects on each person's motives in an effort to reach agreement among all participants.
Stage 5 Social and Conventional System Role Taking (average age range 12–15+)	Level III Post-Conventional or Principled *Stage 5* Social Contract or Utility and Individual Rights
Person realizes mutual perspective taking does not always lead to complete understanding. Social conventions are seen as necessary because they are understood by all members of the group (the generalized other) regardless of their position, role, or experience.	Right is defined in terms of the perspective of the generalized other or the majority. Person considers consequences of actions for the group or society. Orientation to maintenance of social morality and social order.

Source: Alexander, Roodin, & Gorman (1980), pp. 342–343. By permission of the publisher.

not provide much insight as to the interrelationships. Further, as practitioners, classroom teachers must deal with the total individual. Consequently, they are concerned about how cognitive understanding affects attitudes, how behavior is influenced by attitudes or values, and other combinations.

One way to account for interaction is to identify the components that impact on affectivity. In every expression of an attitude or value, there is a manifestation of the cognitive, affective, and behavioral domains. If a student chooses to take something out of another student's locker (the behavior), he or she would recognize this behavior as either right or wrong, prosocial or antisocial (the affect), and think about the consequences of such behavior (the cognition). The extent to which the individual has learned about and internalized these factors is the primary determiner of his or her behavior (Thornburg, 1981b). Students in the primary grades may make such a decision using a reward-punishment model, but, as they move toward early adolescence, they must choose between satisfying personal wants and needs in contexts where the likelihood of punishment is minimal. Early adolescents and adolescents can begin to establish internal rather than external reasons for exercising moral behavior because of the relative contribution and interplay between their affective, cognitive, and behavioral domains.

Readiness for Affective Learning

Affective learning readiness
The developmental maturity or prerequisite learning needed to acquire additional affective content.

The first interaction component is **readiness for affective learning.** This component is designed to determine to what extent a person is ready to acquire affective learning. One factor that affects readiness is development. We have different capacities at different stages of development. Thus, an adolescent could learn more complex affectivity than a child. Another factor that affects readiness is the skills required to learn an affective idea. Some ideas are complex and are made up of simpler components. Teachers cannot assume that students have the prerequisite background. They must analyze the nature of their affective teaching to determine if a lack of skills precludes readiness.

Readiness may be illustrated with a behavior such as dating. To what extent are junior high school students ready to date? Are they physically, socially, and/or emotionally mature enough? Is dating at this age level an outcome of normal development or is it a result of social pressure, such as school-sponsored dances? Children and adolescents use the school environment to develop meaningful relationships with others. This is a common meeting ground for most students. The school must ascertain if its students are ready for its social activities.

Sources for Affective Learning

Affective learning sources
The individuals, institutions, or other avenues from which people learn affective content.

The second interactive component is **sources for affective learning.** Individuals are heavily influenced by parents, peers, teachers, television, literature, religion, and society, to list just a few such sources. These external sources influence decision making in three ways. First, they often functionally tell someone what to do or how to feel. Second, they are sounding boards off which individuals can gain either greater understanding or approval for their feelings. Third, they can influence thinking enough to affect decision making.

Another interactive component is the **cognitive understanding of affectivity.** This is the conceptual aspect of affectivity. Cognitive development has an important influence on affective learning. The rudiments of affectivity are found in childhood and are learned in the same way that academic content is learned. Students learn affective understanding when multiple instances of an affective behavior are presented to them. Just as we may categorize objects by their physical characteristics, so we might categorize affective behavior by common characteristics, such as right or wrong, fair or unfair, just or unjust. Consistent affective behavior will align itself with our affective categories.

The concept category "deception" illustrates this idea. To some individuals, deception means anything from an outright lie to withholding

Cognitive understanding of
affectivity
The capacity to think about the
affective content being learned.

information from another person. In any given classroom, the understanding of deception will vary tremendously among the students. This is one reason teachers see deception manifested in so many different ways. Let us assume this concept has been taught as "any misrepresentation of the truth," examples of which could include lying, cheating, getting another student in trouble, getting help on homework when you should not have, and saying you did something you did not do. The multiple examples broaden the student's understanding of the concept and provide a better cognitive base for making an affective decision. In short, affective concepts can and should be taught in order to help students deal with a myriad of affective decision-making opportunities.

Decision-Making Opportunities

Affective decision-making opportunity
The extent to which people have the opportunity to actually make personal affective decisions.

Affective decision-making opportunities is the fourth interactive component. They present themselves every day in our lives, both within and outside of school. The appropriateness with which individuals make effective decisions is directly proportional to their decision-making skill.

I shall illustrate the decision-making process with the example of stealing. Going home from school, some children steal something from a convenience store. *Readiness*—what was the psychological or sociological motivation that caused them to steal? Are they ready to accept the legal consequences of detection? *Sources*—was the decision to steal their own? Perhaps friends put them up to it. Perhaps they have stolen things before with no negative consequences. Perhaps their parents know of these activities but do nothing about them. *Cognitive understanding*—where did the idea of stealing come from? To what extent do these children understand the concept of stealing? Perhaps they equate cheating with stealing. Perhaps they have heard parents talk about cheating on their income tax. Perhaps they have been watching television shows where stealing and cheating are treated as commonplace events. The adequacy of the individual's decision making is the summation of these multiple factors. Clearly, affective decision making is not as simple as reward and punishment. Students must be taught such skills at more complex levels.

Affective evaluation
The self-determination of whether or not one's affective behavior has been instrumental in meeting one's needs.

Evaluation of the decision is critical to the entire process. Too often the evaluation is also simplistic, that is, appropriate behavior is judged by its consequences. If we do something wrong but do not get caught, such behavior functionally becomes acceptable. Students must be provided with other types of consequences. For example, how does your behavior make you feel about yourself? What effect does your decision have on others? To what extent does your behavior reflect your beliefs? These types of questions enhance the understanding base for decision making as well as facilitate the internalization of the student's own affective standards.

The components of affective decision making are cyclic. The readiness, sources, and understanding individuals have prior to actual decision making heavily affect the adequacy of the decision. The individual's perception of adequacy in making a decision contributes to readiness,

Affective Learning Components	
Component	**Example**
Readiness	The capacity to learn affectivity must exist if instruction is to be effective.
Sources	Affective content is learned from adults, siblings, peers, literature, and media.
Cognitive understanding	Individuals must be able to think out aspects of affectivity.
Decision making	Affective and cognitive skills are used to make behavioral decisions.
Evaluation	To what extent was the decision satisfying? Individuals must also learn new strategies they can use in subseqent decision-making opportunities.

sources, and understanding for subsequent decision making. The interaction of all components enhances the possibility of responsible and productive decision making at all ages of human development.

Affective Instruction

Goals

It is as necessary to plan affective instruction as it is to plan cognitive instruction. Students will use such learning in many ways long after the academic year ends. Because of the long-term ramifications of affective instruction, it is important that it not be made incidental or "off-the-cuff" teaching.

The same internal process is used for learning affective and cognitive material, but the philosophy underlying the two domains differs. For example, the goal of cognitive instruction is student mastery, which can be measured (by a test, for example). For affective instruction, the goal is to learn the process. You cannot expect all students to feel alike, but they should be able to acquire comparable skills that will help them identify their feelings. In cognitive instruction, we diagnose entry behavior in order to adapt teaching-learning situations. In affective instruction, we assume differences; thus, we cannot as readily predict the outcome of affective instruction.

Like cognitive material, affective material has content. It is the content that helps individuals develop cognitive understanding of things that are

primarily affective. If a goal is to help students gain greater respect for the environment, then it is necessary for a student to understand factors that influence the environment. You could make a convincing emotional appeal to protect the environment, but its impact might be limited if students do not understand what constitutes protection. **Content analysis** reduces the possibility of the teacher interjecting personal biases. In this type of instruction, it is virtually impossible to be bias free, but it is a goal toward which teachers should strive. Instructional materials should also be bias and value free. If biases exist but the material must be used, it is the teacher's responsibility to point them out. The goal of understanding is to increase student decision-making potential, which is limited when bias is introduced.

Teachers must distinguish between attitudes and values because they represent different complexities; yet both manifest themselves regularly in the classroom. It is more likely that students are taught attitudes than values in school. Education provides information and exposure to numerous ideas. As a result, students' ranges of attitudes increase as their sources for attitude learning increase. In school, teachers might try to get a student to accept a value. For example, an objective might be "students will learn how they can increase environmental beauty." Such an objective places value on the environment and students' responsibility to it. Teachers often influence values that are perceived as prosocial or desired.

Teachers also teach preferences for values. They might present multiple values and influence students to select one over the other. For example, "students will determine the values portrayed in a documentary compared to a detective show on television" is asking for a choice of one over the other. Teachers often weigh preferences by emphasis or time spent on one aspect of the presentation compared to the other. Thus, when teachers clearly state that one value is more important or better than another, they are introducing the possibility of bias.

Content analysis
The systematic analysis of the content being taught during affective instruction.

Teachers also teach a sense of commitment by stressing how important values are. Teachers can show the relationship between values and behavior. Students can gain a sense of responsibility for their values and actions by learning the decision-making skills required to act upon their beliefs. For example, an objective that is related to commitment might be "students will learn to speak out on issues they believe in."

The following illustration focuses on the importance of affective learning, including major cognitive components. To teach something from a strictly affective position, without consideration of cognitive input, is probably to distort the affective teaching. A classroom situation will best illustrate attitude learning within the cognitive domain.

The teacher is telling students how to attack a social problem and how to use resources to solve it. The following problem is presented to the class: "What might happen to the physical environment of the United States if industry were to discharge waste products uncontrolled?" The class is then divided into small groups, each of which is to present its solution to the entire class. What behavioral objectives should the teacher hope to accomplish? How might the teacher measure the outcomes of this activity? Here is one possible answer.

I. Behavioral objectives
   A. The student will be able to select, gather, and organize appropriate reference material to solve a given problem and to present to the class as a whole.
      1. The student will be able to use reference guides as aids for selecting desired information.
      2. The student will be able to select information that is relevant to a topic and to reject information that is not.
      3. The student will be able to appraise and select sources from which reliable information may be obtained.
      4. The student will be able to collect and organize data from reference reading in several sources.
      5. The student will be able to arrange data in a logical form for presentation.
   B. The student will be able to present attitudinal statements that represent his or her feelings about the topic.
      1. The student will read materials that shape a positive attitude toward uncontrolled disposal of industrial waste products.
      2. The student will read materials that shape a negative attitude toward uncontrolled disposal of industrial waste products.
      3. The student will thoughtfully consider the opposite positions in the process of determining his or her own attitude toward the topic.
      4. The student will consider the attitudes of other group members in formulating his or her attitude toward the topic.
      5. The student will be able to clearly delineate his or her attitudinal position for classroom presentation.
II. Measuring outcomes
   Evaluation of objective A.1 would be accomplished by direct teacher observation during the period of research work. Should it be discov-

ered that a student is lacking any of the desired capabilities, it would be necessary to provide instruction to overcome the deficiency before the student could proceed with the task. Some evaluation of the behaviors described in most of the other objectives could also be carried on during the research preparation. As the teacher supervises the students at work, an effort should be made to determine if they are correctly appraising information, selecting appropriate materials, and providing guidance where deficiencies are found.

Each group presentation could be evaluated according to a prepared checklist that allows the teacher to note such problems as the use of irrelevant or unreliable material, difficulty in synthesizing materials, lack of consideration of other group members' opinions, and lack of logic in forming attitudes toward the issue.

Providing a similar checklist for each student may assist the teacher in determining what learning has taken place. For example, if a student avoids unreliable information in his or her own presentation and recognizes it in the presentation of another student, the teacher has an even better basis for evaluating the student's ability to appraise the reliability of information. Asking each student to appraise personal performance in terms of stated objectives may also prove helpful to the teacher.

Teacher Attitudes

Teachers may create either positive or negative attitudes toward teaching-learning situations in the classroom. As I suggested earlier, planning is all-important in every classroom situation. If certain attitudes are important enough to teach, they are important enough to be planned. Planning enables the teacher to approach an affective topic positively and to present an exemplary model for the students.

Teachers may not expect or want certain affective behavior and make some kind of controlling response. How teachers respond provides social reinforcement for the student, thus shaping attitudes positively or negatively. These situations, too, can and should be planned for. Teachers can anticipate undesirable affective behaviors, determine alternative appropriate behaviors, and teach students the various situations in which the same affective behaviors may be appropriate or inappropriate. This anticipation and planning make it easier for teachers to maintain positive attitudes in the classroom.

Teacher attitudes toward individual students also have an important effect on student affective behavior and the attitude-learning environment of the classroom. Silberman (1969) found four distinct teacher attitudes toward students upon interviewing thirty-two teachers: attachment, concern, indifference, and rejection.

Attachment Teachers form attachments to students they see as sources of pleasure in their work. The affectionate tie with such students is partially a result of the teacher's appreciation for the child's steadfast

conformity to institutional and teacher expectations. For example, one teacher reports, "He's one that I would be very happy to keep. He enjoys school and certainly is never any trouble or difficulty to me." Another teacher speaks of a girl on whom she is "rather dependent; she is kind of an interpreter of my wishes to the class because she responds to me in the way I want my whole class to." The student subject of the teacher's affection is likely to fulfill personal needs for the teacher and/or make few demands on the teacher's energies. Because students expect fairness from teachers, they should not show distinct favoritism toward any student.

Concern   Teachers direct concern toward students they believe make extensive but appropriate demands. The teacher is willing to serve such children, not only because of a sympathetic response to their needs, but also because of a personal satisfaction that is derived from helping children who are receptive and appreciative. One teacher describes such a child as "my project of the year." Another teacher feels that such a child is "very gratifying to work with because she can see what you're trying to show her and really takes off on it." Thus, a candidate for the teacher's concern is a student who, in the teacher's opinion, is a worthy recipient of his or her professional attention.

Indifference   Teachers feel indifferent toward students who neither excite nor dismay them and therefore remain outside the scope of their involvement. For example, one teacher admits, "I really tend to forget he's in the room. I don't really have feelings toward him one way or the other." Another teacher says, "She doesn't strike me as either a goody-goody or a baddy-baddy." Because such students are in the periphery of the teacher's professional vision, their demands tend to go unnoticed.

Rejection Teachers reject students who are not worthy, in their estimation, of any professional energies. Such students make as many demands as students who concern them, but their demands are perceived as illegitimate or overwhelming and are either ignored or attended to in a counterproductive way. As one teacher testifies, "His arrogance makes him impossible to deal with."

Teacher Characteristics

Elaborate questionnaires, such as the *Minnesota Multiphasic Personality Inventory* (MMPI), the *Edwards Personal Preference Schedule*, the *Guilford-Zimmerman Temperament Survey*, the *Sixteen Personality Factor*

Scale, or the *Minnesota Teacher Attitude Inventory,* are usually used to assess teachers' attitudes. Such tests have produced a tremendous amount of literature on the personality characteristics of teachers, but most results tell more about their personal orientation than their effectiveness as teachers. Still, certain characteristics seem to be typical of effective teachers.

Leeds (1954), in analyzing student likes and dislikes regarding teachers, found that students value impartiality, patience, understanding, helpfulness, kindness, and consideration in their teachers. Similarly, research studies with the *Sixteen Personality Factor Scale* found effective teachers to be outgoing and warmhearted, sensitive, intelligent, conscientious, persevering, staid, rulebound and well controlled, socially precise, self-disciplined, and compulsive.

Some of these traits—warmth and understanding and imagination— seem to be especially effective in the classroom. Writing on the subject of teacher warmth, Ausubel (1968, p. 454) states that teachers who exercise some warmth usually help fulfill children's affiliative drives, especially for elementary school children:

> The warm teacher can be identified with ease by students. He provides emotional support, is sympathetically disposed toward pupils, and accepts them as persons. Characteristically, he distributes much praise and encouragement and tends to interpret pupil behavior as charitably as possible. He is relatively unauthoritarian and is sensitive to pupil's feelings and affective responses.

Ausubel's ideas are supported by the research on preferred teacher characteristics cited in Chapter 2. Students can tell which teachers care for them and seem enthused about teaching, and they like these teachers.

Student Self-Concept

Attitudes are often consistently expressed and internalized until they become part of an individual's value structure and are realized in a tendency to act toward or against something in the environment. A very important variable in this process, and in classroom achievement generally, is **self-concept** (attitudes toward self or the perception one has of self) (Shavelson, Hubner, & Stanton, 1976).

Self-concept
The feelings an individual has about the self.

Many theorists have indicated that, in addition to academic success, social and cultural factors play an extensive role in the development of the self-concept; children's self-concepts are directly related to their psychological environment, that is, the sum total of stimulation that has impinged upon them from conception to the present.

The self-concept is social. We evaluate ourselves as others important in our lives evaluate us. Self-concept is our conception of ourselves as it emerges from social interaction and it is thought to be influenced by three primary sociocultural forces: (a) peers within our immediate sociocultural context, (b) peers representative of a larger societal context (schoolmates), and (c) adult figures who represent the larger community (teachers, parents, relatives). Our self-concept guides our behavior.

Academic Self-Concept   Many writers (Bloom, 1976; Brookover et al., 1967; Griffin, Chassin, & Young, 1981; Maslow, 1962; Rogers, 1961; Shavelson & Bolus, 1982) consider an adequate self-concept to be the primary variable in learning and behavior. Bodwin (1957) found a positive correlation between immature self-concept and reading disability among third- and sixth-grade students. Lumpkin (1959) found that the greater the self-concept, the greater the reading achievement level among fifth graders he studied. Research has found similar relationships between self-concept and achievement at the kindergarten level (Wattenberg & Clifford, 1964) through high school (Brookover, Erickson, & Joiner, 1967; Thornburg, 1974). Research on self-concept and achievement may be best represented by Sears (1940), who commented that children's behavior in task situations is affected by success or failure and by the children's feeling about themselves in such situations.

Coopersmith (1967) observed that the theory and research evidence on self-concept is rather vague and intuitive. This is true partly because the dimensions of self are rather difficult to isolate, then empirically research, and partly because the impact of academic events on the self are highly varied among students. Bloom (1976, p. 153) contends that some individuals need more successful or unsuccessful academic experiences than others to affect their self-concept. "Given a sufficient number of unsuccessful learning experiences, almost everyone must eventually succumb to an acceptance of a self view about learning which is negative or inadequate. Similarly, for the successful encounters with learning experiences, given enough of them, one must eventually come to a positive view of oneself as a learner."

Numerous studies have attempted to measure factors influencing self-concept. Bassotti and Bredderman (1979) compared students in high school vocational programs under two conditions: those who enrolled in vocational programs within their regular high school and those who attended a designated vocational high school. Results indicated a stronger self-concept among those students who attended the vocational high school. The researchers thought variations in school programs were a factor in the differences obtained. Brookover et al. (1967) found that, when IQ is controlled, there is significant, positive correlation between self-concept and academic performance. Student behavior within the academic setting was largely determined by academic ability and students' perceptions of how significant others viewed them.

Several studies among elementary school age students by Coopersmith (1959, 1967; Coopersmith & Feldman, 1974) have demonstrated a positive relationship between self-concept and school achievement.

Parsons, Adler, and Kaczala (1982) researched the attitudes and beliefs about math achievement in students in grades five through eleven and their parents. Parent beliefs were more directly related to their children's self-concepts and expectancies than to their past math performance. Parents' perceptions of and expectations for their children were also related to their children's perceptions of parental beliefs and to the children's self- and task-perception.

Strathe and Hash (1979) investigated the effects of the alternative school in enhancing self-concept by comparing junior and senior high students enrolled in such a program. Results indicated an increase in self-concept among the junior high students but not the senior high ones. The authors conclude that early identification of academic problems is essential if alternative school experiences are to facilitate an enhancement of self.

In summary, studies have shown that self-concept is related to academic achievement. Although general self-concept is distinct from academic self-concept, data show they are correlated (Shavelson & Bolus, 1982). A positive general self-concept might influence a student's academic self-concept, which, in turn, might lead to successful academic experiences in school.

Minority Self-Concept   We cannot study behavior outside of its social context. Carroll (1945) found that children from lower socioeconomic positions tend to aspire to ideals of personal beauty and fame, not to the moral and intellectual qualities characteristic of the middle-class child. This finding suggests differences in the self-concepts of these two classes. Hawk (1967) found that a child's socioeconomic status greatly influences academic success, which results in either a positive or negative self-concept.

There is much evidence in the literature on the effects of sociocultural factors on the self-concept, but that regarding the extent and force with which these factors influence the individual appears to be contradictory. Kvaraceus (1965) and Deutsch (1965) declared that the inadequate view disadvantaged children have of themselves is shaped by the reflected appraisals of society. In studies involving the self-concept of minority group students, Coleman et al. (1966) found that the mean self-concept of Mexican-American children was significantly lower than that of both Black and Anglo children. McDaniel's (1967) findings indicated that the self-concept of the Mexican-American child is significantly below that of the White child but not that of the Black child. Studies by Havighurst and Moorefield (1967), Long and Henderson (1968), and Henton and Johnson (1964) found a significantly higher self-concept for White children.

Brookover et al. (1967) studied the relationship of self-concept of ability to school achievement. They define "self-concept of ability" as "those definitions a student holds of his ability to achieve in academic tasks as compared to others" (p. 13). In studying youth in grades seven to eleven, Brookover postulated that, among potentially successful students, academic achievement is artificially limited by the child's self-concept of ability to achieve. Brookover is persuaded that this inadequate self-concept is a consequence of perceived negative evaluations by significant others. Research indicates that self-concept of ability functions independently of measured intelligence in influencing academic adjustment and is a better predictor of academic achievement. He also found that positive changes in evaluations by significant others will raise the child's self-concept of ability and positively influence academic achievement.

Williams and Byers (1968) studied the differences between Black and White self-esteem, using the *Tennessee Self-Concept Scale*. The Black sample exhibited significantly greater defensive distortions of their self-description than did the White students. In general, the results showed that the Black adolescent is negative in self-perception, quite defensive in self-description, and lacking a clear, consistent picture of him or herself.

Awareness of ethnic differences seems to be solidified by age seven; so minority children recognize the cultural and/or social class differences throughout their elementary school years and become more cognizant of them and less sure about themselves than members of the dominant culture as they progress through school. This causes many minority youth to have common, identifiable traits, such as poor self-image, frustration about academic programs, and disillusionment.

Self-Esteem   Although the terms *self-concept* and *self-esteem* are used interchangeably, Anderson (1981) notes that **self-esteem** is the affective component of self-concept. Rosenberg (1965, p.5) defines self-esteem as the "evaluation which an individual makes and customarily maintains with regard to himself; it expresses an attitude of approval or disapproval." In order to distinguish self-esteem from self-concept, keep in mind that self-esteem is the evaluative dimension of the self. In essence, we affectively evaluate our abilities and attributes and consequently form an attitude of approval or disapproval of ourselves (Anderson, 1981; Openshaw, Thomas, & Rollins, 1981; Rosenberg, 1979). In a sense, our self-esteem is an indication of our self-acceptance. Gecas (1971) found that a person's feelings of competence, effectiveness, personal influence, personal virtue, and moral worth are the essence of a positive self-esteem.

Several factors are thought to contribute to self-esteem. The primary contributor is **continuity of experience.** Whatever the avenue of expression, if we can maintain stability, it gives a sense of self-esteem and power and results in a positive affect (Franks & Marolla, 1977; Simmons, Blyth, Van Cleave, & Bush, 1979). Rosenberg (1975) believes that dissonance alters self-esteem and that social class and educational experiences are two major sources of consonance/dissonance. For example, he found that middle- or upper-middle-class children attending lower-class schools had significantly lower self-esteem than middle- or upper-middle-class children attending higher-class schools.

The research in self-esteem has been focused heavily at the secondary school level, particularly in relation to the change processes accompanying changes in organizational structures. In particular, the work of Rosenberg, Simmons, and Blyth (Blyth, Simmons, & Bush, 1978; Blyth, Simmons, & Carlton-Ford, 1983; Savin-Williams & Demo, 1983; Simmons et al., 1979; Simmons, Brown, Bush, & Blyth, 1978; Simmons & Rosenberg, 1975; Simmons, Rosenberg, & Rosenberg, 1973) has created the impetus for examining school structural effects on early adolescent self-esteem. In each of these studies, self-esteem was used as the dependent research variable. Other social or environmental events or perceptions were used to predict the effect they might have on self-esteem. Essentially, the research of Simmons and her colleagues has demonstrated

Self-esteem
The extent to which one approves of his or her own self and actions.

Continuity of experience
The consistent expression of oneself over an extended period of time.

that early adolescents who move into a grade seven through nine school structure experience lower self-esteem than those moving into grade seven in a kindergarten through grade eight school. Simmons et al. (1979) found that almost half (45 percent) of the seventh-grade girls in the junior high had low self-esteem compared to 35 percent of the seventh-grade girls in the kindergarten through grade eight school. Further, only 23 percent of the junior high boys had low self-esteem.

Research by Protinsky and Farrier (1980) and by Thornburg and Jones (Jones, 1981; Jones & Thornburg, 1982; Thornburg & Jones, 1982) has focused more on development than education as the factor affecting self-esteem. Protinsky and Farrier (1980) found the greatest instability in self-esteem to be among nine- to eleven-year-olds, with a gradual increase in stability from ages twelve through eighteen. This finding does not contradict the Simmons research, although it suggests that any change that occurs is likely to occur prior to transition from an elementary to a junior high school.

The Thornburg studies were designed somewhat differently. Age, grade, and sex were all major concerns. These studies investigated overall school structure differences as well as age and grade differences. Five major findings have emerged. First, after investigating students in grades four through nine in several different overall school configurations (such as four through six, seven through eight, and kindergarten through eight), there was no evidence of differences in self-esteem within any structure.

Second, after comparing student self-esteem by grade level, it was observed that self-esteem gradually lowered each year from grade four to

nine. There were slight but nonsignificant gains in self-esteem from grade six to seven for girls and from grade eight to nine for boys.

Third, students who changed school structures between grades five and six and between grades six and seven were investigated. Students moving into a six to eight school experienced lower self-esteem than those sixth graders who remained in a kindergarten through eight school. However, no lowering of self-esteem was found among seventh graders in a seven to nine school, a finding contrary to the Simmons and Blyth studies (Blyth et al., 1978; Thornburg & Jones, 1982).

Fourth, looking at the relationship of age and self-esteem revealed a gradual decrease in self-esteem as students became older. In fact, self-esteem was lower at each successive age than at each successive grade. In essence, eleven-years-olds in the sixth grade had a lower self-esteem than twelve-year-olds in the sixth grade. This can be interpreted as an indication that development more than education is playing a significant role in determining self-esteem.

Fifth, regardless of whether early adolescent self-esteem is compared by age or grade, girls consistently report higher self-esteem, a finding consistent with some research (Protinsky & Farrier, 1980) and in contradiction with others (Blyth et al., 1978, 1983; Simmons et al., 1979).

Affective education is a very important aspect of the school curriculum. It is a difficult dimension to work with because of its magnitude, the limited training teachers have, the belief that the school's only role is academic instruction, and the fear of reprimand from the community if the schools get involved in selected areas of affective instruction. Writing within the context of health education, a major affective area, Ellen Thornburg (1981, p. 160) makes the following observation:

> There are many factors which contribute to and maintain the lack of effective programs. Because of the controversial nature of specific content areas in health education, administrators are often hesitant, even though they recognize the pertinency and immediacy of the need for these programs, to place themselves in a position of vulnerability. They often are concerned about a bombardment from a minority of parents or special interest constituents which inevitably attack any attempt to institute health education programs.
>
> These highly verbal special interest factions attack the teaching of everything from proper nutrition to drug/alcohol education, mental health, personal awareness, and the human body. This, of course, does not even touch on areas dealing with sexuality and family life education. It is interesting to speculate on the process which allows such a small verbal minority to effectively dictate the educational direction of so many others, who because of their lack of organization and verbosity, do not represent themselves adequately in defense of health education programs. The inability to place the intimidating forces in proper perspective is costing us dearly, both monetarily, and in terms of the lives of our young people and their families.

John Naisbitt (1982, p. 53), in his provocative book, *Megatrends,* stresses that, in a highly technological society, the importance of high personal contact is not diminished:

> When we fall into the trap of believing or, more accurately, hoping that technology will solve all our problems, we are actually abdicating the [high touch] of personal responsibility. Our technological fantasies illustrate the

point. We are always awaiting the new magical pill that will enable us to eat all the fattening food we want, and not gain weight; burn all the gasoline we want, and not pollute the air; live as immoderately as we choose, and not contract either cancer or heart disease. In our minds, at least, technology is always on the verge of liberating us from personal discipline and responsibility. Only it never does and it never will. The more high technology around us, the more the need for human touch.

Affective education should not be underplayed. It is an important issue that educators must address, particularly if they are interested in adequately educating students to respond effectively to and live in an increasingly diverse and complex world.

Students' Developmental Characteristics

Since Chapter 6, I have been discussing different aspects of human development that represent major ways people learn to function and interact with their environment. Development follows the same sequence in everyone, although rates may differ. These differential rates create the greatest variance in the school environment. Schools must accommodate all students and effectively instruct them. These varying rates break down into four major shifts in cognitive capacity between kindergarten and twelfth grade. Each shift has its corollary social capacity.

Kindergarten through Second Grade

Students in these early grades have limited reasoning capacities. They are in a precomplete logic stage because all the requirements for conceptual and diverse reasoning are not yet in place. They may intuitively do something, but they rarely can explain their action or why something resulted. For example, some first-grade mathematics texts ask students to compare two sets and tell which is larger. One set may contain four baseballs, the other, three basketballs. Unless the student is instructed to count the number of objects in a set to determine larger or greater than, the student may perceive three basketballs to be larger than four baseballs. Perception is not a property of a set.

Socially, early school children are conforming, generally in relation to accepted school practices. There may be some defiance, however, often because a child may not want to do something. Children at these ages do not reason out behavior and cognitively select an alternative; their intellectual and social development has not yet progressed that far.

Third through Fifth Grade

Logic and reasoning are completed during these school years, although thought depends on concrete examples. The transition from the previous stage to this is relatively easy because it is an extension of concrete language. Students can now build more elaborate concepts and applications. They can explain how phenomena in their environment work. They demonstrate the ability to monitor their own learning when reminded to do so (Brown, Campione, & Day, 1981), although Flavell and Wellman (1977) found that older children monitor their behavior better than younger children. Student capacity in these grades is often greater than teachers' demands.

Students in these grades can now apply their general logic and reasoning to social contexts (social cognition) and engage in discussions on social norms, values, and roles. Because they can construct alternatives, they are now more likely to challenge adults. Not only may they defy, they may honestly believe that a particular behavior being requested of them is inappropriate. General conformity reduces, although it remains dominant.

In grades three through five, students are more likely to ask why something is important for them to learn or how they can use information or skills in nonschool contexts. Enthusiasm for school may wane if students cannot see the importance of what they are doing, particularly because their out-of-school activities are increasing and diversifying.

Sixth through Eighth Grade

Although students' concrete thinking processes are very well defined, this transition is particularly difficult, more so than at any other developmental period or school structural change. Reasons include students' physical growth and cognitive and social development.

Major growth occurs during these grades, the magnitude of which is unequaled during any other school period. Significant increases in height and weight and secondary sex characteristics change the child into an adolescent (Petersen et al., 1983).

Although concrete language and thinking is dominant, there is a gradual acquisition of abstract thought, a second major symbol system. Teachers must realize that students in grades six through eight are not predominately abstract thinkers and avoid making their expectations for them too high. Textbook materials at these grades are also often more abstract than the students' vocabulary. Finally, in regard to learning, many students are mistaught because teachers are not adequately prepared and teaching resources do not match cognitive capacity.

As early adolescents increase their social interests, developing friendships with others is a critical aspect of growth. In contrast to students at earlier grade levels, peers are vital to middle level students. They have learned over the years that friends are important, and what were changeable friendships in the primary grades take on more solidarity by the middle level grades.

Students' behavioral potential has increased tremendously, with most behaviors being adolescentlike rather than childlike. Studies on preteen alcohol and drug use, sexual behavior, preteen pregnancy, runaways, and delinquency all attest to an increasingly complex social and behavioral environment. Their capacity to explore is greater than ever before, and students may perceive school as negative, too confining, more social than academic, and the opportune environment to act out new skills or behavior, particularly when given adequate peer support. The time period of grades six through eight may be the most misunderstood, misprepared, and mismatched of all formal education experiences. Every aspect of education must devote more time to this age range and develop better and more appropriate programs.

Ninth through Twelfth Grade

High school students are complex, highly abstract thinkers who are capable of an unlimited range of functions. Their major limitations are imposed by poor middle level learning of abstract vocabulary and reasoning. Educators must keep in mind that logic and reasoning are the dominant thought structures, which are primarily represented through abstractness. There are generally two thinking modes in high school: one at grades nine and ten, the other at grades eleven and twelve. During the first two years of high school, students are completing their intellectual development and learning how to extend many thoughts into multiple content areas. By the last two years, students are more future oriented and applied thought is important.

Thus, high schools must pursue two major thrusts. First, we must help students complete their diverse and comprehensive intellectual development. Second, we must help them learn how to integrate their thought processes into applied and future settings so they may become competent, functional beings in society. This is an important area that cannot be ignored. Magnet schools in specific skill areas are an attempt to meet this need.

Adolescents are more socially intense than any other school-age child. Although the behavioral domain opens up during middle/junior high school, the consistency and complexity of behavior, including the manifestation of dysfunctional social behavior, is apparent in high school. For example, the average age of the first date is thirteen, but the complexity of dating is a high school phenomenon. Although children may be first arrested for delinquent acts as young as 12.4 years, chronic delinquents are high schoolers. High school students are much more established social beings than ever before, partly due to general earlier socialization. It is important to educate in social skills, interaction processes, and decision making if we expect education to have any impact on adolescent social behavior.

Developing a Student Advisement Program

In recent years, student advisement programs (such as advisor-advisee, homebase, walking advisement, and advisory based) have been developed in secondary schools. These are not career guidance programs, but programs that deal with affective content, how students learn about many aspects of their environment. Their primary purpose is to increase the affective side of education and to provide improved contact with students at the secondary level. This concept is a basic component of the middle school movement.

Several educators have suggested goals for advisement programs, such as to

1. Provide increased opportunities for social and emotional development

2. Enhance interpersonal relationships

3. Provide an adult advocate for every student

4. Aid in improved communication among teachers, students, and parents

5. Establish rapport and a sense of caring

6. Create a feeling of belonging and importance

7. Serve as a rallying point for improving the total school atmosphere

8. Provide referral, advice, and information to students as needed (McEwin, 1981)

These programs add to teacher's duties. In some cases, teachers are unsure about the wide range of affective content with which they may have to deal in such a program. Thus, in some schools, this concept has worked well; in others, it has failed because of teachers' attitudes toward the program. The classroom teacher's role includes the following tasks:

1. Establish a personal, caring relationship with advisees

2. Be available to discuss matters of concern and interest to students

3. Serve as a primary referral source to counselors, nurses, and other specialists

4. Act as a sounding board for student problems

5. Serve as a resource to help students make decisions related to educational planning, personal and social growth, and career planning

6. Have direct input into the social and emotional education of students (Doda, 1976; Tennant, 1981; Toepfer, 1981)

Advisement programs should not be unstructured. Although they are informal learning environments, they must be planned. To carry out such an activity without advanced planning is to increase the risk of students and teachers spending time talking about ideas at a superficial level. This educational dimension should teach affective skills and options as clearly as other areas teach cognitive skills and options. Defining topics that might be discussed during a given two- to three-week period, informing students of topics to be covered, and sending an information sheet home to parents will allow students to think about various topics and possibly even discuss them with their parents before they are discussed in school. Such topics as developing social relationships, dating, divorce, impact of media and technology, alcohol and drug use, marriage, peer pressures, family communication, cultural differences, personal responsibility, sexual behavior, the meaning of life, and respect for others could be discussed in an advisement program.

Assigned readings and occasional projects or papers could be used to involve students in the topics and, when appropriate, evaluate their progress. Students should be taught cognitive information so they can understand topic components, then affective information so they can see how it relates to their lives. In affective education, teachers are essentially looking at the *process* by which students work through ideas, not at the *product* or the end result. Teachers should evaluate the adequacy of a decision, the extent to which students explore or account for alternatives, the extent to which students think an option will fulfill a personal need system, and the logical progression of student thought.

Secondary school students require effective counseling and guidance as they move from the protective environment of the elementary school to the more impersonal secondary school environment and from their childhood dependencies to their adolescent independencies. Well-planned and well-implemented advisory programs can increase students' understanding of the affective dimension of their lives, build a broader context to which to relate all learning experiences, and increase the potential for improving the quality of life.

249

Damon, W., & Hart, D. (1982). The development of self-understanding from infancy through adolescence. *Child Development, 53,* 841–864.

This review constructs from the psychological literature a descriptive account of self-understanding development between infancy and adolescence. It begins by distinguishing self-understanding from other aspects of self-concept, particularly self-esteem. The authors argue that a developmental model of self-understanding is necessary in assessing children's self-esteem. The article also proposes a developmental model that outlines genetic and conceptual relations among different aspects of self-understanding.

Eisenberg, N., Cameron, E., Tryon, K., & Dodez, R. (1981). Socialization of prosocial behavior in the preschool classroom. *Developmental Psychology, 17,* 773–782.

This study investigated the socialization of prosocial behavior in the classroom and reciprocity in young children's social encounters. The naturally occurring behaviors of thirty-three preschool children were videotaped in the classroom. Instances of prosocial, defensive, and social behaviors and peer and teacher reactions to them were coded. Results indicated that peers respond more favorably to each other than the teacher does. Further, teachers were more likely to react positively to girls who exhibit high levels of compliant prosocial behaviors.

Ford, M. E. (1982). Social cognition and social competence in adolescence. *Developmental Psychology, 18,* 323–340.

This research study asked whether social cognition is related to effective social behavior. Students in grades nine and twelve participated in the study. Social behaviors that would propel one toward social goals were defined. Nine measures of social cognition were used to predict this relationship. Results indicate that these predictors (measures) do account for most of the findings regarding social competence. Results indicate that social competence represents a domain of human functioning that is partly distinguishable from a cognitive or general competence domain.

Lazarus, R. S. (1982). Thoughts on the relations between emotion and cognition. *American Psychologist, 37,* 1019–1024.

This paper argues that thought is a necessary condition of emotion. It opposes the position taken by Zajonc, which reflects two widespread misunderstandings about what is meant by cognitive processes in emotion: (1) that a cognitive appraisal of the significance of an encounter for one's well-being must occur in fixed stages through the information processing of initially meaningless inputs from the environment and (2) that such an appraisal is necessarily deliberate, rational, and conscious. Some of the phylogenetic and ontogenetic implications of a cognitive theory are discussed briefly.

Nucci, L. P. (1982). Conceptual development in the moral and conventional domains: Implications for value education. *Review of Educational Research, 52,* 93–122.

This review article focuses on research and theory indicating that individuals' conceptions of social convention and morality are constructed within distinct developmental systems emerging from qualitatively different environmental interactions. The research indicates that people of all ages distinguish between those actions (moral) having an intrinsic effect upon the rights or well-being of others and actions (social convention) whose pro-

priety is determined by the societal context. In addition, the research demonstrates that concepts about morality and convention follow independent and distinct developmental patterns.

Weiner, B., Graham, S., Stern, P., & Lawson, M. E. (1982). Using affective cues to infer causal thoughts. *Developmental Psychology, 18,* 278–286.

Two experiments were conducted to look at the affective reactions of a teacher toward failing students. Linkages between the affect-attribution pairings were anger—lack of effort, guilt—poor teaching, surprise—lack of effort, and pity—low ability. The studies included individuals from age five through college. Findings showed that young children associate anger—lack of effort and older subjects associate pity—lack of ability. These findings were interpreted in light of a person's self-concept.

The Design
of Instruction

Since the 1950s, educators and psychologists have been to trying to discover if behavioral objectives facilitate instruction. Disagreement has focused around two main issues: (1) whether behaviors can be identified as precisely as behavioral objectives imply and (2) whether they stifle teacher-learner interactions. To air current thinking on the issue, Hillside Teachers College sponsored a public debate with three leading educators presenting their views of the role of behavioral objectives in the educational process.

The first presentation was by Dr. Barbara Tokay, an educational researcher at Hillside. She asserted that behavioral objectives are essential to effective instruction and challenged the audience to evaluate the unsystematic way the educational process is carried out. According to Dr. Tokay, behavioral objectives help define content and articulate its instructional sequence. She also emphasized the importance of evaluation, claiming that educators fail to evaluate effectively. Dr. Tokay believes that behavioral objectives give an overall strategy that increases the potential for students to learn.

Dr. Peter Donaldson, a professor of educational psychology at nearby Merriam College, presented the second point of view. He argued that behavioral objectives oversimplify the learning process and attempt to control student behavior. Asserting that the essence of the teaching-learning process is to help students understand and develop strategies for academic and nonacademic encounters, he suggested that it is probably impossible to write behavioral objectives for every academic contingency and surely so for nonacademic situations. Dr. Donaldson thinks that teacher and student initiative decreases if class time is scheduled tightly or systematically and embraces the principles of discovery learning, arguing that students need unstructured time to think and explore the possibilities within a learning environment.

The third speaker, Ms. Jill Steinman, the director of curriculum for the Hillside public school system, took a compromise position. First she stated that both positions have merit within different instructional contexts. Then she suggested that a major limitation of the discussion was that it treated behavioral objectives as the heart of the instructional process. She suggested that, in fact, teacher behavior is the essence of instructional design, and behavioral objectives play a supporting role. Behavioral objectives may serve a more useful role in the planning (preinstructional) phase than in the instructional phase. Ms. Steinman

253

considers teacher flexibility the key to successful teaching. Thus, although behavioral objectives provide a sense of direction, they should not restrict teacher behavior. A broad objective can lend itself to exploratory learning. Teachers cannot and should not observe and monitor everything that occurs in a classroom. Thus, she essentially endorsed the use of objectives as long as teachers understand their purpose and do not feel duty bound to fulfill an instructional objective that is no longer useful.

The debate provided the audience with various opinions of the importance and purpose of behavioral objectives. The moderator did not allow the question and answer session that followed to be dominated by a single point of view; so audience members gained an array of strategies to make more appropriate educational decisions. This chapter considers which teacher behaviors can help students learn. It includes discussions of:

- *Educational theory*
- *Operationalizing instruction*
- *Assessing teacher effectiveness*

Educational Theory

Although theories have been useful in describing the learning process, they cannot help teachers select strategies for instruction. Teachers are assumed to be the primary reason for learner behaviors; so identifying what they do when students learn is seen as the necessary initial step in improving the educational process.

Theory of instruction
Teacher behavior designed to influence student learning.

A **theory of instruction** is the way the teacher influences a pupil to learn. According to Bruner (1966, p. 40), a theory of instruction is *prescriptive* because it establishes rules concerning the best way to teach knowledge and skills, *normative* because it "sets the criteria and states the conditions for meeting [these rules]," and *descriptive* because it tells us what has happened in the instructional process. A theory of instruction provides procedures by which teachers may ensure learning. At a minimum, it should accomplish five tasks.

1. *It should specify the teaching-learning experience that will be most effective in bringing about student learning.* For example, if you are teaching a concept, you must present unfamiliar examples of it in order for the learner to generalize from the familiar to the unfamiliar. If you can apply the concept to the students' environment, it is likely to be more relevant and meaningful.

2. *It should organize a body of knowledge in such a way that it will be learned more easily.* For example, teachers should arrange instructional activities from simple to complex, from nonconceptual to conceptual. If teachers identify the prerequisite skills necessary for learning what is currently being instructed, then the body of knowl-

edge is more likely to be organized in ways to maximize student learning.

3. *A theory of instruction should incorporate basic learning principles.* For example, if you use reinforcement, your strategy should include the types of reinforcement, the frequency and amount of reinforcement, and the extent to which you will encourage learners to be self-reinforcing.

4. *It should assess students' individual differences.* It is important to do some diagnostic testing or pretesting to ascertain the students' entering behaviors. Knowing something about each student's learning rate, demand for reinforcement, motivational level, and general or specific ability will help you adjust the instruction to maximize *every* student's learning potential.

5. *A theory of instruction should systematically evaluate student learning in order to determine when to continue the instructional sequence and when to do supplemental teaching.* For example, relate any form of assessment to the content taught. If a student gets fourteen out of twenty problems right, or 70 percent, on a math test, you might move on to the next unit or concept. But if the test had ten multiplication and ten division problems, you should assess how many of each a student answered correctly. If a student got ten out of ten multiplication problems right, you can assume he or she has mastered the concept. If the student correctly answered only four of the ten division problems, he or she has not mastered this concept and you should reteach it.

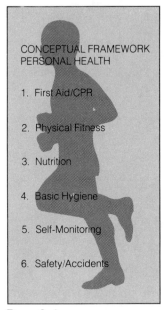

CONCEPTUAL FRAMEWORK
PERSONAL HEALTH

1. First Aid/CPR

2. Physical Fitness

3. Nutrition

4. Basic Hygiene

5. Self-Monitoring

6. Safety/Accidents

Figure 9–1
*Broad conceptual framework for
defining components of personal
health*

Gagne (1977a) has suggested that the goal of programs of instruction is to affect the learners who attend them so that they acquire some new knowledge, skills, or attitudes that increase their behavioral capacity. What events of instruction influence learners? If learning is an internal process and instruction is an external process, how can teaching-learning environments be arranged to maximize teacher effectiveness and learner potential?

There are some essential characteristics of teaching-learning environments that should be in place, whatever instructional model you use. The first is the content of what is being taught. Content is the heart of the curriculum. **Curriculum** is the set of experiences designed to influence learners to accomplish educational goals (Hosford, 1973). Content is the substance of the goals. All subject areas have content. Thus, the specification of appropriate content and an effective delivery system are prerequisites to utilizing instructional design in the classroom.

Articulation of content is a second essential prerequisite characteristic. Articulation is developing a conceptual overview of what should constitute a course of study in a subject area, then sequencing it to effect instruction and learning. Figure 9–1 is a conceptual framework for a personal health component within a health education program. Its topics are comprehensive and serve as the framework for developing the subtopics.

One of the subtopics under personal health is safety. Figure 9–2 illustrates how the general topic of safety can be broken into content areas. In order to articulate this content, a sequence chart is devised to show when a particular content area will be initially taught (I), when extended teaching will occur (E), and when the particular content area should be completed or mastered (M). This scope (content areas) and sequence (grade-level arrangements) facilitate planning instruction at different grade levels. Because most learning has prerequisites (Gagne, 1977a; Reigeluth, Merrill, Wilson, & Spiller, 1980), the better sequenced instruction is, the greater the likelihood that teaching and learning behaviors will build on each other.

Synthesizing is the third important characteristic of the instructional process. **Synthesis of content** pulls things together or demonstrates the interrelationships among content. Reigeluth et al. (1980) address the issue of meaningful learning when they contend that synthesizing helps show the relationship of something to the larger picture, an idea consistent with much of Ausubel's (1968) and Bruner's (1960) perspectives. Reigeluth et al. (1980, p. 196) suggest that meaningful understanding has the following advantages for learners:

1. They will have better long-term retention of those parts.

2. They will gain an additional kind of knowledge, one usually more valuable than segmented information.

3. They will enjoy the learning more.

4. They will be more motivated to learn the subject-matter content.

The fourth prerequisite to engaging in systematic instruction is to be aware of the **interactive effect** of instruction. Teachers not only influ-

**Personal Health
Safety Education**

	K–2	3–5	6–8	9–12
60 Traffic Safety				
Walking	I	E	M	
Riding	I	M		
Operating MV		I	E	M
61 Home				
Home Safety	I	M		
Hazardous Products	I	E	M	
High-Risk Area	I	M		
Fire	I	E	M	
Emergency Procedure and Help	I	E	M	
Child Care	I	E	E	M
62 School				
School Grounds	I	E	M	
Instructional Areas	I	E	E	M
Lunchroom	I	E	M	
Emergency Procedures	I	E	M	
Consideration for Safety of Others	I	E	E	M
63 Recreational				
Poisonous Plants	I	E	E	M
Animals / Insects	I	E	E	M
Weather Conditions	I	E	E	M
Water Safety	I	E	E	M
Hiking / Camping	I	E	E	M
Weaponry	I	E	E	M

Figure 9–2
Delineation of specific content areas in health education across a multigrade-level continuum

Behavioral ecology
Experiences that result from the
interaction of students and teachers
with their environment.

ence students; students also influence students, and students influence teachers. Doyle (1978) has described this process as **behavioral ecology,** the idea that teaching-learning behaviors in a classroom may be seen as the result of interactions among individuals and between individuals and their environment. The interactions are all part of learning; thus, students as well as teachers may facilitate learning in others (Copeland, 1980; Noble & Nolan, 1976; Willems, 1973).

Many factors affect the quality of education a student receives. The ones I have discussed describe the teacher's need to be effective. As Hosford (1973, p. 10) has suggested, the "teacher is still the very heart of the instructional process and therefore must be the *final* concern of a theory of instruction, while the learner remains the *central* concern."

Several approaches to instruction have been advanced in the past few years. They vary considerably because of widely differing opinions of what constitutes instructional design (Carroll, 1963; Glaser, 1962). Gage (1964) contends that we should not search for one approach to instruction because teaching includes too many processes, activities, and behaviors to be narrowed into a single model. He suggests, instead, that we analyze and categorize the various elements of teaching and use these categories, separately and as a whole, as instructional processes. Gage proposes four broad categories for analysis:

1. *Types of teaching activities.* Here Gage includes explaining, demonstrating, guiding, housekeeping, record keeping, assignment making, and curriculum planning.

2. *Types of educational objectives.* These types are classified as cognitive, affective, and psychomotor. Gage suggests that teaching processes can also be classified according to the objectives by analyzing the content and determining which is most relevant.

Concept Summary 9–1

Elements of Teaching		
Element	**Description**	**Example**
Teacher Activity	This aspect involves the variety of things teachers do in the actual instructional process.	The teacher conducts an experiment as a means of helping students learn differences between weight and volume.
Educational Activity	The teacher states what behaviors are expected of students as a result of the day's class session.	The student will be able to explain the effect of weight and volume in the displacement of water.
Analyze Learning	The teacher must learn how to analyze and critique his or her classroom behavior.	Retrospectively, the teacher will evaluate how effectively he or she used reinforcement in teaching a concept.

3. *Types of learning.* Gage contends that, if learning can be analyzed, then so can teaching.

4. *Types of learning theories.* Gage observes that some learning theories conceive learning to be a matter of conditioning, with rewards or punishment serving as reinforcers of independent or response-dependent stimuli. Other theorists, such as Bandura, emphasize that learning consists of identification with a model. Gage believes that each learning theory can suggest a corresponding approach to teaching.

Operationalizing Instruction

Thornburg (1973b) proposed an instructional model that is a pragmatic framework from which to instruct (Figure 9–3). He proposed an initial distinctive step, identifying student needs. This process is important if step two, writing student behavioral objectives, is to be accomplished. Objectives should be based on student need, not just on teacher preference. The third and critical step, developing a teaching strategy, is founded on learning theory. The final step is assessing student behavioral change. Student learning can be measured through teacher-made tests, standardized tests, and teacher observation. I use this model to demonstrate how to design instruction systematically to maximize teacher and learner potential.

Identifying Student Needs

Students bring personal and performance needs into the classroom. **Personal needs** are their internal motives or reasons for learning. Within a teaching-learning environment, most students need to strive for competence (achievement). They may be particularly interested in a specific subject. For example, artistic students may show more interest in the creative aspects of the school environment than in its structured aspects. These types of interests or needs are often labeled "motivation." I discuss

Personal need
The psychological reason for learning that students bring into the classroom.

Figure 9–3
Thornburg's interactive instructional model

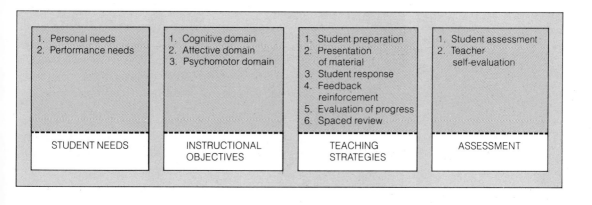

1. Personal needs 2. Performance needs	1. Cognitive domain 2. Affective domain 3. Psychomotor domain	1. Student preparation 2. Presentation of material 3. Student response 4. Feedback reinforcement 5. Evaluation of progress 6. Spaced review	1. Student assessment 2. Teacher self-evaluation
STUDENT NEEDS	INSTRUCTIONAL OBJECTIVES	TEACHING STRATEGIES	ASSESSMENT

them in Chapter 11. Personal needs are an important variable in student learning.

Some writers (Gagne, 1977a; Kibler et al., 1974) think teachers should consider student needs along with their own behavioral objectives for the student. However, this may not be feasible. The process of identifying student needs involves the teacher's attempt to judge whether students have the necessary learning prerequisites—the intellectual skills or concepts—for the ensuing behavioral objectives. In other words, the student needs referred to here are **performance needs**—the deficiencies or sufficiencies of the accumulated knowledge and skills that students bring to the classroom. The primary student need of basic ability is, of course, implicit in the performance needs. Regardless of the student's basic ability, the classroom teacher must assess current attainment and determine that student's needs if he or she is to meet the behavioral objectives of the classroom. It is necessary to identify student needs prior to stating final behavioral objectives, for without this assessment, the objectives would be arbitrary. From this first step of identifying performance needs emerges a decision about instructional procedures and objectives that is based on knowledge of both student needs and teacher goals, rather than just on teacher goals.

Performance needs
The academic capacities students bring into the classroom that will facilitate or hinder learning.

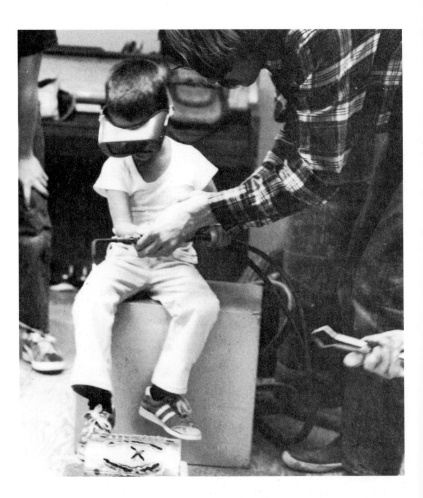

Teachers must periodically evaluate the relevance and effectiveness of their objectives for the student. There are many teaching-learning conditions in which the student fails to perform as expected. If the student is not learning the material as it is instructed, a deficiency exists, and the teacher should evaluate his or her own behavior in terms of the student deficiency rather than the original learning expectancies. Because the objectives are no longer applicable to student performance, the teacher may need to change them. However, continual evaluation may reveal that the student's deficiency can easily be remedied with supplemental instruction or a different instructional strategy. The following example illustrates this principle.

A fifth-grade class has just received math instruction on multiplying using two-digit numbers. Upon giving the students an exam, the teacher observes that several students did poorly on the test items designed to measure the objective "students will be able to multiply two-digit numbers one of which contains a zero to 80 percent accuracy." In order to get at the problem, the teacher must analyze why this learning did not occur.

The two immediate underlying skills necessary to achieve the objective are the abilities to multiply and to understand the concept "zero." A well-designed exam will test both skills. Assume that the teacher looked at the items testing the first skill and found that all students had high mastery. However, most students did not do well on the items designed to test the concept of zero. This type of task analysis helps the teacher identify learning problems and adjust teaching to correct them.

When they discover learning deficiencies, teachers should reteach the skill, concept, or strategy that the students are not learning. Assigning extra work or problems in areas where students show weaknesses without supplemental instruction is not adjusting to individual needs. In this example, the teacher should reteach the concept of zero. He or she then could assign additional problems or a work sheet. Teachers must not lock themselves into inflexible behaviors or abandon student's needs for the sake of time or expediency.

In summary, there are five reasons to identify student needs:

1. The teacher appraises prerequisite student learning to determine if it meets the requirements for the performance needs necessary to the tentative instructional objectives of the class.

2. After considering student performance needs and teacher goals, the teacher writes final student instructional objectives that specify desired learning outcomes.

3. If learning deficiencies exist, the teacher instructs the student in supplemental skills necessary to meet the prerequisite learning.

4. The teacher maintains ongoing assessment of performance needs. When student performance is below the stated objectives, reevaluation of the objectives in terms of student needs is necessary.

5. To align student needs and teacher goals, it may be necessary to restate objectives in more realistic behavioral terms. Further supplemental instruction or a change of strategy may be sufficient to meet the original goal.

Conflict from Multiple Need State	
Personal Need	**Performance Need**
Student had no breakfast. Student experiences distracting hunger in period before lunch.	Class before lunch will have test tomorrow. Student needs to pick up relevant concepts and attend to teacher review.

Writing Behavioral Objectives

Behavioral objective
A teacher-generated statement that describes expected student performance once instruction is completed.

A **behavioral objective** describes what students will be able to do when they complete a teaching unit or instructional materials. Many educators and psychologists advocate their use because they help clarify how the teacher will aid student learning. There are several good reasons for using behavioral objectives, including: (1) they help the classroom teacher plan teaching for the day, (2) they tell students what learning behaviors are expected, (3) they specify what learning behaviors students are responsible for, (4) they provide the teacher with a systematic basis for evaluating student learning, and (5) they align teacher behavior and student behavior.

Characteristics of Objectives   Behavioral or instructional objectives are precise statements designed to provide reference points within the teaching-learning environment. Used effectively, they help both teacher and learner accomplish educational goals. Behavioral objectives have four important characteristics that help define them. First, they specify observable behavior (what is expected of the learner). The statement must contain a behavior that can be observed by either the teacher or the student.

Second, behavioral objectives specify evidence of achievement, that is, they tell the type of intellectual skill required if the objective is to be achieved. If a teacher is presenting factual material, the objective should reflect what he or she expects students to learn (for example, "The student will be able to recall three historic battles of the Revolutionary War."). If the teacher is instructing at a conceptual level, the objective should reflect this (for example, "The student will define the term *democracy*."). If students are learning rules to use in solving problems or drawing conclusions, the objective should reflect this (for example, "The student will be able to provide an example of the functional use of democracy in contemporary society.").

The third characteristic of objectives is that they specify the expected proficiency level, the degree to which they must be achieved if learning is to be considered to have occurred (for example, "The student will be able to recall all the presidents of the United States to 90 percent accuracy.").

Fourth, objectives specify how learning is to be measured. For example, measurement or assessment of student learning may be through teacher observation, peer evaluation, a test, or self-checking.

Behavioral Domains   Objectives belong to one of three behavioral domains: cognitive, affective, or psychomotor (Bloom et al., 1956). The level of complexity of objectives increases as we move from one to the next.

Cognitive Domain   Objectives in the cognitive domain (1) emphasize remembering or reproducing something that has been learned or (2) involve determining the problem to be solved and solving it by combining new and previously learned information. Cognitive objectives vary from simple recall of material to highly original and creative ways of combining and synthesizing new ideas and materials. Because classroom orientation is primarily academic, cognitive objectives tend to be used most frequently. Bloom et al. (1956) arrange the cognitive behavioral objectives that might be required of a student on six operational levels: (1) **knowledge,** (2) **comprehension,** (3) **application,** (4) **analysis,** (5) **synthesis,** and (6) **evaluation.**

Knowledge includes those behaviors and test situations that emphasize remembering, either by recognition or recall, ideas, material, or phenomena (Bloom et al., 1956, p. 52). One aspect of Bloom's knowledge is the recall of specific and isolatable bits of information. Such knowledge operates at a very simple level. Most commonly, the objectives requiring this kind of knowledge are **terminology** (familiarity with meanings of words) and specific facts (dates, events, persons, places, and so on).

The other aspect of the knowledge level of Bloom's taxonomy deals with ways and means of using terminology and facts. The objectives requiring this kind of knowledge include (1) awareness of correct English

Knowledge
The lowest level cognitive objective that requires the recall of information, facts, and so forth.

Comprehension
The ability to interpret information by using one's own words or form.

Application
The ability to use intellectual skills and concepts in applied settings.

Analysis
Breaking down an idea or skill into its component parts.

Synthesis
The formulation of something new or unique by relating heretofore unrelated ideas.

Evaluation
The ability to judge something based on previously defined criteria.

Terminology
The ability to define words that represent environmental phenomena.

form and usage; (2) understanding of processes that dominate any subject field; (3) awareness of the criteria by which facts, principles, opinions, and conduct are tested or judged; and (4) knowledge of the methods of inquiry and other techniques necessary to evaluate social problems and events. Examples of knowledge objectives are

1. The student will be able to recite stanzas from *Morte d'Arthur* accurately.

2. The student will be able to match correctly the dates and places of historic battles of American wars to 95 percent mastery.

3. The student will solve problems containing factorial symbols in mathematics to 100 percent accuracy.

Comprehension includes those objectives, behaviors, and responses that represent an understanding of the literal message contained in a communication. When students are confronted with a communication, they are expected to know what is being communicated and to be able to use the material or ideas contained in it (Bloom et al., 1956, p. 89).

Three basic functions occur within the objectives included in Bloom's comprehension level: **translation, interpretation,** and **extrapolation.** Translation refers to the ability to paraphrase material into a form of communication other than the original. Interpretation is the explanation or summarization of a communication (for example, the ability to analyze and explain data). Extrapolation is the extension of evidence that is apparent in the communication but is not directly supported by the data. Examples of comprehension objectives are

Translation
Paraphrasing or rendering something into a form other than the one originally learned.

Interpretation
Explaining something that is presented in a different form (such as data in a graph).

Extrapolation
Projecting or going beyond the apparent meaning of something.

1. The student will explain the significance of the Battle of the Bulge to the teacher.

2. The student will be able to explain the process of photosynthesis on a written exam.

3. The student will learn to translate visual symbols of works of art into verbal terms to 85 percent accuracy.

Application includes those behaviors in which the student is applying the appropriate abstractions to a given situation without having to be prompted about which abstraction is correct or without having to be shown how to use it in that situation. It is also the use of abstractions in particular and concrete situations (Bloom et al., 1956, p. 20).

At the application level, the objectives include the use of abstractions as general ideas, rules, or methods that help the learner understand or solve a problem or situation. Moore and Kennedy (1971, p. 411) have shown the use of application in the area of language arts. They describe **functional application,** which refers to "the production of oral and written compositions which have as their primary purpose the dispensing of information." Examples of application objectives are

Functional application
Generating a product that transmits relevant information to the receiver.

1. The student will be able to apply Bainton's fever chart to an antinuclear protest.

2. The student will be able to change the infinitive to the *imparfait* 100 percent of the time.

3. The student will be able to use simple, compound, and complex sentences when writing an essay.

Analysis emphasizes the ability to break down the material into its constituent parts and determine their relationship and how they are organized (Bloom et al., 1956, p. 144).

Bloom's three major subheadings at the analysis level are elements, relationships, and organizational principles. The primary objective in analyzing elements is separating and identifying the various elements in a communication (for example, distinguishing fact from hypothesis or theme from plot). Analyzing relationships means discerning the connections and interactions between elements. According to Bloom, much relationship analysis deals with the consistency of elements. The analysis of organizational principles involves understanding the structure and system that hold the communication together (for example, the ability to analyze, in a work of art, the relation of materials and means of production to the elements [color, line, and so on] and to the organization [composition]). Examples of analysis objectives are

1. The student will be able to see the relationship among elements in a sentence by looking at a diagram of the sentence.

2. The student will be able to look at several math problems and decide whether to multiply or divide to 90 percent accuracy.

3. The student will be able to look at an unbalanced ledger sheet and find all the errors.

Synthesis includes those behaviors in which students assemble elements and parts to form a whole—a pattern or structure not clearly there before (Bloom et al., 1956, p. 162).

The synthesis level of cognitive objectives also has three subheadings. First is the production of a unique communication—the development of a communication in which the writer or speaker attempts to convey ideas, feelings, and/or experiences to others. This process may be stated as the behavioral objectives of (1) skill in organizing and writing, (2) ability to tell a personal experience effectively, or (3) ability to make effective extemporaneous speeches.

The second element of synthesis is the development or proposal of a plan of operation (for example, the ability to propose ways of testing hypotheses or the ability to use several rules in writing an essay). Bloom's third subheading for synthesis is the derivation of a set of abstract relations, such as the ability to make mathematical discoveries and generalizations or to formulate appropriate hypotheses based on analysis and then to modify such hypotheses in the light of new factors and considerations. Examples of synthesis objectives are

1. The student will be able to write out a theory about student activism in the 1960s.
2. The student will be able to write a term paper with bibliographic references.
3. The student will be able to propose a research design for determining which of two teaching techniques is more effective.

Evaluation is defined as judging the value, for some purpose, of ideas, works, solutions, methods, or material. It involves using criteria and standards or appraising the extent to which particulars are accurate, effective, economical, or satisfying. The judgments may be either quantitative or qualitative, and either the student or the teacher may determine the criteria (Bloom et al., 1956, p. 185).

Bloom's evaluation level involves two kinds of judgments. One judgment may be viewed in terms of internal evidence, which means evaluating the accuracy of a communication from such direct evidence as logical accuracy and consistency. Bloom suggests that the objectives for this type of evaluation might be the ability to apply given criteria to the judgment of a work and the ability to recognize fallacies in arguments. The second type of evaluation involves judgments in terms of external criteria, which is the process of evaluating material with reference to selected or remembered criteria. A frequent use of this cognitive level is the comparison of major theories, generalizations, or facts about particular cultures. The following are examples of evaluation objectives:

1. The student will develop the ability to formulate judgments about political figures.
2. The student will be able to identify the major characteristics of democracy according to the criteria presented in class to 80 percent accuracy.
3. The student will internalize criteria to recognize artistic quality in contemporary works of art.

Affective Domain   Objectives in the affective domain emphasize an emotion, an appreciation of tone or quality, or a value judgment. Affective objectives range from simple attention to selected phenomena to the attainment of complex and consistent qualities of character, conscience, or criticism. The affective objectives are most commonly used in teaching fine and performing arts, in values education, in interpersonal relations, and in behavior expressed by people in the larger environment. The levels for the affective domain are (1) **receiving,** (2) **responding,** (3) **valuing,** (4) **organization,** and (5) **characterization** by a value or value complex.

At the receiving level, the learner is sensitized to the existence of certain phenomena or stimuli and is aware of, or attending to, the materials (Keathwohl, 1964). For example the student pays attention to what is being said about margins and indentations in typing class. Examples of receiving objectives are

1. The student will attend to teacher directions.
2. The student will indicate interest in joining a club at school when given an activities checklist.

The responding level goes beyond simply perceiving the stimuli or phenomena. However, it is a low level of commitment, and the learner is not expressing or internalizing a value. Responding occurs once the learner begins acting toward some perceived stimulus in the environment. This may be as simple as getting up from an easy chair and taking a beer out of the refrigerator because an advertisement on television promoted the behavior, or it may be as complex as acting out the drama that one feels in a poem or play. Examples of responding objectives are

1. The student will voluntarily seek to be helpful to other members of an organization to which he or she belongs.
2. The student indicates enjoyment in writing by listing personal experiences of reading and writing.

At the valuing level, learners assign worth to something, displaying responsive behavior in situations in which they are not forced to comply or obey. Our concept of worth is in part a result of our own valuing, but it is

Receiving
Attending to any affective phenomenon in the environment.

Responding
Reacting to any affective phenomenon in the environment.

Valuing
Voluntarily selecting beliefs or activities because of their worth.

Organization
Ordering multiple values in a hierarchical way in one's mind.

Characterization
The long-term committment to beliefs and behaviors, often referred to as one's life-style.

much more a social product that we have gradually internalized, accepted, and used as personal criterion. For example, a teacher is looking for valuing response when asking students to express their attitudes about science and the pursuit of a scientific career. This might be in the form of an open-ended response or an attitude questionnaire. Examples of objectives in this category are

1. The student will demonstrate the value of freedom of expression by speaking out on an issue.
2. The student will learn to value the proper care of books by volunteering time in the school library.

As learners successively internalize and express values, they encounter situations for which more than one value is relevant. Thus, they must organize values into a system, determine the interrelationships among them, and establish dominant values. This internally consistent system of values is built gradually and is subject to change as new values are incorporated. Listening to others' opinions about a topic on which we have information is an example of organizing affective behavior. I discussed the ways values are organized in greater detail in Chapter 8. Examples of organization objectives are

1. Given a conflict, the student will articulate techniques for channeling aggression into socially acceptable patterns to his or her classmates.
2. The student reads books about social problems to formulate attitudes toward such problems.

When learners reach the level of characterization by a value or value complex, their values have affected their behavior for so long that they routinely and consistently base affective responses on them. In other words, characterization describes an individual's philosophy of life, which always strongly affects behavior. It may be too complex and developmentally bound (Kohlberg, 1973) to deal with effectively in the classroom. Examples of objectives at this level are

1. The student demonstrates some consistency between personal values and behaviors by his or her classroom behaviors.
2. The student will formulate a model for social justice by writing an essay describing ways to reduce inequalities.

Psychomotor Domain   Objectives in the psychomotor domain emphasize muscular or motor skills, manipulation of materials and objects, and neuromuscular coordination. These objectives are most frequently related to handwriting, speech, physical education, and trade or technical courses. There has been considerably less work and agreement about behavioral factors that constitute the psychomotor domain. Several systems have been devised, but Dave's (1963) is the most comprehensive. The levels for the psychomotor domain are (1) **imitation,** (2) **manipulation,** (3) **precision,** (4) **articulation,** and (5) **naturalization.**

Imitation begins with an internal rehearsal of the muscular system in response to an inner urge to duplicate an observed action. This appears to be the starting point in a psychomotor skill. The overt performance of the

Imitation
The rehearsal in one's mind of a motor behavior observed in a model.

Manipulation
The actual performance of a motor behavior as a result of learning.

Precision
The refinement of a previously learned motor behavior.

Articulation
The ability to integrate multiple motor skills into one sequential activity.

Naturalization
The routine performance of a highly developed motor skill.

action and the capacity to repeat that imitation then follow. However, the performance and its repetitions lack neuromuscular coordination or control and therefore are generally crude and imperfect. Examples of imitation objectives are

1. The student will be able to copy letters of the alphabet as the teacher illustrates them on the board.

2. The student will repeat a sequential complex movement.

At the manipulation stage, the learner is capable of performing an action according to instruction rather than on the basis of observation only. The emphasis at this level is on the development of skills in following directions, in performing selected actions, and in establishing the performances through practice. Examples of manipulation objectives are

1. The student will write the alphabet in response to teacher dictation.

2. The student will be able to kick an object to a specified area.

The proficiency of performance reaches a higher level of refinement at the precision level. Here the objectives of accuracy and proportion become significant. Examples of precision objectives are

1. The student will be able to kick an object so it hits a target.

2. The student will be able to catch objects that have high trajectories.

The articulation level emphasizes the coordination of a variety or a series of actions. The goal is to establish an appropriate sequence and accomplish harmony and consistency among actions. Examples of articulation objectives are

1. The student will demonstrate a variety of gymnastic exercises.
2. The student will throw a ball while running.

At the naturalization stage, the skill of performance attains its highest level of proficiency and the act is performed with the least expenditure of psychic energy. The objective here is to make the action so routine that it is an automatic, spontaneous response. Examples of naturalization objectives are

1. The student will learn to use a T-square routinely in mechanical drawing class.
2. The tennis player will select appropriate strategies while the game is in progress.

Developing a Teaching Strategy

The third phase of the instructional model is the teaching process itself—the development of a teaching strategy. Identifying student needs (phase one) and stating behavioral objectives (phase two) are also strategies of a kind and essential forerunners to instruction, but it is the actual instructional process that finally determines the extent of student learning. Several theorists have attempted to apply their theories of instruction to specific instructional strategies and have heavily influenced the model I present, which is designed to maximize effective teaching and learning. The model has six components: student preparation, presentation of material, student response, feedback/reinforcement, evaluation of progress, and spaced review.

Student Preparation   The first step is to begin preparing the student's mind for the material to be presented. In most cases, this means gaining student attention in some way, which may require no more than the teacher describing the tasks to be learned. The teacher may also wish to make comments that trigger student interest and motivation. Whatever the procedure, the essential task for the teacher is to elicit interest in the immediate teaching-learning situation.

Not all teachers find it easy to gain students' attention and interest. The following devices may assist in this initial phase of the teaching strategy:

1. *Restatement of behavioral objectives.* On some occasions, it is beneficial to bring students back to the general learning objectives. A restatement of teacher-student goals often engages the students' interest and helps in learning as well.

2. *Warm-up.* Students learn the task at hand more readily if the preceding assignments are similar in form or content. Thus, a good way to use the

warm-up effect is to draw the students' attention to the previously learned intellectual skills that will facilitate the acquisition of the skill at hand. This procedure directs students' thoughts, familiarizes them with the content, and provides a working basis for positive transfer in the immediate learning context. Several research studies (Hamilton, 1950; Irion, 1949) have shown warm-up to be effective.

3. *Readiness for learning.* **Readiness** is the degree to which students have the prerequisite knowledge for new learning. Craig (1966, p. 5) suggests that teachers ask two questions: "What must a student need to know or be able to do before he can learn this new thing in the way I plan to teach it?" "To what extent do my students possess the prerequisite knowledge and abilities?" I would add a third question: "Does my proposed plan of instruction fall within the range of my students' abilities as indicated by their prerequisite knowledge?" Gagne (1977a) believes that diagnostic testing is necessary before the teacher can know what course of instruction to take.

Readiness
The extent to which the learner is prepared to engage in an immediate teaching-learning situation.

Presentation of Material   Classroom learning is based primarily on the successful presentation of stimuli (teaching), which elicits the desired responses from students (learning). Thus, it is essential to prepare and present stimuli in a way that will maximize student response. The manner of presentation is determined partly by the behavioral objectives set up for the learning situation and partly by the prerequisite student knowledge. However, the most important factor in stimulus presentation is the **level of response** required of the student. As required responses become increasingly complex, teachers must change the way they present material. For example, if you want the students' response to be a simple fact, then your stimulus statement may be something like, "How far is it from Chicago to St. Louis?" If you want a rule response, your stimulus must be capable of evoking it; for example, "State the method for finding square roots."

Level of response
The capacity to perform learned behaviors with varying degrees of complexity (that is, facts, concepts, rules).

Regardless of the level of instruction, the following two presentation techniques will help direct the learner to the desired objective: (1) The greater the similarity from material to material, the more likely that students will learn; and (2) specific material for specific responses will significantly reduce the likelihood that the student will learn inappropriate responses. Teaching machines, programmed textbooks, and computer-assisted instruction are additional ways to take a learner through a specific learning sequence. Teaching devices are especially helpful in eliminating distracting stimuli and removing negative reinforcement from the classroom. When you use such devices, integrate them into your planning and teaching strategy.

Student Response   Teachers must always give students the opportunity to respond. Unless teachers have some deliberate plan of providing feedback to their responses, they can never know if the students are learning and, in the case of discriminated stimuli, if they are learning the appropriate responses. The response system is inherently tied to the nature of the material being presented in that, as teachers present different information, they will expect different responses that are comparable to the stimuli. This equivalence of presentation of material and student response can best be illustrated by reviewing learning occurring at the factual, conceptual, and relational levels.

Factual material is presented at a nonconceptual level. Instructors must invariably teach some factual material, such as numbers, mathematical facts, places, dates, persons, geographical locations, and events. For example, if you want to tell students when World War I began, you would simply tell them. If you also want to identify where it began and what nations were involved, you would simply tell them Austria and that it involved Austria and Serbia. This information could come from a variety of sources (books, encyclopedias, motion pictures, filmstrips, tape recordings, or television shows). The correspondence is between a factual stimulus and a factual (nonconceptual) response. This type of learning is represented at the knowledge level in Bloom's et al. (1956) behavioral taxonomy.

Conceptual material is what the teacher expects a learner to understand. You would present the concept of a category (for example, the class "balls") and then the objects (stimuli) that represent that class. Student response should be at a conceptual level; that is, they can observe several diverse objects called "balls" and recognize that they all represent the concept category "balls." Students will then be able to generalize understanding of this concept to any new ball you may introduce. Your role is to provide a wide range of stimuli within the class of stimuli being studied so that students have many opportunities to respond conceptually to that class. Whether you use a hierarchical approach, such as Gagne (1977a) describes, or a concept formation approach, such as Ausubel (1968) describes, you expect students to understand. When you ask why the atmosphere is important to the earth, students must understand the concept "atmosphere" well enough to be able to discuss its importance. Bloom et al. (1956) described this level of learning as comprehension within the cognitive taxonomy.

Relational material typically involves verbal stimuli. You may say, for example, "A = 1 × w," which not only verbally represents several concepts but also implies that, if the student understands and uses the formula to solve a problem, the response will be appropriate. Thus, the verbal formula represents a rule that, by its nature, operationally produces appropriate student responses. Bloom et al. (1956) place rules or strategies at the application and analysis objective levels.

Feedback/Reinforcement   Reinforcement is usually described as positive or negative. Positive reinforcement means adding such things as praise, knowledge of results, recognition, or reward to the learner's response, thus increasing the probability of the response recurring. Negative

Aversive control
The withdrawal of a student from an unpleasant situation that reinforced an undesired behavior. Synonymous with negative reinforcement.

reinforcement, referred to as **aversive control**, may similarly strengthen a response, although the probability is less. Do not confuse negative reinforcement, which has not been successfully used to extinguish or eliminate a response, with punishment. (See Chapter 2 for a discussion of these terms.) Reinforcement strengthens behavior, and positive reinforcement is more likely to strengthen than negative reinforcement. Therefore, teaching strategy should include the use of positive reinforcement in the classroom to increase student learning.

Continuous reinforcement involves giving learners feedback when they make a response. This is easily done in individualized instruction, and it is possible in group instruction if all students are learning the same material. Continuous reinforcement is important when students are learning material for the first time.

In intermittent reinforcement, learners are not rewarded for every response. Because of crowded curricula and limited classroom time, this type of reinforcement is advantageous to teachers. Responses learned under partial reinforcement are more likely to persist. Much of school learning is shaped by partial reinforcement.

Teachers can use knowledge of results, originally advanced by Skinner, in two ways: (1) It may be similar to continuous reinforcement in that the teacher provides fairly immediate feedback to the student as to the correctness or incorrectness of the response or (2) it may be a system of self-reinforcement in which the teacher provides the correct responses so students can internalize the reinforcement and therefore be self-motivated to continue to pursue the learning tasks at hand. In complex learning, such as of concepts and rules, feedback need not always come externally; it may arise from the learner's satisfaction at knowing other related concepts or rules that aid in solving the problem or explaining the situation.

Negative reinforcement increases the probability of a response because the undesirable behavior (the response) is followed by the removal, termination, or avoidance of the stimulus that the learner is unable or unwilling to deal with. Examples of negative reinforcement in the classroom are ceasing to monitor a reading group once its members begin reading or removing annoying students from the classroom.

If teachers do not include reinforcement in their teaching strategy,

three consequences may occur: (1) Without any feedback, some students may question the accuracy of their responses. This uncertainty causes them to wonder if they are right or wrong. For this type of student, feedback is important. (2) If a teacher begins with a continuous reinforcement schedule and then withholds reinforcement, student performance may be reduced. This is particularly true in original learning, where continuous reinforcement tends to be used. (3) If the material is conceptual rather than nonconceptual, the demand for reinforcement is less. Thus, teachers must carefully evaluate the type of responses they are asking of students, then determine whether feedback should be continuous, intermittent, or is unnecessary.

Presentation of material, student response, and feedback/reinforcement, the second, third, and fourth components of the teaching strategy, most often occur stimultaneously. In fact, in the best teaching strategies, materials are presented, responses occur, and reinforcement is applied within the same time frame.

Evaluation of Progress   Evaluation is a vital aspect of teaching strategy. It commonly occurs after the teacher has presented a series of problems or a unit and serves two essential functions: student appraisal and teacher analysis.

Perhaps the most crucial function of evaluation is providing learners with feedback about their general progress. If they have some idea of the performance expected of them (behavioral objectives), learners can evaluate their own response level to some extent. However, periodic teacher evaluations are essential for guiding and motivating learners. Evaluation does not mean students must receive a letter grade; tests or exams serve this purpose. Evaluation is used here in the sense of simply providing learners with frequent assessments and guidance.

Teachers need spaced evaluations of student progress in order to adjust their teaching strategy to student needs. If teachers withhold evaluation until the end of a unit of work, valuable instruction time may have been lost while an ineffective strategy was used. Frequent evaluations allow teachers greater flexibility and facilitate teacher-learner goals.

Spaced Review   This final phase of the teaching strategy is important to ensure retention of learning. Students become better in performing some skills with increased practice (**spaced review**). However, continuous practice leads to fatigue and loss of efficiency. Thus, by spacing the times in which students receive additional review materials, the teacher may avoid this negative effect. Spaced review also allows the teacher to recall previous student learning, and such recall-reinforcement may strengthen that learning and its retention. As students move toward complex learning, the practice effect seems to become less valuable. As Gagne (1970a, p. 319) points out, "If a concept or rule has been completely learned, it is entirely possible that conditioned practice may have no appreciable effect on its retention."

If you plan evaluations of student progress in conjunction with reviews of learned materials, you can implement both steps of the teaching

Spaced review
The systematic, intermittent representation of learned material in order to increase its retentive strength.

Mr. Pascouchi has decided to make astronomy a special project this year in his science class. In addition to the standard topics, he feels he can build greater interest and motivation by having a special hands-on assignment. He also hopes to involve parents through this special astronomy assignment.

In the second week of school, Mr. Pascouchi gave his students an orientation to astronomy that included its history, importance, basic terminology, identification skills, and some specific assignments. Because the configurations in the sky change in accordance with the seasons, he decided to have students plot the constellations visible during autumn, winter, and spring, identify them, draw them, and label them. All assignments were to be done with parental help. As a result, many parents and children were out star gazing on clear nights.

Mr. Pascouchi asked his students to turn in their projects the first week of May, although they could seek his assistance on it any time they wanted. The project consisted of four parts: a brief statement as to why the sky is different during the year, four drawings representing constellations of the three seasons, a glossary of new terms learned while pursuing this assignment, and a bibliography of sources used in the project.

Two outcomes really gratified Mr. Pascouchi. First, the students' excitement for the project remained high throughout the year. Many anecdotal stories came up in class that indicated student interest and parental involvement. In addition, some of the projects were extremely well done and artistic. Second, over one third of the parents indicated by phone call, visit, or letter how much they enjoyed helping their child with the assignment. Thus, the goal of parental involvement was apparently met. Mr. Pascouchi's evaluation was that the assignment was relevant, meaningful, and an effective mechanism for helping

parents get involved in their children's learning experiences.

What Do You Think?

1. To what extent did Mr. Pascouchi utilize good instructional design?

2. Do you think parental involvement was a good idea in this assignment?

3. How important is it to extend academic learning to nonacademic contexts?

Elements of a Teaching Strategy

Step 1: *Student preparation*

The teacher directs the students' minds toward the learning tasks at hand.

Step 2: *Stimulus presentation*

The deliberate presentation of specific, identifiable stimuli will ensure more discriminated responses by the students.

Step 3: *Student response*

Two crucial factors in teaching are giving the students time to compose a response to a stimulus and giving them feedback (reinforcement) as to the acceptability of the response.

Step 4: *Reinforcement*

Planning for reinforcement, preferably positive, will strengthen the tendency for students to learn a response and to maintain it when it is subsequently elicited.

Step 5: *Evaluation*

Some assessment of the quality and rate of learning should be undertaken by the teacher. This provides both the student and teacher with awareness as to the effectiveness of the teaching–learning environment.

Step 6: *Spaced review*

A crucial step in the teaching process is the periodic presentation of stimuli that will trigger previously learned responses. Such review ensures retention.

strategy simultaneously. Let the nature of the learning task determine the extent of practice. If students have learned new material, several spaced reviews might ensure retention. Less frequent reviews will be needed with well-established material. Relating learning to life situations adds meaning to reviews. If you can provide fresh and practical situations in which to apply the material under review, students are more likely to benefit from the practice. Occasionally, homework (essentially review on student time) is beneficial to learners. If a homework assignment is to function as a review, you must check the papers in class during the following class session.

Assessment

When students complete a teaching unit, their work should be formally assessed by observation and examination to determine whether the unit objectives were met. Such assessment, of course, provides the teacher with data from which to grade, but assessment is important within an instructional design for other reasons as well.

First, an assessment based on the explicit behavioral objectives for a unit provides the teacher with criteria by which to determine student learning. If the student's ultimate performance level is in line with these criteria, then the student has learned, and the teacher does not need to measure that student's performance against the performance of the other members of the class in order to determine individual learning and the success of the unit. I discuss procedures for effective measurement in Chapter 15.

Second, criteria are designed to help students understand their expected performance level. When a student falls below that level, a learning deficiency exists. Overcoming it may require additional instruction, reading, or practice. As a teacher, you must know if a student is not performing adequately and provide additional attention and direction to help him or her learn the criteria. Two activities, then, are necessary in assessing student learning. One is observing behavioral change. Through evaluation with exams and/or observation, you can detect whether students are progressing toward the goals specified within the instructional objectives. If they are, you can conclude that the behavioral objectives were realistic and that your teaching strategy was effective. If you find that student progress is inadequate, you must analyze your teaching strategy (or the objectives).

The second activity is analyzing learning deficiencies. It could be that students did not have the prerequisite skills necessary to learn the material. In such cases, you may have written inappropriate behavioral objectives or failed to do adequate diagnostic testing in order to determine readiness. Or perhaps your teaching strategy was poorly designed. By diagnosing your behavior, you can assess the effectiveness of each phase of your strategy in terms of student learning. Assessing student behavior is essential to the instructional process.

Assessing Teacher Effectiveness

A corollary assessment component based on criteria and objectives provides the teacher with data on the effectiveness of his or her teaching and the strategies used in meeting teaching-learning goals. Such feedback should help you in future instruction as well as in assessing the effectiveness of the completed instruction. You may find through self-monitoring that you can improve your instructional procedures and thereby increase student learning. Modifying your instructional theory may involve no more than recognizing that reinforcement was not properly given through a particular teaching unit. In this case, rethink the role of reinforcement in the learning of particular material and how you could use it more advantageously. Such ongoing analysis increases your effectiveness.

Flanders (1970) developed a teacher observation procedure that measures the verbal interchange between teacher and pupils. It has been used to study spontaneous teacher behaviors and to design research projects for helping teachers become more aware of and modify their behavior. Flanders's system is based on the verbal interchange between teacher and students. Its premise is that, through self-observation and self-evaluation, teachers gain better understanding and effective control over their behavior. The system utilizes a videotape procedure; thus, its use depends upon schools having the appropriate media equipment.

I have developed a comparable system concerned primarily with teacher behavior. For simplicity and practicality, it is confined to six types of verbal statements. The first is direct teacher statements (teacher statements that tell the student what to do). Evaluation of this verbal behavior is contingent upon the student's understanding, accepting, and pursuing the teacher's directions (for example, "Follow the example on page 42 to work out the problem on the board.").

Problem formation statements (teacher statements that provide direction to the student in an objective, nonthreatening manner) are a second type. In contrast to direct teacher statements, these provide the student with less-structured information. Problem formation statements should clarify a problem and facilitate the student's problem-solving activity (for example, "Are some of our traditions really not as important as we think they are?" "In addition to federal regulations, what can our local government do about pollution?").

Third are reinforcement statements, which give feedback to the student through praise or knowledge of results. They should facilitate student interest and motivation (for example, "Very good." "Right." "Ok." "Yes." "I'm glad to see you followed the example").

Neutral (nonreinforcing) statements are a fourth type. Many statements, such as information or explanation of a classroom procedure, are replies to student inquiry that receive classroom time but have no effect on learning (for example, "In just one week, tryouts for the school play will be held."). One other interaction that can be considered within this category is the event of *not* reinforcing a student when a response is made. This is an **omission statement** and should be recorded as a failure to reinforce.

Fifth are punitive (negative) statements. These statements of disapproval give negative feedback and perhaps even undesirable reinforcement to the student. Withall (1951) sees the intent of such statements as (1) to represent to the learner societal values as the teacher sees them (for example, "But if you become a welfare bum, most people will dislike you." "Sex is not something adolescents can play around with without serious consequences."), (2) to admonish learners for unacceptable behavior and to deter them from repeating it in the future (for example, "You haven't any interest in what we're doing, do you, Jerry?" "If you'd be quiet and pay attention, you wouldn't have to ask such questions."), and (3) to impress on learners the fact that they have not met the teacher's criteria for successful achievement (for example, "If you don't dig in and study, you're going to flunk the test." "I don't think it's relevant to the topic, do you?"). Such statements do not usually facilitate learning and may create social-emotional conflicts within the teaching-learning situation.

The sixth type of verbal statement is teacher centered. In this, the teacher defines or asserts a position. Most such statements have emotional overtones that send messages to the students that the teacher is the authority (for example, "I don't think that legislative policy can be justified.").

Reinforcing, supportive statements produce more student-initiated behaviors and less teacher direction in the classroom. This indicates that the more effective learning takes place when students function within a

Omission statement
No verbal or written activity on the part of a teacher that otherwise might reinforce a student's behavior.

The Thornburg Instructional Model

1. Identify student needs
2. State student behavioral objectives
3. Develop a teacher strategy
   a. Student preparation
   b. Presentation of material
   c. Student responses
   d. Feedback/reinforcement
   e. Evaluation of progress
   f. Spaced review
4. Assess student behavioral change

learner-centered and highly supportive environment (Anderson, 1939; Withall, 1951). Problem formation and reinforcement statements are learner centered and highly supportive. Direct teacher statements are teacher centered, but they can be useful in helping the student learn. Punitive and teacher-centered statements and the omission statement element of neutral statements are teacher oriented and tend not to be conducive to learning.

This system is designed to help teachers create effective instructional strategies so they can approach teaching and predict its results more systematically. They should also evaluate such outcomes in terms of student learning and teacher behavior. Any set of strategies you select should contain the potential for enriched teacher-learning experiences.

A Model for Teaching English Grammar

The following example illustrates the application of an instructional model to teaching English grammar.

- *General subject: Verb tenses*
- *Specific task: Learning the perfect tenses of verbs*
- *Prerequisite skills: Knowing the present, past, and future tenses of verbs*

Identifying Student Needs

To determine if students are ready to learn perfect-tense verbs, the teacher must find out if they have the necessary prerequisite skills. If time has elapsed between their learning the prerequisites and the immediate learning task, a diagnostic test containing some of the following items would be helpful.

1. *Draw two lines under the verb in each of the following sentences.*

2. *In the blank, identify its tense.*

_____ The smallest of the three children swam farthest.

_____ They had written their senator.

_____ Pat is the best player on the softball team.

_____ The show will conclude today.

_____ Every person in the room questioned the waiter.

_____ Has the pianist played that song before?

_____ Both runners were safe on an error the catcher made.

Stating Student Behavioral Objectives

The following objectives must be achieved in order to learn this material satisfactorily:

I. *Knowledge* (Student will be able to recall the meaning of present, past, and perfect verb tenses.)

II. *Comprehension*
   a. Student will be able to discriminate among verb tenses.
   b. Student will learn to conjugate verbs according to the perfect tense.

III. *Application* (Student will be able to use the perfect tense correctly.)

IV. *Analysis* (Student will be able to identify perfect tense verbs in sentences.)

Developing a Teaching Strategy

Student Preparation An alert teacher can point out that some verbs are used to represent action that occurs at an indefinite time before the present (present perfect), that occurred at a fixed point in the past (past perfect), or that will occur before a fixed point in the future (future perfect). When verbs express one of these times, they are called perfect tense verbs. Once the teacher has given some rationale for the continued study of verb tenses, stimuli may be presented. The ma-

terial must be carefully related to the specified behavioral objectives for the student.

Presentation of Material First the teacher introduces the concept "present perfect tense," defines it, and illustrates it by providing contrasting examples of the present perfect and the past tense.

Definition:

Use the present perfect tense to show that something that began in the past is still going on at an indefinite time before the present.

Illustration:

Past tense:	*Mary called Mr. Marshall about a summer job. (Something she did.)*
Present perfect tense:	*Mary has called Mr. Marshall about a summer job. (It is uncertain as to when in the past Mary actually called.)*

Next the teacher introduces the concept "past perfect tense," then the concept "future perfect tense." The teacher is now ready to teach the students to conjugate verbs in the perfect tense. To be able to do this, they must have already learned the auxiliary verbs that specify the time of the perfect tenses. Therefore, the teacher presents the following information:

Present perfect tense:	*has or have + past participle of verb*

Past perfect tense: had + past participle

Future perfect tense: shall have or will have + past participle

Four of the verb tenses have helping (auxiliary) verbs. Knowing these will help students recognize the tense in which the verb is being used. They are shown in the chart below showing the conjugation of the six tenses.

Student Response The materials presented here constitute all the necessary new information that the student needs in order to learn the concepts of present perfect tense, past perfect tense, and future perfect tense and how to conjugate each verb tense. It is now necessary for the teacher to plan for providing opportunities for student response.

Generally, it is best to plan for student responses with each stimulus presentation. Therefore, after presenting the necessary information to learn past-perfect tense verbs, the teacher should give the student a chance to respond, to confirm understanding of what is being taught. Students might supply examples. The continued presentation of similar stimuli to which the students have the opportunity to respond tells the teacher if they have learned the concept.

Students should also have an opportunity to conjugate the verbs. This can be done once the student has learned the auxiliary verbs and has seen them used. Therefore, the teacher's task of providing for student responses is simply to supply new verbs for the students to conjugate.

The ability to identify perfect tense verbs in sentences and use them correctly can be demonstrated within this response component of the teaching strategy. Teachers should provide problems, work sheets, exercises, and so on that give students ample opportunity to apply the materials they have learned. The following is an example of such an exercise:

1. *Draw two lines under the verbs in each of the following sentences.*

2. *In the blank, identify its tense.*

_____ This morning Kris told me that she and her mother had decided to see *Hamlet.*

_____ Because Marty had looked at television all morning, he went for a bicycle ride after lunch.

_____ Fran hasn't taken out the trash yet.

_____ Terry will have played several games of basketball before next weekend.

_____ That's the third time in a row that Dale has beaten you at chess.

The application objective can be realized by providing the students with a series of perfect-tense verbs and requiring them to compose sentences in which they use the verbs correctly.

Reinforcement Once the student has responded, the potential for reinforcement exists. Telling students if their responses are correct will probably be sufficient reinforcement. Because the teacher will probably move from one student to another for responses, it is a good idea to reinforce each student's response. Once the teacher sees that all the students have learned one of the concepts, he or she can move from continuous reinforcement procedures to intermittent ones. This is easily accomplished by allowing the students to work independently on the materials.

Evaluation Once the teacher has presented the designated stimulus material (such as information on the present perfect tense) and has allowed the students to confirm their learning through responses, he or she may want to evaluate the quality of learning that has occurred before moving to new materials. If the teacher has reason to believe that a student or students have not learned the material adequately, he or she should

Present tense	I choose	I go	I write
Past tense	I chose	I went	I wrote
Future tense	I shall choose	I shall go	I shall write
Present perfect	I have chosen	I have gone	I have written
Past perfect	I had chosen	I had gone	I had written
Future perfect	I shall have chosen	I shall have gone	I shall have written

teach further before moving to the new materials. The teacher must also find out where inadequate teaching or learning is occurring and correct the problem before presenting additional stimuli that might depend on previous learning.

For example, assume that the students learned the present perfect tense and past perfect tense adequately but were unable to respond consistently to future perfect tense verbs. The teacher must (1) analyze the difficulty, (2) attempt to correct any inappropriate learning, (3) allow for additional student responses, and (4) reinforce the student's new responses more carefully. When the teacher is sure that learning has occurred, he or she can confirm it by providing additional classroom problems.

Spaced Review   To ensure retention, the teacher should plan to give the students the opportunity to review and use the learning that has taken place. This review could occur one day later, one week later, or even several months later. Perhaps at the end of all the work on verb tenses the teacher would assign a general exercise or test in which students would have to know all six verb tenses.

Assessing Student Behavioral Change

The teacher may use the assessment phase of the instructional process to accomplish three things. First, a general examination may be given to determine how well the students have learned, as well as to provide the teacher with some objective grading information. Second, the teacher could analyze those parts of the examination that were consistently difficult for the students in order to determine what learning deficiencies exist. Third, the assessment of learning deficiencies should tell the teacher whether he or she has been effective in instruction and whether the behavioral objectives were realistic. On the basis of this assessment, the teacher might modify his or her strategy and/or objectives for subsequent classes.

Annotated Readings

Furst, E. J. (1981). Bloom's taxonomy of educational objectives for the cognitive domain: Philosophical and educational issues. *Review of Educational Research, 51,* 441–454.

> *This literature review focuses on the cognitive domain of educational objectives. It covers published and unpublished studies over a twenty-five-year period. The focus is on the following purported characteristics of objectives: neutrality, comprehensiveness, cumulative hierarchical structure, and usefulness.*

Gagne, R. M. (1974). Task analysis—its relation to content analysis. *Educational Psychologist, 11,* 11–18.

> *Gagne discusses the origins, meanings, and elaborations of task analysis in relation to the design of instruction. He describes the purpose of learning task analysis as identifying and classifying the performances that are the outcomes of learning and those subordinate performances that are prerequisite to such learning. Gagne argues that the procedures of task analysis can be employed in analyzing existing content to reveal its probably intended outcomes and discusses interfacing task and content analysis in determining instructional design.*

Kaplan, C. H., & White, M. A. (1980). Children's direction following behavior in grades K–5. *Journal of Educational Research, 74,* 43–48.

> *A sample of over fourteen hundred teachers' classroom directions was obtained from eighteen classrooms in kindergarten through grade five, and each direction was task analyzed for the number of behaviors required to execute it and the number of qualifying statements setting conditions on the response. An instrument composed of fifty-four of these directions was given to 215 kindergarten through fifth-grade children. The results indicated that teachers' directions are very similar in complexity between kindergarten and grade five as measured by the number of behaviors and qualifiers. Over 90 percent of the students could correctly follow teacher directions, indicating that teachers tend to give directions their students can follow.*

Knief, L. M. (1974). Objectives are not the place to begin. *Educational Technology, 14,* 37–39.

> *The author argues that too often teachers or curriculum designers think that the initial starting point in planning instruction is writing objectives rather than devising the overall course configuration, content dimensions, and general goals. Once these have been developed, it is possible to define the course more specifically by objective. In a sense, the overall course configuration provides the broad framework within which to develop relevant course components.*

Peterson, P. P., & Clark, C. M. (1978). Teachers' reports of their cognitive process during teaching. *American Educational Research Journal, 15,* 555–566.

> *Twelve experienced teachers taught a social studies lesson to three groups of junior high students under experimental conditions. After each three-hour lesson, teachers viewed four brief videotaped segments of their teaching and responded to a structured interview concerning their cognitive processes while teaching. Teachers' responses were audiotaped and coded. Reports were characterized most frequently by a sequence of observing student reactions, judging them to be satisfactory, and continuing to teach. Differences in reports were related to teachers' cognitive styles, abilities, and planning statements and to students' achievements and attitudes.*

Rose, J. S., & Medway, F. J. (1981). Measurement of teachers' beliefs in their control over student outcome. *Journal of Educational Research, 74,* 185–190.
This research article describes the development of a scale designed to measure teachers' generalized expectancies for internal-external control over student success and failure in the classroom. Validation studies indicated that the scale predicted teachers' classroom behaviors, including their willingness to adopt new instructional techniques following in-service training.

Transfer and
Retention of Learning

Mr. Longworth complained that his seventh-grade students did not know the difference between an adjective and an adverb. "I don't know why. I guess they weren't taught the difference in elementary school." Ms. Franklin attributed it to summer loss. "It doesn't seem to make much difference how well you have taught because kids forget so much during the summer anyway." These concerns (or complaints) are related to an important, yet often overlooked, educational considera-tion—the extent to which students retain material they have learned.

A chronic problem in education is that most teachers instruct for acquisition of learning rather than for retention. College texts, curriculum specialists, school programs, standardized testing, and pressure for students to achieve tend to focus on the immediate impact of the teaching-learning situation and not on the long-term consequences of teaching and learning. Invariably, students look at their classroom experience in terms of its immediate effect and rarely consider the impact of what they are learning today on future learning. If this "imme-diate perspective" is to be broadened, teachers must understand and impart to students how learning is an ongoing process and how im-mediate and subsequent learning events are related.

Obviously, students do not forget everything they learn. Mr. Longworth can probably help his students recall previously learned material. But sometimes student recall is hazy and needs additional teaching or clarification. To help his seventh-grade students avoid "summer loss" when they enter eighth grade, Mr. Longworth can point out the long-term consequences of learning. This may sharpen their focus on the task at hand and increase their ability to recall the learn-ing in subsequent teaching-learning situations. In other words, Mr. Longworth needs to orient his students as to the purposes of learning by communicating that learning is relevant and ongoing.

I have presented both learning and instructional design principles, which are integrally bound and suggest how to enhance learning retention. Understanding the dynamics of learning and the importance of what is learned to the individual's total life must be an active goal of education if it is to be relevant to the functioning individual within contemporary society. To contribute to this understanding, in this chapter I discuss:

- *Transfer*
- *Retention*
- *Memory*
- *Strategies for increasing retention rate*

Transfer
The effect one learning experience has on another.

Two concepts basic to the process of learning are **transfer** and retention. Transfer is the effect of previous learning on subsequent learning. Retention is the strength, longevity, and potential for retrieval of learning. Both concepts are experimentally proven phenomena of learning: Learning in one situation transfers to performance in another and retention depends on several variables in the learning process, including scheduling of reinforcement and meaningfulness of the learning behavior to previous learning.

Transfer

Whether learning is motor or verbal, previous acquisition tends to influence present acquisition. In most cases, previous learning facilitates additional learning; in some cases, it hinders it. The classroom teacher's strategy should use transfer to its fullest extent to facilitate new learning.

Transfer Theories

Mental discipline theory
The theory that the mind is strengthened by exercise.

Mental Discipline Theory Out of the traditional Aristotelian-based views of learning evolved the nineteenth-century concept that the mind is like a muscle and can be strengthened with continuous, vigorous exercise. The **mental discipline theory** emphasizes the teaching of subjects, such as mathematics, Latin, and Greek, not so much because each will be used in life or in other learning situations but because they are rigorous disciplines that strengthen the mind.

Theory of Identical Elements The writings of William James (1890) and the research of Thorndike and Woodworth (1901) cast the first serious doubts on mental discipline theory. These researchers conclusively demonstrated that the common or identical elements between learning situations, rather than rigor, make learning transferable. This is not to say that the study of mathematics is irrelevant, but that such study cannot be assumed to necessarily increase an individual's general cognitive ability (Thorndike, 1924).

Thorndike's 1924 study discredited mental discipline theory. He compared two groups of high school students, one of which had a heavy concentration of classical studies. He hypothesized that, if classical studies require an intellectual rigor that improves the mind, then those enrolled in such courses would do better in school than those enrolled in less rigorous courses. In his study, the comparison group was enrolled in either drama or home economics. Thorndike found that those enrolled in the classics did only slightly better on a reasoning test than those in the comparison group. Further, when controlling for initial differences attributable to IQ scores, he found that there was no significant difference in the performance levels of the two groups. In other words, intelligence rather than subject matter seemed to explain any differences found between them. A later study by Wesman (1945), which was better designed than Thorndike's 1924 study, bears out his results, thus supporting the idea that the mental discipline theory is inaccurate.

As proposed by Thorndike, the **theory of identical elements** posits that training in one kind of activity transfers to another as long as certain features in both tasks are identical. Thorndike emphasized the stimulus in a learning situation as the vital condition. He suggested that there must be similarity of properties between stimulus 1 and stimulus 2 if transfer is to take place. The following examples focus on this point:

Theory of identical elements
The theory that transfer is increased if the learning of two tasks have similar elements.

- Learning $2 + 2 = 4$ will facilitate learning $II + II = IV$
- Learning $2 + 2 = 4$ will facilitate learning $2 + 4 = 6$
- Learning $4 + 4 = 8$ will facilitate learning $8 - 4 = 4$

The major limitation with Thorndike's theory is its specificity. How could a teacher ensure such a high degree of stimulus similarity in actual classroom practice? Are the Thorndikean demands for transfer so specific that the theory is nonfunctional? Those who tried to answer this question concluded that the theory is not generally applicable to all learning and is an insufficient explanation of transfer. Therefore, the search for a less stringent, more practical theory was begun.

Theory of Generalization   The first researcher to question identical elements was Charles Judd (1908), who contended that transfer is based on an understanding of general principles rather than upon a recognition of identical elements. Judd proposed that the learner who acquires a general principle responds to the principle involved and not to the specific stimulus. This **theory of generalization** may be illustrated as follows:

Theory of generalization
The theory that general principles, rather than specific elements transfer from situation to situation.

- Learning $3 \times 3 = 9$ facilitates learning $7 \times 8 = 56$
- Learning $15 \div 3 = 5$ facilitates learning $96 \div 16 = 6$
- Learning $4\text{-}7/8 - 3\text{-}1/2 = 1\text{-}3/8$ facilitates learning $37\text{-}3/10 - 19\text{-}1/3 = 17\text{-}29/30$

In the multiplication problem, the general principle "multiply" transfers to the new stimulus. Similarly, the principle "divide" transfers to learning the new division problem. These two principles facilitate transfer in the third problem, which involves the multiplication and division of mixed numbers to find the remainder.

Judd's experiment involved two groups of boys who were to throw darts at an underwater target. The experimental group was taught the principle of refraction, but the control group was not. In the initial trial, both groups performed comparably, with knowledge of the principle of refraction being of no apparent value to the experimental group. However, when Judd increased the depth level of the target in a second trial, the experimental group performed more efficiently. Judd concluded that knowledge of the general principle transferred successfully in the experimental group's second trial and the identical elements of the two trials had no bearing on the performance of the control group's second trial.

It is important to remember that the source of departure for generalization theory was the theory of identical elements. Judd's (1939) research was essentially an attempt to develop a more general and functional theory of transfer, but he did not completely break from the notion of identical elements. His theory merely stresses that transfer may occur under less optimal and stringent conditions than those set forth by Thorndike. Some thirty years after Judd's experiment, two psychologists replicated the original study (Hendrickson & Schroeder, 1941) and concluded that an understanding of a principle transferred to new learning situations, and that the more complete the theoretical principle, the more effectively it transferred. The findings supported Judd's original theory of the effectiveness of principle learning in transfer, and no theory of transfer has since been proposed that is any more operational in the classroom.

Transposition Theory   **Transposition theory** originated with Gestalt psychologists in the 1930s and emphasizes that transfer is the learner's perception of relationships between general principles and specific situations. In other words, if the learner can see and understand a learning situation in its appropriate means-end relationship, the learning is transferable. The better the learner understands this relationship, the greater the transfer. This theory is a refinement of Judd's principle in that, if an individual is to hit the deeply underwater target with a dart, he or she must perceive the situation in terms of the relationships among the previously acquired principles of refraction, water depth, darts, and targets.

Transposition theory
The theory that, if a person perceives similarity in learning situations, transfer will occur.

Hierarchical Transfer   Gagne (1965) discusses **lateral transfer** and **vertical transfer.** Lateral transfer is the generalizing of knowledge across a diverse set of situations at roughly the same level of complexity. It is general and does not apply to hierarchical arrangements of learning so much as to functioning in broader life experiences. In other words, when new stimulus situations arise in the general environment, we can generalize previous learning to them. Thus, lateral transfer is a general ability we acquire and internalize by using knowledge in a variety of situations. Teachers can attempt to broaden learners' capability for lateral transfer by presenting a wide variety of different learning situations in which students must use previous knowledge and experience.

Vertical transfer is the underlying concept in a learning hierarchy. It may be defined as the acquisition of new responses contingent on the learning of prerequisite, subordinate capabilities. Learners operate from two reference points when learning in a hierarchical manner. First, for any transfer to take place, original learning must be established; we cannot learn at a particular level on the hierarchy unless we have the prerequisite skills, which serve as an internal reference point. A second, external reference point is provided by the teacher's instructional strategies as learners are guided into more advanced learning stages. Thus, a rule may be learned because the concepts that make it up have previously been established. Table 10–1 uses learning German verbs to demonstrate vertical transfer.

Vertical transfer, as used by Gagne (1965, 1977a), facilitates the

Lateral transfer
A term used by Gagne to describe the generalization of information at the same level of complexity across multiple situations.

Vertical transfer
A term used by Gagne to describe the generalization of information from simple to increasingly complex levels of learning.

Table 10–1   Examples of Vertical Hierarchical Transfer

Learning Level	Prerequisite Capability (Verbal Transfer)
Level 2: Stimulus—response learning. The student learns to sight German verbs and to recognize and pronounce German sounds.	Apprehension of stimuli (level 1) and S–R connections (level 2) for English verbs and sounds.
Level 4: Verbal chains (associative learning). The student learns German and English verb equivalents.	S–R connections (level 2) for German verbs and sounds.
Level 5: Multiple discrimination. The student learns to discriminate among similar verbs and among the conjugated forms of the verbs.	S–R connections (level 2) for German verbs and chaining (associative learning, level 4) of German–English verb equivalents.
Level 6: Concept learning. The student learns the functions of conjugated German verbs based on an understanding of English verb usage.	S–R connections (level 2) for English verb usage and multiple discrimination (level 5) of German forms.
Level 7: Rule learning. The student develops rules for conjugating German verbs according to their use.	Concept learning (level 6) of German verb conjugation and usage.
Level 8: Problem solving. The student translates a paragraph from English to German using appropriate verb forms.	Rule learning (level 7) of German verb conjugation according to use.

Source: Thornburg (1973b), p. 61. By permission.

transfer of relevant skills up the learning hierarchy. If all classroom materials are presented in a logical, sequential, and meaningful manner, then prerequisite knowledge will become relevant (vertically transferable) to the task at hand. Lateral transfer may also function in a classroom learning situation. For example, a learned intellectual skill is probably (1) generally applicable to a variety of classroom contexts at a particular learning level (lateral transfer) as well as (2) a prerequisite for a more advanced skill.

Other research suggests that vertical transfer may not occur as simply as Gagne's hierarchical arrangement implies (Bergan & Jeska, 1980; Gagne & White, 1978; Rosenthal & Zimmerman, 1978). It may have two limitations. First, prerequisite skills have not always transferred automatically to a higher level skill. Second, a higher level skill may be acquired because learners *add* to their response capacity more learning than was purposively taught in order to maximize transfer. These factors establish learner variability to a greater extent than they disprove vertical transfer as a concept. In sum, lateral transfer occurs whenever something learned, regardless of the level of learning, is transferable to a variety of comparable classroom situations. Vertical transfer occurs whenever learning at one level facilitates learning at a higher level.

Transfer in the Classroom

Implicit within transfer is a relationship between two learning events. The learning of one event should influence the learning of another event.

Positive transfer
The learning of a task is facilitated by previous learning.

Positive Transfer In classroom practice, instruction should be designed to facilitate **positive transfer.** If task 2 is facilitated by learning

task 1, positive transfer is occurring. Thus, learning events should be sequenced—for example, presenting nonconceptual material before conceptual. Similarity of events is important (Ellis, 1972), but so is their sequencing (Gagne, 1977a; Rohwer, Rohwer, & Howe, 1980). The combination of similarity and sequence increases the likelihood of positive transfer occurring.

The following example demonstrates how positive transfer can be accomplished by arranging learning activities within the general framework of similarity and sequencing of events. It is a middle school/junior high level general math unit on linear measurement that I developed for a public school system. Intellectual tasks or skills are highly related and are placed in sequence so that each skill to be learned is facilitated by mastery of the immediate prerequisite skills; thus, positive transfer is operating. This is a unit on measurement.

A. Linear Measure
  1. Knowledge
    a. Identify the basic English units of measure
    b. Identify the basic metric units of measure
    c. Define tolerance
  2. Comprehension
    a. Understand English tools of measurement
    b. Understand metric tools of measurement
  3. Application
    a. Estimate line segments using English units
    b. Measure line segments using English units
    c. Estimate line segments using metric units
    d. Measure line segments using metric units
B. Perimeter
  1. Knowledge
    a. Acquire the formula for finding the perimeter of a polygon
    b. Acquire the formula for finding the circumference of a circle
  2. Comprehension
    a. Be able to replace variables with numbers in a formula
  3. Application
    a. Solve perimeter of polygon
    b. Solve problems using circumference
C. Area
  1. Knowledge
    a. Acquire the formula for the area of a triangle
    b. Acquire the formula for the area of a square
    c. Acquire the formula for the area of a rectangle
    d. Acquire the formula for the area of a parallelogram
    e. Acquire the formula for the area of a trapezoid
    f. Acquire the formula for the area of a circle
  2. Comprehension
    a. Equate square units in English and metric
    b. Understand lateral and total surface area
    c. Be able to replace variables with numbers

3. Application
   a. Solve area of triangle
   b. Solve area of square
   c. Solve area of rectangle
   d. Solve area of trapezoid
   e. Solve area of circle
4. Analysis
   a. Solve word problems involving area

D. Volume
   1. Knowledge
      a. Learn the formula for the volume of a prism
      b. Learn the formula for the volume of a pyramid
      c. Learn the formula for the volume of a cylinder
      d. Learn the formula for the volume of a cone
      e. Learn the formula for the volume of a sphere
   2. Comprehension
      a. Equate cubic measure in English and metric systems
      b. Be able to replace variables with numbers
   3. Application
      a. Solve volume of prism
      b. Solve volume of pyramid
      c. Solve volume of cylinder
      d. Solve volume of cone
      e. Solve volume of sphere
   4. Analysis
      a. Distinguish word problems containing volume

E. Protractor
   1. Knowledge
      a. Learn the terms *degree, protractor, initial side*
   2. Comprehension
      a. Understand how to measure an angle
   3. Applications
      a. Measure any given angle
      b. Draw an angle of any given measure

Other Types of Transfer   Other transfer processes can also occur in learning situations. One is **negative transfer.** If task 1 inhibits the learning of task 2, negative transfer occurs. This phenomenon is also referred to as proactive inhibition or interference (discussed later in this chapter). In other words, prior learning makes learning of a new task difficult. Thus, when the learning of a concept inhibits its combination with another learned concept for the emergence of a rule, negative transfer has occurred.

Negative transfer
The learning of a task is inhibited by previous learning.

Neutral (or zero) **transfer** exists when the learning of task 1 neither facilitates nor inhibits the learning of task 2. This happens most often when students move from one type of material to new, unrelated material. We rarely encounter experiences that are completely novel or free from past association; so the concept of neutral transfer is most applicable to the diverse stimulus situations that generate little, if any, transfer.

Neutral transfer
The belief that some learning tasks are unrelated, thus there is no transfer effect.

When task 1 and task 2 are linked by similarities and these similarities are invoked in the teaching of task 2, **specific transfer** is occurring. Early experiments (Bruce, 1933; Hamilton, 1943; Wylie, 1919) tended to equate this phenomenon with positive transfer, but more recent research (Ellis, 1965; Royer, 1979; Weisgerber, 1971) indicates that similarity from one task to another may bring either positive or negative transfer, depending on the material's meaningfulness to the learner.

Nonspecific (general) **transfer** is a fourth type. When the learning of task 1 affects the learning of task 2, but the transfer between the tasks does not involve any specific stimulus situation in these tasks, the transfer is affected by general principles that are broadly applicable to the nature of the task. Learning mathematical sets is an example of nonspecific transfer in that general mathematical principles not specifically tied to the sets nevertheless facilitate understanding and learning. Royer and others (Royer & Cable, 1975, 1976; Royer & Perkins, 1977) have demonstrated considerable general transfer in instructional materials used in classrooms.

The following motor learning situation illustrates the various types of transfer. Byron, a high school senior, decides to try out for his school golf team because he believes he can learn to play the game well and he is becoming increasingly disinterested in baseball, which he has played well in his previous three years of high school. He has no trouble understanding and learning the basic strokes, ball placement, body and foot position, and so on. However, Byron develops trouble in consistently driving the ball well; he has a tendency to hook it. The coach observes that Byron has good foot position, tees the ball correctly, selects the right clubs for distance, and keeps his eye on the ball when driving. In these instances, *positive transfer* is occurring; that is, he successfully applies the techniques he has learned. Yet his problem with hooking the ball persists. Eventually, the coach detects that Byron turns his shoulder away from the ball when swinging, an action similar to batting in baseball. This is an indication of *negative transfer:* the swinging technique Byron learned for baseball inhibits learning the proper swinging technique for golf. How difficult it will be for Byron to overcome this problem will depend on how strong the baseball habit is and how good the corrective instruction is. Examples of *nonspecific transfer* in this situation are Byron's general physical prowess and athletic skill and his interest and desire to do well, which are transferable from the skill already learned (baseball) to the task he now faces (golf), although they are not specifically tied to either learning situation. No *specific transfer* is found between baseball and golf.

Using Transfer in Instruction

The importance of transfer lies in the fact that one learning task facilitates the learning of another. The concept of transfer states that learning is aided when instruction is arranged to maximize the learning of multiple responses. Here are some suggestions for maximizing transfer in teaching-learning situations.

Make Tasks Similar Similar does not mean identical; it means that instruction should be arranged so there is logical progression in teacher behavior and student learning. The more learning tasks fall within the same behavioral domain, the more students will accommodate them. The greater the dissimilarity between learning tasks, the more learners must fill in the gaps (which they may or may not be able to do) and the less efficient learning is.

If you were teaching first graders a science unit on air, similarity in content would be important. For example, you might first describe what air is, then where it can be found. Then you could describe the characteristics of air (for example, weight and pressure). The key is always to present two related topics consecutively, helping students see how they are related.

Teach for Nonspecific Transfer Based on general principles or the understanding of something, nonspecific transfer is a broader base for transfer because it depends on conceptual or figural understanding. The better students understand something, the more generally they can apply that understanding to subsequent learning. Knowing the structure of something (Bruner, 1960) allows the learner to use that same conceptual knowledge when trying to learn subsequent material that has similar structure.

After teaching that air has characteristics, one of which is pressure, you can extend the discussion into conceptual knowledge. Air has pressure; therefore, air has weight. You introduce the concepts "heavier" and "lighter." You could show similarities between these two concepts (science content) and the concepts "greater than" or "less than" (mathematics content). Subsequently, you could set up an experiment that demonstrates

BMOC/LMOC

William Hendershot was a junior in high school and the most outstanding swimmer on the team. He not only held the school record in several events, but three state records as well. In a sense, Bill was Big Man on Campus (BMOC) because he always received lots of attention from the press.

Bill was also a very intelligent person and made straight "A"s in all his classes. In many respects, Bill had two major pluses going for him. In another respect, Bill was the Loneliest Man on Campus (LMOC). In the high school Bill attended, swimming was not ranked very high in the students' minds. Even though Bill was outstanding, he did not gain the peer recognition that athletes in other sports did, even if they were less capable athletes.

Bill felt the loneliest during lunch hour. No one ever ate lunch with Bill or invited him to go with the gang off campus during lunch hour. He was always by himself. Further, some of the school "jocks" nicknamed Bill "egghead" because he was so smart. He also had better manners than most of his adolescent counterparts. Bill never questioned his sense of accomplishment, but he felt very lonely at times. He had some social skills, but they were not on a par or compatible with those of his peers. Their criticism of him was always noticed and always unchecked. Their immaturity was often exercised at Bill's expense. Bill was indeed more LMOC than BMOC.

What Do You Think?

1. Did Bill's general ability transfer into both physical and intellectual excellence?

2. If general ability is transferable, why does Bill lack comparable social skills?

3. Is it the school's responsibility to help Bill and those like him develop in all three areas, physical, intellectual, and social?

Transfer Options			
Strategy	Learning	Potential for Retention	Interference
Isolated Context	High	Low	Low
Multiple Contexts	High	High	Low
General Transfer	High	High	Low
High Task Similarity	High	High	High

that air has weight. These interrelationships are based on general understanding and facilitate learning in many ways.

Make Learning Meaningful and Relevant   Asking students to learn information that has meaning and is relevant maximizes transfer. Meaningful, nonspecific transfer is more likely to facilitate learning than nonmeaningful, nonspecific transfer. You could discuss the idea of expansion and contraction of air, showing how the two concepts are related to the air's temperature. Then you could ask students to find examples of temperature's effects on other objects. The idea of a hot air balloon ascending into the atmosphere illustrates one application of the principle of warm air rising.

Transfer Learning Out of School   Students sometime fail to process learning tasks well because they question their usefulness. One way to minimize this problem is to extend all academic or in-school learning to out-of-school contexts, preferably those students can find in their natural environment. This enhances the meaningfulness and relevance of learning for students.

Once first-graders have working concepts of air, its characteristics and functions, you could apply their knowledge to a broader setting. For example, you could present the "fire triangle" and explain how air is needed if a fire is to burn. Students could learn how to start a fire safely and how to put it out. The ability to use learning in practical settings confirms learning. Relating any learning to life situations maximizes the transfer effects and increases the likelihood of retention.

Retention

Forgetting
The loss in memory of previously learned material.

Storage phase
The coding of information into the mind for subsequent recall.

Retention is the maintenance of a learned response over an extended period of time. It stands in direct contrast to **forgetting,** the tendency of a learned response to fade and disappear over an extended period of time. Gagne (1977a) equates retention to a **storage phase,** during which learned material is retained until subsequently emitted. Recall or recognition of the previously learned responses represents the **retrieval**

phase. Figure 10–1 illustrates this sequence of events in learning and remembering. That Gagne stresses retention and acquisition equally in illustrating the events of learning suggests two points basic to this discussion. First, the emphasis on retention should not lead us to lose sight of the importance of the original learning. Second, the importance of retention in learning affirms the need for classroom teachers to know and use instructional techniques designed to ensure retention.

Retrieval phase
The ability to draw out of memory previously acquired learning.

Research

Ebbinghaus conducted an early study on retention in 1885. After mastering a set of nonsense syllables, he plotted the percentage of the syllables he retained over a month (see Figure 10–2). Upon measuring retention

Figure 10–1

Sequence of events in learning—storage and retrieval. [Source: Gagne (1970b), p. 71. Reprinted by permission of the publisher.]

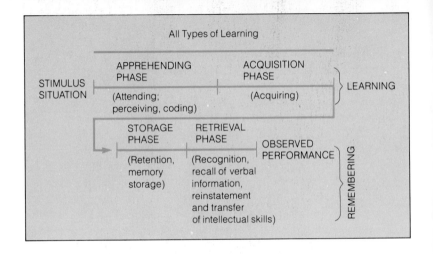

after nineteen minutes, Ebbinghaus found he could recall only 58 percent of the learned responses. A gradual decline in retention followed the drastic drop during the first twenty-four hours, and after thirty-one days, he could recall 21 percent of the original list. The retention rate seemed to plateau at 21 percent. Similar studies focusing on nonsense material were conducted throughout the early part of this century, and in most cases, the retention curves were basically the same.

Figure 10–3 is an example of this later research, which further confirmed the immediate loss of learning with nonsense syllables and demonstrated the higher retention rate of more meaningful material. By

Figure 10–2

Ebbinghaus curve of retention with nonsense syllables

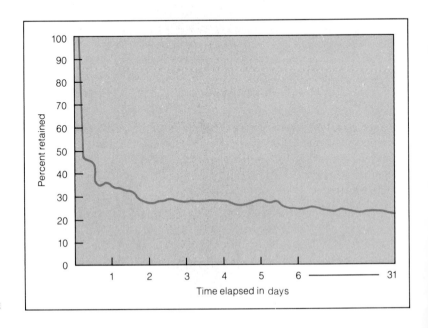

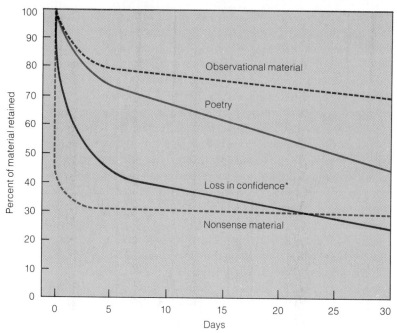

Figure 10–3

Typical retention rates for different kinds of material. [*Source: Gilliland (1948), p. 23. Reprinted by permission of the author and the American Psychological Association.*]

*Observational material was based on a picture of an office scene. Loss in confidence was based on the subject's certainty as to the correctness of his responses.

meaningfulness is meant familiar material or material that can be put into relational or conceptual frameworks for which the learner sees some purpose. What learning variables facilitate retention and what ones do not remains to be investigated. It is likely that some meaningful material will be forgotten, although material presented by the classroom teacher is usually better retained. That is, upon the single presentation of classroom materials, more meaningful material is better learned than less meaningful material, and the retention is higher.

McGeoch and Whitely (1926) tested recall of observed material, which was a sheet of cardboard displaying two photos, a penny, a white button, a one-cent postage stamp, and a red and white label. Immediate recall was almost 100 percent, and the researchers found that, even after fifteen days, there was 95 percent recall. The retention of the observed material seemed to level off at about 65 percent after one hundred or more days. Gilliland (1948) investigated the same phenomenon and found that his subjects still retained 80 percent of the observed material after twenty-five days.

Retention curves for poetry also indicate a much higher rate than for nonsense syllables but a lower rate than for the simple learning of observed material. McGeoch and Whitely (1928) investigated recall of learned stanzas of poetry. Within the first thirty days after learning, retention dropped sharply to just over 40 percent, although it leveled off at that point. Gilliland's (1948) similar study showed a 50 percent retention rate in poetry after thirty days.

Dietze and James (1931) tested recall of factual material subjects read only once. Each subject was presented with a short article and was subsequently asked to recall through a series of multiple-choice questions (a procedure not unlike existing classroom practice). The immediate loss of learning was 30 percent (a 70 percent retention rate), with a gradual decline of retention throughout the first thirty days. Beyond that time, the subjects tended to maintain learning at a 55 percent retention rate.

Bower and Clark (1969) investigated recall of twelve lists of nouns. They presented them to a group of college students with the instructions to learn each list and then to make up a story using the nouns in it. Another group of students was given the same lists to learn, but they were not required to compose a story using the nouns. Immediate recall of each list appeared to be the same for both groups—99 percent. However, the cumulative effects of recall were markedly different for the two groups. When asked to recall all twelve lists, the group that had used the nouns retained 93 percent. Students in the other group retained only 13 percent of the nouns in the twelve lists. Presumably, the practical use of the nouns in stories increased their meaningfulness for the first group. This research is especially significant in that it closely approximates the type of learning behavior characteristic of the classroom.

As researchers have moved into more complex material, such as textual prose, it has become more difficult to specify all that is being learned and thus retained. The relevancy of a prose passage to the learner, its length, the complexity of its content, and the learner's own input into the learning process are variables that affect both learning and retention (Jenkins, 1974; Lee, 1979). If a prose passage is well organized, such as a paragraph in a text, free recall of factual information is generally higher than with less conceptually well organized material (Ceppi, 1973; Frase, 1969; Hirst, 1980; Myers, Pezdek, & Coulson, 1973). A similar finding occurred in retention studies where one group learned summary sentences. This group had higher retention rates than the group that did not learn summary sentences (Glover, Bruning, & Plake, 1982). We might conclude that the better organized and the more conceptual material is, the greater the likelihood of retention (Johnson, 1973; Moors & Clarke, 1981; Shimmerlink, 1978; Yussen & Berman, 1981; Yussen, Matthews, & Knight, 1980).

We can draw four conclusions from the research on retention. First, meaningful materials can be retained better than nonsense materials. Second, highly meaningful material is better retained than less meaningful material. For example, the retention rate for poetry, which is usually learned by the association of words rather than by the meaning of the words, is lower than the rate for materials learned on the basis of their contextual meaning (Mandler & Richey, 1971). Third, contextual materials or lists of words that have associative strength seem to be retained better than the materials or words that have little internal similarity of meaning (Blaubergs, 1976; Schwartz & Humphreys, 1976). Fourth, concrete material is retained better than abstract material (Just & Brownell, 1974; Paivio, 1971).

Nonconceptual Retention   Reinforcement is critical to original non-conceptual learning. Nonconceptual learning is not internally processed the way conceptual learning is; so what happens to it? The process of recall involves emitting previously learned responses under appropriate stimulus conditions. This position is derived from the stimulus-response model. In nonconceptual retention, three conditions may produce recall.

First, response frequency may be a major factor in recall. A response that is used with some regularity (such as a telephone number) is more likely to be recalled than a fact learned in an American HIstory class that has no useful retention function beyond the immediate learning setting. Second, the stimulus that triggers the recall of nonconceptual information may be very powerful; thus, a response that has not been recalled for a long time may suddenly become available. Students who are asked to recall an isolated fact to answer a question on a classroom test may not perceive the stimulus to be as powerful as they would if the recall of the same information were critical to winning an award. Third, if nonconceptual information is organized efficiently, the associative strength might make it more recallable.

Conceptual Retention   Materials learned as concepts or strategies are thought to be better retained than nonconceptual responses. The learner processes understanding, thus develops an internal framework from which to retrieve important learning (Joyce, 1979). Further, the learner processes all attributes relevant to the learning situation, not just specific pieces of information. Conceptual retention focuses on learners' understanding of the material they have learned (Craik & Lockhart, 1972; Kintsch, 1974) and their ability to use such understanding in new and different learning contexts (Kvale, 1977). Because this conceptual learning has high level meaningfulness, it also has high retention rates (Bransford, Barclay, & Franks, 1972). This position is derived from the cognitive learning perspective.

Thornburg (1980b) studied retention with 153 seventh graders enrolled in general math to see how much original learning occurred during the first semester of the seventh-grade year and how well it was retained across the second semester and the summer months between grades seven and eight. Students learned three major topics (whole numbers, decimals, and fractions). A one-hundred-item pretest (form A) was administered to all incoming seventh graders during the first week of school. Table 10–2 summarizes the means of the tests across the four testing periods. All means are based on 116 seventh graders because that is the number that remained in the study across all four testing periods.

The pretest mean was 57.0 points. Although not designed as a retention test, it does give an indirect measure of how well elementary school learning was retained when students moved into a junior high setting. The posttest mean (measured eighteen weeks later) was 76.0, indicating that students, on an average, gained nineteen points as a result

Table 10–2   Retention of General Math Content Across Multiple Retention Periods

Test Period/Form	Mean	S.D.
September, Form A	57.0	15.2
January, Form B	76.0	13.4
May, Form A	81.2	15.7
September, Form B	74.0	15.2

of instruction across one semester. The posttest was also a hundred-item parallel form (B) to the pretest.

The final retention test was given during the first week of the students' eighth-grade year. This testing period was selected because it followed a time of no instruction and could possibly test the effects of learning loss across the summer months. Form B was given as the retention test. Table 10–2 reflects a mean of 74.0, a seven-point drop from the score in May but a nonsubstantial drop when compared with the original posttest in January. It does demonstrate forgetting across the summer, although it also reflects the retention rate from the end of direct instruction to the point of entry into a new grade level (January to September). Although it is inappropriate to overgeneralize from any single study, this one seems to add to an already large number of studies that show that conceptual, contextual, and meaningful material is more likely to be retained than nonconceptual, isolated, and nonmeaningful material (Block, 1982; DiVesta & Gray, 1973; Gagne & Paget, 1980; Taylor, 1982).

Memory

Information Processing

Memory
The ability for humans to store learning in their mind for subsequent use.

The model for **memory** is based on the idea that learning is stored in memory structures through internal operations that not only make storage more efficient but also make the information available for recall. There are several explanations of information processing, primarily because our understanding of retention is incomplete. Most explanations have a cognitive orientation because cognitive processing is essential to the information-processing model (Bransford, 1979; Mayer, 1975; Reese, 1976). Bransford's model, which I discussed in Chapter 1, includes information from the environment or reception of material, sensory storage or input, short-term memory, and long-term memory.

Reception
Attending to learning phenomena within the environment.

Reception is awareness of the environment: What is happening or going on? To what are you attending? Gage and Berliner (1979) describe this process as orienting responses; they are investigative in nature and help us orient and/or adapt to environmental stimuli, to which we then respond. Students who are curious about and explore the school environment are likely to take in more, and as a result learn more, than students who are teacher oriented.

We receive and register stimuli or learning materials in the sensory storage and represent information through verbal, visual, or tactile modes (Bransford, 1979). These representations decay if further processing does not occur. Because the sensory stores are temporary, information must be retrieved from them in order to enter short-term storage. We accomplish this by attending to it. We code items in short-term storage into some type of verbal (phonemic) or visual features or categories. The capacity for short-term storage is very small, and, without rehearsal, the information is

often lost by displacement—that is, new material enters short-term storage and crowds nonrehearsed material out. Long-term memory has an unlimited storage capacity; so information that is highly meaningful or rich in semantic content may be rehearsed and subsequently organized into more complex memory structures. In this way, material leaves short-term memory and becomes part of the large response repertoire stored in long-term memory. When information is moved into long-term storage, we transform it into relevant codes and categories we can retrieve on demand. In a real sense, long-term memory is dominated by conceptually rich material that renders itself meaningful in numerous ways because of how we process it and how it interacts with already stored materials. This makes information-processing approaches to retention a more satisfactory explanation of retention than the associative approaches, where material has limited organization and structure in which to be stored or interact. Thus, both conceptual and information-processing approaches to retention are more complete explanations of human memory than are association theories.

Short-Term Memory

My discussion of retention thus far has been concerned with long-term memory or retention—the ability to recall learned situations in which we are required to retain responses for only a brief period of time. Looking up a phone number and remembering it long enough to dial, remembering outstanding plays in a football game, recalling the names of streets just passed in an unfamiliar town, a waiter's ability to take orders for a large party and subsequently serve each person what he or she ordered, a card player's recall of all the cards that have been played from hand to hand in a game, and remembering someone's name throughout a party are all examples of short-term retention. This type of learning and retention functions well for its purpose, but it is not typical of classroom learning. Classroom learning requires long-term retention and its implications for learning are more diverse than those of short-term retention.

Little is known about the acquisition, retention, and transfer of short-term learning or about the distinctions between short-term and long-term retention. The theory of **trace decay** is an explanation of short-term memory (Brown, 1958; Conrad, 1967). Essentially, it holds that, after we receive a short-term learning stimulus, such as a phone number, we form a cerebral memory trace, which decays rapidly. If we do not use that number again soon, the trace will disappear. If, however, we use the phone number frequently, we will maintain the trace throughout the period of use and often for a relatively brief time after we stop using it.

In trying to equate short-term and long-term retention, some researchers have attempted to explain short-term learning as subject to the same processes of forgetting and extinction as long-term learning. For example, one investigator concluded that a type of interference termed retroactive inhibition operates in both long-term and short-term memory (Murdock, 1961). The amount of new learning intervening between the original use (learning) of material and its subsequent recall is a variable that affects forgetting. Thus, after we learn one phone number, learning several new phone numbers and using them all infrequently will undoubtedly interfere with our retention of the original number. Underwood (1964a) has indicated that short-term memory is not even a function of retention but is a simple type of original learning that is neither internally encoded (stored) nor strengthened by use. Instead, this learning simply carries over from use and must be relearned if use becomes infrequent.

Interference Theory

Interference occurs when one learned response inhibits the learning of another. Rather than attributing forgetting to weakly formed original responses or to an inevitable function of time, most interference theorists believe that certain conditions of new learning affect a learner's ability to recall previous responses. They use two terms to describe this phenomenon of interference: **retroactive inhibition** and **proactive inhibition.** When learning task 2 interferes with retention of task 1, retroactive inhibition occurs. When learning task 1 interferes with retention of task 2, proactive inhibition occurs.

John McGeoch first advanced the theory of retroactive inhibition in the 1930s. Studies caused McGeoch (1942) to propose that forgetting does not occur unless something interferes with the original learning. If a

Trace decay
The gradual fading of learning that has been stored in short-term memory.

Interference
The process whereby one learned response is inhibited by other learning.

Retroactive inhibition
The inability to recall a previous learning task because of the acquisition of a more recent task.

Proactive inhibition
The inability to recall a task because of interference from an earlier learned task.

person learns a list of words, he or she should be able to recall that list indefinitely unless *similar* new learning takes place between the time of the original learning and its recall and thereby interferes with the recall (Weaver, Duncan, & Bird, 1972).

Assume that a teacher has taught one class the intellectual skills necessary for acquiring the concept "proper fractions." Next the teacher teaches the skills necessary for acquiring the concept "improper fractions." After having learned both concepts, the students are tested on proper fractions. Experimentally, the learning task would look like this:

Learns task 1	Learns task 2	Retention test (recall)
Proper fractions	Improper fractions	Task 1, proper fractions

Much to the teacher's surprise, the students do not do well on the test. In some cases, their answers are improper fractions instead of proper fractions. The phenomenon operating here is that the learning of task 2, improper fractions, is interfering with the retroactive recall of task 1, proper fractions.

Now assume that the teacher instructs another class in the same material but gives the students the retention test on proper fractions prior to teaching the concept "improper fractions." Experimentally, the learning task would look like this:

Learns task 1	Retention test (recall)	Learns task 2
Proper fractions	Task 1, proper fractions	Improper fractions

The teacher finds that students in the second class do much better on the test. The lack of retroactive inhibition from the introduction of similar additional learning results in significantly better student recall.

Table 10–3　Retroactive Inhibition

	Learning Conditions			Interference Effect
Class 1	*Learns task 1*	*Learns task 2*	*Retention test (recall)*	
	Proper fractions	Improper fractions	Task 1, proper fractions	Strong
Class 2	*Learns task 1*		*Retention test (recall)*	
	Proper fractions	(Does not learn task 2 prior to retention test)	Task 1, proper fractions	None
Class 1	*Learns task 1*	*Learns task 2*	*Retention test (recall)*	
	Proper fractions	Mixed numbers	Task 1, proper fractions	Mild
Class 2	*Learns task 1*		*Retention test (recall)*	
	Proper fractions	(Does not learn task 2 prior to retention test)	Task 1, proper fractions	None

Source: Thornburg (1973b), p. 73. Used by permission.

Research studies conclusively show that the more similar two tasks are, the greater the interference level. Thus, a similar teaching situation, such as the following, would not be likely to show such a high degree of interference.

Learns task 1	Learns task 2	Retention test (recall)
Proper fractions	Mixed numbers	Task 1, proper fractions

In learning the concept "mixed numbers," the students would be dealing with the combination of a whole number and a proper fraction, the former entirely different from the original learning and the latter identical to it. Task 2 would therefore provide little interference in the recall of task 1. Osgood (1949) observed that, when stimuli are similar but the responses are varied, retroactive interference is also increased. Many learners find it difficult to maintain distinctions between highly similar stimuli that require different responses, especially if they are instructed in verbatim ways but are asked to recall in nonverbatim ways (Ghatala, Levin, & Truman, 1981; Hall, 1955; Levin, Ghatala, & Truman, 1979). Table 10–3 illustrates teaching conditions that generate the potential for retroactive inhibition.

Proactive inhibition exists when task 1 interferes with the recall of task 2. This phenomenon, first emphasized by Underwood (1949), signifies the type of forgetting that occurs every day. We typically acquire new responses that are highly similar to previously acquired responses, and upon recall of the new responses, we often recall components of the first learning situation. To illustrate, if a class first learns the concept "proper fractions" without an opportunity for recall and then learns the concept "improper fractions," proactive inhibition would affect the recall of the improper fractions in a retention test on that subject. The learning task would look like this:

Table 10–4 Proactive Inhibition

	Learning Conditions			Interference Effect
Class 1	*Learns task 1*	*Recalls task 1*	*Learns task 2*	*Retention test (recall)*	
	Proper fractions	No opportunity	Improper fractions	Task 2, improper fractions	Strong
Class 2	*Learns task 1*	*Recalls task 1*	*Learns task 2*	*Retention test (recall)*	
	Proper fractions	Immediate and frequent opportunities	Improper fractions	Task 2, improper fractions	None
Class 1	*Learns task 1*	*Recalls task 1*	*Learns task 2*	*Retention test (recall)*	
	Mixed numbers	No opportunity	Improper fractions	Task 2, improper fractions	Mild
Class 2	*Learns task 1*	*Recalls task 1*	*Learns task 2*	*Retention test (recall)*	
	Proper fractions	Immediate and frequent opportunities	Improper fractions	Task 2, improper fractions	None

Source: Thornburg (1973b), p. 74. Used by permission.

Learns task 1	Learns task 2	Retention test (recall)
Proper fractions	Improper fractions	Task 2, improper fractions

As was true in the case of retroactive inhibition, the similarity or dissimilarity of the two learning tasks is a major variable in the strength of the proactive inhibitory effects. (Table 10–4 illustrates this point.)

A study by Ausubel, Stager, and Gaite (1969) indicates that highly meaningful verbal material does not appear to exhibit proactive inhibitory effects. They presented learners with portions of meaningful verbal materials rather than with the usual lists of serial or paired-associative verbal tasks to be learned by rote. The experimental learning task (task 2) was material regarding Zen Buddhism. The "inhibitory" learning material (task 1) covered two topics: Buddhism and drug addiction. The similarity and relevance of task 1 to task 2 should be apparent. After they had learned the two tasks, the students were given both immediate and delayed retention tests on the Zen Buddhism material. When they analyzed the data, the researchers found no evidence of proactive inhibition effects in the students' recall of the Zen Buddhism material in either test situation. The classroom teacher may want to consider the meaningfulness of verbal materials in planning teaching strategies for the control of proactive inhibitory effects (Butler & Chechile, 1976).

Intelligence and Retention

Several early retention studies (Achilles, 1920; Dietze, 1931; Gillette, 1936; Lyon, 1916; Mulhall, 1917) clearly demonstrate that retention increases as chronological age (CA) and mental age (MA) increase. As chronological age increases, retention strengths are affected by development. Mental age may vary from chronological age. Someone who has an intelligence quotient of 100 has the same CA and MA. As IQ moves upward from 100,

MA increases and retention rate is more affected by MA than by CA. The growth in mental age increases information storage facilities and enhances learning and recall potential. Although these studies reflect biological maturation patterns, they do not allow for the variable of individual differences in basic capability, or intelligence, and its effects on retention of learning.

Klausmeier, Feldhausen, and Check (1959) measured retention tests among children with low, average, and high intelligence. When given the same material to learn, the students with lower intelligence learned less than those with higher intelligence, a factor attributable to basic acquisition ability. However, there was no proportional difference between the acquisition and retention rates of the students of low, average, or high intelligence (see Figure 10–4). Members of each subgroup recalled the materials they were able to learn at a proportionally similar retention rate. Researchers have concluded that, although there are substantial differences in learning rates for various levels of intelligence, there are no significant proportional differences in retention rate. These findings have been substantiated in a number of studies where learning and retention curves are parallel. (Gentile, Monaco, Iheozor-Ehofor, Ndu, & Ogbonaya, 1982; Royer, Hambleton, & Cadorette, 1978; Shuell & Keppel, 1970; Underwood, 1954).

Research on the relationship between intelligence and retention has implications for the teacher. Because studies show that most learners' retention rates are proportionately the same, the teacher's primary concern involves original learning. By making sure that students have the time necessary to respond to teaching, the teacher is in effect increasing the amount of learning that might occur. The students' recall is then related to the amount of information he or she has learned.

Figure 10–4
Retention rates in subtraction problems, by intelligence. [Source: Klausmeier, Feldhausen, & Check (1959), p. 69. Reprinted by permission of the authors.]

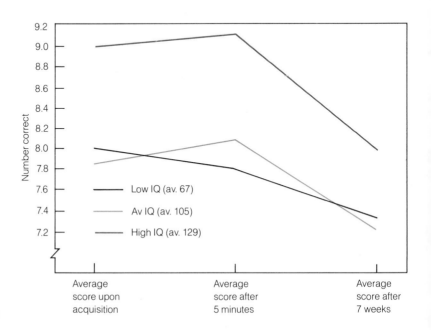

Strategies for Increasing Retention Rate

There are at least three ways for classroom teachers to increase students' retention: **original learning, overlearning,** and **spaced review.** I have continually stressed the importance of the quality of original learning and its effect on recall. The following strategies will help teachers impart intellectual skills that students will retain over long periods of time:

1. Be sure the complexity of the desired response is within the range of the learner's capabilities and previous learning.

2. Provide for some warm-up or practice if the response may be affected positively by the transfer.

3. Make each learning situation clear and specific enough so that the student can learn the desired discriminatory response.

4. Insert relevancy and meaningfulness into the learning situation.

5. Reinforce the learner's response when appropriate.

   Overlearning is the practice of a learned response beyond the point of mastery. Overlearned (frequently recalled) responses tend to be retained for longer periods of time than those not used after mastery (Briggs, 1957; Keppel, 1968). Therefore, teachers should consider the following strategies:

1. Spend additional time on materials that appear to be inherently difficult to learn.

Original learning
The point at which a response is initially acquired.

Overlearning
Practicing a learned response after it is presumably mastered.

Spaced review
The re-presentation of previously learned material for the purpose of enhancing its retention.

2. Once mastery has been assured, provide additional meaningful learning situations in which the student can recall and confirm a newly mastered intellectual skill.

A different, but equally important strategy in facilitating increased retention is spaced review. Spaced review should not be considered synonymous with overlearning or additional practice. In spaced review, previously learned material is periodically re-presented and essentially relearned, with opportunities for the learner to recall and reuse the learned responses. Such relearning reestablishes the conditions of the original learning, thus strengthening the learning in the storage and retrieval stages (retention). The teacher should consider the following strategies:

1. Provide spaced review conditions periodically and systematically throughout a teaching unit or semester.

2. Provide additional teaching-learning situations in which the student not only is learning new material but is required to recall previously acquired responses as well.

3. Use opportunities provided in new learning situations to interrelate relevant existing learning.

Day-After Recall as Retention

Information about human learning has found application outside of, as well as within, educational environments. For example, marketing researchers are very concerned about the effect of commercials and how commercials are retained—an important outcome in product identification. They use the same principles as educational psychologists and teachers and a few additional ones. Perhaps some marketing research strategies could be used in educational settings.

In marketing, an important question is "What is day-after recall?" The history of day-after recall goes back to the late 1940s and the work of George Gallup, Sr., in Princeton, New Jersey. He became intrigued with the problem of measuring commercial effectiveness. In those days, commercials were sixty seconds long. Gallup's experimentation led to a twenty-four-hour recall strategy in which he asked what advertised products could be remembered from the day-before commercials. Different advertisers became interested in his work, and Gallup syndicated the service in 1950. The concept he stressed was "impact."

Compton Advertising began working with a similar system in the 1950s. They started with the forgetting curve work of Herman Ebbinghaus and tested commercials twelve, twenty-four, forty-eight, and seventy-two hours after exposure. Their curves indicated that the greatest impact was within the first twenty-four hours, and Compton subsequently confined their studies to day-after recall.

Extensive testing has been done on the phenomenon of day-after recall. Several variables have been investigated—type of shows, differences from city to city, daytime versus nighttime, commercials at the beginning and end of a show compared to those during a show, and so on. Most field studies indicated that the staying power of the commercial message was the most important thing in people's minds.

Later in the 1950s, Procter and Gamble, the nation's leading advertiser, began studying day-after recall on their own. Their first field study was on the "Loretta Young Show" in Bloomington, Indiana. It was all door-to-door interviewing. Procter and Gamble believed their data provided them with key information that would improve the sale of their products. They were very secretive about their techniques, guarding them like one of their product formulas. They believed they had a considerable advantage over their competition.

The first time Procter and Gamble made any public statements about their research on retention was in February 1972, in the *Journal of Advertising*. John D. Henry, then manager of their research team said:

We do on-air testing and we talk to consumers following exposure without ever having recruited them to look at the advertising. In our judgment, this is the way one should look at advertising. In our judgment, this is the way one should measure communication; as it has to take place in the real world— fighting for attention and memory and reaction against all the advertising which competes for a share of the consumer's mind. That's doing it the hard way, I guess, but that's how it is in the real world as we see it.

At present, there are five major research firms whose primary business is advertising research, a major portion of which is day-after recall. In addition, several major companies have their own research teams. In 1982, an estimated $12 million was spent on studies designed to test day-after recall.

Annotated Readings

Dooling, D. J., & Christiansen, R. E. (1977). Episodic and semantic aspects of memory for prose. *Journal of Experimental Psychology: Human Memory and Learning, 3,* 428–436.

> *Subjects' knowledge about the topic of a prose passage was manipulated to evaluate constructive processes in remembering. Those who knew during comprehension that a passage was about a famous person falsely recognized thematic sentences in two-day and one-week retention intervals. Subjects who learned of the famous person's identity during recall made fewer errors. The study demonstrated that, with the passage of time, individuals have increased difficulty retrieving passage-specific information. They compensate by using related information in memory.*

Gentile, J. R., Monaco, N., Iheozor-Ehofor, I. E., Ndu, A. N., & Ogbonaya, P. K. (1982). Retention by "fast" and "slow" learners. *Intelligence, 6,* 125–138.

> *Several experiments were conducted to test if forgetting would be parallel to learning. Nigerian and American students were given poems and lists of words to learn. Although there were variances between slow and fast learners, both groups recalled a similar proportion of their learning. This study confirms earlier studies that indicate that slow learners can retain as well as fast learners.*

Glass, A. L., Eddy, J. K., & Schwanenflugel, P. J. (1980). The verification of high and low imagery sentences. *Journal of Experimental Psychology: Human Learning and Memory, 6,* 692–704.

> *Experiments were designed to investigate the relationship between imagery and sentence verification. In one experiment, high and low imagery sentences whose subjects and predicates had been matched for frequency and relatedness were rated by subjects for comprehensibility. High imagery sentences were rated as more comprehensible. In other experiments, students were asked to maintain a visual pattern while attempting to verify sentences. Verification of high imagery sentences interfered more with retention of visual patterns than did the verification of low imagery sentences.*

Moors, L., & Clarke, A. M. (1981). The effect of shaping two levels of information processing on children's immediate and delayed retention. *Educational Psychology, 1,* 107–117.

> *Two groups of eighth-grade students listened to a tape-recorded prose passage. Interspersed questions designed to direct attention to either the factual content or arguments and principles resulted in superior retention by the group given principled questions, both immediately and at three-day recall.*

Smith, S. M. (1982). Enhancement of recall using multiple environmental contexts during learning. *Memory and Cognition, 10,* 405–412.

> *Distributing the presentation of sublists of words into multiple learning rooms produced better free recall than a single learning room condition for students who were given a comprehensive recall test in a new environment. The experimenters found that the contextual dependence of recall was nullified by using multiple learning rooms rather than a single room for input.*

Yussen, S. R., & Berman, L. (1981). Memory predictions for recall and recognition in first-, third-, and fifth-grade children. *Developmental Psychology, 17,* 224–229.

Children from the first, third, and fifth grades were administered four different tasks that assessed their accuracy in predicting future memory. In addition, memory was assessed. Two of the tasks required recall; the remaining two required recognition. For each type, one version involved a word list and the other, a sentence list. Accuracy at predicting recall performance improved across grades, but accuracy at predicting recognition did not. Examination of children's predictions revealed that there was no systematic differentiation of task difficulty.

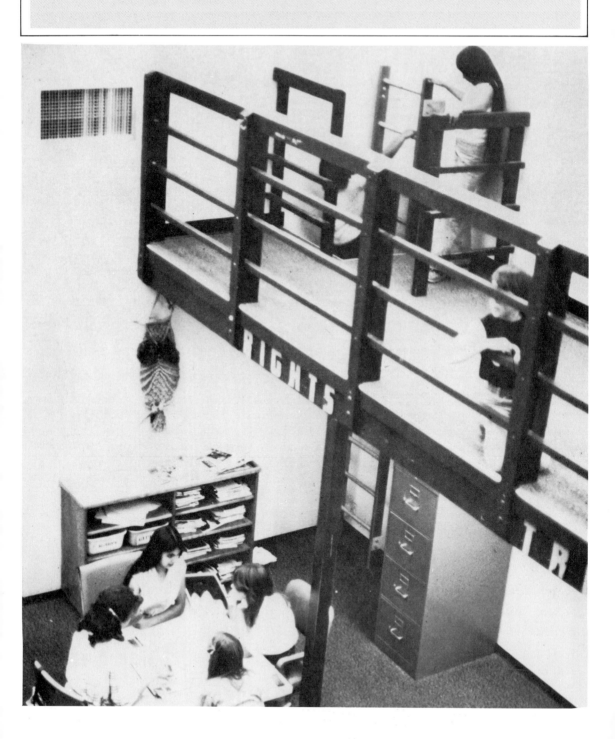

Classroom Motivation

Clem Massey, a well-known football coach, gave a talk on motivation at a youth conference for juniors and seniors in high school. He suggested that a major problem with today's adolescents is a lack of incentive to do things. He argued that "youth culture" interferes with productive behavior that would help adolescents adjust to life. As might be anticipated, many of his analogies were related to football, which he described as "typifying the dreams and goals of American youth because it draws out the energy, discipline, and competitive nature of the individual."

In the question and answer period that followed Massey's talk, several students raised pertinent issues. Some of their inquiries were:

- *In a society controlled by adults, what incentive is there for young people to get involved in the same old things?*
- *I've been trying to find a part-time job for over a year now and can't. I'm tired of looking.*
- *Not everyone is born with athletic talent; thus, many of us aren't offered the same advantages as the high school athletes.*
- *I think you are wrong about youth cultures. Some of my most productive moments have been doing things with friends.*
- *I've tried several different jobs and taken as many different electives in school as I could, but nothing excites me. Any suggestions?*
- *I'm interested in art, but I find most people don't really care about it. Are you suggesting that I have to be like everyone else if I'm going to make it?*
- *Why does society try to make people so dependent on it? Doesn't that enter into a person's motivation?*

Careful analysis of these questions reveals a common thread running through them—the human need system. People are motivated to pursue activities that help meet their needs, whether those needs are academic, social, or economic. To behave in ways that do not meet such needs typically results in an intensification of the need, a dissatisfaction with personal behavior, and a shift in behavior in order to meet the need. Motivation must be considered in relation to needs because this relationship tells us a great deal about human behavior. In this chapter, I discuss:

- *Theories of motivation*
- *Types of motivation*
- *Motivation in the classroom*

317

When we think of motivation, we usually think of what it is that prompts or causes a person to act. In scientific terms, motivation is an "energizing condition of an organism that serves to direct the organism's behavior, usually toward a goal or goals of a certain class" (Wrightsman, Sigelman, & Sanford, 1979, p. 361). The classroom teacher most likely thinks of motivation in more practical terms, such as those factors within a teaching-learning situation that trigger student learning behavior. In this chapter, I first briefly consider motivational research to provide a theoretical framework. Then I explore the practical aspects of motivation to help you recognize and plan classroom situations that motivate learning.

Theories of Motivation

Hedonism

The early works of most stimulus-response psychologists were built around the concept of learning as a process by which organisms reduce their physiological needs by using a new (learned) behavior. Theoretically, the organism's deprived physiological state compelled it to act. This state was termed the *motivation for behavior*. This process of using new behavior to change deprivation to satiation was termed **hedonism**—the tendency of an organism to seek pleasure while avoiding pain.

Hedonism
The deliberate attempt to seek pleasure while avoiding pain.

Such a theory of motivation and behavior was suggested several thousand years ago in classical Greece (Albee, 1901), but it first became formalized in Thorndike's learning laws. His law of effect states that every act is followed by either a satisfying or an annoying state of affairs. Presumably, the actor will perform behavior that produces a satisfying state of affairs; that is, the actor is motivated to behave in a way that brings about a pleasurable state. However, in some cases, despite the actor's intentions, an annoying (painful) state of affairs follows behavior—an occurrence that will later diminish the actor's motivation when reencountering the same situation.

Drive Theory

Drive reduction theory
A theory that states an organism is motivated to act when a need has to be satisfied.

Secondary drive
Secondary drives occur when a primary drive takes on a non-physiological way of being met; e.g., the selection of food.

Hull's **drive reduction theory** grew out of Thorndike's work. Hull concluded that all motives are related to basic physiological needs and that these needs give rise to certain physiological or social drives that the organism learns. Hull termed the physiological needs primary drives, an aroused state of the organism (motivation) produced by basic physiological needs (food, water, elimination, respiration, and sex) that compels the organism to act to reduce the drive and restore equilibrium. He called the psychological or social drives **secondary drives.** Hull postulated that organisms learn these secondary drives along with a primary drive. For example, as you try to reduce the physiological drive of hunger, you may be exposed to social rules for eating behavior. You then associate these rules with the drive reduction of eating and learn them as a secondary drive. Your newly learned social behavior may later determine how you reduce your hunger drive. Thus, you are motivated by hunger not only to eat (primary drive), but also to eat in a socially accepted way (secondary drive).

Since Hull's work in 1943, there have been many questions raised about the effectiveness of drive reduction theory as a satisfactory explanation for motivation. Several writers (McKeachie & Doyle, 1970; White, 1959) have suggested that drive reduction is only a partial explanation of motivation, and many new theories have been proposed to account for psychological and social motivations that may *not* be directly tied to primary physiological needs.

Needs Theory

Needs theory suggests that most of our needs are learned, thus psychological in nature. In other words, as we interact with the environment, we acquire certain needs that allow us to respond to our experiences. Thus, when motivated by a need, we are responding to a psychological condition we have acquired through learning. When motivated by a drive, we are responding to a physiological condition.

Needs theory
The belief that our needs are learned and, as they are met, they motivate us to behave.

A. H. Maslow's (1943) categorization of individual psychological needs is still advanced as a highly satisfactory explanation of motivation by many contemporary writers. Although Maslow recognized physiological needs as strong motivators, he felt that motivation has a broader basis than basic drives. Maslow refers to the physiological needs as deficiencies and contends that, as long as such deficiencies exist, the individual is not free to seek out other needs. In this way, the physiological needs serve as the basis for the other social needs. Yet these other needs enlarge the scope of human functioning and understanding. Maslow ranked the social or psychological needs that motivate us to behave into a hierarchy (see Figure 11-1).

Within Maslow's system, once we satisfy our physiological needs, we seek to satisfy safety needs, which refer to the desire for good health and for security from harm and danger. The major outcome of attaining safety needs is the desire to seek and give love to others. We seek to share with our immediate circle—family, sweetheart, spouse, children, friends—so we may (a) assure ourselves of being loved and (b) know we are accepted by others. An inability to love and belong may motivate persons to act in many different ways to gain such acceptance (for example, trying to use achievement as a substitute for love). However, it is not enough to be loved by others; we must also be respected. We use achievement to gain respect from others as well as self-respect. If we have satisfied all the lower needs on the hierarchy, we become motivated by a strong desire to be ourselves, to be self-actualized. This need concerns developing potential, becoming what we are capable of becoming, or making our behavior consistent with what we are. Maslow contends that, if we have satisfactorily met the other four needs, the need for self-actualization is potent enough to serve as the primary motivation for *all* behavior.

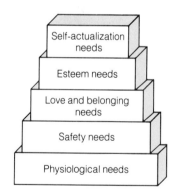

Figure 11-1
Maslow's hierarchy of human needs.
[*Source: Maslow (1943), p. 376.*
Copyright 1943 by the American
Psychological Association and
reprinted by permission.]

319

Examples of Maslow's Needs Hierarchy	
Category	**Example**
Physiological	A man develops a pattern of eating in order to avoid ever feeling hungry.
Safety	A woman watches where she walks on the desert during the summer, because of the increased likelihood of an encounter with snakes.
Love and Belonging	A husband does the evening dishes in order to please his wife.
Esteem	A woman feels good about the advice she gave another person.
Self-Actualization	A man realizes he lives a low stress life and feels secure in his ability to adjust to life situations.

Although only limited empirical research has been done on Maslow's categories of motivation, they are logical constructs and serve as a plausible theory of why we behave as we do. His theory is also widely admired and accepted because it goes beyond a strict physiological explanation for behavior and assumes certain independent psychological and social needs as motivational sources and causes for behavior.

Types of Motivation

Achievement Motivation

In an attempt to measure achievement motives, McClelland, Atkinson, Clark, & Lowell (1953); and Atkinson (1958) adapted the Thematic Apperception Test, (TAT) a projective scale, by using TAT-type pictures (usually four) to elicit stories that they scored against some predetermined system for the presence of desired imagery. The score McClelland derived indicated some measures of the need for achievement (nAch). They showed subjects several ambiguous pictures and asked them to write a story about what is occurring in each. The ambiguity of the pictures allows for many different interpretations. People who develop themes high in achievement relatedness are considered high in nAch. Subjects develop relatively unstructured stories, having been instructed by the examiner to consider the following: (1) What is happening in the picture (including who is doing what), (2) what events, thoughts, and motives have led up to this situation, (3) what events, thoughts, and motives are going on now in the picture, and (4) what is going to happen to these people?

McClelland and his associates found that subjects with high nAch perform better on arithmetic problems, obtain better grades in school, and have higher aspirational levels (Atkinson & Raynor, 1974; McClelland & Liberman, 1949). Other studies (Rosen & d'Andrade, 1959) have supported these findings.

Since McClelland's original work, several studies have been conducted to determine the relationship between **achievement motivation** and other variables. Winterbottom (1958) investigated parental variables. She found that boys with high nAch have mothers who expect self-reliance, independent behaviors, content mastery, and accomplishment from their sons. Such mothers were relatively more demanding than mothers who had sons with low nAch. Teevan and McGhee (1972) found that children who are high in achievement motivation had learned to be independent at an early age and received parental affection as a reward for it. Feather (1966) examined the effects of initial success or failure on students' overt achievement and found that failure experiences produce a lower achievement rate than success experiences. Crootof (1963) found greater nAch scores among bright normal achievers than among bright underachievers.

Achievement motivation
The learned need to achieve or feel competent.

Although each of these studies has shown a correlation between actual achievement and high nAch scores, the following cautions should be observed: (1) Different administrations of the McClelland nAch test (based on the TAT picture test) have not shown consistent results (Birney, 1959); (2) the McClelland approach tends not to assess women's achievement motives as consistently as men's (McClelland et al., 1953); and (3) the nAch test has shown some limitations in that it has not consistently measured all the different motives it attempts to define (Talbert, 1968).

Despite these limitations, most critics feel that McClelland's work on achievement motivation can be considered successful and valuable. Above all, his nAch test has proven to be a good indicator of academic achievement (Maehr & Sjogren, 1971; Uguroglu & Walberg, 1979), and it also seems to have implications for the area of personality development (Frieze, 1979; Maehr & Kleiber, 1981). However, it is likely that a score on McClelland's nAch scale reflects a much broader type of achievement motivation than is necessary for the accomplishment of classroom tasks. What is seen in the classroom is more likely to be **task-oriented motivation,** the term used to designate motivational factors involved in specific classroom behaviors.

Task-oriented motivation
The specific application of achievement motivation to the classroom setting.

Intrinsic and Extrinsic Motivation

When we see people engage in actions to display competency or exercise control over what is happening, we infer they are intrinsically motivated (Deci, 1975; Kukla, 1978; Notz, 1975). **Intrinsic motivation** is what the learner brings into the learning situation. DeCharms (1971) believes that a person's primary motivation is to produce change in the environment. The more internally controlled a person is, the more intrinsically satisfying

Intrinsic motivation
The internal desire to act, which the learner brings into the classroom.

external events are. We maintain intrinsic motivation by being involved in things or events that are internally satisfying. They do not have to lead to extrinsic reward. In contrast, many individuals are **extrinsically motivated.** They are motivated to accomplish certain things if the right incentives are generated for them. An intrinsically motivated student would gain satisfaction from getting a problem correct in class or on an assignment. An extrinsically motivated student would anticipate approval by a teacher in order to be assured that he or she had done well.

Some theorists have assumed that intrinsic and extrinsic motivation are additive. For example, if a person enjoys work (intrinsic) and is paid well for it (extrinsic), they assumed that the combination would increase the work motivation. In contrast, deCharms (1968) suggests that intrinsic and extrinsic motivation may interact, and he concluded that giving someone external rewards for something he or she internally enjoys may actually reduce the effect of the internal satisfaction.

Lepper, Greene, and Nisbett (1973) tested deCharms's ideas. In their study of nursery school children, they gave a preannounced reward to one group for participating in an activity, an unexpected (unpromised) reward to a second group once participation in an activity was completed, and no

Extrinsic motivation
The desire to act if appropriate incentives are created within the environment.

Table 11–1   A Summary of Findings on Two Hypotheses Predicting Interaction between Intrinsic and Extrinsic Motivation

Independent Variable	Experiment	Effect on Intrinsic Motivation
Hypothesis 1: The introduction of extrinsic rewards will decrease intrinsic motivation.		
Expected contingent rewards	Deci (1971)	Decrease
	Deci (1972a)	Decrease
	Lepper, Greene, & Nisbett (1973)	Decrease
Expected noncontingent rewards	Deci (1972b)	No change
	Kruglanski, Freedman, & Zeevi (1971)	Decrease
	Calder & Staw (1975b)	Decrease
	Notz (Note 1)	Decrease
Unexpected rewards	Lepper, Greene, & Nisbett (1973)	No change
	Kruglanski, Alan, & Lewis (1972)	Decrease
Contingent punishment	Deci & Cascio (Note 2)	Decrease
Verbal reinforcement	Deci (1971)	Increase
	Deci (1972a)	No change
	Deci, Cascio, & Krusell (1975)	Increase (males)
		Decrease (females)
Hypothesis 2: Withdrawal of or reduction in extrinsic rewards will increase intrinsic motivation.		
Withdrawal of extrinsic rewards	Weick (1964)	Increase
Reduction in extrinsic rewards	Staw (1974)	Increase

Source: Notz (1975), p. 835. Copyright 1975 by the American Psychological Association. Reprinted by permission.

reward to a third group for completing the activity. In a subsequent experimental session, where children from all three groups were given free choice of play activities, those who had been promised and received a reward in the first part of the experiment indicated less interest in selecting the same activity. Those who had not been motivated to complete the task because of an anticipated reward showed more interest in the task when it was a free choice. Such findings may mean that a preplanned reward has the effect of decreasing intrinsic motivation in children.

Subsequent studies (Calder & Staw, 1975; Deci, 1975; Notz, 1975; Staw, Calder, Hess, & Sandelands, 1980) have demonstrated the same effect in older children, adolescents, and college students. Notz (1975) summarized the research on the relationship between intrinsic and extrinsic motivation (see Table 11–1). Clearly, more studies have been done on adding extrinsic rewards to existing intrinsic motivation. In almost every study, the effect was a decrease in intrinsic motivation. Table 11–1 cites two studies on the effect of withdrawing external rewards, and, in both cases, intrinsic motivation increased. This raises the question of whether external rewards and token economies with school environments actually undermine students' intrinsic motivation.

As we continue to explore the characteristics of motivation in this chapter, a necessary question is whether school learning is primarily intrinsically or extrinsically motivating for students. The concept of extrinsic motivation is tied more closely to reinforcement theory; intrinsic motivation aligns itself more with conceptual learning or cognitive psychology.

Motivation in the Classroom

Do students in the classroom have basic physiological drives that affect their learning behavior? Can we attribute Maslow's need for self-actualization to basic classroom learning behavior? The answer to these questions is yes. All educators would undoubtedly agree that motivation is a very important variable in classroom learning. To increase our understanding of classroom motivation is to increase the probability of student learning. There are eight major factors in classroom motivation:

1. *Task motivation.* The motivational factors involved in student encounters with and mastery of specific classroom tasks and skills

2. *Aspirational motivation.* Behaviors related to the student's long-range goals and/or expectations, which are categorized on an ideal-real continuum

3. *Competition motivation.* The factors of a self-imposed standard of excellence or competition with others in student learning behaviors

4. *Affiliative motivation.* Behaviors that exhibit the need for adult approval and acceptance and peer approval and acceptance

5. *Anxiety motivation.* A common factor that may facilitate learning (minimal anxiety levels) or inhibit it (high anxiety levels)

6. *Avoidance motivation.* Behaviors related to the avoidance of punishment, reprimand, unpleasantness, or guilt within the classroom. (The preferred alternative is always the motive for behaviors that bring teacher approval.)

7. *Reinforcing motivation.* Often teacher approval and grades, may be peer competition and acceptance

8. *Individually guided motivation.* A behavioral scheme developed by Klausmeier, Sorenson, and Ghatala (1971) that categorized self-directed behaviors in a classroom setting and suggests ways for the teacher to utilize these motivational factors within each student.

Task Motivation

When students accomplish a difficult task, achieve success in a learning situation, or use their own initiative to explore learning beyond the limits defined by the teacher, task motivation exists. There is some controversy as to the nature of this type of motivation. Ausubel (1968) contends that successful accomplishment of a task is intrinsically rewarding and will motivate the learner toward additional tasks, regardless of the strength or existence of affiliative (acceptance) and other social motives.

In contrast, Veroff (1969) sees task motivation as varying at different stages of the child's development, with social and other motivational factors performing important functions in task achievement at the different stages. For example, in early stages of development, Veroff suggests that **competence** (an intrinsic need to cope with the environment) is the basic motivational force. The competence drive is represented by such behaviors as grasping, crawling, walking, language acquisition, thinking, manipulating objects, and learning skills. By middle childhood, Veroff sees **social motives,** particularly the needs for affiliation and acceptance from others, as the basic motivational source for much task-learning behavior. By adolescence, an integrated task-achievement pattern exists, built on the motivational forces of the earlier developmental stages (Maehr & Sjogren, 1971; Potter, 1984; Veroff, 1978).

Perhaps the most useful theory of task motivation in the classroom is

Competence
The inherent desire to function successfully in the environment.

Social motive
The need to learn skills that allow a person to relate to, and be accepted by, others.

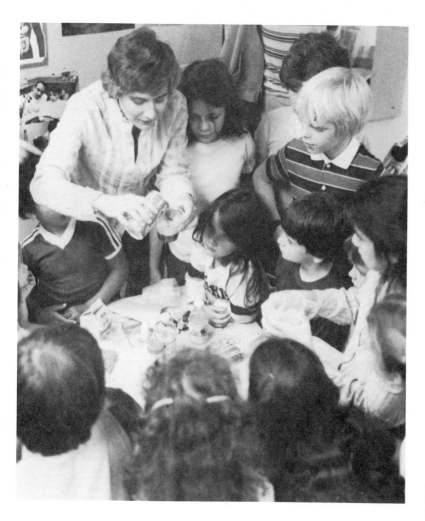

that offered by Atkinson (1965). From the original work by McClelland and his associates, Atkinson has theorized that task motivation is related to either (a) the need to achieve success or (b) the need to avoid failure in learning tasks. When encountering a classroom task, one student may approach it enthusiastically. Another student may use as much energy avoiding an academic behavior if failure on the task is likely. Teachers can facilitate motivation by being cognizant of their students' level of preparedness and of the requirements of each task they assign. Consider the following classroom example. An eighth-grade math instructor is teaching pre-algebra to a group of above-average students. One unit of instruction includes learning the concepts and rules governing the use of commutative property, associative property, and distributive property and applying them not only to addition, subtraction, and multiplication but also to eventual attainment of more complex mathematical behavior. Thus, the primary task involved in this teaching unit focuses on the following instruction objectives:

1. The students will learn the concepts "commutative property," "associative property," and "distributive property."
2. The students will learn the rules governing the use of commutative property, associative property, and distributive property.
3. The students will learn applications of the rules for commutative property, associative property, and distributive property to the mathematical procedures of addition, subtraction, and multiplication.

Students' general desire to achieve should motivate them to proceed with the intellectual tasks at hand. However, this type of learning involves task motivation because three distinct learning behaviors are required within the unit, and each of these behaviors must be motivated if the unit task is to be successfully completed. The distinction being made here between achievement motivation and task motivation is a fine but important one. The essential difference is that task motivation is really the specific application of the more generalized achievement motivation to particular classroom tasks. Thus, achievement motivation refers to a general trait, and task motivation relates to specific content—the successful accomplishment of learning tasks.

In this example from a secondary level mathematics class, and in most academic situations, students may provide and teachers may encourage the following motives for accomplishing specific tasks:

1. Be motivated by the intrinsic satisfaction as a learner
2. See the importance of learning specific materials in terms of a larger learning context
3. See the importance of learning specific material in terms of the student's eventual academic and educational plans
4. Relate knowledge of the material to its practical use in the world
5. Be spurred by competition to do well on the task

Success not only perpetuates setting goals, but also leads to a rise in the level of **aspiration.** In contrast, failure tends to lower the aspirational level. Research by Feather (1962) revealed that success-oriented students have a stronger motivation to succeed when their initial expectation of success is high rather than low. By contrast, failure-oriented students persist longer when the initial expectation of success is low. Other studies (Lewin et al., 1944; Sears, 1940) reach the same conclusion. Matsui, Okada, and Mizuguchi (1981) found that motivation is higher if goals are hard to achieve. The expectation of having to expend greater effort is motivating, as many studies have found (Latham & Yuki, 1975; Steers & Porter, 1974).

Aspirations
Goal-setting behaviors that are self-generated or teacher-facilitated; these behaviors motivate students to move toward their goals.

Although students cannot always experience success and teachers cannot consistently provide students with experiences that lead to success, teachers can and should see that students do not repeatedly fail. Successive prolonged failures cause students to set unrealistic goals and lose interest in the activity (Israel, 1960). Sears (1940) also found a more variable and unrealistic goal-setting pattern among students who experienced failure. Among successful students, goals tend to be slightly higher for the next succeeding task; among unsuccessful students, goals tend to be either distinctly higher or lower for the next succeeding task.

If given the opportunity, many students will set their own goals. They may be long-range, but they are often immediate. One vital aspect of goals students set for themselves is they must be realizable. Research on groups as diverse as retarded adolescents and college students has found that student goal setting increases subsequent performance (Fryer, 1964; Gaa, 1973; Warner & Mills, 1980). Fryer's study (1964) also found that students do better on difficult tasks than on easy ones. Warner and deJung (1971) did not find a differential effect on task difficulty when measuring spelling word acquisition by mentally retarded adolescents. They did, however, find that goal setting improved the performance.

Attribution theory proposes that it is not whether the outcome of students' effort is success or failure that determines whether they will try similar efforts again. Rather, it is their interpretation of why they succeeded or failed. If they believe success was due to ability, they would tend to engage in the task again because they would anticipate subsequent success. It is common to believe that failure is due to lack of effort rather than to lack of ability. If students believe they fail due to lack of effort, they are likely to try harder on subsequent learning tasks. However, if low ability is the reason, most students believe this to be relatively unchangeable and are not as likely to try the task again (Dweck, 1975; Weiner, 1979).

Research suggests that adolescents and college students are better able than children to differentiate ability from effort, and they are more likely to see low ability as unchangeable (Ames & Lau, 1982; Nicholls, 1980; Ruble, 1980). As students become older, they are better able to keep track of success and failure events and to assess whether they want to put out additional effort. Teachers can assist students' classroom efforts by showing them how to work more effectively and helping them succeed rather than fail. Causation and feelings of adequacy are related; so it is

Chapter 11
Classroom Motivation

important to alter student perception in the direction of more fulfilling behavior (Weiner, Russell, & Lerman, 1979).

Thornburg (1971c) used new instructional procedures with a group of high school freshmen considered to be potential dropouts. The students were given one year of special instruction in math and English tasks that were relevant to them and within their ability range. In many cases, this meant figuring interest on automobile loans and doubling or tripling recipes. *Classics Illustrated* was used in preference to standard literature texts. As a result, the students learned, expressed the desire to accomplish additional tasks, and set goals they were capable of accomplishing. They also had a more positive attitude toward school and themselves. This improvement most likely resulted from the fact that these students realized that school did not have to be frustrating and that they could learn. An increased desire to be in school was reflected by a lower absentee rate and dropout rate than among the regular ninth-grade students. Although the number of subjects was small, the study confirms that aspiration and interest levels (motivation) increase with successful experiences.

Factors Contributing to High and Low Aspirations		Concept Summary 11–2

High	Low
Success	Failure
Hard Task	Easy Task
Can Change Behavior	Cannot Change Behavior
Perceive Self-Control	Perceive Others-Control
Homogeneous Group	Heterogeneous Group
Relevant Task	Irrelevant Task
Meaningful Information	Isolated Information
Realistic Goal	Unrealistic Goal

Competition Motivation

Competition permeates every social structure, including the schools. It is motivational if it causes students to engage in an activity in order to do as well as or better than others. Competition can be positive if it helps individuals realize their potential. It is often considered essential in school because it prepares students for competition in "real" life.

Healthy competition can aid social interaction and maturation. If it is handled well, it can benefit those who compete. But too often the demands for success become extreme and the individual gets caught up in unhealthy competitive situations that benefit no one. Early and constant competition may actually cause students to tire of competing, either academically or socially, and the long- m effect may be to decrease motivation (Burke & Kleiber, 1978). Coleman (1961) suggests that a significant amount of adolescents' ene. is spent in jockeying for status. Thus, they expend much motivational energy in the social rather than the academic environment.

Society is diversifying and the range of acceptable behavior is widening. It is becoming increasingly clear that many individuals do not need to be placed in a competitive structure to achieve and that we must devise new models in education to meet these more diverse human needs. One alternative is to instruct students in self-imposed competition or self-imposed standards of excellence, which are associated with the need to achieve competence or mastery in one's environment (Berlyne, 1966; White, 1959). Self-imposed competition may be inferred from the "disposition to strive for the attainment of personally accepted, long-term achievement goals, and by the capacity for satisfaction in the attainment of those goals" (Talbert, 1968, p. 5). Many teachers fail to point out this motivational source. Too often they structure their classrooms around competition with others, creating the risk of one student gaining a sense of achievement and others, a sense of failure. Comparing students to a

standard of excellence avoids the problem of comparing students to each other.

It is unlikely that classroom learning will occur without the influence of student competition. Yet most students would probably benefit from a stress on cooperation rather than on competition because there is not a loser or a sense of failure in a cooperative structure. If the teacher thinks student competition is a useful motivational technique in some circumstances, he or she should take care that students are not put into an unequal competitive situation. An investigation by Clifford (1971) indicated that homogeneous competition—that is, competition among the equally able—with reward is an effective motivational source. Heterogeneous competition—that is, competition among those poorly matched in ability—was found to have less value.

Many students are sufficiently motivated by a self-imposed standard of excellence or self-competition. The idea behind self-imposed standards of excellence is to provide goals or a record of continuing behavior by which learners can measure their success. In such situations, they generate a need to increase personal performance and are not tied to normative comparisons against classmates.

Consider, for example, a physical-fitness test given once in each of four nine-week periods in high school. There are five tasks on the test that each individual must perform: (1) push-ups, (2) pull-ups, (3) sit-ups, (4) squat thrusts, and (5) the 300-yard run. Let us say that a sophomore boy, Otis Brown, performed the test in October and did 12 push-ups, 3 pull-ups, 83 sit-ups, 22 squat thrusts, and ran 300 yards in 69 seconds. The final score for Otis in the May testing was 26 push-ups, 8 pull-ups, 90 sit-ups, 26 squat thrusts, and a 58-second 300-yard run. The fact that he had self-comparative standards from test to test provides motivation for self-improvement.

Jerald and Carl enrolled in Markland Elementary School in the first grade the same year, and by the time they had reached third grade, they were best of friends. In addition to their school experiences, they did things together in evenings and on weekends whenever possible. They had a very good relationship in and out of school, both being high achievers and having pleasant personalities.

In the fourth grade, the two boys started becoming more socially active, and their teacher often reprimanded them for talking in class when they were supposed to be quiet. The boys did not feel they were being unnecessarily noisy and tended to ignore Ms. Yashamoto's comments or, at best, were quieter for only a little while. Finally, the teacher decided to separate them because it was the only way she could get them to stop talking.

During the following weeks, Ms. Yashamoto noticed that Jerald and Carl were doing more poorly in school, sometimes not completing assignments and turning in work of lower quality than they were capable of. In discussing their academic behavior with them, she was not able to get them to see how their behav-

ior had changed, and, in the next week or two, she saw no improvement.

Ms. Yashamoto finally felt she should call a parent-teacher conference and advise both boys' parents of the problems. Carl's parents were particularly intrigued that the quality of the boys' work had declined as a consequence of separation rather than of their talking or disruptive behavior. After exploring several possibilities, Carl's father, who was also a teacher, said that he thought the two boys were really good for each other and believed their achievement would increase if they were put back together in the classroom. Ms. Yashamoto was reluctant to try this, but she and Carl's parents decided they should give it a try for a couple of weeks and see what happened.

The next day, Ms. Yashamoto explained to Carl and Jerald why disruptive behavior was not acceptable in her class, that she was going to put them physically closer to each other again, and that she expected their schoolwork to improve. Much to her surprise, within one week the boys were turning in better papers, completing assignments, and making "A"s on everything they turned in. The spon-

taneous, wholesome competition between the two of them was a strong motivator. Their being in each other's physical proximity was an apparent key to this motivation, and they continued to do well throughout the school year, still being disruptive occasionally.

What Do You Think?

1. What does an example like this tell us about competition as a motivational source?

2. Should Ms. Yashamoto have sought out other motivational sources and kept the boys separated?

3. How important is it for teachers to solicit parental input on school-related matters?

331

Most humans demonstrate a strong need to affiliate with others. We join organizations, clubs, special interest groups, social organizations, and volunteer much time in socially relevant causes in order to carry on effective interaction with others. We are social beings to relieve boredom, to share feelings, to gain social recognition, to express affection, to have support systems, and to alleviate stress.

Students are typically motivated to gain approval from peers and adults within the classroom and home environment. The incentive is the intrinsic need to know we are acceptable to others (Birch & Veroff, 1966). Most young schoolchildren express a strong need for adult affiliation, which is generally evidenced by the tendency to strive to establish, maintain, or restore a positive affective relationship with their teachers. Typically, children see the teacher as controlling the classroom environment. In order to minimize conflict and gain acceptance from the teacher, students usually try to conform to the teacher's expectations. As children grow, they usually tend to shift their affiliations from teachers to classroom peers. Teachers should realize that peer affiliations are important. Peer groupings apparently form a kind of subculture, and students often refuse to violate its norms. For example, students may not achieve beyond what they know their peer group will accept. Goldberg (1960) and Coleman (1961) have shown that intelligent students play down making good grades in order not to receive disapproval from peers. Coleman also found, as did Cawelti (1968) and Friesen (1968), that, when high school students were asked to rank peers in terms of (a) popularity and (b) "who would you like to be most like," they showed a strong preference for socially and athletically oriented students over academically oriented students.

Anxiety refers to the highly unpleasant state of fear or apprehension that painful consequences will ensue. The subjective experience of anxiety is accompanied by such symptoms as dry mouth, pounding heart, trembling, and perspiration. Anxiety is considered a motive because it initiates and sustains goal-directed behavior.

Most fears are learned. We can develop anxieties about a wide variety of presumed dangers (for example, physical injury, rejection, high places, being alone in the dark, or thunderstorms). However, some anxieties facilitate adaptive behavior.

Research on anxiety about testing situations provides valuable information about how we develop anxiety. Sarason et al. (1960) prepared a Test Anxiety Scale for Children to measure children's typical reactions in evaluative and testlike situations. The child is asked to reveal personal anxiety by answering yes or no to questions such as the following: Are you afraid of school tests? When the teacher says she is going to find out how much you have learned, does your heart begin to beat faster? Do you sometimes dream at night that the teacher is angry because you do not know your lessons?

One theory states that test anxiety develops as a result of parental criticism and punishment of the child when he or she fails to perform satisfactorily. If the child reacts to criticisms with fear, parents may forbid the expression of hostility by threatening more extreme punishment. Hostile impulses then come to arouse anxiety about punishment. As a result, the child may defend against the anxiety produced by his or her own aggressive reactions by becoming dependent on parents or unwilling to venture into achievement activities without their aid and may blame himself or herself for not being better.

Raynor and Rubin (1971) checked the effects of achievement motivation and anxiety levels on a three-step arithmetic task in which two different sets of instructions were given. One group was put in a contingency condition (that is, they had to be successful on one test before they could work on a successive test). The conditions for the second group were noncontingent (that is, success on one test was not necessary for work on the other). All subjects were told they had a fifty-fifty chance of success on the task. Subjects high in achievement motivation and low in test anxiety performed significantly better under the contingent conditions than students who were low in achievement motivation and high in test anxiety. Students low in achievement motivation and high in test anxiety performed significantly worse under the contingent than the noncontingent condition. Thus, low anxiety is a better motivational state than high anxiety for classroom test conditions—and particularly for stressful test conditions (the contingency test).

Because anxiety is primarily intrinsic, it is usually beyond the teacher's control. But teachers can at least become aware of the different anxiety states among the students so high-anxiety students can be shown some special concern. For example, if a teacher knows that a student becomes very anxious at the prospect of giving an oral report, he or she could accept

Anxiety
A state of tension, nervousness, or fear that a student brings into the learning environment.

a written one as an alternative. In addition, teachers should strive to avoid creating tension-producing situations within the classroom.

Avoidance Motivation

Sometimes classroom anxiety is severe enough to make students avoid certain learning and behavioral conditions. This is especially true under the threat of punishment or reprimand by the teacher. Such disciplinary techniques frequently produce anxiety, emotional upset, and guilt within students. Even less severe forms of teacher disapproval, such as a student's knowledge that he or she has not met the teacher's expectations, may have detrimental effects on classroom learning conditions.

Lewin et al. (1944) found that knowledge of failure can cause students to avoid setting an aspirational level. He hypothesized three motivational dilemmas that are pertinent to this discussion. Because Lewin considered all behavior goal oriented, there were always either positive or negative forces thrusting a person toward a goal. A state of conflict occurs when a person has two or more competing motives, only one of which can be satisfied. The **approach motive** Lewin described includes situations in which there is positive incentive for moving toward the goal. The **avoidance motive** is when a person encounters a negative incentive. For example, if you were told that you would get a promotion if a certain dollar amount of sales was exceeded in a company, you could perceive this as a positive incentive. If you were told that you must falsify or cover up true sales figures in order to get a promotion, you might perceive that

Approach motive
A term indicating that individuals move toward a goal because the incentives are positive.

Avoidance motive
A term indicating that progress toward a goal is impeded because incentives are negative.

as a negative incentive. To maintain homeostasis, you must resolve the situation.

Lewin contends that sometimes competing motives are both positive and desirable. Which one you select depends on your perception of which will be most rewarding and which will move you toward a goal. Jane, a third-grade pupil, has been asked to do a routine task for her teacher and to help her friend with a problem. Both would fulfill Jane's social needs, but she can do only one at a time. When more than one event will bring satisfaction and help accomplish social or interpersonal needs, the individual has **approach-approach motives.**

Sometimes both of two competing events are unpleasurable, but selecting one will help a person move toward a goal. In school, students often perceive the choices teachers give them as not that desirable. Walter is being punished. He must choose detention or writing a drill exercise. He wants to do neither, but he must select one. Such **avoidance-avoidance motives** may cause students to withdraw from unpleasant situations in the future.

According to Lewin, **approach-avoidance motives** are the most easily resolved. They involve two competing responses, one of which is pleasant and one of which is unpleasant. People usually choose the more pleasant event. Few students in school lunch lines would have any difficulty choosing between an extra helping of vegetables or an extra helping of dessert.

For many students the threat of punishment is enough to cause them to avoid punishing situations or people. For others, they will push teachers to the limit, thinking that punishment is more of a threat than an actuality. Only if such students are reprimanded for their actions are they likely to be motivated to avoid misconduct. The consistency of the classroom teacher becomes a critical variable here.

A great deal has been written about punishment in the classroom, typically in emotionally loaded terms (Gnagey, 1975; Ianni, 1980; Macekura, 1978). As I discussed in Chapter 2, punishment is generally thought to bring about student dissatisfaction as well as some undesirable emotional repercussions. Klausmeier and Ripple (1971, pp. 336–337) present the theoretical, nonemotional view of punishment:

> A punishment by definition brings pain or dissatisfaction to the recipient. Punishment takes many forms, including the withholding or withdrawal of anything that serves as a reward; expressing disapproval, either verbally or in nonverbal ways; threatening, either verbally or in nonverbal ways; giving low grades or other indications of unsatisfactory work or conduct; removal from a desired situation; and depriving of basic needs. Punishment may be administered by groups as well as by individuals. Receiving a punishment immediately after a response may weaken the response; or it may lead to the recipient's temporarily suppressing the response or to his supporting it only in the presence of the punisher, or it may result in evasion of or open aggression against the punisher. Being promised a punishment for not performing a task may lead to performance of the task, but it may lead to avoidance of the task, the punishment and the punisher. Being promised a punishment if a specified

Approach-approach motive
In this mode, an individual must select between two positive incentives that are moving the individual toward a goal.

Avoidance-avoidance motive
In this mode, an individual must select between two negative incentives in pursuit of a goal.

Approach-avoidance motive
In this mode, an individual must select between a positive and negative incentive when moving toward a goal.

anti-social behavior is manifested may lead to nonmanifestation of it, but it may (also) lead to avoidance of the punishment and punisher while still expressing the anti-social behavior. In addition, punishment may result in undesirable anxiety in the child, negative feeling toward the punisher, and negative feelings toward school.

Teachers should be cautious in using punishment. No student should ever be punished because of inability to do an assignment. Such action misuses the purpose and content of the learning situation and affects the student's interest and motivational levels. What does a teacher accomplish by saying, "Either get your assignment finished or you will stay in from recess"? Has the teacher sufficiently motivated the student to get the assignment done? Has the teacher implied that the academic subject is more important than physical activity? Will the student be motivated on subsequent assignments to complete the work on time? Or will the student in fact learn to dislike that academic subject? These are the types of questions a teacher must consider prior to using punishment. Most important, the teacher must assess punishment's long-range effects, even if he or she believes it may effectively motivate the student for the immediate task. Students who cannot complete an assignment generally need additional help rather than punishment.

Reinforcing Motivation

Three reinforcing techniques that can be considered motivational sources are knowledge of results, praise, and tests and grades. Skinner (1938, 1953) contends that knowledge of the correctness of a response is sufficient reinforcement for a learning task. Knowledge of results serves as a motivator probably because it indicates success to the student. It is virtually impossible for the teacher to reinforce every student on every response, but such techniques as programmed learning can provide immediate and consistent reinforcement.

Many learning theorists consider praise a good motivational technique because it encourages achievement, increases aspiration levels, and facilitates learning. The studies I discuss deal with teacher praise, but praise from peers is also highly motivational.

Page (1958) has studied the incentive effects of marking test papers in three ways—test score only, test score with personal teacher comments, and test score with stereotyped teacher comments. The results of the study showed that praise is a motivational source:

1. Students whose papers had personalized comments did better than the other two groups on subsequent testing.

2. Students whose papers had stereotyped comments did better than the no-comment group on subsequent testing.

3. Students whose papers had only the test score showed no significant change in subsequent tests.

Zigler and Kanzer (1962) investigated the effects of verbal praise reinforcers ("good" or "fine") and verbal correct reinforcers ("correct" or "right") upon subsequent academic behaviors of middle- and lower-class children. Assuming that there is a distinct difference between the two reinforcing classifications, the authors found that, among middle-class children, correct reinforcements improved performance better than praise reinforcements. The opposite was true of lower-class children.

Clifford (1971) compared the performances of students at four ability levels, with homogeneous competition and reward (praise) and nonreward conditions. She found the effect of praise to be much greater in the low ability and high average ability groups than in the low average ability and high ability groups.

Zigler, Butterfield, and Capobianco (1970) investigated the motivational effects of praise among institutionalized mentally retarded children. One research variable was the nature of the preinstitutional environment; that is, whether or not it was culturally deprived. Reporting evidence over an eight-year period, the researchers found that the children from highly deprived preinstitutional environments were less motivated by praise reinforcement than their nondeprived counterparts. They also found that the effect of praise as a motivational source decreased among the children from relatively "good" homes as they became more socially deprived from institutionalization. The researchers concluded that social deprivation becomes an integral part of the individual's expectations and thus mediates his or her response to praise and achievement, even ten years later (Zigler, 1963).

Brophy's (1981) comprehensive analysis of praise, its functions and effects on students, attests to the importance of teacher praise as a reinforcement technique. Brophy defined praise as the commendation of worth or expression of approval or admiration. He believes it is more powerful than reinforcement because it represents a deliberate investment of teacher attention and energy beyond the standard verbal praise reinforcers of "okay," "right," or "good."

Tests and grades have always been considered a basic motivational source. Tests typically motivate students to study for the test and not to learn, although this does not preclude learning taking place. Similarly, although grades may serve as good reinforcing motives for study, they often do not motivate students to learn. For example, a semester grade cannot be established as the motivator for ongoing academic performance, and these types of grades certainly do not provide specific feedback for completed work. A daily or weekly grade or a test grade, however, may provide specific feedback and is likely to motivate the student on succeeding work.

Teachers should be cautious not to make grades the primary source of motivation. It is logical to use such reinforcing techniques for motivation for they are powerful conditions for learning, but they should be used as part of the total motivational system and not as the motivational system itself. Too often grades are emphasized as motivators and become associated with classroom competition or with anxiety-producing pressures. Such situations are not conducive to learning.

Klausmeier et al. (1971) have categorized self-directed motivational factors as classroom behavioral objectives for students. Table 11–2 lists student behaviors that indicate individually guided motivation (that is, the activities that the self-motivated student is likely to engage in within the teaching-learning situation). The statements are an outcome of the coordinated research of the Wisconsin Research and Development Center for Cognitive Learning and the Wisconsin Public Schools.

Klausmeier et al. (1971) have also delineated eight principles of motivation by which these objectives can be analyzed. These principles, summarized in Table 11–3, give the teacher an understanding of the basic psychological principles that research has shown to be instrumental in guiding motivation. Note that principles 1 through 4 are specifically related to learning subject matter and principles 5 and 6 relate to conduct, focusing on the learning and maintenance of prosocial behaviors. The latter usually take two forms of expression: (a) those that indicate what the teacher expects the child to do (for example, listening, cleaning up after a project) and (b) those that indicate self-direction (for example, reading in spare time). Principles 7 and 8 may apply to either learning or prosocial behavior.

Table 11–2 Classroom Behaviors Indicative of Self-Motivation

A. The pupil starts promptly and completes self-, teacher-, or group-assigned tasks that together comprise the minimum requirements related to various curriculum areas.
    1. Attends to the teacher and other situational elements when attention is required.
    2. Begins tasks promptly.
    3. Seeks feedback concerning performance on tasks.
    4. Returns to tasks voluntarily after interruption or initial lack of progress.
    5. Persists at tasks until completed.

B. The pupil assumes responsibility for learning more than the minimum requirements without teacher guidance during school hours and outside school hours. In addition to behaviors 1–5, the pupil
    6. Continues working when the teacher leaves the room.
    7. Does additional work during school hours.
    8. Works on school-related activities outside school hours.
    9. Identifies activities that are relevant for class projects.
    10. Seeks suggestions for going beyond minimum amount or quality of work.

C. The pupil becomes self-directive in connection with use of property, relations with other pupils, and relations with adults.
    11. Moves quietly within and about the school building during quiet periods and activities.
    12. Interacts harmoniously with other pupils.
    13. Interacts harmoniously with the teacher and other adults.
    14. Conserves own and others' property.
    15. Tells other pupils to behave in accordance with school policies.

D. The pupil verbalizes a value system consistent with the preceding behaviors.
    16. When asked, gives examples of his own actions illustrative of behaviors 1–15.
    17. When asked, gives reasons for manifesting behaviors 1–15.

Source: Klausmeier, Sorenson, & Ghatala (1971), p. 340. Copyright 1971 by The University of Chicago Press. Reprinted by permission.

Table 11–3 Principles of Motivation and Corollary Instructional Implications

Principle	Instructional Implications
1. Attending to a learning task is essential for initiating a learning sequence.	A. Focus pupil's attention on desired objectives.
2. Desiring to achieve control over elements of the environment and to experience success is essential to realistic goal-setting.	B. Use the individual's need to achieve and other positive motives.
3. Setting and attaining goals requires learning tasks at an appropriate level of difficulty; feelings of success on current learning tasks heighten motivation for subsequent tasks; feelings of failure lower motivation for subsequent tasks.	C. Help each pupil to set and attain goals related to the educational program of the school.
4. Acquiring information concerning correct or appropriate behaviors and correcting errors are associated with better performance on and more favorable attitudes toward the learning tasks.	D. Provide for informative feedback.
5. Observing and imitating a model facilitates the initial acquisition of prosocial behaviors such as self-control, self-reliance, and persistence.	E. Provide for real-life and symbolic models.
6. Verbalizing pro-social values and behaviors and reasoning about them provide a conceptual basis for the development of the behaviors.	F. Provide for verbalization and discussion of pro-social values.
7. Expecting to receive a reward for specified behavior or achievement directs and sustains attention and effort toward manifesting the behavior or achievement. Non-reinforcement after a response tends to extinguish the response. Expecting to receive punishment for manifesting undesired behavior may lead to suppression of the behavior, to avoidance or dislike of the situation, or to avoidance and dislike of the punisher.	G. Develop and use a system of rewards as necessary to secure sustained effort and desired conduct. Use punishment as necessary to suppress misconduct.
8. Experiencing high stress and anxiety is associated with low performance, erratic conduct, and personality disorders.	H. Avoid the use of procedures that create temporary high stress or chronic anxiety.

Source: Klausmeier, Sorenson, & Ghatala (1971), p. 342. Copyright 1971 by The University of Chicago Press. Reprinted by permission.

The concept of individually guided motivation as advanced by Klausmeier provides the teacher not only with a way of capitalizing on the learner's self-motivational conditions but also with a way of assessing student motivation within the classroom setting. By being aware of the student's potential motivational system, the teacher is better able to utilize student motivation within the teaching-learning situation.

The eight types of motivation described in Table 11–3 provide us with insight as to why some individuals engage in the behaviors they do. The strength of motivational sources varies, depending upon the situation. Therefore, it is important to keep in mind five general characteristics of motivation. First, motivated behavior is triggered. The instigator may be a basic need, such as thirst, or a learned need, such as teacher approval. Human behavior is meaningful; thus, as we behave, we are trying to fulfill needs.

Second, motivated behavior gives direction. Children channel their energy to accomplish academic tasks, to develop social relationships, to gain teacher approval, and to increase their sense of competence. When students select a motivational source or strategy, they are fulfilling some goal.

Third, motivation provides intensity. Teachers and students engage in many routine, lackluster behaviors. Other behaviors, however, are pursued with vigor and intensity. A task may be intellectually stimulating; thus it intensifies motivation. A student may be competing for academic or athletic excellence or recognition. As this student moves toward fulfillment, his or her motivation may intensify, thus facilitating accomplishment.

Fourth, motivation is selective. Because human behavior is meaningful and goal directed, we select the behaviors that are likely to fulfill our needs. A high school freshman may dislike general biology and do poorly on assignments and tests. Yet this student may enjoy marine biology and read everything in the school library on the topic. Thus, this student's motivation is selective; that is, the student is attempting to pursue those behaviors that are most fulfilling.

Fifth, motivation is the key to need satisfaction. To be motivated, whether physiologically or psychologically, you must experience some deprivation, be it ever so slight. The concept of satiation implies that an exercised course of action (behavior) has satisfied a need. Thus, all need-related behavior should move us toward greater resolution or satisfaction of personal needs. Remember that satiation implies need satisfaction, not the disappearance of the need. Although it is harder to determine psychological satiation than physiological satiation, we assume that the principle operates in both cases. Thus, the pursuance of goal-directed behavior results in satisfying our needs.

It didn't take Phil Louther long to find out that every student's motivational state is unique. It did take a few years of teaching to develop strategies that would work with various types of students. Some time ago, Phil realized that he could not devise a motivational strategy that would work for all students. He had taught ninth grade social studies for eleven years. During that time he had instructed some 2200 students. The following discussion is an outcome of my conversation with Phil concerning the different types of motivational thrust he had witnessed in his classroom.

Phil divided all of his students into two main types: (a) internally motivated and (b) externally motivated. He felt he could group all students this way, although we did recognize several subtypes within the two main categories.

Intrinsically Motivated

Phil admitted that these were his favorite types because these students bring their own incentives into the classroom. Since such students are self-starters and generally extended their learning beyond the specific given assignment, little effort was required of Phil himself. He used the following teaching strategies with these students:

1. He periodically helped them with their goal setting.

2. He would be sure the ideas they extended were still within the domain of the original learning task.

3. He gave them plenty of leeway in developing their assignments and in using school resources.

4. He would occasionally praise them for their work.

5. He would get them to articulate assignments they would like to do, assignments that were well beyond the work given to all of the students.

Extrinsically Motivated

Phil had observed that there were far more students in this category than in the intrinsic group. These extrinsically motivated students typically sought teacher attention and direction. Often, if they did not receive appropriate or timely feedback, their work pace slowed. Phil realized that these students required a great deal more from him than the intrinsically motivated did. He employed the following motivational strategies, which seemed to work with most of the extrinsically motivated:

1. He stated specific instructional objectives so the students knew exactly what was expected in the teaching-learning situation.

2. He monitored their progress and reinforced intermittently, yet more frequently, than he did with intrinsic students.

3. He graded assignments, generally writing comments on such papers.

4. He occasionally paired an extrinsically motivated student with an intrinsically motivated one, so the former could be exposed to a different learning-style model.

Interestingly, Phil recognized that many of the extrinsic students actually achieved as well as many in the intrinsic group. Still, they demanded considerable teacher energy and, on occasion, Phil wondered if such progress were really worth all the effort he had to put into it.

As mentioned, Phil noticed that there were several subtypes of student motivation. This observation made it impossible to think of all students as just intrinsic or extrinsics demanded considerable these types at length because, with this new insight, it became obvious that teacher behaviors other than the ones just stated were required.

Contemplators

Phil noted that some of the intrinsically motivated students were extremely quiet and thoughtful, not too outspoken. He found himself from time to time drawing responses out of these students, in order to reassure himself that they were progressing accordingly. He found that they were generally innovative and that they sought learning in a variety of ways. He noticed that they were for the most part quite accurate and detailed in their work. Generally, these intrinsic contemplators were quite good achievers. The one strategy Phil found workable for this group involved developing a self-check system, which was kept on his desk. This forced the students to periodically approach his desk, which in turn gave Phil the opportunity to talk with these quieter students.

Activators

Phil noticed that there were a number of students who were generally highly active, who talked a lot, wrote a lot, and made many inquiries. He found these students generated ideas and were motivated to play active, even leadership, roles in the classroom. There were two types of activators—the intrinsic and the extrinsic. The intrinsic activators were extremely active and self-motivated people. The only single additional strategy Phil used with them involved making sure they were channeling their energies in desired ways. He had noticed that some of these students had very high energy levels, but did not always have the self-discipline to channel these energies constructively. Thus, Phil's strategy here was an important one.

The extrinsic activators, on the other hand, constantly required attention, feedback, or teacher explanation to stay motivated. Phil was aware that they were generally good achievers but quite dependent on recognition in order to

stay on top of academic tasks. This group, being extrinsically oriented and generally needing the teacher to initiate a learning activity, was the one subtype of students that required the greatest amount of Phil's energy. The single strategy he used with them was intermittent reinforcement. By attempting to diminish their dependency on constant teacher feedback, Phil hoped to change the balance of their motivation; that is, to teach them to be intrinsically motivated and thus to reduce the constant attention he would have to give these students.

Through analysis, Phil found that student interest was a significant motivational source. Those who liked an academic area or specific academic task were more likely to accomplish an assignment than those students with low interest. Phil discovered that, if a learning task is perceived to help accomplish a goal, then students approach that task more readily. There was yet another factor that caused students to accomplish tasks, and that was if students perceived avoiding a task to be more punishing than actually doing it. Still, Phil had noticed that some students were so disinterested that they either did not accomplish academic learning at all, or learned so slowly that they learned much less than other students in the same classroom.

Overall, the best way to effectively motivate a student is to learn as much about him or her as you can and select strategies that match an individual's needs as much as possible. Classroom teachers themselves should try to

determine how much they are intrinsically motivated or dependent on others for reinforcement and challenges. Some teachers also have deliberate, serious, contemplative teaching styles. How would this affect student motivation in the classroom? Still other teachers are goal oriented and exercise much approach behavior. The motivational state of the classroom teacher is critical in determining what type of motivational strategies will be applied to students. The following scale, which can be administered to students, will yield some idea of their motivational state (e.g., intrinsic vs. extrinsic, contemplative vs. active, approach vs. avoidance.) Try this scale yourself and see if you can gain some insight into your personal motivational level.

Index of Motivation

Directions We are trying to find out how students think and feel about a number of important topics. In order to do this, we would like to ask you to answer some questions. This is not an intelligence test nor an information test. There are no "right" or "wrong" answers. The best and only correct answer is *your personal opinion.* Whatever your answer is, there will be many who agree and many who disagree. What we really want to know is *how you feel* about each statement. Read each statement carefully and then indicate your agreement or disagreement by marking it in the appropriate space on the answer sheet, according to the following scale:

1 – slight support, agreement
2 – strong support, agreement
3 – slight opposition, disagreement
4 – strong opposition, disagreement

The scale items are:

1. School is more fun when teachers let students do things they want to.

2. Pupils who try should get good grades even if they make mistakes.

3. Successful people are those who make the most money.

4. All those who fail have worked in vain.

5. Most young people do not want to go to school.

6. Some new ideas are interesting, but most of them are not.

7. Knowing the right answer is more important than knowing where to get the answer.

8. Many young people feel grouchy.

9. The best people refuse to depend on other persons.

10. We are never really as happy as we think we are.

11. A person's feelings on a topic are not as important as the facts.

12. It does not really help much to study about people from other lands.

13. Life is mostly sorrow with just a little joy.

14. Many youngsters often want to run away from home.

15. Some teachers seem to enjoy making students suffer.

16. Our whole trouble is that we won't let God help us.

17. No one seems to understand young people.

18. Most people would like school better if teachers did not give grades.

19. The world we live in is a pretty lonesome place.

20. Social progress can be achieved only by returning to our glorious past.

21. It is foolish to advocate government support of education.

22. There is nothing new under the sun.

23. Life seems to be one big struggle after another.

24. Most people just don't give a "darn" for others.

25. The best way to achieve security is for the government to guarantee jobs.

26. Many new ideas are not worth the paper they are printed on.

27. It is better to forget than to forgive.

28. Young people should be free to follow their own desires.

29. The present is all too often full of unhappiness.

30. People who dream a lot at night are apt to be crazy.

31. Familiarity breeds contempt, so one should never be too friendly.

32. There is a real limit to man's intelligence.

33. People who are insulted generally deserve to be.

34. Experience may be a good teacher, but schools are better.

35. People who are quick thinkers usually jump to conclusions.

36. Most people do not have good ideas until they grow up.

37. Looking good is just as important as being good.

38. Famous people usually have a lot of money.

39. Most people cannot learn from the experience of others.

40. The dreamer is a danger to society.

41. Most teachers like to drive students if they have the chance.

42. One can never desire too much of a good thing.

43. Being a liar is better than being a gossip.

44. Asking questions usually gets you into trouble.

45. Not many people in the world are really kind.

46. Teachers know more and do less than most other people.

47. Hope is really no better than worry.

48. School is not all that it is cracked up to be.

49. Everything that people do is either right or wrong.

50. Quick thinking is always better than being polite.

Scoring Add all 1–2 responses together; all 3–4 responses together; subtract the difference. The higher the score, the lower the motivation level; the lower the score, the higher the motivation level (Frymier, 1970).

343

Annotated Readings

Maehr, M. L., & Kleiber, D. A. (1981). The graying of achievement motivation. *American Psychologist, 36,* 787–793.

> *The authors contend that, although research and theory related to achievement motivation are generally associated with earlier stages of development, we must now begin looking at the later years for a more complete understanding of motivation. They suggest that cross-cultural work on achievement motivation can provide an appropriate analogue as well as specific procedures for cross-age studies. The authors suggest that, as individuals become older, intrinsic motivation plays a more dominant role than extrinsic motivation.*

Potter, E. F. (1984). Impact of developmental factors on motivating the school achievement of young adolescents: Theory and implications for practice. *Journal of Early Adolescence, 4,* 1–14.

> *Recent writing on school motivation has prescribed techniques to be used but has failed to tailor such techniques to the developmental level of the adolescent. This article addresses the following motivational techniques and indicates aspects of the developmental stage of early adolescence that are relevant to their application: (1) use of behaviorist incentives, (2) evocation of facilitative expectations and causal attributions, (3) use of social incentives, (4) use of competition, and (5) enhancement of intrinsic motivation.*

Staw, B. M., Calder, B. J., Hess, R. K., & Sandelands, L. E. (1980). Intrinsic motivation and norms about payment. *Journal of Personality, 48,* 1–14.

> *Several previous studies have shown that rewarding individuals for performing an interesting task may have an inhibitory effect on task satisfaction and persistence. In this experiment, an extrinsic reward decreased task satisfaction and persistence when a norm for no payment existed, but the inhibitory effect was not found when a norm for payment was associated with the task.*

Tjosvold, D., & Fabrey, L. J. (1980). Motivation for perspective taking: Effects of interdependence and dependence on interest in learning other's intentions. *Psychological Reports, 46,* 755–765.

> *This study looked at the type of dependence college students had on others for rewards/costs. Subjects were led to believe that their outcomes depended upon the combination of their choice and another person's intentions or another person's actions or were unaffected by another person. Participants in an interdependent condition often relinquished a reward to receive information about another person's intentions. Results were interpreted as supporting cognitive developmentalists' and symbolic interactionists' argument that interdependence encourages the use and development of perspective-taking ability.*

Weiner, B. (1980). The role of affect in rational (attributional) approaches to human motivation. *Educational Researcher, 9,* 4–11.

> *This is a most provocative article on the way affective development and learning impact on attribution theory of motivation. The author indicates different types of feeling that motivate action that may facilitate cognitive learning and focuses on how feelings/emotions can guide self-perception. This article adds a useful dimension to motivational theory, particularly in light of the interactive role cognition and affectivity play in human motivation and behavior.*

Winefield, A. H., & Jardine, E. (1982). Effects of differences in achievement motivation and amount of exposure on responses to uncontrollable rewards. *Motivation and Emotion, 6,* 245–257.

Individuals classified as high or low in achievement motivation were given either standard or extended exposure to uncontrollable rewards. Those high in achievement motivation displayed facilitation following standard training that was eliminated after extended training. The researchers claim that their study supports the general contention of achievement motivation theory because the subjects' perception of uncontrollability was independent of learned helplessness or perceived failure.

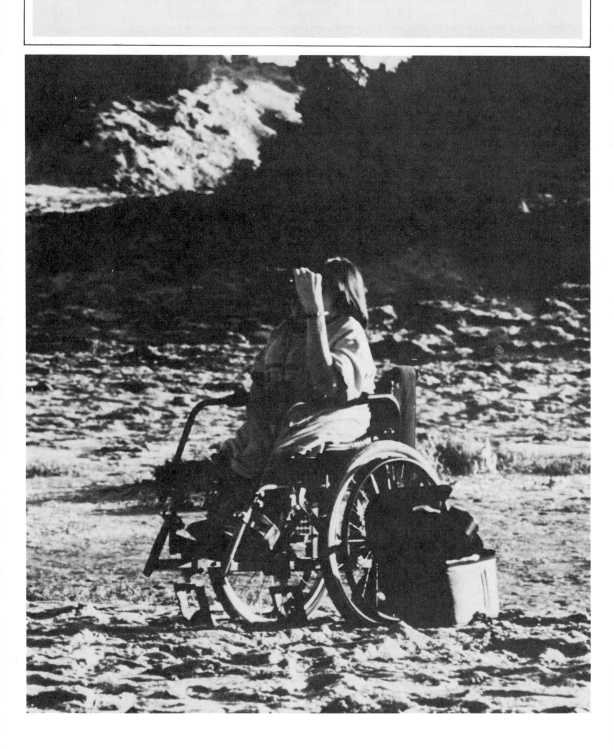

Learners with Special Characteristics

Parkhaven Elementary School was dismissed early for an in-service afternoon for all teachers in the district. The superintendent had titled the program "Educating the Exceptional Child," but the afternoon was actually to be spent discussing the issue of mainstreaming. Mainstreaming had been incompletely implemented in the district, and reactions from the teaching staff had been mixed.

The superintendent brought in Dr. Amy Klatzkin, a national authority, to speak on implementing mainstreaming in the schools. Dr. Klatzkin made several important points regarding this issue and concluded her presentation by reminding the teachers of two things. First, she pointed out that the primary value of mainstreaming is that it gives exceptional students access to a wider range of educational experiences than ever before. Second, she said that schools and classroom teachers must provide the instructional services to these special students; otherwise, the effect will be no more than dumping them into regular classrooms. After her presentation, the faculty divided into small groups to discuss how mainstreaming could be accomplished.

In many of the groups, the discussion centered on teacher attitudes, either toward school programming for the exceptional student or toward the students themselves. The following comments from members of one group are representative:

- I have no trouble in my classroom with these students who have a physical handicap. But I just don't know how to deal with the mentally handicapped student. I think the schools are asking too much of us.
- The classroom is already overcrowded and we are expected to teach so much every day. I just don't have time to give them special attention.
- I have a close friend who is handicapped. This has really helped me learn to work with the youngsters in my class.
- I think it is unjust to put exceptional kids in the regular classroom. They are always frustrated because they can't keep up. They actually learned more when they were in special education classes.
- I'm not sure these students benefit academically, but socially they certainly are more accepted than I thought they would be by the other students.

- *It really makes a difference if you have a strong special services support team. In our school, the speech therapist and school psychologist do everything they can to help teachers better understand and work with these students.*
- *I find myself feeling sorry for the special kids in my class.*
- *However you look at it, these kids are just not equal and can't take advantage of the learning opportunities like the normal students can.*

The facilitator for this group was Dan Kupersmith, a school counselor. He attempted to synthesize the group's ideas regarding mainstreaming in order to provide information to a districtwide committee that is going to reevaluate its mainstreaming efforts and reestablish some priorities and guidelines. He concluded that teachers in this group were hesitant about mainstreaming because they think it creates more problems than it solves, for teachers and students alike. Dan reminded the group of the follow-up meeting in three weeks for which they were to compile a list of strategies to facilitate mainstreaming in their schools.

There are many characteristics that make learners exceptional. Understanding them is the first step in learning to teach special children. Toward that end, I cover the following topics in this chapter:

- *Exceptionality and labeling*
- *Sensory impaired students*
- *Learning disabled students*
- *Emotionally handicapped students*
- *Gifted students*

Exceptionality and Labeling

Some students require special attention in school if they are to learn and realize their potential. Because they bring special learning conditions into the classroom and require some special instruction by teachers, they are referred to as **exceptional children.** Kirk (1972) has defined an exceptional child as anyone who deviates from the average in any of the following ways: (1) mental characteristics, (2) sensory abilities, (3) physical or neuromuscular characteristics, (4) social or emotional behaviors, (5) communication abilities, and (6) multiple handicaps. This broad definition stresses the importance of serving the educational needs of as many students as possible. It is difficult to know exactly how many students fall into Kirk's six categories, although estimates are one in five. Thus, when we are talking about educating exceptional children, we are talking about a significant number of individuals.

A major subcategory of exceptional children is the **gifted,** which includes those individuals with high intelligence or exceptional talent. They do not suffer from impairment, although they often find that the general classroom environment fails to meet their learning needs. Because they are capable of high performance, they often are not challenged. Their exceptional capabilities often lead teachers to assume

Exceptional Child
Any individual who deviates from the average child or normative behaviors.

Gifted child
Any individual with high intellectual or creative ability or talent.

they have no educational problems, a perception that could lead to programs that functionally undereducate them.

Handicapped children have some physical disability that impairs their functioning. Handicaps are usually grouped as **mental retardation, sensory impairment, communication disorders,** and **learning disabilities.** Thus, referring to a child as handicapped implies some physical disorder. Table 12–1 indicates that one school-age child in eight has some form of handicap. Table 12–2 provides a more inclusive set of data because it encompasses all individuals from birth through age nineteen. This table reveals that half of the handicapped people in the United States within these age ranges are being served. Table 12–2 shows that some handicaps have received greater priority and professional attention than others.

As different kinds of exceptionality have been identified, specific terms have been generated to define them. These descriptions should help us understand why a behavior is considered abnormal and how it manifests itself. Labels should be used only to provide a better basis for communication. They should help identify, sort, and describe differences. Unfortunately, this is not always what happens.

Studies designed to determine teacher attitude and behavior toward students labeled "learning disabled" indicate that teachers have lower expectations for these students than for students not so labeled, regardless of ability, sex, socioeconomic background, or residence (Gullung & Rucker, 1977). In a different type of study, Algozzine, Mercer, and Countermine (1977) found that teachers' expectations of student behavior were always influenced by the type of label associated with the student. Goldstein, Arkell, Ashcroft, Hurley, and Lilly (1975) argue that the relationship between labels and instruction is minimal; thus, labeling students has no

Handicapped child
Any individual who has a functional impairment that precludes normal performance in a specific area.

Mental retardation
The development of one's mentality that is below normal, implying limited intellectual capacity.

Sensory impairment
The inability to function normally through one or more of the senses.

Communication disorder
The dysfunctional category that describes any pattern of speech that varies from normal expectations.

Learning disability
Any physically or neurologically based problem that interferes with human potential.

Table 12–1 School-Age Children: Nearly One of Eight Is Handicapped

Among Handicapped Children Ages 6 through 17—

Blind visually impaired	42,800
Deaf, hard of hearing	246,000
Crippled	213,900
Speech-impaired	1,497,100
Emotionally disturbed	855,500
Mentally retarded	983,800
Learning disabled	1,283,200
Multihandicapped	25,700
	5,148,000
Handicapped children in private schools	516,000
Total	5,664,000

Source: U.S. Departments of Health, Education and Welfare, and Commerce, 1978.

Table 12–2 Number and Percent of Children Needing and Receiving Special Education in the United States

Categories	Percentage Overall[a]	Estimated Number	Percent in Programs
Speech impaired	3.3	2,293,000	81
Learning disabled	2.8	1,966,000	16
Mentally retarded	2.2	1,507,000	83
Intellectually gifted	2.2[b]	1,507,000[b]	40[b]
Emotionally disturbed and socially maladjusted	1.9	1,310,000	18
Crippled and other health problems	0.5	328,000	72
Hard of hearing	0.5	328,000	18
Deaf	0.1	49,000	71
Visually handicapped	0.1	66,000	59
Multi-handicapped	0.1	40,000	33
Total	13.4	9,394,000	49 (mean)

[a] Based on U.S. Census figures for 1975.
[b] Estimated from 1971 data.

Source: U.S. Bureau of the Census, 1977.

educational value at all. Although many would argue that labels are useful descriptors and necessary to the intervention and education process, few studies have tested the advantages of using labels with exceptional children. Lilly (1979, p. 29) summarizes the issues surrounding the use of labels. He suggests that labels have the following advantages:

1. They reduce ambiguities and allow professionals to communicate information more clearly.
2. Some labels describe physical conditions that have important educational implications.
3. They help identify the number of students who need special services.
4. They provide a focus for legislative and public support for special educational programs.
5. They assist school districts in obtaining funds from state and federal agencies for special education services.

According to Lilly (1979, p. 31) labels have the following disadvantages:

1. They encourage stereotyping and overgeneralization.
2. They imply that instructional difficulties stem solely from the students and not from instruction itself.
3. The information they provide teachers is largely irrelevant to instruction.
4. Labels are often a school life sentence for students with little chance to escape.
5. They discriminate against minorities and the poor.

Whatever the problems inherent in labeling exceptional children, it is increasingly clear that students with special needs are being provided with better individual educational programs designed to facilitate their academic and social growth. Many children historically considered uneducable are now in school and benefiting from educational experiences.

Most children can learn if they are given the appropriate instructional environment. Some handicapped children may not be able to handle as much content as nonhandicapped children within the same time frame, but they can and do learn content. They require different instructional approaches. Teachers may need to explicate their methodology more carefully than with regular students. Some handicapped students may even need special facilities not always available or practical within most classroom settings. By and large, however, most special students require only slight modifications of teacher behavior and time to learn. Gallagher (1974) has summarized the sorts of adaptations required to meet the needs of exceptional students (Table 12–3).

Table 12–3 Adapting the School To Meet the Needs of Exceptional Children

| Categories | Aspects of Educational Program To Be Modified[a] | | |
	Content (What Is Taught)	Methodology (How Content Is Taught)	Learning Environment (Where Content Is Taught)
Severe-Chronic (Required for entire school career)			
Moderate and severe mental retardation	XX	XX	XX
Deafness and severe hearing loss	XX	XX	XX
Blindness and severe visual impairment	X	XX	X
Schizophrenia and autism	XX	XX	XX
Orthopedically handicapped	—	X	XX
Severe communication problems (cleft palate, cerebral palsy)	—	XX	X
Transitional (Needs may be met by limited, intensive treatment)			
Educable mentally retarded	XX	XX	X
Hard of hearing	X	XX	X
Partially sighted	—	X	X
Articulation problems in speech	—	X	X
Emotionally disturbed	X	X	X
Specific learning disabilities (for example, reading handicaps)	XX	XX	X
Intellectually gifted	X	X	X

[a] Key: XX, major change needed; X, minor change needed; —, no change needed.

Source: Gallagher (1975c), p. 517.

Sensory Impaired Students

The sensory impaired account for 35.3 percent of all categories of school-age exceptionality. Sensory impairment includes communication disorders (74.9 percent of this category), hearing disabilities (12.3 percent), physical impairments (10.7 percent), and visual impairments (21 percent). Table 12–1 indicates that almost twenty-six thousand school-age children have multiple handicaps. Undoubtedly, some of these have one or more sensory impairments; thus, the actual number of exceptional children with sensory impairments is slightly higher than 35.3 percent.

Communication Disorders

Speech disorder
The inability to effectively articulate sounds or verbally communicate with others.

Receptive speech problem
Difficulty in encoding and interpreting things in the environment.

Expressive speech problems
Difficulty in communicating information to others.

Delayed speech
Deviation from the expected ability to speak due to personal development.

Stuttering
A break in the rhythmic pattern of vocalizing that causes nonfluent speech.

A speech disorder is a behavior "sufficiently deviant from normal or accepted speaking patterns that it attracts attention, interferes with communication, and adversely affects communication for either the speaker or the listener" (Gelfand, Jenson, & Drew, 1982, p. 161). Estimates of sensorimotor speech impairments have ranged from 12 to 15 percent of children in grades kindergarten through four to 4 to 5 percent in grades five through eight. Only planned intervention reduces the problem in high school–age adolescents (Milisen, 1971). Speech problems are often compounded by the fact that they are symptomatic of multiple handicaps; thus, they are not always overcome. Speech problems tend to be either **receptive** or **expressive.** Receptive speech problems concern the intake and interpretation of information. Expressive speech problems imply an inability to communicate information to others. My discussion focuses on **delayed speech** and **stuttering.**

Delayed Speech When speech does not develop at the expected age, there may be communication problems. There is some variation in what could be called normal speech development, which is summarized in Box 12–1, but some children develop little expressive speech, with their limited speech being dominated by nouns. Undoubtedly, limited expression is linked to reception. Nonstimulating environments, poor language models, sensory loss (such as hearing), or mild to severe emotional disturbance can all contribute to delayed speech.

Few parents know how speech should develop; so, unless the problem is severe, it is likely to go unnoticed until the child enters school. Even then the problem is not always detected. In preschoolers, incomplete sounds or words are often reinforced because parents think such "baby talk" is cute.

Deficiencies that result from delayed speech can be overcome in two ways. First, classroom teachers should be consistently good speech models and help their students learn vocabulary and ways of expression. Second, teachers, like parents, often anticipate students' needs and respond rather than letting children articulate for themselves. By "forcing" the student to communicate, the teacher facilitates speech development and increases the student's experiences in using speech.

Box 12–1   The Pattern of Normal Speech Development

Child's Chronological Age	Child's Normal Speech Development	Child's Chronological Age	Child's Normal Speech Development
6 months	Repeats self-produced sounds; imitates sounds; vocalizes to other people; and uses about 12 different speech sounds (known as phonemes).	36 months	Commonly uses up to 900 words in simple sentences averaging 3 to 4 words per sentence; averages 15,000 words per day and 170 words per hour; uses words such as when, time, today, not today and can repeat three digits, name one color, say name, give simple account of experiences, and tell stories that are understandable; begins to use plurals and some prepositions; uses commands such as you make it, I want, and you do it; verbalizes toilet needs.
12 months	Commonly uses up to 3 words besides mama and dada; may vocalize such words as bye-bye, hi baby, kitty, and puppy; and uses up to 18 different phonemes.		
18 months	Commonly uses up to 20 words and 21 different phonemes; jargon words or phrases are present and often automatically repeats words or phrases said by others (echolalia); uses names of objects that are familiar, one-word sentences such as go or eat, and uses gestures; uses words such as no, mine, good, bad, hot, cold, nice, here, where, more, and expressions such as oh-oh, what's that, and all gone; the use of words at this age may be quite inconsistent.	42 months	Commonly uses up to 1200 words in mostly complete sentences that average between 4 and 5 words in length; 7 percent of the sentences are compound or complex and averages 203 words per hour; rate of speech is faster; relates experiences and tells about activities in sequential order; can say a nursery rhyme; asks permission (such as Can I? or Will I?).
24 months	Commonly uses up to 270 words and 25 different phonemes; jargon and echolalia are infrequent; averages 75 words per hour during free play; speaks in words, phrases, and 2- to 3-word sentences; averages 2 words per response; first pronouns appear such as I, me, mine, it, who, and that; adjectives and adverbs begin to appear; names common objects and pictures; enjoys Mother Goose; refers to self by name such as Bobby go bye-bye; and uses phrases such as I want, go bye-bye, want cookie, up daddy, nice doll, ball all gone, and where kitty.	48 months	Commonly uses up to 1500 words in sentences averaging 5 to 5½ words in length; averages 400 words per hour; counts to 3, repeats 4 digits, names 3 objects and repeats 9-word sentences from memory; names the primary colors, some coins, and relates fanciful tales, enjoys rhyming nonsense words and using exaggerations; demands reasons why and how; questioning is at a peak, up to 500 a day; passes judgment on own activities; can recite a poem from memory or sing a song and uses such words as even, almost, now, something, like, and but.
30 months	Commonly uses up to 425 words and 27 different phonemes; jargon and echolalia no longer exist; averages 140 spoken words per hour; says words that name or identify items such as chair, can, box, key, and door; repeats 2 digits from memory; average sentence length is about 2½ words; uses more adjectives and adverbs; demands repetition from others (such as do it again); almost always announces intentions before acting; begins to ask questions of adults.	54 months	Commonly uses up to 1800 words in sentences averaging 5½ to 6 words but now averages only 230 words per hour and is satisfied with less verbalization; does little commanding or demanding; about 1 in 10 sentences is compound or complex and only 8 percent of the sentences are incomplete; can define 10 common words and count to 20; asks questions for information and learns to control and manipulate persons and situations with language.

(Continued on page 354.)

Box 12–1 continued

60 months	Commonly uses up to 2200 words in sentences averaging 6 words; can define ball, hat, stove, policeman, wind, and can count five objects and repeat 4 or 5 digits; definitions are in terms of use—can single out a word and ask its meaning; makes serious inquiries (such as what is this for, how does this work, etc.); uses all types of sentences, clauses, and parts of speech; reads by way of pictures and prints simple words.		length; grammatical errors continue to decrease as sentences and vocabulary become more sophisticated.
		72 months	Commonly uses up to 2500 words in sentences averaging 7 words in length; relates fanciful tales, recites numbers up to 30; asks the meaning of words; repeats five digits from memory; can complete analogies such as: A table is made of wood, a window of _____ . A bird flies, a fish _____ .
66 months	Commonly uses up to 2300 words in sentences that average 6½ words in		

Source: Adapted and abridged from Weiss & Lillywhite (1976), pp. 56–58.

Stuttering   This speech disorder may receive the greatest amount of attention from professionals. Stuttering is a timing disorder that affects about 30 percent of those with a speech disorder (Dupuy, 1977). Behaviors classified as stuttering include the prolongation of sounds or words, disturbed fluency, and an imbalance in speech rhythm. Stuttering is not well understood and it may have several causes. Three explanations are generally offered for stuttering: (1) It is a neurological problem that is not easily resolved. (2) It is symptomatic of emotional or psychological disturbance. (3) People learn to become stutterers.

The third explanation offers classroom teachers an approach to correcting the problem. If stuttering is learned, then a successful intervention with school-age children includes offering alternative learning. The other two explanations, which undoubtedly apply to many individuals, place help outside the scope of most school personnel's skills. Thus, setting up behavioral alternatives may be a partial solution for many stutterers.

Hearing Disorders

Deaf
The inability to fully hear or not hear verbal information.

Hard-of-hearing
A person who cannot hear without the use of a hearing aid.

Hearing-impaired students include those who are **deaf** or partially **hard-of-hearing.** A deaf person is one whose hearing disability precludes successful processing of linguistic information through audition with or without a hearing aid. A hard-of-hearing person is one who, with the assistance of a hearing aid, has sufficient residual hearing to process linguistic information through audition.

Heredity is a major cause of deafness. Almost half the individuals with hearing loss have a relative with a hearing loss (Reis, 1973). Two other well-established causes of hearing disorders are rubella and meningitis. When a woman contracts rubella or German measles in her first trimester of pregnancy, the potential for birth defects, including deafness, is increased. Meningitis is a viral infection that can destroy the acoustic apparatus of the inner ear. Finally, fluid buildup in the middle ear contributes to hearing loss, a situation that affects speech, hearing, and perceptual skills. Techniques for identifying and solving hearing difficulties due to fluid buildup do exist. Early diagnosis can alleviate many problems for children.

Karchmer and Trybus (1977) report that approximately half the deaf school-age children are in special educational environments, such as residential or day schools. The other half attend public schools. A comprehensive survey by Jordan, Gustason, and Rosen (1979) revealed that, of those attending public schools, only 37 percent were being mainstreamed. This percentage includes any type of mainstreaming, whether it be a class period or an entire day. No significantly greater percentages of mainstreaming were found at the elementary, middle, and high school levels. The researchers also found that the number of interpreters available is proportionally low for those being mainstreamed. This implies that more careful research needs to be done in order to determine how well educational needs are being met.

Deaf children generally are underachievers, presumably because their language acquisition is inferior to nondeaf children's. Rarely has a systematic symbol system been modeled or shared with them during their early language acquisition years (Tomlinson-Keasy & Kelly, 1978). Studies have been done in virtually all academic areas to compare the achievement of deaf children and hearing children. Most studies show lower achievement among deaf children, as much as one to two grade levels below expectancy (Furth, 1966a; Meadow, 1975). Educational programs that compensate for this lack of language are neither well developed nor widespread.

Use of individual intelligence tests with deaf people has clearly shown a range of normal intelligence among the hearing impaired (Birch & Birch, 1951; Hiskey, 1956). This finding supports the contention that cognitive ability and language facility are not functionally related (Furth, 1966b;

Robertson & Youniss, 1969). But language is the major way of representing academic content. Furth (1971) contends that the deaf are "linguistically deficient" because the symbol system available to them during formative periods is at best limited. Educators must help the deaf acquire language and represent thought processes in nonlanguage ways. If deaf students fall within the range of normal intelligence, they deserve the opportunity to have educational experiences that increase the likelihood of their achieving all they can.

Physical Impairments

Physical impairment
Physical impairment
Any disability or health disorder that interferes with physical functioning.

Physical disability
The inability to function physically due to loss of limb, muscle control, or damage.

Physical health disorder
The curtailment of normal physical functions because of a chronic health problem.

Physical impairments include **physical disabilities** and **physical health disorders.** Physical disabilities include the loss of a limb, lack of muscle control, crippling, or any other physical or psychomotor impairment that precludes normal physical functioning. According to Suran and Rizzo (1979, p. 175), a physical health disorder is any "identified physical health problem that (a) requires intensive medical attention or hospitalization, (b) cannot be easily and completely cured and is therefore long-standing, and (c) places severe demands on the child's ability to lead a normal life." Technically, any physical disability is a physical health disorder, but they are often perceived as different problems. For example, a crippled child (physical disability) is often treated differently from a child who has cancer (physical health disorder).

Educational programs for children with physical impairments are not that different, although most physical plants require modifications to accommodate the physically handicapped. A child with epilepsy may be given no special treatment at all unless an epileptic attack occurs at school. The stress that accompanies physical disability or chronic illness typically goes unnoticed by classroom teachers. Ironically, this lack of teacher awareness may add to the student's stress, thus interfering with learning. Farrell (1982) has pointed out that a child with cancer invariably has alternating periods of remission and relapse and as a result tends to focus on the uncertainty and ambiguity of living rather than on dying. The education of such children is complicated by the fact that they have alternating periods of low stress, hope, and achievement with high stress, despair, and withdrawal. Table 12–4 summarizes the physical health disorders of childhood.

Visual Impairments

The problems of visually handicapped students, who for years have been excluded from public school environments, are now beginning to be dealt with in regular classroom environments. Teachers must adapt methods and materials in order to help the visually impaired learn. When learners cannot perform common visual tasks, individualized instruction may be necessary in order for them to master certain learning tasks (Collins & Barraga, 1980).

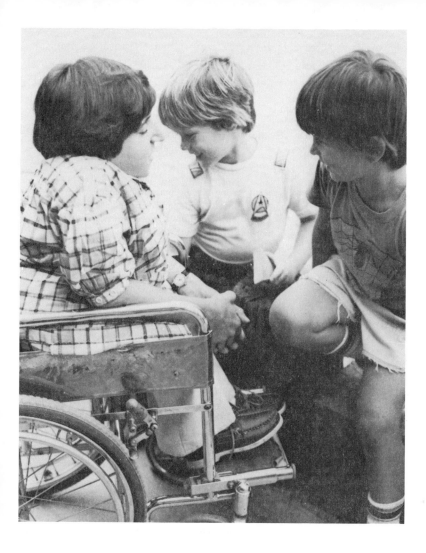

Visual acuity refers to the accuracy of distance vision, which is measured by the Snellen chart, a standardized series of letters, numbers, or symbols that are read from a distance of twenty feet. A person who can read a designated letter at twenty feet is said to have 20/20 vision. A person who can distinguish a letter at twenty feet that a person of normal vision can see at eighty feet has 20/80 vision. A person with 20/200 vision is considered legally blind.

Field of vision is another means of determining legal blindness. A person whose angle of vision is less than 20 degrees is legally blind. This narrow band of vision results in the person not seeing the array of objects or events with a normal visual field.

As with other types of sensory impairment, the visually handicapped may learn less than the nonsensory impaired student, although this should not be equated with less intelligence. The functionally blind student generally has a more restricted range of experiences than the sighted student. Generally speaking, a blind student has more restricted concepts, cannot

Visual acuity
The accuracy of a person's distance vision.

Field of vision
The angle or breadth of a person's vision.

Table 12–4   Common Physical Health Disorders of Childhood

Name	Diagnostic Description	Important Characteristics
Cerebral palsy	A crippling condition of the neuromuscular system; disorder of movement and posture; central characteristic is neurological motor dysfunction caused by brain damage (birth injury, congenital defect, infection); not a clear-cut syndrome but includes children with a variety of symptoms, such as muscle weakness or involuntary muscle movements.	Brain damage involved in CP may also affect IQ but not inevitably; however, a greater proportion of CP children are mentally retarded than is case with general population; since condition involves brain damage, it cannot be cured, but physical therapy and surgery can improve function.
Epilepsy	A condition of the neuromuscular system involving recurring attacks of loss of consciousness, convulsive movements, or disturbances of feeling and behavior; also known as *seizure* or *convulsive disorder;* caused by as yet undetermined brain damage.	Focus of treatment is the control of seizures; many effective anticonvulsant medications are now available; although many mentally retarded individuals suffer from seizures, the seizures themselves do not seem to cause mental retardation.
Spina bifida	A congenital defect of the spinal column; in its more severe forms, paralysis of lower limbs is virtually inevitable without surgical intervention; condition is evident at birth; most severe form is termed *myelomeningocele.*	Typically involves mental retardation; although the lives of these children can usually be saved by surgery, many such youngsters will have considerable physical and intellectual disabilities.
Muscular dystrophy	A degeneration of the muscles; disease is progressive and grows worse with age.	These children typically require a wheelchair in the normal course of the disease; cognitive abilities are not affected.
Limb deficiencies	Caused by genetic birth defects, amputations due to disease, or accidents.	Mechanical limbs (prosthetic devices) can frequently be fitted, but considerable training in use of limb as well as supportive attitudes are necessary.
Cystic fibrosis	Symptoms include generalized dysfunction of the exocrine glands, very high salt concentrations in sweat, and chronic pulmonary dysfunction with repeated episodes of pneumonia (with severe bouts of coughing); most lethal hereditary disorder of children in U.S.; specific cause unknown; no known cure, and illness is inevitably fatal; many patients, however, survive into adolescence and young adulthood.	These youngsters are encouraged to lead active lives and no physical restrictions are placed on behavior; cognitive development is normal and they typically remain in regular school placement; extensive therapeutic regimen is required in the home; patients frequently feel emotionally inhibited due to mucous excretions, chronic coughing, and breathing difficulty.
Leukemia	A group of diseases characterized by sudden increases of white blood cells in the bone marrow and peripheral blood; most common form of childhood cancer; a decade ago, the disease was considered fatal; recent advances in chemotherapy have made it possible to expect cure or at least long-term leukemia-free survival.	Many children can be treated with drugs on an outpatient basis; others require surgery, radiation therapy, or bone marrow transplantation; fear of death is frequent concern of child and family, even in remission, and an atmosphere of normalcy should be stressed with emphasis on positive aspects of living.
Asthma	Causes unclear; involves both psychological and somatic factors; often described as *psychophysiologic* illness; characterized by difficulty in breathing due to narrowing of airways; involves severe and life-threatening attacks of wheezing; may cause death due to inability to breathe.	Sometimes described as the "vulnerable child syndrome"; breathing attacks are frightening and parents may tend to overprotect the child; drug therapy can be very effective in preventing attacks and aerosol (fine mist spray) can be helpful in controlling attack.
Diabetes	Characterized by an inability to store sugar in the blood due to dysfunction of the pancreas; symptoms include loss of weight, frequent urination, and excessive thirstiness; treatment involves diet management and insulin therapy as needed.	With proper management, diabetes can be brought under control; risks involve diabetic coma (excess of sugar in blood causing nausea, abdominal pain, labored breathing) and insulin reaction (lack of sugar causing hunger, sweating, tremors, drowsiness).

Source: Suran & Rizzo (1979), pp. 179–180.

The Jackie Steiner Story

Sometimes a student is so different or unique that you simply cannot ignore him or her, even though that is exactly what has happened in school in the past. Such is the case of Jackie Steiner, a sixteen-year-old, 6'3" boy in the eighth grade. Although Jackie had been held back three times in elementary school, he entered the eighth grade unable to read and labeled "mentally retarded."

Jackie was of special interest to his eighth-grade language arts teacher, Mr. Whiteall. Something about Jackie suggested to Mr. Whiteall that he had more potential than previously thought. Mr. Whiteall also thought Jackie would probably drop out of school after eighth grade and should be taught enough skills to be able to function in society.

Jackie was started on a pre-primer series the third week of school. Mr. Whiteall set aside fifty minutes a week to work with Jackie. This special attention caused Jackie to begin to respond, sounding out words and learning vocabulary. Very soon Jackie was through a first level preprimer, then on to more advanced material.

One evening Mr. Whiteall took Jackie home from school and was invited in to meet his parents. The teacher was surprised to learn that Jackie's parents were deaf-mutes and had been so since before Jackie's birth. In reality, Jackie had lived for sixteen years without any parental language models, a fact that appeared nowhere in the school records even though Jackie had been in the same school for eleven years.

This new insight about Jackie convinced the teacher that Jackie could learn and was not retarded. With ongoing tutoring sessions, Jackie made continuous progress. By the time school was out, Jackie had a functioning vocabulary, was reading at a fifth-grade level, and, with the help of Mr. Whiteall, had a part-time summer job.

As predicted, Jackie did drop out of school after the eighth grade, and, by the end of the summer, he had worked himself into a full-time job. But Jackie also had better language skills and could better interact with people in his environment. Just fifty minutes of special attention a week, combined with the teacher's discovery of Jackie's background, allowed

Jackie to learn enough to function in society.

What Do You Think?

1. What kind of school conditions might cause a student to be ignored as long as Jackie was?

2. Identify things school personnel can do to avoid this type of problem.

3. To what extent can teachers help students who are victims of long-term neglect?

use touch to mediate two-dimensional representation of three-dimensional objects, and is more dependent on secondhand experiences (those verbally transmitted by others).

Barraga (1964) has documented that a planned learning program can improve visual efficiency in students with seriously impaired but usable vision. She found that planned instructional materials increase the students' visual perceptual development in a sequence similar to that found in children with no impairment. Several subsequent studies using both teacher-made and commercial materials have substantiated the effectiveness of planned learning experiences to promote efficiency in visual functioning (Barraga & Collins, 1979; Holmes, 1967; Tobin, 1973).

Hallahan and Kauffman (1978, p.367) offer the following suggestions for teachers with visually impaired students:

1. The visually handicapped child should be required to care for his or her own materials as part of the teacher's effort to foster a sense of independence.
2. A sighted child in the class can at times act as a guide, as long as the visually disabled pupil does not become too dependent upon him or her.
3. The blind child should be treated the same as sighted children; the same expectations should be maintained for all the children.
4. Interpersonal interaction between the blind child and his or her sighted peers should be encouraged.
5. The child should be encouraged to participate in as many activities as possible. Alternative activities should be arranged if it is not possible for the blind child to join in with the rest of the class.
6. ·The visually impaired child should be given the same kind of special tasks (such as watering plants) that are given to other children.

Concept Summary 12–1

Impairment Categories		
Category	**Label**	**Characteristics**
Speech	Delayed Speech	Speech patterns develop at a slower rate than in others of same age
	Stuttering	Break in rhythmic pattern
Hearing	Deaf	Total loss of audible sound
	Hard-of-Hearing	Partial loss, which can be corrected with hearing aid
Physical	Disability	Loss of limb, muscle control, malformation
	Health Disorder	Chronic, debilitating disease, often requiring hospitalization
Visual	Acuity	Ability to see things at normal ranges, 20/20
	Field	Lack of peripheral vision, impairing total visual field

Learning Disabled Students

Few labels encompass so wide a range of behavior as that of "learning disabilities." The term is designed to identify those students whose academic achievements fall below their intellectual potential. Yet the term has been applied so broadly that it often has little significance in educational decision making. As a result, numerous subcategories have been added.

Kirk (1972) has grouped one set of terms around disorders that have a biological causation or etiology. These terms include *brain injury, minimal brain damage, cerebral palsy, cerebral dysfunction, organic behavior disorders,* and *psychoneurological disorders.* Sometimes these terms are grouped under the broader category of **learning disorders.** The second group of terms Kirk uses centers around deviant behavioral manifestations and does not necessarily have a biological basis. Terms include *hyperkinetic behavior, perceptual disorders, conceptual disorders, social dyspraxia, catastrophic behavior, disinhibition, dyslexia, and aphasia.*

In 1966, a task force summarized the labels most often used in the literature. Thirty-eight terms prevailed in the literature, but the following ten are most frequently used (Clements, 1966, p.9):

1. Hyperactivity
2. Perceptual-motor impairments
3. Emotional liability
4. General orientation defects
5. Attention disorders
6. Impulsivity
7. Memory and thinking disorders
8. Disabilities in reading, arithmetic, spelling, and writing
9. Speech and hearing disorders
10. Equivocal neurological signs and EEG irregularities

In an attempt to arrive at some labels or terms, the National Advisory Committee to the Bureau of Education for the Handicapped (1968, p. 34) provided the following definition:

> Children with special learning disabilities exhibit a disorder in one or more of the basic psychological processes involved in understanding or in using spoken or written language. These may be manifested in disorders of listening, thinking, talking, reading, writing, spelling, or arithmetic. They include conditions which have been referred to as perceptual handicaps, brain injury, minimal brain dysfunction, dyslexia, developmental aphasia, etc. They do not include learning problems which are due primarily to visual, hearing, or motor handicaps, to mental retardation, emotional disturbance or to environmental deprivation.

The popular use of some terms has resulted in mislabeling as well as justification by parents and teachers for many behaviors that are either unexplainable or unacceptable when observed in children. For example, nail biting, poor eating habits, playing loud rock music, not being concerned with personal hygiene, being disrespectful, and being involved in drugs are not symptomatic of a learning disability. Teachers must understand this term and not apply it broadly and unfairly.

Dyslexia

Dyslexia
The inability to properly encode into the mind phenomena that are seen or heard.

Dyslexia is a reading disability. Some children cannot learn and remember letters they see, which is visual dyslexia. Others cannot learn and remember letters they hear, which is auditory dyslexia. Bryant (1964, p. 196) has identified the following primary characteristics of dyslexia:

1. Extreme difficulty in associating the sounds with the visual symbols of letters
2. Lack of attention to the details within words (Word recognition might be based on initial letter or length of the word rather than on vowels and consonants or patterns.)

3. Problems with reverse images, such as "b" and "d", which may be a result of spatial confusion
4. Confusion of right and left, sizes and shapes, and directions

Many children, when first learning to read, make sensory or spatial errors. This may be due to incomplete learning, misunderstanding the teacher, lack of attention, or task difficulty. Children with no specific disability will overcome such deficiencies rather quickly as a result of additional help. If a child is dyslexic, these behaviors will persist and routine reteaching will not be enough to help him or her overcome the problem.

Minimal Brain Dysfunction (MBD)

MBD is widely used to describe students with learning disabilities. In fact, minimal brain dysfunction and learning disabilities are often used interchangeably, especially within the medical profession. In actuality, MBD is a type of learning disability. It has been used to "designate a condition in children in which the neurological impairment is *minimal;* behavior and learning are affected without lowering the general intellectual capacity" (Waugh & Bush, 1971, p. 6).

Strauss (1939) and his associates (Strauss & Kephart, 1955; Strauss & Lehtinen, 1947) first studied this problem because they believed there were children who were dysfunctional due to brain injury and children who were dysfunctional for cultural-familial reasons. They described the former as those who, before, during, or after birth, received an injury to the brain. Such children were thought to have problems with perception, thinking, or emotional behavior that could prevent or impede normal learning.

Hyperactivity, impulsivity, and short attention span are common manifestations of MBD in the classroom. Lubin (1977) suggests that about 5 percent of all elementary school children are hyperactive. Havighurst (1976) notes that 1 percent of all elementary school children are prescribed drugs as therapy for their hyperactivity. Although it is presumed that appropriate drugs can control hyperactivity, they have been found to suppress normal physical growth. Up to one-third less than the expected gains in height and weight occurred with long-term treatment in some children. There is also the potential for excessive use of dextroamphetamine sulfate (Dexedrine) or methylphenidate hydrochloride (Ritalin) (Hollister, 1972). Research has begun to question if there is a unitary syndrome such as MBD, thus suggesting that treatment may be oversimplified or inappropriate (Crinella, 1973; Routh & Roberts, 1972).

Minimal brain dysfunction
Mild neurological damage that interferes with an individual's ability to function normally.

Perceptual Handicaps

Perception describes the process through which individuals become aware of things or events in the environment. These processes primarily are visual, auditory, and tactile. The term *perceptual-motor* refers to how we coordinate visual perception with motor behavior (Suran & Rizzo, 1979). Because the major emphasis in public education is on visual learning, a student's inability to perceive and integrate such perception with motor behavior may restrict his or her learning. Children who misperceive a numeral or letter are going to reproduce it incorrectly. Because of the dominance of perceptual-motor coordination in classrooms, problems in this area may be a major form of learning disability.

Diagnosis of perceptual-motor functions is very important. Kephart (1960) considers the inability to acquire basic motor skills during infancy an early indicator of perceptual-motor problems. He believes a perceptual-motor disability exists if a motor experience and a perceptual experience are misaligned. Consequently, he sees a direct relationship between a perceptual disability and poor academic achievement in subject-matter areas where perception is important to the learning task. Frostig (Frostig, Lefever, & Whittlesey, 1964) developed the *Frostig Developmental Test of Visual Perception,* to diagnose visual perceptual abilities that she thought were central to most learning tasks. Once a learner's problems are assessed, the teacher can remediate and help the student acquire academic skills.

Perceptual handicaps involve more than just perceptual-motor disabilities. Auditory, tactile, and kinesthetic abilities are rarely taught, although, if they are not normal, they will interfere with learning. All the senses must work in relation to each other to have maximal learning. Hurst (1968, p. 267) summarizes several indicators of perceptual handicaps:

1. Specific learning deficits—reading, spelling, and so forth
2. Perceptual-motor deficits—poor printing, drawings, and so forth
3. General coordination—awkwardness, clumsiness
4. Hyperkinesis—constant motion, restlessness
5. Impulsivity—inability to keep from touching and handling objects, speaking without checking himself or herself
6. Emotional instability—irritability, aggression, or tearfulness
7. Short attention span

Language Disabilities

Auditory perception is important to language, but language itself involves more than perceptual abilities. It involves cognitive processes, such as verbal facility, language expression, memory, and understanding verbal symbols. Suran and Rizzo (1979) describe three types of language disabilities that help educators realize the importance of language deficits:

1. *Inner-language disorder.* This is the preverbal inability to internalize and organize experiences. For example, the student may have difficulty organizing concrete experiences with a more general concept (may not associate the sound of thunder with the general concept of a thunderstorm).

2. *Receptive language disorder.* This is difficulty in understanding verbal symbols. The most common example of this is the inability to use the same word in contexts where the meanings are different. A child may understand the word *gang* when applied to adolescents who live in the neighborhood but not to a gang of garden implements in the garage.

	Learning Disability Categories	
Category	**Type of Disorder**	**Characteristic of Disorder**
Dyslexia	Visual	Inability to learn what is seen
	Auditory	Inability to learn what is heard
MBD	Neurological	Inability to learn because of hyper-activity, impulsivity, or short attention span
Perceptual	Motor	Inability to align perceptual and motor ability
Language	Cognitive	Inability to associate experiences with their underlying meaning

3. *Expressive language disorder.* This is difficulty in producing spoken language. "Children with expressive language disorders tend to avoid the use of words in communicating and may rely extensively on pointing or gesturing or overusage of certain words that have become comfortable" (Suran & Rizzo, 1979, p. 253). A student may point to an upsetting event rather than verbalize the feeling to the teacher.

A commonly used test for assessing language disabilities is the *Illinois Test of Psycholinguistic Abilities* (ITPA). Devised by Kirk and McCarthy (1968), it measures language, motor and perceptual skills, memory, and concept formation (see Table 12–5). The ITPA helps determine what type of remedial program a student needs by focusing on strengths and identifying weaknesses. The test is not appropriate for students beyond approximately grade four.

The assessment of learning disabilities through standardized or norm-referenced tests seems to fulfill the task of diagnosis. However, as several writers have pointed out, diagnosis and prescription differ in their intent; therefore, a test should not be used for prescriptive purposes (Kratochwill, 1977; Schlieper, 1982). Prescription means finding ways to help the learner overcome the deficiencies discovered in diagnosis. Specifying learning experiences, monitoring time on task, and articulating subject matter at a level within the learner's grasp are necessary components of helping students overcome learning problems and increase their response potential (Gaskins, 1982; Rosenshine & Berliner, 1978). Tasks must be designed around diagnosed learning or perceptual deficiencies.

Emotionally Handicapped and Mentally Retarded Students

There is no universal agreement as to what constitutes an emotionally disturbed child. According to Bower and Lambert (1971), emotionally

Table 12–5 Summary of ITPA Subtests

	Test Description*	Examples of Classroom Observations
Auditory reception	The child indicates "yes" or "no" to such questions as "Do babies drink?" "Do barometers congratulate?"	Does the child understand what is said? Can he follow written directions but not verbal ones? Can he take down dictated sentences? Can he identify common animal sounds? musical instruments? classroom noises?
Visual reception	The child must select from a group of pictures the one of an object that is used in a same or similar way as a stimulus picture.	Can the child get specific requested information from pictures or films? Does he have a wide acquaintance with everyday objects, such as tools?
Manual expression	The child must show through gesture how an object (e.g., a phone, a toothbrush) is used.	Can the child express action through movement? Can the child play charades? Is he hesitant and awkward when the class does creative movement?
Verbal expression	The child is asked to describe a familiar object, such as a ball.	How well does the child express himself? How many different concepts does he use? Is he creative and imaginative?
Auditory association	The child is required to make analogies in completing sentences: e.g., "Cotton is soft; stones are (hard)."	Does the child understand the concepts of "same" and "different?" Can he understand math relationships? Does he have difficulty in classifying?
Visual association	The child must associate pictures on the basis of relationships such as functional usage (sock and shoe) and conceptual categories (horse and cow, both animals; bread and cheese, both foods).	How large is the child's store of concepts? Does he make logical connections between ideas? Does he understand that the same object can be classiffed in different ways?
Grammatic closure	The child is asked to complete sentences using the correct inflection: e.g., "Here is a dog; here are two (dogs)." "The man is painting. He is a (painter)."	Does the child speak correctly?
Auditory sequential memory	The child is requested to repeat a series of digits presented rapidly.	Can the child, after hearing a spoken sentence or number fact or a word spelled orally, repeat the information?
Visual sequential memory	The child is shown a sequence of geometric forms; it is removed, and the child is asked to reproduce the sequence by placing chips in proper order.	Can the child focus his attention? Can he discriminate among similar geometric forms? Can he copy a pattern? Can he reproduce it from memory?
Visual closure	The child is asked to identify all the partially obscured pictures of common objects against a distracting background; he must do so in 30 seconds.	Does he scan pictures? Can he work rapidly? Is he easily distracted? Can he locate specific information on a printed page? Does he have special difficulty in reading hyphenated words or blurry ditto copies?
Auditory closure (optional)	The child is asked to repeat words or phrases in which certain sounds have been omitted: e.g., "Easter unny" (Easter bunny).	Does the child understand a speaker with a different accent? Does he understand phone conversations? Can he understand speech in a noisy room? Does he leave off word endings?
Sound blending (optional)	Sounds are spoken at half-second intervals, and the child must blend them into a word: e.g., "f-oo-t, f-u-n, wh-e-n."	Can the child decode unfamiliar words in reading if he can associate the sound with the individual letter? Can he blend sounds into words, as in the test?

*The questions used as examples are not those actually used in the ITPA.

Source: Kirk, S., McCarthy, J., & Kirk, W. *Illinois test of psycholinguistic abilities.* (Examiner's manual), rev. ed. Champaign: IL: University of Illinois Press, 1968.

disturbed children have moderate to marked reduction in behavioral freedom that consequently affects their ability to function effectively when learning or interacting with others. Rhodes (1970) views disturbance as resulting from the interface between behavior and the reactions

others have to that behavior. Algozzine and Sherry (1981) point out that it is the child's behavior, and not the child, that constitutes the problem. Behavioral disabilities include chronic, excessive, and/or deviant behaviors that range from impulsive and/or aggressive to those indicating depression and withdrawal. Bower and Lambert (1971, pp. 142–143) suggest that children with emotional problems may manifest one or more of the following behavior patterns:

1. Inability to learn that cannot be adequately explained by intellectual, sensory, neurophysiological, or general health factors
2. Inability to build or maintain satisfactory interpersonal relations with peers and teachers
3. Inappropriate or immature types of behavior or feelings under normal conditions
4. General pervasive mood of unhappiness or depression
5. Tendency to develop physical symptoms, such as speech problems, pains, or fears, associated with personal or school problems

Many interpretations, misconceptions, and prejudices surround mental retardation. Few terms in education or medicine have been so variously defined. Attitudes toward mental retardation are related to society's attitude toward the handicapped, and only recently have these attitudes begun to change (Morris & Hoschouer, 1980). The following three criteria have been widely used in diagnosing mental retardation:

1. An IQ under 70 as measured by an individual intelligence test (Educable mentally retarded [EMR] fall within an IQ range of 50 to 75. Trainable mentally retarded [TMR] fall within an IQ range of 25 to 49.)
2. Deficiencies in social maturity to the extent that an independent life is difficult or impossible

3. Structural defects of the central nervous system if congenital or acquired impairments occurring from the embryonic period through the third to fourth year of life

Numerous studies have been done on educable mentally retarded students. Blatt (1958) researched the differences in physical development, academic status, and personality characteristics of EMR children in special and regular classes. With the exception of the special class students being underweight, the EMR children were not different in physical development. In terms of personality, those in special classes were assessed as being more socially mature and emotionally stable. The two groups were not different in arithmetic, language, and reading achievement, although, within the time frame of the study, those in special classes did make greater gains in reading.

Meyerowitz (1963) found that EMRs were more self-derogatory than nonretarded students, but EMR children in regular classrooms were less self-derogatory than those in special classes. Lewis (1973) measured self-concept, attitude toward school, academic achievement, and social adaptive behavior among EMR students in four settings: regular classrooms, self-contained classrooms, special classes, and resource rooms or learning centers. There were no significant differences among the four groups in self-concept, achievement, or attitudes toward school. Students in the nonintegrated self-contained classrooms had the most difficulty with adaptive behavior.

Bradfield, Brown, Kaplan, Rickert, and Stannard (1973) compared EMR students in regular classrooms modified to address their needs with those in self-contained classrooms. The modified classrooms were designed around individual instruction through the use of learning centers. They found no differences in academic achievement in the two settings in the third grade, but students in the regular class gained significantly in reading and arithmetic in grade four. Those in regular classrooms demonstrated less disruptive social behaviors in grades three and four.

The numerous studies on EMR children in a variety of educational settings do not demonstrate that any particular setting results in greater academic achievement. However, several studies demonstrate effects on their social development. Because studies are designed so differently and may be based on teacher perceptions of EMR students, rather than self-perceptions, it is difficult to generalize these results. However, it appears that EMR students integrated into regular classrooms make the best social adjustments and gain greater acceptance by their nonretarded peers. With the Education for All Handicapped Children Act of 1975 (Public Law 94-142), integrating or **mainstreaming** EMR students into the regular classroom has become more common. Some have cautioned, however, that mainstreaming does not automatically help EMR students or make their nonretarded peers accept them (Blatt, 1981; Childs, 1979).

Mainstreaming
The integrating of a special education student, regardless of handicap, into the regular classroom.

Screening and Assessment

Assessment of emotional disturbance is most difficult. It is so easy to judge observable behavior on a "normal-abnormal" continuum. If parents, teachers, or school behavioral consultants are to describe and identify emotional problems, they must first know the range of "normal" human development. Studies have shown that one behavior may disturb some people and not others (Algozzine, 1977; Quay & Peterson, 1975). Algozzine (1976) reports that regular classroom teachers are more bothered than special education teachers by student behaviors. Similarly, in nonschool settings, therapists, who report they find many behaviors unacceptable at the beginning of a series of therapy sessions, do not hold the same perceptions at the conclusion of the sessions (Gullotta & Adams, 1982).

A comprehensive screening procedure can help reduce relative judgments of what is disturbed behavior. Again, Bower and Lambert (1971, p. 144) have carefully addressed this issue. They suggest the following screening criteria:

1. It should be possible to complete the screening procedure with only such information as the teacher can obtain without outside technical or professional assistance.
2. The procedure should be sufficiently simple and straightforward so the average teacher can undertake it without long training or daily supervision.
3. The results of the procedure should be tentative identification of children with emotional problems—leading the teacher to refer to competent specialists those children who could benefit most from thorough diagnosis.
4. The procedure should not encourage the teacher to diagnose emotional problems, to draw conclusions about their causes, or to label or categorize children. In fact, the procedure should actively discourage the teacher from undertaking any of these highly technical interpretations.
5. The procedure should neither invade the individual's privacy nor violate good taste.
6. The procedure should not threaten any child.
7. The procedure should be inexpensive to use.

The importance of effective, nonstigmatized screening procedures cannot be overestimated, especially because teachers often diagnose and label, and behavioral consultants and physicians often accept their judgments (Doke, 1976; Wallace, 1976). Several studies show that the label "emotionally disturbed" brings out the most negative attitudes in teachers toward students, even more so than the labels "mentally retarded" and "learning disabled." Emotional disturbance is a less acceptable handicap. It is difficult within school environments to avoid labels, particularly when using them is such a common practice. Nevertheless, it is the school's responsibility to upgrade teachers' understanding of emotionally disturbed students.

Instructing

Educational techniques for working with the emotionally handicapped vary; but whatever approach is used, it is important they be given adequate individual instruction, which usually occurs in one of three treatment settings. The first is regular classrooms. Students are placed with all other students and are assigned work that falls within their range of ability. Children placed in this setting are usually only mildly disturbed. Occasionally, they will need some crisis intervention from the teacher, school counselor, school psychologist, or other qualified personnel.

A second setting is the resource classroom. Some school systems are large enough to have several teachers who have resource rooms in which the emotionally disturbed child may spend several minutes to hours a week. Teachers in resource classrooms use their specialty area as a means of teaching and helping the student learn and make personal adjustments. Moderately disturbed children are often placed in this treatment mode.

Self-contained classrooms are a third treatment setting. One teacher is responsible for the student all day, a format generally used with the severely emotionally disturbed. Although these classrooms are individualized, they are often highly structured and task oriented. Behavioral contingencies are typically in effect; that is, children must accomplish specific tasks in order to earn play time or unstructured learning time.

Mainstreaming

In November 1976, Public Law 94-142 went into effect, creating the potential for a new educational era for exceptional handicapped children capable of benefiting from education. The law gave these children the same rights to education and related services as the nonhandicapped. Some eight million handicapped children suddenly became eligible for more diverse and comprehensive education.

PL 94-142 requires that all public schools (1) identify all handicapped children between the ages of four and twenty-one, (2) assess their educa-

tional needs, (3) give them a written document for learning expectations known as an **individual education plan** (IEP), (4) provide due process to students and their parents (schools must develop safeguards and give parents access to their child's records), (5) not discriminate against students in any classification of disability, and (6) provide education in the least restrictive environment (presumably the regular classroom) that meets the student's needs.

Individual education plan (IEP)
A written statement that prescribes the course of intervention for a special education student within a given time period.

There are varying opinions as to the extent to which PL 94-142 has been fulfilled. Some would contend that a significant portion of those students has not really been properly identified or given appropriate IEPs. Several have suggested that the existing limitations are primarily the result of PL 94-142 being developed on legal, philosophical, and social equity, rather than educational principles (Hundert, 1982; Zigler & Muenchow, 1979). This has led to poor or incomplete implementation as well as different interpretations of what constitutes mainstreaming. In attempting to assess mainstreaming, Linton and Juul (1980) suggest four basic assumptions were made that have yet to be verified by research data.

The first is that the setting of the regular classroom is less isolating for the handicapped. Studies have not demonstrated that mainstreaming reduces feelings of isolation. The assumption that interactions would automatically improve seems to be erroneous. Robinson and Robinson (1976) suggest that isolation is related to the severity of the handicap. Students with nonphysical and mild handicaps seem to have the least stigma attached to them.

A second assumption is that the handicapped child will benefit academically and socially from integration with regular students. There is little evidence to demonstrate that mainstreamed special education students perform better academically than isolated special education students (Abramson, 1981; Budoff & Gottlieb, 1976). Linton and Juul (1980) caution that the criteria for achievement for special education and regular classroom students are not the same. Among regular students, teacher expectancy is higher, there is emphasis on mastery of substantive material, and competition generally prevails. Special education students in that same classroom can rarely compete, are generally on individualized programs, and are not as likely to gain as much teacher time as they would in a special class.

A third assumption is that regular students in a mainstreamed class will come to understand and accept handicapped students in a more positive, normal manner. Again, several studies have not sufficiently demonstrated this (Goodman, Gottlieb, & Harrison, 1972; Iano, Ayers, Heller, McGettigan, & Walker, 1974). Gottlieb and Davis (1973) found that overt name-calling and labeling lessened, but negative attitudes toward the handicapped students remained.

The fourth assumption is that the teacher is the key. The assumption that teachers will automatically accept any mainstreamed child may also be erroneous. The law, a directive change, was mandated giving teachers few choices and presuming that it would not affect teacher behavior in the classroom. Individual districts would have to do any in-service training to help teachers acquire the new skills required to teach the handicapped. In

Table 12–6 Teachers' Reasons, Classified by Type of Handicap, for Not Voluntarily Mainstreaming Handicapped Children

	Number of Teachers Who Chose the Reason			
General Content of Item	Physically Handicapped	Learning Disabled	Socially/ Emotionally Disturbed	Educable Mentally Retarded
1. Too much time from other students	27	50	86	105
2. Not enough patience to instruct such children	9	16	32	26
3. Not enough technical ability to instruct such children	26	68	90	95
4. No support personnel in district	15	26	44	44
5. Previous experiences were not successful	3	17	22	1
Obtained Q	124.39*	107.03*	45.59*	207.96*

*$p < .01$.

Source: From Williams, R. J. & Algozzine, B. *Elementary School Journal*, 1979, p. 66. By permission of the University of Chicago Press.

addition, different handicaps require different teaching skills, and not all teachers have the interest or feelings of personal competence to meet these educational needs (Stoner, 1980).

A study of teachers' attitudes toward mainstreaming by Williams and Algozzine (1979) yielded a significant set of reasons for working or not working with the handicapped. Table 12–6 summarizes the responses of teachers who did not volunteer to teach mainstreamed students. Williams and Algozzine (1979, pp. 66–67) suggest the following reasons why teachers volunteered to have handicapped children placed in their rooms:

1. They had had successful experiences with handicapped children.
2. Specialized support services gave them confidence.
3. They felt that programming for physically handicapped children was not different from regular programming.

PL 94-142 requires that each handicapped child receiving special education services have an individual education plan (IEP). The plan is designed to specify the goals of the educational services and the methods for achieving them. The IEP is developed at a planning meeting that includes parent, student, if appropriate, classroom teacher, a person(s) who has recently evaluated the student, and other significant people, at the discretion of the parent and the school.

The IEP is a written statement based on a complete developmental assessment of the student. It must indicate the extent to which the child will participate in regular classroom activities and what specific special education services will be provided (for example, physical therapy, medical services, or transportation). Prepared annually, the IEP must indicate when services will begin and terminate, specify instructional objectives, and list the evaluation criteria that will be used to determine if the goals are being met. If parents question any part of the IEP, they have the right to obtain an independent evaluation.

In order to ensure parental participation in their child's IEP, PL 94-142 requires that:

1. Parents receive written notice in their native language that indicates the purpose, time, place, and attendees of an IEP meeting.

2. The meeting must be scheduled at a mutually agreeable time.

3. The meeting must be conducted free of jargon that parents might not understand.

4. If parents cannot attend an IEP meeting, the school must clearly demonstrate that they made every reasonable attempt to reach the parents.

5. Parents must receive a copy of the IEP if they request.

An IEP is a mutual agreement between all parties concerned that this is the best educational program the schools can give the handicapped student at this point in time. It is subject to revision by the mutual parties throughout any given school year. It is an important document because it reflects attention and concern for the student involved. An IEP appears in the *Application* section of this chapter.

Gifted Students

Defining Giftedness

Interest in giftedness may have started with Sir Francis Galton's *Study of Genius* in 1862. The forty-year longitudinal study begun by Lewis Terman and his associates (Terman, 1925; Terman & Merrill, 1937; Terman & Oden, 1947, 1951, 1959) not only identified characteristics of the gifted but established that they maintain their giftedness throughout their lives. Interest in giftedness was very high in the 1920s (Henry, 1920; Whipple, 1924) and has recurringly waned and resurged. Over the years, definitions of giftedness have become increasingly more inclusive, particularly when compared with the early designation of gifted persons as being extremely high in intelligence.

Hollingsworth (1942) defined gifted individuals as those in the top 1 percent of the population in general intelligence. Literacy and abstractness were the hallmarks of this. In 1931, she wrote:

> By a gifted child, we mean one who is far more educable than the generality of children are. This greater educability may lie along the lines of one of the arts, as in music or drawing; it may lie in the sphere of mechanical aptitude; or it may consist in surpassing power to achieve literacy and abstract intelligence. It is the business of education to consider all forms of giftedness in pupils in reference to how unusual individuals may be trained for their own welfare and that of society at large. (Pritchard, 1951, p. 49)

The Portland, Oregon, Public Schools (1959) broadly define gifted persons as including approximately the upper 10 percent of the most

talented pupils in each of seven aptitude areas: art, music, creative writing, creative dance, creative dramatics, mechanical talent, and social leadership.

In 1971, the Advisory Panel on the Education of the Gifted and Talented defined as gifted any child in the upper 3 to 5 percent of his or her group who singly or in combination possesses the following abilities:

- General intellectual
- Specific academic
- Creative or productive
- Leadership
- Visual and performing arts
- Psychomotor

The Gifted and Talented Education Act of 1978 included many of these characteristics. The national definition of giftedness is:

The term "gifted and talented children" means children, and whenever applicable, youth, who are identified at the preschool, elementary, or secondary level as possessing demonstrated or potential abilities that give evidence of high performance responsibility in areas such as intellectual, creative, specific, academic, or leadership ability, or in the visual and performing arts, and who by reason thereof, require services and activities not ordinarily provided by the school. (Council for Exceptional Children, 1978, p. 16)

Renzulli (1978) defines giftedness in a way he believes is supported by research and is useful to school practitioners. Giftedness includes three elements. First, a person should be of *above average ability,* although Renzulli does not designate a cutoff score as measured by an IQ test. Second, *task commitment* is required. By this, Renzulli means that gifted people demonstrate a refined or focused form of motivation. Third, *creativity* is part of giftedness.

Maker (1981) has summarized characteristics of the gifted, particularly in relation to the national definition. In addition to her own work, she used three basic references in her compilation: *Scales for Rating the Behavioral Characteristics of Superior Students* by Renzulli, Smith, White, Callahan, and Hartman (1976), *Classroom Cues: A Flip Book for Cultivating Multiple Talent* by Eberle (1974), and the nontest indicators of creative talent among the disadvantaged as constructed by Torrance (1973). Box 12–2 lists characteristics of children with outstanding abilities in seven areas.

Educating the Gifted

The task of providing relevant educational programs for the gifted is not as easy as it may seem. Just as many school systems have found it difficult to maintain programs for the handicapped, so they also have had trouble maintaining programs for the gifted. Schools do not always have the personnel and other resources to implement special programs. In fact, some systems do not see the need for them. Those that do usually employ one or a combination of three strategies: enrichment, ability grouping, and acceleration.

Enrichment   Gifted students can be educated within the regular classroom. **Enrichment** involves providing special content or activities that are more complex or involved than regular classroom instruction. Gallagher (1975a) asserts this involves modifying the content and the instructional demands to challenge students to think productively and resolve complex problems and issues. What must be assured is that students are learning new and challenging content and are not simply being given additional work at the same level of complexity.

Most enrichment programs require independent study and exploration. If gifted students find their classrooms too structured, then opportunities to be engaged in special activities will be extremely limited. Several content specialists in areas such as math, language arts, social studies, and the humanities have suggested programs or ideas that would work in

Enrichment
The acceleration of subject matter within a classroom for gifted or talented students.

Box 12–2　Characteristics of Children of Exceptional Ability

Intellectual/Academic Ability

1. Possess a large storehouse of information about a variety of topics (beyond the usual interests of youngsters their age)

2. Have quick mastery and recall of factual information

3. Are keen and alert observers; usually "see more" or "get more" out of a story or film than others

4. Read a great deal on their own; usually prefer adult-level books; do not avoid difficult material; may show a preference for biography, autobiography, encyclopedias, and atlases

5. Try to understand complicated material by separating it into its respective parts; reason things out for themselves; see logical and commonsense answers

6. Become absorbed and truly involved in certain topics or problems; are persistent in seeking task completion (It is sometimes difficult to get them to move on to another topic.)

7. Are easily bored with routine tasks

8. Need little external motivation to follow through in work that initially excites them

9. Strive toward perfection; are self-critical; are not easily satisfied with their own speed or products

10. Are more interested in many "adult" problems—such as religion, politics, sex, race—than is usual for age level (Renzulli et al., 1976)

Visual and Performing Arts Ability

Artistic Characteristics

1. Like to participate in art activities; are eager to express ideas visually

2. Incorporate a large number of elements into artwork; vary the subject and content of artwork

3. Arrive at unique, unconventional solutions to artistic problems

4. Concentrate for long periods of time on art projects

5. Willingly try out different media; experiment with a variety of materials and techniques

6. Tend to select art media for free activity or classroom projects

7. Are particularly sensitive to the environment; are keen observers—see the unusual, which others may overlook

8. Produce balance and order in artwork

9. Are critical of own work; set high standards of quality; often rework creation in order to refine it

10. Elaborate on ideas from other people—use them as a "jumping off point," as opposed to copying them

Dramatic Characteristics

1. Volunteer to participate in classroom plays and skits

2. Effectively use gestures and facial expressions to communicate feelings

3. Are adept at role playing, improvising, acting out situations "on the spot"

4. Can readily identify themselves with the moods and motivations of characters

5. Handle body with ease and poise for their age

6. Command and hold the attention of a group when acting

7. Are able to evoke emotional responses from listeners—can get people to laugh, frown, feel tense, and so forth

8. Can imitate others—are able to mimic the way people walk, gesture (Renzulli et al., 1976)

Planning Ability

1. Clearly identify the objective, goal, or outcome they hope to achieve

2. Know how to get the information and materials they need

3. Gain the involvement and support of others

4. Display an understanding of sequence and order in their work

5. Visualize their plan and the desired outcome; see it

6. Check their plan with others; seek criticism and suggestions for improvement

7. Use symbols, drawings, and notations to clarify and elaborate

8. Systemize well; understand the need for a step-by-step procedure

9. Grasp the relationship of individual steps to the whole process

10. Allow time to execute all steps involved in a process

11. Foresee consequences of actions

12. Organize their work well

13. Take into account the details necessary to accomplish a goal

Box 12–2, continued

14. Are good at games of strategy where it is necessary to anticipate several moves ahead

15. Establish priorities when organizing activities

16. See alternative ways to distribute work or assign people to accomplish a task (Eberle, 1974)

Forecasting/Predicting Ability

1. Anticipate effects and outcomes

2. Evaluate past knowledge and experiences

3. Reorganize past knowledge and experiences

4. View situations objectively

5. Take into consideration and display empathy for human reactions

6. Are attuned to their feelings and hunches

7. Are not overly concerned about being right in their predictions

8. Are socially aware; know what is going on around them

9. Are sensitive to actions that would affect the situation and others

10. Clearly perceive situations of cause and effect (Eberle, 1974)

Leadership Ability

1. Carry responsibility well; can be counted on to do what they have promised and usually do it well

2. Are self-confident with children their own age as well as with adults; seem comfortable when asked to show their work to the class

3. Seem to be well liked by classmates

4. Are cooperative with teacher and classmates; tend to avoid bickering and are generally easy to get along with

5. Adapt readily to new situations; are flexible in thought and action and do not seem disturbed when the normal routine is changed

6. Seem to enjoy being around other people; are sociable and prefer not to be alone

7. Tend to dominate others when they are around; generally direct the activity in which they are involved

8. Participate in most social activities connected with the school; can be counted on to be there if anyone is

Decision-Making Ability

1. Remain emotionally apart from the problem

2. Weigh consequences; withhold early judgment

3. Consider more than one course of action

4. Pose many influential questions and seek out the answers

5. Engage in experimental evaluation; ask "What if?"

6. Have data to support their decisions

7. Apply evaluative criteria in making choices

8. Are willing to make a decision

9. Stick with their decision and act accordingly (Eberle, 1974)

Creative/Productive Ability

1. Can express feelings and emotions

2. Can improvise with commonplace materials

3. Can be articulate in role playing and storytelling

4. Enjoy and are good in visual art

5. Enjoy and are good in creative movement, dance, dramatics, and so forth

6. Enjoy and are good in music, rhythm, and so forth

7. Speak expressively

8. Are fluent and flexible in nonverbal media

9. Enjoy and are good in small group activities, problem solving, and so forth

10. Respond to the concrete

11. Respond to the kinesthetic

12. Are expressive in gestures, "body language," and so forth

13. Are humorous

14. Use rich imagery in informal language

15. Are original in problem solving

16. Are problem centered

17. Are emotionally responsive

18. Are quick to warm up (Torrance, 1973)

enrichment settings, although invariably their success hinges on challenging materials and time flexibility (Perry & Hoback, 1982; Treffinger, 1980).

Ability grouping
The placement of students with comparable abilities within the same academic classroom; sometimes called homogeneous grouping.

Ability Grouping   **Ability grouping** refers to placing students of comparable ability in the same classroom—homogeneous rather than heterogeneous placement. The immediate advantage is that instruction can be developed around a narrower range of student abilities. The one limitation is that teacher planning may not be significantly different, thus students may not be adequately challenged. Ability grouping requires more effort on the part of the teacher than does a regular classroom.

Educationally different experiences are important. Content should not only be more complex; it should be different than that received in the regular classroom. The variety of learning experiences should be challenging and innovative, perhaps even focusing on issues broader than the school context itself. For example, Schug (1981, p. 22) has suggested that, in the area of citizenship education, the content could come from the community itself.

> Curriculum materials can be developed specifically for gifted students based on public issues in the community. This enables students to identify community problems, analyze data from local sources, study alternatives facing the community, consider their own goals in relationship to the problems under study, make decisions about local issues, and take action on their decisions by attempting to influence policy decision by direct means (such as testifying at a community hearing) or indirect means (such as writing a letter to the editor).

Acceleration
The advancement of a gifted or talented student to a higher grade level.

Acceleration   The third major way of handling gifted students is by **acceleration,** the most common way being skipping a grade in school. Terman (1925) provides sufficient evidence that children can be accelerated in school without any deleterious academic effects. This position is supported by the more recent findings of Getzels and Dillon (1973). However, many educators feel that letting students skip a grade or two places them at a disadvantage physically, socially, and emotionally. This concern may be legitimate in specific instances, but, as a generalization, it is unfounded. Several studies on acceleration have not demonstrated negative effects intellectually, physically, socially, or emotionally (Gallagher, 1966; McEwin & Cross, 1982; Terman & Oden, 1947; Tidwell, 1980).

Because of the expanding definitions of giftedness, meeting the education needs of the upper 3 to 5 percent of a school's student body is an overwhelming task, particularly because these upper percentages in nine areas of giftedness or talent may make up one-fourth or more of all students. Keating (1980) makes five suggestions for effectively implementing gifted education. The first is that we disavow clearly nonsubstantive or diversionary programs that claim to benefit the gifted but actually do not. The temptation is to applaud any efforts on behalf of these students, justifying poorly conceived programs by saying that any beginning is better than none. In fact, inadequate programs are more often counterproductive, generating skepticism and losing the support of key groups inside and outside the educational community.

Second, Keating says that, to distinguish among programs for the gifted, we should welcome, and even insist upon, rigorous evaluations with clearly defined achievement criteria. Solidly conceived and executed programs will show clear, positive effects. On this basis, efforts on behalf of the intellectually underserved can continue and expand.

Third, we should consider the full range of educational alternatives, whether they are called enrichment or acceleration or something else. Teachers are sometimes urged to find something to do with these students, as long as it does not involve moving ahead in a core area and impinging upon next year's curriculum. Such recommendations are pedagogically unethical. The educational priorities are or ought to be primary; administrative convenience is a priority far down on the list.

Keating's fourth suggestion is that, whenever possible, we should clarify misconceptions about the nature of ability and abandon unnecessary assumptions. Many issues that are interesting and important as research topics are irrelevant in terms of educational planning.

Fifth, the educational responsibilities toward the intellectually underserved should be asserted on a firm, rational basis. At a minimum, explanations for assigning a low priority to this problem, when that situation exists, should be required from school officials. The arbitrary definition of such programs as luxury items in the school budget rather than as necessities should be cogently contested. Advocates will be in a better position to make those arguments if they have theoretically and practically defensible alternatives available.

Developing an IEP

Every school district in the United States is required by law to develop an IEP on all students who are evaluated as handicapped. Figure 12–1 is a standard IEP provided by the federal govern- ment, but local districts have been encouraged to develop their own forms. Figure 12–2a is one district's adaptation of the IEP. Figure 12–2b shows notes from an actual case in a school. The IEP is a useful document for all parties involved, and, when used as intended, it should facilitate student learning.

Figure 12–1
The federal IEP form

INDIVIDUALIZED EDUCATION PROGRAM

Child's Name _____

School _____

Date of Program Entry _____

Prioritized Annual Goals
(Terminal Behavior)

_____

_____

_____

Summary Statement of Present Levels of Educational Performance (Strengths and Weaknesses)

_____

_____

_____

_____

Short Term Instructional Objectives (Measurable)	Specific Educational and Support Services; Procedures/Techniques and Materials	Person(s) Responsible	Amount of Time	Beginning Date	Ending Date

Figure 12-1 continued

What evaluation procedures are to be used, on at least an annual basis, to determine whether objectives are being achieved?

Amount of time in regular classroom	Student present: _____ _____ Yes No	Participants in IEP Development & Review
	Comments: _____ _____ _____	Parent: _____ Spec. Teacher: _____ Reg. Teacher: _____
	Date of annual IEP review: _____	Admin. Rep.: _____ Plan written by: _____

Figure 12–2a
A school district's IEP form

Mary Belle Public Schools
125 Prince Road

INDIVIDUAL EDUCATIONAL PLAN

Student's Name: _Cheryl Thomas_ Birthdate _10/27/72_ Sex _F_

School _Belleweather Elem._ Grade _5_ Primary language _English_

Special Education
Placement Program _L.D. Resource Room_

Present Level of
Performance _C.A. = 10 yr 3 mo ; M.A. = 8 yr 7 mo ; WISC – R Verbal ; IQ = 80_
Performance = 91 ; Full Scale = 84. Information, comprehension and Vocabulary is 1 S.D. below
the mean. Reading Discrepancy = 2.11 Woodcock (L.I. = 12.9 ; W.I. = 2.3 ; W.A. = 1.8 ;
W.C. = 2.4 ; P.C. = 2.7) Good Visual Memory & Discrimination.

Long-range Goals _____ (see attached sheet) _____

Services to Be Provided:

	AMOUNT OF TIME	BEGINNING DATE	REVIEW DATE	PROJ. ENDING DATE
Reading	120 min/week	10/17	3/1	5/19
Math	100 min/week	11/4	3/1	5/19
Spelling	40 min/week	10/29	3/1	5/28

Amount of Time in Regular Classroom
One-half day

IEP Committee Members:

T.R. Macdonald Date _____

S.P. Moore Date _____

A.E. Vaughan Date _____

P.R. Brown Date _____

Contact Person _S.P. Moore_

I approve the Individual Educational Plans written above.

Eleanor Thomas Date _10/1/82_
(Parent or guardian)

382

Figure 12-2b
Section of a school district's IEP for one student

GOALS

School Year ___1982-3___

Student's Name ___Cheryl Thomas___

Birthdate ___10/27/72___

LONG-RANGE GOALS ARE:

PRIORITIZE GOALS THAT ARE APPROPRIATE.

___✓___ 1. The student will complete reading readiness skills that are appropriate for his level.

___✓___ 2. The student will complete decoding skills that are appropriate for his level.

___✓___ 3. The student will complete the reading comprehension skills that are appropriate for his level.

___✓___ 4. The student will complete the math readiness skills that are appropriate for his level.

___✓___ 5. The student will complete the math computation skills that are appropriate for his level.

___✓___ 6. The student will complete the problem solving math skills that are appropriate for his level.

_____ 7. The student will complete remediation of information processing skill deficits.

_____ 8. The student will complete the remediation for the development of gross motor skills.

_____ 9. The student will complete the remediation for the development of fine motor skills.

___✓___ 10. The student will complete the spelling skills that are appropriate for his level.

___✓___ 11. The student will complete the writing skills that are appropriate for his level.

_____ 12. Appropriate behavior will be shaped through the use of a behavior management program.

___✓___ 13. The student's self-image will be improved through the use of positive teaching and/or behavior management techniques.

_____ 14. The student's language skills will be developed to a level appropriate for his age.

_____ 15. Other goals as needed:

Annotated Readings

Beckwith, A. H. (1982). Use of the Ross test as an assessment measure in programs for the gifted and a comparison of the Ross test to individually administered intelligence tests. *Journal for the Education of the Gifted, 5*, 127–140.

This study examined the Ross Test of Higher Cognitive Processes as an appropriate instrument to assess critical thinking skills in programs for gifted students. Evidence suggests that the measure is a useful instrument because it supports the idea that more concentrated methods of teaching critical thinking skills are as effective as more extensive teaching approaches.

Blackman, S., & Goldstein, K. M. (1982). Cognitive styles and learning disabilities. *Journal of Learning Disabilities, 15*, 106–115.

Research relating the cognitive style dimensions of field dependence and reflection-impulsivity to underachievement, process deficits (minimal brain dysfunction), and hyperactivity is reviewed. In general, field independence and a reflective cognitive style are associated with better performance. The importance of modifying the learner's cognitive style and matching the learning environment to the learner's cognitive style also are examined.

McEwin, C. K., & Cross, A. H. (1982). A comparative study of perceived victimization, perceived anonymity, self-esteem, and preferred teacher characteristics of gifted and talented and nonlabeled early adolescents. *Journal of Early Adolescence, 2*, 247–254.

This study compared results from gifted and talented and nonlabeled early adolescents on measures of self-esteem, victimization, anonymity, and preferred teacher characteristics. A total of 260 nonlabeled and 115 gifted and talented students (grades five through eight) were in the study. Significant differences were found between the groups on perceived anonymity and preferred teacher characteristics, with gifted and talented students preferring person-oriented teachers and feeling less anonymous than nonlabeled students. Still, there were more similarities than differences between the two groups, particularly with self-esteem and victimization. Generally, self-esteem was high and victimization was low.

Shinn, M., Algozzine, B., Marston, D., & Ysseldyke, J. (1982). A theoretical analysis of performance of learning disabled students on the Woodcock-Johnson Psycho-educational Battery. *Journal of Learning Disabilities, 15*, 221–226.

Two studies were conducted to analyze the subtest characteristics of the Woodcock-Johnson Psycho-educational Battery and apply those results to an analysis of learning disabled students' performance on the battery. Analyses indicated that poorer performance of LD students on the test compared to their performance on the Wechsler Intelligence Scale for Children-Revised (WISC-R) is better explained in terms of the kinds of behaviors sampled in the Woodcock-Johnson battery.

Valencia, R. R. (1982). Predicting academic achievement of Mexican American children: Preliminary analysis of the McCarthy scales. *Educational and Psychological Measurement, 42*, 1269–1278.

This study examined the effectiveness of the McCarthy Scales of Children's Abilities in predicting school achievement, as measured by the Comprehensive Tests of Basic Skills for English-speaking, second-grade Mexican-American children. High validity between the two tests was found on most subscales, although the McCarthy verbal scale did not predict reading achievement too strongly. In view of all the analyses run, the researcher concluded that the McCarthy scale appears to be a promising way to assess English-speaking, Mexican-American children.

Yeh, J. W., & Rie, E. D. (1982). An abstraction test for normal and learning disabled children. *Journal of Learning Disabilities, 15,* 326–330.

The performance of eighteen neurocognitively impaired learning disabled children on visual abstraction was compared to that of twenty intact learning disabled and twenty normal students. The two comparison groups were matched for age and IQ. The Abstraction Test for Children *was developed and standardized as the measure of abstraction. When IQ among the three groups was controlled, the results indicated that neurocognitively impaired LD children are not specifically deficient in abstraction.*

Individualized Instruction

Preview

A rather heated discussion surfaced when members of the Roseville Teachers Association sat down to discuss things they should seek in contract negotiations for the next school year. Surprisingly, the disagreements did not focus on salaries, but on teaching resources. Eventual consensus was that there were not enough resources to bring about desired student learning and that the teachers felt the school administration had its priorities out of order in regard to teaching resources.

Several teachers said they lacked the resources to meet their students' diverse needs. Ms. Faulkner observed, "We are expected to mainstream handicapped students, provide enrichment for the gifted, and at the same time meet the individual differences of the rest of the class. Yet I don't have any more resources than I had five years ago."

Ms. Koff, an eighth-grade language arts teacher, had a similar complaint, although the composition of her class was quite different. Her class was a homogeneous group consisting of approximately the upper 20 percent of the eighth-grade students. She stated, "My students completed their eighth-grade literature book in six weeks. I started them on American and British literature. Then I received a call from the district curriculum supervisor telling me to stop using those resources because I would ruin the tenth-grade literature class. Still, he had no suggestions as to what I should do." The teachers felt they should have more diverse resources if they were going to teach successfully.

In regard to priorities, Mr. Kent was really hostile about all the money the school had allocated for microcomputers. He remarked, "They have no instructional value. If the kids want to play games, let them do it on their own time. This is education's newest boondoggle." Others disagreed, pointing out that we live in the age of computers and microcomputers. Still others argued that they did not mind the purchase of microcomputers; they just thought other resources, which were much less expensive and could serve a greater number of students, should be bought first.

There was general agreement that the quantity and quality of educational resources impacted heavily on their work load more significantly than their salary increase would offset. Thus, their resolution to the Roseville School Board placed educational resources as their top priority in the new contract negotiations.

387

Demands for individualized instruction of children with diverse needs and ability levels and the impact of modern technology on education are two topics that come together in this chapter. Key concepts include:

- *Classroom organization*
- *Mastery learning*
- *Models for individualizing instruction*
- *Educational technology*

Individualized instruction
Instructional activity designed specifically for an individual or small groups of students.

Individualized instruction has multiple meanings because it refers to maximizing student learning potential. Gage and Berliner's (1979, p. 511) definition of individualized instruction provides a solid framework: "Individualized instruction occurs when the goals of instruction, learning materials, subject matter, and methods of instruction are especially chosen for a particular student or a small group of students with common characteristics." Gronlund (1974a, p. 2) suggests the following ways to implement such instruction:

1. Individualized instruction may range from minor modifications in group instruction to completely independent learning.

2. Individualized instruction may permit variation in any of the following: rate of learning, the objectives pursued, the methods and materials of study, and the required level of achievement.

3. Individualized instruction may be used in all subjects, in some subjects, in parts of some subjects, or only with particular students.

Inasmuch as individuals come into classrooms with different learning histories and interests, to individualize instruction to match these diversities would be a Herculean task. In this chapter, I discuss ways to accomplish this task.

Social changes over the past thirty years have increased the importance of individualized instruction. Educators have been required to build compensatory programs for the underprivileged, bilingual programs to accommodate ethnic and cultural minorities, enrichment programs for the gifted and talented, and mainstreaming programs for the handicapped in order to give them access to broader educational experiences. Each of these requires new educational philosophies and increased teacher skills.

At the same time, the media have altered the learning and skills that children bring into school. No single teaching approach will meet these individual needs; so educators must begin developing more diverse and effective instructional models.

Classroom Organization

Individualized instruction need not mean one-on-one correspondence; there are several ways to organize the classroom. Teachers must develop classroom management skills that allow them to implement more than one educational goal or objective simultaneously with diverse groups of students (see Figure 13–1).

Large Group Instruction

Most public school classrooms have from twenty to thirty-five students assigned to them, with the national average hovering at twenty-six (Statistical Abstract, 1982). This is the most common grouping of students. Teachers generally teach to the average student, anticipating that this level of presentation will meet the greatest number of needs. The assumption is that there is a common block of content in any subject-matter area that all students must and can learn and that **large group instruction** is the best format for teaching it.

Those who criticize regular group instruction contend that it is the most restrictive environment in which to meet individual needs. In this instructional format, teachers tend to lecture and dominate the instructional environment, and discussion seldom occurs. McKeachie and Kulik (1975) studied the advantages of lecture and discussion methods. They found that the lecture method is superior when factual material is presented and that the discussion method is superior if the instructional criteria are retention and higher level thinking, attitudes, or motivation. Other researchers have demonstrated that, if the instructional environment allows for student-initiated learning, better learning occurs (Amidon & Flanders, 1961; Soar, 1967).

Rounds, Ward, Mergendoller, and Tikunoff (1981) investigated the differences in classroom group size and composition in sixth- and seventh-grade classrooms. They found that sixth-grade teachers used more varied strategies than seventh-grade teachers. In fact, they found virtually no variation in instructional style among seventh-grade teachers, regardless of their subject-matter area. Several other educators (Clark & Clark, 1981; Wiles & Bondi, 1981) have expressed concern about reduced teacher flexibility as students become increasingly older.

Large group instruction
The presentation of classroom material to all the students in a classroom at any given time.

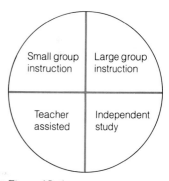

Figure 13–1
Possible group procedures in classrooms with emphasis on individual instruction

Small Group Instruction

A small group operates within the context of the regular classroom. Small groups, which generally are composed of ten or fewer students, are organized around specific needs. In this sense, they typically receive individualized instruction. **Small group instruction** also provides greater opportunity for students to become actively engaged in the learning process. As teachers monitor student progress in small groups, they can better discern how each person is responding and apply motivational or reinforcement strategies when appropriate.

Teachers usually organize small groups either to extend or better refine the subject-matter content they present in large groups or to allow for remedial work in specific areas. Many teachers are not organized well enough to run three to five groups simultaneously in a classroom. They

Small group instruction
The presentation of classroom material to a group of students, usually 6 to 10, who have been specifically targeted for instruction.

Chapter 13
Individualized Instruction
389

may need specific training in small group techniques to function well. Hauge (1980, p. 376) makes the following suggestions to help teachers plan for small group instruction:

1. Effective small group instruction depends on carefully determined goals and objectives. What is the teacher trying to teach or help the students learn?

2. Careful consideration is given to which mode or modes of small group instruction can best help students meet objectives.

3. Once the grouping mode or modes have been established, the room is arranged and materials obtained to realize the teaching strategy.

4. The teacher has carefully worked out specific directions to be given to students.

5. The teacher has carefully considered his or her role in working with the various groups.

Hauge (1980) has formatted five types of instructional modes that should be related to teacher goals and objectives and the type of role the teacher wants to play at any given time with any given group.

One-to-One Instruction

One-to-one instruction
Direct instruction to only one individual in a classroom.

One-to-one instruction involves the teacher working directly with one student on some content area. Although this is not the primary mode of instruction for teachers, there invariably are students who need this focused learning from time to time. Prior to such instruction, teachers should adequately assess a student's learning needs and develop a strategy that will meet them. In this process, students cannot only make academic progress, but they will develop a sense of independence, the ability to stick with a task and learn on their own.

One-to-one teaching can also be achieved through **tutoring** programs, where another student or a teacher's aide directs a student. Tutoring programs also require considerable diagnosis and planning if they are to be effective. Generally, tutoring has proven to be an effective means of instruction (Lippitt & Lippitt, 1968).

Tutoring
One-to-one instruction to a student by someone other than the classroom teacher, e.g., teacher's aide or another student.

Independent Study

Another type of individualized instruction is **independent study,** wherein students choose a subject-matter area in which to work. For independent study to be successful, students must be self-directed and self-disciplined, although the teacher should help them set their goals and objectives and serve as the primary resource person.

Independent study
The opportunity for one student to work on his or her own within the classroom environment.

Student Input

One indication of effective instruction is that students take responsibility for their own learning. This is most likely to occur if the teacher creates a classroom environment that encourages self-initiative. One of the useful designations in the Rounds et al. (1981) study was **student control,** the extent to which students regulate or control aspects of their school environment. As students become older, they should begin acquiring the skills necessary to work independently with minimal teacher supervision. Thus, teachers should begin providing greater opportunities for students to

Student control
The opportunity given students to regulate or pace some aspect of their learning experience.

Instructional Presentation Modes		Concept Summary 13–1
Type	**Characteristic**	
Large group	Basic presentation of material to all students in the classroom	
Small group	Breaking the class into smaller working groups, occasional direct instruction by teacher	
Individualized	Additional diagnosis of student learning warranting special attention, usually fulfilled in tutorial role by teacher or peer tutor	
Independent study	Diagnosis of additional learning, either remedial or enrichment, assumes self-pacing and self-motivation without direct teacher involvement	

exercise some control over their classroom assignments, a process that may be more difficult to set in motion in the large group lecture method.

Based on the work of Bossert (1979) and Tikunoff, Ward, and Mergendoller (1979) within the Rounds et al. (1981) study, student control has been defined as consisting of any one or more of the following characteristics:

1. *Order in which prescribed tasks will be completed.* This may range from the teacher or situation demanding a particular task order to students selecting any of several possible task orders.

2. *Pacing, or the amount of time to be devoted to a particular task.* In some classroom settings, pacing may be completely under the teacher's control. In others, the amount of time devoted to a task may be negotiable, with a specified deadline. The student determines the speed with which to do the work within the time frame.

3. *Procedures used to complete the assigned work.* Procedures may vary from being set by the teacher to being set by the student.

4. *Products to be achieved.* Choices in this category may range from none (the teacher prescribes the content and form of product) to students being free to select the content and form of the product. However, students are rarely free to select both the content and form of the outcomes of schoolwork.

5. *Participation in classroom activities.* In some classes, participation in an activity may be voluntary; in others, students may have to participate but be free to choose when and where to do so. Often such choices are contingent upon the student obeying class norms. For example, in a typical class recitation session, students have the opportunity to choose whether or not to volunteer for an answer. At a more tacit level, they may pretend to read during silent reading or sit silently while their group works on a social studies project.

6. *Materials to be used.* Areas of choice in this category include such items as instructional materials (for example, textbooks, encyclopedias, films, or filmstrips), arts and crafts materials, and resource persons.

Rounds et al. (1981) studied the extent of student control in sixth-grade **self-contained classrooms** and classrooms organized around the **team-teaching** concept. The seventh-grade classrooms investigated were all departmentalized around subject specialties. In comparing the three structures, the researchers found that students in the self-contained class-room had more control over their learning experiences and those in the departmentalized seventh grade had the least.

Across the subject areas, several options were given to students in self-contained classrooms. These ranged from selecting which assignment to do from among several alternatives the teacher offered to pacing when to do which parts of an assignment in a given day or week. In some classrooms, students developed contracts with teachers stating what they planned to do each week in the various subjects.

Because they spent part of the school day with different teachers, students in team-teaching classrooms could pace their work in some subject areas (math, reading, and language arts). In others, they had nothing to say about their school day, assignments, or responsibility for learning. Thus, although there was some flexibility in this arrangement, it did not delegate as much student control as the self-contained structure.

In the departmentalized environment, students were given some control over pacing (the opportunity to decide where and when to complete assignments). Some assignments were due one week after they were given. Having some control over pacing allowed students to use nonlecture class time in ways other than always working on their assignment. The research team observed that, as due dates for assignments neared, students spent more time on assignments and less time talking or doing assignments for other classes. In all, this structure was the least flexible.

Self-contained classroom
A classroom wherein one teacher instructs all subject areas to the same group of students.

Team teaching
The effort by two or more teachers to combine subject matter when instructing students.

Mastery Learning

Bloom (1968) contends that the existing educational system is too content to accept degrees of learning rather than **mastery.** He sees no reason students cannot learn more and be expected to learn more. He and others (Block, 1971; Carroll, 1963; Keller, 1968) propose mastery

Mastery
Learning or performing academic and social tasks at or beyond the designated level of expectation.

Norm-referenced instruction
The comparison of all students
against one another on some
specified task or assessment.

learning as the desired educational goal for all levels and areas of the educational system. This is different from **norm-referenced instruction,** which compares students and their achievements to each other.

Carroll (1963) has made two important points regarding mastery learning. First, if students are distributed in the normal curve in their aptitudes for some academic subject and if they are provided with the same instruction, the results of the instruction will be a normal distribution of achievements. Second, if students are normally distributed by aptitude for some academic subject, but are provided instruction appropriate to their individual characteristics and needs, the majority should achieve mastery of the subject.

In order for mastery learning to be effective, an instructional program should allow for (1) instruction, (2) testing, (3) analysis of learning, (4) relearning where necessary, and (5) retesting. Such processes rarely occur in traditional learning environments. Carroll (1963) notes that the amount

of learning that occurs is directly related to the time students spend learning compared to the time they actually need to learn. He believes that both learner characteristics and instructional strategies are essential to mastery learning.

Carroll strongly believes that the amount of learning is related to the student's *perseverance* and *opportunity to learn*. Perseverance refers to the amount of time a person is willing to spend in learning. If a student does not spend time to learn a task or skill, he or she is not likely to master it. Within any given classroom, students will vary considerably in their perseverance, and there will even be variance from task to task for the same student. Teachers have less control over this learner variable than they do over the variable of opportunity to learn. Virtually all students can achieve if given enough time. Group instruction does not accommodate varying rates of learning as well as individualized instruction. Teachers will find it necessary to monitor student learning rates in order to individualize for mastery. Thus, teachers must find some flexibility in time, often a most difficult task, given the inflexibility of many school organizational structures.

The time needed for learning is related to learner *aptitude*, the third component in Carroll's model. Students with higher general intelligence or aptitude generally require less time for learning. *Quality of instruction,* a teacher component, and *ability to understand instruction,* the learner component, are also related to mastery. High quality instruction should facilitate the student's ability to understand, and well-defined instruction can minimize the range of student aptitudes.

To maximize learning to the point of mastery, the teacher must ensure that the student understands instruction. "The ability to understand instruction may be defined as the ability of the learner to understand the nature of the task he is to learn and the procedures he is to follow in the learning of the task" (Bloom, 1968, p. 5). The greater students' understanding of what is expected and how they may meet these expectations, the greater the chances that mastery learning will occur. In short, the teacher must provide a sense of direction, which often means adapting instruction to individual student needs.

Mastery learning is not always easy to implement, and it places additional responsibility on the teacher. Block (1973) has observed that mastery learning shifts the responsibility to the school. Schools must adapt to students, rather than students adapting to the school. In order to do this, teachers must consider three questions:

1. Do I know where each student is in relation to a predetermined sequence?

2. Do I know what skills each student is working on now?

3. Do I know what skills each student has mastered?

Answering these questions requires systematic evaluation of student learning, which I discussed in Chapter 9. Mastery learning has helped teachers organize their materials more effectively and has helped students become more task oriented (Abrams, 1979; Block & Burns, 1976; Hyman & Cohen, 1979).

Factors Affecting Student Mastery
1. Clear statement of instructional objectives
2. Required performance criteria
3. Student understanding of teacher expectation
4. High quality of instruction
5. Adequate time for students to learn
6. Analysis of student performance
7. Reinstruction when necessary
8. Reevaluation when necessary

Models for Individualizing Instruction

In the past two decades, several systematic models for individualizing instruction have been advanced. Some use teachers as the primary instructional resource; others use computer technology. But all programs are systematically designed to maximize learning based upon what is known from research.

Learning for Mastery

Learning for mastery
An instructional design that compares individual student expectations, instructional criteria, and assessment of actual performance against the criteria rather than against other students.

Learning for mastery (LFM) is an approach that has come out of the work of Carroll (1963), Bloom (1968), and Block (1971). Intended to change the teaching-learning environment by altering both teacher and pupil performance, LFM is based on seven techniques (Hyman & Cohen, 1979):

1. Instructional objectives must be behaviorally defined so both teachers and learners know where they are in their content area.

2. Teachers should directly teach the behavior or attitude they expect of students.

3. Learners must receive immediate feedback, which facilitates learning.

4. The level of instruction must be planned so the feedback will be positive.

5. Learning should be modularized by dividing it into small, self-contained units. Closure is the most potent of all positive feedback techniques. The smaller the unit of information, the more immediate the closure.

6. The stimulus must be controlled so that the teacher knows exactly what the student is responding to.

7. The learner's critical response must be reinforced. The critical response is to the appropriate stimulus defined by the instructional objective.

Numerous studies have compared LFM strategies to other instructional techniques. The actual implementation of such strategies may have varied from teacher to teacher or researcher to researcher, although the techniques central to the LFM approach were the same. Most studies demonstrated that LFM is an effective individualized instructional approach (Block, 1979; Bloom, 1973; Burns, 1979; Hyman & Cohen, 1979; McKeachie & Kulik, 1975).

Block and Burns (1976) reviewed ninety-seven studies. They found that 61 percent of them statistically favored mastery-taught students, and only 3 percent favored nonmastery-taught students. The other 36 percent yielded no statistically significant results in either direction. Nevertheless, Burns (1979) has noted that mastery-taught students scored higher in 82 percent of the nonsignificant studies. In summary, three generalizations seem warranted in light of all the studies done on LFM:

1. Learning for mastery strategies are consistently more effective than traditional instruction.

2. Learning for mastery learners acquire more instructional objectives in a specified time frame than students in nonmastery or traditional classrooms.

3. Mastery learning strategies designed around individual learners bring about more learning than those based on a group design.

Instructional Program for Mastery

The **Instructional Program for Mastery** (IPM) is an instructional approach developed by Thornburg in 1974 that has been implemented in some public school systems. Like LFM, this strategy is concerned with maximizing student learning; so it uses a systematic approach. The second major concern of IPM is increasing teacher effectiveness, which is also more likely if a systematic self-evaluation of a teacher behavior is employed. Such self-evaluations require teachers to rethink their instructional behavior, an essential task if teachers are to keep instructional content relevant, meaningful, and contemporary.

Instructional program for mastery A variation of the *Learning for Mastery* technique that also evaluates individual performance against specified criteria.

The development phase of IPM consists of four components:

1. Subject-matter framework (scope and sequence)

2. Instructional units

3. Instructional objectives

4. Unit evaluations

The instructional phase has six steps:

1. Preassess by objective

2. Instruct

3. Evaluate learning

4. Analyze evaluation

5. Reinstruct deficiencies

6. Reevaluate reinstructions

Development Phase

Subject-Matter Framework   The first step in defining effective instruction is to develop the subject-matter framework for the academic year. What are the major content areas that should be covered? This overview of what an academic year should consist of provides the teacher with a working knowledge of what he or she should try to accomplish in a given year. In order to make instruction more consistent and ensure essential student learning, teams of teachers should decide on the conceptual overview. Thus, all teachers should be working to accomplish the same instructional content.

The subject-matter framework should specify the major topics and subtopics to be taught. This relationship is presented in Figure 13–2, which illustrates the major topics and subtopics for a high school English class. Subtopics help articulate the major topic in a logical, cohesive fashion.

The subject-matter framework for any grade level must be related to the total (kindergarten through twelfth-grade) subject-matter framework. It is important to articulate the major topics within a school year, but it is equally important to see how any particular grade level builds on previous learning and sets the base for subsequent learning. This process is usually viewed within a scope and sequence. **Scope** refers to the range of topics; **sequence** refers to the grade level at which the various topics are to be instructed. Figure 13–3 demonstrates how parts of a sentence should be taught across multiple grade levels. Some subtopics are initially taught as early as third grade; others may not be introduced until tenth grade. The scope and sequence should be a districtwide function that exists prior to developing units of instruction. It is important because it emphasizes looking at the overall curriculum plan when building units of instruction.

Scope
The range of topics to be instructed within a specified time frame.

Sequence
The grade level or order at which various topics are to be presented.

Figure 13–2
Subject-matter framework by major topics with emphasis on parts of sentence subtopics

```
  I.   Parts of Speech
 II.   Simple Subject and Predicate
III.   Parts of Sentence
        A.   Learning the Concept
        B.   Subjects
        C.   Simple Predicate
        D.   Direct Object
        E.   Indirect Object
        F.   Predicate Nominative
        G.   Predicate Adjective
        H.   Object of the Preposition
        I.   Appositive
        J.   Object Complement
 IV.   Phrases
  V.   Clauses
 VI.   Kinds of Sentences
VII.   Usage
```

Figure 13-3
Scope and sequence for parts of sentence, K–12

Parts of sentence	K	1	2	3	4	5	6	7	8	9	10	11	12
1. Subject													
a. Simple				I	E	E	E	M					
b. Compound						I	E	M	M				
2. Predicate													
a. Simple				I	E	E	E	M					
b. Compound						I	E	E	M				
3. Complements													
a. Direct object							I	E	E	M			
b. Indirect object								I	E	M			
c. Predicate nominative							I	E	E	M			
d. Predicate adjective							I	E	E	M			
e. Objective complement											I	E	M
4. Appositive							I	E	E	E	M		
5. Prepositional Phrase						I	E	E	E	E	M		
6. Nominative Adverb											I	E	M
7. Nominative Absolute											I	E	M
8. Expletive Adverb											I	E	M

Instructional Units   The next step is to organize subject matter into **units of instruction,** which is the organization of instructional objectives and activities that cover the same academic content. Units are developed around major topics and include (1) relevant subtopics, (2) specific instructional objectives, and (3) the unit's evaluation procedure. Figure 13-2 shows the full year's high school English topics organized by units. The units represent a sequence of instruction; thus, mastery of unit two implies mastery of unit one. Whenever there is a major shift in content emphasis, one unit should be completed and another unit should be designed. For example, unit four, "phrases," and unit five, "clauses," are separated into two distinct units of instruction because the nature of the content is significantly different.

Instructional Objectives   In order for units of instruction to meet mastery criteria, they must specify expected student outcomes. To do so, these subtopics within a unit must be developed by objective. Within the IPM, objectives are specified in the cognitive domain, the affective domain, and the psychomotor domain (see Chapter 9). A unit of instruction should clearly specify what constitutes adequate coverage of a major topic. In a sense, specification of objectives under each subtopic is an outline for instruction because objectives should build on each other (that is, from simple to complex and from nonconceptual to conceptual).

Unit of instruction
A predetermined instructional sequence that is restricted to an academic content area and that specifies expected student learning.

Unit Evaluation   It is also possible to evaluate by objective within the unit. It is extremely important to develop a systematic evaluation package that measures student performance and helps determine mastery. The relationship between unit objectives and unit evaluation makes it possible to develop reliable and valid assessment techniques. **Measurement by objective** (criterion) is the key to an effective evaluation package wtihin the IPM. I present evaluation techniques in Chapter 15. Box 13–1 provides some examples of instructional objectives and test items to measure them at the knowledge, comprehension, application, and analysis levels of the cognitive domain.

Instructional Phase

Preassessment by Objective   The purpose of preassessing by unit objectives is to determine how much learning the student has already mastered. Thus, the preassessment must be representative of the unit's objectives. Mastery level may vary, depending upon the skill level indicated by the objective. For example, in spelling words, the mastery level may be very high, perhaps 100 percent, because the objective level is knowledge. In contrast, the mastery level for using a rule to find the circumference of a circle may be lower, perhaps 80 percent, because the rule is at the application level, a higher intellectual skill. Furthermore, the rule is built on concepts; so to have learned the rule, the student must have learned the concepts. In contrast, there is no prerequisite learning required to spell a word. Once the preassessment is done, the teacher can determine which objectives can be fulfilled using large group or individual instruction techniques.

Instruction   The instruction phase involves delivering content to students. Unit objectives influence instructional plans. In every instructional endeavor, teachers must ask themselves two questions: "What is it I want my students to know once I have completed my teaching?" "Do they have the requisite skills necessary to learn what I am about to teach?"

Critics of systematic instructional programs have contended that this structure interferes with, rather than facilitates, learning. They have attacked hierarchical and taxonomic systems. However, students do not learn complex skills before they learn simple ones or conceptual skills prior to nonconceptual ones. Also, objectives are only as rigid as the teacher makes them. A specific objective is designed to identify what students should be learning. If teacher assessment indicates students are not ready to learn the objective at hand, then the teacher should cover supplemental or prerequisite skills before trying to fulfill the designated objective. The classroom teacher is writing the objectives; thus, nothing really precludes making necessary adjustments.

Evaluation of Learning   Once a unit of instruction is taught, the teacher should evaluate student learning by objective. An effective posttest will evaluate all objectives taught, but the teacher must set the mastery level. When an individualized instructional technique is used, the mastery level

may vary from student to student. Whatever the level, the teacher must make sure he or she has adequately assessed, which means that, once the evaluation is complete, the teacher must know that mastery, rather than chance, is being reflected in the results.

If a teacher sets a mastery level of 80 percent on a particular objective but asks only three questions on the unit test, the teacher has actually set 100 percent mastery on that objective because students must correctly answer all questions in order to achieve mastery. A minimum of four questions correct out of five would be needed to achieve 80 percent mastery. Thus, there must be enough questions to set a reasonable mastery level that also minimizes chance.

Analysis of Evaluation   The analysis phase of the IPM is designed to look at student progress on the unit test. Such analysis must be by objective and not by unit. If a teacher sets a unit mastery level at 80 percent, it is possible for a student to achieve that level yet not master specific objectives within the unit. This is a critical distinction because an unmastered objective may be essential to the mastery of other objectives. For example, assume a student took a thirty-item test that contained fifteen questions each over two objectives: identifying action verbs and identifying linking verbs. The results were fourteen correct for the first objective and ten correct for the second. If these two objectives are added, the student would have obtained the 80 percent mastery. Obtained mastery was 93 percent for the first objective and 67 percent for the second. The understanding of linking verbs will be very important to subsequent grammar usage. Evaluation by objective allows the teacher to better identify those skills students have or have not mastered.

I. Knowledge Level
   A. Subject Area: Health
      1. Topic: Immunology
      2. Grade Level: Upper elementary
      3. Objective: The student will know the definition of naturally acquired passive immunity to 100 percent accuracy as measured by test questions.
      4. Sample Item:
         Naturally acquired passive immunity is obtained
         a. From a balanced diet and regular exercise
         b. By coming in contact with a sick person
         *c. From antibodies in a mother's breast milk
         d. From having a disease and recovering from it
   B. Subject Area: Science
      1. Topic: The microscope
      2. Grade Level: Junior high
      3. Objective: The student will be able to define magnification to 100 percent accuracy as measured by test questions.
      4. Sample Item:
         Magnification of a microscope means
         *a. Enlargement   c. Intensification
         b. Clearness   d. To heighten
II. Comprehension Level
   A. Subject Area: French
      1. Topic: Partitive
      2. Grade Level: First-year French
      3. Objective: The student will be able to translate changes in partitive after negatives to 85 percent accuracy as measured by test questions.
      4. Sample Item:
         Complete the sentence with the appropriate item.
         Je prends _____ limonade.
         a. du   c. de l'
         *b. de la   d. des
   B. Subject Area: Mathematics
      1. Topic: Rounding
      2. Grade Level: Third
      3. Objective: The student will identify a number nearest a given number to 90 percent accuracy as measured by test questions.
      4. Sample Item:
         826 is >
         a. 827   *c. 825
         b. 828   d. 829

Box 13–1, continued

III. Application Level
   A. Subject Area: Social studies
      1. Topic: Time zones
      2. Grade Level: Junior high
      3. Objective: The student will be able to determine time in another time zone to 70 percent accuracy using a world time map.
      4. Sample Item:
         Use your world time zone map to answer the following question. If the time is 5 P.M. Wednesday in Sydney, Australia, the time in New York City is
         a. 2 A.M. Wednesday   *c. 2 A.M. Thursday
         b. 2 P.M. Wednesday   d. 2 P.M. Thursday
   B. Subject Area: Algebra
      1. Topic: Symbolism
      2. Grade Level: First-year algebra
      3. Objective: The student will apply his or her understanding of variables to problems at 80 percent accuracy as measured by actual problems.
      4. Sample Item:
         Complementary angles are two angles whose sum is 90 degrees. If one of the angles is 40 degrees greater than the other, how many degrees are in each angle? Find the correct equation.
         a. $(X + 40) + X = 180$ c. $2X = 90 + 40$
         b. $X + 40 = 90$ *d. $2X + 40 = 90$
IV. Analysis Level
   A. Subject Area: Social studies
      1. Topic: American Revolution
      2. Grade Level: High school
      3. Objective: Given a problem, the student will be able to analyze a political evolution.
      4. Sample Item:
         Which of the following situations best exemplifies the concept that people can legally withdraw from an undesirable political agreement
         a. The agreement of the Pueblo Indians to join together to fight the Spanish in the 1680s   c. The U.S. Constitution
         *b. The Mayflower Compact   d. The 1871 Constitutional Amendment
   B. Subject Area: English
      1. Topic: Parts of sentence
      2. Grade Level: High school
      3. Objective: The student will be able to recognize a simple predicate in context to 90 percent accuracy.
      4. Sample Item:
         Last year I *rented* a french horn for several months.
         a. Object of preposition   *c. Verb
         b. Predicate adjective   d. Predicate nominative

Reinstruction Analysis by objective provides the basis for determining what type of unit objectives must be retaught, to whom, and the grouping structure in which reteaching should occur. A lack of mastery set up specific learning deficiencies in students. A teacher must reteach to these deficiencies, not simply give students additional problems or work sheets. This is an important step in IPM because it pays attention to those areas not learned during the initial instruction phase.

Reevaluation of Reinstruction The initial evaluation phase is formal, that is, a unit test is built proportional to the unit objectives. The evaluation of reinstruction does not necessarily have to be formal; sometimes additional work on specific objectives is sufficient. This may be verified by teacher observation, work sheets, quizzes, or formal evaluation. Whatever reevaluation is done, it is essential that the student conclusively demonstrate mastery of the retaught objectives. This sets the stage for advancing to additional units of subject matter.

Research with IPM Thornburg (1979a, b, 1980a) has conducted research studies using the IPM in math, social studies, music, and health. In nine studies, the experimental groups (those being instructed with the IPM) made significantly greater gains than the control groups (who were traditionally instructed). In one of the studies, the results were also analyzed by objective level. The experimental and control groups were compared on how well they achieved at the knowledge, comprehension, and application levels.

In each analysis, the experimental group outachieved the control group at statistically significant levels (Thornburg, 1980a). Two factors make this finding significant. First, the greatest gain made by the experimental group was the application level, the highest skill level being tested. Second, the control group measured significantly higher in intelligence and math achievement on standardized tests at the onset of the eighteen-week study. Still, they did not achieve as well as the IPM-taught students.

Individually Guided Education

Individually guided instruction
The development of an instructional team that cooperatively plans and fulfills classroom instruction in multiple ways, depending on the situational demands.

The concept of **individually guided instruction** (IGE) came out of the work of Herbert Klausmeier at the University of Wisconsin Research and Development Center. This approach works around the concepts of team teaching and student self-pacing and includes nongraded classrooms, meaning that any class may have students from different grade levels and of different ages. IGE is particularly effective in middle school/junior high school environments.

Teachers' roles in IGE are different from those in self-contained or single-subject classrooms. IGE teachers work as team members and cooperatively plan instructional activities. Within the content of both large and small group instruction, they perform a variety of instructional tasks. Different teachers assume leadership roles, depending on their compe-

tencies and interests. A team leader assumes coordination responsibilities and serves as the team liaison with other instructional teams, the administration, and special services personnel.

Klausmeier (Klausmeier, Quilling, Sorensen, Way, & Glasrud, 1971a) identified the following basic components to the IGE approach:

1. A unique set of organizational-administrative arrangements and processes

2. Instructional programs designed for the individual student

3. Evaluation of student learning based upon individual instructional programs

4. Curriculum materials that are compatible with individual instructional programs

5. A program of school-home-community relations

6. Facilitative environments in the school district and state

Klausmeier et al. (1971a) believe the two primary components are the development of instructional programs for individual students and the organizational-administrative conditions that make it possible. The emphasis on this latter point makes this approach somewhat different from the other instructional programs. Figure 13–4 shows the steps in designing instruction for each student. Specification of expected student learning and evaluation of the extent to which such skills are mastered are critical steps in the program.

Figure 13–4

Steps in designing instruction for each student. [Source: Adapted from Klausmeier, Quilling, Sorensen, Way, & Glasrud (1971), p. 19.]

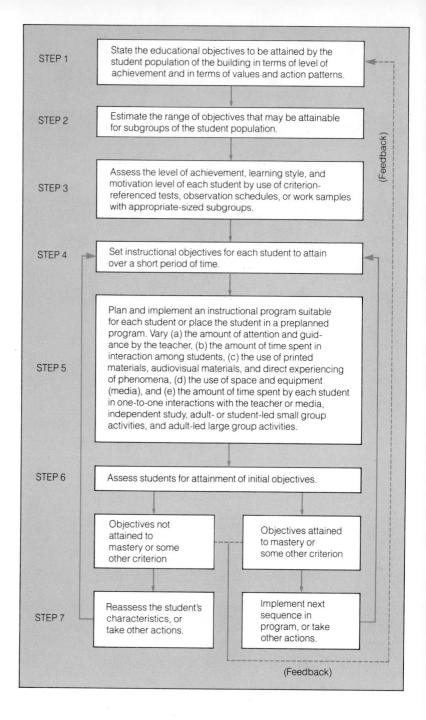

IGE is more than an individualized system of instruction; it is a new instructional philosophy that embraces school, home, and community. In order to be effective, it requires the involvement of the entire administrative and instructional staff, particularly if the nongraded and multi-age grouping components are to be implemented. The advantage to this system is total school involvement.

IGE programs have been successfully implemented in hundreds of U.S. schools. However, IGE is not as versatile as the previous two instructional approaches. The advantage of the LFM and IPM is that any teacher can implement the strategy within his or her classroom or with specific students in the classroom, whether the entire school is committed to an individualized concept or not. Thus, they have the potential to be more widely used. Jeter (1980, p. 31) has suggested that schools with the following characteristics will find the IGE approach compatible:

1. Willingness to exchange the traditional, age-graded structure for the multiunit school organization.

2. Commitment to a comprehensive staff development program

3. Resources to hire instructional and clerical aides and to invest in materials and consultative help during the initial years of implementation

4. Desire for accountability

Educational Technology

Educational psychologists have looked to technology for years in their search for more effective ways to increase learning rates. Thus far, educational technology's major contributions have been more effective research tools for better understanding learning theory and its application to education and instructional systems and devices that produce more effective learning and simpler and more efficient teaching procedures.

Teaching Machine

Although the earliest **teaching machine** was advanced by Pressey in 1926, Skinner (1958) is appropriately credited with the modern teaching machine and the subsequent development of **programmed** and **computer-aided instruction.** Skinner's machine was a simple device, based on established learning principles, which could be used for a systematized instructional procedure. Essentially, the teacher directed a student or class through a series of instructional sequences (**frames**), and the student gradually learned the desired response. Although the machine lacked flexibility, it did bring about systematic student learning. Two additional outcomes of the teaching machine were also important. First, it precluded aversive teacher comments; so the student learned in a positively controlled environment. Second, it proved to be a particularly effective technique for individualizing instruction.

Shortly after the teaching machine became well known, it fell under heavy criticism, usually on moral grounds. Fear was expressed that the teacher would be replaced, that teaching and learning would become

Teaching machine
A mechanical device that is used in the presentation of carefully sequenced instructional material to students.

Programmed instruction
The development of software designed to present learning in a step/sequence order, accompanied by reinforcement.

Computer-aided instruction
The utilization of carefully designed hardware and software that contain academic content that can be presented to students.

Frame
The designation of a specific piece of information that students should learn. Frames are sequentially arranged to maximize learning.

dehumanized, and that the children would become unsuspecting victims of manipulation. With greater knowledge, these fears dissipated, and the use of the machine proved programmed instruction to be a useful teaching technique. Occasionally, someone still writes a moralistic plaint about educational technology, but most educators recognize and are quick to point out that technology itself is value free. It merely provides tools to facilitate teaching and learning.

Programmed Instruction

Programmed instruction has proved effective, probably because it is built around established educational principles. As Hilgard (1961) has pointed out:

1. It recognizes individual differences by beginning where learners are and by permitting them to proceed at their own pace.
2. It requires that learners be active.
3. It provides immediate knowledge of results.
4. It emphasizes the organized nature of knowledge by requiring continuity between the easier (earlier) concepts and the harder (later) ones.
5. It provides spaced review in order to guarantee a high order of success.
6. It reduces anxiety because learners cannot be threatened by the task. They know that they can learn and are learning at their own pace, and they gain the satisfaction that this knowledge brings.

Programmed textbooks today are written for every grade level and in every academic subject. Undoubtedly, most readers of this text will have been exposed to some type of programmed material by now. The Skinnerian-type program, called **linear programming,** is characterized by four features:

Linear programming
A simple programming technique that focuses on small bits of information that, when sequenced, complete a learning task.

1. It uses small units of information, generally one or two sentences in length.
2. It forces student answers, which must be composed rather than selected.
3. It presents information and problems in a series of sequential, easily grasped steps (shaping).
4. It uses a linear format; that is, the student must proceed from step to step, without skipping or deviating for remedial work.

Branching program
A programming technique that utilizes multiple pieces of information in learning although the learner must respond in appropriate sequence for learning and reinforcement to occur.

Loop
A mechanism within branching that presents corrective feedback to the learners if they select the incorrect response.

A second type of program, which uses multiple-choice questions, is called **branching.** This technique typically presents a paragraph or two of information and then asks a series of questions about the information (Crowder, 1960). If learners select the correct response to a question, they are allowed to go to the next question or source of information. If not, they are told, in a remedial section or **loop,** why they were wrong and are referred back to the original question to select an alternative response. As with the linear technique, students move from step to step as they select the

Sylvia is an identical twin. Until recently, her sister, Dolores, and she were good students, always receiving "A"s and "B"s in school. But in the fifth grade, Sylvia became very outgoing, made many friends, and enjoyed the social environment of the school more than her academic studies. Her social skills improved, but her academic grades dropped.

By the second fifth-grade report card, Sylvia's parents noticed that her grades were lower than Dolores's and began to question Sylvia. She explained that her friends were more important than schoolwork right now, but this was not acceptable to her parents. In fact, they decided to restrict her after-school social activities until her grades improved. For the first time in her life, Sylvia felt she was being treated differently from her sister, which resulted in mixed feelings, especially because she was having the most important thing taken away from her for a while—her friends.

Mr. Blackard, the twins' teacher, noticed that Sylvia's work continued to be poor and that she seemed less happy than he had ever seen her. He talked to her and learned about her parents' decision. Without interfering with parental authority, Mr. Blackard decided to come up with a possible solution to this problem.

The school had several microcomputers that students could use. Mr. Blackard decided that he would have Sylvia do much of her low performance schoolwork on the micro. His strategy was based on three rationales. First, to use the microcomputer, Sylvia would have to concentrate on the lessons; thus, she would not be as free to interact with friends during class. Second, Sylvia's concentration should result in better academic performance, thus increasing her grades. Third, increased performance would help her better match parental expectations and possibly change the rules they had imposed on her, which, Mr. Blackard hoped, would change her overall attitude in school. Mr.

Blackard's strategy worked. Sylvia enjoyed working on the micro, improved her school performance, began reestablishing positive interaction with her school friends, and had her restrictions removed by her parents.

What Do You Think?

1. Did Sylvia's parents take appropriate action when her grades declined?

2. Should Mr. Blackard have discussed this situation with her parents or does his strategy seem acceptable?

3. Is it possible that Sylvia wanted to be different from her twin sister, regardless of how she had to do it?

correct responses. Boxes 13–2 and 13–3 are examples of programmed materials.

The success of programmed instruction has been responsible in part for the growth of an educational technology into an industry that now produces billions of dollars worth of hardware (equipment such as projectors, recorders, videotape machines, interactive videodiscs, and computers) and millions of dollars worth of accompanying software (films, filmstrips, records, slides, videotapes, and specially written computer programs) every year. The popularity of technological materials, combined with advances in computer technology, has also paved the way for research.

Computer-Assisted Instruction

I have suggested that many of the technological techniques of instruction used in recent years have failed to meet expectations because insufficient learning theory precludes their use. Computer-assisted instruction (CAI)

Box 13–2   Linear Programming

Stimulus and Response

Before we study the empirical definitions for "stimulus" and "response," let us consider their simplest dictionary definitions. These two words are words taken into English from Latin. "Goad" and "spur" are synonyms for the word "stimulus." "Answer" and "reply" are synonyms for the word (14) "_____."

When we say that "answer" and "reply" are synonyms for the word "response," we mean that "answer" and "reply" have the same or nearly the same meaning as (15) "_____."

Response means any change in an individual that is an (16) _____, or reply, to a stimulus.

In the quotation at the beginning of this lesson, Watson says that every (17) _____ (*response* or *stimulus?*) is called out by some (18) _____ (*response* or *stimulus?*)

Most psychologists assume that every response, everything that an individual does, is dependent upon some stimulus. Thus, "stimulus" is a very basic term in the science of psychology. It is important to study its exact empirical meaning. In these lessons, you will learn definitions for *four* different usages of the term "stimulus." We shall study two of these definitions in this lesson.

When we refer to *more than one* stimulus, we use the plural form, which is "stimuli." Thus we say "two (19) _____," not "two stimulus."

Source: Barlow (1968), pp. 6–7. Reprinted by permission of Harper & Row, Publishers, Inc.

---

systems are not only based on learning principles, but also provide an instructional approach that is flexible enough to meet each student's academic needs (Hilgard, Atkinson, & Atkinson, 1975).

Computers are used for record keeping and retrieval—a service that provides the classroom teacher with more time for instruction—but the simplest use of computers in instructional settings is what Suppes (1968) calls the **individualized drill and practice systems.** Using this system, teachers teach academic knowledge and concepts in a conventional manner, then use the computer to provide students with regular review and practice on important skills and concepts.

A second type of computer instruction is the **laboratory computing device,** which has been used successfully in mathematics and science classes. With this device, the students are allowed to develop their own programs for their course work. Developing the procedures is educational

Drill and practice systems
Simple computer programs that present additional instances of already learned material to students in order for them to continue their learning.

Laboratory computing device
A computer program that allows students to develop their own learning program in any given subject-matter area.

Chapter 13
Individualized Instruction

411

Box 13–3   Branching Programming

Frame 1

When issued a driver's license, the driver is granted the privilege of using Wisconsin streets and highways as long as he obeys the traffic laws and drives in a safe manner.

Question 1

Upon obtaining a Wisconsin driver's license, the driver

(a) is permitted to drive in any manner he chooses. (p. 5)
(b) should remember his responsibilities for safety. (p. 7)
(c) is obligated to renew his license periodically. (p. 6)

Student Answers

(p. 5) Upon obtaining a Wisconsin driver's license, the driver is permitted to drive in any manner he chooses.

Whoops! Obviously, this is wrong. Whether a driver has just received his license or is an experienced driver, he never has the right to drive as he pleases. One of the remaining two answers is better than this one. Go back to the question on page 1 and see if you can find it.

(p. 6) Upon obtaining a Wisconsin driver's license, the driver is obligated to renew his license periodically.

While this is true, it is not the answer for which you are looking. Return to page 1 and select a better answer.

(p. 7) Upon obtaining a Wisconsin driver's license, the driver should remember his responsibilities for safety.

Right you are! A driver must always assume responsibility when operating a motor vehicle. This means obeying the traffic laws and driving in a safe manner. Now you are ready to go to additional information in Frame 2 (page 2).

Box 13-3, continued

Frame 2

Special attention must be given to traffic violators, to drivers involved in accidents, and to those whose physical condition makes safe driving questionable. The Driver Improvement Bureau was created to deal with such people. If this cannot be achieved, the Bureau has no alternative but to suspend or cancel the driver's license.

Question 2

The agency created to deal with drivers whose physical condition is questionable is the

(a) Highway Patrol. (p. 8)
(b) Department of Public Safety. (p. 10)
(c) Driver Improvement Bureau. (p. 9)

Student Answers

(p. 8) The agency created to deal with drivers whose physical condition is questionable is the Highway Patrol.

No, not in this case. Of course, the Highway Patrol will apprehend a driver whose physical condition obviously is interfering with safe driving. But this agency was not created for the improvement of the individual's driving. With this clue you should return to page 2 and select another response.

(p. 9) The agency created to deal with drivers whose physical condition is questionable is the Driver Improvement Bureau.

Excellent! This is the correct answer. The Driver Improvement Bureau was specifically created to deal with traffic violators, drivers involved in accidents, and with those whose physical condition is in question. The basic purpose of this agency is to create self-improvement in the licensed driver. Now that you have successfully answered this question, let's try Frame 3 (page 3).

(p. 10) The agency created to deal with drivers whose physical condition is questionable is the Department of Public Safety.

Incorrect! This answer is too general. The Department of Public Safety has many functions, but it was not specifically created to deal with drivers whose physical condition is questionable. Go back to page 2 and select a more appropriate answer.

in and of itself, and students learn to handle and understand academic material.

Tutorial systems assume teaching responsibility by presenting instructional material at a conceptual or skill level. The stimuli require students to respond in conceptual and meaningful ways rather than by rote. In this sense, they are different from drill and practice systems, which maintain student behavior. Rather, they actually instruct and require responses that are more complex than simpler computer systems.

Suppes (1968) mentions the potential of **dialogue systems,** which permit students to conduct a genuine dialogue with the computer. These are a more complex level of computer functioning and represent a conceptual level of learning. Several hardware problems must still be worked out within this system.

Another promising area is the **simulation system,** which has already been used extensively in medical science to simulate pathological conditions. This use of a computer is a good learning device and could become quite functional in the classroom for appropriate academic material. The simulation of reality by computer may someday provide learners with clear and vividly memorable applications of issues and problem solving.

Perhaps one of the greatest contributions that CAI will make to education is the individualization of instruction. The age-old problem in the conventional classroom is adjusting the rate of the teaching-learning process to each student's various needs and abilities. Because computers provide systematized and repeatable educational programs, they are adaptable to students' needs. It is simply impossible for a classroom teacher to do this as consistently, efficiently, and effectively.

Research with CAI has confirmed its benefits:

1. Students can learn as well by CAI as within the regular classroom and, in most cases, have a greater learning and retention rate.

2. CAI makes logical decisions and adjustments to individual differences with regard to learning sequence, depth and mode of material, and rate of progress.

3. The computer is capable of recording a variety of learning data about the student during instruction. This feedback can tell how well students are learning and what adjustments in the computer programming may be necessary.

4. Diverse academic materials can be incorporated into CAI programs. There seems to be no area where CAI cannot function.

I discuss the impact of high technology on society in greater detail in the Epilogue.

Tutorial system
The presentation of new information or skills by a computer for the express purpose of facilitating student learning.

Dialogue system
Software programs that allow the student to interact with the computer in the learning process.

Simulation system
The presentation of classroom like or life like information under simulated conditions designed to increase the meaningfulness of what is being learned.

A sixth-grade classroom teacher was interested in developing a systematic way to monitor student behavior, get quick feedback on performance, and address observed learning deficiencies. With the assistance of a high school teacher who taught microcomputer education, she developed a program that would expedite scoring student papers and diagnosing student deficiencies. Because the sixth-grade math program was already broken down by units and objectives, it was an easy program to develop.

They designed the system to analyze each student by objective. The teacher was interested in mastery teaching; so it made more sense to diagnose each student's learning behavior in relation to the criteria and not in relation to other students. They built a total class diagnosis into the program to assist the teacher in grouping students where learning problems indicated it to be most appropriate.

By the time the two teachers worked the "bugs" out of the computer program, the sixth-grade teacher was ready to instruct a unit entitled "Subtraction with and without regrouping." The following objectives made up the unit. The numerical system that precedes each objective is a coding system that allows the teacher to place information in and retrieve it from the microcomputer.

A   Subtraction without Regrouping

A1A   The student will know the terms related to subtraction.

A2A   The student will identify a problem involving checking by addition.

A3A   The student will be able to solve two-place subtraction problems without regrouping.

A3B   The student will be able to solve subtraction problems and equations involving multiple-digit numbers.

A3C   The student will be able to find the difference of a subtraction problem and check it by addition.

B   Subtraction with Regrouping

B1A   The student will know the terms related to subtraction with regrouping.

B2A   The student will identify a problem involving borrowing.

B3A   The student will be able to solve a two-place subtraction problem with regrouping.

B3B   The student will be able to solve subtraction problems and equations involving multiple-digit numbers.

B3C   The student will be able to find the difference of a subtraction problem and check it by addition.

C   Estimating Differences

C1A   The student will learn the terms *estimated difference* and *rounded addends*.

C2A   The student will identify correctly rounded addends.

C2B   The student will identify correctly estimated differences.

C3A   The student will solve problems using rounded addends and estimated differences.

Once the teacher had instructed this math unit, she gave the students a sixty-item test that covered the unit objectives. Table 13–1 provides the computer analysis of Karen Goodfellow's performance on the test. The teacher also had the computer analyze and print an individual analysis for the other twenty-six students in her class.

There were fourteen objectives on the test. By referring to Table 13–1, you can see that Karen mastered twelve of them. Karen mastered all the material related to subtraction without regrouping and subtraction with regrouping. Her weakest performance was on the material that covered estimating differences. She did not master objective C2A, which was identifying rounded addends, or objective C3A, which was solving problems using rounded addends and estimated differences. The teacher recognized that she would have to work with Karen on rounded addends.

You will notice that Karen did not achieve mastery to the same level. Her teacher believed that

Table 13–1   Individual Student Performance Analysis

Student ID: 41223   *Teacher: S. Barnhill*
Test File Name: Subtraction   *Date: October 17, 1983*

Objective	No. of Items	Number Correct	Percent Correct	Below Mastery
A1A	3	2	67	
A2A	4	4	100	
A3A	5	5	100	
A3B	5	4	80	
A3C	5	5	100	
B1A	3	3	100	
B2A	4	3	75	
B3A	5	4	80	
B3B	5	4	80	
B3C	5	4	80	
C1A	3	2	67	
C2A	4	2	50	•••
C2B	4	4	100	
C3A	5	3	60	•••

Table 13–2   Class Performance Analysis

Number of Students: 27   *Teacher: S. Barnhill*
Test File Name: Subtraction   *Date: October 17, 1983*

Objective	No. of Items	Number Correct	Percent Correct	Below Mastery	Number Below
A1A	3	2.2	67		6
A2A	4	3.0	75		5
A3A	5	4.4	88		4
A3B	5	4.1	82		7
A3C	5	4.3	86		6
B1A	3	2.8	93		3
B2A	4	3.5	88		5
B3A	5	3.8	76	•••	8
B3B	5	3.0	60	•••	11
B3C	5	3.4	68	•••	10
C1A	3	2.3	77		5
C2A	4	3.1	78		4
C2B	4	3.2	80		7
C3A	5	3.1	62	•••	12

higher level skills were more important than lower level skills and asked more questions on them. Because the program allowed the teacher to set a different mastery level for each objective, she did exactly that. She used the following criteria on this subtraction test:

1. Knowledge level objectives (1) were set at 67 percent.

2. Comprehension level objectives (2) were set at 75 percent.

3. Application level objectives (3) were set at 80 percent.

Table 13–2 shows that the entire class did quite well on this subtraction unit. As a whole, the class mastered ten out of fourteen objectives, although there were individual variations. By looking at her class analysis, the teacher observed that the greatest number of problems were at the application level, the level she felt was most important to master. Virtually all students had no trouble with subtraction without regrouping. However, at the point where it is required to regroup, multiple concepts are required in order to solve problems. It was here that the students had the greatest problem. The teacher decided to reteach the concept of borrowing and estimating to all the students; beyond that point, she decided to group students into smaller teams to teach. She decided that she would not individualize any of this material unless some student continued to perform poorly after small group instruction had been completed.

Systematic monitoring systems such as this one are important to the classroom teacher. Diagnosing student learning after every formal evaluation is crucial. To do so quickly is also important. Karen's teacher had all this information from the computer in fourteen minutes, from the time of scoring the students papers to getting the individual printouts. She estimated that it would have taken two hours to do all this by hand, in addition to which, she would then have to decide appropriate small group placement. The computer not only gives individual profiles, but tells the teacher what objectives were missed by the same students. Thus, it does the preliminary placement for additional instruction.

417

Annotated Readings

Berliner, D. C. (1983). Developing conceptions of classroom environments: Some light on the T in classroom studies of ATI. *Educational Psychologist, 18,* 1–13.

> *The author describes a procedure for analyzing the impact of activity structures in classrooms. Activity structures such as reading circle or seatwork have different functions and contain rules and norms to guide individuals' behavior within them. A taxonomy and description of eleven activity structures was derived from observations of over twelve hundred activity structures in elementary classrooms. The activity structures perspective allows for a more precise description of classrooms than has previously been possible, a factor important to Aptitude Treatment Interaction research in the classroom.*

Cox, W. F., Jr., & Dunn, T. G. (1979). Mastery learning: A psychological trap? *Educational Psychologist, 14,* 24–29.

> *The authors challenge the announced advantages of implementing mastery learning instruction in classrooms. They claim that such strategies often fall short of expectations. The authors summarize factors that contribute to mastery learning being less than "proclaimed."*

Gall, M. D., Ward, B. A., Berliner, D. C., Cahen, L. S., Winne, P. H., Elasoff, J. D., & Stanton, G. C. (1978). Effects of questioning techniques and recitation on student learning. *American Educational Research Journal, 15,* 175–199.

> *Two experiments were done in which sixth-grade students participated in ten ecology lessons, each involving reading/viewing of curriculum materials plus a teaching treatment. The first experiment compared the presence/absence of recitation and presence/absence of probing (a follow-up question to improve a student's initial response) and redirection (asking another student to respond to the question). The second experiment asked a percentage of higher cognitive questions (25 percent, 50 percent, 75 percent). In both studies, recitation substantially improved learning, particularly information recall and higher cognitive responding. Probing and redirection (experiment 1) had no effect on improving student behavior.*

Marshall, H. H. (1981). Open classrooms: Has the term outlived its usefulness? *Review of Educational Research, 51,* 181–192.

> *The author reviews the effectiveness of open education research and determines that studies are inconclusive, even though research methodologies have improved. She cites the fact that few studies distinguish between the classification of open classrooms and the actual implementation of open education in them. The conclusion is drawn that better conceptualization of research studies is necessary if the data they yield is to be meaningful.*

Slavin, R. E. (1980). Cooperative learning. *Review of Educational Research, 50,* 315–342.

> *Research on classroom cooperative learning techniques, in which students work in small groups and receive rewards or recognition based on their group performance, has been increasing. This review summarizes the results of twenty-eight field projects lasting at least two weeks in which cooperative learning methods were used in classrooms. The pattern of research findings supports the utility of cooperative learning methods in general for increasing student achievement, positive race relations in desegregated schools, mutual concern among students, and student self-esteem. Steps for additional research in this area are outlined.*

Thompson, S. B. (1980). Do individualized mastery and traditional instructional systems yield different course effects in college calculus? *American Educational Research Journal, 17,* 361–375.

> *The effects of an individualized mastery instructional system similar to the Keller plan were compared with a conventional lecture-discussion-recitation system in a variety of ways, including mathematics achievement and fail rate in the comparison course and subsequent mathematics courses, mathematics reading comprehension, facilitation of performance in other disciplines, student study time, faculty time required for instructional system operation, students' and instructors' preferences, and student propensity for continued math-related studies. In general, the superiority of achievement and attitude outcomes claimed for the Keller plan in many other studies was not observed in this one.*

Classroom Management Techniques

In 1942, I trotted off to school with all the exuberance and naïveté becoming of an aspiring eager learner. That afternoon, during an innocent jaunt down the slide, an equally exuberant and naïve first-grade girl became the unsuspecting victim of my affection. I kissed her! The teacher saw me and I was paddled. Self-initiative or discipline?

In 1952, when I was a high school sophomore, my inappropriate mixture of chemicals brought on an unanticipated reaction. The teacher took offense at the smoke-filled room. I took offense at the teacher kicking me out of the room. The vice-principal took offense at seeing the teacher and me in his office. My reward—kicked out of school for one week. The operative chemical concept—synthesis. Somehow that punishment was supposed to entice me to return to science class highly motivated and eager to learn. Incentive or discipline?

In 1962, as an assistant principal of a junior high school, I was summoned by the eighth-grade math teacher to witness a paddling, a state law requirement. When I arrived at his room, I found the teacher and eleven reluctant boys standing in the hallway. Each received three swats for not learning the mathematical equations assigned on the previous day. Achievement motivation or discipline?

In 1972, I read in the newspaper a request from teachers in a small Arizona town to the school board that they be given the authority to use corporal punishment as the primary means of discipline in the classroom. Educators or disciplinarians?

In 1982, I was commencement speaker for a high school graduation in a small Arizona town. Prior to the exercise, the school superintendent, high school principal, and school board were all apprehensive about how unruly the graduating class would be. The seniors were well behaved, enjoying their sense of accomplishment. The school officials were relieved when it was all over. A recognition for their accomplishment or greater concern with a well-disciplined graduation ceremony?

These ancedotes show that my school-related experiences over this forty-year span reveal a uniform response to misconduct in the school environment—resort to discipline! The question of how to manage the classroom or school environment is not easily resolved. However, discipline is only one of several techniques for working with

421

students. Managing school environments is the subject of this chapter, in which I discuss the following topics:

- *Optimal learning environments*
- *Discipline*
- *Causes of misbehavior*
- *Behavior modification as a management technique*
- *Behavioral self-management*

Optimal Learning Environments

There are many different opinions as to what constitutes the best classroom environment for successful teaching and learning. These varying opinions are justified because each classroom, with its diverse teacher and pupil personalities, has its own unique makeup. Research will shed little light because there are no universal phenomena to study. Nevertheless, there are some commonalities that warrant discussion because they provide insight into learning environments and classroom management.

Optimal learning environments are generated from two sources: the academic nature of the classroom and the social interactions within the classroom. Teachers invariably perceive the social interaction source as generating most problems. However, these interactions may be heavily affected by the academic nature of the classroom. Teachers functionally control their academic classroom, but students influence its social nature.

Jacob Kounin (1970) tried to determine the nature of academic environments and their effects on disruptive and nondisruptive student behavior. His findings show how teachers either purposely or inadvertently create many conditions that result in classroom management problems. The six key outcomes of Kounin's research concern smoothness, student involvement, optimal classroom movement, variety, "with-it-ness," and the ripple effect.

Smoothness

Kounin (1970) found that some teachers do not keep a steady flow in the classroom activities. Teachers should strive to make an easy transition from one topic to the next. Some teachers are **stimulus-bound;** that is, they carefully plan out and do not vary a sequence of instructional activities. Kounin found many such teachers tended to "get off track" by introducing irrelevant information or responding to irrelevant questions. Some teachers interrupt learning activities; others switch content areas rather abruptly. Kounin found that classroom management was easier when teachers maintained smoothness once they had established it.

Stimulus-bound
The tendency for a teacher to adhere strictly to instructional material with minimal flexibility.

Student Involvement

Keeping students actively engaged in classroom activities is another way to reduce the potential for misbehavior. Kounin found that, if students are involved, their tendency toward disruptive behavior is reduced. Some strategies that seem effective are picking students randomly to respond, presenting unusual material, and asking students to demonstrate their knowledge or skills.

Optimal Classroom Movement

Kounin suggests that classes that have little momentum or lose their momentum result in disinterest. **Behavior overdwelling** is excessive attention, usually perceived by the students as negative (for example, nagging or moralizing), to an academic skill that does not need that much time and attention. For example, the teacher may discuss how complex a complex task is rather than actually instructing it.

Fragmentation involves having individuals do something one at a time when they could learn it better as a group. An elementary school teacher who is dismissing a class for recess could simply tell students to line up in the room or hall. This teacher fragments if he or she sets conditions that have nothing to do with lining up to go out to recess (such as asking students to put all their books in their desks and sit up straight, then letting them line up according to how neat their desks are and how straight they are sitting). This unnecessary, lengthy process can cause students to be restless and disruptive, particularly when they are being kept from a pleasant activity.

Behavior overdwelling
The tendency for a teacher to stress a point to the extent of fatigue or redundancy.

Fragmentation
The tendency for a teacher to tell something to several students individually that could have been told effectively to the entire class.

Variety

Within the classroom, Kounin observed that some teachers were highly predictable, presenting materials in rather boring, uninteresting ways. At the other extreme are those teachers who are very interesting and introduce variety into their teaching. Variety in content and mode of presentation seems to engage students' interest and reduce disruptiveness and discipline problems. Teachers need to be enthusiastic about their classroom, its pupils and academic content. Kounin observed that variety may be more likely in self-contained classrooms, where there is greater content and time flexibility.

"Withitness"

Kounin used the term *withitness* to describe the teacher's general perception of the classroom. Effective teachers focus on the real problems, ignore trivial problems, and have a sense of what is the heart of the classroom. Good classroom managers recognize the need for student interaction and do not focus on those aspects of human behavior that do not really affect the classroom environment.

Ripple Effect

A teacher's behavior toward one student affects the rest of the class. A teacher's personality conflicting with that of even one student can result in each being oversensitive to the other, causing unnecessary conflict.

Teacher interactions should reflect fairness and respect for students. In instances where students perceive teachers as unfair, negative perceptions or attitudes often emerge. For example, Rounds et al. (1981) found that teachers tend to ridicule or punish students publicly (in front of others). But, when students do something worthy of teacher praise, teachers tend to indicate approval in private. The researchers found students disliked teachers who publicly criticized and privately praised them. This is an example of teacher behavior that can cause students to become difficult to manage.

Potential Teacher Causes of Classroom Management Problems		Concept Summary 14–1
Kounin's Category	**Symptom**	
Smoothness	Jumping from topic to topic, interjecting irrelevant material	
Student Involvement	Minimizing student involvement in actual school-work, leaving students time to do other distracting things	
Optimal Classroom Movement	Focusing on an issue that creates negative reactions or attitudes in students, even though the issue is not that important	
Variety	Following the same old routine or standard way of doing things	
Withitness	Lacking awareness of how classroom tasks, both academic and social, are interrelated to create an overall positive learning environment, providing fragmented rather than integrated activities	
Ripple Effect	Using students as examples for others, especially in the area of discipline, which often backfires if students think the teacher is unfair or student can elicit peer sympathy	

Discipline
An externally imposed control on students.

Permissiveness
A lack of classroom control or regulation of student behavior.

Authoritarianism
Excessive or arbitrary control of students by teachers.

Discipline

There is no common acceptable definition of **discipline.** Therefore, disciplinary practices run the gamut from strict authoritarianism to high permissiveness. In considering the school environment, discipline might be defined as the imposition of external standards and controls on individual conduct. **Permissiveness** implies the absence of such standards and controls. **Authoritarianism** can be viewed as a type of excessive, arbitrary, and autocratic control.

Positive Aspects

There are at least four positive aspects to discipline. First, it is necessary for socialization. It is very important that children and adolescents learn socially approved standards of conduct. Second, discipline is necessary for normal personality development. It may foster such traits as self-reliance, self-regulation, persistence, and the ability to tolerate frustration, and such skills as problem solving and individually initiated learning. Third, discipline is necessary to the internalization of moral standards. Individuals internalize standards by interacting with their external form. The classroom is a good environment for such interaction. Fourth, discipline may promote emotional security in children. A reference point provides the basis for learning self-control. Without it, children often experience ambiguity and uncertainty (Ianni, 1980).

Teachers who take a positive, democratic approach to discipline believe in imposing minimal control. They do not regard discipline and

obedience as ends in themselves, but as means to these ends. **Democratic discipline** is as rational, nonarbitrary, and bilateral as possible. It is not a winner-loser situation, but a teacher-learner one. A positive approach to discipline is likely better than a negative attitude. Cuban (1978) has pointed out that most students want to do well in school, to be accepted, and to go along with rules. He contends that they will respond favorably to reasonable, competent teachers.

Democratic discipline does not, however, imply freedom from external controls or classroom decorum, presuppose the eradication of distinctions between the roles of pupil and teacher, or suggest that teachers abdicate responsibility for making the final decisions in their classroom. It provides the mechanism for teachers to set limits and controls while helping students meet learning goals through intellectual exploration and mastery of new situations. Thus, limits breed trust, promote learning, and nurture self-control. If limits are fair and consistently upheld, students may be less likely to test them.

Typical Problems

The support base for handling disciplinary problems in the schools is often defined either too ambiguously or too narrowly. On the one hand, teachers may feel insecure about the nature and extent of administrative support, perhaps because they do not know whether the behavior warrants administrative attention and perhaps because they do not want to reveal their ineffectiveness in handling disciplinary problems. On the other hand, teachers are sometimes reluctant to call a problem to an administrator's attention because the traditional methods of discipline are not those the teacher would prefer to employ. Detention, corporal punishment, and school suspension, for example, are being increasingly questioned (Glickman & Tamashiro, 1980; Ratliff, 1980).

Fontein (1978) discusses one primary source of disciplinary problems—underachievers' behavior patterns. She contends that combining an underachiever with a learning situation that is too difficult results in disruption. Based on her experiences as a classroom teacher, she asserts that one out of every four to five adolescents has this disruptive potential. Fontein (1978, p. 106) has used the following nine student characteristics to anticipate and counteract problems:

1. Short attention span, easily distracted

2. Inability to deal with the abstract without very gradual transition from the concrete

3. Short memory of abstractions or isolated items (dates, causes, events)

4. Much greater interest in their limited personal world than in abstract academics

5. Great need for recognition of self, of *success*

6. Academic inadequacies (low ability in reading, spelling, and other areas, with little self-confidence in the school setting)

7. Inability to establish satisfactory interpersonal relations

8. Great need for constant direction and reassurance that they are doing the job correctly

9. Many strengths that have usually gone unrecognized and unappreciated

Teachers may have difficulty with discipline because they frequently lack support from the school system and the community fosters antisocial behaviors. In stressing the inherent rights of children to receive due consideration by the teacher, we have ignored the equally important facts of the teacher's age and maturity. By respect for age, I do not mean that students should give uncritical veneration to teachers, but rather that consideration is due to all human beings, regardless of their stage in life. Student disrespect seems to be socially bound. Youth tend to rate adults negatively and to be patronizing and somewhat contemptuous. Too often this general social attitude is transferred to the classroom teacher.

Our society has tended to put teachers, as authority figures, in an anomalous position. They are expected to command respect, exercise authority, and inculcate prosocial behaviors and attitudes in students. Yet it is not uncommon to find weak community support. Many teachers have been intimidated and their jobs threatened because they were too punitive, authoritarian, or antisocial.

Perhaps the key to potential disciplinary problems does rest in teachers' instructional strategies. They should attempt to make learning meaningful and relevant to as many students as possible. The diversity of student skills, interests, and behaviors is challenging and often requires more energy and versatility than classroom teachers can generate.

Alternatives

Many teachers, not knowing what else to do, adopt traditional methods of discipline. For instance, what do you do when a student refuses to do homework or punches a classmate? Should a teacher view this as a defiance of authority, as a lack of self-control, as a learning disability, or as a form of emotional disturbance? How might a teacher respond to these student behaviors without being punitive, defensive, or authoritarian? There are at least three alternatives to traditional discipline.

First, the teacher must always consider the idea that student misconduct may be symptomatic of underlying needs or feelings. There is a tendency to interpret student misbehavior literally, in a direct cause-and-effect way. As the child develops toward adolescence, however, the arena for acting out broadens. Thus, the teacher's inferences may be less accurate.

Two illustrations may serve my point. Children who are handled too permissively at home tend to regard themselves as privileged persons. Their behavior may not conform to normative standards and expectations because they have never learned them. They may make unrealistic demands on other students and the teacher. Yet their classroom behavior may be a natural extension of their home behavior. Rather than punish-

ing these students, the teacher should help them learn more realistic expectations, thus socializing them.

Another common classroom problem is disruptive students. Underlying much disruptive behavior is the need for attention. The students may not receive enough attention at home and may find that the teacher pays any attention to them only when they are disruptive. Whatever form of discipline the teacher uses, it reinforces the disruptive behavior, because the students have gained the teacher's attention. As an alternative strategy, the teacher should find ways to recognize the students when they display prosocial behavior. As the students gain attention for acceptable behavior, their need to disrupt diminishes.

Second, it is important for the teacher to view classroom behavior as a function of perception. Students need to perceive that they have some control over the environment and are not always under the teacher's control. Some research evidence relates this perceptual variable to both achievement and conduct (Duke & Nowicki, 1974). The more students perceive control, the greater their achievement and the more accepting their conduct. Therefore, improvement in classroom environments will have an effect on the student's behavior, whether these improvements are changes in the teacher's perception of or interaction with the student or changes in the student's perception of and interaction with the teacher.

Third, teachers should consider the extent of the problem—the frequency and intensity of the misbehavior, the individual(s) it affects, and the importance of stopping the behavior immediately. For example, is the class disrupted or is the teacher offended? Is it an isolated incident or persistent behavior? Perhaps, when an undesirable behavior surfaces, the teacher's skill in sorting out its effects is an alternative to traditional discipline in itself.

Uses in Classroom Control

Discipline is the most common classroom control technique used in the schools. Strom and Bernard (1982, p. 395) have defined classroom discipline as the "maintenance of order in a school by both teachers and pupils so that conditions are conducive to the achievement of stated educational objectives." Implicit in this definition is the idea that teachers and students alike are responsible for classroom behavior. Strom and Bernard have suggested that the nature of discipline varies, depending upon the student's age. The diverse behavioral capacities of students in grade one and in high school must be considered. Strom and Bernard have summarized the implications for discipline at different developmental stages (see Table 14–1).

When the balance between teacher and student shared responsibility is not maintained, it ultimately falls upon the teacher to restore it. Some externally imposed discipline seems essential to maintain or restore classroom order and to facilitate positive student growth. Whether children or adolescents, students do need the perspective that experience and adulthood can bring into classrooms.

Many teachers administer discipline in front of other students, believing it serves to "shape up the student" as well as present an example for the others. There is no question but that such an effect does occur, although the manner is which the teacher goes about it will determine the nature of the effect. Research indicates that broad, general statements have virtually no effect on student behavior, but a specific statement does (Kounin, 1970; Rounds et al., 1981). A general statement is "I wonder if I'm going to have to give someone detention. When you disturb this class

Table 14–1 Discipline and Age Stages

All Ages	Age Stages	Considerations
Because there are different lifestyles and experiences, causes or contributing factors for each individual transgression must be sought. Often the cause will suggest a remedial approach.	Preschool	Teacher in control. Conditioning, immediate reward for desired conduct.
	Kindergarten Primary grades	Conditioning continues; peers taught to bring social pressure.
Disciplinary techniques must vary with teachers' styles and personalities. Techniques cannot be uniform, either for teachers or for children at different age stages. Tendencies toward teacher-centered or pupil-centered methods should vary with age stages.	Upper elementary Junior high school	As children approach moral-reasoning age, clear-cut rules should be stipulated and periodically restated. Use contracts and agreements.
	High school	As the stage of formal-operational thinking is reached, pupils should have input into rules, and more dependence on peers should be encouraged.
	College adult	Reasoned, responsible, self-government.

Source: From *Educational Psychology* by R. D. Strom and H. W. Bernard, p. 395. Copyright © 1982 by Wadsworth, Inc. Reprinted by permission of Brooks/Cole Publishing Company, Monterey, CA 93940.

you're asking for detention." A specific statement would be "Judy, you know if you don't want detention you must ask permission before going to the pencil sharpener."

Research by Kounin (1970) and Rounds et al. (1981) also found that teacher firmness and consistency were keys to classroom discipline, particularly when discipline was public. The element of fairness, combined with teacher concern for student behaviors, seems to be an effective strategy for classroom management.

Students can adjust to teacher controls and disciplinary actions if they are not excessive and if they feel teachers care for them. Students gain a sense of support if they perceive they are in reasonable learning environments, have positive interactions with teachers, and sense that teachers care about them as individuals. A recent study focused on the teacher characteristics students preferred (Thornburg, McEwin & Jones, 1982). Each question was set up as a dichotomy, eliciting student perceptions toward teacher competency versus teacher affectivity. A summary of the questions given to twenty-four hundred North Carolina students in grades four through nine is presented in Table 14–2. Students overwhelmingly perceived teacher support to be more important than teacher competency. This type of student perception impacts on their receptivity to teachers in discipline situations.

Other Discipline Sources

Peers are another source for discipline. If classroom norms that meet the students' needs are established, they themselves can exert pressure on a student who is misbehaving. Students often internalize discipline their peers impose so that on subsequent occasions, they exhibit self-regulation or self-imposed discipline. This type of student behavior is highly desirable because it indicates the student's ability to control himself or herself.

Table 14–2 Percentage of Early Adolescent Responses to Items Measuring Preferred Teacher Characteristics

Item	SA	A	D	SD	NA
A person who is smart is better than one who accepts me as a person.	5.7	12.7	42.6	38.5	.5
A teacher who thinks logically is better than one who is concerned about the welfare of others.	7.9	22.6	43.8	24.6	1.1
Logical thinking for a teacher is more important than being concerned about the class.	5.2	12.9	43.4	37.4	1.1
It is more important for a teacher to know the subjects we study than to be friendly.	10.4	21.4	31.2	20.2	16.8
In order to be good, a teacher has to be strict.	10.6	20.7	29.0	23.0	16.6
Teachers who do not put up with nonsense in class are best.	15.2	30.6	26.4	11.0	16.8
Teachers should accept students as people.	68.7	26.9	2.4	1.0	.4
First of all, teachers should be smart.	21.4	43.6	21.4	13.2	.3
Teachers who tell stories in class are better than those who let the students tell stories.	10.9	32.4	44.4	11.5	.8
I like a teacher who asks me questions even though I might not know the answers.	14.9	40.6	31.2	12.9	.4

Note: SA = Strongly Agree, A = Agree, D = Disagree, SD = Strongly Disagree, NA = No Answer.

Source: Thornburg et al. (1982), p. 5.

A second discipline source is nonpersonal. Mouly (1982) has cited **task-imposed discipline** as the need to act responsibly in performing tasks by exercising the willpower and constraints to accomplish the task within certain time frames. This task-imposed discipline seems particularly dependent on student capacity. It is difficult to imagine that a student who has little classroom behavioral control would have the capacity to be highly task oriented because the ability to exercise discipline is generalizable to a variety of circumstances.

Corporal Punishment

Historically, **corporal punishment** was used as a means of altering behavior. Although it is now used much less, it has not totally disappeared. A study in the state of Pennsylvania by Reardon and Reynolds (1978) among 292 school districts indicated that 92 percent officially approved the use of physical punishment. Within these districts, they surveyed six groups as to whether they favored it. Table 14–3 reports that the group most favoring it was school board presidents (81 percent) and the group least favoring it was students (25 percent).

Levine (1978) reported on a survey among teachers in which one-third were opposed to corporal punishment under any conditions; another 46 percent opposed its use except in response to bodily assault by students. Elrod (1979) reports on an Indiana study in which nearly all the junior high schools and two-thirds of the high schools approved or used physical punishment.

I discussed the limitations on punishment in Chapter 2. Several others have cited these limitations (Bongiovanni, 1977; Haviland, 1979; Ratliff, 1980; Sloan, Young, & Marcusen, 1977). In general, they find punishment aversive, counterproductive, and in direct conflict with the goals of education. The most serious limitation is that physical punishment does not result in improved behavior. The result of punishment is to repress behavior or subdue students. However, the long-term results show no appreciable change in behavior. In the past two decades, strategies that do produce behavioral change have emerged. One of the best is behavior modification, which I discuss later in this chapter.

Causes of Misbehavior

Classroom misbehavior may result from characteristics students bring into classrooms or from those they learn there, particularly as a result of interaction with other students and the teacher. How children and adolescents are socialized may also affect classroom behavior. The school, through the curriculum, its teachers, and the administration, also influences student misbehavior.

Students

Many children do not know how to behave consistently in appropriate ways. Much of this is due to a lack of teaching, poor socialization, or inappropriate modeling. Students are generally influenced by their families, the media, and society. Variations in child-rearing practices mean that children enter school functioning in different ways. They often do not

Table 14–3 **Attitudes Toward Corporal Punishment**

	Percent Favor	Percent Opposed	Percent Not Sure
School Board Presidents	81	12	6
Principals	78	13	8
Administrators	68	25	6
Teachers	74	16	9
Parents	71	21	7
Total Adults	75	17	8
Students	25	51	25

Source: Reardon & Reynolds (1975), pp. 7–8.

understand why they should behave in certain ways in the classroom. The media, particularly television, also influence behavior. Students may believe they are watching acceptable behaviors when they see lack of respect and aggressiveness on television. Social change sets up different behavioral norms. As the range of acceptable behavior increases, students' behavioral potentials also increase. In short, many classroom misbehaviors may be what students have been taught or perceive as acceptable.

Schools

Several writers have cited three primary ways that schools contribute to student misbehavior: the curriculum, teachers, and the administration. These sources have to do with how schools operate, the components are interrelated, and students' needs are met.

Curriculum   As student needs become increasingly diverse, the school curriculum must also. Otherwise, an increasing number of student needs simply does not get met. Chapter 13 pointed out the importance of individualized instruction. In addition, schools should make sure their curriculum is relevant and contemporary. As students become older, they begin to construct more complex representations of the world. If they find school unchallenging or irrelevant, they may become disruptive, especially if their peers approve of such behavior.

Teachers   As I discussed earlier in this chapter, Kounin (1970) observed several teacher-initiated factors that resulted in student classroom misbehavior. Teachers may initiate, contribute to, or reinforce disruptive situations. Johnson (1979, pp. 87–88) believes that poor teacher organization is a major cause of discipline problems. A lack of organization wastes time, does not keep students engaged in schoolwork, and may be viewed by students as an indication of teacher incompetence. Recognizing that poor organization can lead to classroom disruption, Johnson suggests that the following factors are important to diminishing disruption:

1. Classroom materials should be organized so the teacher can find them when needed.

2. The teacher should be time conscious. Class should begin and end punctually.

3. The teacher should not panic easily. When unexpected events happen, the teacher and the class should know what to do immediately.

4. Short- and long-term objectives should be planned. Objectives should be developed for pupils who need immediate feedback as well as for those who can work on projects over a longer period of time.

5. Good records should be kept. A unique system, one that is easy to interpret, should be developed for each student.

6. Materials should be prepared before class. Objectives should be developed and materials secured before the class begins.

7. Teachers should utilize other resources. Volunteers and other resource persons should be invited to class to expand a class objective or to impart new knowledge.

Administration   A lack of leadership and a failure to define rules and regulations within the school environment have been recognized as sources for disruptive behavior. School principals should demonstrate the leadership to organize the school in a way that maximizes both teacher and learner effectiveness. Responsibilities and the mechanism for handling disruptive behavior should be clearly defined. The principal must be concerned about what happens in classrooms, being supportive of teachers and students alike. Concern for the curriculum, instructional process, teacher satisfaction, and student needs are all primary concerns.

Invariably, there are situations where teacher-student conflict is brought to the principal's attention. In such cases, teachers feel a strong need for administrative backing. At the same time, the student must be treated fairly. Two factors may facilitate resolution. First, school rules and regulations covering many disruptive student behaviors should be estab-

lished. They should be written out and made known to teachers and students. Knowing the consequences of infractions places the responsibility on the student and maintains a sense of fairness.

Second, controversial areas must be discussed by administrators and teachers. Teachers, for example, vary tremendously in how much classroom noise they permit. In such cases, each teacher must resolve any potential conflict with the principal. In any cases of discrepancy between the principal and teacher, the possibility always exists that students will get caught in the middle. The principal's leadership ability should circumvent this as often as possible. It is a difficult but necessary task for the principal to define and actively maintain an optimal balance.

Teaching and the Exercise of Control

Mrs. Banister is the art teacher in a small town high school with about four hundred students. She teaches five sections of art each day, consisting mostly of freshmen and sophomores, although she does have one advanced class of juniors and seniors. Now sixty-eight years old, Mrs. Banister has been teaching since she was twenty, and everyone is looking forward to her fiftieth anniversary (seventieth birthday) and an already announced retirement.

Mrs. Banister advocates self-expression. She does not believe teachers should control students and feels that students can be creative only if they have the opportunity to express themselves. She strongly believes that students should not be treated like "animals" and has on several occasions criticized behaviorism as a means of student control, both intellectually and physically.

In spite of Mrs. Banister's beliefs, her behavior toward students often betrays her. She has a basic mistrust of adolescents and a tendency to accuse students unjustifiably of inappropriate behavior. For example, she makes a ritual of getting everyone's attention, putting her purse in her desk, locking her desk, and telling everyone to be quiet when she has to leave the classroom. When she returns, she unlocks her desk, takes out her purse, and goes through it to see if anything is missing.

On more than one occasion, she has accused her students of breaking into her desk and taking things out of her purse when she was out of the room. Mrs. Banister's ritual became a source of aggravation for many students and a way to play jokes on her and keep her upset. One day the joke backfired. Three boys decided to fake breaking into her desk. They succeeded in setting the trap for accusation.

As a result of Mrs. Banister's persistence, the three boys admitted to the behavior in order to see what she would do. Her punishment was totally unexpected. She took the three fifteen-year-old boys into the hallway, discussed their "sinful act," told them God would punish them for it, and had them get down on their knees while she prayed for their forgiveness.

The superintendent and the principal received phone calls from irate parents. Upon being questioned, Mrs. Banister proclaimed that the aim of education is to teach students morality; thus, she was unable to tolerate such student behavior. As you might

imagine, she also often disapproved of the content of students' art. There was no resolution. The principal only warned Mrs. Banister not to let such a thing happen again. The superintendent, principal, parents, and students were probably all praying for the next two years to pass rapidly.

What do you think?

1. How effective do you think Mrs. Banister's strategy was in reducing disruptive behavior in her classroom?

2. Do you think Mrs. Banister modeled the feeling of distrust or is it more likely that the students would dismiss her as an "old fogey" or "senile"?

3. Should school boards take action on teachers who display such behavior, even to the point of dismissal?

Behavior modification
The direct application of learning
principles with the expressed intent
to alter behavior.

Behavior modification is an attempt to apply the general principles of learning in order to achieve desired changes in an individual's behavior. Although behavior modification procedures vary considerably according to the types of behavioral problems they deal with, all such techniques usually share the following characteristics:

1. They seek to change only those responses that are observable or measurable.
2. They require specification of the particular behavioral goal.
3. They require detailed specification of the probable conditions responsible for the response that is to be changed or introduced.
4. They involve continual data collection to assess the effect (the success) of the modification.

For an in-depth discussion of the technical aspects of behavior modification and for literature on the modification of markedly deviant behaviors, see Bandura (1969), Rimm and Masters (1974), Sulzer-Azaroff and Mayer (1977), and Wolpe (1969).

Strategies

Most social behaviors are controlled by their effect on the environment. Walking, talking, and book-writing behaviors are not directly elicited by stimuli; they are emitted in hope of some favorable consequences. Such behavior is called operant behavior (see Chapter 2). It is acquired, modified, or eliminated as a result of events that follow it.

In discussing operant conditioning and behavior in terms of its modification, we must briefly reconsider reinforcement and punishment. *Reinforcement* is the stimulus event that when presented immediately following a response, increases the probability of that response occurring again in the same or a similar situation. *Punishment* is the identical process that accounts for decreasing the probability of a response. In *positive reinforcement,* the strength of a response is increased as a result of the behavior being followed by a stimulus presentation (the reinforcer). *Negative reinforcement* increases the probability of a response as a result of the behavior being followed by the removal or avoidance of a stimulus. Punishment can take two forms. It may be the infliction of a painful experience, such as spanking, sarcasm, or ridicule, or it may be taking away something the student likes, such as a loss of privilege. In most cases, punishment tends to create aversive attitudes and conflict problems between the teacher and the student; thus, most educators reject it as a viable alternative for behavior modification.

Methods of Response Management

Reinforcement theorists use the term *reinforcement* to mean any consequences that increase the likelihood of a behavior occurring. Because individuals differ from one another, and even within themselves from situation to situation, the effects of reinforcement vary greatly, especially when applied in a group setting. This has led to the interpretation that all reinforcers should be contingent upon the student emitting the correct response.

Operant Extinction   Any response that has been established through reinforcement may be reduced and eventually eliminated by **operant extinction.** In this procedure, the reinforcement for the undesirable response is discontinued, effecting a gradual (or, in some cases, rapid) reduction in the strength of that behavior. For example, a child who continuously whines because whining has been reinforced by attention from his or her mother will eventually stop the behavior if the parent never again attends to the whining. Similarly, a teacher who feels that disapproving attention may be maintaining some disruptive behavior from a student might eliminate that behavior by changing his or her response to one of neutral recognition. If, in fact, the student was being reinforced by the teacher's disapproving looks, the replacement of the disapproving look with a noncommittal one may reduce the undesirable behavior.

Operant extinction
The purposeful withholding of any reinforcing event that has previously established or maintained an undesirable behavior.

    The problem in applying operant extinction procedures is the difficulty of identifying or isolating the reinforcer. Many behaviors are reinforced by a number of different events. Even when the probable reinforcer is identifiable, as in the case of children who cry when put to bed until mother comes in and holds them, extinction is difficult to employ. In such cases, it might be more effective simply to substitute (**countercondition**) a different type of response (such as turning on a bedside lamp) rather than attempt to make no response at all.

Counterconditioning
The substitution of one response for another in order to alter behavior.

Shaping   In many cases, when a teacher desires to instill an appropriate behavior by applying reinforcement, the desired behavior may not exist in the student's repertoire. How can a behavior be reinforced if it does not exist? One possibility is to reinforce an existing behavior that most closely approximates the desired behavior. Then, as the strength of the response increases, only closer and closer approximations of the desired terminal behavior are reinforced. This procedure is known as *shaping*—the application of differential reinforcement to successive approximations of a desired response (Skinner, 1953).

    Shaping could be used in the classroom to teach a child to raise his or her hand and be recognized by the teacher before talking. First, the teacher should avoid recognizing the student when he or she speaks in class without first raising his or her hand (extinction). Second, the teacher should reinforce any of the student's behavior that approximates the teacher's expectation. Shaping can be a slow and laborious procedure, but it can be facilitated by coupling it with other procedures, such as verbal instruction.

Reinforcement of Competing Responses   **Competing responses** are responses that cannot occur at the same time. You cannot stand up and sit down at the same time. Because competing responses cannot coexist, if one of them is increased in strength, the other must decrease. Therefore, if a response that competes with an unwanted behavior can be

Competing responses
The presentation of two or more response options, only one of which is possible to perform prior to a reinforcer.

identified and increased by positive reinforcement, the unwanted response will decrease. In an educational setting, the behavior that most logically competes with undesired behavior is that of doing academic work. Classroom behavioral problems often disappear when a child's academic efforts are put under a reinforcement program.

Brown and Elliott (1965) report a practical application of the combination of operant extinction and reinforcing competing responses. They dramatically reduced physical and verbal aggressive behavior for twenty-seven male nursery school students by having the teacher ignore (whenever possible) any occurrence of physical aggression and provide positive reinforcement (attention, praise) for cooperative, nonaggressive behavior.

Token Economy Systems Another type of reinforcing procedure especially effective for students who are unresponsive to "regular" school reinforcers is the *token economy system*. It involves using reinforcers that are originally neutral but that acquire strength when they are established as stimuli for responses leading to existing backup reinforcers. These include intangibles, such as privileges, or tangibles, such as money, food, and toys.

Initially, a token system involves selecting certain behaviors (academic tasks, appropriate social acts, and so on) and assigning them a value in tokens (such as poker chips, checkmarks, gold stars, or play money). A procedure is then set up whereby the student may "cash in" accumulated tokens for the existing backup reinforcers. The advantages of a token system are that it uses a reinforcer (the token) that (1) can be quickly and easily delivered following an appropriate response, (2) will not lose its effect as long as the backup reinforcers are desirable, (3) can be applied to a variety of appropriate behaviors, and (4) provides a way of reinforcing students for whom recognition and praise are not effective reinforcers.

Phillips (1968; Phillips, Phillips, Fixsen, & Wolf, 1971) used a rather elaborate token system in modifying social behavior with a group of predelinquent boys in a home-type environment. They utilized scorecard points, supported by backup reinforcers (privileges, activities, tangible goods) to change a variety of behaviors, including schoolwork, personal habits, swearing, and neatness. An interesting aspect of this program was that the boys did all their own record keeping, adding points for appropriate behaviors and subtracting points for rule infractions.

Token economies are a useful way to increase academic and social behaviors when nothing else has worked. Thus, within the context of school, the teacher must develop a functional exchange system. If students are allowed to earn many tokens but not convert them into something desirable or usable, after a while, the token economy loses its strength as a reinforcer (Baer & Sherman, 1969). If tokens can be converted into free time, extended play periods, special privileges, or field trips, then students are more likely to maintain learning or modify a behavior in order to gain the reinforcement. An example comes from a middle school in Florida where teachers wanted to reduce the incidence of gum chewing, restroom abuse, and talking at inappropriate times among the seventh-grade students (Hall & Phelps, 1979). Students were able to earn a field trip at the end of a five-week period. Those students who had six violations of these three behaviors within the five-week period would remain in class on field trip day. Students were not reprimanded verbally. Rather, teachers kept a record of violations, which students could monitor by coming to the teacher's desk. Table 14–4 demonstrates how this simple procedure was

Intangible reinforcers
Application of reinforcers, such as free time or special privileges, following a student behavior.

Tangible reinforcers
Application of reinforcers, such as food or money, following a student behavior.

Table 14–4   Incidence of First Group Misbehaviors

Week	Chewing Gum		Restroom Abuse		Talking While the Teacher Was Talking	
I	118	100%	53	100%	168	100%
II	93	78%	34	64%	127	69%
III	61	52%	17	32%	83	50%
IV	38	32%	20	37%	60	45%
V	29	24%	7	13%	32	19%
VI	36	30%	16	30%	44	26%

Identifying Behavioral Change Reinforcers

Match each of the following reinforcers with its appropriate category.

_____ 1. Candy
_____ 2. Checkmarks
_____ 3. Erase the blackboard
_____ 4. Extra recess time
_____ 5. Food
_____ 6. Free time
_____ 7. Gold stars
_____ 8. Grade on paper
_____ 9. Industrial tour
_____ 10. Money
_____ 11. Praise
_____ 12. Prizes
_____ 13. Run errand
_____ 14. Run movie projector
_____ 15. S & H Green Stamps
_____ 16. Teacher recognition
_____ 17. Trip to zoo

A. Backup Reinforcer
B. Intangible Reinforcer
C. Tangible Reinforcer

instrumental in significantly reducing inappropriate behavior. You will observe that at week six the incidence of inappropriate behavior rose slightly. At the beginning of this week, the first school day following the field trip, the teachers started new record-keeping. Thus, the effect was to temporarily increase the behaviors. However, if weeks one and six are compared, it is easier to see how effective the token economy system was in reducing inappropriate student behavior.

Response cost
Taking away part of a reinforcement that has already been earned through previous behavior.

Response Cost In **response cost,** something a person has already received or earned is taken away. It is the withdrawal of a reinforcer (or part of a reinforcer). When an inappropriate behavior occurs, the withdrawal of an already earned reinforcer has been a useful strategy to stop or alter behavior. A parent may give a child an allowance at the beginning of each week and take back ten cents every time the child leaves clothes on the floor. Parents may give an adolescent use of the family car twice a week and take it away on any subsequent occasion if curfew has been violated. A teacher may give points to students who always ask for permission to sharpen their pencils and take back points when a student sharpens a pencil without first asking for permission.

Response cost may seem to be the same as punishment, but although it is an aversive procedure, it differs from punishment in that the event that follows the undesired response is withdrawing a reinforcer. Punishment adds something aversive, such as teacher reprimand.

For example, a teacher may establish the rule that there will be absolutely no talking when students are taking a test. Bill inadvertently breaks a pencil lead and asks another student for a pencil. The teacher notices Bill's behavior. How can he handle this situation? In using response cost, he could deduct points from the final score on Bill's test. In using punishment, the teacher might do several things. First, he could verbally reprimand Bill while the test is in progress. Second, he could have Bill hand in the test at that point and base the grade on the number correct to the point when he was disruptive. Third, the teacher could automatically give Bill a zero on the test. Fourth, the teacher could send Bill to the principal's office. Let us assume in this case that the teacher gave Bill a zero. Figure 14-1 illustrates this.

In situations like this, teachers often do not know what the student is actually doing. Although Bill's request was not test related, the teacher may have thought Bill was seeking an answer. In Chapter 2, I talked about *time out* as another reinforcement strategy. If the teacher used time out here instead of response cost, he would move Bill to another part of the room or away from other students, thus taking away the opportunity for him to talk. This presumably would reduce the likelihood of Bill's talking to others, whatever the reason, in subsequent testing situations. The use of time out in this instance is also illustrated in Figure 14-1.

Response cost strategies have proven to be very effective in producing behavioral change (Abrhamson & Crocker, 1978; Kazdin, 1973). Their success depends on two primary factors, however. First, the teacher must use a token economy system. Obviously, if there are no reinforcers for the teacher to take away, the strategy is inoperable. Second, students need to have a reinforcement reserve prior to using the strategy. In response cost, the idea is not to withdraw reinforcement until you deplete the supply (tokens). Rather, it is the withholding that creates incentive for the student to behave differently. If students can cash in accumulated tokens for special privileges or objects, these tokens are highly prized. Pulling away prized reinforcers provides strong incentives for change.

Premack Principle Premack's (1959, 1965) animal and human research established that, when a response that is less likely to occur (low frequency) is paired with a response that is more likely to occur (high frequency), the likelihood of the low frequency response recurring is increased. Arranging such learning events is quite simple. A teacher identifies an activity that a student enjoys and makes the participation of that activity contingent upon first performing a less desired activity. Essentially, the teacher arranges learning within the classroom by using the preferred activity to motivate students to perform the less preferred activity.

If a teacher has a science filmstrip that illustrates some pages within the text, she may observe that students prefer learning from the filmstrip to reading the book. However, if the filmstrip is designed to supplement the book, the teacher will hold the position that reading the text first, followed by the filmstrip, is the way to maximize learning. From time to time, students may implore the teacher to show them the filmstrip first. Using Premack's findings, the text (less desired activity) would be read prior to observing the filmstrip (more desired activity). The teacher who shows the

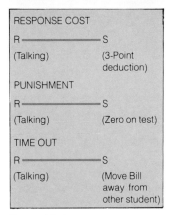

RESPONSE COST

R ——————— S
(Talking)   (3-Point deduction)

PUNISHMENT

R ——————— S
(Talking)   (Zero on test)

TIME OUT

R ——————— S
(Talking)   (Move Bill away from other student)

Figure 14-1
Student disruption during an exam

filmstrip first may increase the likelihood that the students will not read the text and will base their comprehension of the text upon what they saw rather than on what they read.

This principle has been demonstrated to be effective in working with people on an individual basis (Homme, 1966; Homme, DeBaca, Devine, Steinhorst, & Rickert, 1963; Hosie, Gentile, & Carroll, 1974). Whether it is academic or social behavior, determining what a student enjoys doing and pairing another behavior that occurs with less frequency is an effective way to increase the less frequent activity. Study time-play time, homework-television, and vegetables-dessert are all dichotomous types of things that, when arranged properly, can increase the likelihood of the less frequent response occurring.

In light of the discussion in this chapter, a desirable reinforcer for classroom use would be one that (1) is effective for a particular child, (2) can be delivered quickly, (3) is economical for the teacher in cost and time, and (4) is a natural part of the classroom environment. Special duties (such as taking roll, leading the flag salute, taking messages to other rooms, being a crossing guard, and feeding the fish) or preferred positions (such as committee chair, lunch-line leader, and captain of recess games) have all been used effectively as reinforcers in specific cases. Perhaps students are the most useful source. Ask them what activity or privilege is most reinforcing. In one case where a potential reinforcer had been tried unsuccessfully, the child, when asked, indicated that a powerful reinforcer would be to pick up trash from the playground (Moore, 1969). When ten minutes of this activity was made contingent on the desired behavioral change, the strength of that new behavior increased rapidly.

Behavioral Self-Management

One outcome of students' educational experiences should be the capacity to regulate or control their own behavior, which they learn by interacting with other students and teachers in formal and informal contexts. The student who may not shove another student in the classroom because of fear of teacher reprimand (external control) should learn that such behavior is not any more appropriate in the hallway. When the student learns that it is the behavior, and not its consequences, that determines whether it will or will not occur, then self-control is being exercised.

Although some self-control is learned incidentally, most is learned when a purposeful attempt is made to modify behavior. Mahoney and Thorensen (1972) have stated that **self-control** involves (1) describing the behavior one wishes to increase or decrease, (2) identifying the stimulus that precedes a behavior and the consequences that follow, and (3) changing the antecedent stimulus and/or consequences. Self-control is the person's use of behavior modification principles to change his or her own behaviors.

If a person is to exercise self-control, he or she must be aware of

Self-control
The individual use of any behavior modification principle to change personal behavior.

personal behavior and recognize that some aspects of such behavior need to be changed. Mahoney and Thorensen (1972) describe this as self-observation. A person must act upon personal awareness, placing himself or herself in a different situation or changing expectancies. Another change process is evaluating the consequences of personal behavior and altering them or the behavior so that the consequences are no longer reinforcing (Rimm & Masters, 1974). Evaluating the relationship between behavior and its consequences is very important in the change process.

Teachers often must help students identify misbehavior and select an appropriate alternative response. Although many students are aware that their behavior is not acceptable to either themselves or their teacher, they may not know what their options are. Gagné (1975, p. 29) suggests the following strategies for classroom teachers:

1. Describe the misbehavior clearly so students know exactly what they have been doing. Be sure students have just as clear a picture of what they should do instead.

2. Ask students to count the times they break the rule and note what happens just before and right after the misbehavior.

3. Help students change the stimuli that come just before the misbehavior and punish themselves immediately afterward.

4. Ask students to count and record the times they do the preferred action and reward themselves immediately afterward.

5. By explaining the principles and using many illustrations, help students learn this general sequence for other situations calling for self-control.

Although these suggestions are useful in producing change, two additional factors heavily influence behavior. First, self-control procedures are more easily implemented early in the response pattern. This is consistent with the conept of extinction. The earlier a teacher helps the student identify a misbehavior, the more likely it will be alterable. Second, the teacher must help a student select a response alternative that is feasible and falls within the student's response capability. The more unrealistic or stringent the alternative, the less likely behavior is to change. The psychodynamics between a teacher and a student during episodes of misbehavior often result in guilt. To compensate for such feelings, students may make unrealistic promises or set unachievable alternatives. It requires teacher awareness and sensitivity to students to neutralize this effect so that guilt-free and achievable alternatives are explored.

Contingency Contracts

A practical strategy for self-control is a behavioral contract between a student and a teacher wherein the student receives approval for achieving specific tasks within the contract. The reinforcers are always contingent upon the student fulfilling mutually agreed upon components within the contract (Homme, Csanyi, Gonzales, & Rechs, 1970).

Homme et al. (1970) suggest that reinforcers should be immediate and come early in the contract so the learner experiences an immediate sense of fulfillment. They also suggest using the shaping technique wherein each success builds progressively toward total contract fulfillment.

It is particularly important to use reinforcement only when the expected (agreed upon) behavior is emitted. The teacher who says, "You can spend ten more minutes on your special project; then you must finish your grammar assignment" is putting the reinforcer before the behavior and violating the terms of the contract.

As Homme et al. (1970) have stressed, the contract must be fair and clear, written in such a way that neither the student nor the teacher can violate it. Within behavior management, contract violations render the effort ineffective and minimize the chances of producing desired change.

Contingency contracts are good ways to modify student behavior because they are designed around positive contingencies and they are mutually developed by the student and the teacher. Sometimes it is to the teacher's advantage to have parents involved in a contract as well.

Contracts should focus specifically on the desired behavior change area, the ways for change to occur, the consequence for the student as a result of change, and the conditions under which the contract is fulfilled. They should be void of irrelevant behaviors or conditions.

Contracts offer a strong alternative to punishment or discipline because they increase the individual's behavioral capacity while they modify undesirable behavior. The following contract is an example of what a classroom teacher can do.

Alexander was a disruptive student who fought at school every time he did not get his way or became frustrated. Ms. Greene, his third-grade teacher, met with Alexander and his parents and explained why this behavior was unacceptable to her within her classroom. The parents and teacher agreed that Alexander should stop his fighting in the school environment. Although initially reluctant to go along with his parents and teacher, after continued discussion Alexander agreed with Ms. Greene that he would work on his behavior. Ms. Greene developed a jigsaw puzzle that contained twelve pieces. This puzzle was made of construction paper and, once the twelve pieces came together, it ended up in a multicolored, meaningful picture. She knew that Alexander loved animals; so she constructed a picture of a scene at the zoo. As Alexander's behavior improved, he was allowed to paste one of the pieces of the puzzle on some corkboard. Once he had completed the puzzle, he was entitled to a special event (reward). As a bonus, Ms. Greene said she would let Alexander frame his puzzle and put it up in the classroom for one month. They sat down and mutually developed the following contract:

Date: _____

Contract No: _____

Ms. Greene will give Alexander a piece of the jigsaw puzzle each time he does one of the following:

1. Comes into the classroom, hangs up his coat, and takes his seat without causing any disturbance in the morning.
2. Stands in lunch line and eats his lunch without annoying or fighting with any other student.
3. Participates in morning and afternoon recesses without fighting with any other student.
4. Puts away his school things, straightens his desk, and gets on the bus without fighting with anyone.

When Alexander has completed his puzzle, he may choose any one of the following rewards:

1. Collect milk money in the morning for the teacher for one week
2. Be first in line for lunch for one week
3. Read a story aloud in class
4. Be hall monitor for passing to and from recesses for three days
5. Have one hour to spend in the library as free time
6. Choose to play an academic game with a friend
7. Run an errand for the teacher to the school office
8. Erase the board for the teacher for one week

Alexander may frame his puzzle and place it in the room once he has completed his selected activity.

I, Alexander, agree to the above statements. I also agree that my selected behavior will be discontinued if I am arguing or fighting with anyone while the activity is going on.

Alexander Verdi

THIS CONTRACT IS TERMINATED ONCE ALL THE CONDITIONS WITHIN IT HAVE BEEN MET.

Annotated Readings

Cairns, L. (1981). Classroom management and discipline: An alternative model to "survival" courses. *South Pacific Journal of Teacher Education, 9*, 22–28.

> *The author presents a model for more effective preservice instruction on classroom management and student discipline. He focuses on effective management, which includes teacher awareness, group focus, and clear direction of the teaching-learning task, and pupil disruption and the strategies teachers can use to correct it. The article presents a positive perspective to more effective classroom environments and behavioral management.*

Connis, R. T., & Dwinell, M. A. (1981). An evaluation of response maintenance with self-monitoring procedures. *Behavioral Engineering, 7*, 45–49.

> *The authors evaluated self-monitoring as a method of treatment to determine its effects on the response maintenance of a retarded adult. Extended time periods of self-monitoring for on-time task completion were probed for maintenance by removing treatment for a few days at a time. Results of two maintenance probes suggested that the one-time task completion behavior the subject learned would not maintain in the absence of self-monitoring. The need for maintenance programming and self-monitoring seemed apparent.*

Kazdin, A. E. (1982). The token economy: A decade later. *Journal of Applied Behavioral Analysis, 15*, 431–445.

> *This is a review of how token economy systems have changed across the 1970s. They have been extended widely across populations and behaviors in treatment, rehabilitation, educational, and community settings. This article discusses recent advances in research and reviews progress on major issues surrounding token economies. The demands for maintaining the integrity of treatment, the ability to integrate token economies within existing institutional constraints, and the ability to disseminate the procedures on a large scale are major issues that will continue to influence the future of token economy use.*

Miller, A. J., & Kratochwill, T. R. (1979). Reduction of frequent stomachache complaints by time out. *Behavior Therapy, 10*, 211–218.

> *Time out was employed to treat a ten-year-old girl's report of stomach pains at home and at school. Time out involved removing the girl from adult attention and activities for verbal pain episodes. Pain complaint episodes were treated sequentially across home and school environments. The treatment rapidly reduced pain over both settings. A one-year follow-up indicated there were no further problems with stomach pain episodes.*

Thomas, J. W. (1980). Agency and achievement: Self-management and self-regard. *Review of Educational Research, 50*, 213–240.

> *A research review and a discussion of the interrelationship of student self-management behaviors, academic motivation, and basic skills achievement are presented. Results from recent training studies in self-management, attribution, and achievement motivation are presented as providing important qualifications for the view that basic skills instruction requires teacher control and structure. It is concluded that giving students some degree of control over their learning and some sense of responsibility for their successes and failures can result in the continued disposition to achieve.*

Wolpe, J. (1981). Behavior therapy versus psychoanalysis: Therapeutic and social implications. *American Psychologist, 36,* 159–164.

This article compares the public images of psychoanalysis and behavior therapy as contrasting therapy approaches. Wolpe suggests that behavior therapy has been presented as "inhuman" treatment, and he attempts to correct these misperceptions. He also draws attention to the suffering imposed on many by years of psychoanalysis. This is an interesting article to evaluate and compare major behavioral change systems.

Assessing Behavior

Preview

It was just after Thanksgiving break when Mr. Watkins, the Lincoln Middle School principal, called a conference to discuss the academic and behavioral progress of Freddie Conners, a seventh-grade student. He called the conference because of severe disparities in Freddie's grades at the end of the first nine weeks, his excessive absence from school, and too frequent referrals to the principal's office. All of Freddie's teachers, Ms. Mizan, the counselor, and the principal attended the conference.

Mr. Watkins first reported Freddie's grades to the group: Language Arts, "C—"; Math, "A"; Science, "F"; Social Studies, "D"; Physical Education, "D"; and Industrial Arts, "B". He reported that Freddie was absent one out of every three school days.

Mr. Watkins asked Ms. Mizan to provide the group with standardized testing data. She reported that Freddie's scores on the Iowa Tests of Basic Skills (taken in October of this school year) ranged from the sixtieth percentile in science to the ninety-second percentile in math. His overall battery was the eighty-first percentile. The Otis Quick-Scoring intelligence test, which was administered in the fifth grade, was the most recent group IQ test Freddie had taken. His IQ score was 97 on that test. However, Ms. Mizan had administered the Wechsler Intelligence Scale for Children-Revised (WISC-R) the week before Thanksgiving in order to get a more recent IQ measure on Freddie. The WISC-R is an individual intelligence test that yields a verbal and performance IQ as well as an overall score. Freddie's scores were verbal IQ, 117; performance IQ, 129; overall IQ, 121.

After the information was provided, Mr. Watkins asked the teachers to discuss why these discrepancies were occurring and some possible solutions to the problem. Several comments followed, with the explanations generally falling into one of three areas.

Mr. Kohl said that Freddie did quite well in math class, was attentive, and always completed assignments. The science teacher indicated just the opposite. An individual's general reasoning ability should indicate closer performance between math and science. However, Mr. Kohl was a 6-foot-4-inch, 280-pound man who appeared intimidating to most junior high students. Ms. Mizan suggested that this might be a critical factor in Freddie's behavior. The subject in which Freddie did best, other than math, was industrial arts. Mr. Segabarth did not cite any particular behaviors that contributed to Freddie's *grade, although he thought Freddie would have received an "A" if his attendance had been better.*

After considerable discussion, there was consensus that Freddie was better in performance or manipulative skills than in verbal skills. This consensus is partly supported by Freddie's performance IQ score on the WISC-R, where he exceeded nearly 98 percent of his peers.

The third focus of discussion concerned Freddie's attendance, attitudes, and self-direction or discipline. His grade was low in language arts because he never made up missed assignments. In physical education, grades were affected by attendance. Further, Mr. Kenny indicated that Freddie would fail to bring his gym clothes or shoes and, as a result, often could not participate as he should. The social studies teacher concluded that "Freddie uses my class to dream in." In all, each teacher thought Freddie could do better if he were more motivated and interested in what was going on.

Individuals like Freddie are common in school environments. He is moving toward adolescence, changing schools, and exploring new situations and ideas. Conferences are often necessary and should result in strategies that teachers can use to alter undesirable and maintain desirable behavior. In Freddie's case, Ms. Mizan decided to talk to each teacher about ways for Freddie to improve his behavior in his or her classroom, followed by a conference with Freddie. What did seem clear, however, was that ability was not as much of a factor in Freddie's academic behaviors as was his interest in school.

Such conferences and discussions are often part of a teacher's work load. Teachers should know how to interpret, if not how to use, behavior assessment techniques. Key concepts in this chapter include:

- *Measurement practices and problems*
- *Intelligence testing*
- *Planning for a test*
- *Test item selection*
- *Criterion-referenced or norm-referenced measurement*

Measurement Practices and Problems

The learning process is a complex array of forces acting on and interacting with the student, with the end result of a change in behavior (intellectual, affective, or psychomotor) in the direction of the educational objectives established by the instructor. **Measurement** is an attempt to describe quantitatively the behavior or, more specifically, the change of behavior. Many believe it is impossible to quantify human behavior and argue that paper and pencil tests are artificial, removed from learning, psychologically stressful (because of student fear and misuse of test results), and noninterpretable. But some level of either qualitative or quantitative assessment of behavioral change is necessary for the individual and society, because both positive and corrective feed-

Measurement
The quantitative assessment (objective) of behavior.

back (praise and redirection) are necessary to learning. Each person needs to know how well he or she is doing compared to others. Thus, measurement is an essential part of the learning process.

By definition, the term *measurement* is restricted to quantitative assessment in which ordinal numbers are applied to data. *Ordinal numbers* indicate rank order only, as opposed to numbers that indicate categories or numbers that assume equal interval units, as found on rulers. The item or person that is rated highest is given the rank of one, the second highest, the rank of two, and so on. Usually, qualitative assessment is closely tied to **evaluation,** which is a more comprehensive term than *measurement.* Evaluation is measurement plus a value judgment; the teacher makes decisions about the degree of "goodness" or "importance" of certain behavioral changes as a result of careful study of all the available data. Most of these evaluative data are also quantitative in nature—the teacher may even quantify feelings about a student in an attempt to make that data compatible with other measurement information. Grading systems are simply translations of these often complex evaluations into meaningful symbols.

Evaluation
The qualitative assessment (subjective) of behavior.

At all levels of education, the determination and the meaning of marks have become serious issues. Today there is pressure from students, teachers, school boards, and state legislators to create real and meaningful learning situations that are evaluated in real and meaningful ways.

Educational Levels

Elementary School In addition to teaching basic skills, elementary school teachers are directly involved with the social development of the child in the classroom. They must plan activities to encourage group interaction in games as well as in work projects and change these activities frequently to keep the children interested. They must often subtly cloak academic training within a game setting. Attention spans are relatively short; so there are few lectures of any length. There is constant oral communication between teacher and student and between the child and other students. Teachers face the problem of trying to react constructively to several active, boisterous, and inquisitive youngsters at the same time. When the children are neglected, or when proper individual attention is temporarily or permanently denied, behavioral problems of various kinds may result. What about the resulting measurement problems? How can teachers quantify accurately all the behaviors they observe, measure the academic and social changes, and then make the required evaluations?

Because of the nature of the elementary school curricula, teachers prepare only a limited number of written tests. Instead, the tests are printed and standardized by test companies or come from workbooks. Scoring may be done by the test company for the former and by simple totals or percentages for the latter. Exact translation of these scores into letter grades is seldom expected or requested in most elementary schools. Some schools still use a marking system and send home the traditional

report card, but many more employ periodic oral or written progress reports that provide general aptitude test scores, grade-level achievement scores, averages from work sheets in various areas (word skills, fractions, social studies, and so on), analyses of sociograms, and miscellaneous comments related to behavioral patterns. Therefore, the major problems of trying to reduce a complex array of observations and data to a single meaningful mark is eliminated.

These progress reports have proven to be a very time-consuming procedure for the teacher, but they are also rewarding in that parents have an opportunity to learn much more about their children's school activities and learning progress than a single series of marks could possibly convey. Likewise, the teachers have a chance to listen to the parents' concerns and reports of specific home experiences, which, in turn, help the teacher better understand each child's total learning environment. Of course, parent-teacher conferences are also found, on a somewhat more limited scale, in those schools that retain the traditional, more formal marking and report card system.

It would seem, then, that, with this increasingly popular progress report system, the needs for communication of results of student learning to parents and for simpler and more flexible evaluative procedures for grade school teachers are being successfully met. There will always be the continuing debate about whether parents should be told aptitude scores and how precise teachers should be in reporting test scores or percentiles. Nevertheless, the children quickly learn how they are doing in the various subjects; they know who is best, second best, and worst in arithmetic, spelling, and baseball. Competition is keen. Children also sense within themselves and through the reactions of peers, teachers, and parents when they are learning more quickly or more thoroughly than others.

Secondary School   In the secondary school, a different set of problems and needs must be met in the evaluation procedures. First, the curriculum is more subject oriented than at the elementary level, and the measurement and evaluation procedures must be more precise. Second, students are taught and evaluated by many different people, instead of one teacher. Although the school system may try to encourage some form of consistency in measuring and evaluating student progress, there is inevitably a divergence of thought and approaches among the various teachers. Third, the use of teacher-made tests is much higher in secondary schools, even though publisher-prepared achievement tests and workbook drills are used. In some secondary schools, there is also an attempt to measure such behaviors as pleasantness, cooperativeness, promptness, interest, and attendance—usually summarized in a separate mark for "citizenship." A single mark that represents this composite of academic work and social behavior is always rather difficult to measure and interpret. The better procedure is to give separate marks for the two main areas of academic and social behavior.

Because testing is more frequent in high school, and quarterly grade reports to students and parents are generally part of the evaluative procedure, high school students frequently become preoccupied with grades and begin to value them above learning. Teachers may contribute to this preoccupation because of their need for a precise evaluation of achievement. Grades are especially emphasized for those students following the college preparatory programs, because competition for college entrance and scholarships is keen. The fact that high school grades (or rank in class, which is based directly on those grades) predict college success only about 25 percent of the time suggests that there are other important aspects of high school achievement that are either not being measured or that are being measured inadequately.

Being able to make effective testing instruments is one of the most important skills for high school teachers to acquire. Because of the time-consuming nature of test preparation, it is often given much less attention than is required. Teachers frequently consider tests necessary evils and prepare and give them without sufficient thought to their contribution to students' total learning experience. The general result is that students acquire negative feelings about the abstractness and artificiality of tests and grading procedures, and teachers often make judgments from tests that do not really measure established educational objectives.

College At the college level, courses and evaluative procedures and standards are as individually different as the professors who teach them. The majority of classroom tests are teacher made and tend to be as sophisticated and effective as the professor's understanding of the subject matter. Indeed, professors are characteristically known by their tests rather than by their teaching.

Grades themselves are often given more emphasis at the college level because survival is at stake. Doing poorly or flunking out has very significant social implications. Many college teachers and administrators who are concerned about the inequities and negative effects of this emphasis are attending workshops and seminars on improving assessment techniques. In addition, some colleges are experimenting with alternative grading systems that range from the very simple pass-fail to a complex grade-point system. Others are attempting to do without grades entirely by merely certifying completion of academic programs. The problems that arise from these different systems are mostly in the articulation of student achievement to other schools. Colleges that institute new approaches to evaluation must deal with the question of their responsibility in giving qualitative evaluations to other colleges, graduate schools, and employers.

Test Types

Standardized Tests   Both teachers and counselors in the public schools commonly use standardized aptitude and achievement tests. The word *standardized* refers to a professional test developed by a publisher and usually accompanied by a set of norms that helps the teacher interpret student scores by comparing them with the scores of many other similar students. The primary advantage of using **standardized tests** is that they are developed by experts to measure common educational objectives. They are most useful when measuring or comparing student progress across an extended time frame, such as a semester or school year. Many teachers feel they can rely more on the completeness and fairness of the score results of such tests than they could on their own tests. The test publishers also stress the **reliability** and **validity** of their tests—that is, how accurately and consistently the tests measure the objectives. Two other advantages of standardized tests are the fact that comparative scores are available to aid in the interpretation of students' scores and that most test publishers offer scoring services, which relieve teachers of the burden of correcting papers and transforming scores into meaningful charts or percentiles.

There are also some disadvantages to using standardized tests. One is that the objectives that teachers want to measure may not be included in any standardized test. Another is that the tests may cover topics that were not included in a subject-matter area. It is rather difficult to tailor a standardized test to fit a particular learning situation. A teacher who wants to approach certain subject areas differently from the standardized test has little choice but to devise his or her own testing instrument. There is always the temptation for the teacher to give professionally made tests, regardless of the particular classroom situation, because these tests remove the burden of item writing and scoring for the teacher. However,

Standardized test
A test that compares students on its norms regardless of the school or location in which the test is taken.

Reliability
The dependability or consistency of a test upon repeated administration.

Validity
The extent to which a test actually measures what it was designed to measure.

standardized tests that do not relate directly to educational objectives are likely to be *invalid* measures of the student learning. For this reason, score results from standardized achievement tests should not be used to determine student grades. Teachers and counselors should use the results primarily for diagnostic purposes and academic counseling. This is true for aptitude and intelligence tests. My discussion of standardized intelligence tests later in this chapter demonstrates the purpose for which they were designed.

Despite these limitations and problems, the standardized achievement test does have an important role to play in education. It is helpful to teachers at the end of each year for evaluating students' general progress, and it is useful to both the teacher and the school administrator in evaluating the effectiveness of the school's curricula. Comparing ability or intelligence scores with achievement scores will also help teachers and counselors diagnose learning difficulties of students.

Teachers should acquaint themselves thoroughly with reliability, validity, and normative data in test manuals. In addition, school systems should consider the development of their own local norms from year to year for comparison with the national norms found in test manuals. Local norms may be preferred over national norms because they have more direct interpretive value for a specific school or community. The following section focuses on standardized intelligence tests because they are stressed so heavily in schools and regarded so highly nationally. This section will address the structure of such tests and how students are comparatively measured on them. Limitations of such tests will also be reviewed.

Measurement of Intelligence

The number and variety of concepts and definitions of intelligence are reflected in the plethora of intelligence tests that are available. Buros' *Tests in Print* (1974) lists around 280 standardized tests of intelligence or scholastic ability. Not each of these has an individualized definition of intelligence, of course, but, still, such a large number of different tests indicates the often bewildering array of conceptual possibilities for measuring intellectual capability.

Single-Factor Tests

Single-factor tests
An intelligence test designed around one single human trait or characteristic, usually verbal ability.

Individual intelligence test
An IQ test specifically designed to be orally administered to people on an individual basis.

The **single-factor theory** of intellgence was the first concept to be applied to intellectual measurement. This theory is exemplified in the testing scales developed in France by Alfred Binet and Theodore Simon in 1905. These **individual intelligence** scales were further developed and revised by Lewis Terman in 1916 in the United States and have been revised three times, the latest in 1972. Terman defined intelligence as the ability to think in abstract terms, and this ability (the single factor) is the primary emphasis in the test items of what is now called the *Stanford-Binet Intelligence Scale*. Examples of questions from the Stanford-Binet are illustrated in Figure 15–1. The number of questions that the examinee is able to answer correctly represents **mental age** (MA), which serves as the measure of intellectual status. The score is reported in terms of years and months of *mental growth;* that is, a child who scores X-3 has correctly answered the same number of questions as the *average* child with a chronological age of 10 years, 3 months. Then with the child's chronological age (CA), the MA can be converted to an intelligence quotient (IQ), which represents a rate of mental growth. Thus, the quotient reflects a *relative* degree of "brightness," or intellectual growth. A child who is 8 years, 4 months of age and demonstrates a mental age of 10 years, 5 months would have an IQ of 125, which indicates that he is growing mentally at the rate of 1¼ years for each year of chronological growth.

Until the 1960 revision of the Stanford-Binet scales, the intelligence quotient was computed by the formula $IQ = MA/CA \times 100$. The 1960 revision reports **deviation intelligence scores,** which are scores that are statistically more accurate than those based on the earlier formula.

The Binet tests were first developed in France to screen out those children who could not benefit from regular academic school experiences. In America, they were revised to assist the schools in predicting and preparing for the capabilities of individual children in classroom learning. Since schools were then (and still are) highly oriented toward verbal and abstract learning, and since the test questions on the Stanford-Binet are highly verbal in content, the single-factor intelligence score of the Stanford-Binet serves adequately for predicting a child's success in school.

However, we cannot assume that the single-factor intelligence measure of the Stanford-Binet will be reflected in the whole range of activities or learning behaviors that the child will perform within and outside of the classroom. If the child is "average" in intelligence according to the Stanford-Binet, he is not necessarily capable of showing an average performance in arithmetic or mechanics or any other less verbal school activity.

Mental age (MA)
The relative development of an individual mentally when compared with chronological age.

Deviation IQ
The statistical computation of an IQ test score that takes into account measurement error.

YEAR II-6   IDENTIFYING PARTS OF THE BODY

The child is shown a large paper doll and is asked to point to the hair, mouth, feet, ear, nose, hands, and eyes.

YEAR VI   DIFFERENCES

What is the difference between a bird and a dog?

YEAR VIII   VERBAL ABSURDITIES

A man had flu (influenza) twice. The first time it killed him but the second time he got well quickly. What is foolish about that?

YEAR XIV   VOCABULARY

Examinee must define 17 words correctly.

Figure 15–1
Sample questions from Stanford–Binet Scale, Form L–M. [*Source: Reprinted from the Stanford–Binet Intelligence Scale, Form L—M, by permission of Riverside Publishing Company.*]

This test predicts quite well for performances on tasks that are verbally oriented, but it will not serve as well in predicting achievement on nonverbal intellectual tasks.

The need to administer a test to large groups of people in a single setting emerged during World War I. A panel of psychologists were asked to construct a **group intelligence test** for the Army. Terman was part of that group, and he heavily influenced the test's development. Known as the *Army Alpha,* its constructural underpinnings were actually the work of Arthur Otis, a student of Terman's. The test was subsequently constructed in 1917 and administered to thousands of individuals throughout the war. Following World War I, the test became of interest to commercial publishers. The first major group intelligence test, which was essentially a paper-and-pencil form of the Stanford-Binet, was the *Otis Group Intelligence Test* published in 1922. This test was administered to millions of school-aged students across the United States. It underwent revisions and subsequently became known as the *Otis-Lennon Mental Ability Test,* which remains in print and measures at six levels, ranging from kindergarten through grade twelve.

Group intelligence test
An IQ test specifically designed to be administered to a large group of people simultaneously in a paper-and-pencil format.

Two-Factor Tests

Two-factor test
An IQ test designed to measure two aspects of a person's behavior:

The most popular approach in **two-factor testing** is reflected by the three Wechsler Scales: (1) Wechsler Pre-School and Primary Scales of Intelligence (WPPSI), (2) Wechsler Intelligence Scale for Children, revised in 1974 (WISC), and (3) Wechsler Adult Intelligence Scale (WAIS). David Wechsler (1944, p. 3) defines intelligence as "the aggregate or global capacity of the individual to act purposefully, to think rationally, and to deal effectively with his environment." Wechsler cites the concept of an *aggregate* or **global intelligence,** which refers to the idea that there are several components of the mind that, as a whole, make up an individual's intellectual capacity. His individual intelligence tests were designed to yield three measures of intelligence: The *verbal IQ,* the **performance IQ,** and the *total IQ,* which is a combination of the other two scales.

The verbal score within the WISC and WAIS tests is measured in subtests that are termed *General Information, General Comprehension, Arithmetic, Similarities,* and *Vocabulary,* with *Digit Span* as an alternate test. The performance scale in these tests is found through subtests called *Picture Completion, Picture Arrangement, Block Design,* and *Object Assembly,* with *Coding with a Maze Test* as an alternate. The WPPSI taps the

Global intelligence
The belief that several components in the mind collectively make up a person's intelligence.

Performance IQ
A standardized IQ score that is based solely on a person's performance or nonverbal behavior.

same abilities, but the names and subject matter of the subtests are slightly different. Each subtest of the various scales yields a standard score, which is then combined with other subtest scores to produce the verbal IQ or performance IQ. The total IQ is computed from the combination of these two measures. Sample questions paraphrased from selected subtests are shown in Figure 15–2.

The verbal and total IQs relate highly with the results of a Stanford-Binet test. The correlation of the performance scale of the Wechslers with Stanford-Binet results is somewhat lower, of course. One advantage of two-factor testing is that significant differences between subtest scores and between verbal and performance IQs may assist the teacher in recognizing certain intellectual strengths or weaknesses within a student.

Group intelligence tests representative of the two-factor approach are the *Lorge-Thorndike Intelligence Test,* the *Kuhlmann-Anderson Intelligence Test* (seventh edition) and the *Henmon-Nelson Test of Mental Ability* (revised edition). The Lorge-Thorndike test reflects a concept of intelligence much like that of the Wechslers. Two different kinds of abilities are measured: (1) *verbal*—knowledge and ability to work with symbols, and (2) *nonverbal*—ability to work with figural and spatial relations. The Kuhlmann-Anderson and Henmon-Nelson scores are called *verbal* and *quantitative.* Their tests for verbal ability are similar in nature to the Lorge-Thorndike and appear to tap the same abilities. However, the quantitative score represents a somewhat different orientation—the examiner's ability to work with, manipulate, and see relations between numbers. The Kuhlmann-Anderson tests are designed for kindergarten through twelfth grade, while the Lorge-Thorndike tests begin at grade three and extend through the college freshman year. The Henmon-Nelson tests also begin at grade three and extend through the college sophomore year.

Multifactor Tests

Multifactor test
Measures of human intelligence that determine capability to function in several dimensions, not just in one or two.

Factor analysis
A statistical procedure that verifies the relationship between several behaviors representative of the same ability, e.g., numerical ability.

The Thurstone test of *Primary Mental Abilities* is perhaps the most representative of several **multifactor tests** that expand the global IQ concept of the two-factor tests. Through a statistical procedure called **factor analysis,** L. L. Thurstone (1938) analyzed 60 IQ subtests and was able to isolate 7 abilities that in his opinion comprise a person's intelligence: *number, word fluency, verbal meaning, associative-memory, reasoning, space,* and *perceptual speed.* The *Thurstone Primary Mental Abilities Test,* with subtests representing each of these seven factors, was derived from this research. In order to make his test marketable, Thurstone shortened it by eliminating the entire *Memory* subtest and by reducing the number of questions in the other subtests. Unfortunately, as a result of the fewer questions, the reliability of the subtests decreased, and prediction on the basis of the differential scores on the separate subtests is extremely risky. However, the total test score for the Thurstone subtests gives an adequate prediction of future academic achievement.

Figure 15–2
Questions similar to those found on Wechsler tests

VERBAL IQ SUBTESTS

General Information

1. How many wings does a bird have?
2. How many nickels make a dime?
3. What is steam made of?
4. Who wrote ''Paradise Lost''?
5. What is pepper?

General Comprehension

1. What should you do if you see someone forget his book when he leaves his seat in a restaurant?
2. What is the advantage of keeping money in a bank?
3. Why is copper often used in electrical wires?

Arithmetic

1. Sam had three pieces of candy and Joe gave him four more. How many pieces of candy did Sam have altogether?
2. Three men divided eighteen golf balls equally among themselves. How many golf balls did each man receive?
3. If two apples cost 15¢, what will be the cost of a dozen apples?

Similarities

1. In what way are a lion and a tiger alike?
2. In what way are a saw and a hammer alike?
3. In what way are an hour and a week alike?
4. In what way are a circle and a triangle alike?

Vocabulary

This test consists simply of asking questions like ''What is a _____?'' or ''What does _____ mean?'' The words cover a wide range of difficulty and familiarity.

PERFORMANCE IQ SUBTESTS

The various performance tasks in these subtests involve the use of blocks, cut-out figures, paper and pencil puzzles, etc.

These paraphrased Wechsler-type test items were prepared by The Psychological Corporation and are printed with their permission.

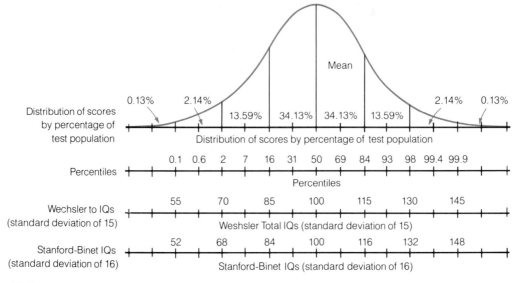

Distribution of scores by percentage of test population

0.13%   2.14%   13.59%   34.13%   34.13%   13.59%   2.14%   0.13%

Mean

Distribution of scores by percentage of test population

Percentiles

0.1   0.6   2   7   16   31   50   69   84   93   98   99.4   99.9

Percentiles

Wechsler to IQs (standard deviation of 15)

55   70   85   100   115   130   145

Weshsler Total IQs (standard deviation of 15)

Stanford-Binet IQs (standard deviation of 16)

52   68   84   100   116   132   148

Stanford-Binet IQs (standard deviation of 16)

Figure 15–3
Normal curve of measured IQs among the population

Curve
The way all scores derived from giving an IQ test are shown in relation to each other.

Mean
The arithmetical average score. In the case of IQ testing, one would add up all scores and divide by the number of people taking the test to find the mean score.

Standard deviation
A statistical measure that systematically describes how any single IQ score may vary from the mean score.

Distribution of Intelligence

The distribution of measured intelligence, like many other measured human traits and characteristics, tends to fall in a normal distribution pattern, or **curve,** among the population. The **mean** of this distribution curve is an IQ score of 100, and the **standard deviation** from the mean is usually 15 or 16 score points (see Figure 15–3), although in certain IQ tests, the distribution of scores may vary somewhat from these standard deviations.

In order to interpret a test score, a teacher must first know which test has been administered. The importance of this is that, as we have seen, (a) the test maker defines the concept of intelligence by the kinds of questions asked, and (b) a test for which the standard deviation differs from the usual 15 or 16 percent will produce a markedly different IQ figure than a test that complies to this "normal" standard deviation. As an example, assume that we have IQ scores for one student from three different tests on which he or she performed equally well. Assume also that the means are all 100. However, the standard deviations of tests X, Y, and Z vary at 15, 16, and 20 points respectively. The differences in recorded IQs for the student are illustrated in Table 15–1.

Such differences between IQ scores on tests with different standard deviations have been the main reason that many teachers have lost confidence in intelligence scores. If a student has taken two IQ tests, X and Z, and the teacher sees that one test scores the student 115, while the other scores the student 120, the teacher is naturally confused and concerned about the different results. As a student scores further from the mean, the differences in the two test results become greater and more bewildering. The conflict is resolved if teachers are aware of the differences in standard deviations in the distribution curves of different IQ tests.

Another important consideration for a teacher in the interpretation of student scores on intelligence tests is the **error factor.** In any testing situation, there are uncontrolled factors that tend to detract from the student's true score. These factors are represented as the error factor, which is normally standardized and published in the technical manual that accompanies each test. For most intelligence tests, the standard error of measurement is around 5 IQ points. The meaning and use of this standard error of measurement are illustrated in the following example.

Error factor
The amount of error that possibly occurs as a function of test administration. It is calculated and reported as the standard error of measurement.

Suppose a teacher has 30 children in class who have been administered an intelligence test, and the teacher wishes to take the error factor into consideration in studying their scores. Using the test's published standard error of measurement of 5 IQ points and following the mean and standard deviations of the normal curve, the teacher could compute that if the test were to be administered a second time, 20 of the students (68 percent) would probably score within 5 points of their IQ score on the first test. Eight students (27 percent) might vary as much as 10 points from their first test, and two (5 percent) could vary as much as 25 IQ points. Thus, if the teacher takes one student's test score, say 103, and adds and subtracts 5 IQ points (98–108), she or he could assume that 68 percent of the time this range of 98–108 includes the student's *true* IQ rank. By adding and subtracting 10 IQ points to the test score (93–113), the teacher could assume a 95 percent probability that this range includes the student's true IQ; and by adding and subtracting three standard errors of measurement, or 15 IQ points, to the student's test score of 103, the teacher could be virtually certain—a 99.8 percent probability—that the range of 88–118 includes the student's true IQ score.

The important point here is that if IQ scores are reported as **ranges,** the variations in scores from one test to another will not be so alarming to a teacher. It is also likely that the use of IQ ranges would eliminate such comparisons as the too-common conclusion that a child with an IQ of 104

Range
The likely upper and lower limits of a person's IQ based on his or her IQ score, its deviation from the mean, and the standard error of measurement.

Table 15–1   **Equivalent IQ Scores for Tests with Different Standard Deviations**

Percentile Scores*	0.1	2	16	50	84	98	99.9
Test X (stand. deviation of 15)	55	70	85	100	115	130	145
Test Y (stand. deviation of 16)	52	68	84	100	116	132	148
Test Z (stand. deviation of 20)	40	60	80	100	120	140	160

*The *percentile* score measures the percent of the test population that an examinee surpasses.

is "brighter" than a child with an IQ of 100. (Table 15–2 presents one classification system of IQ score ranges according to comparative capability among the general population.)

Table 15–2   Intelligence Classifications

IQ Score Range	Classification	Percent of Population
130 and above	Very superior	2.2
120–129	Superior	6.7
110–119	Bright normal	16.1
90–109	Average	50.0
80–89	Dull normal	16.1
70–79	Borderline	6.7
69 and below*	Mental defectives	2.2

*For educational purposes regarding the mentally retarded, the lower end of the distribution has been further subdivided into the following classifications: 50–75, Educable Mentally Retarded; 25–49, Trainable Mentally Retarded; and 0–25, Institutionalized.

Reprinted from the *Wechsler Intelligence Scale for Children*, 1949, p. 16. Used by permission of The Psychological Corporation.

Concept Summary 15–1

Plotting an IQ Score on the Curve

Key Definitions

1. *Normal curve*—the way all scores distribute themselves above and below the mean.

2. *Mean*—The average score on a test after taking all individual scores into account.

3. *Standard deviation*—A measurement unit that tells how far from the mean each individual's score is.

4. *Percentile*—The reporting of a score in terms of what percent of other students one exceeded on a particular test.

Problem Statements

1. Jim had an IQ of 121 on the Stanford-Binet. How many standard deviations above the mean was Jim? What percent of the other students did Jim exceed?

2. Susan was .6 standard deviations below the mean on the WISC-R. What was her IQ score?

3. Wade had an IQ of 103 on the WAIS. Everyone describes this as an average IQ score. Why?

Limitations/Criticisms of Intelligence Testing

There have been countless reactions to intelligence testing and the issues relevant to it. Many psychologists and educators feel that the importance of intelligence testing has been overemphasized. This argument is well made in light of the broader concept of cognitive functioning. Simply stated, individuals function in more diverse ways than intelligence tests can assess; thus, they do not comprehensively measure a person's intelligence. Six common criticisms appear in the literature.

1. *Intelligence tests do not really measure intelligence.* Critics state that intelligence tests only measure what an individual has learned. They only assess ability on a specified, somewhat limited number of mental tasks. The most popular theory of intelligence, Piaget's, is considered to be more qualitative than quantitative, and no satisfactory group intelligence test has been developed from his theory. Further, adequate cognitive functions include individual characteristics, such as interest, motivation, problem solving, creativity, affectivity, values, and social cognition. Intelligence tests make no attempt to assess these dimensions (White & Hall, 1980).

2. *Intelligence tests do not account for cultural differences.* Culture is the sum of the knowledge, beliefs, morals, customs, and ideologies acquired by a member of society. Within any society, many cultures emerge that are both unique and meaningful. People define their culture through an interactive process. Of necessity, they learn about their culture through association with others; therefore, it is appropriate to say that culture is socially created, not instinctively determined. Culture is socially shared as well; individuals collect into groups, or social units, in order to share culturally acceptable behaviors.

   Invariably, within any society one culture surfaces or dominates. It shares a common history, common value structure, and common language (Marden & Meyer, 1978). When an intelligence test is developed to compare individuals within such a culture, it must reflect those commonalities if it is to fairly assess individuals in relation to each other. This is why most standardized intelligence tests do not adequately measure individuals with diverse cultural backgrounds. Thus, IQ comparisons across cultures not only violate the assumptions of generalizability, but are scientifically incorrect as well. To compare ethnic or minority groups against the dominant culture is a misinterpretation of assessment data and a violation of the cultural distinctiveness of nondominant cultures.

3. *Intelligence tests and their norms are **biased.*** Most group intelligence tests are normed on a middle-class, white population. In recent years, norms have been developed on some ethnic populations, specifically Blacks and Hispanics. Intelligence test performance must be interpreted on a normative scale. Any individual's performance is difficult to interpret if there is no normative group to which to compare. The

Bias
The belief that items on an IQ test might favor one subgroup within society.

critics believe that to compare ethnic populations against middle-class norms is inappropriate. As previously indicated, if a test does not represent the culture it is measuring, then the measure is of limited value. This issue has focused on test item bias. Items should represent a common set of knowledge with a minimal dependency on content-specific questions. For example, an item such as "What direction would you travel if you went from Chicago to New York?" may be too **content-specific.** The rural child in Wyoming may know what direction to travel from Laramie to Denver or the Hispanic student may know what direction Mexico City is from Houston, but neither may know the Chicago to New York answer. Conversely, many who could answer the Chicago-New York questions correctly might answer the Laramie-Denver question incorrectly.

Some individuals would argue that tests are not biased and you cannot criticize a test for the ways in which it may be misused. Nevertheless, those who cite test bias as an intelligence test limitation can argue convincingly because of the normative groups and content-specific questions.

4. *Intelligence tests perpetuate stereotypes or labeling.* Critics believe that labels are assigned to individuals as a result of an IQ score that may "haunt" an individual throughout life. The categories listed in Table 15–2 illustrate this point. There are two major problems surrounding this issue. First, intelligence test scores are often misinterpreted. This occurs because the norms from test to test may vary and because interpreters often do not know the meaning or significance of an IQ score. A teacher may think an IQ of 119 is better than 115 and consequently view the two students differently. You will recall from our earlier discussion on intellectual measurement that such a difference is not significant and labeling one individual inferior to the other would be unfair.

Second, IQ scores can be misleading because the calculated score is an estimate of capacity rather than a precise measure of it. Several researchers have urged reporting a range of ability instead (Anastasi, 1967; Ebel, 1963). White and Hall (1980, p. 213) argue that

> an intelligence score, like other test scores, is based on a work sample of specific test items, administered under a specific set of conditions and at a particular point in time. In light of these factors, it would be more justified to report performance as a band of scores, as is done for some achievement tests. This practice also might highlight the fact that a test score also can vary according to changes in the life experience of an individual.

These positions suggest that labeling could be reduced if a broader interpretation of test results were made.

One final argument should be cited in regard to the issue of **stability** of IQ across time. Scores are thought to remain rather stable from approximately 8 years of age on (Bayley, 1949, 1965; Bloom, 1963; Thorndike, 1940). In a well-designed comprehensive study by Hopkins and Bracht (1975, p. 476), where group IQ scores were compared across 10 years of test administration, the following conclusions were drawn:

Content-specific questions
An item within an IQ test that is so specific, its correct answer may be more attributable to learning than to intelligence.

Stability
The extent to which one's IQ remains highly similar across time.

a. Verbal IQ scores are much more stable than nonverbal IQ scores, especially prior to grade seven.

b. At grades one and two, verbal and nonverbal IQs from group tests reflect relatively little lasting variance, even over short intervals.

c. By grade four, verbal IQs show a high relationship (above .7) with subsequent scores. There is substantial change in verbal scores prior to grade four but considerable stability thereafter.

d. Total IQs have a pattern of stability quite similar to that of verbal IQs.

e. Verbal IQs from group tests are considerably less stable than Stanford-Binet IQs prior to grade seven. After grade seven, there is little difference in the stability of IQ scores from individual and group verbal tests.

f. There is a trend for the scores of girls to be slightly more stable than boys' scores.

Each of the issues cited here mitigate against labeling or stereotyping individuals because of IQ scores. If such labeling is reduced, a conscious plan must be developed that gives interpreters a viable alternative way of expressing such scores.

5. *Intelligence tests discriminate against minorities.* Several ideas presented thus far in this discussion of intelligence test limitations overlap with this common charge. Essentially, the charge of discrimination states that intelligence tests unfairly punish minority students because they focus on information that may be irrelevant to minority students. Perhaps the argument would be fairer and more forceful if the charge of discrimination were more selective.

The issue of discrimination has been well stated. Lennon (1970, p. 42) summarized the problem succinctly when he stated:

> There is a deep-seated conviction that the performance of poor black, Puerto Rican, Mexican-American, or just poverty stricken examinees on these tests will be relatively poor: That because of this poor performance, inferences will be made as to the ability of these examinees; which inferences will lead to treatment, either in school or on the job, that will in effect constitute a denial of opportunity.

The issue really is whether we want to develop skills to *equate* performance of individuals from different cultural groups. There is no doubt that test constructors can do so. It is, truly, a matter of whether that is a desirable outcome of the testing movement. Translated versions of tests are a partial solution. Scholars from various ethnic groups point out, however, that individuals in different cultures do not always structure their thought processes in the same way. Aguirre (1979) has pointed this out in regard to Hispanics:

> Concerning Chicano intelligence scores, it has been recognized that language is a factor contributing to lower scores (Padilla & Garza, 1975). A subsequent movement has been the translation of intelligence tests into Spanish. However, instead of creating a more equitable relationship between the Chicano child and the intelligence test, the translations have proven quite problematic. On the one hand, the basis of the problem of translated intelligence tests is that more concern has been placed on

facilitating the testing of Chicano children rather than making the test more comprehensible to them. On the other hand, translated tests are often dominated with supposedly equivalent words that have different connotations for the child. In brief, where the flaw in IQ tests has earlier been the Chicano student's inability to read and understand English, the flaw in the translated tests came to be the Chicano student's inability to understand fully the translated concepts (Garcia, 1977, p. 7).

In terms of educational decision-making, we have evolved beyond the point of convincing each other that intelligence tests discriminate against multiple components of the total population and we need to engage in dialogue of what we shall do about it.

6. *Intelligence test outcomes are influenced by* **examiner bias.** There have been numerous studies conducted since the mid-1960s to investigate the effect the examiner may have on examinee scores. The general assumption has been that examiners of different ethnic origin will depress the scores of examinees. Like so many other educational issues, there have been a number of studies that support such a position and a number of studies that demonstrate no negative effect. As a result, it is difficult to know exactly how to interpret all these findings. The greater the examinee's dependence on vocabulary, the more examiner influence seems to affect results. The key to reducing or eliminating any negative effects that might occur does not lie simply in becoming highly skilled in test administration. Rather, it involves a greater awareness of the total testing situation in which an examiner finds himself or herself (Mishra, 1980).

Teacher-Made Tests   For measurement of specific academic achievement in the classroom, teachers have to devise their own testing instruments. Teacher-made tests are of all kinds and lengths and are used not only for measurement of learning but also for motivation and reinforcement. The main purpose of these tests is the determination of student grades.

There are many problems directly related to this purpose, not the least of which is preparing the test items. Before writing items, teachers need to know what behaviors to measure. If a statement of the objectives and conditions of the learning is made before any instruction takes place, writing tests becomes a relatively easy task. The statement of instructional objectives also ensures that subsequent tests measure not only areas of content but also the levels of thinking involved in the learning situation. The latter are difficult to include in a test, but they are very important in the measurement and evaluation of learning. Gronlund (1981) has provided a conceptual framework within which to place testing or student evaluation. He, too, stresses the importance of systematic evaluation that is, in part, facilitated by instructional objectives. His overview is depicted in Figure 15–4.

The most common type of cognitive test items are true-false, multiple choice, matching, completion, short answer, and essay. Although the first of these is still used on a small scale in elementary grades, it has been replaced by the more sophisticated multiple-choice variety at all other levels.

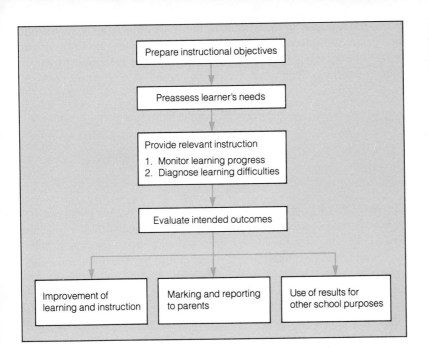

Too frequently true-false tests are made up of statements lifted verbatim from textbooks; when these are used out of context, they often are ambiguous. The true-false test also restricts measurement to the knowledge level of thinking—rote memory of facts (knowledge level objectives). The well-constructed multiple-choice test is easy to mark and can cover a large number of thinking levels, but it is limited to measurement of recognition abilities. This test type should be replaced by the completion or short-answer type if recall of information is desired. If analysis, synthesis, and evaluation are desired, the essay question is preferable. It gives the student freedom in which to develop an answer. One problem with short-answer and essay tests is the care with which teachers prepare each item. It takes serious thought to express precisely the response that is expected from the student. Words can be misunderstood and students frequently misinterpret questions.

Another problem with essay tests is grading. It is difficult for a teacher to be objective and not be influenced by extraneous factors, such as neatness, modes of expression, or knowledge of a student's previous work. Having a clearly outlined key and reading the answers *seriatim* will help to ensure consistent evaluations. Other techniques can be useful in essay grading, but the main thing to realize is that it will take no longer to do a good job of grading essay papers than it would have taken to prepare an equally long multiple-choice test. In the latter case, the preparation time is long and the scoring time is short, which allows for quick return of tests to students. In the former, the preparation time is relatively short and the scoring time is long.

No one test type is ideal for all occasions. Teachers should offer a variety of tests because the level and kind of behavioral objective should dictate the test type. In most courses, there is a wide variety of levels and types of desired behavioral objectives. Students may have special skills with certain types of tests—for example, skill in writing (essay) or skill in logically figuring out the correct given answer by careful elimination of poor distractors (multiple choice). Therefore, using only one type of test throughout a course can work to the advantage or disadvantage of individual students.

Planning for a Test

Two major factors influence how a test will be developed: (1) the number and levels of instructional objectives being pursued within a specified time frame and (2) the content areas covered in that time frame. These factors can be represented in a two-way grid of intersecting content and objectives. Table 15–3 illustrates a fifth-grade science unit on plants. The instructor developed a unit with several content areas, ranging from the classification of plants to how plants affect a changing environment. The range of unit complexity is represented by knowledge, comprehension, and application objectives, as described in Bloom's (1956) taxonomy. The numbers at each intersecting cell represent the number of objectives taught in each content area. For example, there were four knowledge level objectives taught in regard to classification, five comprehensive objectives on tropism, and three application objectives on photosynthesis. This particular unit is rather extensive, consisting of seventy-seven objectives.

The **test blueprint** or table of specifications was devised several decades ago to systematically evaluate classroom learning. With the specification of instructional objectives and the advent of **criterion-referenced measurement,** this strategy seems more important today than it has ever been. The table of specifications consists of the following:

Test blueprint
A measurement device that is a systematic description of how students should be assessed following designated instruction. Often this is referred to as a table of specifications.

Criterion-referenced measurement
The assessment of student behavior against predetermined performance criteria.

Table 15–3 Instructional Objectives for Fifth-Grade Science Unit on Plants

Objectives/ Content	Knowledge	Comprehension	Application
Classification	4	1	1
Cellular Structure	5	3	4
Photosynthesis	2	3	3
Transpiration	2	1	2
Respiration	2	2	1
Digestion	2	2	0
Circulation	1	1	0
Reproduction	4	2	2
Tropism	7	5	6
Changing Environment	2	3	4
Total Objectives	31	23	23

Table 15–4   Table of Specifications for Multiple-Choice Exam on Life Processes in Plants, Fifth-Grade Level

Objectives/Content	Know	Comp.	Applic.	Percent	Item
Photosynthesis	2	3	5	25	10
Transpiration	2	2	2	15	6
Respiration	2	3	1	15	6
Digestion	2	4	0	15	6
Circulation	2	2	0	10	4
Reproduction	4	2	2	20	8
Total Items by Objective	14	16	10	100	40

1. The content being taught in a unit of work
2. The instructional objectives designed to teach that content
3. The number of items the test will contain

The number of items written for each objective is variable. It depends upon the weight assigned to each content area, the importance given to each objective level, the amount of class time devoted to each topic, the number of items considered minimal to adequately test each objective, and the overall length of the test. The table of specifications implies proportionality of the five variables that determine the number of items written for each objective. Bloom (1956) contends that, when the number of test items written to measure each objective in the intersecting cells approximates the value assigned each cell, **content validity** exists.

Content validity
The analysis of sample test items to determine adequate representation of the items.

Within the plant unit described in Table 15–3, it is easy to see that the number of objectives being covered are too many to evaluate in one sitting. Even at the ratio of one question per objective, a seventy-seven-item test is generally too exhaustive for fifth-grade students. A teacher would have to determine if all objectives are to be measured, the number of items appropriate for each objective, the number of items students can legitimately respond to within a given time frame, and the logical place to break an extensive instructional unit into measurement segments.

Let us assume that a teacher wants to give a forty-item test over the material on life processes in plants. These processes include six content areas: photosynthesis, transpiration, respiration, digestion, circulation, and reproduction. The hypothetical table of specifications (Table 15–4) reflects the relative amount of time to be spent on each content area and the number of questions on each area. The number of objectives, the time spent on them, and the number of test items should be relatively proportional. Table 15–4 also gives a proportionality of time spent at the various objective levels. The table of specifications implies that approximately 35 percent of the instructional time was spent on knowledge level content, 40 percent on comprehension, and 25 percent on application. The test items should reflect these varying levels of emphasis.

Format

No single test item format is appropriate to the measurement of all student learning. Classroom teachers must know the various types of test items available, the learning levels they most appropriately assess, and the extent to which they help achieve teaching-learning purposes. Test items have been categorized as highly structured versus unstructured, supply versus select, and objective versus subjective.

Highly structured response
The development of a test item that elicits very specific, non-interpretable answers.

Highly Structured versus Unstructured **Highly structured responses** are very specific and require a noninterpretable answer. Such items fall within multiple-choice, true-false, and matching formats. There is greater latitude in completion and short-answer items. Although such items are limited in their expectations, students can compose some of their own answers, present multiple meanings or synonyms, or interpret the question somewhat differently without being incorrect. Unstructured or free responses represent the greatest latitude.

Essay questions represent the maximum opportunity for latitude in student responses. Which type of question should be used depends on the type of response the student is expected to emit. If it is very specific information, then a structured question would be appropriate. If it is a conceptual idea, primarily dependent on high level thought processes, then an unstructured question is more appropriate.

Supply items
Test items wherein the student must provide the correct answers, e.g., completion, short-answer, essay.

Select items
Test items wherein the student must choose the correct answer from given alternatives.

Objective items
Test items written with enough specificity that the answer is clearly correct or incorrect.

Subjective items
Test items that permit variation in student responses that are still acceptable answers.

Problem items
A specific test item wherein the answer is not readily apparent. Students must provide the answer that is specific rather than varied.

Supply versus Select The determination of whether a student should supply the answer to a test item or select among provided alternatives also depends on the nature of the response desired from the student. The terms *supply* and *select* are generally confined to objective tests. **Supply items** would be either short answers or completion, those allowing for restricted student latitude in answering. **Select items** are highly specific, allowing for no student latitude in the answer; one gets the item either right or wrong. None of these items is likely to get into the higher level thinking processes. Multiple-choice items, if written well, can measure some complex reasoning skills and are clearly preferable to the other item types in that regard (Brown, 1976; Gronlund, 1981).

Objective versus Subjective A distinction is made between test items students answer objectively and test items they answer subjectively, that is, where the response may vary from student to student and be evaluated differently by the teacher. Objective tests are considered fairer, although subjective tests are necessary to comprehensive evaluation. Multiple-choice, true-false, matching, completion, and short-answer items are classified as **objective**. Essay items are classified as **subjective**. Although there is greater variability in student responses to essay questions, they are the most effective in eliciting higher level skills. A newer classification is **problem items**. This refers to items where a student is given a specific problem to solve but the solution is not implied by the statement of the problem. In a subject such as math, such problems are constantly being presented. In a sense, problem items do not fit my classification scheme. They are very much like short-answer items, yet there is only one correct solution.

Item Writing

It is important to construct test items carefully. For tests to reflect student learning, items must be written clearly and simply. Because teacher-constructed tests have greater potential for measuring student learning than standardized tests, they must be carefully put together. There are six types of test items: essay, multiple choice, true-false, matching, completion or short-answer, and problems.

Essay Items An **essay item** is designed to draw out a free response in which the answer can be organized and written out in as much detail as the students desire. Its primary advantage is that it taps higher level cognitive skills, allowing students to demonstrate their understanding more completely than they could in any other format. Travers (1979, p. 442) cites three advantages to essay items:

Essay items
Items that provide stimulus information necessary for students to compose a response in some detail.

1. They are fairly easy to construct.
2. They may be administered simply; questions may be written on the blackboard.
3. They emphasize wholes rather than parts.

Several writers (Gronlund, 1981; Lien, 1980; Thorndike & Hagen, 1977) have offered suggestions on how to construct essay items and tests. I have summarized them in Box 15–1.

To broadly sample student knowledge, increase the total number of questions but reduce the comprehensiveness of each. Gronlund (1981) has distinguished between restricted and extended response questions. In restricted questions, the scope of the topic is limited; in extended questions, more integrated responses emerge. You can cover more content areas with restricted questions, but you limit the depth. Examples of restricted response essay questions are:

1. Define assimilation and accommodation and explain the difference between them.
2. Describe why short story writers prefer to use complex sentence structures rather than simple and compound ones.
3. Compare a coach's versus parents' influence on a high school athlete's decision to attend college.

Examples of extended response essay questions are:

1. Identify the sociocultural factors of the 1960s and 1970s that may have contributed to the accelerated increase in female juvenile delinquency.

1. Determine the cognitive skills you want the student to use in the answer. Key words or phrases such as "compare and contrast," "summarize," or "show the relationship," are indicators that a complex level of thinking is required.

2. Use essay items only for those academic responses that cannot be written as objective items. In effect, objective items have more discriminatory power and a general rule would be never to write anything in a subjective format that can be tested in an objective format.

3. Write the question clearly enough that the student has no difficulty knowing what the question is asking. If a question is too ambiguous, it has different meaning for different students. The purpose of an essay question is to get at higher level cognitive skills in all students, rather than different skills among students.

4. Write questions that can be answered within the time frame given. Specify the approximate time a student should spend on an item as well as the point value of each item.

5. Require all students to answer the same questions. If optional questions are given (for example, "Answer any five of the following eight questions"), it is difficult to say that the content domain of the total exam is equivalent.

2. Describe the definitive characteristics of the Ming dynasty. Discuss how it was influenced by the dynasty that immediately preceded it.

3. Explain the difference between behavioral subcultures and value subcultures. Which do you think is more characteristic of American adolescents? Carefully state the reasons why.

Essay tests have been heavily criticized because of the difficulty involved in grading them. Teachers must accept this limitation if they decide to give essay tests. It is not possible to apply scoring criteria consistently to multiple papers. There is a tendency for teachers to grade on such factors as spelling, handwriting, and overall neatness in addition to content. This is particularly problematic because of the highly subjective nature of essay tests. Teachers must attempt to reduce subjectivity, which can partially be accomplished by developing scoring criteria for each test item and by focusing only on the *content* of each question. A teacher should analyze each question and write down the minimum requirements for passing the item. If a question has multiple parts, a relative weight (points) should be given to each part. This increases the chance that criteria will be systematically applied from paper to paper.

Gronlund (1981) suggests that teachers not know which student's paper they are grading because they form many impressions about students that may affect scoring. Gronlund also suggests evaluating all student answers to the same question before moving on to the next test item. This is likely to increase the consistency of applying the scoring criteria to each question.

Multiple-Choice Items   The most popular objective test item is **multiple choice.** It is more versatile, contains more information, and can measure a wider range of content than any other objective format. Multiple-choice tests are written in either of two ways: as a question ("Which of the following events was the key to westward expansion?") or as an incomplete sentence ("The definition of photosynthesis is . . . "). It is suggested that each item be followed by four alternatives, only one of which is correct. The student selects the alternative that answers the question or completes the sentence. If each alternative is a plausible answer, the item will tend to discriminate between the high and low achievers. Box 15–2 summarizes guidelines for writing multiple-choice items from several sources (Brown, 1976; Ebel, 1980; Gronlund, 1981).

Multiple-choice items
An objective test item that supplies the student with several plausible answers from which the student must choose.

True-False Items   As educators have learned more about the range of student learning, it has become increasingly clear that **true-false items** tap the lower end of that range. Gronlund (1981, p. 157) has observed that the most common use of true-false items is in measuring the ability to "identify the correctness of statements of fact, definitions of terms, statements of principles, and the like." True-false items are simply declarative sentences to which the student must respond true (T) or false (F). They are used to recall nonconceptual information.

True-false items
The presentation of a statement as fact to which a student must agree or disagree.

There are several limitations to true-false items. First, the response is very low level and easily forgotten. Second, because a true-false question has two options, the chance factor is high. A good item should get at whether the student answers a question correctly because of knowledge and not because of chance. Third, true-false items are often unclear or ambiguous, which further increases the chance factor. Fourth, a goal of a good item is to reinforce and help retain learning. With true-false items, every false item focuses on something we do not want the student to retain. This is a serious limitation of this type of item. Fifth, true-false items are unduly dependent on specific determiners, such as "never" or "always." Such clues often help students respond correctly even if they do not know the answer. Examples of acceptable true-false items are:

T or F   1. Ronald Reagan is the first president of the United States who had previously served as a governor.

T or F   2. When a liquid is changed into a solid, it shrinks; thus, its total volume is reduced.

T or F   3. Babe Ruth hit sixty home runs in 1927.

T or F   4. The first capital of the United States was New York City.

T or F   5. The only undefeated heavyweight boxing champion in the history of boxing was Joe Louis.

Box 15–2   How to Write Multiple-Choice Questions

A. The stem or question must present one idea clearly and succinctly. Avoid nonfunctional and ambiguous words.

> *Examples:* 1. Which of the following is a complex sentence?
> 2. Topic sentences may appear _____.

B. The stem should avoid catch words or phrases that either give the answer away or are perceived as tricks. If a particular word (such as "never") is the key to the answer, underline it.

> *Examples:* 1. Which of the following conditions <u>never</u> exists during the summer months?
> 2. The moon is <u>almost always</u> full on the first _____.

C. There may be occasions when the stem will ask for incorrect information. When using "not" or other negatives in the stem, underline them for emphasis.

> *Examples:* 1. The subtraction algorithm is <u>not</u> correctly expressed in which example?
> 2. The seventeenth-century Spanish explorers <u>never</u> sailed west of _____.

D. There should be only one correct response to each question. This alternative should be clearly distinguished from the other options.

> *Examples:* 1. Which of the following is an idiom?
> a. hot as a pistol
> b. fall in love
> c. cool
> d. Tijuana special
> 2. The movement along the San Andreas fault is a result of
> a. vulcanism
> b. continental drift
> c. ecological destruction
> d. erosion

E. List the alternatives in a logical sequence (for example, small to large or earliest to latest).

> *Examples:* 1. In which year did the Spanish-American War begin?
> a. 1879
> b. 1886
> c. 1894
> d. 1898
> 2. The first Americans could have come from Siberia as early as
> a. 25,000 years ago
> b. 40,000 years ago
> c. 55,000 years ago
> d. 70,000 years ago

F. If a stem states a controversial or research-based idea, cite the authority or source.

> *Examples:* 1. Which of the following conclusions was drawn from Bandura's research on television violence?
> a. There is no direct relationship between television violence and human violence.
> b. Children under age eight are most susceptible to negative effects from television violence.
> c. People with high intelligence are not susceptible to television violence.
> d. Television violence actually has a cathartic effect on people.
> 2. According to Gagne, rules cannot be learned unless
> a. reinforcement is given
> b. a learner is highly motivated
> c. the prerequisite concepts are learned
> d. the teacher models appropriate behavior

Box 15–2, continued

G. Avoid irrelevant clues to answers. Such factors as length of alternatives, key words in both the stem and the correct response, and nonsense choices break down the power of the item.

H. Randomly select the placement of the correct response. Do not use any one response choice with disproportionately high frequency.

I. Use *all of the above* or *none of the above*

sparingly as an alternative. Do not use either as the answer.

J. Make all alternatives as brief as possible. It is to students' advantage if they can keep the options in immediate memory span until they make their selection. Questions that are too lengthy require students to reread information prior to selecting the answer.

Matching Items **Matching questions** consist of a list of stimulus words or statements and a list of responses to which they can be matched. If an instructor is trying to get students to exercise the ability to identify the relationships between two things, a matching exercise may be appropriate. Matching items suffer the same limitations as true-false items because they also tap the lower end of a person's response repertoire. Brown (1976, p. 257) provides some suggestions for constructing matching exercises that I list in Box 15–3.

The following example illustrates a perfect match, that is, where the stimulus words (stem) on the left and the response words on the right are the same:

Matching items
The presentation of multiple pieces of information that the student must discriminate among and pair correctly.

Box 15–3 How to Write Matching Questions

1. All parts of a single matching item should be homogeneous in content; that is, all should refer to dates, all to names, all to places, and so on. Be sure that the student knows the basis on which the terms should be matched.
2. If the two lists contain phrases of different lengths, have the longer phrases serve as the stems and the shorter ones as the responses.
3. Each list should contain no more than five to seven items. When possible, include more responses than stems. Instruct students as to whether each response can be used more than once.
4. Each stem should have one, and only one, response associated with it; that is, there should be only one correct response for each stem.
5. Arrange responses in a logical order—for example, alphabetically. Avoid response patterns.

A. On the line to the left indicate which major city is in which country.

_____	1. Australia	A.	Tripoli
_____	2. Brazil	B.	Stockholm
_____	3. Denmark	C.	Rio de Janeiro
_____	4. Libya	D.	Lima
_____	5. Peru	E.	Copenhagen
_____	6. Scotland	F.	Melbourne
_____	7. Sweden	G.	Glasgow

The following example illustrates an imperfect match, that is, where the stimulus words on the left and the response words on the right are uneven. In such cases, the response words should be greater in number.

B. On the line to the left, indicate which psychologist is identified with which system of thought.

_____	1. Reinforcement theory	A.	David Ausubel
_____	2. Social learning theory	B.	Albert Bandura
_____	3. Hierarchical learning	C.	John Bransford
_____	4. Cognitive-field psychology	D.	Robert Gagne
_____	5. Information processing	E.	Kurt Lewin
		F.	O. H. Mowher
		G.	B. F. Skinner

Completion / short-answer items
The presentation of questions that require the student to supply information. They are not as objective as multiple-choice or true-false; not as subjective as essay.

Completion / Short-Answer Items All **completion / short-answer items** require that the student supply the correct answer to the question. They are far more objective than an essay item, but not as precise as an objective item. If the question is written ambiguously, students may supply more than one answer. In such cases, credit must be given even if it was not the precise answer the teacher was looking for. In completion, there is usually a blank left in the sentence. The student is to fill in the blank in order to complete the sentence and answer the item. This usually involves a word or phrase. In short-answer items, the student may need to provide a sentence or two. The short answer usually is more interpretive than the completion item. In either case, they do not require as much organization as the essay item. Scoring is also easier and more objective. Lien (1980, pp. 107–108) has provided several suggestions for constructing recall (supply) items (see Box 15–4).

Too often completion items are written as variations to true-false and matching items. Thus, they are often used to test low level skills and not higher level processes. The short-answer item potentially involves higher level skills. Teachers need to be aware of the fact that short-answer items fall within the range of simple to complex and structured to unstructured. Examples of completion items are:

1. The congressional document that protects the individual's rights within the democratic society is _____ .

2. The presidential election in the United States is held every _____ years.

Box 15–4   How to Write Recall Questions

1. The simple recall item can be written in either a question or a statement form, but the question form is preferable.
2. State the item in special terms so that pupils have no difficulty knowing the kind of answer desired.
3. Be sure to retain key words that are necessary for pupils to know what is required in their answer.
4. Begin by asking for only one word in lower grades and progress to asking for more words or a phrase or sentence in higher grades.
5. Make minimum use of textbook language—refrain from listing sentences from the text.
6. Avoid *a* and *an* or similar words before the blank.
7. The question should be worded so that there is only one correct response.
8. A single blank should be provided for each idea, not for each word in the response.
9. The important word or words to be entered by the pupil should be at the end or near the end of the question.
10. Blanks should be of uniform length, providing no clue to the correct response.

---

3. Dwight Eisenhower was first elected president of the United States in

_____ .

Examples of short-answer items are:

1. What are the minimum requirements in order to run for president of the United States?
2. What is the *best* definition of altruism?
3. State Thorndike's law of effect.

Problem Items   There are many different ways to measure learning, some of which do not really fall into the objective or subjective formats. Solving problems in math class, conducting scientific experiments, using map-reading skills in social studies, and reading tables, graphs, or charts are examples of student performance that is commonly measured. These testlike items call upon problem-solving or informational skills. They are basically objective in that the end result is discrete and observable. Yet they are subjective in the sense that they may evaluate the process the student undertakes as well. In fact, there are numerous learning experiences where the process clearly outweighs the product in importance. Although many problem items do not fit the standard test format, they should be considered as another way to measure student performance.

Criterion-Referenced or Norm-Referenced Measurement

Since the appearance of Glaser's (1963) article that pointed to the inadequacy of existing measurement instruments and the need to develop both theory and tests based on performance, an increasing number of educators' articles have discussed the merits of criterion-referenced tests. Criterion-referenced tests are used to identify a student's performance in relation to a specified expectation or standard. Such tests are usually constructed on the basis of specific instructional objectives and content areas to measure the degree of mastery. Although criterion-referenced measurement is proposed for its ability to evaluate qualities not being measured by traditional **norm-referenced measurement** techniques (Glaser & Nitko, 1971), there is still some question as to whether it is the inadequacy of norm-referenced tests to measure outcomes that has promoted the change or the new instructional approaches in the schools that require new measurement techniques.

Norm-referenced measurement The assessment of student performance by comparing any individual with all other students taking the same measure.

Intelligence tests, achievement tests, aptitude tests, and most teacher-made tests are norm-referenced. Norm-referenced tests have established means and standard deviations, and an individual's performance is assessed by comparing it to the norm. In criterion-referenced measurement, a performance level is specified for an individual student somewhere on a continuum from no learning to mastery learning (Nitko, 1980). If the learner meets the designated level, he or she has mastered the task and met the criterion.

The following example is useful to our discussion. A classroom teacher has specified two behavioral objectives for a teaching-learning task:

1. The student will be able to multiply whole numbers to find distance.

2. The student will be able to find the area of an object.

The students were taught the following two rules:

1. To find a product, multiply the two factors available; that is, $f \times f = p$.

2. To find area, multiply length times width; that is, $l \times w = A$.

The students were then given the following problem: A swimming pool is 75 feet long and 40 feet wide. How many square feet are in the swimming pool? How far does Mark travel in swimming twice the length of the pool?

To measure learning outcomes, the teacher will grade the correctness of the two answers each student computes. Would the teacher use norm-referenced or criterion-referenced measurement? Either may be used, although criterion-referenced technique is preferable.

It is very impractical to attempt to grade an assignment with two answers on a norm-referenced basis; so, for illustrative purposes, let us assume that these two rules are to be applied in twenty problems. First, the teacher plots each score to determine the range of student responses within the class of thirty-two:

Total Scores	Number of Students
19	3
18	2
17	4
16	4
15	6
14	6
13	3
11	2
10	2
	32

This mean score for the class is found to be 15.0, and individual grades could be computed from this figure. But what does this tell the teacher about each student's learning? One student correctly answered fourteen problems, which approximates the mean, and the teacher might then give that student a "C" and proceed to the next learning task. But suppose this student applied rule 1 correctly to all ten problems representing that rule but used rule 2 correctly only four times. Has the student sufficiently learned? Obviously, the teacher could be satisfied with his learning of rule 1 and its relevant concepts. But what about rule 2? Without such diagnosis, it is easy for the teacher to assume that the student has learned all the material at an average level and to proceed to the next task, leaving the student inadequately prepared.

Considering this same student's performance using a criterion-referenced measurement, the student's test is analyzed first in reference to criteria and not to the entire class. The test is analyzed in terms of whether the stated performance objectives were met. This second procedure would reveal that rule 1 was sufficiently mastered and rule 2 was not. This analysis tells the teacher not only that the student was unable to find area, but also that the student may not have learned the necessary prerequisite concepts for formulating the rule. In other words, the reason the student did not apply rule 2 correctly is that he or she had not really learned the rule. The instructional implications for the teacher are to go back over the material and make sure that the student acquires the relevant skills and knowledge, then remeasure the student's ability.

In using criterion-referenced measurement, the teacher must be cautious not to equate mastery with perfection. Because criterion-referenced performance is on a continuum, it is logical that teachers specify certain percentages as acceptable for mastering a specified performance objective. If, for instance, the learning of the two rules in the previous example was the expected performance, the teacher might specify 100 percent mastery. Certainly, the teacher would expect 100 percent mastery of the relevant concepts that went into the rules. However, if the terminal behavior is to memorize a list of words, the criterion level might be set at a lower level. The end product of criterion-referenced measurement is the same as that of norm-referenced measurement—a score or percentage that must usually be translated into conventional symbols or marks. Table

Table 15–5 Comparison of General Characteristics of Norm-Referenced and Criterion-Referenced Evaluation Systems

Norm-Referenced System	Criterion-Referenced System
1. The main function of norm-referenced evaluation is to ascertain the student's relative position within a normative group.	1. The main function of criterion-referenced evaluation is to assess whether the student has mastered a specific criterion or performance standard.
2. Either general conceptual outcomes (usually done) or precise objectives may be specified when constructing norm-referenced evaluation.	2. Complete instructional objectives are specified in the construction of criterion-referenced evaluation.
3. The criterion for mastery is not usually specified when using norm-referenced evaluation.	3. The criterion for mastery must be stated (i.e., instructional objectives) for use in criterion-referenced evaluation.
4. Test items for norm-referenced evaluation are constructed to discriminate among students.	4. Test items for criterion-referenced evaluation are constructed to measure a predetermined level of proficiency.
5. Variability of scores is desirable as an aid to meaningful interpretation.	5. Variability is irrelevant; it is not a necessary condition for a satisfactory criterion-referenced evaluation.
6. The test results from norm-referenced evaluation are amenable to transposition to the traditional grading system (A, B, C, D, F).	6. The test results from criterion-referenced evaluation suggest the use of a binary system (i.e., satisfactory-unsatisfactory; pass-fail). However, criterion-referenced evaluation test results can be transposed into the traditional grading system by following a set of specifically constructed rules.

Source: Smythe, Kibler, & Hutchings (1973), p. 4. Reprinted by permission of the authors and the Speech Communication Association.

15–5 provides an overview of the general characteristics of norm- and criterion-referenced evaluation.

Criterion-Referenced Testing

The underlying principles in a criterion-referenced test are directed toward observing student behavior that can be expressed in relationship to educational objectives. Glaser and Nitko (1971, p. 653) have described a criterion-referenced test as one that is "deliberately constructed to yield measurements that are directly interpretable in terms of specified performance standards." A test samples tasks drawn from the instructional domain and is related to the instructional domain designated for each learner. Gronlund (1973) has identified several essential characteristics of criterion-referenced testing:

1. *Criterion-referenced testing requires a clearly defined and delimited domain of learning tasks.* As I discussed in Chapter 9, behavioral objectives are one primary way to define appropriate learning tasks. Tasks may be nonconceptual or conceptual, simple or complex; in any case, they must be observable to be measurable.

2. *Criterion-referenced testing requires that performance standards be clearly specified.* Because criterion-referenced testing does not use an averaging effect, the basis for determining whether an objective has been mastered must be specified prior to instruction and evaluation. High level performance, such as applying a principle to a problem, requires mastery or understanding in order to solve the problem. In first aid, one either knows how to tie a tourniquet or not. There is no such thing as being "average" in tying a tourniquet. Whatever the standards, they are necessary if evaluation is to occur.

3. *Criterion-referenced testing requires a scoring and reporting system that adequately describes student performance on clearly defined learning tasks.* Because criteria are independent of each other, a different reporting system could be used from objective to objective. Nevertheless, some indication of whether a student accomplished a particular objective must be made. This could be a percentage score or

absolute mastery. The teacher and student alike should have no diffi-culty in determining whether an objective was successfully mastered.

Criterion-referenced measurement may be easily accommodated within several current teaching-learning trends:

1. Within a learning hierarchy, mastery from one level to the next is necessary for advanced learning to occur. Recognition of learning deficiencies at any level provides the teacher with an instructional direction.

2. Within the theory of instruction, behavioral objectives are an important procedure. They are, in fact, performance objectives because they specify the desired terminal behavior of the student.

3. Because computer-assisted instruction is highly individualized and based on mastery learning, criterion-referenced feedback is essential to effective computer programming.

4. With all individualized instruction, the student must be at least initially evaluated on some basis other than norm-referenced measurement if individualization is to be meaningful.

Marking Systems

A grade or mark is an established symbol that represents the final mea-surement of a given set of educational objectives. A marking system is useful as a means of communication so long as the marks are based on

---

Norm or Criterion Statements

Place a check mark in front of each criterion-referenced statement:

1. Freddie can balance a ledger sheet in business class.
2. Marcella ran the half-mile faster today than ever before.
3. Phil has the second highest average on the high school bowling team.
4. Marilyn knows the names of all the presidents of the United States.
5. Sally received the second highest grade on the science test.
6. Perry was the shortest player on the basketball team.
7. Ms. Reardon placed the lower fourth of the class in a special reading group.
8. Joel can skip count by 10 to 500.
9. Elbert exceeded 75 percent of his classmates on the achievement test.
10. Jessica transcribes dictation at 50 words a minute.

Clue:

Norm-referenced statements compare a person against all other persons.

Criterion-referenced statements compare a person against an established standard.

valid evaluation and have meaning for the persons involved. In the section on scores, I emphasized the problem of interpretation of scores and, specifically, the recognition of errors of measurement, for marks cannot be more accurate than the score data from which they are derived.

The most common method of grading in schools today is the **five-point system,** with letter grades of "A," "B," "C," "D," and "F." There are variations that involve pluses and minuses and other marks for incompletes or withdrawals, but essentially, there is this single set of five marks to measure classroom achievement. Because the factors that influence the evaluation of achievement vary from teacher to teacher, it is likely that, if different teachers were to evaluate the same learning experiences in the classroom, the students would receive different sets of final marks. In some cases, only test scores would be used to determine grades; in others, student interest, personality, attention, and participation would strongly influence the evaluation. The differences in evaluations would also depend on the teacher's sophistication in norm- and criterion-referenced measurement. The point is that the actual educational objectives are different for each teacher in each classroom, and the method of measuring them is likely also to be different. Marks reflect these differences and, therefore, cannot be considered meaningful and valid for comparisons from classroom to classroom.

In an attempt to resolve this difficulty, many schools have established two or more sets of marks for each course. One set is designed to reflect only the student's academic achievement; the other reflects the nonintellectual factors that are considered relevant. As helpful as this division of objectives has been, many serious problems remain. How do teachers prevent nonintellectual behaviors from influencing their evaluations of academic areas? How are ability and aptitude separated from achievement? Is progress or growth during the course more important than the achievement level reached at the end of the course? Is achievement to be measured by comparison with other student achievement in the same class, all previous classes that the instructor has had, or some ideal class of students? Further complications are involved when some students are placed in special curricula, such as honors or remedial. What are the grading standards to be for these situations? If the standards are different, and they usually are, what effect do these marks have when other educational institutions and employers compare these students' credentials with other students' marks?

As I noted earlier, many professional educators today feel that the present grading system needs to be changed. Experimental approaches range widely, from one extreme of increased subdivisions in marks to the other of no marks at all, just a statement of completion. For example, some colleges are reporting grades by using **grade points** only. In a 4-point system, in which an "A" is 4 points, a "B," 3 points, and so on, marks such as 3.3 or 2.7 are entered on the grade reports for each course. The rationale is that grade-point marks are more flexible and grade-point averages are more precise. It sounds logical enough, but the main difficulty still remains in the precision or accuracy of the original course mark. Knowing what we do about measurement errors connected with class-

Five-point system
The distribution of grades across a scale of high to low performance, usually, A, B, C, D, and F.

Grade point
The distribution of grades across a point system, usually a four-point scale. It differs from the five-point system in that it is more flexible because a grade may fall between any two given points, e.g., 3.2.

room testing, how can we believe that a grade-point mark is really accurate? Even professional test writers cannot claim such accuracy.

More moderate attempts to gain precision in marking systems are found in the use by many secondary schools and colleges of pluses and minuses on letter grades so that the number of letter grades can be increased to fifteen. The obvious problem with this approach is again one of consistency in interpretation. Are the intervals between all consecutive marks equal, or is "B—" closer to "B" than it is to "C+"? Teachers naturally view these grades differently; so we still have ambiguity. However, even with these problems of accuracy and consistency of meaning, this system has important psychological advantages for both teachers and students. Students usually feel a lot better about earning a "C+" rather than just a "C," especially if they think they deserved a "C." Similarly, teachers feel they can give a little more meaning to their marks by using the plus and minus. However, teachers often have a considerable problem in justifying to a student the evaluation process that leads to a "C+" rather than a "B—."

Recognizing the obvious faults in these attempts to make marking systems more definitive, many schools are going in the opposite direction and suggesting the use of only two marks—satisfactory-unsatisfactory or **pass-fail.** This type of marking is a simple approach and takes care of some of the measurement problems mentioned earlier, but it usually does not satisfy students and parents. Students want to know how *well* they passed a course, not just that they passed it, and parents share their concern. What frequently happens is that a third category—high pass or honors—is added to make a three-mark system.

Extending the pass-fail trend somewhat further, a few institutions are initiating the **competency approach** (Gronlund, 1974b). When a certain competency level of achievement has been reached, the student's academic record will show that he or she has satisfied that requirement or completed that part of the curriculum. This approach appears to satisfy all the measurement and scoring problems previously discussed, but, in actuality, it does not. In the classroom, the teacher still has to determine the point at which minimum competence is reached, and the likelihood that all teachers will agree in all classes as to that point of competence is remote.

The field of educational measurement will continue to investigate ways to make classroom evaluation more precise, valid, and reliable. As such attempts continue to be made, three important dimensions will be germane to the work:

1. *Students and their needs.* Measurement must focus not only on educational objectives that are more meaningful to students' lives and society, but that also satisfy students' motivational and reinforcement needs. In one way or another, students must be given the means to understand and gain insight into life processes and world problems and to acquire the necessary academic and professional skills to survive in and contribute to this world.

2. *Society and its needs.* Education is required in any modern society, and society has to have some way of knowing who can fill what positions. School systems have a responsibility to train and educate and to be able to communicate when and to what degree the training and education has been accomplished. Rapid and accurate articulation from school to school and from school to employer is necessary if adequate evaluations of a person's qualifications are to be made. Minimally, this requires accurate reporting of student achievement and progress, multiple levels of qualitative achievement, and consistent and meaningful use of symbols.

3. *Recognition of measurement and evaluation problems.* In addition to the measurement errors associated with test scores and the subjective elements that affect evaluations, there is the question of what the mark really means. If quantitative techniques are to be used in the assessing process, then educational institutions must modify their methods of communicating evaluations to students, parents, and the outside world. Marking symbols must represent evaluations as accurately as possible.

If these considerations are taken seriously and improved measurement and evaluation techniques are developed, important strides will be made in increasing this aspect of the educational process.

Although this chapter has focused on teacher-made tests that measure achievement, there are occasions when classroom teachers may wish to assess a student's attitudes or self-perceptions. Many different types of instruments are used to measure the ways individuals feel about themselves. These self-report instruments focus on personal perceptions, which are a major way we construct reality. They may focus on self-worth, self-derogation, perception of power or helplessness, personality dimensions, and responses to social phenomena. Classroom teachers may find such scales useful under two conditions: helping students become more aware of their affective responses to things and helping students broaden their own or consider an alternative point of view.

It is often difficult to ensure consistently valid responses from students on such scales. There is a tendency for students to respond in socially desirable ways that may not always reflect their true feeling or perception of something. Anderson (1981) has suggested that there are three ways to reduce this potential to answer in socially desirable ways:

1. By using favorable conditions to administer a scale

2. By using instructions that clearly state that there is no right or wrong answer to each question

3. By ensuring anonymity of the respondent

This last point can be fulfilled if the teacher is going to give general feedback to the students. It cannot be fulfilled if the teacher intends to give specific feedback to individual students.

The following items that measure *self-esteem* are taken from the *Rosenberg Self-Esteem Scale* (Rosenberg, 1965):

1. I feel I do not have much to be proud of.

2. I certainly feel useless at times.

3. At times I think I am no good at all.

4. I wish I could have more respect for myself.

5. On the whole, I am satisfied with myself.

6. I feel I have a number of good qualities.

7. I take a positive attitude toward myself.

The following items reflect a way to measure a student's perception of *victimization,* the feeling that one is vulnerable in the school environment, particularly to theft, assault, and intimidation. These items were originally constructed by Simmons et al. (1979):

1. It's always younger kids who get "picked on" most in this school.

2. It is a shame that we all have to be so careful about protecting our personal property here at school.

3. There are too many students who threaten others here at school.

4. In this school, one has to worry about being "picked on."

5. Girls are more threatening to me than boys.

6. The school authorities don't do enough about kids who "shake down" other kids.

In scales such as these, the statements are specifically structured and students are expected to respond to some scaling technique. The most common are the following:

1. Yes-no or agree-disagree

2. A range of agreement to disagreement such as:
   a. Strongly agree
   b. Agree
   c. No opinion, don't know, cannot say
   d. Disagree
   e. Strongly disagree

3. An indication of frequency such as:
   a. All of the time
   b. Most of the time
   c. Some of the time
   d. Not very often
   e. Never

A different type of self-perception scale forces test takers into a choice. This type of scale reduces ambiguity and often provides the teacher with a better sense of what the results mean. Sample items from the *Intellectual Achievement Responsibility Questionnaire* (Crandall, Katkovsky, & Crandall, 1965) illustrate forced choice questioning:

1. Suppose you did better than usual in a subject at school. Is this likely to happen
    a. Because you tried harder
    b. Because someone helped you

2. When you forget something you heard in class, is it
    a. Because the teacher didn't explain it very well
    b. Because you didn't try very hard to remember

3. If your parents tell you that you are bright or clever, it is more likely
    a. Because they are feeling good
    b. Because of something you did

Which scaling technique teachers use depends on why they administered the scale and how they will use the results. For example, if teachers want to collect data on students from class to class, even year to year, they must use a quantifiable scale that provides scores that have interpretative meaning. If they intend to use an affective scale to determine a social/citizenship grade, then the scale must not only be precise but must cover content (validity) specifically taught in the classroom. In most cases, an overall reported grade on a student's affective development should not be determined by a scale or series of scales that measures different affective characteristics. Affectivity is a subjective evaluation that is difficult to measure precisely; thus, any attempt by the teacher to turn such data into a meaningful grade is likely to fail.

If teachers are interested in gathering factual information about students so they have more insight into the group, rather than for comparing or grading purposes, they can use virtually any type of questionnaire or scale, highly structured or open-ended. Teachers must decide why they are developing a scale, how they will use the data, and how precise a measurement is needed. Rarely do affective measures have the same strength as cognitive measures, and teachers should remember that they yield different types of information.

Annotated Readings

Graziano, W. G., Varca, P. E., & Levy, J. C. (1982) Race of examiner effects and the validity of intelligence tests. *Review of Educational Research, 52,* 469–498.

> *The authors review recent evidence for the influence of examiner's race on examinee's performance on intelligence tests. They classify studies as either adequate or inadequate and as either complete or incomplete, based on design and sampling procedures. In general, the current literature offers little support for the hypothesis that examiner's race, per se, has a systematic effect on examinee's performance on intelligence tests. Conceptual and methodological issues are presented, as well as suggestions for future research.*

Lucas, P. A., & McConkie, G. W. (1980). The definition of test items: A descriptive approach. *American Educational Research Journal, 17,* 133–140.

> *This article describes an approach for characterizing test questions in terms of (1) the information in a passage relevant to answering them and (2) the nature of the relationship of this information to the questions. The approach offers several advantages over previous proposals based on the specification of algorithms for the production of all possible members of a class of test items. Among these are the ability to consider information in a passage that relates to a question but is not part of the text segment from which it was generated and a lack of reliance on procedures for uniquely assigning a structural description to the text.*

Nevo, D. (1983). The conceptualization of educational evaluation: An analytical review of the literature. *Review of Educational Research, 53,* 117–128.

> *Recent work has been productive in the conceptualization of educational evaluation, trying to clarify its meaning and exposing the distinction between evaluation and other related concepts. This article reviews the literature through an analytical framework, representing issues addressed by major evaluation approaches in education. The article includes discussion of the definition of evaluation, the process of doing evaluation, its methods of inquiry, and the standards that should be used to judge the worth and merit of an evaluation. Some implications for the advancement of evaluation theory and practice are summarized.*

Pedulla, J. J., Airasian, P. W., & Madaus, G. F. (1980). Do teacher ratings and standardized test results of students yield the same information? *American Educational Research Journal, 17,* 303–307.

> *Teachers rated students on IQ, mathematics, and English, as well as on twelve social and academic classroom behaviors. Analysis of IQ, math, and English standardized test scores and teacher ratings showed that there is overlap between ratings and test results but that the information obtained is not redundant. Three factors were identified: One was primarily social behaviors; a second was of the academic classroom behaviors and teacher ratings on IQ, mathematics, and English; the third was comprised of the test scores on IQ, math, and English, with corresponding teacher ratings.*

Roid, G., & Haladyna, T. (1980). The emergence of item-writing technology. *Review of Educational Research, 50,* 293–314.

> *The authors review the emerging technology for item writing for achievement and discuss several approaches to item development. They propose a continuum of item-writing methods ranging from informal, subjective methods to algorithmic, objective methods. Examples of techniques include objective-based item writing, domain-referenced concept testing, and*

computerized techniques. Each item-writing technique is critically reviewed and empirical studies of methods are described.

Tesser, A., & Campbell, J. (1982). A self-evaluation maintenance approach to school behavior. *Educational Psychologist, 17,* 1–12.

According to a recent self-evaluation maintenance model, three variables act in concert to affect self-evaluation: our relative level of performance in school, the relevance of school to our self-definition, and the psychological closeness of comparison to others in the classroom. By assuming that individuals behave so as to maximize self-evaluation, researchers can use knowledge of any two variables to predict behavior on the third. These predictions are articulated for relevance, performance, and closeness. A review of literature for each of these components is included.

The Future of Education

There is a nationwide cry for education to be more relevant and have higher academic content. On the one hand, there are back-to-basics advocates who think children's abilities in math and science are deficient; on the other, there are individuals who plead for greater understanding of human behavior and human interaction in an increasingly complex society. The developmental nature of schoolchildren causes different capacities to emerge at different points. Thus, instructional strategies must shift. The environment is becoming increasingly complex, and individuals must learn to respond to multiple options and diverse problem-solving situations. Researchers are learning that context (a behavior is more likely to occur in one situation than another) is a significant factor in human learning and behavior. Thus, existing learning may not always manifest itself because the context is not appropriate.

Broader Learning Base

Students learn from numerous sources: parents, peers, the media, electronics, community groups, and organizations. Their total response capacity is much greater than what they learn in school. Because of differences in what students bring into schools, teachers cannot assume the same instructional starting point for all students. This impacts on what teachers can do. For example, television has a major effect on learning. Proponents claim that it builds vocabulary, models behavior, and exposes viewers to wider roles. Opponents say that it interferes with problem solving, shortens attention span, sets up an expectation for being entertained in school, and interferes with homework. Television is a pervasive and powerful influence on children from preschool on; the average viewing time is four or more hours a day.

Broader Experiential Base

Individuals are engaging in a wider range of behaviors at all age levels, often pursuing personal goals without considering their impact on

495

others. Many children and adolescents have been socialized to different norms and social expectations than those of their teachers. They do not always have the same inhibitions or perceptions of behaviors. Age distinctions have diminished. Society today is more individualistic and behaviorally diverse, and educational systems must recognize this fact and accommodate to it.

Broader Societal Context

Teachers must focus on the changing context in which education occurs. We live in a rapidly changing society that both facilitates and demands different behaviors of individuals throughout their life span. The issue here is not philosophical; we must identify how to fulfill underlying educational premises in contemporary society. As society and networks within it change, different outcomes are demanded. Simple responses to complex problems do not satisfy either human or societal needs. Substantive changes have occurred in the last twenty years, and, in education, we are learning that different performance or attitudes can be expected in different contexts. If educators perceive human diversity and multiple societal change as faddish, they will not give substantive change the attention it deserves.

Broader Social Behavior

Behavior is defined within the context of three criteria: values, norms, and roles. The understanding and interaction of these expectations are the primary guidelines for most social behaviors. *Values* are beliefs that are at the center of an individual's behaviors. They are what people perceive to be important in their lives and are derived through learning. Parents, teachers, peers, and the media are the primary value sources. They model behavior, teach morality, share experiences, and interact intellectually at all ages of the individual's development. We can often infer students' values from their behavior.

Norms are behaviors that are expected of large groups of people. When a teacher sets a rule or expectation in the classroom, this becomes a norm for the students because it is the standard behavior.

Roles are more individualized than norms because they describe what is expected in a variety of contexts. Various roles do have norms, particularly in school contexts.

Educators must realize that, in contemporary society, values are more diverse, norms are more open, and roles are more numerous. For example, the norm is to have your first date at age thirteen. It is related to age and not to sexual development. As children get older, they apply

more situational criteria to personal behaviors. It may be acceptable for a twelve-year-old to drink wine at family dinner, but not to drink in any other context. With increasing diversity in families, increased roles must be played. Thus, a teenage girl may be a student, class officer, athlete, sweetheart, babysitter, and cook.

Several factors have contributed to social change. Since the 1960s, we have had significant shifts in social behavior because of the following factors:

1. *Affluence.* The increase in income and purchasing power that upgraded the worth of millions of people in society contributed to the upper-middle-class population.

2. *Automation.* The utilization of technological advancements to manufacture large quantities of products at low costs significantly reduced the number of workers needed.

3. *Urbanization.* The accelerated shift from a rural to urban society created massive population centers.

4. *Increased education.* The greater participation in high school and college educations has particularly increased the number of women and minorities pursuing education.

5. *Communications technology.* The increase in all forms of media provides people worldwide with large quantities of information within any given day.

6. *Medical technology.* Breakthroughs in many aspects of medicine

have contributed to greater general health, the prevention of many diseases, and the prolongation of life.

7. *Equal rights movement.* The wide-scale movement in the United States to establish a human role system devoid of unfair treatment and discrimination has had a tremendous impact.

8. *Sex role alternatives.* The expansion of options for women and men within society has opened up opportunities for women and increased opportunities for men.

9. *Family structures.* The development of diverse family units has been particularly facilitated by increased divorce rates and a reduction in the stigma of multiple-family structures.

10. *Individualism.* The thrust has been toward increasing the importance of the individual over the unit, be it the family, occupation, or society.

11. *Information age.* The reduction of societal dependence on industry and an accompanying need to process and respond to massive amounts of information has shifted society's educational and occupational needs.

A New Educational Model

A contemporary educational model places students and teachers, not subject matter, at the core. It defines educationally relevant experiences as those that meet individual and societal needs rather than those that produce high marks or increase standardized test scores. Students' interactions in school assume added importance. As society's needs change, schools must change in order to prepare individuals for better functioning within that society. Effective instruction should include the following:

1. *Mutually supportive environments.* Research indicates that students cannot be controlled, but need teacher support in the things they do. This requires that students and teachers learn mutual respect. Teachers must listen to students' concerns and interests.

2. *Student involvement.* Students need to be involved in the learning environment. If the classroom is structured too tightly, students have little time or motivation to put much of themselves into the teaching-learning situation. Although they may respond to teacher demands, they also need the opportunity to plan some of their own learning experiences and the time to fulfill them.

3. *Student responsibility.* Students often feel that whatever they do will be accepted. Many teachers who use norm-referenced evaluation essentially do accept whatever a student does. Many students could perform better if expectations were higher. Using criterion statements helps students understand their responsibility for learning. Again, the

more tightly structured the classroom, the more the teacher takes on the responsibility for student learning.

A Better Understanding of the Dynamics of Human Behavior

Schoolteachers are often so overwhelmed by the immediacy of their role that they do not look at the broader picture. They may have a limited understanding of human behavior and not see how to relate human dynamics to their classroom. Greater awareness could be achieved if educational systems would value and help people gain an understanding of human behavior within the educational context. This could be facilitated by establishing working groups, study groups, and research teams.

Working Groups

Within school structures, there is a strong need for effective educational implementers. Such groups must deal with the routine decisions that make the school viable for instruction and socialization. Such working groups should not be dominated by any specific strata of the educational system, but should be composed of individuals from central administration, building administration, classroom teachers, and special services. In some areas, consultants or parents should be added to working groups.

This strategy has two advantages. First, it provides input from diverse sources assigned distinctly different roles. Second, it decentralizes power by increasing those contributing to decision making. Schools today need greater grass-roots input and social consciousness.

Study Groups

Multistrata study teams can establish, maintain, and reevaluate policies and practices. School systems cannot afford to have all their employees so concerned with the specific demands of their jobs (short-term goals) that they cannot continuously reevaluate educational practices and policies (long-term goals). The working groups are designed for implementing practices. The study groups are designed to do *content analysis* to determine if educational practices are representative of educational needs, individual needs, and societal needs. This process enhances the quality of the educational environment.

Research Teams

School districts must identify their own research needs. The purpose of doing research is to gather information on how to optimize the growth/

learning potential in a specific educational environment. In a decentralized structure, educational decision making rests heavily in the hands of principals. Data are needed to increase their effectiveness. Principals, like teachers, often become overwhelmed by the immediacy of their roles. Sometimes they need a broader perspective, and research data has the potential for generating new conceptualizations and decision-making strategies. Regardless of the size of a school district, it should do some data collection and base many of its educational decisions on its own findings.

This process can be enhanced by better dialogue between school personnel and researchers from either the private or public sector. There are many researchers who would be willing to help schools identify needs and design studies that could yield important information about their school environment. Sometimes research in the schools is designed to benefit the researcher only; however, researchers and school personnel could design relevant research studies that benefit both. There must be a deliberate attempt to share interests and concerns. Marotz (1983, p. 165) had noted that researchers have a unique opportunity to assist school personnel in developing studies and answering questions. Reflecting upon his own junior high school, Marotz indicated that some pressing, yet unanswered, questions include:

1. Should students be taught in interdisciplinary blocks or single subject courses?

2. What is the impact of cocurricular activities on students?

3. How do students acquire basic skills such as language arts, math, social studies, and science?

4. How much daily physical activity should students have?

5. What learning and teaching styles should be employed?

6. To what extent should students explore and clarify values at school or is this appropriately done elsewhere?

7. What impact do minority or handicapped students have when infused into a new setting because of a court order or state mandate?

8. How do we deal with or what should we expect from single-parent families or multiple families?

9. How should schools plan on research in the area of computer technology? Is this another fad?

10. Are teachers being adequately prepared in colleges today?

11. What type of teachers exist today as compared with those of twenty or ten years ago? What will they need to be like in the future?

Studying Those Who Work with Students

It is important to study the interactions between adults and students. Many school-related problems are administrative/organizational or

teacher problems, and not student problems. Yet they impact on student behavior. Recent research on school climate has provided some insight into what constitutes effective schooling and teaching. This research is very important because we must know more about school environments and the nature of individuals working within them.

Mackenzie (1983) has summarized the dimensions of effective schooling. He points out that increased research on teaching and learning has resulted in a new context for thinking about school as a total learning environment. He conceptualizes the dimensions of this total environment as leadership, efficacy, and efficiency.

School leadership falls under the jurisdiction of the principal. The intuitive belief, supported by some studies, is that more effective leadership will generate a better overall school climate. Efficacy dimensions may tell us more about effectiveness. The reconceptualization of school philosophy and the redesign of implementation strategies may help educators meet their goals. In a society where increased pressure is being applied to the schools, careful consideration of educational goals and strategies must be undertaken. School personnel are the change agents and can effect change if they develop more contemporary goals, update curriculum, recommit to excellence, and create greater incentives for teachers in their work environment.

The efficiency dimension relates to how educational goals and objectives are carried out. Recent innovations such as mastery learning, direct instruction, and cognitive instructional strategies all point to the fact that teachers must be more efficient in delivering instruction. In order to do this, colleges of education must develop more contemporary and intense preservice programs, local school districts must support in-service education, and teachers must carry a stronger sense of dignity and professionalism. I present Mackenzie's summary of school climate dimensions in Box E–1.

If educators work from the assumption that effective schools should be based on bottom-up input, then networks must be established to gather and analyze information. Schools that incorporate these basic school-

Facilitating Elements

Emphasis on homework and study
Positive accountability; acceptance of responsibility for learning outcomes
Strategies to avoid nonpromotion of students
Deemphasis of strict ability grouping; interaction with more accomplished peers

Efficiency Dimensions:

Core Elements

Effective use of instructional time; amount and intensity of engagement in school learning
Orderly and disciplined school and classroom environments
Continuous diagnosis, evaluation, and feedback
Well-structured classroom activities
Instruction guided by content coverage
Schoolwide emphasis on basic and higher order skills

Facilitating Elements

Opportunities for individualized work
Number and variety of opportunities to learn

Source: Mackenzie (1983), p. 5. By permission of the American Educational Research Association.

climate dimensions will find a vital and fresh approach surfacing. When school districts themselves are innovative and develop the mechanism for all involved to have input, they tell both the beginning teacher and the twenty-year veteran that their ideas are important, that they have an effect on educational decision making. Further, bottom-up input provides the mechanism for input from all levels and exchanges of information at all levels. Implementing these strategies becomes a matter of reallocating priorities and developing a workable plan that will not be neutralized by immediate demands, personnel changes, or diverse administrative leadership. It is a successful strategy for getting at the academic and social goals critical to effective schooling.

New School Curricula

There is a tendency to focus on traditional educational processes and problems. Contemporary emphasis from external pressure groups to

return to the basics and to upgrade math and science instruction endorses the idea that if we return to the more traditional method of doing things, we can reduce problems facing education. The failure to recognize social and individual complexities is a serious shortcoming of these advocates of tradition.

What is needed in contemporary education is a curriculum that impacts on the individual in the educational and total environments. As structures change, so does the human behavior related to them. The need to identify contemporary phenomena affecting relevant education is important to educational researchers and practitioners alike. If we are going to meet student needs, we must understand factors impacting upon them. The traditional model—that all students must adjust to the needs or agenda of the schools—will not be successful in educating students today to function in a changing world.

In response to societal change, educationally relevant experiences must bring about self-fulfillment within the new frameworks. We have shifted from an industrial to an information society, and school curricula must shift as well. Using the context of the economy, Naisbitt (1982, p. 13) has stated, "It makes no sense to reindustrialize an economy that is not based on industry, but on the production and distribution of information. Without an appreciation of the larger shifts that are restructuring our society, we act on assumptions that are out of date. Out of touch with the present, we are doomed to fail in the unfolding future." Naisbitt could have been describing education. Most school curricula were developed to educate individuals to function within an industrial society. Just as education changed its curriculum at the turn of the twentieth century from meeting the needs of an agricultural society to meeting those of the emerging industrial society, so it must now shift its curriculum to meet the needs of a rapidly emerging information society.

When developing a new curriculum, educators must be aware that knowledge, not products or property, is the key resource. Learning will become a central feature of the new society because it is self-generating, renewable, and capable of meeting the needs of diverse individuals in a complex world. Table E–1 overviews differences between educational goals in an industrial society and an informational society. The Westrend Group believe such goals are evolutionary, that is, they extend rather than replace current emphases (New Directions, 1983).

The Computer as a Change Mechanism

Computer literacy is a new catch phrase today. The emphasis on microcomputers in homes, industry, and schools is clearly substantive in nature; yet many educators do not take it seriously. Few schools in the

Table E–1   Contrasting Educational Goals

Goal Areas	Industrial Society	Information Society
Cognitive Goals	Basic skills	Higher order skills
	Specific training	Generalizable skills
	Right to read	Right to excel
	U.S. citizenship	Global community citizenship
	Literacy as survival skill	Many literacies, more than one language
Affective Goals	Competition dominant	Collaboration dominant
	Organization dependent	Independent, entrepreneurial
	Single family oriented	Support group oriented
	Large organization skills	Small group skills
Curriculum Areas	Mathematical computation	Mathematical reasoning and application
	Science appreciation	Science utilization
	Print oriented	Computer literacy and use of computer tools
	Social studies	Global and multicultural education and understanding
	Physical education	Physical/mental well being
	Arts appreciation	Aesthetic education/creativity
Career Preparation	Single career preparation	Multiple career preparation
	Distinct vocational education programs	Integrated academic/vocational programs

Source: From New Directions for Education Goals, 1983, p. 5. By permission.

United States have a workable or comprehensive plan for developing computer literacy (Pogrow, 1982a). School districts have limited money to purchase microcomputers and accompanying software packages. Educators may perceive this shift as just another fad—but it is not!

Education is the last major structure where computers are impacting. For example, of all computers sold in 1978, 75.5 percent were sold for home use, 17.8 percent for the workplace, and only 6.7 percent for schools (Nilles, 1980). Computers have had some impact with business/personnel management and student records, but most computer literate students have learned on their own home computers. I am not advocating that computer literacy be the major educational goal, but it is a need to which educators must respond.

Pogrow (1983) sees computers rapidly emerging as both a cultural technology and primary work tool. A cultural technology innovation is defined as one that is found in at least 10 percent of the homes. A primary work tool is designed to changed the nature of work and is required in 25 percent of the jobs. Using these criteria, Pogrow (1983, p. 22) suggests that the greater the extent to which computers become "both a cultural and work-tool technology, the greater will be the demand and need for their use in schools." Table E–2 demonstrates the technological impact microcomputers have had and shall continue to have in the future. Schools must be prepared by 1985–1986 to respond to these technological advances if education is to meet a basic societal need (Pogrow, 1982b; Porat, 1977).

Whereas 15,000 microcomputers were sold to schools in 1978, 538,000 is the projected 1990 sale. School use will increase dramatically. Table E–3 shows the change in the number of schools having microcomputers between 1980 and 1983. It is projected that every school in the United States will have at least one microcomputer before the decade is over.

Several factors contribute to an increase in microcomputer use in the public schools:

1. *Awareness.* There is increased awareness that high technology is a substantive change in society that education must address.

Table E–2   Technology Assessment (TA) of Societal Use of Microcomputers

	1980–1985	1985–1990	1999–
Cultural Technology	Increasing use for entertainment and simple applications.	Found in about 40 percent of homes, increasingly used for accessing electronic data bases and home education.	Extensive use accessing electronic data bases and home education. Found in a majority of homes.
Primary Work Tool	Extensive use for technicians and clerks. Minor implications for blue collar work.	Growing use by nontechnician managers; some replacement of blue collar work.	Basic tool used for managing communications and conferences. Large scale replacement of blue collar and other routine work.

Source: From S. Pogrow, *Education in the Computer Age,* 1983, p. 51.

Table E–3   Number of Public Elementary/Secondary Schools with Computers Available for Instruction and Major Uses of Computers, by Grade Level: School Year 1981–82

Item	All Schools	Elementary Schools	Junior High Schools	Senior High Schools	Combined and Other
Total number of schools	81,970	50,800	11,184	14,113	5,874
Schools with computers:					
Number	29,027	11,364	5,822	10,445	1,396
Percent of total	35	22	52	74	24
Schools with microcomputers:					
Number	27,501	11,050	5,774	9,504	1,173
Percent of total	34	22	52	67	20
Percent indicating as major uses:					
Compensatory and remedial	14	18	20	6	19
Basic skills	19	29	11	12	6
Learning enrichment	19	21	19	18	4
Computer literacy	33	29	30	39	34
Computer science	23	7	10	49	15
Schools with terminals:					
Number	5,898	958	978	3,620	343
Percent of total	7	2	9	26	6
Percent indicating as major uses:					
Compensatory and remedial	12	23	28	6	0
Basic skills	13	20	10	13	0
Learning enrichment	24	28	23	21	50
Computer literacy	22	0	23	28	15
Computer science	34	0	14	47	45

Source: From *The Condition of Education*, 1983 ed. National Center for Educational Statistics, p. 40.

2. *Hardware availability.* There has been a dramatic decrease in cost of hardware. There are many different types of microcomputers, all of which cost a fraction of their price a few years ago. Noyce (1977) has noted that today's computers are 1/30,000 the volume of the first computers and 1/10,000 the cost.

3. *Software availability.* For education, software development has not kept pace with hardware development. Although hardware costs are decreasing, software costs are increasing because the development of quality materials takes considerable time and staff. Still, as microcomputers become more prevelant, so will software, and it will eventually drop in cost.

4. *Allocated spending.* Local school boards will have to increase budget allocations for purchasing hardware and software. Because these initial investments are high, careful planning by school personnel is essential to ensure the purchase of high quality and versatile equipment. Nevertheless, if education is to respond to the broad societal need, additional spending must occur.

5. *Teacher training.* Colleges of education must make computer education courses part of their basic preservice curricula. Because of the dominance of microcomputers in the home and workplace, numerous

students will bring computer skills into school. Educators must be able to respond to these students' needs.

6. *Continued innovations.* Across this decade, additional information designed to represent vision, hearing, and touch will surface. New technology will advance the currently primitive voice input devices and speech synthesizers (Pogrow, 1983). Such new technologies will reach an even broader segment of the school population, such as special education students.

Various task forces and commissions on education have pointed out the deficiencies in the current educational system, particularly in regard to math, science, and computer literacy. The assertion is that scientific and technical literacy is necessary in our society, but high school graduates have limited, if any, literacy in these areas. Such deficiencies are often placed in the world context; an increase in computer understanding and efficiency is presumed to secure a stronger national defense and maintain world dominance in the electronics field. Few point out the importance of computer literacy in everyday functioning.

Although the study of computers is intrinsically valuable, educators should also develop an awareness of the advantages of computers both in interdisciplinary problem solving and as an aid to instruction. Educational decision makers, including classroom teachers, should seek to make computers readily available as an integral part of the education program. Thus, computers can go far beyond the drill-and-practice technology discussed in Chapter 13. They can also be used in problem solving, programming concepts, and simulating life events. We still do not know the full capacity of computers.

Educators face classrooms full of academically and socially complex individuals. Students' options are increasing and their ability to make choices or decisions must increase as well. Educators must provide students with the understanding and skills for effective choice selection and decision-making. Cognitive mastery in a world that generates stimuli far faster than we can sort them out depends upon strategies for reducing the complexity and clutter (Bruner, 1960).

Throughout this decade, education must be increasingly upgraded and relevant. To fail to identify important human and societal needs is to undereducate students. We simply cannot afford to *undereducate* America's schoolchildren. The long-term consequences are too costly.

Ability grouping The placement of students with comparable abilities within the same academic classroom; sometimes called homogeneous grouping.

Acceleration The advancement of a gifted or talented student to a higher grade level.

Accommodation The intellectual process whereby individuals increase their internal symbol system in order to derive meaning from external events.

Achievement motivation The learned need to achieve or feel competent.

Active avoidance learning The pursuit of an alternative behavior to avoid punishment.

Adaptation The process of adjusting to internal or external conditions that affect intelligence.

Affective evaluation The self-determination of whether or not one's affective behavior has been instrumental in meeting one's needs.

Affective learning The process through which we acquire emotions, drives, or temperament associated with our feeling state instead of our thought processes.

Affective learning readiness The developmental maturity or prerequisite learning needed to acquire affective content.

Affective learning sources The individual, institutions, or other avenues from which people learn affective content.

Anal stage The second of Freud's stages, characterized by control over elimination of body wastes.

Analysis The process of breaking down an idea or skill into its component parts.

Annoyer A term used by Thorndike to describe something that is unpleasant or punishing to an organism.

Anxiety A state of tension, nervousness, or fear that a student brings into the learning environment.

Apperception Relating newly learned information, skills, or feelings to existing ones.

Application The ability to use intellectual skills and concepts in applied settings.

Appreciation The involvement in a high-interest activity because of one's feeling and understanding of it.

Approach-approach motive A term describing a situation in which an individual must select between two positive incentives that are moving one toward a goal.

Approach-avoidance motive A term describing a situation in which an individual must select between a positive and negative incentive when moving toward a goal.

Approach motive A term indicating when individuals move toward a goal because the incentives are positive.

Articulation The ability to integrate multiple motor skills into one sequential activity.

Articulation of content Preparation of a well-planned and integrated course of study.

Aspirations Goal-setting behaviors that are self-generated or teacher-facilitated; these behaviors motivate students to move toward their goals.

Assimilation The intellectual process whereby individuals modify or translate external events into internal symbol systems in order to acquire them.

Association The process of establishing connections between events in the mind.

Associative ability The input of information that is straightforward, requiring little or no interpretation—such as learning a fact.

Attention According to social learning theory, the learner focuses on aspects of the model's behavior that the learner desires to imitate.

Attitudes The emotional disposition to behave in some way.

Auditory information The term used in Bransford's information-processing model to describe learning that is initially received through hearing.

Authoritarianism In classrooms, the excessive or arbitrary control of students by teachers.

Autonomic process The ability to function independently, thus gaining muscle control.

Autonomous moral development The internalization of external rules to the point that they can be modified in special situations.

Aversive control The withdrawal of a student from an unpleasant situation that reinforced an undesired behavior. Synonymous with negative reinforcement.

511

Avoidance-avoidance motive A term describing a situation in which an individual must select between two negative incentives in pursuit of a goal.

Avoidance learning The deliberate avoidance of a situation or individual that has been punishing.

Avoidance motive A term indicating that progress toward a goal is impeded because incentives are negative.

Behavior The observable responses of an organism or any of its parts.

Behavior modification The direct application of learning principles with the expressed intent to alter behavior.

Behavior overdwelling The tendency for a teacher to stress a point to the extent of fatigue or redundancy.

Behavioral ecology Experiences that result from the interaction of students and teachers with their environment.

Behavioral objective A teacher-generated statement that describes expected student performance once instruction is completed.

Bias The belief that items on an IQ test might favor one subgroup within society.

Branching program A programming technique that utilizes multiple pieces of information in learning, although the learner must respond in appropriate sequence for learning and reinforcement to occur.

Castration complex The Freudian position that male children abandon cross-sex attachment because of the fear of being castrated.

Categorization The ability to process information into the mind, integrating it with already existing information.

Characterization The long-term commitment to personal beliefs and behaviors, often referred to as one's life-style.

Classical conditioning The substitution of a neutral stimulus for the stimulus that naturally elicits the response.

Class inclusion The ability to see that something is complete within itself but is also a member of a larger classification system.

Coding The translation of information, either verbally or visually, into the mind so it may be stored.

Cognition A general term describing all the ways in which people think, for example knowledge, concepts, reasoning.

Cognitive growth A general term used to describe the way in which intellectual development unfolds over time.

Cognitive psychology The study of new patterns, knowledge, or ideas in a dynamic and meaningful way.

Cognize The ability to think about the rightness or wrongness of something.

Communication disorder The dysfunctional category

that describes any pattern of speech that varies from normal expectations.

Competence In motivational theory, the inherent desire to function successfully in the environment.

Competence approach A grading system based strictly on mastering pre-designated criteria.

Competing responses The presentation of two or more response options, only one of which is possible to perform prior to a reinforcer.

Completion/short-answer terms The presentation of questions that require the student to supply information. They are not as objective as multiple-choice or true-false; not as subjective as essay.

Complex learning The acquisition of information of skills that contain multiple components, thus multiple behavioral potential.

Comprehension The ability to interpret information by using one's own words or form.

Computer-aided instruction The utilization of carefully designed hardware and software that contain academic content that can be presented to students.

Concept The internal representation of multiple ideas and attitudes by classifying them into previously established categories.

Concept assimilation The process of learning the attributes of a concept or proposition, usually through abstract verbal representation.

Concept mapping The method of showing the relationship between concepts or ideas within the structure of subject matter.

Conceptual ability The input of information that requires internal processing or transformation—such as explaining something.

Concrete concept The categorization of an object or event that is characterized by physical properties.

Concrete operations period The developmental period wherein emerges all the components required to carry out logical reasoning and to offer verbal verification of such reasoning.

Conditioned response A response that is controlled by its specific pairing with a conditioned stimulus.

Conditioned stimulus The deliberate pairing of a neutral stimulus with an unconditioned stimulus in order to condition a response.

Conjunctive concept utilization The ability to place multiple objects in the same category because they have similar attributes.

Connectionism The reinforced association of a stimulus and response in the mind.

Connotative understanding Learning the meaning of something in affective and personal ways, beyond any literal meaning.

Conservation The recognition that something remains

the same in quantity although it may be manifested in different ways.

Consistency The extent to which a person's behavior is repeatedly the same or similar.

Content The ideas that go into an experience a person is having in school; subject matter makes up the experience.

Content analysis The systematic analysis of the content being taught during affective instruction.

Contents of thought Guilford's description of the kinds of things individuals think about, for example, school subject matter, experiences.

Content-specific questions An item within an IQ test that is so specific that its correct answer may be more attributable to learning than to intelligence.

Content validity The analysis of sample test items to determine adequate representation of the items.

Contiguity The theoretical position that holds that if two or more events occur in the same time frame, learning will result.

Contiguity of experience The consistent expression of oneself over an extended period of time.

Continuous reinforcement schedule The application of a reinforcer following every response.

Conventional level According to Kohlberg, the ability to describe moral behavior in terms of what is right or wrong regardless of one's action.

Corrective feedback Providing information to the learner on how to improve on a reproduced behavior that is less than optimal.

Counterconditioning The substitution of one response for another in order to alter behavior.

Criterion-referenced measurement The assessment of student behavior against predetermined performance criteria.

Crystallized general ability Cattell's theoretical construct that accounts for the environmental influences on mental functioning.

Culture The dominant social influences on the lives of people.

Curriculum The designation of specific academic content intended to provide a comprehensive education to learners.

Curve The way all scores derived from administering an IQ test are shown in relation to each other.

Deaf The ability to partly hear or not hear verbal information.

Decenter The intellectual ability to look at more than one property of a physical event.

Decision making opportunity The extent to which people have the opportunity to actually make personal affective decisions.

Delayed speech Deviation from the expected ability to speak due to personal development.

Democratic discipline The development of classroom rules and regulations that promotes order but is not arbitrary or capricious.

Denotative understanding The verbal representation of a physical object.

Development The gradual increase in size and capacity of humans over time.

Dialogue system Software programs that allow the student to interact with the computer in the learning process.

Differentiation of fields The perceptual ability to discriminate among phenomenon in the environment.

Direct instruction The maintenance of student involvement in a learning task; sometimes called *engaged time* or *time-on-task*.

Discipline An externally imposed control on students.

Discovery learning Awareness or understanding of objects, events, or symbols in our environment gained through personal exploration.

Discriminated stimulus The presentation of a specific event in order to establish a specific response.

Disinhibition The reproduction of a previously inhibited behavior because an observer sees the behavior in a model without negative consequences.

Disjunctive concept utilization The understanding of multiple meaning in any phenomenon that represents the concept category.

Drill and practice systems Simple computer programs that present additional instances of already learned material to students in order for them to continue their learning.

Drive The motivational state of an organism set up by deprivation in the organism.

Drive reduction theory A theory stating that an organism is motivated to act when a need has to be satisfied.

Dyslexia The inability to properly encode into the mind phenomena that are seen or heard.

Ego The personality dimension of the individual that tries to construct reality in the world, tempering both the id and the superego.

Ego integrity The ability to interact with the social environment while maintaining a sense of self by perceiving both the self and society in a balanced perspective.

Electra complex A cross-sex attachment in the direction of a daughter toward a father that results in pleasure.

Empathic content Expression of personal thinking in social contexts.

Emotional development The emergence of the capacity to feel and express oneself in emotional ways.

Empirical law of effect Kenneth Spence's theory that

responses that reduce drive are more likely to reoccur than those that do not.

Enactive representation   The ability to represent environmental phenomenon through one or more of the senses.

Enrichment   The acceleration of subject matter within a classroom for gifted or talented students.

Epigenetic principle   The belief that as genetically determined human capacity increases it is influenced by the prevailing social environment.

Equivalence category   The ability to respond to different objects, events, or other phenomena as if they were the same.

Error factor   The amount of error that possibly occurs as a function of test administration. It is calculated and reported as the standard error of measurement.

Essay item   An item that provides stimulus information necessary for students to compose a response in some detail.

Evaluation   The qualitative assessment (subjective) of behavior. In regard to cognitive behavioral objectives it is the ability to judge something based on previously defined criteria.

Examiner bias   The belief that test examiners of one ethnicity may discriminate against examinees of a different ethnicity, either purposefully or inadvertently.

Exceptional child   Any individual who deviates from the average child or normative behaviors.

Excitatory potential   The strength of the likelihood that a specific stimulus will trigger a specific response.

Expressive speech problems   Difficulty in communicating information to others.

Extinction   The reduction of a response tendency by the withholding of reinforcement.

Extrapolation   Projecting or going beyond the apparent meaning of something.

Extrinsic motivation   The desire to act if appropriate incentives are created within the environment.

Facilitation   The exercise of a learned response that has not previously been reproduced because the learner now sess it reproduced by a model.

Factor analysis   A statistical procedure that verifies the relationship between several behaviors representative of the same ability, e.g., numerical ability.

Field of vision   The angle or breadth of one's vision.

Figural content   The ability to perceive through the senses.

Figure   A Gestalt term used to describe phenomena in our environment that perceptually stand out.

Five-point system   The distribution of grades across a scale of high-to-low performance, usually, A, B, C, D, and F.

Fixed internal schedule   Applying reinforcement after a predetermined time has elapsed.

Fixed ratio schedule   Reinforcing the learner after a predetermined number of responses has occurred.

Fixed schedule   Giving reinforcers in a specific, regular pattern.

Fluid general ability   Cattell's theoretical construct that accounts for heredity's influence on mental functioning.

Forgetting   The loss in memory of previously learned material.

Formal operations   The emergence of abstract and theoretical thought throughout adolescence.

Form quality   The quality of a whole but not of its component parts.

Fragmentation   The tendency for a teacher to tell something to several students individually that could have been told effectively to the entire class.

Frame   The designation of a specific piece of information that students should learn. Frames are sequentially arranged to maximize learning.

Frequency   The more frequently an organism makes a response to a stimulus, the more likely that it will respond to that stimulus again.

Functional application   Generating a product that transmits relevant information to the receiver.

Generative grammar   Language is composed of a large set of potential combinations although only a few words/sentences are used in any specific setting.

Genital period   The resurgence of sexual energy triggered by physical and sexual maturation at the onset of adolescence.

Gestalt   A configuration or pattern of a psychological phenomena that is a whole entity.

g factor   The construct designed to explain a general basis for intellectual functioning.

Gifted child   Any individual with high intellectual or creative ability or talent.

Global intelligence   The belief that several components in the mind collectively makes up a person's intelligence.

Grade point   The distribution of grades across a point system, usually a four-point scale. It differs from the five-point system in that is is more flexible because a grade may fall between any two given points, i.e., 3.2.

Ground   A Gestalt term used to describe the total environment of which we are aware at any given time.

Group intelligence tests   An IQ test specifically designed to be administered to a large group of people simultaneously in a paper-and-pencil format.

Growth   Quantitative change in human body characteristics.

Growth readiness   The belief that biological growth

must occur prior to an individual having the capacity to learn or behave in certain ways.

Habit   The tendency to repeat or maintain a behavior.

Habit-family hierarchy   The ordering of response tendencies in an organism by their likelihood to ccur.

Handicapped child   Any individual who has a functional impairment that precludes normal performance in a specific area.

Hard-of-hearing   A person who cannot hear without the use of a hearing aid.

Hedonism   The deliberate attempt to seek pleasure while avoiding pain.

Heteronomous moral development   The acceptance of external rules learned from an authority.

Hierarchical learning   The arrangement of acquired responses into a hierarchy from simple to complex.

Hierarchical structures   The arrangement of learning in a way where lower level skills are prerequisite to and facilitate the acquisition of higher level skills.

Higher order concept   According to Gagné, the ability to relate rules to each other in order for a more complex cognitive strategy to emerge.

Highly structured response   The development of a test item that elicits very specific, noninterpretable answers.

Hypothesis   A theoretical statement designed to explain observed behavior.

Iconic representation   According to Bruner, an awareness of the concrete representation of phenomena in the environment.

Id   The personality dimension of the individual that seeks pleasure or basic satisfaction.

Identity category   The ability to classify events that represent the same category.

Imitation   The rehearsal in one's mind of a motor behavior observed in a model.

Implicit grammar   The formation of pre-vocal language environment.

Incentive   The increase in the motivational state of an organism due to the reinforcement of an emitted response.

Independent study   The opportunity for one student to work on his/her own within the classroom environment.

Individual education plan (IEP)   A written statement that prescribes the course of intervention for a special education student within a given time period.

Individual intelligence test   An IQ test specifically designed to be orally administered to people on an individual basis.

Individualized instruction   Instructional activity designed specifically for an individual or small groups of students.

Individually guided instruction   The development of an instructional team that cooperatively plans and fulfills classroom instruction in multiple ways, depending on the situational demands.

Information processing   The storing and retrieving of information in the mind. While in storage, information may interact, thus forming new capacities.

Inhibition   The suppression of the reproduction of behavior because the observer sees its negative consequences on a model.

Insight   The sudden awareness of relationships between things.

Insight learning   The theory that through perception people can put things together, which results in learning and problem solutions.

Instructional program for mastery   A variation of the Learning for Mastery technique that also evaluates individual performance against specified criteria.

Intangible reinforcers   Application of reinforcers, such as free time or special privileges, following a student behavior.

Intellectual development   Gradual increase in thought processes.

Intelligence   A hypothetical construct that describes ways of behaving in lower organisms and humans.

Interactive effect   In classrooms, the understanding that teachers and students alike influence each other.

Interests   The behavior a person chooses from freedom of choice.

Interference   The process whereby one learned response is inhibited by other learning.

Intermittent schedule   The application of reinforcers at varying frequencies following responses or time intervals.

Interpretation   Explaining something that is presented in a different form—such as data in a graph.

Interval schedule   The systematic application of a reinforcer following a given time period.

Intrinsic motivation   An inner drive to explore and acquire without dependency on external incentives.

Intuitive stage   According to Piaget, the ability to carry out simple problem solving without the corollary capacity to explain what one has just done.

Intuitive thinking   The self-generated initiative to explore the environment and learn on our own.

Invariate functions   The belief that an aspect of development occurs in all humans in the same way without variance.

Knowledge objective   The lowest level cognitive objective that requires the recall of information, facts, and so forth.

Knowledge structure   The arrangement of concepts that makes each one part of a more encompassing concept.

Laboratory computing device   A computer program that allows students to develop their own learning program in any given subject matter area.

Language acquisition device   The universal, inherent ability to be linguistically competent.

Large group instruction   The presentation of classroom material to all the students in a classroom at any given time.

Latency period   The period roughly equivalent to the elementary school years during which a child abandons attempts at sexual pleasure and learns the mores, customs, and expectations of society.

Lateral transfer   A term used by Gagné to describe the generalization of information at the same level of complexity across multiple situations.

Law of association   The idea that learning occurs by the contiguous pairing of a stimulus and a response.

Law of closure   The theory that things perceived to be complete are complete.

Law of common direction   The belief that geometric shapes will be grouped together if they complete an object or concept.

Law of effect   The theoretical position that holds that a reinforced response is learned and will likely reoccur.

Law of exercise   The concept that the stimulus-response bond in the mind is strengthened by use, weakened by disuse.

Law of proximity   The concept that our perception that things in the environment go together.

Law of similarity   The grouping together of objects or events in the environment that are perceived to go together.

Law of simplicity   The Gestalt explanation of symmetry in the environment. Environment is viewed as simple, regular patterns.

Learning   The acquisition or modification of a response that results from experience.

Learning disability   Any physical or neurological based problem that interferes with human potential.

Learning for Mastery   An instructional design that compares individual student expectations, instructional criteria, and assessment of actual performance against the criteria rather than against other students.

Learning hierarchy   The organization of a set of learned capabilities so they have logical relationships with each other.

Level of response   The capacity to perform learned behaviors with varying degrees of complexity (that is, facts, concepts, rules).

Libido   A person's sexual energy that strives for pleasure throughout the lifespan.

Life space   The totality of the individual in his or her perceived physical and psychological environment at any given time.

Linear programming   A simple programming technique that focuses on small bits of information that, when sequenced, complete a learning task.

Logical meaningfulness   According to Ausubel, material to be learned must fall within the learner's capacity to comprehend.

Long-term memory   The retention of learned material for an extended time through encoding of information into the mind.

Loop   A mechanism within branching that presents corrective feedback to the learners if they select the incorrect response.

Mainstreaming   The integrating of a special education student, regardless of handicap, into the regular classroom.

Manipulation   In psychomotor behavioral objectives, the actual performance of a more behavior as a result of learning.

Mastery   Learning or performing academic and social tasks at or beyond the designated level of expectation.

Matching items   The presentation of multiple pieces of information that students must discriminate among and pair correctly.

Maturation   The nonobservable changes in human body characteristics.

Mean   The arithmetical average score. In the case of IQ testing, one would add up all scores and divide by the number of people taking the test to find the mean score.

Meaningful learning set   The learner's intent to integrate new learning into his or her existing cognitive structure.

Meaningfulness   The extent to which learning is useful or purposeful in a person's life.

Meaningful reception learning   The ability to combine, relate, or reorganize ideas, concepts, and rules in order to generate new learning.

Measurement   The quantitative assessment (objective) of behavior.

Measurement by objective   Assessment of student behavior in relation to specific criteria.

Memory   The ability of humans to store learning in the mind for subsequent use.

Mental discipline theory   The theory that the mind is strengthened by exercise.

Mental retardation   The development of one's mentality that is below normal, implying limited intellectual capacity.

Minimal brain dysfunction   Mild neurological damage that interferes with an individual's ability to function normally.

Monogenetic   The belief that intelligence is based on a single factor that is inherited.

Motivation   The term Bandura uses in place of reinforcement because he views the effects as facilitating motivation and not learning.

Multi-factor tests   Measures of human intelligence that determine capability to function in several dimensions, not just in one or two.

Multiple-choice items   An objective test item that supplies several plausible answers from which the student must choose.

Naturalization   The routine performance of a highly developed motor skill.

Natural unfoldment   The idea that individuals, as they develop, unfold the capacity to learn without undue dependence on the environment.

Needs theory   The belief that our needs are learned and, as they are met, they motivate us to behave.

Negative reinforcer   The strengthening of behavior by removing an unpleasant event following the behavior.

Negative transfer   The learning of a task is inhibited by previous learning.

Neutral stimulus   Any event in the environment that is incapable of eliciting a response from an organism.

Neutral transfer   The belief that some learning tasks are unrelated, thus there is no transfer effect.

Nonspecific transfer   The acquisition of a general trait or learning process that might be applied in a variety of subsequent learning situations.

Norms   Expectations of human behavior that emerge from such sources as the family, school, religion, and society.

Norm-referenced instruction   The comparison of all students against each other on some specified task or assessment.

Norm-referenced measurement   The assessment of student performance by comparing any individual with all other students taking the same measure.

Objective items   Test items written with enough specificity that the answer is clearly correct or incorrect.

Observational learning   The acquisition of behavior through the vicarious observation of that behavior in another.

Oedipus complex   A cross-sex attachment in the direction of a son toward a mother that results in pleasure.

Omission statement   No verbal or written activity on the part of a teacher that otherwise might reinforce a student's behavior.

One-to-one instruction   Direct instruction to only one individual in a classroom.

Ontogeny   The evolution or development of the individual.

Operant conditioning   The voluntary behavior of an organism that acts upon the environment. The result is that the organism learns.

Operant extinction   The purposeful withholding of any reinforcing event that has previously established or maintained an undesirable behavior.

Operation of thought   Guildford's description of the way in which the mind functions that includes types of thinking, memory, and logic.

Oral stage   The first of Freud's developmental stages that is characterized by gaining pleasure through stimulation of the mouth.

Organization   Ordering multiple values in a hierarchical way in one's mind.

Original learning   The point at which a response in initially acquired.

Overlearning   Practicing a learned response after it is presumably mastered.

Pass fail   A grading system that avoids numerical weighting by indicating a student either passed or failed on a designated task, test, or course.

Passive avoidance learning   Purposefully not responding in order to avoid punishment.

Perception   Awareness of one of the senses by external stimulation.

Performance   The actual exercise of a behavior that has been learned and is in a person's response repertoire. In Bandura's theory, it is known as reproduction.

Performance IQ   A standardized IQ score that is based solely on a person's performance or nonverbal behavior.

Performance needs   The academic capacities students bring into the classroom that will facilitate or hinder learning.

Permissiveness   A lack of classroom control or regulation of student behavior. It typically reinforces irresponsible student behavior by not establishing clear expectations.

Personal need   The psychological reason for learning that students bring into the classroom.

Phallic stage   The developmental period in which pleasure is derived by stimulation of the genital area.

Phylogeny   The evolution of a species or race.

Physical disability   The inability to physically function due to loss of limb, muscle control, or damage.

Physical health disorder   The curtailment of normal physical functions because of a chronic health problem.

Physical impairment   Any disability or health disorder that interferes with physical functioning.

Postconventional level The understanding of morality in relation to individual rights and specific situations.

Positive reinforcer Any event following a response that is rewarding to an individual and increases the probability of the response recurring.

Positive transfer The process by which learning of a task is facilitated by previous learning.

Postlanguage position The belief that language is necessary if concepts are to be learned.

Potential meaningfulness The capacity to relate new learning to what the learner already knows.

Precision The refinement of a previously learned motor behavior.

Preconceptual stage A substage of the preoperational period that occurs in early childhood in which mental symbols are formed to represent absent objects, people, or events.

Preconventional level The description of moral development that is based on one's perceptions of the physical consequences of action.

Prelanguage position The belief that children attach meaning to objects or events in the environment even though they cannot verbally represent them.

Preoperational period The stage in childhood wherein individuals learn to symbolically represent objects, people, and events in the environment.

Primary reinforcement Responses are paired to stimuli if they are capable of reducing the drive.

Principle of association The concept that the combined strength of ideas in the mind increases their chances of entering consciousness.

Principle of frequency The belief that ideas that enter consciousness with high frequency are better retained than those that enter with low frequency.

Proactive inhibition The inability to recall a task because of interference from an earlier learned task.

Problem items A specific test item wherein the answer is not readily apparent. Students must provide the answer that is specific rather than varied.

Problem solving The ability to make decisions or choices by using multiple pieces of learned information.

Products of thought Guilford's description of the different types of intellectual experiences people have and how these experiences facilitate thinking.

Programmed instruction The development of software designed to present learning in a step sequence order, accompanied by reinforcement.

Proximal goals The ability to move toward goals that we have a desire to achieve.

Psychological development Nonbiological aspects of humans that change over time.

Psychological environment The objects, events, or attitudes within a person's environment that are perceived as important.

Psychosocial development The capacity to function resulting from the interaction of one's instinctual urges with the social and physical environment in which one finds himself or herself.

Punishment Any event that follows a response that is aversive to an individual.

Range The likely upper and lower limits of a person's IQ based on their IQ score, its deviation from the mean, and the standard error of measurement.

Ratio schedule The systematic application of a reinforcer following a number of responses.

Readiness The extent to which the learner is prepared to engage in an immediate teaching-learning situation.

Receiving Attending to any affective phenomenon in the environment.

Recency The morr recently an organism has made a response to a stimulus, the more likely that the response will reoccur.

Reception Attending to learning phenomena within the environment.

Receptive speech problem Difficulty in encoding and interpreting speech in the environment.

Reflex An inherent behavioral predisposition found in organisms as described by Pavlov.

Reinforcer Any event that follows a response that increases the likelihood of its recurring.

Relational concept The ability to draw relationships between two or more concrete objects, commonly known as a "rule."

Reliability The dependable consistency of a test upon repeated administration.

Representational learning The attachment of symbolic meaning to objects in the environment.

Representational equivalence The ability to process new information or experiences by relating them to existing concept categories.

Respondent conditioning The term used by Skinner to describe the phenomenon Pavlov discovered in classical conditioning.

Responding Reacting to any affective phenomenon in the environment.

Response cost Taking away part of a reinforcement that has already been earned through previous behavior.

Response generalization The ability of one stimulus to elicit more than one response.

Retention The maintenance of a learned response across time.

Retrieval phase The ability to draw out of memory previously acquired learning.

Retroactive inhibition The inability to recall a previous learning task because of the acquisition of a more recent task.

Reversibility The ability to retrace one's steps in an intellectual operation.

Roles Behavior that is expected of an individual in a specific situation.

Satisfier A term used by Thorndike to describe something that is pleasant or rewarding to an organism.

Schedule of reinforcement The arrangement of reinforcements and responses in a systematic way that ensures response maintenance.

Schemes Piaget's description of the way individuals represent things in their minds. Schemes are variant in that they change as a result of experience.

Scope The range of topics to be instructed within a specified time frame.

Secondary drive Secondary drives occur when a primary drive takes on a nonphysiological way of being met; e.g., the selection of food.

Select items Test items wherein the student must choose the correct answer from given alternatives.

Self-concept The feelings an individual has about the self.

Self-contained classroom A classroom wherein one teacher instructs all subject areas to the same group of students.

Self-control The individual use of any behavior modification principle to change personal behavior.

Self-motivation The process by which, due to the application of self-reinforcement, we are motivated to engage in or avoid performance of behavior.

Self-reinforcement The recognition and satisfaction of our own behavior.

Self-regulation The ability to monitor our own behavior by understanding its consequences.

Semantic content The ability to attach meaning to concrete and abstract words.

Sensorimotor period The initial stage of intellectual development wherein infants perceive environmental events through the senses.

Sensory impairment The inability to function normally through one or more of the senses.

Sequence The grade level or order at which various topics are to be presented.

Serial ordering The ability to assign value or structure to something—such as ranking or alphabetizing.

s factor The construct designed to explain a wide range of specific traits that affect intellectual functioning.

Shaping The reinforcing of a behavior that most closely approximates the desired response.

Short-term memory The retention of learned material for a very specific purpose for a short duration.

Simulation system The presentation of classroom-like or life-like information under simulated conditions designed to increase the meaningfulness of what is being learned.

Single-factor tests An intelligence test designed around one single human trait or characteristic, usually verbal ability.

Small group instruction The presentation of classroom material to a group of students, usually 6 to 10, who have been specifically targeted for instruction.

Social cognition The ability to understand social phenomena in the environment because of the way they are cognitively presented.

Social development The increased capacity to relate to others and the environment.

Socialization Ways in which individuals learn about and act consistently with social norms, values, and roles.

Socialized anxiety The anticipation of punishment if behavior is not according to social expectations.

Social learning theory The formal term used to describe the various processes by which Albert Bandura postulates human learning occurs.

Social motives The need to learn skills that allows a person to relate to and be accepted by others.

Socio-emotional adjustment The totality of one's feelings and expressions, often referred to as one's lifestyle.

Spaced review The systematic, intermittent representation of learned material in order to increase its retentive strength.

Specific transfer The deliberate relating of two tasks in order to maximize learning.

Speech disorders The inability to effectively articulate sounds or verbally communicate with others.

Spiral effect The organization of a school curriculum in progressively complex ways so that students increasingly learn at higher conceptual levels.

Stability The extent to which one's IQ remains highly similar across time.

Standard deviation A statistical measure that systematically describes how any single IQ score may vary from the mean score.

Standardized test A test that compares students on its norms regardless of the school or location in which the test is taken.

Stimulus bound The tendency for a teacher to adhere strictly to instructional material with minimal flexibility.

Stimulus generalization The ability of multiple stimuli to elicit one response.

Storage phase The coding of information into the mind for subsequent recall.

Structural development   Characteristics of humans that are directly related to biological development.

Student control   The opportunity given students to regulate or pace some aspect of their learning experience.

Stuttering   A break in the rhythmic pattern of vocalizing that causes nonfluent speech.

Subculture   Social beliefs and behaviors that influence the lives of people to a lesser extent than does the dominant culture.

Subjective items   Test items that permit variation in student responses that are still acceptable answers.

Successive approximation   The strategy used in shaping whereby an individual is reinforced for a series of responses, each gradually getting closer to the desired response.

Superego   The personality dimension of the individaul that is known as one's conscience. It incorporates social values and expectations.

Supply items   Test items wherein the student must provide the correct answers, e.g., completion, short-answer, essay.

Symbolic content   Something in the environment that is designated to represent the real things, for example, cartoon characters or situation comedies.

Symbolic representation   The ability to represent environmental phenomena through symbols, primarily language.

Synthesis   The formulation of something new or unique by relating heretofore unrelated ideas.

Synthesis of content   The ability to interrelate relevant educational experiences into a conceptual whole.

Tangible reinforcers   Application or reinforcers, such as food or money, following a student behavior.

Task imposed discipline   Self-regulated student behavior that facilitates the accomplishment of a specific learning task.

Task-oriented motivation   The specific application of achievement motivation to the classroom setting.

Teaching machine   A mechanical device that is used in the presentation of carefully sequenced instructional material to students.

Team teaching   The effort by two or more teachers to combine subject matter when instructing students.

Terminology   The ability to define words that represent environmental phenomena.

Test blueprint   A measurement device that is a systematic description of how students should be assessed following designated instruction. Often this is referred to as a table of specifications.

Theory   A principle of generalization that explains phenomena.

Theory of generalization   The theory that general principles, rather than specific elements transfer from situation to situation.

Theory of identical elements   The theory that transfer is increased if the learning of two tasks have simialr elements.

Theory of instruction   Teacher behavior designed to influence student learning.

Threshold variable   Jensen's term to explain that, unless the environment is severely restricted, environmental impact on intellectual ability is almost imperceptible.

Time out   The withholding of a positive reinforcer for a specific time in order to reduce the tendency to respond.

Token economy system   A reinforcement system wherein tokens of assigned point value are given for exercising certain behaviors.

Trace decay   The gradual fading of learning that has been stored in short-term memory.

Transducive reasoning   The belief that because two things are alike in one way, there are like in all ways.

Transfer   The effect one learning experience has on another.

Translation   Paraphrasing or rendering something into a form other than the one originally learned.

Transposition theory   The theory that, if a person perceives similarity in learning situations, transfer will occur.

True-false items   The presentation of a statement as fact to which a student must agree or disagree.

Tutorial system   The presentation of new information or skills by a computer for the expressed purpose of facilitating student learning.

Tutoring   One-to-one instruction to a student by someone other than the classroom teacher, e.g., teacher's aide or another student.

Two-factor tests   IQ tests designed to measure two aspects of a person's behavior; verbal and performance.

Unconditioned response   The automatic response to a natural, external stimulus.

Unconditioned stimulus   An environmental event capable of eliciting an unconditioned response, for example, food eliciting salivation.

Unit of instruction   A predetermined instructional sequence that is restricted to an academic content area and that specifies expected student learning.

Validity   The extent to which a test actually measures what it was designed to measure.

Values   The internal belief system of an individual that directly affects behavior.

Valuing   Voluntarily selecting beliefs or activities because of their worth.

Variable interval schedule   Applying reinforcement randomly, after an unspecified time lapse.

Variable ratio schedule   Reinforcing the learner after several responses have occurred, the ratio being set around an arbitrary mean.

Variable schedule   Giving reinforcers in a random, irregular pattern.

Verbal coding   The internal representation of an observed behavior into memory.

Vertical transfer   A term used by Gagné to describe the generalization of information from simple to increasingly complex levels of learning.

Visual Acuity   The accuracy of distance vision within a person.

Visual imagery   An impression that registers through the visual sense that accompanies learning.

Visual information   The term used in Bransford's information processing model to describe learning that is initially received through seeing.

Abrams, J. D. (1979). Mastery learning in a smaller school system. *Educational Leadership, 37,* 136–139.

Abrahmson, E. E., & Crocker, R. W. (1978). Rapid elimination of out-of-seat behavior by the cause of response cost and reinforcement. *Behavioral Engineering, 4,* 103–105.

Abramson, M. (1981). Implications of mainstreaming: A challenge for special education. In L. Mann & D. A. Sabatino (Eds.), *Fourth Review of Special Education.* New York: Grune & Stratton.

Achilles, E. M. (1920). Experimental studies in recall and recognition. *Archives of Psychology, 6*(44), 1–32.

Adler, M. J. (1982). *The Paideia proposal: An educational manifesto.* New York: Macmillan.

Aguirre, A. (1979). Chicanos, intelligence testing, and the quality of life. *Educational Research Quarterly, 4,* 3–12.

Albee, E. (1901). *A history of English utilitarianism.* London: Allen & Unwin.

Alexander, T., Roodin, P. & Gorman. B. (1980). *Developmental psychology.* New York: D. Van Nostrand.

Algozzine, B. (1976). What teachers perceive—children receive? *Communications Quarterly, 24,* 41–47.

Algozzine, B. (1977). The emotionally disturbed child: Disturbed or disturbing? *Journal of Abnormal Child Psychology, 5,* 205–211.

Algozzine, B., Mercer, C. D., & Countermine, T. (1977). The effects of labels and behavior on teacher expectations. *Exceptional children, 44,* 131–132.

Algozzine, B., & Sherry, L. (1981). Issues in the education of emotionally disturbed children. *Journal of the Council for Children with Behavioral Disorders, 6,* 223–237.

Ames, R., & Lau, S. (1982). An attributional analysis of student helpseeking in academic settings. *Journal of Educational Psychology, 74,* 414–423.

Amidon, E. J., & Flanders, N. A. (1961). The effect of direct and indirect teacher influence on dependent-prone students learning geometry. *Journal of Educational Psychology, 52,* 286–291.

Anastasi, A. (1967). Psychology, psychologists, and psychological testing. *American Psychologist, 22,* 297–306.

Anderson, H. H., & Brewer, J. E. (1946). Studies of teachers' classroom personalities. II. Effects of teachers' dominative and integrative contacts on children's classroom behavior. *Applied Psychology Monographs,* No. 8.

Anderson, L. W. (1981). *Assessing affective characteristics in the schools.* Boston: Allyn & Bacon.

Anderson, R. C., Goldberg, S. R., & Hidde, J. L. (1971). Meaningful processing of sentences. *Journal of Educational Psychology, 62,* 395–399.

Arlin, P. K. (1975). Cognitive development in adulthood: A fifth stage? *Developmental Psychology, 11,* 602–606.

Arlin, P. K. (1980). Test of formal reasoning. Unpublished paper.

Aronfreed, J. (1968). *Conduct and conscience.* New York: Academic Press.

Atkinson, J. W. (1958). *Motives in fantasy, action, and society.* New York: Van Nostrand Reinhold.

Atkinson, J. W. (1964). *An introduction to motivation.* Princeton, NJ: Van Nostrand.

Atkinson, J. W. (1965). The mainsprings of achievement oriented activity. In J. D. Krumboltz (Ed.), *Learning and the educational process.* Chicago: Rand McNally, 25–26.

Atkinson, J. W., & Raynor, J. O. (1974). *Motivation and achievement.* Washington: Winston.

Atkinson, R. C., & Shiffrin, R. M. (1971). The control of short-term memory. *Scientific American, 224,* 82–90.

Ausubel, D. P. (1960). The use of advance organizers in the learning and retention of meaningful verbal learning. *51,* 267–272.

Ausubel, D. P. (1968). *Educational psychology: A cognitive view.* New York: Holt, Rinehart and Winston.

Ausubel, D. P. (1977). The facilitation of meaningful verbal learning in the classroom. *Educational Psychologist, 12,* 162–178.

Ausubel, D. P., & Ausubel, P. (1966). Cognitive development in adolescence. *Review of Educational Research, 3,* 403–413.

Ausubel, D. P., & Robinson, F. G. (1969). *School learning: An introduction to educational psychology.* New York: Holt, Rinehart and Winston.

Ausubel, D. P., Stager, M., & Gaite, A. J. H. (1969). Proactive effects in meaningful verbal learning and retention. *Journal of Educational Psychology, 60,* 59–64.

Ayllon, T., & Azrin N. H. (1965). The measurement and reinforcement of behavior of psychotics. *Journal of the Experimental Analysis of Behavior, 8,* 357–383.

Ayllon, T., & Azrin, N. H. (1968). *The token economy: A motivational system for therapy and rehabilitation.* New York: Appleton-Century-Crofts.

Baer, D. M., & Sherman, J. A. (1969). Aprraisal of operant therapy techniques with children and adults. In C. M. Franks (Ed.), *Behavior therapy: Appraisal and status.* New York: McGraw-Hill, 190–221.

Bandura, A. (1965a). Behavior modification through modeling procedures. In L. P. Ullman & L. Krasner (Eds.), *Research in behavior modification*. New York: Holt, Rinehart and Winston, 310–340.

Bandura, A. (1965b). Influence of models' reinforcement contingencies on the acquisition of imitative responses. *Journal of Personality and Social Psychology, 1*, 589–595.

Bandura, A. (1967). Behavioral psychotherapy. *Scientific American, 216*, 78–86.

Bandura, A. (1969). *Principles of behavior modification*. New York: Holt, Rinehart and Winston.

Bandura, A. (1971). *Social learning theory*. New York: General Learning Press.

Bandura, A. (1976a). Effecting change through participant modeling. In J. D. Krumboltz & C. E. Thorensen (Eds.), *Counseling methods*. New York: Holt, Rinehart and Winston, 248–264.

Bandura, A. (1976b). Self-reinforcement: Theoretical and methodological considerations. *Behaviorism, 4*, 135–156.

Bandura, A. (1977a). *Social learning theory*. Englewood Cliffs, NJ: Prentice-Hall.

Bandura, A. (1977b). Self-efficacy: Toward a unifying theory of behavioral change. *Psychological Review, 84*, 191–215.

Bandura, A. (1978). The self-system in reciprocal determinism. *American Psychologist, 33*, 344–358.

Bandura, A. (1982). Self-efficacy mechanism in human agency. *American Psychologist, 37*, 122–147.

Bandura, A., Grusec, J. E., & Menlove, F. L. (1966). Observational learning as a function of symbolization and incentive set. *Child Development, 37*, 499–506.

Bandura, A., & Kupers, C. J. (1964). The transmission of patterns of self-reinforcement through modeling. *Journal of Abnormal and Social Psychology, 69*, 1–9.

Bandura, A., & Menlove, P. (1968). Factors determining vicarious extinction of avoidance behavior through symbolic modeling. *Journal of Personality and Social Psychology, 8*, 99–108.

Bandura, A., & Mischel, W. (1965). Modification of self-imposed delay of reward through exposure to live and symbolic models. *Journal of Personality and Social Psychology, 2*, 698–705.

Bandura, A., & Perloff, B. (1967). Relative efficacy of self-monitored and externally-imposed reinforcement systems. *Journal of Personality and Social Psychology, 7*, 111–116.

Bandura, A., Ross, D., & Ross, S. A. (1961). Transmission of aggression through imitation of aggressive models. *Journal of Abnormal and Social Psychology, 63*, 575–582.

Bandura, A., Ross, D., & Ross, S. A. (1963a). Imitation of film-mediated aggressive models. *Journal of Abnormal and Social Psychology, 66*, 3–11.

Bandura, A., Ross, D., & Ross, S. A. (1963b). A compartive test of the status envy, social power, and secondary reinforcement theories of identificatory learning. *Journal of Abnormal and Social Psychology, 67*, 527–534.

Bandura, A., Ross, D., & Ross, S. A. (1963c). Vicarious reinforcement and imitative learning. *Journal of Abnormal and Social Psychology, 67*, 601–607.

Bandura, A. & Walters, R. H. (1963). *Social learning and personality development*. New York: Holt, Rinehart and Winston.

Bandura, A., & Whalen, C. K. (1966). The influence of antecedent reinforcement and divergent modeling cues on patterns of self-reward. *Journal of Personality and Social Psychology, 3*, 373–382.

Barlow, J. A. (1968). *Stimulus and response*. New York: Harper & Row.

Barraga, N. D. (1964). *Increased visual behavior in low vision children*. New York: American Foundation for the Blind.

Barraga, N. D., & Collins, M. E. (1979). Development of efficiency in visual functioning: Rationale for a comprehensive program. *Visual Impairment and Blindness, 73*, 121–126.

Bart, W. M., Frey, S., & Baxter, J. (1979). Generalizability of the ordering among five formal reasoning tasks by an ordering-theoretic method. *Child Study Journal, 1979, 9*(4), 251.

Bar-Tal, D., Raviv, A., & Shavit, N. (1981). Motives for helping behavior: Kibbutz and city children in kindergarten and school. *Developmental Psychology, 17*, 766–772.

Barth, R. (1979). Home-based reinforcement of school behavior: A review and analysis. *Review of Educational Research, 1979, 49*, 436–458.

Baskett, L. M., & Johnson, S. M. (1982). The young child's interactions with parents versus siblings: A behavioral analysis. *Child Development, 53*, 643–650.

Bassotti, R. A., & Bredderman, T. (1979). Self-concept and attitudinal differences between B.O.C.E.S. and home-school vocational students. *Adolescence, 14*(56), 709–714.

Bayley, N. (1949). Consistency and variability in the growth of intelligence from birth to eighteen. *Journal of Genetic Psychology, 75*, 165–196.

Bayley, N. (1965). On the growth of intelligence. *American Psychologist, 10*, 811.

Becker, W. C. (1971). *Parents are teachers*. Champaign, IL: Research Press.

Belin, H. (1975). *Studies in the cognitive bases of language development*. New York: Basic Books.

Belson, W. A. (1978). *Television violence and the adolescent boy*. Hampshire, England: Saxon House.

Benton, A. A. (1967). Effects of the timing of negative response consequences on the observational learning of resistance to temptation in children. *Dissertation Abstracts, 2*, 2153–2154.

Bergan, J. R., & Jeska, P. (1980). An examination of prerequisite relations, positive transfer among learning tasks, and variations in instruction for a seriation hierarchy. *Contemporary Educational Psychology, 5*, 203–215.

Berliner, D. C. (1980). Using research on teaching for the improvement of classroom practice. *Theory into Practice, 19*, 302–308.

Berliner, D. C. (1983). The executive functions of teaching. *Instructor, 93*, 29–38.

Berliner, D. C., & Rosenshine, B. V. (1977). The acquisition of knowledge in the classroom. In R. C. Anderson, R. J. Spiro, & W. E. Montague (Eds.), *Schooling and the acquisition of knowledge*. Hillsdale, NJ: Erlbaum, 375–396.

Berlyne, D. E. (1966). Notes on intrinsic motivation and intrinsic reward in relation to instruction. In J. Bruner (Ed.), *Learning about learning*. Washington, DC: Office of Education, 105–110.

Biehler, R. F., & Snowman, J. (1982). *Psychology applied to teaching* (4th ed.). Boston: Houghton Mifflin.

Bigge, M. L., & Hunt, M. P. (1962). *Psychological foundations of education.* New York: Harper & Row.

Birch, D., & Veroff, J. (1966). *Motivation: A study of action.* Monterey, CA: Brooks/Cole.

Birch, J. R., & Birch, J. W. (1951). The Leiter International Performance Scale as an aid in the psychological study of deaf children. *American Annals of the Deaf, 96,* 502.

Birney, R. C. (1959). The reliability of the achievement motive. *Journal of Abnormal and Social Psychology, 58,* 266–267.

Blatt, B. (1958). The physical, personality, and academic status of children who are mentally retarded attending special classes compared with children who are mentally retarded attending regular classes. *American Journal of Mental Deficiency, 62,* 810–818.

Blatt, B. (1981). *In and out of mental retardation.* Baltimore: University Park Press.

Blaubergs, M. S. (1976). Encoding self-embedded sentences. *Language and Speech, 19,* 1–8.

Block, J. H. (Ed.) (1971). *Mastery learning.* New York: Holt, Rinehart and Winston.

Block, J. H. (April, 1973). *Mastery learning in the classroom: An overview of recent research.* Paper presented at the American Educational Research Association annual meeting.

Block, J. H. (1979). Mastery learning: The current state of the craft. *Educational Leadership, 37,* 114–117.

Block, J. H., & Burns, R. B. (1976). Mastery learning. In L. S. Shulman (Ed.), *Review of research in education* (Vol. 4). Itasca, IL: Peacock, 3–49.

Block, R. A. (1982). Temporal judgments and contextual change. *Journal of Experimental psychology: Learning, memory, and cognition, 8,* 530–544.

Bloom, B. S. (1964). *Stability and change in human characteristics.* New York: Wiley.

Bloom, B. S. (1968). Learning for mastery. *UCLA Evaluative Comment, 1*(2), 1–12.

Bloom, B. S. (1973). *Time and learning.* Thorndike Award Address at the American Psychological Association annual convention, September 1973.

Bloom, B. S. (1974). An introduction to mastery learning theory. In J. H. Block (Ed.), *Schools, society and mastery learning.* New York: Holt, Rinehart and Winston, 4–14.

Bloom, B. S. (1976). *Human characteristics and school learning.* New York: McGraw-Hill.

Bloom, B. S., Englehart, M. D., Hill, W. H., Furst, E. J., & Krathwohl, D. R. (1956). *Taxonomy of educational objectives: Cognitive domain.* New York: McKay.

Blyth, D. A., Hill, J. P., & Smyth, C. K. (1981). The influence of older adolescents on younger adolescents: Do grade-level arrangements make a difference in behaviors, attitudes, and experiences? *Journal of Early Adolescence, 1,* 85–110.

Blyth, D. A., Simmons, R. G., & Bush, D. M. (1978). The transition into early adolescence: A longitudinal comparison of youths in two educational contexts. *Sociology of Education, 51,* 149–162.

Blyth, D. A., Simmons, R. G., & Carlton-Ford, S. (1983). The adjustment of early adolescents to school transition. *Journal of Early Adolescence. 3,* 105–120.

Bodwin, R. F. (1957). The relationship between immature self-concepts and certain educational disabilities. *Dissertation Abstracts, 17,* 564.

Bohannan, P. (1970). *Divorce and after.* Garden City, NY: Doubleday.

Bolles, R. C. (1967). *Theories of motivation.* New York: Harper & Row.

Bongiovanni, A. F. (1977). A review of research on the effects of punishment: Implications for corporal punishment in the schools. In J. Wise (Ed.), *Proceedings: Conference on corporal punishment in the schools.* Washington, DC: National Institute of Education, 61–77.

Bossert, S. T. (1979). *Tasks and social relationships in classrooms: A study of classroom organization and its consequences.* New York: Cambridge University Press.

Bovet, M. (1969). Cognitive processes among illiterate children and adults. In J. W. Berry (Ed.), *Culture and cognition: Readings in cross-cultural psychology.* London: Methuen, 190–218.

Bower, E. M., & Lambert, N. M. (1971). In-school screening of children with emotional handicaps. In N. J. Long, W. C. Morse, & R. G. Newman (Eds.), *Conflict in the classroom.* Belmont, CA: Wadsworth, 142–148.

Bower, G. H. (1974). *Development in infancy.* San Francisco: Freeman.

Bower, G. H., & Clark, M. C. (1969). Narrative stories as mediators for serial learning. *Psychonomic Science, 14,* 181–182.

Bower, G. H., & Hilgard, E. R. (1981). *Theories of learning* (5th ed.). Englewood Cliffs, NJ: Prentice-Hall.

Bowerman, C. E., & Kinch, J. W. (1959). Changes in family and peer orientation of children between the fourth and tenth grades. *Social Forces, 37,* 206–211.

Bowlby, J. (1969). *Attachment.* New York: Basic Books.

Bradfield, R. H., Brown, J., Kaplan, P., Rickert, E., & Stannard, R. (1973). The special child in the regular classroom. *Exceptional Children, 39,* 384–390.

Brainerd, C. J. (1978). *Piaget's theory of intelligence.* Englewood Cliffs, NJ: Prentice-Hall.

Bransford, J. D. (1979). *Human cognition.* Belmont, CA: Wadsworth.

Bransford, J. D., Barclay, J. R., & Franks, J. J. (1972). Sentence memory: A constructive versus interpretive approach. *Cognitive Psychology, 3,* 193–209.

Bransford, J. D., McCarrell, N. S., Franks, J. J., & Nitsch, K. E. (1977). Toward unexplaining memory. In R. Shaw & J. D. Bransford (Eds.). *Perceiving, acting, and knowing: Toward an ecological psychology.* Hillsdale, NJ: Erlbaum.

Brazee, E. N. (1981). Student response to a language arts test of cognitive functioning. *Journal of Early Adolescence, 1,* 373–384.

Brazelton, T. B. (1977, November). The infant's world. *Redbook,* pp. 24–28.

Briggs, G. E. (1957). Retroactive inhibition as a function of the degree of original and interpolated learning. *Journal of Experimental Psychology, 53,* 60–67.

Bronowski, J. (1975). Technology and culture in evolution. In H. D. Thornburg (Ed.), *Contemporary adolescence: Readings* (2nd ed.) (pp. 17–26). Monterey, CA: Brooks/Cole.

Brookover, W. B., Erickson, E. L., & Joiner, L. M. (1967). *Self-*

concept of school ability and school achievement (Vol. 3). East Lansing: Educational Research Series, No. 36, Cooperative Research Project No. 2831, Michigan State University.

Brophy, J. (1981). Teacher praise: A functional analysis. *Review of Educational Research, 51,* 5–32.

Brophy, J. E., & Good, T. L. (1979). Teachers' communication of differential expectations for children's classroom performance: Some behavioral data. *Journal of Educational Psychology, 61,* 365–374.

Brown, A., Campione, J., & Day, J. (1981). Learning to learn: On training students to learn from texts. *Educational Researcher, 16,* 14–21.

Brown, F. G. (1976). *Principles of educational and psychological testing* (2nd ed.). New York: Holt, Rinehart and Winston.

Brown, P., & Elliott, R. (1965). Control of aggression in a nursery school class. *Journal of Experimental Child Psychology, 16,* 343–361.

Brown, R. (1958). How shall a thing be called? *Psychological Review, 65,* 14–21.

Brown, R., & Berko, J. (1960). Word association and the acquisition of grammar. *Child Development, 31,* 1–14.

Bruce, R. W. (1933). Conditions of transfer of training. *Journal of Experimental Psychology, 16,* 343–361.

Bruner, J. S. (1956). *A study of thinking.* New York: Wiley.

Bruner, J. S. (1960). *The process of education.* New York: Vintage Books.

Bruner, J. S. (1961). The act of discovery. *Harvard Educational Review, 31,* 21–32.

Bruner, J. S. (1966). *Toward a theory of instruction.* New York: Norton.

Bruner, J. S. (1971). *The relevance of education.* New York: Norton.

Bruner, J. S., Goodnow, J. J., & Austin, G. A. (1956). *A study of thinking.* New York: Wiley.

Bryan, J. H., & Walbek, N. (1970). Preaching and practicing generosity: Children's actions and reactions. *Child Development, 41,* 329–353.

Bryant, N. D. (1964). Characteristics of dyslexia and their remedial implication. *Exceptional Children, 31,* 195–199.

Budoff, M., & Gottlieb, J,(1976). Special class students mainstreamed: A study of an aptitude (learning potential) treatment interaction. *American Journal of Mental Deficiency, 81,* 1–11.

Burke, E. J., & Kleiber, D. (1978). Psychological and physical implications of highly competitive sports for children. *Physical Educator, 33,* 63–70.

Burns, R. B. (1979). Mastery learning: Does it work? *Educational Leadership, 37,* 110–113.

Buros, O. K. (1978). *The eighth mental measurements yearbook.* Highland Park, NJ: Gryphon Press.

Butler, K., & Chechile, R. (1976). "Acid bath" effects on storage and retrieval PI. *Bulletin of the Psychonomic Society, 8,* 349–352.

Calder, B. J., & Staw, B. M. (1975). The interaction of intrinsic and extrinsic motivation: Some methodological notes. *Journal of Personality and Social Psychology, 31,* 76–80.

Carroll, J. B. (1963). A model of school learning. *Teachers College Record, 64,* 723–733.

Carroll, J. B. (1964). Words, meanings, and concepts. *Harvard Educational Review, 34,* 178–202.

Carroll, R. E. (1945). Relation of the school environment to the moral ideology and personal aspirations of Negro boys and girls. *School Review, 53,* 30–38.

Cattell, R. (1940). A culture-free intelligence test. *Journal of Educational Psychology, 64,* 723–733.

Cattell, R. (1963). Theory of fluid and crystallized intelligence: A critical experiment. *Journal of Educational Psychology, 54,* 1–22.

Cattell, R. (1968). Are IQ tests intelligent? *Psychology Today, 1*(10), 56–62.

Cawelti, G. (1968). Youth assess the American high school. *PTA Magazine, 62,* 16–19.

Ceppi, C. M. (1973). *Effects of presented and requested organization on children's recall of semantically-categorized sentences.* Unpublished doctoral dissertation, Columbia University, New York.

Child, I. L., & Whiting, J. W. M. (1949). Determinants of levels of aspiration: Evidence from everyday life. *Journal of Abnormal and Social Psychology, 44,* 303–314.

Childs, R. E. (1979). A drastic change in curriculum for the educable mentally retarded child. *Mental Retardation, 21,* 299–301.

Chomsky, N. (1965). *Aspects of the theory of syntax.* Cambridge, MA: M.I.T. Press.

Christen, A. G. (1980). The case against smokeless tobacco: Five facts for the health professional to consider. *Journal of the American Dental Association, 101,* 464–469.

Christen, A. G., McDaniel, R. D., & Doran, H. (1979). Snuff dipping and tobacco chewing in a group of Texas college athletes. *Texas Dental Journal, 97,* 6–12.

Clark, S. N., & Clark, D. C. (1981). Continuous progress: A curriculum responsive to the needs of early adolescents. *Contemporary Education, 52,* 142–145.

Clements, S. D. (1966). *Minimal brain dysfunction in children.* Monograph #3, Public Health Service Bulletin #1415. Washington, DC: U.S. Department of Health, Education and Welfare.

Clifford, M. M. (1971). Motivational effects of competition and goal setting in reward and non-reward conditions. *Journal of Experimental Education, 39,* 11–16.

Clifford, M. M. (1981). *Practicing educational psychology.* Boston: Houghton Mifflin.

Coates, T. J., & Thoresen, C. E. (1979). Behavioral self-control and educational practice or do we really need self-control? In D. C. Berliner (Ed.), *Reveiw of Research in Education* (Vol. 7). Itasca, IL: Peacock.

Cohen, S. A., & Hyman, J. (1976). *The reading house series.* New York: Random House.

Cole, M., & Scribner, S. (1974). *Culture and thought.* New York: Wiley.

Coleman, J. S. (1961). The competition for adolescent energies. *Phi Delta Kappan, 42,* 231–236.

Coleman, J. S., et al. (1966). *Equality of educational opportunity.* Washington, DC: U.S. Department of Health, Education and Welfare.

Collins, A. M., & Quillian, M. R. (1969). Retrieval time from semantic memory. *Journal of Verbal Learning and Verbal Behavior, 8,* 240–247.

Collins, M. E., & Barraga, N. C. (1980). Development of efficiency in visual functioning: An evaluation process. *Visual Impairment and Blindness, 74,* 93–96.

Combs, A. W. (1979). Humanistic education: Hope or hazard? *Educational Forum, 44,* 115–116.

Condry, J., & Siman, M. L. (1974). Characteristics of peer- and adult-oriented children. *Journal of Marriage and the Family, 36,* 543–554.

Conrad, R. (1967). Interference or decay over short retention intervals? *Journal of Verbal Learning and Verbal Behavior, 6,* 49–54.

Coopersmith, S. (1959). A method for determining types of self-esteem. *Journal of Educational Psychology, 59,* 87–94.

Coopersmith, S. (1967). *The antecedents of self-esteem.* San Francisco: Freeman.

Coopersmith, S., & Feldman, R. (1974). Fostering a positive self-concept and high self-esteem in the classroom. In R. H. Coop & K. White (Eds.), *Psychological concepts in the classroom.* New York: Harper & Row, 192–225.

Copeland, W. D. (1980). Teaching-learning behaviors and the demands of the classroom environment. *Elementary School Journal, 80,* 163–177.

Council for Exceptional Children. (1978). *The nation's committment to the education of gifted and talented children and youth.* Washington, DC: United States Office of Education, Office of Gifted and Talented.

Cowan, P. A. (1978). *Piaget with feeling.* New York: Holt, Rinehart and Winston.

Craig, R. C. (1966). *The psychology of learning in the classroom.* New York: Macmillan.

Craik, F. I. M., & Lockhart, R. S. (1972). Levels of processing: A framework for memory research. *Journal of Verbal Learning and Verbal Behavior, 11,* 671–684.

Crandall, V. C., Katkovsky, W., & Crandall, V. J. (1965). Children's beliefs in their own control of reinforcement in intellectual-academic achievement situations. *Child Development, 36,* 91–109.

Crinella, F. M. (1973). Identification of brain dysfunction syndromes in children through profile analysis: Patterns associated with so-called "minimal brain dysfunction." *Journal of Abnormal Psychology, 82,* 35–45.

Crootof, C. (1963). *Bright underachievers' acceptance of self and their need for achievement.* Unpublished doctoral dissertation, New York University, New York.

Crowder, N. A. (1960). Automatic tutoring by intrinsic programming. In A. A. Lumsdaine & R. Glaser (Eds.), *Teaching machines and programmed learning.* Washington, DC: National Education Association, 286–298.

Cuban, L. (1978). Discipline and American students. *Social Education, 42*(2), 98–99.

Danner, F. W., & Day, C. M. (1977). Eliciting formal operations. *Child Development, 48,* 1600–1606.

Dave, R. H. (1963). *The identification and measurement of environmental process variables that are related to educa-tional achievement.* Unpublished doctoral dissertation, University of Chicago.

Davidson, H. H., & Greenberg, J. W. (1967). *Traits of school achievers from a deprived background.* New York: City College of New York.

Davis, A. (1944). Socialization and adolescent personality. In *Adolescence: Yearbook of the National Society for the Study of Education,* 43 (Part I). Chicago: University of Chicago Press, 198–216.

Day, C. M. (1981). Thinking at Piaget's stage of formal operations. *Educational Leadership, 38,* 44–46.

deCharms, R. (1968). *Personal causation: The internal affective determinants of behavior.* New York: Academic Press.

deCharms, R. (1971). From pawns to origins. Toward self-motivation. In G. Lesser (Ed.), *Psychology and educational practice.* Glenview, IL: Scott, Foresman, 380–409.

Deci, E. L. (1975). *Intrinsic motivation.* New York: Plenum.

Deci, E. L., Sheinman, L., Wheeler, L., & Hart, R. (1980). Rewards, motivation, and self-esteem. *Educational Forum, 44,* 429–433.

DeCorte, E. (1980). Processes of problem solving: Comparison of an American and a European view. *Instructional Science, 9,* 1–13.

Denham, C., & Lieberman, A. (Eds.) (1980). *Time to learn.* Washington, DC: National Institute of Education.

Dennis, W., & Dennis, M. G. (1940). The effect of cradling practices upon the onset of walking in Hopi children. *Journal of Genetic Psychology, 56,* 77–86.

Deutsch, M. (1967). Minority groups and class status as related to social and personality factors in scholastic achievement. In M. Deutsch (Ed.), *The disadvantaged child.* New York: Basic Books, 89–131.

Deutsch, M. (1965). Some psychological aspects of learning in the disadvantaged. In E. P. Torrance and R. D. Strom (Eds.). *Mental health and achievement.* New York: Wiley, 320–326.

Dewey, J. (1903). *Ethical principles underlying education.* Chicago: University of Chicago Press.

Dewey, J. (1933). *How we think: A restatement of the relation of thinking to the educative process.* Boston: Heath.

Dietze, A. G. (1931). The relation of several factors to factual memory. *Journal of Applied Psychology, 15,* 563–574.

Dietze, A. G., & James, H. E. (1931). Factual memory of secondary school pupils for a short article which they had read a single time. *Journal of Educational Psychology, 22,* 667–676.

DiVesta, F. J., & Gray, S. G. (1973). Listening and note-taking. *Journal of Educational Psychology, 63,* 8–14.

Doda, N. (1976). Affective education and the advisor-advisee program. *Middle School Journal, 7,* 8–10.

Doke, L. A. (1976). Assessment of children's behavioral deficits. In M. Hersen & A. S. Bellack (Eds.), *Behavioral assessment: A practical handbook.* Elmsford, NY: Pergamon Press, 161–180.

Dooling, D. J., & Christiansen, R. E. (1977). Levels of encoding and retention of prose. In G. H. Bower (Ed.), *The psychology of learning and memory.* New York: Academic Press, 310–335.

Doyle, W. (1978). Paradigms for research on teacher effectiveness. In L. S. Shulman (Ed.), *Review of research in education*. Itasca, IL: Peacock, 163–198.

Drever, J. (1964). *A dictionary of psychology*. Baltimore: Penguin Books.

Duke, M. P., & Nowicki, S. (1974). Locus of control and achievement: The confirmation of a theoretical expectation. *Journal of Psychology, 87,* 263–267.

Dupuy, H. J. (1977). *The construction and utility of three indexes of intellectual achievement.* Department of Health, Education, and Welfare Publication No. (HRA) 78-1343. Washington, DC: U.S. National Center for Health Statistics.

Dweck, C. S. (1975). The role of expectations and attributions in the alleviation of learned helplessness. *Journal of Personality and Social Psychology, 31,* 674–685.

Ebbinghaus, H. (1913). *Memory* (H. A. Ruger & C. E. Bussenius, Trans.). New York: Teachers College, Columbia University. (Original work published 1885)

Ebel, R. L. (1963). The social consequences of psychological testing. *Proceedings of the 1963 Invitational Conference on testing problems.* Princeton, NJ: Educational Testing Service.

Ebel, R. L. (1980). *Practical problems in educational measurement.* Lexington, MA: Heath.

Eberle, B. (1974). *Classroom cues: A flip book for cultivating multiple talent.* Buffalo, NY: DOK Publishers.

Eisenberg, N. (1979a). Relationship of prosocial moral reasoning to altruism, political liberalism, and intelligence. *Developmental Psychology, 15,* 87–89.

Eisenberg, N. (1979b). Development of children's prosocial moral judgment. *Developmental Psychology, 15,* 128–137.

Eisenberg, N., Cameron, E., Tryon, K., & Dodez, R. (1981). Socialization of prosocial behavior in the preschool classroom. *Developmental Psychology, 17,* 773–782.

Elkind, D. (1975). Recent research on cognitive development in adolescence. In S. Dragastin & G. H. Elder (Eds.), *Adolescence in the life cycle.* Washington, DC: Hemisphere Publishing, 49–61.

Elkind, D., & Weiner, D. B. (1978). *Development of the child.* New York: Wiley.

Elliott, R., & Vasta, R. (1970). The modeling of sharing: Effects associated with vicarious reinforcement, symbolization, age, and generalization. *Journal of Experimental Child Psychology, 10,* 8–15.

Ellis, H. C. (1965). *The transfer of learning.* New York: Macmillan.

Ellis, H. C. (1972). *Fundamentals of human learning and cognition.* Dubuque, IA: Brown.

Elrod, W. T. (1979, April 1). Paddles still swing in Indiana schools. *Hartford Courant.*

Englemann, S. (1969). *Conceptual learning.* San Rafael, CA: Dimensions Press.

English, H. B., & English, A. C. (1958). *A comprehensive dictionary of psychological and psychoanalytical terms.* New York: McKay.

Epstein, H. T. (1974). Phrenoblysis: Special brain and mind growth periods: II. Human mental development. *Developmental Psychobiology, 7,* 217–224.

Epstein, H. T. (1978). Growth spurts during brain development: Implications for educational policy and practice. In J. S. Chall & A. R. Mirsky (Eds.), *Education and the brain.* Chicago: National Society for the Study of Education Yearbook.

Epstein, H. T. (1979). Brain growth and cognitive functioning. *Colorado Journal of Educational Research, 19*(1), 3–4.

Erikson, E. H. (1950). *Childhood and society.* New York: Norton.

Erikson, E. H. (1959). Identity and the life cycle. *Psychological Issues, 1,* 18–164.

Erikson, E. H. (1963). *Childhood and society* (2nd ed.). New York: Norton.

Erikson, E. H. (1968). *Identity: Youth and crisis.* New York: Norton.

Estes, W. K. (1944). An experimental study of punishment. *Psychological Monographs, 57,* No. 263.

Estes, W. K., & Skinner, B. F. (1941). Some quantitative properties of anxiety. *Journal of Experimental Psychology, 29,* 390–400.

Farrell, F. (1982). The reaction to an adolescent's own illness and impending death, reactions to a parent's illness and death, and reactions to the illness and pending death of a sibling. *High School Journal, 65,* 198–204.

Feather, N. T. (1962). The study of persistence. *Psychological Bulletin, 59,* 94–114.

Feather, N. T. (1966). Effects of prior success and failure on expectations of success and subsequent performance. *Journal of Personality and Social Psychology, 3,* 287–298.

Ferguson, L. R. (1970). *Personality development.* Monterey, CA: Brooks/Cole.

Ferster, C. B., & Skinner, B. F. (1957). *Schedules of reinforcement.* New York: Appleton-Century-Crofts.

Fisher, C. W., Berliner, D. C., Filby, N. N., Marliave, R., Cahen, L. S., Dishaw, M., & Moore, J. E. (1978). *Teaching and learning in the elementary schools.* San Francisco: Far West Laboratory for Educational Research and Development, Report VII-I.

Flanders, N. A. (1970). *Analyzing teacher behavior.* Reading, MA: Addison-Wesley.

Flavell, J., & Wellman, H. Metamemory. (1977). In R. Kail & J. Hagen (Eds.), *Perspectives on the development of memory and cognition.* Hillsdale, NJ: Erlbaum.

Fontein, H. (1978). Re discipline: An ounce of prevention. *Social Education, 42*(2), 105–108.

Foster, G. G., Schmidt, C. R., & Sabatino, D. (1976). Teacher expectations and the label "learning disabilities." *Journal of Learning Disabilities, 9,* 11–114.

Franks. D. D., & Marolla, J. (1977). Efficacious action and social approval as interacting dimensions of self-esteem: A tentative formulation through construct validation. *Sociometry, 39,* 234–240.

Frase, L. T. (1969). Paragraph organization of written materials: The influence of conceptual clustering upon the level and organization of recall. *Journal of Educational Psychology, 60,* 394–401.

Frase, L. T. (1977). Instructional research: The enlargement of understanding. *Educational Psychologist, 12,* 128–137.

Freud, S. (1923). *The ego and the id* (rev. ed.). New York: Norton.

Freud, S. (1948). *The ego and the mechanism of defense*. New York: International Universities Press.

Freud, S. (1949). *An outline of psychoanalysis*. New York: Norton.

Friesen, D. (1968). Academic-athletic-popularity syndrome in the Canadian high school society (1967). *Adolescence, 3,* 39–52.

Frieze, I. H. (1979). Beliefs about success and failure in the classroom. In H. H. McMillian (Ed.), *The social psychology of school learning*. New York: Academic Press, 39–78.

Frostig, M., Lefever, D. W., & Whittlesey, J. R. B. (1964). *The Marianne Frostig developmental tests of visual perception*. Palo Alto, CA: Consulting Psychologists Press.

Fryer, F. W. (1964). *An evaluation of level of aspiration as a training procedure*. Englewood Cliffs, NJ: Prentice-Hall.

Frymier, J. R. (1970). Motivation: The mainspring and gyroscope of learning. *Theory into Practice, 9,* 23–32.

Fryrear, J. L., & Thelen, M. H. (1969). Effect of sex of model and sex of observer on the imitation of affective behavior. *Developmental Psychology, 1,* 298.

Furth, H. G. (1966a). A comparison of reading test norms of deaf and hearing children. *American Annals of the Deaf, 111,* 461–462.

Furth, H. G. (1966b). *Thinking without language: Psychological implications of deafness*. New York: Free Press.

Furth, H. G. (1971). Linguistic deficiency and thinking: Research with deaf subjects, 1964–1969. *Psychological Bulletin, 76,* 58–72.

Gaa, J. P. (1973). Effects of individual goal-setting conference on achievement, attitudes, and goal-setting behavior. *Journal of Experimental Education, 42,* 22–28.

Gage, N. L. (1964). Theories of teaching. In E. R. Hilgard (Ed.), *Theories of learning and instruction*. Sixty-third Yearbook of the National Society for the Study of Education. Chicago: National Society for the Study of Education, 268–285.

Gage, N. L. (1968). An analytical approach to research on instructional methods. *Phi Delta Kappan, 49,* 601–606.

Gage, N. L., & Berliner, D. (1979). *Educational psychology* (2nd ed.). Boston: Houghton Mifflin.

Gage, N. L., & Berliner, D. (1984). *Educational Psychology* (3rd ed.). Boston: Houghton Mifflin.

Gagne, E. D., & Middlebrooke, M. S. (1977). Encouraging generosity: A perspective from social learning theory and research. *Elementary School Journal, 77,* 281–291.

Gagne, E. D., & Paget, K. D. (1980). Eight-month retention of stance and definition recognition for educational psychology concepts. *Journal of Experimental Education, 49,* 76–83.

Gagne, R. M. (1965). *Conditions of learning*. New York: Holt, Rinehart and Winston.

Gagne, R. M. (1968). Contributions of learning to human development. *Psychological Review, 75,* 177–191.

Gagne, R. M. (1970a). Some new views of learning and instruction. *Phi Delta Kappan, 51,* 468–472.

Gagne, R. M. (1970b). *Conditions of learning* (2nd ed.). New York: Holt, Rinehart and Winston.

Gagne, R. M. (1973). Observations of school learning. *Educational Psychologist, 10*(3), 112–116.

Gagne, R. M. (1977a). *Conditions of learning* (3rd ed.). New York: Holt, Rinehart and Winston.

Gagne, R. M. (1977b). Instructional programs. In M. H. Marx & M. E. Bunch (Eds.), *Fundamentals and applications of learning*. New York: Macmillan, 404–428.

Gagne, R. M. (1980). Preparing the learner for new learning. *Theory into Practice, 19,* 6–9.

Gagne, R. M., & Briggs, L. J. (1974). *Principles of instructional design*. New York: Holt, Rinehart and Winston.

Gagne, R. M., & Briggs, L. J. (1979). *Principles of instructional design* (2nd ed.). New York: Holt, Rinehart and Winston.

Gagne, R. M., & Weigand, V. K. (1968). Some factors in children's learning and retention of concrete rules. *Journal of Educational Psychology, 59,* 355–361.

Gagne, R. M., & White, R. T. (1978). Memory structures and learning outcomes. *Review of Educational Research, 48,* 187–222.

Gallagher, J. J. (1966). *Research summary on gifted child education*. Springfield, IL: Office of Superintendent of Public Instruction.

Gallagher, J. J. (1974). Phenomenal growth and new problems characterize special education. *Phi Delta Kappan, 55,* 516–520.

Gallagher, J. J. (1975a). *Teaching the gifted child* (2nd ed.). Boston: Allyn & Bacon.

Gallagher, J. J. (1975b). The prospects for governmental support of educational research. *Educational Researcher, 4,* 13–14.

Gallagher, J. J., Wright, R. W., & Noppe, L. (1975). Piagetian conservation tasks and concepts attainment: Educational implications. In G. I. Lubin, J. F. Magary, & M. K. Poulsen (Eds.), *Piagetian theory and the helping professions*. Los Angeles: University of Southern California Press, 93–99.

Gander, M. J., & Gardiner, H. W. (1981). *Child and adolescent development*. Boston: Little, Brown.

Garcia, J. (1977). Intelligence testing: Quotients, quotas, and quackery. In J. L. Martinez (Ed.), *Chicano psychology*. New York: Academic Press.

Gaskins, I. W. (1982). Let's end the reading disabilities/learning disabilities debate. *Journal of Learning Disabilities, 15,* 81–83.

Gecas, V. (1971). Parental behavior and adolescent self-evaluation. *Sociometry, 34,* 466–482.

Gecas, V. (1972). Parental behavior and contextual variations in adolescent self-esteem. *Sociometry, 35,* 332–345.

Gelfand, D. M. (1962). The influence of self-esteem on rate of verbal conditioning and social matching behavior. *Journal of Abnormal and Social Psychology, 65,* 259–265.

Gelfand, D. M., Jenson, W. R., & Drew, C. J. (1982). *Understanding child behavior disorders*. New York: Holt, Rinehart and Winston.

Gelman, R. (1969). Conversation acquisition: A problem of learning to attend to relevant attributes. *Journal of Experimental Child Psychology, 7,* 167–187.

Gentile, J. R., Monaco, N., Iheozor-Ehofor, I. E., Ndu, M., & Ogbonaya, P. K. (1982). Retention by "fast" and "slow" learners. *Intelligence, 6,* 125–138.

Gesell, A. (1928). *Infancy and human growth.* New York: Macmillan.

Gesell, A. (1954). The ontogenesis of infant behavior. In L. Carmichael (Ed.), *Manual of child psychology* (2nd ed.). New York: Wiley.

Gesell, A., & Ilg, F. L. (1949). *Child development.* New York: Harper & Row.

Gesell, A., & Thompson, H. (1929). Learning and growth in identical infant twins: An experimental study by the co-twin method. *Genetic Psychology Monographs, 6,* 1–124.

Getzels, J. W. (1966). The problem of interests: A reconsideration. In H. A. Robinson (Ed.), *Reading: Seventy-five years of progress.* Supplementary Education Monographs, *66,* 97–106.

Getzels, J. W., & Dillim, J. T. (1973). The nature of giftedness and the education of the gifted. In R. Travers (Ed.), *Second handbook of research on teaching.* Skokie, IL: Rand McNally.

Gewirtz, J. L., & Stingle, K. C. (1968). The learning of generalized imitation as the basis for identification. *Psychological Review, 75,* 374–397.

Ghatala, E. S., Lewin, J. R., & Truman, D. L. (1981). Sources of interference when testing students' learning from sentences. *Contemporary Educational Psychology, 6,* 46–58.

Gillette, A. L. (1936). Learning and retention: A comparison of three experimental procedures. *Archives of Psychology,* No. 198.

Gilliland, A. R. (1948). The rate of forgetting. *Journal of Educational Psychology, 39,* 19–26.

Glaser, R. (1962). Psychology and instructional technology. In R. Glaser (Ed.), *Training research and education.* Pittsburgh: University of Pittsburgh Press.

Glaser, R. (1976). Cognitive psychology and instructional design. In D. Klahr (Ed.), *Cognition and instruction.* New York: Wiley.

Glaser, R., & Nitko, A. J. (1971). Measurement in learning and instruction. In R. L. Thorndike (Ed.), *Educational measurement* (2nd ed.). Washington, DC: American Council on Education, 625–670.

Glass, A. L., Holyoak, K. J., & Santa, J. L. (1979). *Cognition.* Reading, MA: Addison-Wesley.

Glickman, C. D., & Tamashiro, R. T. (1980). Clarifying teachers' beliefs about discipline. *Educational Leadership, 37*(6), 459–466.

Glover, E. D., Christen, A. G., & Henderson, A. H. (1982). Smokeless tobacco and the adolescent male. *Journal of Early Adolescence, 2,* 1–14.

Glover, E. D., Christen, A. G., & Plake, B. S. (1981). Just a pinch between the cheek and the gum. *Journal of School Health, 51,* 415–418.

Glover, J. A., Bruning, R. H., & Plake, B. S. (1982). Distinctiveness of encoding and recall of text materials. *Journal of Educational Psychology, 74,* 522–534.

Gnagey, W. J. (1975). *Maintaining discipline in classroom instruction.* New York: Macmillan.

Goldberg, M. L. (1960). Studies in underachievement in the academically talented. In A. Frazier (Ed.), *Freeing the capacity to learn.* Washington, DC: American Society of Curriculum Development.

Goldstein, H., Arkell, C., Ashcroft, S. C., Hurley, O. L., & Lilly, M. S. (1975). Schools. In N. Hobbs (Ed.), *Issues in the classification of children* (Vol. 2). San Francisco: Jossey-Bass.

Goodman, H., Gottlieb, J., & Harrison, R. H. (1972). Social acceptance of EMRs integrated into a nongraded elementary school. *American Journal of Mental Deficiency, 76,* 412–417.

Gottlieb, J., & Davis, J. E. (1973). Social acceptance of EMR children during overt behavioral interactions. *American Journal of Mental Deficiency, 78,* 141–143.

Gough, H. G. (1964). Academic achievement in high school as predicted from the California Psychological Inventory. *Journal of Educational Psychology, 55,* 174–180.

Graham, C. H. (Ed.) (1965). *Vision and visual perception.* New York: Wiley.

Greenberg, B. S., & Reeves, B. (1976). Children and the perceived reality of television. *Journal of Social Issues, 32*(4), 86–97.

Griffin, N., Chassin, L., & Young, J. D. (1981). Measurement of global self-concept versus multiple role-specific self-concepts in adolescents. *Adolescence, 16*(61), 49–56.

Grimes, J. W., & Allinsmith, W. (1961). Compulsivity, anxiety and school achievement. *Merrill-Palmer Quarterly, 7,* 247–269.

Gronlund, N. E. (1973). *Preparing criterion-referenced tests for classroom instruction.* New York: Macmillan.

Gronlund, N. E. (1974a). *Individualizing classroom instruction.* New York: Macmillan.

Gronlund, N. E. (1974b). *Improving marking and reporting in classroom instruction.* New York: Macmillan.

Gronlund, N. E. (1981). *Measurement and evaluation in teaching* (4th ed.). New York: Macmillan.

Guilford, J. P. (1956). Three faces of intellect. *American Psychologist, 14,* 469–479.

Guilford, J. P. (1967). *The nature of human intelligence.* New York: McGraw-Hill.

Guilford, J. P. (1972). Thurstone's primary mental abilities and structure-of-intellect abilities. *Psychological Bulletin, 77,* 129–143.

Guilford, J. P. (1973). Theories of intelligence. In B. B. Wolman (Ed.), *Handbook of general psychology.* Englewood Cliffs, NJ: Prentice-Hall, 617–650.

Guilford, J. P., & Hoepfner, R. (1971). *The analysis of intelligence.* New York: McGraw-Hill.

Gullotta, T. P., & Adams, G. R. (1982). Minimizing juvenile delinquency: Implications for prevention programs. *Journal of Early Adolescence, 2,* 105–118.

Gullung, T. B., & Rucker, C. N. (1977). Labels and teacher expectation. *Exceptional Children, 43,* 464.

Guthrie, E. R. (1940). Association and the law of effect. *Psychological Review, 47,* 127–148.

Guthrie, E. R. (1942). Conditioning: A theory of learning in terms of stimulus, response, and association. In *Forty-first Yearbook of the National Society for the Study of Education, Part II.* Bloomington: Public School Publishing.

Guthrie, E. R. (1952). *The psychology of learning* (rev. ed.). New York: Harper & Row.

Guttman, N., & Kalish, H. I. (1956). Discriminality and stimulus generalization. *Journal of Experimental Psychology, 51,* 79–88.

Hall, G. S. (1904). *Adolescence*. New York: Appleton.

Hall, G. S. (1921). *Aspects of child life and education*. New York: Appleton-Century-Crofts.

Hall, J. E., & Phelps, M. S. (1979). Improving behavior at Crab Orchard School. *Middle School Journal, 10,* 10–30.

Hall, J. F. (1955). Retroactive inhibition in meaningful material. *Journal of Educational Psychology, 46,* 47–52.

Hallahan, D. P., & Kauffman, J. (1978). *Exceptional children*. Englewood Cliffs, NJ: Prentice-Hall.

Hamilton, C. E. (1950). The relationship between length of interval separating two learning tasks and performance on the second task. *Journal of Experimental Psychology, 40,* 613–621.

Hamilton, R. J. (1943). Retroactive facilitation as a function of degree of similarity between tasks. *Journal of Experimental Psychology, 32,* 363–376.

Harper, S. (1980, June 23). In tobacco, when there's smokeless fire. *Advertising Age,* 61.

Hauge, J. (1980). A second look at small group instruction. *Clearing House, 53,* 376–378.

Havighurst, R. J. (1976). Choosing a middle path for the use of drugs with hyperactive children. *School Review, 85,* 61–77.

Havighurst, R. J., & Moorefield, T. E. (1967). The disadvantaged in industrial cities. *The Educationally Retarded and Disadvantaged, 66* (Part I).

Haviland, J. M. (1979). Teachers' and students' beliefs about punishment. *Journal of Educational Psychology, 71,* 563–570.

Hawk, T. L. (1967). Self-concepts and the socially disadvantaged. *Elementary School Journal, 67,* 196–206.

Hawkes, G. R., Burchinal, L. G., & Gardner, B. (1957). Measurement of preadolescents' views of family control of behavior. *Child Development, 28,* 387–392.

Hendrickson, G., & Schroeder, W. (1941). Transfer of training in learning to hit a submerged target. *Journal of Educational Psychology, 32,* 206–213.

Henry, N. B. (Ed.) (1950). *The education of exceptional children*. Chicago: NSSE Yearbook.

Henry T. S. (Ed.) (1920). *Classroom problems in education of gifted children*. Chicago: National Society for the Study of Education, 19th Yearbook.

Henton, C. L., & Johnson, E. E. (1964). *Relationships between self-concept of Negro elementary children and their academic achievement, intelligence, interests and manifest anxiety*. Washington, DC: U.S. Office of Health, Education, & Welfare, Project No. 1542.

Hicks, D. J. (1971). Girls' attitudes toward modeled behavior and the content of imitative private play. *Child Development, 42,* 139–147.

Hilgard, E. R. (1961). Teaching machines and programmed learning: What support from the psychology of learning? *NEA Journal, 50,* 20–21.

Hilgard, E. R., Atkinson, R. C., & Atkinson, R. L. (1975). *Introduction to psychology*. New York: Harcourt Brace Jovanovich.

Hilgard, E. R., & Bower, G. H. (1975). *Theories of learning* (4th ed.). Englewood Cliffs, NJ: Prentice-Hall.

Hill, W. F. (1977). *Learning: A survey of psychological interpretations* (3rd ed.). New York: Crowell.

Hirst, W. (1980). The locus of constructive activity in memory for mathematical proofs. *Journal of Experimental Psychology: Human Learning and Memory, 6,* 119–126.

Hiskey, M. (1956). A study of the intelligence of the deaf and hearing. *American Annals of the Deaf, 101,* 329.

Hoffman, M. L. (1975). Moral internalization, parental power, and the nature of parent-child interaction. *Developmental Psychologist, 11,* 228–239.

Hoffman, M. L. (1980). Fostering moral development. In M. Johnson (Ed.), *Toward adolescence: The middle school years*. Chicago: NSSE Yearbook, 161–185.

Hollingsworth, L. (1942). *Children above 180 IQ*. New York: World Book.

Hollister, L. E. (1972). Stimulant drugs and the hyperactive child. *Wisconsin Journal of Education, 105*(1), 14–15.

Holmes, R. B. (1967). *Training residual vision in adolescents' education previously as non-visual*. Unpublished master's thesis, Illinois State University, Normal, IL.

Holt, J. (1969). *The underachieving school*. New York: Pitman.

Homme, L. E. (1966). Human motivation and environment. *Kansas Studies in Education, 16,* 30–39.

Homme, L. E., Csanyi, A. P., Gonzales, M. A., & Rechs, J. R. (1970). *How to use contingency contracting in the classroom*. Champaign, IL: Research Press.

Homme, L. E., DeBaca, P. C., Devine, J. V., Steinhorst, R., & Rickert, E. J. (1963). Use of the Premack principle in controlling the behavior of nursery school children. *Journal of the Experimental Analysis of Behavior, 6,* 544.

Hopkins, K. D., & Bracht, G. H. (1975). Ten-year stability of verbal and nonverbal IQ scores. *American Educational Research Journal, 12,* 469–478.

Hosford, P. L. (1973). *An instructional theory: A beginning*. Englewood Cliffs, NJ: Prentice-Hall.

Hosie, T. W., Gentile, J. R., & Carroll, J. D. (1974). Pupil preferences and the Premack principle. *American Educational Research Journal, 11,* 241–247.

Hovland, C. I., Janis, I. L., & Kelley, H. H. (1953). *Communication and persuasion*. New Haven, CT: Yale University Press.

Hull, C. L. (1943). *Principles of behavior*. New York: Appleton-Century-Crofts.

Hultsch, D. F., & Pentz, C. A. (1980). Research on adult learning and memory: Retrospect and prospect. *Contemporary Educational Psychology, 5,* 298–320.

Hundert, J. (1982). Some considerations of planning the integration of handicapped children in the mainstream. *Journal of Learning Disabilities, 15,* 73–80.

Hurst, W. A. (1968). A basis for diagnosing and treating learning disabilities within the school system. *Journal of Learning Disabilities, 1,* 263–275.

Hyde, T. S., & Jenkins, J. J. (1973). Recall of words as a function of semantic, graphic, and syntactic orienting tasks. *Journal of Verbal Learning and Verbal Behavior, 12,* 471–480.

Hyman, J. S., & Cohen, S. A. (1979). Learning for mastery: Ten conclusions after 15 years and 3,000 schools. *Educational Leadership, 37,* 104–109.

Ianni, F. A. J. (1980). A positive note on schools and discipline. *Educational Leadership, 38,* 457–458.

Iano, R. P., Ayers, D., Heller, H. B., McGettigan, J. F., & Walker,

V. S. (1974). Sociometric status of retarded children in an integrative program. *Exceptional Children, 40*, 267–271.

Ilg, F. L., & Ames, L. B. (1955). *Child behavior.* New York: Harper.

Inhelder, B., & Piaget, J. (1958). *The growth of logical thinking from childhood to adolescence.* New York: Basic Books.

Irion, A. L. (1949). Reminiscence in pursuit-motor learning as a function of length of rest and amount of pre-rest practice. *Journal of Experimental Psychology, 39*, 492–499.

Irwin, O. G. (1960). Infant speech: Effect of systematic reading of stories. *Journal of Speech and Hearing Research, 4*, 187–190.

Isakson, R. L., & Ellsworth, R. (1979). The measurement of teacher attitudes toward educational research. *Educational Research Quarterly, 4*, 12–18.

Israel, J. (1960). The effect of positive and negative self-evaluation on the attractiveness of a goal. *Human Relations, 13*, 33–47.

Jackson, P. W., Silberman, M. L., & Wolfson, B. J. (1969). Signs of personal involvement in teacher's descriptions of their students. *Journal of Educational Psychology, 60*, 22–27.

James, W. (1980). *Principles of psychology.* New York: Holt, Rinehart and Winston.

Janicki, T. C. (1979). *Aptitude-treatment interaction effects of variations in direct instruction.* Unpublished doctoral dissertation, University of Wisconsin, Madison.

Jarcho, H. D., & Peterson, A. C. (1981). Cognitive development and the ability to infer others' perceptions of self. *Journal of Early Adolescence, 1*, 155–162.

Jeffrey, R. W. (1976). The influence of symbolic and motor rehearsal on observational learning. *Journal of Research in Personality, 10*, 116–127.

Jenkins, G. G., Shacter, H. S., & Bauer, W. W. (1966). *These are your children* (3rd ed.). Glenview, IL: Scott, Foresman.

Jenkins, J. J. (1974). Remember that old theory of memory? Well forget it! *American Psychologist, 29*, 785–795.

Jensen, A. R. (1969). How much can we boost IQ and scholastic achievement? *Harvard Educational Review, 39*, 1–123.

Jensen, A. R. (1974). The effect of race of examiner on the mental test scores of white and black pupils. *Journal of Educational Measurement, 11*, 1–14.

Jensen, A. R. (1982). Level I/level II: Factors or categories? *Journal of Educational Psychology, 74*, 868–873.

Jeter, J. (1980). Individualized instructional programs. In J. Jeter (Ed.), *Approaches to individualized instruction.* Alexandria, VA: Association for Supervision and Curriculum Development, 24–44.

Johnson, R. D., & Downing, L. L. (1979). Deindividuation and valence of cues: Effects on prosocial and antisocial behavior. *Journal of Personality and Social Psychology, 37*, 1552–1538.

Johnson, R. E. (1973). Meaningfulness and the recall of textual prose. *American Educational Research Journal, 10*, 49–58.

Johnson, S. O. (1979). Better discipline for middle school students. *Clearing House, 53*, 86–89.

Jones, R. M. (1981). Social characteristics of early adolescents upon entering a middle school. *Journal of Early Adolescence, 1*, 283–292.

Jones, R. M., & Thornburg, H. D. (1982, October). *The relationship between development, schooling, and self-esteem.* Paper presented at the National Middle School Association annual meeting, Kansas City, MO.

Jordan, I. K., Gustason, G., & Rosen, R. (1979). An update on communication trends at programs for the deaf. *American Annals of the Deaf, 124*, 350–357.

Joyce, B. (1979). Toward a theory of information processing in teaching. *Educational Research Quarterly, 3*, 66–77.

Judd, C. H. (1908). The relation of special training and general intelligence. *Educational Review, 36*, 42–48.

Judd, C. H. (1939). *Educational psychology.* Boston: Houghton Mifflin.

Just, M. A., & Brownell, H. H. (1974). Retrieval of concrete and abstract prose descriptions from memory. *Canadian Journal of Psychology, 28*, 339–350.

Kagan, J. (1966). A developmental approach to conceptual growth. In H. J. Klausmeier & C. W. Harris (Eds.), *Analysis of concept learning.* New York: Academic Press, 190–219.

Kagan, J., Moss, H., & Siegel, I. (1963). Basic processes in children. *SRCD Monograph, 28*(2).

Kalish, P. W. (1966). Concept attainment as a function of monetary incentives, competition, and instructions. *Technical Report from the Wisconsin Research and Development Center for Cognitive Learning* (No. 8). Madison: University of Wisconsin.

Kandel, D. B., & Lesser, G. S. (1972). *Youth in two worlds.* San Francisco: Jossey-Bass.

Kanfer, F. (1965). Behavioral diagnosis. *Archives of General Psychiatry, 12*, 529–538.

Karchmer, M. A., & Trybus, R. J. (1977, October). Who are the deaf children in "mainstream" programs? *Research Bulletin, Series R.* Washington, DC: Gallaudet College.

Karoly, P. (1977). Behavioral self-management in children: Concepts, methods, issues, and directions. In M. Hersen, R. M. Eisler, & P. M. Miller (Eds.), *Progress in behavior modification* (Vol. 5). New York: Academic Press, 197–262.

Kazdin, A. E. (1973). The effect of response cost and aversion stimulation in suppressing punished and non-punished speech disfluencies. *Behavior Therapy, 4*, 73–82.

Keating, D. P. (1978). A search for social intelligence. *Journal of Educational Psychology, 70*, 218–223.

Keating, D. P. (1980). Four faces of creativity: The continuing plight of the intellectually underserved. *Gifted Child Quarterly, 24*, 56–61.

Keating, D. P., & Caramazza, A. (1975). Effects of age and ability on syllogistic reasoning in early adolescence. *Developmental Psychology, 11*(6) 837–842.

Keating, D. P., & Clark, L. V. (1980). Development of physical and social reasoning in adolescence. *Developmental Psychology, 16*(1), 23–30.

Keller, F. S. (1968). Good-bye teacher. *Journal of Applied Behavioral Analysis, 1*, 79–84.

Kellogg, W. N., & Kellogg, L. A. (1933). *The ape and the child.* New York: McGraw-Hill.

Kephart, N. C. (1960). *The slow learner in the classroom.* Columbus, OH: Merrill.

Keppel, G. (1968). Retroactive and proactive inhibition. In T. R. Dixon & D. L. Norton (Eds.), *Verbal behavior and general behavior theory*. Englewood Cliffs, NJ: Prentice-Hall, 172–213.

Kerlinger, F. N. (1973). *Foundations of Behavioral Research* (2nd ed.). New York: Holt, Rinehart and Winston.

Kibler, R. J., Barker, L. L., & Miles, D. T. (1974). *Behavioral objectives and instruction* (2nd ed.). Boston: Allyn and Bacon.

Kimble, G. A. (1961). *Hilgard and Marquis' "Conditioning and learning."* New York: Appleton-Century-Crofts.

Kintsch, W. (1974). *The representation of meaning in memory*. Hillsdale, NJ: Erlbaum.

Kirk, S. A. (1972). *Educating exceptional children*. Boston: Houghton Mifflin.

Kirk, S. A., McCarthy, J., & Kirk, W. (1968). Illinois test of psycholinguistic abilities. (Examiners Manual), rev. ed. Champaign, IL: University of Illinois Press.

Klausmeier, H. J., Feldhausen, J., Check, J. (1959). *An analysis of learning efficiency in arithmetic of mentally retarded children in comparison with children of average and high intelligence*. U.S. Office of Education, Research Project No. 153. Maidson, WI: University of Wisconsin.

Klausmeier, H. J., & Ripple, R. E. (1971). *Learning and human abilities* (3rd ed.). New York: Harper & Row.

Klausmeier, H. J., Ghatala, E., & Frayer, D. (1974). *Conceptual learning and development*. New York: Academic Press.

Klausmeier, H. J., Sorenson, J. S., & Ghatala, E. S. (1971). Individually guided motivation: Developing self-direction and prosocial behaviors. *Elementary School Journal, 71*, 339–350.

Klausmeier, H. J., Quilling, M., Sorenson, J., Way, R. S., & Glasurd, G. R. (1971). *Individually guided education and the multiunit elementary school: Guidelines for implementation*. Madison, WI: Wisconsin Research and Development Center for Cognitive Learning.

Knafle, J. D. (1972). The relationship of behavior ratings to grades earned by female high school students. *Journal of Educational Research, 66*(3), 106–110.

Koffka, K. (1925). *The growth of the mind*. New York: Harcourt Brace & World.

Koffka, K. (1935). *Principles of gestalt psychology*. New York: Harcourt, Brace, & World.

Kohlberg, L. (1964). Development of moral character and moral ideology. In M. L. Hoffman & L. W. Hoffman (Eds.). *Review of child development research* (Vol. 1). New York: Russell Sage, 383–441.

Kohlberg, L. (1971). Indoctrination versus relativity in value education. *Zygon, 6*(4), 385–390.

Kohlberg, L. (1975). The cognitive-developmental approach to moral education. *Phi Delta Kappan, 56*, 670–677.

Kohler, W. (1925). The mentality of apes (E. Winter, Trans.). New York: Harcourt, Brace & World.

Kohnstamm, G. A. (1967). *Piaget's analysis of class inclusion: Right or wrong?* The Hague: Mounton.

Kolesnik, W. B. (1970). *Educational psychology* (2nd ed.). New York: McGraw-Hill.

Kolesnik, W. B. (1976). *Learning: Educational application*. Boston: Allyn & Bacon.

Konopka, G. (1973). Requirements for healthy development of adolescent youth. *Adolescence, 8*(31), 291–316.

Kounin, J. S. (1970). *Discipline and group management in classrooms*. New York: Holt, Rinehart and Winston.

Krathwohl, D. R., Bloom, B. S., & Masia, B. B. (1964). *Taxonomy of educational objectives: Affective domain*. New York: McKay.

Krathwohl, D. (1977). Improving educational research and development. *Educational Researcher, 6*, 8–14.

Kratochwill, T. R. (1977). The movement of psychological extras into ability assessment. *Journal of Special Education, 11*, 299–311.

Krypsin, W. J., & Feldhusen, J. F. (1974). *Developing classroom tests*. Minneapolis: Burgess.

Kukla, A. (1978). An attributional theory of choice. In L. Berkowitz (Ed.), *Advances in experimental and social psychology*. New York: Academic Press, 141–170.

Kulik, H., Kulik, C., & Cohen, P. (1979). A metaanalysis of outcome studies of Keller's Personalized System of Instruction. *American Psychologist, 34*, 307–318.

Kurdek, L. A., & Krile, D. (1982). A developmental analysis of the relation between peer acceptance and both interpersonal understanding and perceived social self-competence. *Child Development, 53*, 1485–1491.

Kvale, S. (1977). Dialectics and research on remembering. In N. Datan & H. W. Reese (Eds.), *Life-span developmental psychology: Dialectical perspectives on experimental research*. New York: Academic Press, 391–422.

Kvaraceus, W. C. (Ed.) (1965). *Negro and self-concept*. New York: McGraw-Hill.

Latham, G. P., & Yuki, G. A. (1975). A review of researches on the application of goal setting in organizations. *Academy of Management Journal, 18*, 824–845.

Lazarus, R. S. (1980). The stress and coping paradigm. In C. Eisdorfer, D. Cohen, A. Kleinman, & P. Maxim (Eds.), *Theoretical bases of psychopathology*. New York: Spectrum, 163–182.

Lee, S. S. (1979). Memory span, IQ, and memory aids effects on learning of logico-conceptual rules. *Contemporary Educational Psychology, 4*, 334–347.

Leeds, C. H. (1954). Teacher behavior liked and disliked by pupils. *Education, 75*, 29–36.

Lennon, R. T. (1970). Testing: The question of bias. In T. J. Fitzgibbon (Ed.), *Evaluation in the inner city*. New York: Harcourt, Brace & World, 410–443.

Lepper, M. R., & Greene, D. (Eds.) (1978). *The hidden costs of reward: New perspectives on the psychology of human motivation*. Hillsdale, NJ: Erlbaum.

Lepper, M. R., Greene, D., & Nisbett, R. E. (1973). Understanding children's intrinsic interest with extrinsic rewards. *Journal of Personality and Social Psychology, 38*, 129–137.

Lepper, M. R., Sagotsky, J., & Mailer, J. (1975). Generalization and persistence of effects of exposure to self-reinforcement models. *Child Development, 46*, 618–630.

Levin, J. R., & Allen, V. (Eds.) (1976). *Cognitive learning in children*. New York: Academic Press.

Levin, J. R., Ghatala, E. S., & Truman, D. L. (1979). Reducing

533

intersentence interference via contextual aids. *American Educational Research Journal, 16,* 249–256.

Levine, D., & Linn, M. C. (1977). Scientific reasoning ability in adolescence: Theoretical viewpoints and educational implications. *Journal of Research in Science Teaching, 14,* 371.

Levine, M. A. (1978). Are teachers becoming more humane? *Phi Delta Kappan, 59,* 353–354.

Lewin, K. (1935). *A dynamic theory of personality.* New York: McGraw-Hill.

Lewin, K. (1951). *Field theory in social science.* New York: Harper & Row.

Lewin, K., Dembo, T., Festinger, L., & Sears, P. S. (1944). Levels of aspiration. In J. McV. Hunt (Ed.), *Personality and the behavior disorders.* New York: Ronald Press.

Lewis, M. M. (1959). *How children learn to speak.* New York: Basic Books.

Lewis, M. M. (1963). *Language, thought and personality.* New York: Basic Books.

Lewis, M. M. (1973). *A comparison of self-concept, academic achievement, attitude toward school and adaptive behavior of elementary school children identified as educable mentally retarded in four different school environments.* Unpublished doctoral dissertation, University of Michigan, Ann Arbor.

Lien, A. J. (1980). *Measurement and evaluation of learning.* Dubuque, IA: W. C. Brown.

Lilly, S. (1979). *Children with exceptional needs.* New York: Holt, Rinehart, and Winston.

Lindgren, H. C. (1980). *Educational psychology in the classroom* (6th ed.). New York: Oxford University Press.

Linn, M. C. (1983). Content, context, and process in reasoning during adolescence: Selecting a model. *Journal of Early Adolescence, 3,* 63–82.

Linn, M. C., & Pulos, S. (1983). Male-female differences in predicting displaced volume: Strategy usage, aptitude relationships and experience influences. *Journal of Educational Psychology, 75,* 85–96.

Linton, T. E., & Juul, K. D. (1980). Mainstreaming: Time for reassessment. *Educational Leadership, 37,* 433–437.

Lippitt, P., & Lippitt, R. (1968). The peer culture as a learning environment. *Childhood Education, 47,* 135–138.

Lipsett, L. (1975). The synchrony of respiration, heartrate and sucking in the newborn. In *Biological and clinical aspects of brain development.* Evansville, IN: Mead and Johnson.

Lipsitz, S. (1969). *The effect of the race of the examiner on results of intelligence and performance on Negro and white children.* Unpublished master's thesis, Long Island University, New York.

Lipton, A. (1963). Cultural heritage and the relationship to self-esteem. *Journal of Educational Sociology, 36,* 211–212.

Loewenstein, S. F. (1980). The passion and challenge of teaching. *Harvard Educational Review, 50,* 1–12.

Logan, F. A. (1959). The Hull-Spence approach. In S. Koch (Ed.), *Psychology: A study of science* (Vol. 2). New York: McGraw-Hill.

Long, B. H., & Henderson, E. H. (1968). Self-social concepts of disadvantaged school beginners. *Journal of Genetic Psychology, 133,* 41–51.

Lubin, J. S. (1977, June 6). The way we eat: American diets today are high in proteins, fats and controversy. *Wall Street Journal.*

Lumpkin, D. D. (1959). Relationship of self-concept to achievement in reading. *Dissertation Abstracts, 20,* 204–205.

Lyon, D. O. (1916). The relation of quickness of learning to retentiveness. *Archives of Psychology, 5*(34).

Maccoby, E. E. (1959). Role taking in childhood and its consequences for social learning. *Child Development, 30,* 229–252.

Macekura, J. (1978). Building discipline in a "tough" school. *Social Education, 42,* 100–104.

Mackenzie, D. E. (1983). Research for school improvement: An appraisal of some recent trends. *Educational Researcher, 12,* 5–16.

Maehr, M. L., & Kleiber, D. A. (1981). The graying of achievement motivation. *American Psychologist, 36,* 787–793.

Maehr, M. L., & Sjogren, D. D. (1971). Atkinson's theory of achievement motivation: First step toward a theory of academic motivation? *Review of Educational Research, 41,* 143–161.

Mahoney, M. J., & Thorensen, C. E. (1972). Behavioral self-control—power to the person. *Educational Researcher, 1,* 5–7.

Maier, H. W. (1978). Piagetian principles applied to the beginning phase in professional helping. In R. Weizmann, R. Brown, P. J. Levinson, & P. A. Taylor (Eds.), *Piagetian theory and the helping professions.* Los Angeles: University of Southern California Press, 1–13.

Maker, C. J. (1981). The gifted hearing-impaired student. *American Annals of the Deaf, 126,* 631–645.

Malinowski, B. (1927). *Sex and repression in savage society.* New York: Harcourt, Brace.

Mandler, J. M., & Richey, G. H. (1971). Long-term memory for pictures. *Journal of Experimental Psychology, 3,* 386–396.

Marden, C. F., & Meyer, G. (1978). *Minorities in American society* (5th ed.). New York: Van Nostrand.

Markle, S. M. (1977). *Teaching conceptual networks.* Paper presented at the annual convention of the Association for Educational Communications and Technology.

Markle, S. M., & Tiemann, P. W. (1969). *Really understanding concepts.* Chicago: Itemann Associates.

Markle, S. M., & Tiemann, P. W. (1970). "Behavioral" analysis of "cognitive" content. *Educational Technology, 10,* 41–45.

Marland, S. (1972). *Education of the gifted and talented.* Washington, DC: U.S. Government Printing Office.

Marotz, L. W. (1983). Adolescent research from the practitioner's point of view. *Journal of Early Adolescence, 3,* 163–166.

Maslow, A. H. (1943). A theory of human motivation. *Psychological Review, 50,* 370–396.

Maslow, A. H. (1962). *Toward a psychology of being.* New York: Van Nostrand Reinhold.

Maslow, A. H. (1968). *Toward a psychology of being.* (2nd ed.). Princeton, NJ: Van Nostrand.

Massler, M., & Schour, I. (1958). *Atlas of the mouth.* Chicago: American Dental Association.

Matsui, T., Okada, A., & Mizuguchi, R. (1981). Expectancy theory prediction of the goal theory postulate, "The harder the goals, the higher the performance." *Journal of Applied Psychology, 66,* 54–58.

Mausner, B. (1953). Studies in social interactions: III. Effect of variation in one partner's prestige on the interaction of observer pairs. *Journal of Applied Psychology, 37,* 391–393.

Mayer, R. E. (1975). Information processing variables in learning to solve problems. *Review of Educational Research, 45,* 525–542.

McClelland, D. C., Atkinson, J. W., Clark, R. A., & Lowell, E. L. (1953). *The achievement motive.* New York: Appleton-Century-Crofts.

McClelland, D. C., & Liberman, A. M. (1949). The effect of need for achievement on recognition of need-related words. *Journal of Personality, 18,* 236–251.

McEwin, C. K. (1981a). Interscholastic sports and the early adolescent. *Journal of Early Adolescence, 1,* 123–134.

McEwin, C. K. (1981b). Establishing teacher-advisory programs in middle level schools. *Journal of Early Adolescence, 1,* 337–348.

McEwin, C. K., & Cross, A. H. (1982). A comparative study of perceived victimization, perceived anonymity, self-esteem, and preferred teacher characteristics of gifted and talented and non-labeled early adolescents. *Journal of Early Adolescence, 2,* 247–254.

McGeoch, J. A. (1942). *The psychology of human learning.* London: Longmans.

McGeoch, J. A., & Whitely, P. L. (1926). The recall of observed material. *Journal of Educational Psychology, 17,* 419–425.

McGreal, T. L. (1980). Helping teachers set goals. *Educational Leadership, 37,* 414–419.

McKeachie, W. J., & Doyle, C. L. (1970). *Psychology* (2nd ed.). Reading, MA: Addison-Wesley.

McKeachie, W. J., & Kulik, J. A. (1975). Effective college teaching. In F. N. Kerlinger (Ed.), *Review of research in education* (Vol 3). Washington, DC: American Educational Research Association, 165–209.

McKenzie, G. R. (1980). Improving instruction through instructional design. *Educational Leadership, 37,* 664–669.

McMains, M. J., & Liebert, R. M. (1968). Influences of discrepancies between successively modeled self-reward criteria on the adoption of a self-imposed standard. *Journal of Personality and Social Psychology, 8,* 166–171.

McNeill, D. (1966). Development of psycholinguistics. In F. Smith & G. A. Miller (Eds.), *The genesis of languages: A psycholinguistic approach.* Cambridge, MA: M.I.T. Press.

Meadow, K. P. (1975). The development of deaf children. In E. M. Hetherington (Ed.), *Review of child development research* (Vol 5). Chicago: University of Chicago Press.

Mechner, F. (1967). Behavioral analysis of instructional sequencing. In *Programmed Instruction, Part II.* Chicago: NSSE Yearbook 81–103.

Meeker, M. N. (1969). *The structure of intellect, its interpretation and uses.* Columbus, OH: Merrill.

Menyuk, P. (1971). *The acquisition and development of language.* Englewood Cliffs, NJ: Prentice-Hall.

Mergendoller, J. R., Packer, M. J., Osaki, S. Y., Rounds, T. S., Mitman, A. L., Ward, B. A., & Tikunoff, W. J. (1981). *The junior high school transition study: Students' definitions of teachers.* San Francisco: Far West Laboratory.

Merrill, M. D., & Tennyson, R. D. (1978). Concept classification and classification errors as a function of relationships between examples and nonexamples. *Improving Human Performance, 7,* 351–364.

Meyerowitz, J. H. (1962). Self-derogations in young retardates and special class placement. *Child Development, 33,* 443–451.

Midlarsky, E., Bryan, J. H., & Brickman, P. (1973). Aversive approval, interactive effects of modeling and reinforcement on altruistic behavior. *Child Development, 44,* 321–328.

Milisen, R. (1971). The incidence of speech disorders. In L. E. Travis (Ed.), *Handbook of speech pathology and audiology.* New York: Appleton, 619–633.

Miller, N. E., & Dollard, J. C. (1941). *Social learning and imitation.* New Haven: Yale University Press.

Mishra, S. P. (1980). The influence of examiners' ethnic attributes on intelligence test scores. *Psychology in the Schools, 17,* 117–122.

Mishra, S. P. (1983). Cognitive processes: Implications for assessing intelligence. *Theory into Practice,* 145–150.

Mitman, A. L., & Packer, M. J. (1982). Concerns of seventh-graders about their transition to junior high school. *Journal of Early Adolescence, 2,* 319–338.

Montemayor, R., & Eisen, M. (1977). The development of self-conceptions from childhood to adolescence. *Developmental Psychology, 13,* 314–319.

Montessori, M. (1972). *The discovery of the child.* New York: Ballantine.

Moore, G. (1969). Untitled, unpublished case study, Arizona Center for Early Childhood Education.

Moore, W. J., & Kennedy, L. D. (1971). Evaluation of learning in the language arts. In B. S. Bloom, J. T. Hastings, & G. F. Madaus, *Handbook on formative and summative evaluation of student learning.* New York: McGraw-Hill, 399–446.

Moors, L, & Clarke, A. M. (1981). The effect of shaping two levels of information processing on children's immediate and delayed retention. *Educational Psychology, 1,* 107–117.

Morris, R. J., & Hoschouer, R. L. (1980). Current issues in applied research with mentally retarded persons. *Applied Research in Mental Retardation, 1,* 85–93.

Mouly, G. J. (1982). *Psychology for teaching.* Boston: Allyn & Bacon.

Mowrer, O. H., & Solomon, L. N. (1954). Contiguity versus drive-reduction in conditioned fear: The proximity and abruptness of drive-reduction. *American Journal of Psychology, 67,* 15–25.

Mulhall, E. F. (1917). Tests of the memories of school children. *Journal of Educational Psychology, 8,* 294–302.

Munn, N. L. (1965). *The evolution and growth of human behavior* (2nd ed.). Boston: Houghton Mifflin.

Murdock, B. B., Jr. (1961). The retention of individual items. *Journal of Experimental Psychology, 62,* 618–625.

Mursetin, B. I. (1965). The relationship of grade expectation and grades believed to be deserved to actual grades received. *Journal of Experimental Education, 33,* 357–362.

Muuss, R. E. (1976). The implications of social learning theory for an understanding of adolescent development. *Adolescence, 11,* 61–65.

535

Myers, J. L., Pezdek, K., & Coulson, D. (1973). Effects of prose organization upon free recall. *Journal of Educational Psychology, 65,* 313–320.

Nagy, P., & Griffiths, A. K. (1982). Limitations of recent research relating Piaget's theory to adolescent thought. *Review of Educational Research, 52,* 513–556.

Naisbitt, J. (1982). *Megatrends.* New York: Warner.

National Advisory Committee (1968). *First annual report: Special education for handicapped children.* Washington, DC: U.S. Office of Education.

Neimark, E. D. (1975). Intellectual development during adolescence. In F. D. Horowitz (Ed.), *Review of child development research* (Vol. 4). Chicago: University of Chicago Press, 541–587.

Nelson, K. (1977). Acquisition of concepts. In R. C. Anderson, R. J. Spiro, & W. E. Montague (Eds.), *Schooling and the acquisition of knowledge.* Hillsdale, NJ: Erlbaum, 215–240.

New directions for educational goals (1983). *Learning Trends, 1,* 5.

Nicholls, J. G. (1980). A re-examination of boys' and girls' causal attributions for success and failure based on New Zealand data. In L. Fyans (Ed.), *Achievement motivation: Recent trends in theory and research.* New York: Plenum, 289–311.

Nickerson, R. S. (1981). Thoughts on teaching thinking. *Educational Leadership, 38,* 21–25.

Nilles, H. (1980). *A technology assessment of personal computers.* Los Angeles: University of Southern California, Office of Interdisciplinary Programs.

Nitko, A. J. (1980). Distinguishing the many varieties of criterion-referenced tests. *Review of Educational Research, 50,* 461–485.

Noble, C. G., & Nolan, J. D. (1976). Effect of student verbal behavior on classroom teacher behavior. *Journal of Educational Psychology, 68,* 343–346.

Notz, W. W. (1975). Work motivation and the negative effects of extrinsic rewards. *American Psychologist, 30,* 884–891.

Novak, J. (1979). Applying psychology and philosophy to the improvement of laboratory teaching. *American Biology Teacher, 41,* 466–471.

Novak, J. (1980a). *Handbook for the learning how to learn program.* Ithaca: New York State College of Agriculture and Life Sciences.

Novak, J. (1980b). Learning theory applied to the biology classroom. *American Biology Teacher, 42,* 280–285.

Novak, J. (1980c). Progress in application of learning theory. *Theory into Practice, 19,* 58–65.

Nowicki, S., & Walker, C. (1974). The role of generalized and specific expectancies in determining academic achievement. *Journal of Social Psychology, 94,* 275–280.

Noyce, R. (1977). Microelectronics. *Scientific American, 237,* 63–69.

O'Connor, R. D. (1969). Modification of social withdrawal through symbolic modeling. *Journal of Applied Behavioral Analysis, 2,* 15–22.

O'Connor, R. D. (1972). Relative efficacy of modeling, shaping, and the combined procedures for the modification of social withdrawal. *Journal of Abnormal Psychology, 79,* 327–334.

Ohanian, V. (1971). Educational technology: A critique. *Elementary School Journal, 71,* 183–197.

Olson, D. R. (1970). Language and thought: Aspects of a cognitive theory of semantics. *Psychological Review, 77,* 257–273.

Openshaw, D. K., Thomas, D. L., & Rollins, B. C. (1981). Adolescent self-esteem: A multidimensional perspective. *Journal of Early Adolescence, 1,* 273–282.

Osgood, C. E. (1949). The similarity paradox in human learning: A resolution. *Psychological Review, 56,* 132–143.

Osgood, C. E. (1961). Comments on Professor Bousfield's paper. In C. N. Cofer & B. S. Musgrave (Eds.), *Verbal learning and verbal behavior.* New York: McGraw-Hill.

Padilla, A. M., & Garza, B. M. (1975). I.Q. tests: A case of cultural myopia. *National Elementary Principal, 54,* 53–58.

Page, E. B. (1958). Teacher comments and student performance. *Journal of Educational Psychology, 49,* 175–181.

Paivio, A. (1971). *Imagery and verbal processes.* New York: Holt, Rinehart and Winston.

Palermo, D. S. (1978). *Psychology of language.* Glenview, IL: Scott, Foresman.

Parsons, J. E., Adler, T. F., & Kaczala, C. M. (1982). Socialization of achievement attitudes and beliefs: Parental influences.

Pavlov, I. P. (1903). *Lectures on conditioned reflexes.* Moscow: Foreign Languages Publishing House.

Pavlov, I. P. (1927). *Conditioned reflexes: An investigation of the activity of the cerebral cortex.* London: Oxford University Press.

Peel, E. A. (1978). Generalizing through the verbal medium. *British Journal of Educational Psychology, 48,* 36–46.

Perry, P. J., & Hoback, J. R. (1982). The cart before the horse: A frequent danger in gifted and talented programs. *Middle School Journal, 13,* 18–19.

Petersen, A. C., Tobin-Richards, M., & Boxer, A. (1983). Puberty: Its measurement and meaning. *Journal of Early Adolescence, 3,* 47–62.

Peterson, P. L. (1979). Direct instruction: Effective for what and for whom? *Educational Leadership, 37,* 46–48.

Phillips, E. L. (1968). Achievement Place: Token reinforcement procedures in a home-style rehabilitation setting for "predelinquent" boys. *Journal of Applied Behavior Analysis, 1,* 213–223.

Phillips, E. L., Phillips, L. A., Fixsen, D. L., & Wolf, M. M. (1971). Achievement Place: Modification of the behaviors of predelinquent boys within a token economy. *Journal of Applied Behavior Analysis, 4,* 45–49.

Piaget, J. (1948). *The moral judgment of the child.* Glencoe, IL: Free Press. (Original work published 1932)

Piaget, J. (1950). *The psychology of intelligence.* London: Routledge & Kegan Paul.

Piaget, J. (1951). *Play, dreams, and imitation in childhood.* New York: Norton.

Piaget, J. (1952). *The origins of intelligence in children.* New York: International University Press.

Piaget, J. (1960). *The child's conception of physical causality.* Totowa, NJ: Littlefield, Adams.

Piaget, J. (1969). The intellectual development of the adolescent. In G. Caplan & S. Lebovici (Eds.), *Adolescence: Psychosocial perspectives.* New York: Basic Books.

Piaget, J. (1971). The theory of stages in cognitive development. In D. R. Green (Ed.), *Measurement and Piaget.* New York: McGraw-Hill.

Piaget, J. (1972). Intellectual evolution from adolescence to adulthood. *Human Development, 19,* 1–12.

Piaget, J., & Inhelder, B. (1958). *The growth of logical thinking from childhood to adolescence.* New York: Basic Books.

Piaget, J., & Szeminska, A. (1952). *The child's conception of number.* London: Routledge & Kegan Paul.

Pogrow, S. (1982a). On technological relevance and the survival of U.S. public schools. *Phi Delta Kappan, 68,* 610–611.

Pogrow, S. (1982b). Micro-computerizing your paperwork. *Electronic Learning, 1,* 55–59.

Pogrow, S. (1983). *Education in the computer age.* Beverly Hills: Sage Publications.

Porat, M. (1977). *Information economy: Definition and measurement.* Washington, DC: U.S. Department of Commerce, Publication No. 77-12.

Portland Public Schools (1959). *The gifted child in Portland.* Portland: Portland Public Schools.

Posner, G. J., & Rudnitsky, A. N. (1982). *Course design* (2nd ed.). New York: Longmanns.

Potter, E. F. (1984). Impact of developmental factors on motivating the school achievement of young adolescents: Theory and implications for practice. *Journal of Early Adolescence, 4,* 1–14.

Premack, D. (1959). Toward empirical behavior laws: I. Positive reinforcement. *Psychological Reports, 66,* 219–233.

Premack, D. (1965). Reinforcement theory. In D. Levine (Ed.), *Nebraska symposium on motivation* (Vol. 13). Lincoln: University of Nebraska Press, 123–180.

Pritchard, M. C. (1951). The contribution of Leta S. Hollingworth to the study of gifted children. In P. Witty (Ed.), *The gifted child.* New York: Heath, 47–85.

Protinsky, H. O., & Farrier, S. (1980). Self-image changes in pre-adolescents and adolescents. *Adolescence, 15*(60), 887–894.

Protinsky, H. O., & Hugston, G. (1980). Adolescent volume conservation abilities: A comparison of three tests. *Journal of Psychology, 104,* 27–30.

Public perceptions of television and other mass media: A twenty-five year review (1979). New York: Television Information Office.

Pulos, S., deBenedictis, T., Linn, M. C., Sullivan, P. A., & Clement, C. A. (1982). Modification of gender differences in the understanding of displaced volume. *Journal of Early Adolescence, 2,* 61–74.

Pulos, S., & Linn, M. (1981). Generality of the controlling variables scheme in early adolescence. *Journal of Early Adolescence, 1,* 26–37.

Quay, H. D., & Peterson, D. (1975). *Manual for the behavior problem checklist.* Miami: University of Miami (mimeographed).

Quillian, M. R. (1967). Word concepts: A theory and simulation of some basic semantic capabilities. *Behavioral Science, 12,* 410–430.

Rappoport, L. (1972). *Personality development.* Glenview, IL: Scott, Foresman.

Raths, L. E., Harmin, M., & Simon, S. B. (1966). *Values and teaching.* Columbus, OH: Merrill.

Ratliff, R. (1980). Physical punishment must be abolished. *Educational Leadership, 37,* 474–476.

Raynor, J. O., & Rubin, I. S. (1971). Effects of achievement motivation and future orientation on level of performance. *Journal of Personality and Social Psychology, 17,* 36–41.

Razran, D. (1951). Experimental semantics. *Transactions of the New York Academy of Sciences, 13,* 171–177.

Reardon, F. J., & Reynolds, R. N. (1978). *Corporal punishment in Pennsylvania.* Harrisburg: Pennsylvania State Department of Education.

Reese, H. W. (1976). Models of memory development. *Human Development, 19,* 201–303.

Reigeluth, C. M., Merrill, M. D., Wilson, B.G., & Spiller, R. T. (1980). The elaboration theory of instruction: A model for sequencing and synthesizing instruction. *Instructional Science, 9,* 195–219.

Reis, R. (1973). What is a resource room program? *Journal of Learning Disabilities, 6,* 609–614.

Renzulli, J. S. (1978). What makes giftedness: Reexamining a definition. *Phi Delta Kappan, 60,* 180–184.

Renzulli, J. S., Smith, F. H., White, A. J., Callahan, C. M., & Hartman, C. K. (1976). *Scales for rating the behavioral characteristics of superior students (SRBCSS).* Wethersfield, CT: Creative Learning Press.

Resnick, L. B., & Glaser, R. (1976). Problem solving and intelligence. In L. B. Resnick (Ed.), *The nature of intelligence.* Hillsdale, NJ: Erlbaum, 205–230.

Rhodes, W. C. (1970). A community participation analysis of emotional disturbance. *Exceptional Children, 36,* 307–314.

Ricciuti, H. (1965). Object grouping and selective ordering behavior in infants 12–24 months old. *Merrill-Palmer Quarterly, 11,* 129–148.

Rice, F. P. (1978). *The adolescent: Development relationships and culture* (2nd ed.). Boston: Allyn & Bacon.

Rimm, D. C., & Masters, J. C. (1974). *Behavior therapy: Techniques and empirical findings.* New York: Academic Press.

Robertson, A., & Youniss, J. (1969). Anticipatory visual imagery in deaf and hearing children. *Child Development, 40,* 123–135.

Robinson, N. M., & Robinson, H. B. (1976). *The mentally retarded child.* New York: McGraw-Hill.

Rogers, C. R. (1961). *On becoming a person.* Boston: Houghton Mifflin.

Rohwer, W. D., Rohwer, C. P., & Howe, J. R. (1980). *Educational psychology: Teaching for student diversity.* New York: Holt, Rinehart and Winston.

Rosen, B. C., & d'Andrade, R. (1959). The psychosocial origins of achievement motivation. *Sociometry, 22,* 185–218.

Rosenberg, M. (1965). *Society and the adolescent self-image.* Princeton, NJ: Princeton University Press.

Rosenberg, M. (1975). The dissonant context and the adolescent self-concept. In S. E. Dragastin & G. H. Elder (Eds.), *Adolescence in the life cycle: Psychological change and social context*. Washington, DC: Hemisphere, 335–361.

Rosenberg, M. (1979). *Conceiving the self*. New York: Basic Books.

Rosenhan, D. L. (1969). The kindness of children. *Young Children, 25*, 30–44.

Rosenkoetter, L. J., Alderman, M. K., Nelson, J. R., & Ottaviano, M. (1982). Moral education: An evaluation of the effect of moral dilemma discussions for sixth graders. *Journal of Early Adolescence, 2*, 75–82.

Rosenkrans, M. A., & Hartup, W. W. (1967). Imitative influences of consistent and inconsistent response consequences to a model on aggressive behavior in children. *Journal of Personality and Social Psychology, 7*, 429–434.

Rosenshine, B. (1976). Classroom interaction. In N. L. Gage (Ed.), *Psychology of teaching methods*. Chicago: University of Chicago Press, 212–240.

Rosenshine, B. V. (1979). Content, time, and direct instruction. In P. L. Peterson & H. J. Walberg (Eds.), *Research on teaching: Concepts, findings, and implications*. Berkeley, CA: McCutchan, 28–56.

Rosenshine, B. V. (1980). How time is spent in elementary classrooms. In C. Denham & A. Liberman (Eds.), *Time to learn* (pp. 107–126). Washington, DC: National Institute of Education.

Rosenshine, B. V., & Berliner, D. C. (1978). Academic engaged time. *British Journal of Teacher Education, 4*, 3–16.

Rosenthal, T. L., & Zimmerman, B. J. (1973). Organization, observation, and guided practice in concept attainment and generalization. *Child Development, 44*, 606–613.

Rosenthal, T. L., & Zimmerman, B. J. (1978). *Social learning and cognition*. New York: Academic Press.

Ross, R. J. (1974). The empirical status of the formal operations. *Adolescence, 9*(35), 413–420.

Rosser, R. A., & Brody, G. H. (1981). Acquisition of a concrete operational rule through observational learning: How abstract is the acquired abstraction. *Merrill-Palmer Quarterly, 27*, 3–13.

Rosser, R. A., & Horan, P. F. (1982). Acquisition of multiple classification and seriation from the observation of models: A social learning approach to horizontal decalage. *Child Development, 53*, 1229–1232.

Rotter, J. B. (1966). Generalized expectancies for internal versus external control of reinforcement. *Psychological Monographs, 80* (1, Whole No. 609).

Rounds, T. S., Ward, B. A., Mergendoller, J. A., & Tikunoff, W. J. (1981). *Junior high school transition study, Vol. 2: Organization of instruction*. San Francisco: Far West Laboratory.

Routh, D. K., & Roberts, R. D. (1972). Minimal brain dysfunction in children: Failure to find evidence for a behavioral syndrome. *Psychological Reports, 31*, 307–314.

Royer, J. M. (1979). Theories of the transfer of learning. *Educational Psychologist, 14*, 53–69.

Royer, J. M., & Cable, G. W. (1975). Facilitated learning in connected discourse. *Journal of Educational Psychology, 67*, 116–123.

Royer, J. M., & Cable, G. W. (1976). Illustrations, analogies, and facilitative transfer in prose learning. *Journal of Educational Psychology, 68*, 205–209.

Royer, J. M., Hambleton, R. K., & Cadorette, L. (1978). Individual differences in memory: Theory, data, and educational implications. *Contemporary Educational Psychology, 3*, 182–203.

Royer, J. M., & Perkins, M. R. (1977). Facilitated transfer in prose learning over an extended time period. *Journal of Reading Behavior, 9*, 185–188.

Ruble, D. N. (1980). A developmental perspective on theories of achievement motivation. In L. Fyans (Ed.), *Achievement motivation: Recent trends in theory and research*. New York: Plenum, 31–54.

Rumelhart, D. E., & Ortony, J. A. (1977). The representation of knowledge in memory. In R. C. Anderson, R. J. Shapiro, & W. E. Montague (Eds.), *Schooling and the acquisition of knowledge*. Hillsdale, NJ: Erlbaum.

Salomon, G. (1979). *Interaction of media, cognition, and learning*. San Francisco: Jossey-Bass.

Salomon, G. (1980). The use of visual media in the service of enriching mental thought processes. *Instructional Science, 9*, 327–339.

Sarason, S. B., Davidson, K. S., Lighthall, F. F., Waite, R. R., & Ruebush, B. K. (1960). *Anxiety in elementary school children*. New York: Wiley.

Sattler, J. M., & Theye, F. (1967). Procedural, situational, and interpersonal variables in individual intelligence testing. *Psychological Bulletin, 68*, 347–360.

Savin-Williams, R. C., & Demo, D. H. (1983). Conceiving or misconceiving the self: Issues in adolescent self-esteem. *Journal of Early Adolescence, 3*, 121–140.

Schlieper, A. E. (1982). A note on frames of reference in the assessment of learning disabilities. *Journal of Learning Disabilties, 15*, 84–85.

Schoettle, Y. C., & Cantwell, D. P. (1980). Children of divorce: Demographic variables, symptoms, and diagnoses. *Journal of the American Academy of Child Psychiatry, 19*, 453–475.

Schug, M. C. (1981). Using the local community to improve citizenship education for the gifted. *Roeper Review, 4*, 22–23.

Schwartz, R. M., & Humphreys, M. S. (1976). Further examinations of the category-recall function. *Memory and Cognition, 4*, 655–660.

Sears, P. S. (1940). Levels of aspiration in academically successful and unsuccessful children. *Journal of Abnormal and Social Psychology, 35*, 498–536.

Sears, R., Maccoby, E., & Levin, H. (1957). *Patterns of child rearing*. Evanston, IL: Row, Peterson.

Selman, R. (1976). Toward a structural analysis of developing interpersonal relations concepts: Research with normal and disturbed preadolescent boys. In A. Pick (Ed.), *Minnesota Symposia on Child Development* (Vol. 10). Minneapolis: University of Minnesota Press, 156–200.

Selman, R. (1980). *The growth of interpersonal understanding*. New York: Academic Press.

Shatz, M., & Gelman, R. (1973). The development of communication skills: Modification in the speech of young children as a function of listener. *Monograph of the Society for Research in Child Development, 38.*

Shavelson, R. J., & Borko, H. (1979). Research on teachers' decisions in planning instruction. *Educational Horizons, 57,* 183–189.

Shavelson, R. J., & Bolus, R. (1982). Self-concept: The interplay of theory and methods. *Journal of Educational Psychology, 74,* 3–17.

Shavelson, R. J., Hubner, J. H., & Stanton, J. C. (1976). Self-concept: Validation of construct interpretations. *Review of Educational Research, 46,* 407–441.

Shimerlink, S. M. (1978). Organization theory and memory for prose: A review of the literature. *Review of Educational Research, 48,* 103–120.

Shuell, T. J., & Keppel, G. (1970). Learning ability and retention. *Journal of Educational Psychology, 61,* 59–65.

Silberman, M. L. (1969). Behavioral expression of teachers' attitudes toward elementary school students. *Journal of Educational Psychology, 60,* 402–407.

Simmons, R. G., Blyth, D. A., VanCleave, E. F., & Bush, D. M. (1979). Entry into early adolescence: The impact of school structure, puberty, and early dating on self-esteem. *American Sociological Review, 44,* 948–967.

Simmons, R. G., Brown, L., Bush, D. M., & Blyth, D. A. (1978). Self-esteem and achievement of black and white early adolescents. *Social Problems, 26,* 86–96.

Simmons, R. G., & Rosenberg, F. (1975). Sex, sex roles, and self-image. *Journal of Youth and Adolescence, 4,* 229–258.

Simmons, R. G., Rosenberg, F., & Rosenberg, M. (1973). Disturbances in the self-image at adolescence. *American Sociological Review, 38,* 553–568.

Skinner, B. F. (1938). *The behavior of organisms: An experimental analysis.* New York: Appleton-Century-Crofts.

Skinner, B. F. (1953). *Science and human behavior.* New York: Free Press.

Skinner, B. F. (1958). Teaching machines. *Science, 128,* 969–977.

Skinner, B. F. (1968). *The technology of teaching.* New York: Appleton-Century-Crofts.

Skinner, B. F. (1971). *Beyond freedom and dignity.* New York: Knopf.

Sloan, H. N., Young, K. R., & Marcusen, T. (1977). Response cost and human aggressive behavior. In B. C. Etzel, J. M. LeBlanc, & D. M. Baer (Eds.). *New developments in behavioral research.* Hillsdale, NJ: Erlbaum.

Smith, C. P. (1966). *Child development.* Dubuque, IA: W. C. Brown.

Smith, M. E. (1926). An investigation of the development of the sentence and the extent of vocabulary in young children. *University of Iowa Studies in Child Welfare, 3,* No. 5.

Smythe, M. J., Kibler, R. J., & Hutchings, P. W. (1973). A comparison of norm-referenced and criterion-referenced measurement with implications for communication instruction. *The Speech Teacher, 22,* 4.

Snow, R. E. (1980). Intelligence for the year 2001. *Human Intelligence International Newsletter,* No. 4, 1–2.

Soar, R. S. (1967). Pupil needs and teacher-pupil relationships: Experiences needed for comprehensive reading. In E. J. Amidon & J. B. Hough (Eds.), *Interaction analysis: Theory, research, and application.* Reading, MA: Addison-Wesley, 243–250.

Solomon, R. L. (1964). Punishment. *American Psychologist, 19,* 239–253.

Spearman, C. (1927). *The abilities of man.* New York: Macmillan.

Spearman, C., & Jones, L. W. (1950). *Human ability.* London: Macmillan, 1950.

Spence, K. W. (1951). Theoretical interpretations of learning. In S. S. Stevens (Ed.), *Handbook of experimental psychology.* New York: Wiley, 690–729.

Spence, K. W. (1956). *Behavior therapy and conditioning.* New Haven, CT: Yale University Press.

Spence, K. W., & Lippitt, R. (1940). "Latent" learning of a simple maze problem with relevant needs satiated. *Psychological Bulletin, 37,* 429.

Spence, K. W., & Lippitt, R. (1946). An experimental test of the sign-gestalt theory of trial-and-error learning. *Journal of Experimental Psychology, 36,* 491–502.

Statistical abstract of the United States (1982). Washington, DC: U.S. Department of Commerce.

Staw, B. M., Calder, B. J., Hess, R .K., & Sandelands, L. E. (1980). Intrinsic motivation and norms about payment. *Journal of Personality, 48,* 1–14.

Steers, R. M., & Porter, L. W. (1974). The role of task-goal attributes in employee performance. *Psychological Bulletin, 81,* 434–452.

Stein, G. M., & Bryan, J. H. (1972). The effects of a television model upon rule adoption behavior of children. *Child Development, 43,* 268–273.

Sternberg, R. J. (1981). Intelligence as thinking and learning skills. *Educational Leadership, 38,* 18–20.

Stewart, J., VanKirk, J., & Rowell, R. (1979). Concept maps: A tool for use in biology teaching. *American Biology Teacher, 41,* 171.

Stoner, M. (1980). Education in mainstreaming. *Clearing House, 55,* 39–42.

Strathe, M., & Hash, V. (1979). The effect of an alternative school on adolescent self-esteem. *Adolescence, 14*(53), 185–190.

Strauss, A. A. (1939). Typology in mental deficiency. *American Journal of Mental Deficiency, 44,* 83–90.

Strauss, A. A., & Kephart, N. C. (1955). *Psychopathology and education of the brain-injured child* (Vol. 2). New York: Grune & Stratton.

Strauss, A. A., & Lehtinen, I. E. (1947). *Psychopathology and education of the brain-injured child* (Vol. 1). New York: Grune & Stratton.

Strickland, B. R. (1965). The prediction of social action from a dimension of internal-external control. *Journal of Social Psychology, 66,* 353–358.

Strom, R. D., & Bernard, H. W. (1982). *Educational psychology.* Monterey, CA: Brooks/Cole.

Sulzer-Azaroff, B., & Mayer, G. R. (1977). *Applying behavior analysis procedures with children and youth.* New York: Holt, Rinehart and Winston.

Suppes, P. (1968). Computer technology and the future of education. *Phi Delta Kappan, 49,* 420–423.

Suran, B. G., & Rizzo, J. V. (1979). *Special children: An integrative approach.* Glenview, IL: Scott, Foresman.

Taba, H. (1967). *Teacher's handbook for elementary school studies*. Reading, MA: Addison-Wesley.

Taffel, S. J., O'Leary, K. D., & Armel, S. (1974). Reasoning and praise: Their effects on academic behavior. *Journal of Educational Psychology, 66*, 291–295.

Talbert, E. G. (1968). *Story preferences: A technique for assessing children's motives*. Unpublished doctoral dissertation, University of Oklahoma, Norman.

Taylor, B. M. (1982). Text structure and children's comprehension and memory for expository material. *Journal of Educational Psychology, 74*, 323–340.

Teevan, R. C., & McGhee, P. (1972). Childhood development of fear of failure motivation. *Journal of Personality and Social Psychology, 21*, 318–326.

Tennant, J. (1981). Student advisement: Who cares? *Dissemination Services on the Middle Grades, 7*, 1–6.

Tennyson, R. D., & Park, O. (1980). The teaching of concepts: A review of instructional design research literature. *Review of Educational Research, 50*, 55–70.

Terman, L. M. (1918). *The Stanford revision and extension of Binet-Simon scale for measuring intelligence*. Baltimore: Warwick & York.

Terman, L. M. (1925). *Mental and physical traits of a thousand gifted children. Vol. 1: Genetic studies of genius*. Stanford, CA: Stanford University Press.

Terman, L. M., & Merrill, M. (1937). *Measuring intelligence*. Boston: Houghton Mifflin.

Terman, L. M., & Oden, M. (1947). *The gifted child grows up. Vol. 4: Genetic studies of genius*. Stanford, CA: Stanford University Press.

Terman, L. M., & Oden, M. (1951). The Stanford studies of the gifted. In P. Witty (Ed.), *The gifted child* (pp. 20–46). New York: Heath.

Terman, L. M., & Oden, M. (1959). *The gifted group at mid-life. Vol. 5: Genetic studies of genius*. Stanford, CA: Stanford University Press.

Thelen, M. H. (1969). Modeling of verbal reactions to failure. *Developmental Psychology, 1*, 297.

Thoresen, C. E., & Mahoney, M. J. (1974). *Behavioral self-control*. New York: Holt, Rinehart and Winston.

Thornburg, E. E. (1981). Why the lack of health education programs in the middle school? *Contemporary Education, 52*, 160–163.

Thornburg, E. E., & Thornburg, H. D. (1974). The key to success in preventive dentistry. *Journal of the American College of Dentists, 40*, 226–234.

Thornburg, H. D. (1971a). *Attitudes toward school and self: Indians, Blacks, and Mexican-Americans*. Paper presented at the meeting of the Pacific Division, AAAS, San Diego, CA.

Thornburg, H. D. (1971b), *Minority youth families: A comparative analysis of attitude between self and family*. Paper presented at the meeting of the Southwestern and Rocky Mountain Division, AAAS, Tempe, AZ.

Thornburg, H. D. (1971c). *An investigation of attitudes among potential dropouts from minority groups during their freshman year in high school*. Final Report, U.S. Department of Health, Education and Welfare, Office of Education, Bureau of Research, Contract No. OEC-9-71-9992 (057).

Thornburg, H. D. (1973a). *School learning and instruction: Readings*. Monterey, CA: Brooks/Cole.

Thornburg, H. D. (1973b). *School learning and instruction*. Monterey, CA: Brooks/Cole.

Thornburg, H. D. (1973c). *Child development*. Dubuque, IA: W. C. Brown.

Thornburg, H. D. (1974). An investigation of a dropout program among Arizona's minority youth. *Education, 94*(3), 249–265.

Thornburg, H. D. (1977). *You and your adolescent*. Tucson, AZ: HELP Books.

Thornburg, H. D. (1979a, April). *A preliminary analysis of an experimental criterion-referenced math program*. Paper presented at the Rocky Mountain Psychological Association annual meeting, Las Vegas.

Thornburg, H. D. (1979b, April). *Increasing students' music awareness through criterion-referenced instruction*. Paper presented at the Rocky Mountain Psychological Association annual meeting, Las Vegas.

Thornburg, H. D. (1979c). *Performance accountability through computer help*. Santa Fe: New Mexico State Department of Education, Final Report, ESEA, Title IV-C, Los Alamos Schools.

Thornburg, H. D. (1980a). *Performance accountability through computer help: II*. Santa Fe: New Mexico State Department of Education, Final Report, ESEA, Title IV-C, Los Alamos Schools.

Thornburg, H. D. (1980b, August). *Effective outcomes in a criterion-referenced junior high math program*. Paper presented at the American Psychological Association annual meeting.

Thornburg, H. D. (1981a). Developmental characteristics of middle schoolers and middle school organization. *Contemporary Education, 52*, 134–139.

Thornburg, H. D. (1981b). Moral development in the middle-school-aged adolescent. *Journal of North Carolina League of Middle/Junior High Schools, 3*, 8–10.

Thornburg, H. D. (1982a). *Development in adolescence* (2nd ed.). Monterey, CA: Brooks/Cole.

Thornburg, H. D. (1982b). *Health and living: K–12 approach*. Santa Fe: New Mexico State Department of Education, Final Report, ESEA, Title IV-C, Los Alamos Schools.

Thornburg, H. D. (1982c, December). *Academic implications of the developmental capacity of school children within a changing social environment*. Address given to Tucson Schools Administrators.

Thornburg, H. D., & Gould, A. W. (1980). The role of the middle school in peer group socialization. *Michigan Middle School Journal, 6*, 18–20.

Thornburg, H. D., & Jones, R. M. (1982). Social characteristics of early adolescents: Age versus grade. *Journal of Early Adolescence, 2*, 229–240.

Thornburg, H. D., McEwin, C. K., & Jones, R. M. (1982, March). *School structure effects on early adolescent perceived preferred teacher characteristics*. Paper presented at the American Educational Research Association annual meeting, New York.

Thornburg, H. D., & Thornburg, E. E. (1974). Motivational aspects of teaching patients dental home care. *American Society for Preventive Dentistry Journal, 4,* 14–24.

Thorndike, E. L. (1898). Animal intelligence: An experimental study of the associative process in animals. *Psychological Review Monograph Supplement, 2,* 1–109.

Thorndike, E. L. (1903). *Educational psychology.* New York: Lemcke & Buchner.

Thorndike, E. L. (1913). *The psychology of learning* (Vol. 2). New York: Teachers College Press.

Thorndike, E. L. (1924). Mental discipline in high school studies. *Journal of Educational Psychology, 15,* 83–98.

Thorndike, E. L. (1932). *The fundamentals of learning.* New York: Teachers College Press.

Thorndike, E. L. (1935). *The psychology of wants, interests, and attitudes.* New York: Appleton-Century-Crofts.

Thorndike, E. L. (1940). "Constancy" of the IQ. *Psychological Bulletin, 27,* 167–186.

Thorndike, E. L., & Woodworth, R. S. (1901). The influence of improvement in one mental function upon the efficiency of other functions. *Psychological Review, 8,* 247–261.

Thorndike, R. L., & Hagen, E. (1977). *Measurement and evaluation in psychology and education* (3rd ed.). New York: Wiley.

Thurstone, L. L. (1928). Attitudes can be measured. *American Journal of Sociology, 33,* 529–544.

Tidwell, R. (1980). A psycho-educational profile of 1,593 gifted high school students. *Gifted Child Quarterly, 24,* 63–68.

Tikunoff, W. J., Ward, B. A., & Mergendoller, J. R. (1979). *Technical proposal: Ecological perspectives for successful schooling practice, program #2.* San Francisco: Far West Laboratory.

Tobin, M. J. (1973). *A study in the improvement of visual efficiency in children registered as blind.* Birmingham, England: University of Birmingham Research Centre for the Education of the Visually Handicapped.

Toepfer, C. F. (1981). Advisor-advisee programs: A requisite for effective middle school guidance. *Dissemination Services on the Middle Grades, 7,* 1–4.

Tolman, E. C. (1938). *Purposive behavior in animals and men.* New York: Appleton-Century-Crofts.

Tomlinson-Keasey, C. (1972). Formal operations in females from eleven to fifty-four years of age. *Developmental Psychology, 6,* 364.

Tomlinson-Keasey, C., & Kelley, R. R. (1978). The deaf child's symbolic world. *American Annals of the Deaf, 123,* 452–459.

Torrance, E. P. (1973). Non-test indicators of creative talent among disadvantaged children. *Gifted Child Quarterly, 17,* 3–9.

Travers, J. F. (1970). *Fundamentals of educational psychology.* Scranton, PA: International Press.

Travers, J. F. (1979). *Educational psychology.* New York: Harper & Row.

Treffinger, D. J. (1980). Fostering independence and creativity. *Journal for the Education of the Gifted, 3,* 214–215.

Turiel, E. (1983). *The development of social knowledge.* New York: Cambridge University Press.

Uguroglu, M. E., & Walberg, H. J. (1979). Motivation and achievement: A quantitative synthesis. *American Educational Research Journal, 16,* 375–390.

Underwood, B. J. (1948). Retroactive and proactive inhibition after five and forty-eight hours. *Journal of Experimental Psychology, 38,* 29–38.

Underwood, B. J. (1949). Proactive inhibition as a function of time and degree of prior learning. *Journal of Experimental Psychology, 39,* 24–34.

Underwood, B. J. (1954). Speed of learning and amount retained: A consideration of methodology. *Psychological Bulletin, 51,* 276–282.

Underwood, B. J. (1964a). Degree of learning and the measurement of forgetting. *Journal of Verbal Learning and Verbal Behavior, 3,* 112–129.

Underwood, B. J. (1964b). Laboratory studies of verbal learning. In E. R. Hilgard (Ed.), *Theories of learning and instruction.* Chicago: National Society for the Study of Education, 133–152.

U.S. Commission on Civil Rights (1967). *Racial isolation in the public schools* (Vol. 1). Washington, DC: U.S. Government Printing Office.

Veroff, J. (1969). Social comparison and the development of achievement motivation. In C. P. Smith (Ed.), *Achievement-related motives in children.* New York: Russell Sage Foundation, 46–102.

Veroff, J. (1978). Social motivation. *American Behavioral Scientist, 21,* 709–729.

Violent schools—safe schools (2 vols) (1978). Washington, DC: National Institute of Education.

Vye, N. J., & Bransford, J. D. (1981). Programs for teaching thinking. *Educational Leadership, 38,* 26–28.

Vygotsky, L. S. (1962). *Thought and language.* Cambridge, MA: M.I.T. Press.

Wallace, C. J. (1976). Assessment of psychotic behavior. In M. Hersen & S. Bellack (Eds.), *Behavioral assessment: A practical handbook.* Elmsford, NY: Pergamon Press, 110–139.

Walters, R. H., & Parke, R. D. (1964). Influence of response consequences to a social model on resistance to deviation. *Journal of Experimental Child Psychology, 1,* 269–280.

Walters, R. H., Parke, R. D., & Cane, V. A. (1965). Timing of punishment and the observation of consequences to others as determinants of response inhibition. *Journal of Experimental Child Psychology, 2,* 10–30.

Ward, B. A. (1982). Changes in student participation in different instructional settings. *Journal of Early Adolescence, 2,* 363–388.

Ward, B. A., Rounds, T. S., Packer, M. J., Mergendoller, J. R., & Tikunoff, W. J. (1981). *Junior high school transition study: Volume 4: Students experience during response to transition to junior high school.* San Francisco: Far West Laboratory.

Warner, D. A., & deJung, J. E. (1971). Effects of goal setting upon learning in educable retardates. *American Journal of Mental Deficiency, 75,* 681–684.

Warner, D. A., & Mills, W. D. (1980). The effects of goal setting on the manual performance rates of moderately retarded adolescents. *Education and Training of the Mentally Retarded, 15,* 143–147.

Watson, J. B. (1926). Experimental studies on the growth of emotions. In C. Murchison (Ed.), *Psychologies of 1925.* Worcester, MA: Clark University Press, 37–57.

Watson, J. B. (1928). *Psychological care of infant and child.* New York: Norton.

Watson, J. B., & Raynor, R. (1920). Conditioned emotional reactions. *Journal of Experimental Psychology, 3,* 1–14.

Wattenberg, W. W., & Clifford, C. (1964). Relationship of self-concept to beginning achievement in reading. *Child Development, 35,* 461–467.

Waugh, K. W., & Bush, W. J. (1971). *Diagnosing learning disorders.* Columbus, OH: Merrill.

Wechsler, D. (1944). *The measurement of adult intelligence.* Baltimore: Williams & Wilkins.

Wechsler, D. (1949). *Wechsler intelligence scale for children, manual.* New York: Psychological Corporation.

Weaver, G. E., Duncan, E. M. & Bird, C. P. (1972). Cue-specific retroactive inhibition. *Journal of Applied Learning and Verbal Behavior, 11,* 362–366.

Weiner, B. (1979). A theory of motivation for some classroom experiences. *Journal of Educational Psychology, 71,* 3–25.

Weiner, B., Russell, D., & Lerman, D. (1979). The cognition-emotion proceeds in achievement-related contexts. *Journal of Personality and Social Psychology, 47,* 1211–1220.

Weintraub, D. J., & Walker, E. L. (1966). *Perception.* Monterey, CA: Brooks/Cole.

Weisgerber, R. A. (Ed.) (1971). *Developmental efforts in individualizing learning.* Itasca, IL: Peacock.

Weiss, C. D., & Lillywhite, H. S. (1976). *A handbook for prevention and early intervention: Communicative disorders.* St. Louis, MO: Mosby.

Wertheimer, M. (1938). Laws of organizations in perceptual forms. In W. D. Ellis (Ed.), *A source book of Gestalt psychology,* Trans., 71–88). New York: Harcourt, Brace & World. (Original work published 1923)

Wesman, A. G. (1945). A study of transfer of training from high school subjects to intelligence. *Journal of Educational Research, 39,* 254–264.

Whipple, G. M. (Ed.) (1924). *The education of gifted children.* Chicago: National Society for the Study of Education.

White, G. M. (1967). The elicitation and durability of altruistic behavior in children. *Research Bulletin.* Princeton, NJ: Educational Testing Service.

White, M. B., & Hall, A. E. (1980). An overview of intelligence testing. *Educational Horizons, 58,* 210–216.

White, R. W. (1959). Motivation reconsidered: The concept of competence. *Psychological Review, 66,* 297–333.

Whitely, P. L., & McGeoch, J. A. (1928). The curve of retention for poetry. *Journal of Educational Psychology, 19,* 471–479.

Wiles, J., & Bondi, J. (1981). *The essential middle school.* Columbus, OH: Merrill.

Willems, E. P. (1973). Behavioral ecology and experimental analysis: Countship is not enough. In J. R. Nesslroade & H. W.

Reese (Eds.), *Life-span developmental psychology.* New York: Academic Press.

Williams, P. B., & Carnine, D. W. (1981). Relationship between range of examples and of instructions and attention in concept attainment. *Journal of Educational Research, 74,* 144–148.

Williams, R. J., & Algozzine, B. (1979). Differential attitudes toward mainstreaming: An investigation. *Alberta Journal of Educational Research, 23,* 207–212.

Williams, R. L., & Byers, H. (1968). Negro self-esteem in a transitional society: Tennessee Self-concept Scale. *Personnel and Guidance Journal, 46,* 120–125.

Winograd, T. (1972). Understanding natural language. *Cognitive Psychology, 3,* 1–191.

Winterbottom, M. R. (1958). The relation of need for achievement to learning experiences in independence and mastery. In J. W. Atkinson (Ed.), *Motives in fantasy, action, and society.* New York: Van Nostrand Reinhold.

Withall, J. (1951). The development of a climate index. *Journal of Educational Research, 45,* 93–99.

Wolf, T. M. (1972). A developmental investigation of televised modeled verbalizations of resistance to variation. *Developmental Psychology, 6,* 537.

Wolpe, J. (1969). *The practice of behavior therapy.* Elmsford, NY: Pergamon.

Woodworth, R. S. (1918). *Dynamic psychology.* New York: Columbia University Press.

Wright, R. J., & DuCette, J. P. (1976). *Locus of control and academic achievement in traditional and nontraditional educational settings.* Unpublished manuscript. (ERIC Document Reproduction Service No. ED 123 203)

Wrightsman, L. S. (1977). *Social psychology* (2nd ed.). Monterey, CA: Brooks/Cole.

Wrightsman, L. S., Silegman, C. K., & Sanford, F. H. (1979). *Psychology* (5th ed.). Monterey, CA: Brooks/Cole.

Wylie, H. H. (1919). An experimental study of transfer of response in the white rat. *Behavioral Monographs, 3*(16).

Yussen, S. R., & Berman, L. (1981). Memory predictions for recall and recognition in first-, third-, and fifth-grade children. *Developmental Psychology, 17,* 224–229.

Yussen, S. R., Matthews, S., & Knight, J. W. (1980). Performance of Montessori and traditionally schooled nursery children on social cognitive tasks and memory problems. *Contemporary Educational Psychology, 5,* 124–137.

Zigler, E. (1963). Social reinforcement, environmental conditions, and the child. *American Journal of Orthopsychiatry, 33,* 614–623.

Zigler, E., Butterfield, E. C., & Capobianco, F. (1970). Institutionalization and social reinforcement. *Developmental Psychology, 3,* 255–263.

Zigler, E., & Kanzer, P. (1962). The effectiveness of two classes of verbal reinforcers on the performance of middle- and lower-class children. *Journal of Personality, 30,* 157–163.

Zigler, E., & Muenchow, S. (1979). Mainstreaming: The proof is in the implementation. *American Psychologist, 34,* 993–996.

Zimmerman, B. J. (1977). Modeling. In H. L. Hon, Jr., & P. A. Robinson (Eds.), *Psychological processes in early education*. New York: Academic Press.

Zimmerman, B. J., & Ghozeil, F. S. (1974). Modeling as a teaching technique. *Elementary School Journal, 74,* 440–446.

Zimmerman, B. J., & Kleefeld, C. F. (1977). Toward a theory of teaching: A social learning view. *Contemporary Educational Psychology, 2,* 158–171.

551